D1473646

Law, Lawyers and Social Change

CASES AND MATERIALS ON THE
ABOLITION OF SLAVERY, RACIAL
SEGREGATION AND INEQUALITY
OF EDUCATIONAL OPPORTUNITY

Harold W. Horowitz

and

Kenneth L. Karst

Professors of Law
University of California
Los Angeles

THE BOBBS-MERRILL COMPANY, INC.
A SUBSIDIARY OF HOWARD W. SAMS & CO., INC.
PUBLISHERS • INDIANAPOLIS • KANSAS CITY • NEW YORK

To Lizzie, Lisa and Adam,
and
To Smiley, Ken, Dick, Leslie and Laura

Acknowledgments

To the late Henry Hart, "who first opened our minds to these problems," and to Albert Sacks, our intellectual debt is obvious. Their materials on *The Legal Process* (1958) have inspired much of the content of this book. We should like to think that what we do here is what they might have done in the doctrinal area we have chosen to study. We have also profited from two other casebooks on the legal process: *On Law In Courts,* by Mishkin and Morris (1965), and *The Legal Process,* by Auerbach, Garrison, Hurst and Mermin (1961).

We appreciate the support of our colleagues in the UCLA law faculty, and particularly the confidence implicit in their experimental adoption of this course in the first-year curriculum. Murray Schwartz not only helped to conceive the course, but also contributed a number of ideas for its content relating to the legal profession. Richard Wasserstrom taught the course from a tentative edition of these materials; his many valuable suggestions have been adopted in the present volume. Dean Richard Maxwell, whose devotion to his faculty and students is strong, cheerful and unfailing, gave us the kind of institutional aid and personal encouragement that he has trained us all to expect as our due.

For the typing and processing of the manuscript, we are grateful to Mrs. Helen Jeffares and her staff, and especially to Mrs. Pauline Kosche.

Finally, we thank the students of the Class of 1971 of the UCLA School of Law, who taught us this course while we were purporting to teach it during its experimental offering.

H.W.H.
K.L.K.

Summary Table of Contents

Table of Contents

Table of Cases

Principal cases are italicized and their page references are also in italics. Cases which are excerpted or discussed at some length are in roman and their page references are in italics. Other cases are in roman with page references in roman.

INTRODUCTION TO AN INTRODUCTION

This course is an introduction to the American legal system, through the study of some materials that have been produced as the legal process has shaped (and been shaped by) the movement toward racial equality. The course is designed as an overview of the legal process—the totality of governmental instrumentalities and processes by which the functions of law in society are performed. So Olympian an objective, and so grandiose a course title, demand an explanation.

Every course in law school is a course in the legal process, reflecting the entire legal system as it comes to bear on a single subject area. Most courses, however, emphasize the development of the legal doctrine that governs their fields, and not the institutional process that produces the doctrine. (Even that rather hedgy statement contains some exaggeration, but the general point is accurate enough.) In this course, we shall study some doctrine, but always for the purpose of analyzing the way courts, legislatures, administrative officers and lawyers contribute to the growth of law. Our focus is institutional, not doctrinal; any subject would serve this purpose of the course.

Yet the choice of slavery, racial segregation, and inequality of educational opportunity as our subject areas is not accidental. The course has the additional purpose of demonstrating to the law student some of the ways in which the legal system can be made an instrument for effecting changes in society. In the long view of history, it is true that the theme of racial equality has only sporadically claimed the center of our national attention. During the professional lifetime of today's law student, though, racial equality will be The Theme that dominates all others in our society, in both its domestic and its foreign manifestations. Law and lawyers have not created the black revolution. But they have played a critical part in institutionalizing the gains of that movement—and thereby making the movement acceptable to the Nation's white majority. No revolution, however revolutionary its goals, seeks the destruction of all social controls. The very continuation of social organization implies that much that bears the name of revolution turns out to be accommodation. And much of the accommodation is carried out by lawyers through legal institutions. Mr. Justice Thurgood Marshall, when he was

Solicitor General, made the point we wish to make: "that lawyers, through their everyday work in the courts, may become social reformers."[1] We would add only that the courts are merely one arena in which lawyers have that opportunity.

The first chapter is devoted to the uses of law as an instrument to achieve the abolition of slavery in England, in the British colonies, and in the United States. Since the rest of the course is devoted to the problems of racial segregation and inequality of educational opportunity, it may seem curious to start with slavery. A too-easy answer would be that, after all, the enslavement of black people was the foundation on which racial distinctions in America were originally based. A better answer, given the purposes of this course, is that the efforts to achieve the two abolitions—of slavery and of segregation—have raised parallel institutional issues in the legal process. (Besides, the editors both regret having completed law school without having studied the *Dred Scott* case, surely one of the most important judicial decisions an American court ever made.)

Five aspects of the legal process will take most of our attention:

(i)   the judicial process: the role of courts in resolving disputes and declaring law;
(ii) the role of legislatures as lawmakers;
(iii) the role of judges in interpreting statutes and constitutions;
(iv) the role of the administrative process in the making and application of law;
(v)   the role of the legal profession.

Our chapters are not organized around these topics. Instead, we shall consider the various working parts of the legal process as they come to bear on a complex of social problems. But the student should keep in mind that these topics are the basic subject of the course; they should not be lost among the doctrinal trees. The ground we expect to cover in the first two chapters is summarized in a three-page "anticipatory epilogue," p. 235 *infra*.

Even in examining the legal system as a process, there is room for the eye of the reformer. With respect to the existing institutions for making and applying law, as with the existing professional obligations of lawyers, it is always appropriate to ask, "Why do it this way?" Questions like that not only lead toward the exploration of alternative solutions; they also help us understand

---

[1] Marshall, *Law and the Quest for Equality*, 1967 WASH. U.L.Q. 1, 7; cf. Wasserstrom, *Lawyers and Revolution*, 30 U. Pitt. L. Rev. 125 (1968).

how the existing institutions work, and how they have reached their present forms. Additionally, such questions help to create and maintain the critical, questioning frame of mind that is an important part of the lawyer's stock in trade.

Of course the legal process is not an end in itself. Ultimately, no legal system can be evaluated apart from the substantive social product that emerges from it. But it is precisely this interconnection of process and output that makes the legal process a fit subject for special attention. In our society, lawyers are the experts on these matters of process. For that reason, lawyers have a special obligation to see that the end product of the system is just. And justice normally depends on making the right institutional choices. Means have a way of swallowing up ends, as Camus knew: "There is no justice; there are only limits."

The materials relating to the legal profession are included in order to begin the student's critical examination of the profession *as* a profession. By long tradition the law has been considered a "learned profession," with special responsibilities to society. Our final objective is to demonstrate the validity of this statement by Professor Herbert Wechsler: "Those of us to whom it is not given to 'live greatly in the law' are surely called upon to fail in the attempt."[2]

---

[2] Wechsler, *Toward Neutral Principles of Constitutional Law*, 73 HARV. L. REV. 1, 35 (1959).

Chapter 1

THE ABOLITION OF SLAVERY

Our own generation is not morally neutral about slavery. It is hard, therefore, for us to comprehend the discussion of slavery by some lawyers and some judges of the eighteenth and nineteenth centuries, who treated the ownership of a human being as if it were not fundamentally different from other forms of ownership. But that comprehension is precisely what we must seek, if we are to understand how the legal process was involved in the abolition of slavery. Every law, every judicial decision, is the product of its own time. We shall be concerned with the way in which the social context of a decision, or the moral-intellectual climate surrounding it, conditions the result. But we shall be concerned also with the way in which the institutional structure of the legal system shapes what judges and legislators do. The latter task places a strain on the intellectual and emotional resources of both teacher and student, for it requires a rather cool look—a lawyer's look—at some features of a legal system that first created and protected slavery, and only later abolished it.

A. ABOLITION OF SLAVERY IN ENGLAND AND THE BRITISH COLONIES

No legal landmarks are to be found in the development of slavery in the British colonies of the Western Hemisphere. The institution began early in the seventeenth century, and was encouraged in various ways from England. Eventually legislation by Parliament regulated the slave trade and recognized the legal validity of slavery in the colonies. By the third quarter of the eighteenth century slavery was firmly established. By this time, also, the abolition movement was underway in England and in some of the colonies. Myriad forces—economic, social, political, philosophical, moral, religious—contributed to the ultimate abolition of slavery under English and American law in the nineteenth century. But in the last analysis enforcement of the master-slave relationship rested on law, and the abolition of slavery required changes in the law.

The germinal legal event in the progress under English law toward abolition was Lord Mansfield's decision in *Somerset v. Stewart,* in 1772. The background of the case was described by Thomas Clarkson, a leading English abolitionist.

T. CLARKSON, HISTORY OF THE RISE, PROGRESS, & ACCOMPLISHMENT OF THE ABOLITION OF THE AFRICAN SLAVE-TRADE BY THE BRITISH PARLIAMENT 54-65 (1808)

Before the year 1700, planters, merchants, and others, resident in the West Indies, but coming to England, were accustomed to bring with them certain slaves to act as servants with them during their stay. The latter, seeing the freedom and the happiness of servants in this country, and considering what would be their own hard fate on their return to the islands, frequently absconded. Their masters of course made search after them, and often had them seized and carried away by force. It was, however, thrown out by many on these occasions, that the English laws did not sanction such proceedings, for that all persons who were baptized became free. The consequence of this was, that most of the slaves, who came over with their masters prevailed upon some pious clergymen to baptize them. They took of course godfathers of such citizens as had the generosity to espouse their cause. When they were seized they usually sent to these, if they had an opportunity, for their protection. And in the result, their godfathers, maintaining that they had been baptized, and that they were free on this account as well as by the general tenour of the laws of England, dared those, who had taken possession of them, to send them out of the kingdom.

The planters, merchants, and others, being thus circumstanced, knew not what to do. They were afraid of taking their slaves away by force, and they were equally afraid of bringing any of the cases before a public court. In this dilemma, in 1729 they applied to York and Talbot, the attorney and solicitor-general for the time being,[3] and obtained the following strange opinion from them: "We are of opinion, that a slave by coming from the West Indies into Great Britain or Ireland, either with or without his master, does not become free, and that his master's right and property in him is not thereby determined or varied, and that baptism doth not bestow freedom on him, nor make any altera-

---

[3] York and Talbot, as attorney-general and solicitor-general, occupied high governmental positions. York later became Lord Hardwicke, and, as Lord Chancellor, stated as dictum in a case in 1749 the same opinion he had stated as attorney-general in 1729. Pearne v. Lisle, 27 Eng. Rep. 47, Ambler 75 (1749). [*Eds.* note.]

tion in his temporal condition in these kingdoms. We are also of opinion that the master may legally compel him to return again to the plantations."

This cruel and illegal opinion was delivered in the year 1729. The planters, merchants, and others, gave it of course all the publicity in their power. And the consequences were as might easily have been apprehended. In a little time slaves absconding were advertised in the London papers as runaways, and rewards offered for the apprehension of them, in the same brutal manner as we find them advertised in the land of slavery. They were advertised also, in the same papers, to be sold at auction, sometimes by themselves, and at others with horses, chaises, and harness. They were seized also by their masters, or by persons employed by them, in the very streets, and dragged from thence to the ships; and so unprotected now were these poor slaves, that persons in nowise concerned with them began to institute a trade in their persons, making agreements with captains of ships going to the West Indies to put them on board at a certain price. . . .

These circumstances then, as I observed before, did not fail of producing new coadjutors in the cause. And first they produced that able and indefatigable advocate Mr. Granville Sharp. This gentleman is to be distinguished from those who preceded him by this particular, that, whereas these were only writers, he was both a writer and an actor in the cause. In fact, he was the first labourer in it in England. By the words "actor" and "labourer," I mean that he determined upon a plan of action in behalf of the oppressed Africans, to the accomplishment of which he devoted a considerable portion of his time, talents, and substance. . . . The following is a short history of the beginning and of the course of his labours.

In the year 1765, Mr. David Lisle had brought over from Barbados, Jonathan Strong, an African slave, as his servant. He used the latter in a barbarous manner at his lodgings in Wapping, but particularly by beating him over the head with a pistol, which occasioned his head to swell. When the swelling went down, a disorder fell into his eyes, which threatened the loss of them. To this an ague and fever succeeded, and a lameness in both his legs.

Jonathan Strong, having been brought into this deplorable situation, and being therefore wholly useless, was left by his master to go whither he pleased. He applied accordingly to Mr. William Sharp the surgeon for his advice, as to one who gave up a portion of his time to the healing of the diseases of the poor. It was here that Mr. Granville Sharp, the brother of the former, saw him.

Suffice it to say, that in process of time he was cured. During this time Mr. Granville Sharp, pitying his hard case, supplied him with money, and he afterwards got him a situation in the family of Mr. Brown, an apothecary, to carry out medicines.

In this new situation, when Strong had become healthy and robust in his appearance, his master happened to see him. The latter immediately formed the design of possessing him again. Accordingly, when he had found out his residence, he procured John Ross keeper of the Poultry-compter and William Miller an officer under the lord mayor, to kidnap him. This was done by sending for him to the public house in Fenchurch-street, and then seizing him. By these he was conveyed, without any warrant, to John Kerr, for thirty pounds.

Strong, in this situation, sent, as was usual, to his godfathers, John London and Stephen Nail, for their protection. They went, but were refused admittance to him. At length he sent for Mr. Granville Sharp. The latter went, but they still refused access to the prisoner. He insisted, however, upon seeing him, and charged the keeper of the prison at his peril to deliver him up till he had been carried before a magistrate.

Mr. Sharp, immediately upon this, waited upon Sir Robert Kite, the then lord mayor, and entreated him to send for Strong, and to hear his case. A day was accordingly appointed. Mr. Sharp attended, and also William M'Bean, a notary public, and David Laird, captain of the ship Thames, which was to have conveyed Strong to Jamaica, in behalf of the purchaser, John Kerr. A long conversation ensued, in which the opinion of York and Talbot was quoted. Mr. Sharp made his observations. Certain lawyers, who were present, seemed to be staggered at the case, but inclined rather to recommit the prisoner. The lord mayor, however, discharged Strong, as he had been taken up without a warrant. . . .

Mr. Sharp, having been greatly affected by this case, and foreseeing how much he might be engaged in others of a similar nature, thought it time that the law of the land should be known upon this subject. He applied therefore to Doctor Blackstone, afterwards Judge Blackstone, for his opinion upon it.[4] He was, however, not satisfied with it, when he received it; nor could he obtain any satisfactory answer from several other lawyers, to whom he afterwards applied. The truth is, that the opinion of York and Talbot, which had been made public and acted upon

---

[4] Blackstone warned that "it would be uphill work in the Court of King's Bench." E. LASCELLES, GRANVILLE SHARP AND THE FREEDOM OF SLAVES IN ENGLAND 23 (1928). [*Eds.* note.]

by the planters, merchants, and others, was considered of high authority, and scarcely any one dared to question the legality of it. In this situation, Mr. Sharp saw no means of help but in his own industry, and he determined immediately to give up two or three years to the study of the English law, that he might the better advocate the cause of these miserable people. The result of these studies was the publication of a book in the year 1769, which he called "A Representation of the Injustice and dangerous Tendency of Tolerating Slavery in England." . . .

. . . [S]oon after the work just mentioned was out . . . [another] case occurred. This happened in the year 1770. Robert Stapylton, who lived at Chelsea, in conjunction with John Malony and Edward Armstrong, two watermen, seized the person of Thomas Lewis, an African slave, in a dark night, and dragged him to a boat lying in the Thames; they then gagged him, and tied him with a cord, and rowed him down to a ship, and put him on board to be sold as a slave in Jamaica. This base action took place near the garden of Mrs. Banks . . . . Lewis, it appears, on being seized, screamed violently. The servants of Mrs. Banks, who heard his cries, ran to his assistance, but the boat was gone. On informing their mistress of what had happened, she sent for Mr. Sharp, who began now to be known as the friend of the helpless Africans, and professed her willingness to incur the expense of bringing the delinquents to justice. Mr. Sharp, with some difficulty, procured a habeas corpus, in consequence of which Lewis was brought from Gravesend just as the vessel was on the point of sailing. An action was then commenced against Stapylton, who defended himself, on the plea, "That Lewis belonged to him as his slave." In the course of the trial, Mr. Dunning, who was counsel for Lewis, paid Mr. Sharp a handsome compliment, for he held in his hand Mr. Sharp's book on the injustice and dangerous tendency of tolerating slavery in England, while he was pleading; and in his address to the jury he spoke and acted thus: "I shall submit to you," says Mr. Dunning, "what my ideas are upon such evidence, reserving to myself an opportunity of discussing it more particularly, and reserving to myself a right to insist upon a position, which I will maintain (and here he held up the book to the notice of those present) in any place and in any court of the kingdom, that our laws admit of no such property."[5]

---

[5] It is lamentable to think, that the same Mr. Dunning, in a cause of this kind, which came on afterwards, took the opposite side of the question. [Footnote in original, renumbered.]

The result of the trial was, that the jury pronounced the plaintiff not to have been the property of the defendant, several of them crying out, "No property, no property."[6]

After this, one or two other trials came on, in which the oppressor was defeated, and several cases occurred, in which poor slaves were liberated from the holds of vessels, and other places of confinement, by the exertions of Mr. Sharp. . . .

But though the injured Africans, whose causes had been tried, escaped slavery, and though many who had been forcibly carried into dungeons, ready to be transported into the Colonies, had been delivered out of them, Mr. Sharp was not easy in his mind. Not one of the cases had yet been pleaded on the broad ground, "Whether an African slave coming into England became free?" This great question had been hitherto studiously avoided. It was still, therefore, left in doubt. Mr. Sharp was almost daily acting as if it had been determined, and as if he had been following the known law of the land. He wished therefore that the next cause might be argued upon this principle. Lord Mansfield too, who had been biased by the opinion of York and Talbot, began to waver in consequence of the different pleadings he had heard on this subject. He saw also no end of trials like these, till the law should be ascertained, and he was anxious for a decision on the same basis as Mr. Sharp. In this situation the following case offered, which was agreed upon for the determination of this important question.

James Somerset, an African slave, had been brought to England by his master, Charles Stewart, in November 1769. Somerset, in process of time, left him. Stewart took an opportunity of seizing him, and had him conveyed on board the Ann and Mary, captain Knowles, to be carried out of the kingdom, and sold as a slave in Jamaica. The question was "Whether a slave, by coming into England, became free?"

In order that time might be given for ascertaining the law fully on this head, the case was argued at three different sittings. First, in January, 1772; secondly, in February, 1772; and thirdly, in May, 1772. And that no decision otherwise than what the law warranted might be given, the opinion of the Judges was taken on the pleadings. The great and glorious result of the trial was, That as soon as ever any slave set his foot upon English territory, he became free.

---

6 ". . . [T]he jury found that there was no evidence of Lewis being Stapylton's property, some of them evidently wishing to go farther and express the view that no such property could exist." E. LASCELLES, GRANVILLE SHARP AND THE FREEDOM OF SLAVES IN ENGLAND 29 (1928). [*Eds.* note.]

SOMERSET v. STEWART
Court of King's Bench
98 Eng. Rep. 499, 1 Lofft 1 (1772)[7]

[Easter Term, May 14, 1772]

On return to a habeas corpus, requiring Captain Knowles to show cause for the seizure and detainure of the complainant Somerset, a negro—the case appeared to be this—

That the negro had been a slave to Mr. Stewart in Virginia, had been purchased from the African coast, in the course of the slave-trade, as tolerated in the plantations; that he had been brought over to England by his master, who intending to return, by force sent him on board of Captain Knowles's vessel, lying in the river; and was there, by the order of his master, in the custody of Captain Knowles, detained against his consent; until returned in obedience to the writ. And under this order, and the facts stated, Captain Knowles relied in his justification. . . .

[Eminent counsel represented Somerset and Stewart. Somerset's counsel did not accept fees.[8] One of the attorneys appearing for Stewart was Dunning, who had represented the slave in the 1770 case described in the preceding extract from Clarkson. The arguments for Stewart were "that villeinage,[9] or slavery, had been permitted in England by the common law; that no statute had ever passed to abolish this *status*; that although *de facto* villeinage by birth had ceased, a man might still make himself a villein by acknowledgment in a court of record; that at any rate the rights of these parties were to be decided according to the

---

[7] At the time of the decision in *Somerset v. Stewart,* it was not yet the practice for judges to write their opinions for publication. Opinions were delivered orally from the bench, and were recorded by lawyers, whose names were given to the volumes of reports. "Capel Lofft, man of letters, country gentleman, and Whig politician, was called to the bar in 1775 [having previously been a solicitor], and in 1776 published his reports of cases decided in the court of King's Bench and Chancery between the years 1772 and 1774. To the book was appended a wordy preface, and at the end the author printed a collection of 652 maxims, to which he prefixed a Latin preface. The reports are not of very great authority—Park, J., in 1821 said that though they filled the gap between the ending of Burrow and the beginning of Cowper, he had never heard them quoted three times in his life. But Lofft's reports are not without value, if only for the reason that he is the only reporter of *Sommersett's Case* sub nomine *Somerset v. Stewart.*" 12 W. HOLDSWORTH, A HISTORY OF ENGLISH LAW 139-40 (1938). What does Holdsworth mean when he says that Lofft's reports are "not of very great authority"?

[8] E. LASCELLES, GRANVILLE SHARP AND THE FREEDOM OF SLAVES IN ENGLAND 30 (1928). [*Eds.* note.]

[9] For a discussion of villeinage in medieval England and its possible relevance in *Somerset v. Stewart* see 3 W. HOLDSWORTH, A HISTORY OF ENGLISH LAW 491-508 (3d ed. 1923).

law of Jamaica, where they were domiciled; and as there could not be the smallest doubt that the voyage to England did not amount to emancipation, so that if Somerset were again in Jamaica he would still be considered the property of his master, the relation between them could not be considered suspended in England. Various instances were stated in which negro slaves, brought over here from the West Indies, had been [carried] back again against their will by their masters; and *dicta* of Lord Talbot and Lord Hardwicke were cited to the effect that this might lawfully be done." J. CAMPBELL, LIVES OF THE CHIEF JUSTICES OF ENGLAND 320 (1851).]

LORD MANSFIELD.—The question is, if the owner had a right to detain the slave, for the sending of him over to be sold in Jamaica. In five or six cases of this nature, I have known it to be accommodated by agreement between the parties; on its first coming before me, I strongly recommended it here. But if the parties will have it decided, we must give our opinion. Compassion will not, on the one hand, nor inconvenience on the other, be to decide; but the law: in which the difficulty will be principally from the inconvenience on both sides. Contract for sale of a slave is good here; the sale is a matter to which the law properly and readily attaches, and will maintain the price according to the agreement. But here the person of the slave himself is immediately the object of enquiry; which makes a very material difference. The now question is, whether any dominion, authority or coercion can be exercised in this country, on a slave according to the American laws? The difficulty of adopting the relation, without adopting it in all its consequences, is indeed extreme; and yet, many of those consequences are absolutely contrary to the municipal law of England. We have no authority to regulate the conditions in which law shall operate. On the other hand, should we think the coercive power cannot be exercised: 'tis now about fifty years since the opinion given by two of the greatest men of their own or any times, (since which no contract has been brought to trial, between the masters and slaves); the service performed by the slaves without wages, is a clear indication they did not think themselves free by coming hither. The setting 14,000 or 15,000 men at once free loose by a solemn opinion, is much disagreeable in the effects it threatens. There is a case in Hobart, (*Coventry and Woodfall,*) where a man had contracted to go as a mariner; but the now case will not come within that decision. Mr. Stewart advances no claim on contract; he rests his whole demand on a right to the negro as slave, and mentions the purpose of detainure to be the sending of him over to be sold in Jamaica. If the parties will have judgment, fiat justitia, ruat cœlum, let justice be done whatever be the consequence. 50£ a head may not be a high price; then a loss follows to the proprietors of above 700,000£ sterling. How would the law stand with respect to their settlement; their wages? How many actions for any slight coercion by the master? We cannot in any of these points direct the law; the law must rule us. In these particulars, it may be matter of weighty consideration, what provisions are made or set by law. Mr. Stewart may end the question, by discharging or giving freedom to the negro. I did think at first to put the matter to a more solemn way of argument: but if my brothers agree, there seems no occasion. I do not imagine, after the point has been discussed on both sides so extremely well, any new light could be thrown on the subject. If the parties chuse to refer it to the Common Pleas, they can give them that satisfaction whenever they think fit. An application to Parliament, if the merchants think the question of great commercial concern, is the best, and perhaps the only method of settling the point for the future. The Court is greatly obliged to the gentlemen of the Bar who have spoke[n] on the subject; and by whose care and abilities so much has been effected, that the rule of decision will be reduced to a very easy compass. I cannot omit to express particular happiness in seeing young men, just called to the Bar, have been able so much to profit by their reading. I think it right the matter should stand over; and if we are called on for a decision, proper notice shall be given.

[Trinity Term, June 22, 1772]

LORD MANSFIELD.—On the part of Somerset, the case which we gave notice should be decided this day, the Court now proceeds to give its opinion. I shall recite the return to the writ of habeas corpus, as the ground of our determination; omitting only words of form. The captain of the ship on board of which the negro was taken, makes his return to the writ in terms signifying that there have been, and still are, slaves to a great number in Africa; and that the trade in them is authorized by the laws and opinions of Virginia and Jamaica; that they are goods and chattels; and, as such, saleable and sold. That James Somerset, is a negro of Africa, and long before the return of the King's writ was brought to be sold, and was sold to Charles Stewart, Esq. then in Jamaica, and has not been manumitted since; that Mr. Stewart, having occasion to transact business, came over hither, with an intention to return; and brought Somerset, to attend and abide with him,

and to carry him back as soon as the business should be trans-
acted. That such intention has been, and still continues; and that
the negro did remain till the time of his departure, in the service
of his master Mr. Stewart, and quitted it without his consent; and
thereupon, before the return of the King's writ, the said Charles
Stewart did commit the slave on board the "Ann and Mary," to
save custody, to be kept till he should set sail, and then to be
taken with him to Jamaica, and there sold as a slave. And this
is the cause why he, Captain Knowles, who was then and now is,
commander of the above vessel, then and now lying in the river
of Thames, did the said negro, committed to his custody, detain;
and on which he now renders him to the orders of the Court. We
pay all due attention to the opinion of Sir Philip Yorke, and
Lord Chief Justice Talbot, whereby they pledged themselves to
the British planters, for all the legal consequences of slaves coming over to this kingdom or being baptized, recognized by Lord
Hardwicke, sitting as Chancellor on the 19th of October 1749,
that trover would lie:[10] that a notion had prevailed, if a negro
came over, or became a Christian, he was emancipated, but no
ground in law; that he and Lord Talbot, when Attorney and
Solicitor-General, were of opinion, that no such claim for freedom
was valid; that tho' the Statute of Tenures had abolished villains
regardant to a manor, yet he did not conceive but that a man
might still become a villain in gross, by confessing himself such
in open Court. We are so well agreed, that we think there is no
occasion of having it argued (as I intimated an intention at first,)
before all the Judges, as is usual, for obvious reasons, on a return
to a habeas corpus; the only question before us is, whether the
cause on the return is sufficient? If it is, the negro must be
remanded; if it is not, he must be discharged. Accordingly, the
return states, that the slave departed and refused to serve; where-
upon he was kept, to be sold abroad. So high an act of dominion
must be recognized by the law of the country where it is used.
The power of a master over his slave has been extremely different, in different countries. The state of slavery is of such a nature, that it is incapable of being introduced on any reasons,
moral or political; but only positive law, which preserves its force
long after the reasons, occasion, and time itself from whence it
was created, is erased from memory: it's so odious, that nothing
can be suffered to support it, but positive law. Whatever inconveniences, therefore, may follow from a decision, I cannot say this

---

[10] The reference is to *Pearne v. Lisle*, referred to n.3 *supra*. A decision
of the Lord Chancellor, sitting in the High Court of Chancery, was not a
binding precedent in the Court of King's Bench. [*Eds*. note.]

case is allowed or approved by the law of England; and therefore the black must be discharged.

QUESTIONS

1. The judicial function.—*Somerset v. Stewart* is an excellent example of the decision by a court in the Anglo-American legal system, in a lawsuit involving two private litigants, of an issue involving wide-ranging social consequences. Under the doctrine of *stare decisis* the courts' decisions on such issues carry great weight in resolution of similar issues in the future. As Thomas Clarkson summed up his description of the *Somerset* case, "Thus ended the great case of Somerset, which, having been determined after so deliberate an investigation of the law, can never be reversed while the British Constitution remains." (p. 65) We will consider later in these materials the question of when, if ever, a court should depart from an earlier precedent. We turn now to some more basic inquiries concerning the nature of the judicial function, as suggested by Lord Mansfield's disposition of the case.

a. Resolving disputes and declaring the law.—In his opinion Mansfield said, "We cannot . . . direct the law; the law must rule us." At the end of his opinion he said, "this case is [not] allowed or approved by the law of England. . . ." What was the "law of England" on the validity of slavery in Great Britain *before* the decision in *Somerset v. Stewart*? As Mansfield's opinion suggests, there were no clear statements of principle on that issue from Parliament or the courts. Is it not fair then to observe that despite his protestations to the contrary Mansfield did indeed "direct" the "law" here? Could he have decided the dispute between Somerset (and Sharp) and Stewart without deciding what the law of England was on the issue of slavery?

What we have here is an illustration of the dual role of a court in our legal system: an official mechanism, *i.e.*, an instrumentality of government, to perform the function of resolving disputes in society, and, in the process, declaring the legal principles by which the disputes will be resolved. In the great mass of disputes, of course, applicable legal doctrine is relatively firmly settled; partly for that reason most disputes do not become lawsuits. But in cases like *Somerset*, and in many cases which make their way into law school casebooks, the law-declaring function of the courts involves the exercise of a creative role. Over the centuries of development of the Anglo-American legal system jurists have debated whether courts "make" law, or, in a less activist role, only "find" the law in cases like *Somerset*. Why, recognizing the necessity that the court somehow determines the principle by which to resolve the previously undecided case, should it make a difference whether the court is viewed as "making" or "finding" the law? In considering this question, think about the role of the legislature: does it "make" or "find" law?

b. Can there be "no law" governing the case?—Is it accurate to describe Mansfield's decision as having declared that slavery was illegal in England? Or did he purport to say only that there was "no law" on the question, and therefore that Stewart lost? Given the creation of courts to resolve disputes, is it sound to conclude that on any aspect of relationships among people there is "no law"? If there were "no law" on the question of the validity of slavery should not the slave Somerset have lost, since he was the moving party? In other words, if there were "no law" on the subject, should not the court be required to leave the parties as they were?

c. Alternative mechanisms for settling disputes.—Courts are one possible institutional means for resolving disputes in society. Is some such official mechanism implicit in the concept of an organized society? The alternative, of leaving the resolution of disputes to private mechanisms and self-help, was suggested in the events preceding *Somerset v. Stewart*. As a result of Granville Sharp's efforts in bringing about the release of the slave Jonathan Strong (see Clarkson, p. 7 *supra*), David Lisle, the slave owner, sued Sharp for damages for depriving him of his property. When Lisle's action for damages failed, he challenged Sharp to a duel. Sharp later wrote:

> David Lisle, Esq., (a man of the law) called on me in Mincing Lane, to demand *Gentlemanlike satisfaction*, because I had procured the liberty of his slave, Jonathan Strong. I told him that as he had studied law so many years, he should want no satisfaction that the law could give him.[11]

Are there other official mechanisms that might be used to resolve disputes such as that in *Somerset v. Stewart*? Consider, for example, the opinion of the Attorney-General and Solicitor-General, in 1729, referred to in the Clarkson extract and Mansfield's opinion, that slavery was valid in England in circumstances like those

---

11 E. Lascelles, Granville Sharp and the Freedom of Slaves in England 22 (1928). Presumably the word "want" is used in the sense of "lack." Sharp later published a pamphlet attacking duelling.

in the *Somerset* case. Mansfield paid "all due attention" to that opinion, but found its conclusion not controlling in his decision. That opinion was rendered by the two chief law officers of the kingdom, in response to inquiries from slave owners. Which mechanism do you prefer as a way to provide for official settlement of disputes: the slave owners' applying to a government official for an opinion, as was done in 1729, or presentation of the dispute to a court, in an adversary proceeding with each party represented by counsel, as was done in 1772? Which of these mechanisms is likely to produce the more thorough exploration of disputed questions of fact? The more exhaustive and disinterested consideration of the competing interests asserted by the parties? Which of these mechanisms is more likely to produce a result that will be acceptable to the losing party and to society generally? Is there not a relationship between the answers to these questions and one's judgment about whether Mansfield could soundly depart from the conclusion which the Attorney-General and Solicitor-General had reached almost half a century before?

2. The grounds for decision.—Considering the nature of the judicial function, should a judge feel obliged to explain his decision? That is, should he give an opinion that can be reduced to writing?

Consider counsel's arguments for Stewart, set forth above. What was Mansfield's reasoning, in coming to the opposite conclusion? Did he adequately respond to those arguments? Should he have provided a more detailed explanation of his conclusions than he did? Should we conclude that Mansfield's decision was, at least insofar as his opinion offers any explanation, based on not much more than his feeling as a private citizen that slavery was "odious"? Is that an adequate basis for a court's declaration of the controlling legal principle in a case before it, or must a court be able to demonstrate reasoned grounds for its decision— *i.e.*, decide the case by reasoning based on underlying principle? The foregoing questions are critical to an understanding of the nature of the judicial function. If a court ought to decide a case on the basis of reasoned elaboration of principle, what are the sources of such principle? The concept of *stare decisis* leads courts to apply principles declared in earlier cases. Statutory principles are also controlling in the courts. But what should a court do in a case like *Somerset v. Stewart*, where there was no controlling judicial precedent or statutory doctrine? If the court had to declare the legal principle in order to decide the case, what factors should the court have considered, and perhaps have articulated in its opinion, in developing the principle which justified the result in *Somerset v. Stewart*? For example, was the consensus of public opinion in England, if it could have been ascertained, relevant? Consider the following extract from Justice Benjamin Cardozo's THE NATURE OF THE JUDICIAL PROCESS 112-13 (1921):*

> My analysis of the judicial process comes then to this, and little more: logic, and history, and custom, and utility, and the accepted standards of right conduct, are the forces which singly or in combination shape the progress of the law. Which of these forces shall dominate in any case, must depend largely upon the comparative importance or value of the social interests that will be thereby promoted or impaired. One of the most fundamental social interests is that law shall be uniform and impartial. There must be nothing in its action that savors of prejudice or favor or even arbitrary whim or fitfulness. Therefore in the main there shall be adherence to precedent. There shall be symmetrical development, consistently with history or custom when history or custom has been the motive force, or the chief one, in giving shape to existing rules, and with logic or philosophy when the motive power has been theirs. But symmetrical development may be bought at too high a price. Uniformity ceases to be a good when it becomes uniformity of oppression. The social interest served by symmetry or certainty must then be balanced against the social interest served by equity and fairness and other elements of social welfare. These may enjoin upon the judge the duty of drawing the line at another angle, of staking the path along new courses, of marking a new point of departure from which others who come after him will set out upon their journey.

Did Mansfield adequately deal with the issue posed by the presence, at that time, of 14,000-15,000 slaves in England, and the apparent reliance by slave owners for almost fifty years on the 1729 opinion of the Attorney General and Solicitor General? Would it have been a wise exercise of the judicial function to hold that from the date of the decision in the *Somerset* case a slave brought to England under the circumstances of the *Somerset* case would be free, but that Stewart and all other slave owners who had brought slaves to England before the decision in the case would retain their slave-ownership rights? Might a judge's

---

response to this question be affected by his attitude toward the question whether he is "making" or "finding" law?

3. Refraining from decision: "deferring" to the legislature.—
Did Lord Mansfield's decision perhaps rest less on a determination of the issue of slavery's validity under English law than on institutional considerations in the legal process? "An application to Parliament," he said, "if the merchants think the question of great commercial concern, is the best, and perhaps the only method of settling the point for the future." And, at the end of his opinion: "The state of slavery is of such a nature, that it is incapable of being introduced on any reasons, moral or political; but only positive law [*i.e.*, apparently, statutory law], which preserves its force long after the reasons, occasion, and time itself from whence it was created, is erased from memory: it's so odious, that nothing can be suffered to support it, but positive law."

There are two possible interpretations of this language in Mansfield's opinion: (a) that the issue before the court, the validity of slavery in England, was an issue which should be resolved by the legislative branch of government, and not by the courts; or (b) that only the legislative branch of government could declare slavery valid, while the courts shared power with the legislative branch to declare slavery invalid (and, on the merits, slavery should be held to be invalid). Can it ever be an appropriate exercise of the judicial function for a court to "defer" to the legislature, saying "We cannot decide this issue; if there is to be law to govern the case, the legislature must be the source of that law"? Is this question only a variation of the question, raised earlier, whether a court ever should conclude that any aspect of relationships among people lacks law to govern it? We now ask whether the very existence of the legislature as a lawmaking institution can justify a court's refusal to decide a case and to declare the governing legal principle. Compare the manner in which Parliament and the Court of King's Bench might alternatively have dealt with the issues related to *Somerset v. Stewart*. Which agency, legislature or court, was better equipped to inform itself about all of the factual data relevant to a decision on the validity of slavery? Which agency could better respond to the slave owners' claim that they should be compensated if slavery were to be invalidated? (Could the court in *Somerset* have dealt with the latter issue at all?) Which agency could better deal with the question whether persons held as slaves in England would now have claims for damages against their former masters? Which agency could better devise solutions for related issues, such as the effect of a ruling of invalidity of slavery in England on the validity of slavery in the colonies? (Could the court in *Somerset* have dealt with that issue?) If a court is convinced that while it might decide an issue before it, the legislature could do a "better" job of dealing with the issue, is it then wise for the court to refrain from deciding the issue? Or would the court then be abdicating its function to decide the case? If a court is to conclude that, until the legislature declares otherwise, the result in a specific case before the court is that a specific party wins, should the court be convinced that that party should prevail on the merits of his case? If a court does "defer" to the legislature, is there any mechanism by which the litigant seeking declaration of a legal principle can require the legislature to consider the issue and vote on it? If such mechanisms do not exist, should they be established?

4. The court as conciliator.—Contrary to Clarkson's statement, in the extract above, that Mansfield was "anxious" to resolve the issue of the validity of slavery in England, the Lord Chief Justice appears to have sought to avoid having to decide the case. In his first opinion, he noted that he had "recommended" that the issue "be accommodated by agreement between the parties." Later in that opinion he noted that "Mr. Stewart may end the question, by discharging or giving freedom" to Somerset. Once the parties bring a dispute before an appropriate court, is it proper for the judge to seek to bring about a settlement of the dispute, or to seek to induce either party to abandon his position?

5. Mr. Dunning's professional ethics in representing first a slave and then a slave owner: the lawyer's ethical obligation to agree to represent a client.—In the 1770 case involving the slave Thomas Lewis (see Clarkson, p. 9 *supra*), John Dunning was counsel for Lewis (and relied in his argument on Granville Sharp's book). Two years later, in *Somerset v. Stewart,* Dunning was one of the attorneys for the slave owner, Stewart. "[H]e was doubtless retained, that his formidable powers might not be called into action" for Somerset.[12] Granville Sharp was indignant at Dunning's representing the master, and "recorded his condemnation of 'an abominable and insufferable practice in Lawyers, to undertake causes diametrically opposite to their own declared opinions of law and common justice.' "[13] Sharp's indignation was

---

[12] 2 H. WOOLRYCH, LIVES OF EMINENT SERJEANTS-AT-LAW 617 (1869).

[13] E. LASCELLES, GRANVILLE SHARP AND THE FREEDOM OF SLAVES IN ENGLAND 30 (1928).

Abraham Lincoln was involved in a similar incident in 1847. Six years before, Lincoln had successfully argued in the Illinois Supreme Court that

perhaps based on two grounds: (a) Dunning's advocacy of a position with which he, Dunning, disagreed ("How can a lawyer defend an individual whom he believes to be guilty?"); (b) Dunning's turnabout, representing a slave owner two years after he had represented a slave on the same issue.

The practices of the legal profession supported Dunning's action, for in England a barrister has traditionally had an obligation to accept a client unless the barrister was otherwise retained. Should a lawyer be obliged to represent a client if he disagrees with the client's position? The American Bar Association Canons of Ethics provide, in Canon 31: "No lawyer is obliged to act either as adviser or advocate for every person who may wish to become his client. He has the right to decline employment."[14] Which approach is the sounder: that of Canon 31 or that of the English rule, under which a barrister "can refuse a brief only if the fee offered is not properly professional, in view of the length and difficulty of the case, . . . [or] under special circum-

---

an alleged slave was free under a presumption of Illinois law that a person was free unless proved to be a slave. Bailey v. Cromwell, 4 Ill. 70 (1841). In 1847 an Illinois farm owner, who annually brought slaves from Kentucky to Illinois to work his farm, sued in an Illinois court, charging the defendant with hiding the slaves and refusing to turn them over to him. The defendant asked Lincoln to represent him.

    As Rutherford told his troubles, he noticed Lincoln growing sober, sad, looking far off, shaking his head in a sorry way. "At length, and with apparent reluctance, Lincoln answered that he could not defend me, because he had already been counselled with in Matson's interest," said Rutherford later. "This irritated me into expressions more or less bitter. He seemed to feel this, and endeavored in his plausible way to reconcile me to the proposition that, as a lawyer, he must represent and be faithful to those who counsel with and employ him. Although thoroughly in earnest I presume I was a little hasty. The interview and my quick temper made a deep impression on Mr. Lincoln, I am sure, because he dispatched a messenger to me followed by another message, that he could now easily and consistently free himself from Matson and was, therefore, in a position if I employed him to conduct my defense. But it was too late; my pride was up. Instead, I employed Charles H. Constable." C. SANDBURG, ABRAHAM LINCOLN: THE PRAIRIE YEARS AND THE WAR YEARS 90 (1954). The court decided against Lincoln's client, apparently concluding that the alleged slaves were not in transit through the state, but had been there long enough to be freed under Illinois law. See Chroust, *Abraham Lincoln Argues a Pro-Slavery Case*, 5 AM. J. LEGAL HIST. 299 (1961).

14 The canons of professional ethics of the American Bar Association were adopted in 1908. Since then they have been added to and amended in substantial part. They have been expressly adopted in the majority of states. Other states maintain their own sets of rules, on occasion commending the canons to members of the bar as a general guide. *See generally* H. DRINKER, LEGAL ETHICS 23-30 (1953). Violations of the canons can result in professional discipline.

stances of conflict of interest, embarrassment, and the like?"[15] Can
a lawyer perform adequately if he disagrees with his client's
position?

Did Sharp have a justifiable grievance with respect to Dunning's doctrinal turnabout? Should lawyers always take consistent positions regardless of the interests of their clients? That is,
should lawyers restrict their services to clients whose interests and
legal positions are similar? In the American bar, at present,
many lawyers are known as plaintiffs' personal injury lawyers, or
"defense" (insurance-company) lawyers, or union lawyers, etc.
Has this been a desirable development?

Assume that a lawyer has two clients whom he is simultaneously representing in wholly separate legal actions. Is there
anything improper about his making one argument in one of
the cases and the exact opposite argument in the other? Does it
make any difference whether the two cases are at the trial stage
or are on appeal to the state's supreme court? Is the problem—
if there is one—that of a possible psychological inability of a lawyer to argue two contradictory positions equally well? Is it the
concern that, no matter what else happens, the lawyer will be
forced to eat his own words? That he will be doing his opposing
counsel's work? That he will confuse the court? Or is the problem simply that a client will not be able to understand his counsel's arguing against his position, even in another case? Does this
latter consideration explain what troubled Sharp?

Dunning did not simultaneously represent conflicting interests.
Should it make any difference that the lawyer *successively* represents conflicting interests? Should it be improper for a lawyer to
take the second case? What factors are relevant in deciding the
propriety of such conduct: The reaction of the first or second
client? The extent to which the lawyer has been privy to confidential disclosures of the first client? General public acceptance?

These questions raise, in a preliminary way, some fundamental
issues about the adversary system of adjudication, and about the
lawyer's function and responsibility within that system. In addi-

---

[15] Rostow, *The Lawyer and His Client*, 48 A.B.A.J. 25, 29 (1962).
WOOLRYCH, n.12, *supra*, at 617-18 n.1, said of the alleged "professional
apostasy" of Dunning:

  The criticisms . . . were made in ignorance of the strict etiquette
  of the Bar. That etiquette is based upon constitutional liberty, for
  every subject in the realm has a right to avail himself of the services
  of any lawyer, unless he be otherwise retained, or unless in office
  under the Crown. Such is the pact under which a barrister enters the
  profession. How far it may be prudent to employ a counsel of decided
  opinions to support particular points, is quite another question. "It is
  my misfortune," said Mr. Dunning, "to address an audience, much the
  greater part of which, I apprehend, wish to find me in the wrong. . . ."

tion to Canon 31, two other A.B.A. canons are relevant here: No. 37: "It is the duty of a lawyer to preserve his client's confidences. This duty outlasts the lawyer's employment, and extends as well to his employees; and neither of them should accept employment which involves or may involve the disclosure or use of these confidences, either for the private advantage of the lawyer or his employees or to the disadvantage of the client, without his knowledge and consent, and even though there are other available sources of such information. A lawyer should not continue employment when he discovers that this obligation prevents the performance of his full duty to his former or to his new client." No. 6: "It is unprofessional to represent conflicting interests, except by express consent of all concerned given after a full disclosure of the facts. Within the meaning of this canon, a lawyer represents conflicting interests when, in behalf of one client, it is his duty to contend for that which duty to another client requires him to oppose. The obligation to represent the client with undivided fidelity and not to divulge his secrets or confidences forbids also the subsequent acceptance of retainers or employment from others in matters adversely affecting any interest of the client with respect to which confidence has been reposed."

6. Was Anglo-American legal history shaped by an inaccurate report of Mansfield's opinion?—It may be that Lord Mansfield never said what Lofft's Reports attributed to him in *Somerset v. Stewart.* Holdsworth's comment (p. 11 *supra,* n.7) that Lofft's Reports "are not of very great authority" may have been borne out in the reporting of the *Somerset* case. Writing in 1934, Edward Fiddes analyzed Mansfield's various statements in *Somerset* (as reported by Lofft) in relation to the report of his statements during the argument of a later case, The King v. The Inhabitants of Thames Ditton, 99 Eng. Rep. 891, 4 Douglas 300 (1785). In that case—so Douglas tells us—Mansfield commented, in response to counsel's argument that the court had never decided that a slave brought to England was still bound to serve his master, "The determinations go no further than that the master cannot by force compel him to go out of the kingdom." Mansfield gave this historical explanation: "In the case relating to villeins, it was held that the lord could not by force take them out of the country." After mentioning *Somerset* in a neutral way, Mansfield added: "Where slaves have been brought here, and have commenced actions for their wages, I have always nonsuited the plaintiff." 99 Eng. Rep. at 892, 4 Douglas at 301. Fiddes concluded: "If the various pronouncements of Mansfield are collated it is clear that he had no thought of proclaiming a complete emancipation of the slave as soon as he touched English soil." Fiddes, *Lord Mansfield and the Sommersett Case*, 50 L.Q. REV. 499, 506 (1934). See also Nadelhaft, *The Somersett Case and Slavery: Myth, Reality and Repercussions*, 51 J. NEGRO HISTORY 193 (1966), noting that another contemporary report of the *Somerset* decision—in *Gentleman's Magazine*, published in 1772—stated the same narrower ground that Mansfield later stated for *Somerset*. (Lofft's Reports were not published until 1776; Nadelhaft suggests that Lofft garbled his transcription, putting into Mansfield's mouth the words of counsel for Somerset.)

But Lofft's report may have been accurate, for Fiddes's conclusions as to what Mansfield said in *Somerset* are not necessarily inconsistent with a declaration by Mansfield of the legal principle that slavery was invalid in England:

> . . . Fiddes . . . gives a good account of . . . Lord Mansfield's fluctuations of opinion; it may be true that Lord Mansfield's decision was, not that the slave was free, but that the master could not forcibly remove him from England . . .; but his decision involved the consequence which Blackstone had previously drawn . . . that "the law will protect him in the enjoyment of his person and his property," so that in effect he was free . . .; the fact that he might be obliged to serve his master was no proof that he was not free; for that was an obligation to which an apprentice was subject; therefore though Lord Mansfield put this limited construction on his own decision, the popular view of its consequences is substantially correct. 11 W. HOLDSWORTH, A HISTORY OF ENGLISH LAW, 247 n.1 (1938).

The preceding interpretations of what Mansfield said and did in his opinion in *Somerset* are illustrative of an ever-present question when courts perform the function of making law. It is at least clear that Mansfield ordered that Stewart not transport Somerset to Jamaica. The question is the scope of the holding— *i.e.*, the content of the principle of law declared by Mansfield—in coming to that decision. Did he declare, without deciding the validity of slavery in England, simply that Somerset could not be sent to Jamaica; or that slavery was valid in England, but a slave held in England could not be sent to Jamaica; or that slavery was invalid in England and, of course, a free man in England could not be sent to Jamaica to be a slave? As we shall see in these materials it is often difficult to agree on what a court has held, even where there is no doubt about the accuracy of the reporter. For purposes of our study of *Somerset v. Stewart* we have taken Lofft's version as the "true" statement of Mansfield's decision, not because we think Lofft was accurate but because his version is the one that came to be accepted. Judges and laymen in England consistently treated the case as if it declared slaves in England to be emancipated, as we shall see in the next case.

After the decision in *Somerset v. Stewart* the next and final steps in the abolition of slavery in England and the British colonies were taken by the legislature. Abolitionist activity intensified, and in 1807 Parliament outlawed the African slave trade. This enactment did not deal with the validity of slavery in the colonies; that was left for an act of Parliament in 1833. But six years before that final statutory abolition there was a judicial opinion which merits study.

THE SLAVE, GRACE
High Court of Admiralty
166 Eng. Rep. 179 (1827)

In 1822, Mrs. Allan of Antigua came to England, bringing with her a female attendant, by birth and servitude a domestic slave, named Grace. She resided with her mistress in this country until 1823, and accompanied her voluntarily on her return to Antigua. . . . She continued with Mrs. Allan, in the capacity of a domestic slave, till August 8th, 1825, when she was seized by the waiter of the customs at Antigua "as forfeited to the King, on suggestion of having been illegally imported in 1823." . . . Mr. Allan then made an affidavit of claim, as sole owner and proprietor of Grace, as his slave. . . . [T]he judge of the Vice-Admiralty Court of Antigua decreed, after argument, that the woman Grace be restored to the claimant. . . .

From this sentence an appeal was prosecuted on the part of the Crown, and the principal question made, was—whether, under the circumstances, slavery was so divested by landing in England that it would not revive on a return to the place of birth and servitude?[16] . . . .

---

16 R. Hildreth, Despotism in America: An Inquiry into the Nature, Results, and Legal Basis of the Slave-Holding System in the United States 208 (1854), described why this action, determining the status of an alleged slave, was brought in a court of admiralty:

The circumstance, however, that she had been in England, was presently set up as having made her free; and since the local courts would not recognize the claim, to give her and others in her condi-

LORD STOWELL.—This case commences with an information against a woman named Grace, who attended her mistress as a domestic servant to England, and returned with her to Antigua; and consists, in the first place, of various counts charging omissions of regulations imposed upon the importation and exportation of slaves to and from the West India colonies; and in consequence thereof, condemnation, or forfeiture to His Majesty, is contended for. . . . The objection, therefore, which constitutes the foundation of this suit and the ground of unlawful treatment is, that she was a free subject of His Majesty and under that character unlawfully imported as a slave and was so treated. Now this averment must be proved: it must be shewn that she was so, for otherwise she has no right to prefer this complaint to the Court; and if that assertion fails, there is no ground whatever for the insinuation of her being unlawfully treated; for that assertion of her freedom is the foundation of the wrong of which she complains: if she cannot plead with truth that she was a free subject there is no ground of complaint in her being treated as a slave: her rights are not violated and she has no injured rights to represent. It may be a misfortune that she was a slave; but being so, she in the present constitution of society had no right to be treated otherwise.

I have looked with the utmost attention to discover, if possible, the foundation of her complaint—that she being a free person is treated as a slave. The truth of that complaint depends upon the nature of that freedom, if any, which she enjoyed before the institution of this suit; and I can find nothing that warrants any such assertion of a freedom so conferred. The sole ground upon which it appears to have been asserted is, that she had been resident in England sometime as a servant waiting upon her mistress, but without the enjoyment of any manumission that could alone deliver her from the character of a slave which she carried with her when she left Antigua; for I think it demonstrable that she could derive no character of freedom that could entitle her to maintain a suit like this (founded upon a claim of permanent freedom) merely by having been in England, without manumis-

---

tion the chance of an English adjudication, without the heavy expenses of an ordinary appeal, (if indeed it were possible by the ordinary course of appeal, to carry such a case to England), she was libelled in the Vice Admiralty Court of Antigua, as having been introduced into that island as a slave, contrary to the acts abolishing the slave trade; and the local admiralty judge having decided against her, the case came before Lord Stowell by appeal. Thus, while the alleged owner was making a claim against the customs official, the real dispute in this case was between the alleged owner and the alleged slave. [*Eds.* note.]

sion; for a manumission is a title against all the world. The mode of treatment applied to such persons is a strong illustration between the effect produced by a residence in England and that conferred by a manumission; for manumissions are not uncommon in England and always granted where there is an intention of giving the party an absolute title to freedom. This suit, therefore, fails in its foundation: she was not a free person; no injury is done her by her continuance in a state of slavery, and she has no pretentions to any other station than that which was enjoyed by every slave of the family. If she depends upon such a freedom, conveyed by a mere residence in England, she complains of a violation of right which she possessed no longer than whilst she resided in England, but which had totally expired when that residence ceased and she was imported into Antigua; and that is the proposition which I propose to make good in the course of the following observations. . . .

The question has been argued as depending upon the interpretation of the well-known case of *Sommersett* . . . in which a *habeas corpus* was granted, directed to Capt. Knowles, to bring up the body of Sommersett, a negro, which was in his possession in irons, with the cause of his detention. The affidavits stated, that Sommersett had been bought in Virginia and brought to England by Mr. Steuart, his master; and on his refusing to return was sent by his master on board Knowles's ship to be carried to Jamaica and sold as a slave. It appears that, some time before, this case was argued upon a question addressed to Lord Talbot and to Mr. Yorke, whilst Attorney and Solicitor-General. They gave it as their opinion, that a slave coming from the West Indies, either with or without his master, to Great Britain, doth not become free, and that his master's property or right in him is not thereby determined or varied; and they were also of opinion that the master might legally compel him to return to the plantations; and, as Lord Mansfield expresses it, "they both pledged themselves to the merchants in London to save them harmless from all inconvenience on such a subject," which pledge was afterwards very fully confirmed by a similar judgment pronounced in 1749 by Sir Philip Yorke, then become Lord Chancellor Hardwicke, sitting in the Court of Chancery (STATE TRIALS, vol. xx, pp. 4, 81): both of these persons being great men of that age, and, as Lord Mansfield admits, great men in any age. This judgment so pronounced in full confidence, and without a doubt upon a practice which had endured universally in the colonies, and (as appears by those opinions) in Great Britain, was, in no more than twenty-two years afterwards, reversed by Lord Mansfield. The personal traffic in slaves resident in England had been as public and as authorised in London as in any of our West India islands. They were sold on the Exchange and other places of public resort by parties themselves resident in London, and with as little reserve as they would have been in any of our West India possessions. Such a state of things continued without impeachment from a very early period up to nearly the end of the last century.

It appears that Lord Mansfield was extremely desirous of avoiding the necessity of determining the question: he struggled hard to induce the parties to a compromise, and said, he had known five cases so terminated out of six; but the parties were firm to their purpose in obtaining a judgment, and Lord Mansfield was at last compelled after a delay of three terms to pronounce a sentence, which, followed by a silent concurrence of the other judges, discharged this negro; thereby establishing that the owners of slaves had no authority or control over them in England, nor any power of sending them back to the colonies. Thus fell, after only two-and-twenty years, in which decisions of great authority had been delivered by lawyers of the greatest ability in this country, a system, confirmed by a practice which had obtained without exception ever since the institution of slavery in the colonies, and had likewise been supported by the general practice of this nation and by the public establishment of its Government, and it fell without any apparent opposition on the part of the public. The suddenness of this conversion almost puts one in mind of what is mentioned by an eminent author, on a very different occasion, in the Roman History, *"Ad primum nuntium cladis Pompeianæ populus Romanus repente factus est alius"*: the people of Rome suddenly became quite another people.

The real and sole question which the case of *Sommersett* brought before Lord Mansfield, as expressed in the return to the *mandamus*, was, whether a slave could be taken from this country in irons and carried back to the West Indies, to be restored to the dominion of his master? And all the answer, perhaps, which that question required was, that the party who was a slave could not be sent out of England in such a manner and for such a purpose; stating the reasons of that illegality. It is certainly true that Lord Mansfield in his final judgment amplifies the subject largely. He extends his observations to the foundation of the whole system of the slavery code; for in one passage he says, that "slavery is so odious that it cannot be established without positive law." Far from me be the presumption of questioning any *obiter dictum* that fell from that great man upon that occasion; but I trust that I do not depart from the modesty that belongs to my situation, and I hope to my character, when I observe, that ancient custom is generally recognised as a just foundation of all law; that villenage of both kinds, which is said by some to be the prototype of slavery, had no other origin than ancient custom; that a great part of the common law itself in all its relations has little other foundation than the same custom; and that the practice of slavery, as it exists in Antigua and several other of our colonies, though regulated by law, has been in many instances founded upon a similar authority. Much occurs in the discussion of the advocates on that question respecting villenage, but little appears in the decision of Lord Mansfield upon that point. . . .

It may, perhaps, be doubted whether the emancipation of slaves in England, pronounced at the end of the last century, was not rather more owing to the increased refinement of the sentiments and manners of the age than to the decay of the two systems of villenage, one of which had expired two hundred years before, and the other one hundred and fifty years at least, and which then only slumbered in the memory of a few antiquaries. The opinion of Lord Mansfield upon this immediate subject makes a very small part of his celebrated speech; it is almost confined to a particular portion of it. There is hardly anything else that is expressed, save several well-merited civilities to the gentlemen of his bar, and some expressions of contempt for the danger and jealousy that might be encountered, but of which none ever appear to have occasioned any reasonable alarm. Thus fell a system which had existed in this country without doubt, and which had been occasionally forced upon its colonies and has continued to this day—that is, above fifty years—without further interruption. . . .

It is very observable, that Lord Mansfield, when he struggles hard to decline the office of determining the question, confines that question almost in terms to this country; he limits it expressly to *this country,* for he says, "the *now* question is, Whether any dominion, authority, or coercion can be exercised on a slave in this country according to the American laws, meaning thereby the laws of the West Indies? The service performed by the slaves without wages is a clear indication that they did not consider themselves free by coming here." In the final judgment he delivers himself thus: "The state of slavery is so odious that nothing can be suffered to support it but positive law": that is, the slavery as it existed in the West Indies; for it is to that he looks, considering that many of the adjuncts that belonged to it there were not admissible under the law of England.

Lord Mansfield very justly observes, that "if the merchants consider the prohibition of slavery in this country of sufficient commercial concern, an application to Parliament is the best, and, perhaps, the only method of settling the point for the future." In conformity with this advice, it is much to be lamented that application was not made to Parliament to settle the question upon a right footing, if it were still to be considered as a *dependent* question. It might have saved a world of trouble and suffering to both parties, which is now to be produced by the springing up of this question at a very late hour of the day. Persons, though possessed of independence and affluence acquired in the mother-country, have upon a return to the colony been held and treated as slaves; and the unfortunate descendants of these persons, if born within the colony, have come slaves into the world, and in some instances have suffered all the consequences of real slavery; and the proprietors of these slaves are now called upon to give up to the public all the slaves that they have thus acquired; and this not only in Antigua, but most probably in all the islands of the Archipelago: for it cannot be supposed that this claim, if maintained with respect to *this* island, will not be extended to all the others. These are matters that might have cost at that time of day comparatively little expense and little suffering; but which now cannot be settled without a gross violation of important interests on one side or the other. . . .

The public inconvenience that might follow from an established opinion that negroes became totally free in consequence of a voyage to England, without any express act that declared them to be so, is not altogether to be overlooked. It is by no means improbable that, with such a temptation presented to them, many slaves might be induced to try the success of various combinations to procure a conveyance to England for such purpose; and, by returning to the colony in their newly-acquired state of freedom, if permitted, might establish a numerous population of free persons, not only extremely burdensome to the colony, but, from their sudden transition from slavery to freedom, highly dangerous to its peace and security. . . . The fact is, that in England, where villenage of both sorts went into total decay, we had communication with no other country; and, therefore, it is triumphantly declared, as I have before observed, "once a freeman ever a freeman," there being no other country with which we had immediate connection, in which, at the time of suppressing that system, we had any occasion to trouble ourselves about. But slavery was a very favoured introduction into the colonies: it was deemed a great source of the mercantile interest of the country; and was, on that account, largely considered by the mother-country as a great source of its wealth and strength. Treaties were made on that account and the colonies compelled to submit to those treaties by the authority of this country. This system continued entire. Instead of being condemned as *malus usus*, it was regarded as a most eminent source of its riches and power. It was at a late period of the last century that it was condemned in England as an institution not fit to exist here, for reasons peculiar to our own condition; but it has been continued in our colonies favoured and supported by our own Courts, which have liberally imparted to it their protection and encouragement. To such a system, whilst it is so supported, I rather feel it to be too strong to apply the maxim, *malus usus abolendus est*. The time may come when this institution may fall in the colonies, as other institutions have done in other flourishing countries; but I am of opinion that it can only be effected at the joint expense of both countries; for it is in a peculiar manner the crime of this country; and I rather feel it to be an objection to this species of emancipation, that it is intended to be a very cheap measure here by throwing the whole expense upon the colony.

It has been said that the law of England discourages slavery, and so it certainly does within the limits of these islands; but the law uses a very different language and exerts a very different force when it looks to her colonies; for to this trade in those colonies it gives an almost unbounded protection, and it is in the habit of doing so at the present time in many exercises of public authority; and even since slavery has become odious in England, it has been fully supported by the authority of many statutes for the purpose of carrying it into full effect in the colonies. All the efforts of the persons who have contended for the abolition of slavery in the colonies, and who have obtained many Acts of Parliament for the regulation of it therein, have in no degree weakened the force of those English statutes which so powerfully support it in the mother-country.

It has been observed, that the sovereign state has declared, that all laws made in the colonies, contradicting its own law, shall be null and void, and cannot be put in execution; but is that the character of the laws in the colonies for the encouragement of the proprietors of slaves? Has it not, since the declaration of its judgment against slavery, declared, in the most explicit and authentic manner, its encouragement of slavery in its colonial establishments? Have not innumerable Acts passed which regulate the condition of slaves, and which tend to consider them, as the colonists themselves do, as *res positae in commercio*, as mere goods and chattels, as subject to mortgages, as constituting part of the value of estates, as liable to be taken in execution for debt—to be publicly sold for such purposes; and has it not established Courts of the highest jurisdiction for the carrying into execution provisions for all these purposes; and these its most eminent Courts of Justice—its Court of the King's Privy Council, and its Courts of Chancery, where all these regulations are carried into effect with most scrupulous attention and under the authority of Acts of Parliament? Can any man doubt that at this time of day slaves in the colonies may be transferred by sale made in England, and which would be affirmed without reference to the Court so empowered; for the Acts of Parliament, including the recent Consolidation Act (5 G. IV, c. 113, s. 37),[17] prescribe and regulate the manner in which these transfers of slaves are to be securely made in this kingdom, and the mode to be adopted where money is lent on mortgage upon the security of slaves; and how, under the guarantee of such protection, can it be asserted that the law of England does not support, and in a high degree favour, the law of slavery in its West India colonies, however it may discourage it in the mother-country? Is it not most certain that this trade of the colonies has been the very favourite trade of this country, and so continues, so far as can be judged from encouragement given in various forms—the making of treaties, the institution of trading companies, the devolution of property from one company to another, the compulsion of the colonies to accept this traffic, and the recognition of it in a great variety of its laws? If it be a sin, it is a sin in which this country has had its full share of the guilt, and ought to bear its proportion of the redemption. How this country can decline to perform the act of justice, in performing the act of charity, men of great wisdom and integrity have not been able to discover. . . .

That persons brought up with the expectation of considerable wealth, acquired in this or other countries, should be subjected to the reverses of fortune which may befall them, upon visiting the country of their parents at an advanced period of life, is a most severe hardship; that they should be compelled to submit to the humiliation which may attend them in any acquired situations, upon such return, is to be much lamented; but these are matters happily within the power, and certainly within the justice, of Parliament to remedy by some general correctives. Lord Mansfield, I observe, recommended to the merchants to make application to Parliament for any purposes which they might deem requisite on the subject. It cannot, I think, be de-

---

17 The Consolidation Act of 1824 amended and consolidated previous statutes dealing with the abolition of the slave trade. Section 37, referred to by Lord Stowell, reenacted an 1819 statute that required the registration of slaves (see n.20 infra), specifying in some detail how sales and mortgages of slaves were to be formalized. This legislation surely does give Parliament's recognition to slavery in the colonies. Does it also decide the case before Lord Stowell? [Eds. note.]

nied, that there are purposes for which such an application might be deemed eminently useful. Cases in which the representatives of families, who have acquired property in England or elsewhere, and who have returned at a very mature age to those islands, are certainly very fit objects to be relieved from a state of interminable slavery; for a return to a condition of slavery must operate upon them and others, who are at all under similar circumstances, with an unjust severity; and, at any rate, the humanity of Parliament could not be employed to a more beneficent effect, if the colonists themselves should neglect to interfere. . . .

These are the conclusions to which I have arrived, after a very full and mature consideration of the subject. I can truly say that I arrived at those conclusions with a mind free from any prepossession upon the subject, and with the determination to attend to nothing but the fair result of the evidence which applies to it. I am sensible that other opinions may be formed upon the question; but, in affirming the sentence of the Judge of the Court below, I am conscious only of following that result which the facts not only authorise but compel me to adopt.

Sentence affirmed, with costs.

QUESTIONS

1. The court's evaluation of the competing interests in The Slave, Grace.—Lord Stowell's opinion identifies, to a far greater extent than did Mansfield's opinion in *Somerset v. Stewart,* some of the factors to be considered in deciding the case. The precise issue before the court—assuming the invalidity of slavery in England and its validity in Antigua—was whether the petitioner, formerly resident in England, could be held as a slave in Antigua. Parliament had not spoken on this issue, and in Lord Stowell's view *Somerset* was not a controlling precedent.

Facing what he considers to be a "new" issue, Lord Stowell points out on the one hand the "severe hardship" imposed on individuals again to be held in slavery upon return to a colony, and on the other hand such factors as reliance interests of masters who had invested in such slaves for fifty years after the decision in *Somerset,* the dangers to peace and security in the colony from a large population of persons recently and suddenly emancipated, and the significance of slavery in the colonies to the mercantile welfare of England and the colonies. Can the court soundly appraise and weigh these social interests in the context of the precise issue before it? Is Lord Stowell's reasoning clear, in explaining why he reached the result he did? Consider the

following extract from B. CARDOZO, THE NATURE OF THE JUDI-
CIAL PROCESS 113-15 (1921):*

> If you ask how [the judge] is to know when one interest
> outweighs another, I can only answer that he must get his
> knowledge just as the legislator gets it, from experience
> and study and reflection; in brief, from life itself. Here,
> indeed, is the point of contact between the legislator's
> work and his. The choice of methods, the appraisement of
> values, must in the end be guided by like considerations
> for the one as for the other. Each indeed is legislating
> within the limits of his competence. No doubt the limits
> for the judge are narrower. He legislates only between
> gaps. He fills the open spaces in the law. . . . [W]ithin the
> confines of these open spaces and those of precedent and
> tradition, choice moves with a freedom which stamps its
> action as creative. The law which is the resulting product
> is not found, but made. The process, being legislative, de-
> mands the legislator's wisdom.

"The legislator's wisdom" is normally informed from such sources
as testimony in committee hearings. Does it appear from the
opinion in *The Slave, Grace* that Lord Stowell was adequately
informed about the factual background for his lawmaking? How
can a court acquire such information?

Lord Stowell's careful discussion of the interests at stake in his
legislative decision omits any consideration of the interest of a
slave in freedom. (He does mention the injustice of enslaving a
freeman.) Is that omission consistent with the proper performance of the judicial function? Why do you suppose Lord Stowell
failed to discuss the point?

2. The precedent of Somerset v. Stewart.—To what extent
should Lord Stowell have considered the case before him to be
governed by the decision in *Somerset v. Stewart*? At the very least
the declaration of law in *Somerset* that slavery was invalid in
England, and that a slave brought to England from a colony
which recognized slavery could not be held as a slave in England,
was a declaration on one issue which was involved in *The
Slave, Grace*. Arguably, *Somerset* even held that a slave brought
to England was thereby emancipated, *i.e.*, free thereafter both
in England and in the colonies. Why should a judge in deciding

---

* Copyright 1921, Yale University Press.

a case consider giving weight to a decision of an earlier court on the same or an analogous issue? A number of reasons are often suggested. Mansfield's decision, though not so articulated in his opinion, presumably had been the product of his evaluation of social interests similar to those now involved in *The Slave, Grace,* and the wisdom and experience of the past may be of value in deciding a current issue. And reliance on earlier decisions can relieve a court from the wasteful necessity of redetermining every issue which comes before it. But more important than these considerations are others related to the function of courts and the role of law in society: (a) Consider the infinite number of transactions in which people plan their affairs in reliance on what they understand will be the legal consequences of their actions. (b) Recall the statement, p. 18 *supra,* in an extract from Cardozo's, *The Nature of the Judicial Process,* that "One of the most fundamental social interests is that law shall be uniform and impartial." How does the doctrine of *stare decisis* advance that social interest? (c) Consider, finally, the lawmaking roles of the legislature and of the courts. Does the doctrine of *stare decisis* serve a needed function in setting limits to the judge's lawmaking function? See generally R. WASSERSTROM, THE JUDICIAL DECISION (1961).

Somerset *v.* Stewart was then, under the doctrine of *stare decisis,* of great relevance to the decision of *The Slave, Grace.* Unless Lord Stowell was ready to reopen the issue of the validity of slavery in England, *Somerset* had settled that issue for the case now before him. The remaining question was whether *Somerset* also had settled the issue whether a slave brought to England was, by virtue of that fact, emancipated throughout the British colonies.

In *The Slave, Grace* it was contended on behalf of the alleged slave that she had been emancipated by being in England. The authority for this contention, of course, was *Somerset v. Stewart.* Did Mansfield decide (a) that Somerset had been emancipated, so that he was a free man throughout the British Empire, or (b) simply that the status of master and slave, valid under colonial law, had been suspended while Somerset and Stewart were in England? How would you argue that *Somerset* stands for the legal principle that a slave brought to England by his master is emancipated? The specific assertion of dominion over Somerset as a slave which was attacked was a physical seizure of him in order to return him to the colonies. If Mansfield were holding only that the master-slave relationship was suspended while the parties were in England, would it not have been consistent for him to decide that it was permissible for the

owner to assert dominion over Somerset for the purpose of taking
him to Jamaica? Would that not be the one right of a slave owner
most likely to survive in England if, as Mansfield's opinion assumed, slavery was valid in the colonies but not in England?
Since *Somerset* held that not even that form of dominion of the
owner over the slave was permissible in England, does that holding also imply that the slave was emancipated? There is language
in Mansfield's opinion on this issue:

> The now question is whether any dominion, authority or
> coercion can be exercised in this country, on a slave ac-
> cording to the American laws? The difficulty of adopting
> the relation, without adopting it in all its consequences, is
> indeed extreme; and yet many of those consequences are
> absolutely contrary to the municipal law of England. We
> have no authority to regulate the conditions in which law
> shall operate.

Would it have made any sense to limit the exercise of dominion
by an owner over a slave in England to cases involving the purpose of returning the slave to a colony? If that limited dominion
were accepted, would it not be necessary to give the owner full
powers over the slave during the entire time the parties were in
England, so as to assure that the owner would be able to return
the slave to the colonies whenever he chose to do so? The decision that Somerset was not subject to Stewart's control in order
to return him to a colony may then be not necessarily a recognition of emancipation, but rather a practical decision that if *any*
rights of the master under colonial law were to be given effect
in England, then *all* such rights would have to be vindicated.
Should we conclude, then, that no compelling answer can be
given as to the implications of *Somerset v. Stewart* on the issue
of emancipation of Somerset? The specific issue in *The Slave,
Grace* was not before the court in *Somerset,* and the prohibition
of exercise of control over Somerset is consistent either with a
conclusion that Somerset was emancipated or a conclusion that
he was not.

Lord Stowell commented on his opinion in *The Slave, Grace*
in a letter to Justice Joseph Story of the United States Supreme
Court in May, 1828:

> I desire to be understood as not at all deciding the
> question upon the lawfulness of the slave trade, upon
> which I am rather a stern Abolitionist, but merely this nar-
> row question, whether the Court of King's Bench, in the

case of Sommersett, meant to declare that our non-execution of the slave code in England was a new suspension of it as respected England, but left it in full operation with respect to the colonies,—which some of our Abolitionists here and some of our Judges resolutely contend for. My clear opinion is for its limited effect. The execution of the Code laws is suspended in England, as being thought inconsistent with the nature as well as the institutions of this country. So far as it goes, but no farther, it does not at all derogate from the law of the colonies upon the return of the party so partially liberated here; this is the whole of the question which I had occasion to consider, and is a question which has nothing to do with the general legality of the slave trade in the colonies. How the laws in respect of that trade made in England and enforced by our courts of law, the King's Privy Council, and the Court of Chancery, to their utmost extent, can consist with any notion of its entire abolition here, is, in my view of it, an utter impossibility.

I am a friend to abolition generally, but I wish it to be effected with justice to individuals. Our Parliaments have long recognized it and have not only invited, but actually compelled our colonies to adopt it, and how, under such circumstances it is to be broken up at the sole expense of the colonist, I cannot see consistent with either common reason or common justice; it must be done at the common expense of both countries; and upon that part of the case very great difficulties exist. Our zealots are for leaping over them all, but in that disposition I cannot hold them to be within the wise or the just part of this nation. W. STORY, LIFE AND LETTERS OF JOSEPH STORY 554-55 (1851).

THE ACT ABOLISHING SLAVERY IN THE COLONIES

The final step in the abolition of slavery in the British colonies occurred in 1833, with the enactment by Parliament of "An Act for the Abolition of Slavery throughout the British colonies; for promoting the Industry of the manumitted Slaves; and for compensating the Persons hitherto entitled to the Services of such Slaves." 3 & 4 Will. 4, c. 73 (1833). This was legislatively declared law, as compared with the judicially declared law in *Somerset v. Stewart* which, in effect, invalidated slavery in England.

1. The content of the Act: an early use of the administrative process, and a contrast to judicially declared abolition.—The emancipation pattern adopted in the 1833 English statute was complex. The bill's draftsmen sought to deal (a) with concerns that emancipation should be gradual rather than abrupt, because the slaves were not prepared for sudden freedom, and (b) with what Lord Stowell, in his letter to Justice Story, had called the "very great difficulties" in avoiding placing the "sole expense" of the loss of their slaves on the owners. The legislative response to these arguments focused on use of the administrative process. Parliament set forth general guidelines for emancipation, and charged administrative officers with filling in details and carrying out the legislatively-declared principles. The Act thus turned over much of the substance of the system of emancipation to administrators, who were to declare or make law, and apply that law in the resolution of specific disputes—all within the Parliamentary guidelines.

The statute was enacted in August 1833, and took effect in August 1834. It abolished slavery in the British colonies, and changed the status of persons who were then slaves to "apprenticed Labourers." The status of "apprentice" was to end in 1840. (In Chapter 2 we shall see an analogous use of gradualism by the United States Supreme Court in its "all deliberate speed" formula in *Brown v. Board of Education.*) A fund of twenty million pounds sterling was established to pay compensation for the loss of the services of the emancipated slaves. A commission was created to inquire into and decide claims to compensation. The commissioners were to be appointed by the King. No compensation was to be paid to anyone in a colony until a finding had been made that the colony had made adequate legal provision to give effect to the Act, and particularly the Act's requirement that the colonial legislature adopt standards to regulate the new form of apprenticeship. The commissioners were to apportion the twenty million pounds among the colonies according to the number of slaves in each colony and the average price at which slaves had been sold in each colony during a specified period. The commissioners were to frame rules "for securing the just and equitable distribution" of the funds so apportioned, considering such matters as joint ownership, the ownership rights of married women and children, the rights of mortgagees of slaves, and the like. These rules were to be published in the *London Gazette*,[18] and an appeal to His Majesty in Council was available

---

18 "The official publication of the English government. . . . It is evidence of acts of state, and of everything done by the king in his political capacity." BLACK'S LAW DICTIONARY 839 (3d ed. 1933).

to anyone "interested in or affected by" such rules who wished to contest the validity of any of the rules, *i.e.*, to contend that the commissioners had exceeded their statutory authority. The rules, once final, were to have the same force and effect as if they had been enacted by Parliament. The commissioners were also to adjudicate individual claims to compensation, with an appeal for a claimant whose claim was rejected to His Majesty in Council. At the appellate stage new evidence could not be introduced.

This scheme, placing both legislative and adjudicatory functions in the commissioners, was a precursor of the way in which a vast portion of lawmaking and law-applying takes place in the United States today. Some functions of the National Labor Relations Board, the Securities and Exchange Commission, and the Federal Trade Commission are examples. This use of the administrative process to adjudicate massive numbers of individual claims today finds parallels in the United States, *e.g.*, the Department of Health, Education, and Welfare, which adjudicates old-age and survivors' insurance claims, and claims for disability insurance under the federal Social Security Act; and state agencies that adjudicate claims for public assistance and unemployment insurance. Some American lawyers and law firms specialize in representing clients in the administrative process.

Think again about Lord Mansfield's opinion in *Somerset v. Stewart,* where the court declared a rule of emancipation that applied to 14,000-15,000 slaves in England. No effort was made in that decision to deal either with the claim of the slave owners to compensation or with the asserted need for gradualism in granting the slaves freedom. When the legislature dealt with the emancipation of approximately 750,000 slaves in the colonies,[19] the result was the complex plan described above. Would it have been appropriate for Mansfield, as part of his decision in *Somerset,* to have declared that Stewart should have compensation from the public treasury, ordering that such compensation be paid? And to have added, perhaps, an order that an administrative agency be created, with powers and functions similar to those provided in the 1833 Act, to determine how much Stewart, and any others with claims of ownership in Somerset, should receive? Or to have ordered some type of intermediate "apprentice" status for Somerset to be in effect for a specific period, as the 1833 Act did? Are there some kinds of law which courts are not empowered to declare, even in the context of decision of a specific case? What are the criteria for identifying that type of law? Is it appropriate, then, for a court to "defer" to the legislature for

---

[19] F. KLINGBERG, THE ANTI-SLAVERY MOVEMENT IN ENGLAND 293 (1926).

declaration of this type of law? Assume that in *Somerset v. Stewart* Lord Mansfield was of the view that Stewart should receive compensation from the public treasury and that Somerset should be an "apprentice" for a specified period. If Mansfield, as a judge, could not deal effectively with those issues, how should he have disposed of *Somerset v. Stewart?* Should he, for example, have said, "I am of the opinion that slavery is contrary to the law of England. I am of the opinion, too, that Stewart should be compensated from public funds, and that Somerset should occupy the intermediate status of apprentice for a period of years. Since I cannot, as a judge, effectuate the latter conclusions, I have no choice but to return Somerset to Captain Knowles, for shipment to Jamaica or such other disposition of him that Stewart may wish to make, including continuing to hold him as a slave in England"?

2. The role of lawyers in the legislative process.—Lawyers made significant contributions to the action of Parliament in 1833. Three names stand out:

> . . . James Stephen, . . . and his two sons, Sir James and Sir George. James Stephen fought for the abolition of the slave trade; he devised the system of registration;[20] he wrote the leading treatise on slavery. Sir James became the most influential man in the colonial office and drafted the emancipation act. Sir George organized the agency committee of the Anti-Slavery Society and conducted the whirlwind campaign during the two years prior to the emancipation act of 1833. The services of these high spirited men, all of them lawyers, were invaluable. . . . F. KLINGBERG, THE ANTI-SLAVERY MOVEMENT IN ENGLAND 185 (1926).

The activities of the Stephens illustrate a role of lawyers in the legal system other than as representatives of litigating parties in the judicial process. Sir James Stephen, as a government official, drafted the 1833 statute, a typical task for a lawyer in government. James and Sir George Stephen were advocates, in various ways, of legislative action. Issues concerning the ethical obligations of lawyers arise with respect to their role in the legislative process as they do in the judicial process. Consider A.B.A. Canon 26: "A lawyer openly and in his true character may render pro-

---

20 The Registration Act, which took effect in 1820, was designed to control illicit traffic in slaves by registering all the slaves in the West Indies. No slave could be transferred without a certificate of registration; an unregistered slave was presumed to be free. [*Eds.* note.]

fessional services before legislative and other bodies, regarding proposed legislation and in advocacy of claims before departments of government, upon the same principles of ethics which justify his appearance before the Courts; but it is unprofessional for a lawyer so engaged to conceal his attorneyship, or to employ secret personal solicitations, or to use means other than those addressed to the reason and understanding to influence action."

Would Canon 26 be violated—and what should an attorney's ethical obligations be regardless of Canon 26—in the following situations: (a) advocating, before a legislative committee, on behalf of a client, legislation which would be contrary to the interests of a present or former client; (b) meeting alone with individual legislators to urge, on behalf of a client, favorable action on a bill before the legislature; (c) seeking, on behalf of a client, to persuade a legislator to support a bill before the legislature by arguing that a contrary vote will be unpopular in the legislator's district and will likely lead to his defeat at the next election; (d) appearing, on behalf of a client, before a legislative committee in support of a bill being considered by the committee, and making only arguments in favor of the client though the attorney feels that some features of the bill significantly conflict with the "public interest"?

B.   ABOLITION OF SLAVERY IN THE UNITED STATES

At the time of the adoption of the Constitution some of the original states in the United States had already acted to abolish slavery. The Vermont Constitution of 1777, for example, in its "Declaration of Rights of Inhabitants of Vermont," provided that "no male person, born in this country, or brought from over sea, ought to be holden by law, to serve any person, as a servant, slave or apprentice, after he arrives to the age of twenty-one years, nor female, in like manner, after she arrives at the age of eighteen years, unless they are bound by their own consent. . . ." Pennsylvania, in 1780, and Rhode Island, in 1784, enacted statutes for the "gradual abolition of slavery." The Pennsylvania statute, Act of March 1, 1780, c. 146, provided that no person born in the state after the date of enactment should be deemed a slave. Slaves' children were to be considered as indentured servants, until age twenty-eight, of the master of their parents. Rhode Island's statute, Acts and Resolves, p. 6 (Feb. 1784), similarly provided that no children born in the state after the date of enactment should be deemed to be slaves. In order that such children could remain with their mothers a "convenient time" after birth and that those who claimed the services of the mothers could support the children in a "becoming manner," the support of such children was made an obligation of the towns in which the mothers and children resided. Importation of slaves into the state was prohibited. New York abolished slavery in two statutory steps, in 1799 and 1817. The 1799 statute, Act of March 29, 1799, c. 62, provided that any child born of a slave in the state after July 4, 1799, was "born free." Such a child was considered to be a servant of the legal proprietor of the mother in the same manner as if the child had been apprenticed to service by the overseers of the poor, until the age of twenty-eight for males and twenty-five for females. The 1817 statute, Act of March 31, 1817, c. 137, declared every Negro within New York born before July 4, 1799, to be free from and after July 4, 1827. Importation of slaves was prohibited, and any slave illegally imported became free.

The abolition of slavery in Massachusetts occurred by state constitutional provision in 1780, as interpreted by a judicial decision in 1783. In 1781, the Massachusetts Superior Court of Judicature had held that a Negro, Quock Walker, was free. His putative master, Nathaniel Jennison, had accused Walker's employers of enticing him away. Walker's former master had promised to manumit him. Yet his attorney, Levi Lincoln,[21] argued on the broader ground that slavery was contrary to natural law, and could not exist in the absence of positive law—the ground that Lord Mansfield had stated for his decision in *Somerset v. Stewart*. In holding that Walker was free, the Massachusetts court did not state a reason for its ruling. Then in 1783, Jennison was charged with an assault on Walker, made in order to require him to return to service:

> Chief Justice William Cushing, in his charge to the jury in this case, rejected Jennison's plea that his actions merely constituted legitimate correction of a runaway slave. Cushing held that Walker was a freeman because of the promised manumission. He went further. The chief justice held that although slavery had been tolerated in Massachusetts, it was incompatible with the new spirit "favorable to the natural rights of mankind." The new constitution declared all men to be free and equal and guaranteed their liberty and their right to life and property. Therefore, "without resorting to implication in constructing the constitution, slavery is . . . as effectively abolished as it can be by the granting of rights

---

[21] Later Attorney General of the United States and Governor of Massachusetts. [*Eds.* note.]

and privileges wholly incompatible and repugnant to its existence." A. ZILVERSMIT, THE FIRST EMANCIPATION: THE ABOLITION OF SLAVERY IN THE NORTH 114 (1967).[22]

In the southern states there was, at the time of the adoption of the Constitution, a considerable body of legal doctrine concerning slavery, and this doctrine was afterward expanded, by statutory and case law. We shall not here attempt to study this body of law. In general, state law set forth the owner's right to the slave's "time, labor and services," and to his obedient compliance with all lawful commands. The owner had legal duties to provide the slave with food and clothing, and with care in sickness and in old age. Legal doctrine covered such matters as: who was a slave; the owner's right to sell the slave or his labor; the denial to slaves of rights to own property, to be parties to contracts, or to enter into binding marriages; criminal penalties for the theft of slaves; aspects of sales of slaves, such as misrepresentation of the condition of a slave; civil liability to the owner for injuring a slave; and prohibitions against teaching slaves to read or write. See K. STAMPP, THE PECULIAR INSTITUTION 192-236 (Vintage ed. 1956). A comprehensive collection of judicial decisions on slavery is contained in the five volumes of H. CATTERALL, JUDICIAL CASES CONCERNING AMERICAN SLAVERY AND THE NEGRO (1926). The Constitution of the United States as originally adopted contained three provisions which represented a compromise position, for the new Nation, on the question of the validity of slavery. Article I, section 2 provided that members of the House of Representatives and direct taxes should be apportioned by population, counting as three-fifths of a person each person other than "free Persons, including those bound to Service for a Term of Years, and excluding Indians not taxed." Article I, section 9 precluded Congress from prohibiting prior to the year 1808 the "Importation of Such Persons as any of the States now existing shall think proper to admit." And Article IV, section 2, provided that "No Person held to Service or Labour in one State, under the Laws thereof, escaping into another, shall, in Consequence of any Law or Regulation therein, be discharged from such Service or Labour, but shall be delivered up on Claim of the Party to whom such Service or Labour may be due."[23] The result of the adop-

---

22 *See also* Cushing, *The Cushing Court and the Abolition of Slavery in Massachusetts: More Notes on the "Quock Walker Case,"* 5 AM. J. LEGAL HIST. 118 (1961). [*Eds.* note.]

23 For development of the argument that these provisions of the Constitution did not acknowledge the legal validity of slavery under the laws of

tion of the Constitution was to leave to each state the development of its own position on the validity of slavery. For a discussion of early decisions of the United States Supreme Court relating to slavery, see Roper, *In Quest of Judicial Objectivity: The Marshall Court and the Legitimation of Slavery*, 21 STAN. L. REV. 532 (1969). Within the federal union, the dominant legal issues concerning slavery during the first half of the nineteenth century were raised by the fugitive-slave question. We shall explore only the aspects of those issues that paralleled the issues in *Somerset v. Stewart* and *The Slave, Grace.*

COMMONWEALTH v. AVES
Supreme Judicial Court of Massachusetts
35 Mass. (18 Pick.) 193 (1836)

SHAW, C.J., delivered the opinion of the Court. The question now before the Court arises upon a return to a habeas corpus, ... for the purpose of bringing up the person of a colored child named Med,[24] and instituting a legal inquiry into the fact of her detention, and the causes for which she was detained. . . . [The owner] claims to have the child as master, and carry her back to New Orleans, and . . . to hold and return her as a slave. . . .

The precise question presented by the claim of the respondent is, whether a citizen of any one of the United States, where negro slavery is established by law, coming into this State, for any temporary purpose of business or pleasure, staying some time, but not acquiring a domicil here, who brings a slave with him as a personal attendant, may restrain such slave of his liberty during his continuance here, and convey him out of this State on his

---

the slave states, see R. HILDRETH, DESPOTISM IN AMERICA: AN INQUIRY INTO THE NATURE, RESULTS, AND LEGAL BASIS OF THE SLAVE-HOLDING SYSTEM IN THE UNITED STATES 230-39 (1854). At the end of his book Hildreth made the following comment on the bar: "Assuming and conscientiously believing, as no doubt all of those who have consciences do,—though conscience is not commonly regarded as indispensable to a 'consummate lawyer,'—that slavery is one of 'the public institutions of their country,' guaranteed and endorsed by the Federal constitution, . . . all their skill and subtlety is employed, not in reforming the tyranny of darker ages, but in twisting new whips and forging new fetters, to perpetuate that tyranny to the latest times, and to diffuse it over the whole face of the country. What I have written on the subject of the legal basis of slavery, I have not written with the least expectation of producing any effect upon lawyers or judges already committed to different views; or, indeed, upon any lawyer more than forty years of age. Harvey did not convert a single physician above that age to his view of the circulation of the blood; and as to new views, whether true or false, lawyers and doctors, for obvious reasons, are very much alike." *Id.* at 300.

24 The child's age was six years. [*Eds.* note.]

return, against his consent. It is not contended that a master can exercise here any other of the rights of a slave owner, than such as may be necessary to retain the custody of the slave during his residence, and to remove him on his return.

Until this discussion, I had supposed that there had been adjudged cases on this subject in this Commonwealth; and it is believed to have been a prevalent opinion among lawyers, that if a slave is brought voluntarily and unnecessarily within the limits of this State, he becomes free, if he chooses to avail himself of the provisions of our laws; not so much because his coming within our territorial limits, breathing our air, or treading on our soil, works any alteration in his *status*, or condition, as settled by the law of his domicil, as because by the operation of our laws, there is no authority on the part of the master, either to restrain the slave of his liberty, whilst here, or forcibly to take him into custody in order to his removal. There seems, however, to be no decided case on the subject reported.

It is now to be considered as an established rule, that by the constitution and laws of this Commonwealth, before the adoption of the constitution of the United States, in 1789, slavery was abolished, as being contrary to the principles of justice, and of nature, and repugnant to the provisions of the declaration of rights, which is a component part of the constitution of the State.

It is not easy, without more time for historical research than I now have, to show the course of slavery in Massachusetts. . . . Slavery to a certain extent seems to have crept in; not probably by force of any law, for none such is found or known to exist; but rather, it may be presumed, from that universal custom, prevailing through the European colonies, in the West Indies, and on the continent of America, and which was fostered and encouraged by the commercial policy of the parent states. That it was so established, is shown by this, that by several provincial acts, passed at various times, in the early part of the last century, slavery was recognized as existing in fact, and various regulations were prescribed in reference to it. . . .

How, or by what act particularly, slavery was abolished in Massachusetts, whether by the adoption of the opinion in Sommersett's case, as a declaration and modification of the common law, or by the Declaration of Independence, or by the constitution of 1780, it is not now very easy to determine, and it is rather a matter of curiosity than of utility; it being agreed on all hands, that if not abolished before, it was so by the declaration of rights. . . .

Without pursuing this inquiry farther, it is sufficient for the purposes of the case before us, that by the constitution adopted in 1780, slavery was abolished in Massachusetts, upon the ground that it is contrary to natural right and the plain principles of justice. The terms of the first article of the declaration of rights are plain and explicit. "All men are born free and equal, and have certain natural, essential, and unalienable rights, which are, the right of enjoying and defending their lives and liberties, that of acquiring, possessing, and protecting property." It would be difficult to select words more precisely adapted to the abolition of negro slavery. According to the laws prevailing in all the States, where slavery is upheld, the child of a slave is not deemed to be born free, a slave has no right to enjoy and defend his own liberty, or to acquire, possess, or protect property. That the description was broad enough in its terms to embrace negroes, and that it was intended by the framers of the constitution to embrace them, is proved by the earliest contemporaneous construction, by an unbroken series of judicial decisions, and by a uniform practice from the adoption of the constitution to the present time. The whole tenor of our policy, of our legislation and jurisprudence, from that time to the present, has been consistent with this construction, and with no other.

Such being the general rule of law, it becomes necessary to inquire how far it is modified or controlled in its operation; either,

1. By the law of other nations and states, as admitted by the comity of nations to have a limited operation within a particular state; or

2. By the constitution and laws of the United States.

In considering the first, we may assume that the law of this State is analogous to the law of England, in this respect; that while slavery is considered as unlawful and inadmissible in both, and this because contrary to natural right and to laws designed for the security of personal liberty, yet in both, the existence of slavery in other countries is recognized, and the claims of foreigners, growing out of that condition, are, to a certain extent, respected. Almost the only reason assigned by Lord *Mansfield* in Sommersett's case was, that slavery is of such a nature, that it is incapable of being introduced on any reasons moral or political, but only by positive law; and, it is so odious, that nothing can be suffered to support it but positive law. . . .

But although slavery and the slave trade are deemed contrary to natural right, yet it is settled by the judicial decisions of this country and of England, that it is not contrary to the law of nations. . . . The consequence is, that each independent community, in its intercourse with every other, is bound to act on the principle, that such other country has a full and perfect authority to make such laws for the government of its own subjects, as its own judgment shall dictate and its own conscience approve, provided the same are consistent with the law of nations; and no independent community has any right to interfere with the acts or conduct of another state, within the territories of such state, or on the high seas, which each has an equal right to use and occupy; and that each sovereign state, governed by its own laws, although competent and well authorized to make such laws as it may think most expedient to the extent of its own territorial limits, and for the government of its own subjects, yet beyond those limits, and over those who are not her own subjects, has no authority to enforce her own laws, or to treat the laws of other states as void, although contrary to its own views of morality. . . .

Upon a general review of the authorities, and upon an application of the well established principles upon this subject, we think they fully maintain the point stated, that though slavery is contrary to natural right, to the principles of justice, humanity and sound policy, as we adopt them and found our own laws upon them, yet not being contrary to the laws of nations, if any other state or community see fit to establish and continue slavery by law, so far as the legislative power of that country extends, we are bound to take notice of the existence of those laws, and we are not at liberty to declare and hold an act done within those limits, unlawful and void, upon our views of morality and policy, which the sovereign and legislative power of the place has pronounced to be lawful.

. . . So, in pursuance of a well known maxim, that in the construction of contracts, the *lex loci contractus* shall govern, if a person, having in other respects a right to sue in our courts, shall bring an action against another, liable in other respects to be sued in our courts, upon a contract made upon the subject of slavery in a state where slavery is allowed by law, the law here would give it effect. . . .

The conclusion to which we come from this view of the law is this:

That by the general and now well established law of this Commonwealth, bond slavery cannot exist, because it is contrary to natural right, and repugnant to numerous provisions of the constitution and laws, designed to secure the liberty and personal rights of all persons within its limits and entitled to the protection of the laws.

That though by the laws of a foreign state, meaning by "foreign," in this connection, a state governed by its own laws, and between which and our own there is no dependence one upon the other, but which in this respect are as independent as foreign states, a person may acquire a property in a slave, such acquisition, being contrary to natural right, and effected by the local law, is dependent upon such local law for its existence and efficacy, and being contrary to the fundamental laws of this State, such general right of property cannot be exercised or recognized here.

That, as a general rule, all persons coming within the limits of a state, become subject to all its municipal laws, civil and criminal, and entitled to the privileges which those laws confer; that this rule applies as well to blacks as whites, except in the case of fugitives, to be afterwards considered; that if such persons have been slaves, they become free, not so much because any alteration is made in their *status,* or condition, as because there is no law which will warrant, but there are laws, if they choose to avail themselves of them, which prohibit, their forcible detention or forcible removal.

That the law arising from the comity of nations cannot apply; because if it did, it would follow as a necessary consequence, that all those persons, who, by force of local laws, and within all foreign places where slavery is permitted, have acquired slaves as property, might bring their slaves here, and exercise over them the rights and power which an owner of property might exercise, and for any length of time short of acquiring a domicil; that such an application of the law would be wholly repugnant to our laws, entirely inconsistent with our policy and our fundamental principles, and is therefore inadmissible.

Whether, if a slave, voluntarily brought here and with his own consent returning with his master, would resume his condition as a slave, is a question which was incidentally raised in the argument, but is one on which we are not called on to give an opinion in this case, and we give none. From the principle above stated, on which a slave brought here becomes free, to' wit, that he becomes entitled to the protection of our laws, and there is no law to warrant his forcible arrest and removal, it would seem to follow as a necessary conclusion, that if the slave waives the protection of those laws, and returns to the state where he is held as a slave, his condition is not changed. . . .

The question has thus far been considered as a general one, and applicable to cases of slaves brought from any foreign state or country; and it now becomes necessary to consider how far this result differs, where the person is claimed as a slave by a citizen of another State of this Union. As the several States, in all matters of local and domestic jurisdiction are sovereign, and independent of each other, and regulate their own policy by their own laws, the same rule of comity applies to them on these subjects as to foreign states, except so far as the respective rights and duties of the several States, and their respective citizens, are affected and modified by the constitution and laws of the United States.

In *art*. 4, § 2, the constitution declares that no person held to service or labor in one State, under the laws thereof, escaping into another, shall in consequence of any law or regulation therein, be discharged from such service or labor, but shall be delivered up on claim of the party to whom such service or labor may be due.

The law of congress made in pursuance of this article provides, that when any person held to labor in any of the United States, &c. shall escape into any other of the said States or Territories, the person entitled, &c. is empowered to arrest the fugitive, and upon proof made that the person so seized, under the law of the State from which he or she fled, owes service, &c. Act of February 12, 1793, c. 7, § 3.

In regard to these provisions, the Court are of opinion, that as by the general law of this Commonwealth, slavery cannot exist, and the rights and powers of slave owners cannot be exercised therein; the effect of this provision in the constitution and laws of the United States, is to limit and restrain the operation of this general rule, so far as it is done by the plain meaning and obvious intent and import of the language used, and no further. The constitution and law manifestly refer to the case of a slave escaping from a State where he owes service or labor, into another State or Territory. He is termed a fugitive from labor; the proof to be made is, that he owed service or labor, under the laws of the State or Territory *from which he fled*, and the authority is given to remove such fugitive to the State *from which he fled*. This language can, by no reasonable construction, be applied to the case of a slave who has not fled from the State, but who has been brought into the State by his master.

The same conclusion will result from a consideration of the well known circumstances under which this constitution was formed. Before the adoption of the constitution, the States were to a certain extent, sovereign and independent, and were in a condition to settle the terms upon which they would form a more perfect union. It has been contended by some overzealous philanthropists, that such an article in the constitution could be of no binding force or validity, because it was a stipulation contrary to natural right. But it is difficult to perceive the force of this objection. It has already been shown, that slavery is not contrary to the laws of nations. It would then be the proper subject of treaties among sovereign and independent powers.

Suppose instead of forming the present constitution, or any other confederation, the several States had become in all respects sovereign and independent, would it not have been competent for them to stipulate by treaty that fugitive slaves should be mutually restored, and to frame suitable regulations, under which such a stipulation should be carried into effect? Such a stipulation would be highly important and necessary to secure peace and harmony between adjoining nations, and to prevent perpetual collisions and border wars. It would be no encroachment on the rights of the fugitive; for no stranger has a just claim to the protection of a foreign state against its will, especially where a claim to such protection would be likely to involve the state in war; and each independent state has a right to determine by its own laws and treaties, who may come to reside or seek shelter within its limits, and to prescribe the terms. Now the constitution of the United States partakes both of the nature of a treaty and of a form of government. It regards the States, to a certain extent, as sovereign and independent communities, with full power to make their own laws and regulate their own domestic policy, and fixes the terms upon which their intercourse with each other shall be conducted. In respect to foreign relations, it regards the people of the States as one community, and constitutes a form of government for them. It is well known that when this constitution was formed, some of the States permitted slavery and the slave-trade, and considered them highly essential to their interest, and that some other States had abolished slavery within their own limits, and from the principles deduced and policy avowed by them, might be presumed to desire to extend such abolition further. It was therefore manifestly the intent and the object of one party to this compact to enlarge, extend and secure, as far as possible, the rights and powers of the owners of slaves, within their own limits, as well as in other States, and of the other party to limit and restrain them. Under these circumstances the clause in question was agreed on and introduced into the constitution; and as it was well considered, as it was intended to secure future peace and harmony, and to fix as precisely as language could do it, the limit to which the rights of one party should be exercised within the territory of the other, it is to be presumed that they selected terms intended to express their exact and their whole meaning; and it would be a departure from the purpose and spirit of the compact to put any other construction upon it, than that to be derived from the plain and natural import of the language used. Besides, this construction of the provision in the constitution, gives to it a latitude sufficient to afford effectual security to the owners of slaves. The States have a plenary power to make all laws necessary for the regulation of slavery and the rights of the slave owners, whilst the slaves remain within their territorial limits; and it is only when they escape, without the consent of their owners, into other States, that they require the aid of other States, to enable them to regain their dominion over the fugitives. . . .

The constitution and laws of the United States, then, are confined to cases of slaves escaping from other States and coming within the limits of this State without the consent and against the will of their masters, and cannot by any sound construction extend to a case where the slave does not escape and does not come within the limits of this State against the will of the master, but by his own act and permission. The provision is to be construed according to its plain terms and import, and cannot be extended beyond this, and where the case is not that of an escape, the general rule shall have its effect. It is upon these grounds we are of opinion, that an owner of a slave in another State where slavery is warranted by law, voluntarily bringing such slave into this State, has no authority to detain him against his will, or to carry him out of the State against his consent, for the purpose of being held in slavery.

This opinion is not to be considered as extending to a case where the owner of a fugitive slave, having produced a certificate according to the law of the United States, is *bona fide* removing such slave to his own domicil, and in so doing passes through a free State; where the law confers a right or favor, by necessary implication it gives the means of enjoying it. Nor do we give any opinion upon the case, where an owner of a slave in one State is *bona fide* removing to another State where slavery is allowed, and in so doing necessarily passes through a free State, or where by accident or necessity he is compelled to touch or land therein, remaining no longer than necessary. Our geographical position exempts us from the probable necessity of considering such a case, and we give no opinion respecting it. . . .

QUESTIONS

1. **The analogy to Somerset v. Stewart.**—The issue in *Commonwealth v. Aves* was similar to that in *Somerset v. Stewart,* and the Massachusetts court reached the same result as the Court of King's Bench: slavery was invalid in Massachusetts, and an out-of-state slave owner could not in this case exercise dominion over the slave in Massachusetts in order to return the slave to another state where slavery was valid. In *Somerset* the issue arose

within the British Empire, with a central government and subordinate colonies. Was the issue the same in *Aves*, where two
states were involved, each of them an equal member of a federal
union of states, each having power under the Constitution to
determine the validity of slavery for itself?

2. Chief Justice Shaw's constitutional interpretation.—The *Aves*
opinion refers to earlier decisions of the Massachusetts court, interpreting the state constitution of 1780, that slavery was invalid
in that state. In *Aves* it was argued that a provision of the United
States Constitution required Massachusetts to permit the owner
to exercise dominion over the slave in order to return her to
Louisiana, and Chief Justice Shaw's opinion includes an interpretation of that section of the Constitution in order to decide
the case. These are illustrations of a court's performing the function of interpreting, in the context of a specific case, a written
instrument in which controlling legal principle for decision of
the case is presumably to be found. In these cases the written
instruments were constitutions, state and federal—the highest
sources of law in the American legal system. Courts perform a
similar interpretive function with respect to statutory law enacted by legislatures, and, in an analogous sense, with respect to
the "law" that private parties make to govern themselves in contractual transactions. Chief Justice Shaw's handling of the federal constitutional issue in *Aves* is an excellent starting place for
consideration of this function of courts. In reflecting upon the
questions which follow it should be kept in mind that the court's
function in *Aves* was, in a general way, the same as that performed by the courts that decided *Somerset v. Stewart* and *The
Slave, Grace*, and, indeed, by all courts: The court had a specific
dispute before it; in order to resolve that dispute, the court had
to declare the applicable legal principle. In *Aves* the court had
to consider whether the Federal Constitution, among other potential sources of doctrine, provided the governing rule on the
owner's asserted right to exercise dominion over the slave in
Massachusetts, invalidating the Massachusetts common-law rule,
declared in *Aves*, which otherwise would free the slave.

The federal constitutional provision was Article IV, section 2:

> No Person held to Service or Labour in one State, under
> the Laws thereof, escaping into another, shall, in Conse-
> quence of any Law or Regulation therein, be discharged
> from such Service or Labour, but shall be delivered up on
> Claim of the Party to whom such Service or Labour may be
> due.

In *Commonwealth v. Aves,* the court decided that this section of the Constitution did not compel Massachusetts to recognize the owner's rights under the laws of Louisiana. The common law of Massachusetts, declared by the court in this case (that the owner could not assert dominion over the slave in Massachusetts for the purpose of returning the slave to Louisiana), therefore could be given effect.

The constitutional issue in *Aves* centered on interpretation of the words "escaping into" in the above-quoted clause from Article IV, section 2. Chief Justice Shaw concluded that these words referred only to slaves "coming within the limits of this State without the consent and against the will of their masters," and did not include slaves who came to Massachusetts by the "act and permission" of the owner.

What was the reasoning that justified Chief Justice Shaw's conclusion? Was his reasoning consistent with a sound exercise of the judicial function in interpreting a written Constitution?

a. **The purposes behind Article IV, section 2.**—One approach to understanding a court's function in interpreting a written instrument like the Federal Constitution can begin with this language in Chief Justice Shaw's opinion in *Commonwealth v. Aves,* p. 50 *supra:* ". . . it would be a departure from the purpose and spirit of the compact to put any other construction upon it, than that to be derived from the plain and natural import of the language used." Presumably there was some purpose or reason, or combination of purposes or reasons, for including each provision of the Constitution. In giving meaning to the words "escaping into" in Article IV, section 2, should not the court seek to implement the purposes of that provision? Part of Shaw's opinion examined into those purposes. Article IV, section 2, he said, was one of the compromises of the Constitution, reflecting the interests of slave states and free states. Restoration of fugitive slaves "would be highly important and necessary to secure peace and harmony. . . . Besides, this construction of the provision in the constitution, gives to it a latitude sufficient to afford effectual security to the owners of slaves. The States have a plenary power to make all laws necessary for the regulation of slavery and the rights of the slave owners, whilst the slaves remain within their territorial limits; and it is only when they escape, without the consent of their owners, into other States, that they require the aid of other States, to enable them to regain their dominion over the fugitives." Pp. 50, 51 *supra.* After considering the consequences of a decision either way on the meaning of "escaping into," Shaw concluded that the purposes of Article IV, section 2, would be better served if the section were limited to fugitive slaves.

Perhaps this analysis of the purposes of Article IV, section 2, could have been spelled out more fully. Would it be useful, in making such an analysis, to state the issue in *Aves* this way: Article IV, section 2, clearly includes the case of the fugitive slave who flees into another state. We must now decide whether the reasons for the rule in Article IV, section 2, with respect to a fugitive slave are sufficiently present in the case of a slave taken by his owner to a free state so that the latter case should be decided in the same way as that of the fugitive slave. Shaw suggested at least two reasons for the rule in Article IV, section 2, about fugitive slaves: (a) advancement of peace and harmony among the states, and (b) provision of effectual security for the owners of slaves who might run away to other states. To what extent were these two reasons present where the owner voluntarily took the slave into a free state? Certainly the case of the fugitive slave was a more serious one for both the slave owner and the slave state; if owners could not recapture slaves who fled north, it was believed, a threat of some magnitude was posed to the entire institution of slavery. The depth of this feeling was demonstrated in the southern insistence on a strong federal fugitive-slave law. The threat to the system was far less serious if a slave owner were prevented from asserting dominion over a slave whom he had brought into a free state. Any threat in the latter case could be controlled by refraining from taking slaves into free states. The interests of free states in the fugitive and non-fugitive cases were arguably different as well. As had been suggested by Lord Mansfield in *Somerset v. Stewart,* recognition of a right in the owner to assert dominion within the state over a slave he had brought into the state, in order to return the slave to another state, might, in a practical sense, require recognition of other aspects of the master-slave relationship, so as to protect the owner's right to return the slave whenever he wished to do so. The case of the fugitive slave, however, would not raise, to the same extent, the possibility of the continued presence of owner and slave within the free state, with the ever-present issue as to what their relationship should be during the time before the owner might attempt to return the slave. If we consider Article IV, section 2, as a compact between free states and slave states—an effort to accommodate fundamentally opposed positions—was not Chief Justice Shaw's interpretation of the words "escaping into" the meaning of the words which better effectuated the purposes of that delicate compromise in the Constitution? In the remainder of these materials, we give the name "purpose-oriented approach" to this analysis of a court's function in interpreting written declarations of law.

b. The "plain meaning" of the words.—In his opinion, Chief Justice Shaw used other language frequently used by courts in interpreting constitutions, statutes, and other documents. Shaw said that he was seeking to determine the "plain meaning and obvious intent and import of the language used." The "plain and natural import" of the words in Article IV, section 2, led to his conclusion: "This language can, by no reasonable construction, be applied to the case of a slave who has not fled from the State, but who has been brought into the State by his master." Pp. 49, 50 *supra*.

Perhaps all that Chief Justice Shaw meant was that a consideration of the purposes of Article IV, section 2, led to the conclusion the court reached, and the words of the Constitution "plainly" meant that. But a court's reference to "plain meaning" sometimes connotes something else: a process of interpretation which does not profess to implement the purposes of the legal standard involved, but limits itself to study of the words alone. One way to point up the distinction is to consider this question: Assume that a purpose-oriented interpretation of Article IV, section 2, led to the conclusion that the principle of that provision applied also in the case of a slave who had been brought to a free state by his owner. Would an interpretation of Article IV, section 2, to reach that result strain the words to an impermissible degree? That is, could the words "escaping into" permissibly carry that meaning? If they could, then there is no single "plain meaning" of those words. The word "escape" has been used to convey meanings other than "to flee from detention or confinement." Among other meanings, the word "escape" has been used to convey "to get safely out of," "to avoid." And the word "into" has occasionally been used to mean "in." All of these we learn from dictionaries. 3 A NEW ENGLISH DICTIONARY ON HISTORICAL PRINCIPLES 283 (1897); 5 *Id.* at 430; WEBSTER'S NEW INTERNATIONAL DICTIONARY 871, 1302 (2d ed. 1948); WEBSTER'S NEW INTERNATIONAL DICTIONARY 774, 1184 (3d ed. 1961). Among the linguistically permissible meanings (among the "reasonable constructions") of Article IV, section 2, could have been these: no person held as a slave in one state, who (a) flees to another state, or (b) gets safely out of or avoids his condition of slavery by traveling with his owner to a free state, or (c) flees from the master while both are in the free state, shall be made free by application of the laws of the free state. If the words of Article IV, section 2, could reasonably bear these meanings, judicial determination of the controlling meaning must rest on more than an attempt to discover the one "plain meaning" of the words. The governing meaning should be selected, should it not, by determining which of the competing meanings will more faithfully carry out the purposes of the general principles declared in the written instrument?

c. The "intent" of the framers.—Chief Justice Shaw referred also to the "obvious intent" of the language used. Language of this kind is often found in judicial opinions interpreting written instruments, particularly in this form: "What did the founding fathers (legislature) (contracting parties) intend?" It is useful to make a distinction between what we have described as a purpose-oriented approach and one meaning which courts may have in mind in using this "intent" terminology. A judge may be using this "intent" language as if he were determining the meaning the men who adopted the words "intended" them to bear in the specific fact situation now before the court. Such an analysis raises problems of great difficulty. For one thing, *whose* intent matters? With respect to Article IV, section 2, of the United States Constitution, would the court seek to determine the intent of the committee which drafted the section? All those in the Constitutional Convention who voted to include the section as drafted? All those who participated in one way or another in the ratification of the Constitution in each of the states? More importantly, phrasing the issue of interpretation in terms of "intent" of the lawmaker may lead a court to try to ascertain a collective subjective intent that never existed. For example, there appears to be nothing in the records of the Constitutional Convention, not to mention the records of ratification proceedings in the states, to demonstrate that anyone even considered whether "escaping" slaves would include slaves whose owners took them temporarily to a free state, much less decided that question.

It may seem odd to conclude that the search for "the intent of the lawmaker" with respect to the specific case before the court may be doomed to failure, and at the same time to take seriously a search for legislative "purposes." The important point here does not relate to definitions, but to function. The "purposes" of a constitutional provision or of a statute, as we use the term, are also a construct of the judicial mind; they may, in fact, be "purposes" that no one had in view when the constitution or statute was adopted. The inquiry into "purpose" may lose some of its metaphysical quality if we focus on the task that faces the judge: to decide the concrete case before him. The lawmakers

who produced the written declaration of law may not have foreseen the specific case; indeed, if the constitutional or statutory
provision does clearly specifically dispose of the case, it is surprising that the issue has survived until the stage of litigation.
The harder and more typical case is that in which it cannot be
confidently concluded that the lawmakers have expressed themselves on the specific issue before the court. What we have called
a purpose-oriented approach will permit the judge to interpret
the legislative language in such a case. With the concrete case
before him in mind, the judge must articulate a set of "reasons
for the rule" in cases where the constitutional or statutory provision clearly applies, in order to determine whether the rule
applies now. In this analysis, interpretation of a written declaration of law takes on the character of reasoning by analogy, not
unlike a judge's reasoning when he considers prior judicial precedent.

In any case, it seems fair to say that when a judge uses the
"intent" of the legislative body as the basis for his interpretation,
he may not, in fact, be relying on a discovered collective subjective intent, but may instead be rationalizing the result he has
reached. Why does a court, called upon to decide which of the
possible meanings of words in a written declaration of law shall
prevail, resort to this "intent" terminology in explaining its
decision? For a careful analysis of the various possible questions
suggested by an inquiry into legislative intent, and a comprehensive discussion of the classical literature on the subject, see
MacCallum, *Legislative Intent,* 75 YALE L.J. 754 (1966).

**3. Chief Justice Shaw's comments on the issues he was not de-
ciding.**—At the end of his opinion Chief Justice Shaw said that
the court was not giving "any opinion upon the case, where an
owner of a slave in one State is *bona fide* removing to another
State where slavery is allowed, and in so doing necessarily passes
through a free State, or where by accident or necessity he is compelled to touch or land therein, remaining no longer than necessary." Earlier in the opinion Shaw referred to the question
whether a slave voluntarily brought to Massachusetts who consents to return with the slave owner to a slave state would resume
his condition as a slave. This issue, Shaw said, was one "on
which we are not called on to give an opinion in this case, and we
give none." But in the following sentence Shaw suggested the
"necessary conclusion" that "would seem to follow in such a
case"—that he would resume his condition as a slave. Should
Shaw also have opined about the status of a slave who was brought
into Massachusetts in transit to a slave state, or who, with the

slave owner, was in Massachusetts "by accident or necessity" for a transitory period? Does it serve any constructive purpose for a judge to *identify* issues he is not deciding? Compare Shaw's treatment of the slave who voluntarily returns with the slave owner to a slave state. There he expressed his view on how that issue ought to be resolved, though he disclaimed giving an opinion (*i.e.,* deciding the issue). Does it serve any constructive purpose for a judge to *express his thoughts* about an issue he is not deciding?

An insight into why Shaw, having identified two issues he was not deciding, gave his thoughts about one and not the other, is suggested by his general views about slavery. In 1820, when he was a practicing lawyer, and 16 years before *Aves*, he wrote an article in which he argued for gradual abolition of slavery in the slave states. He emphasized the importance of due recognition by states in the United States of the laws and policies of other states:

> The question whether slavery shall continue in those states, or whether it shall in any way be modified or limited, we consider as exclusively a question of local jurisdiction belonging to those states respectively; and whatever may be our wishes and our hopes upon the subject, we expressly disclaim any legal or constitutional authority on the part of any other state or of the United States, to interfere in any arrangements respecting slavery, which those states respectively may think fit to adopt. *Slavery and the Missouri Question,* 10 No. Am. Rev. 137, 141 (1820).

Perhaps his statement in *Aves* on the issue of the slave who consents to return to the slave state was an effort to make clear that the result in *Aves* would have only a limited effect on slave states. But as his opinion in *Aves* indicates, he was firmly of the view that the status of slavery should not be enforced *in* Massachusetts. If he had expressed his views on the issues of slaves and slave owners in transit through the state or in the state "by accident or necessity," perhaps he would have suggested that the slave owner could not exercise dominion over the slave in order to return him to a slave state. And that view might have appeared to him to suggest too great a negation of the policies of slave states to be articulated in a case in which it was not necessary to opine on the issue. In short, perhaps Shaw, having isolated two issues which need not have been decided in order to decide *Aves,* went on to opine only about the issue in which his opinion would be less inflammatory to the south. Shaw later was called upon to decide a case involving the transitory presence in Massachusetts of a slave owner and slave, analogous to the cases on which he expressed no opinion in *Aves*. A United States naval officer from a slave state arrived in Boston harbor aboard a naval vessel with a slave as his personal servant. The ship had been on a Pacific voyage, and Boston was the first port it entered upon its return. Shaw, sitting as a trial judge in a habeas corpus proceeding, held that the officer could not assert his rights as a slave owner in Massachusetts, and the slave was in effect freed. "Where," he said, "a slave is in Massachusetts casually, not being a runaway, whether he is brought here voluntarily by his master or not, there is no law here to authorize his restraint." L. LEVY, THE LAW OF THE COMMONWEALTH AND CHIEF JUSTICE SHAW 70 (1957).

One year after *Commonwealth v. Aves*, a closely similar issue came before the Connecticut Supreme Court of Errors. The Connecticut decision, which turned on interpretation of statutes enacted by the Connecticut legislature, raises additional questions about a court's function in interpreting a written instrument which declares legal principles.

JACKSON v. BULLOCH
Supreme Court of Errors of Connecticut
12 Conn. 39 (1837)

WILLIAMS, Ch. J. The question in this case is, whether *Nancy Jackson*, the petitioner, can, by the laws of this state be detained here longer, in a state of slavery; and it is a question of deep interest to this community, how far our laws tolerate slavery within our limits.

That every human being has a right to liberty, as well as to life and property, and to enjoy the fruit of his own labour; that slavery is contrary to the principles of natural right and to the great law of love; that it is founded on injustice and fraud, and can be supported only by the provisions of positive law, are positions, which it is not necessary here to prove. Indeed, a discussion of many of the principles contended for, on the part of the applicant, has become unnecessary, in this case, in consequence of the admissions made by the counsel for the respondent. It was expressly conceded that slavery was a system of such a character, that it can claim nothing by the law of comity, which prevails among friendly states upon subjects of a different class;

that it was local, and must be governed entirely by the laws of the state, in which it is attempted to be enforced. We do not, therefore, propose to examine the authorities, which have been cited, but refer to the able opinion of the supreme court of Massachusetts, in the case of *The Commonwealth v. Aves*, decided in *August*, 1836, and the authorities there cited. *Somerset's* case. . . .

It was further admitted, by the counsel for the respondent, that there is nothing in the constitution of the United States applicable to this case: That the article in that instrument providing, that persons held to service in one state, *escaping* into another state, shall not thereby be discharged, but shall be delivered up, upon claim of the party to whom such labour or service was due, applied only to slaves escaping from their masters, and not to those voluntarily brought in by them. . . .

In England, it is well settled, that slavery does not exist in that country; that a slave coming from another country—even their own colonies—was free, the moment he placed his feet upon English ground. *Somerset's* case. . . .

It is said, however, this is not our law; because slavery exists here, to a certain extent. It cannot be denied, that in this state, we have not been entirely free from the evil of slavery; and a small remnant still remains to remind us of the fact. So far as slavery is sanctioned by law, so far those who are to expound the law, are to give it effect, but no further. How or when it was introduced into this state, we are not informed. We find no traces of it in our earliest statutes. It probably crept in silently, until it became sanctioned, by custom or usage. Did it depend entirely upon custom or usage, perhaps it would not be too late to enquire, whether a custom so utterly repugnant to the great principles of liberty, justice and natural right, was that *reasonable* custom, which could claim the sanction of law. But we find, that for nearly a century past, the system of slavery has been, to a certain extent, recognized, by various statutes, designed to modify, to regulate, and, at last, abolish it; and thus, we think, it has received the implied sanction at least of the legislature.

The question, however, arises, to what extent was slavery permitted; and how far is it now tolerated? The counsel for the petitioner contend, that slavery does not exist at all in Connecticut, or, if it exists at all, it is only as to persons born before the year 1784, and, of course, not as to this woman. This they attempt to show from the constitution of this state, and from legislative enactments. . . .

[W]e feel bound to declare, as the result of our examination of the constitution of this state, that its provisions do not, and were not intended to vary the relation of master and servant, as by law established, at the time of the adoption of that instrument. And in this opinion, the court are unanimous.

This brings us to the question, what was the state of our law upon this subject, at the time of the adoption of the constitution of this state; for it has not since been varied.

The first step taken for the suppression of slavery was at a time when the public pulse beat high in favour of liberty; when our fathers were smarting under the oppressive acts of the British government; a short time after the decision in Somerset's case, which proclaimed liberty to the slave in England; and a few months before the first blood was shed for liberty in this country, *viz.* in *October*, 1774. A law was then passed to prevent the importation of slaves into this state, by sea or land. And almost as soon as the war, which gave to us liberty and peace, had terminated, another law was enacted, declaring, that no negro or mulatto, born in this state after the first of *March*, 1784, should be held in servitude longer than until they arrived to the age of 25 years; which was subsequently reduced to 21 years.

Thus, it would seem, that ample provision was made for the final extinction of slavery in this state, as soon as the slaves then alive had passed from the stage. No attempt, indeed, was made to set at liberty those who were then in bondage; but public opinion and the influence of these laws led to the voluntary emancipation of many. No general proclamation was made, that slavery was abolished. But as slaves could neither be imported into the state, nor raised within its limits, it would seem as if a foundation was laid for its final extinction, by these simple provisions. And such was the understanding at the time. . . .

Unless then, there is some defect in those statutes, which will prevent their operating in the manner intended, slavery in the state of Connecticut, (except as it respects the few born before the act of [1784],) is abolished. It may then become necessary to examine these statutes more in detail.

The first statute was as follows: "And whereas the increase of slaves in this state is injurious to the poor and inconvenient; *Be it enacted*, that no indian, negro, or mulatto slave shall, at any time hereafter, be brought or imported into this state, by sea or land, from any place or places whatsoever, to be disposed of, left or sold within this state." . . .

. . . [I]t is the business of the court to give such construction to the statute as to suppress the mischief and advance the remedy;

or, in the language of Lord *Coke*, to "suppress subtle inventions and evasions for continuance of the mischief, and *pro privato commodo*, and to add force and life to the cure and remedy according to the true intent of the makers of the act, *pro bono publico.*" *Heydon's* case, 3 Co. 7. If, then the construction claimed by the respondent, would go, in a considerable degree, to impair or defeat the object in view; if it would suffer the mischief, at which the statute was aimed to increase; we may well doubt, whether such a construction can be a correct one.

What then would be the consequences of that construction? It cannot be denied, that this statute prohibits the importation of slaves, by citizens of other states, as well as by our own citizens; and that our own citizens have at least equal privileges on the subject with others. The claim here attempted to be supported, is, that persons may bring into this state, negro or mulatto slaves, in any number, and for any time their owners shall choose; (not to sell or dispose of)—provided they do not intend to remain here permanently, themselves; and do not mean that the slave shall remain here for life: that is to say, if the person who brings the slave here, can show, that he did not intend to remain here permanently, and did not mean his slave should remain here permanently, but that he intended, at some time, when it should suit his convenience or pleasure, to return with his slaves, then it would not be within the statute. Now, unless an inhabitant of another state or nation can, by comity, claim some privilege of this sort, which our citizens cannot, then any inhabitant of this state may also bring from abroad his negro slaves; or he may go abroad and hire slaves, and bring them to labour in this state; and if he may do it, in one instance, he may do it in another; and if he may hire one slave, to wait upon him, or cultivate his grounds, what prevents his hiring a hundred? The slave indeed could not be left here for life; but he may be hired for a term of years; and the contract of hiring for a term, would always prove that he was not to be permanently left. If this is a correct exposition of this statute, we see not why, under its operation, slaves may not again become the cultivators of our soil; and why we may not take from the slave-growing states, for a term of years, the crops of slaves which some of the new slave states have, by their recent laws, excluded. Surely, such a construction of the statute is not one which would tend to suppress the mischief in view.

Does the language of the statute require, or even admit, such a construction? It provides, that no indian, negro or mulatto slave shall, at any time hereafter, be brought or imported into this state, by sea or land, from any place or places whatsoever. Language can hardly be more comprehensive. No slave from the slave stock shall be brought or imported, at any time, by sea or by land, from any place or places, into the state. It seems as if the legislature were anxious that no loop-hole should be left. And had they stopped here, no doubt could have existed that the words of the act were as broad as the intent. But it is added, "to be disposed of, left or sold within this state." These words, it is contended, qualify the preceding enactment, in such a manner, as to shew, that the case of the respondent is not within the statute. These words forming a part of the statute, are to be construed in connexion with the other part of the enactment, in such a manner as to give a full and fair effect to the intent of the legislature. It is not claimed, that *Nancy Jackson* was brought into this state to be sold or disposed of; and the respondent also insists upon it, she was not brought here to be *left*. On the other side, it is contended, that as she was brought here, and has been suffered to remain, for nearly two years, she has been *left* here, within the true intent and meaning of this statute. This brings us to the question, how far does this word "left" qualify and limit the previous provisions of this statute? Must it be shewn, that the slave imported was to be *permanently* left in this state? Such a construction would greatly enervate the statute; and ought not, therefore, to be given, unless the language imperiously demands it.

How then is the term "left" to be understood? The word *leave*, from which this is derived, is used in a variety of senses; as to forsake, to abandon, to depart from, to suffer to remain, not to carry away. These, it is believed, are the only significations, which can be considered applicable to this case. The word "left" cannot have been used in the first sense; for it cannot be believed, that any one would bring his slaves here, merely to abandon or forsake them; or that such an event could have been thought so likely to happen, as to require this extraordinary interposition. . . . Nor can the term mean to depart from, or not to carry away his slave, unless it can be shewn, that so long as the owner remains in the state, as well as the slave, this statute cannot be violated. And if this construction is correct, it follows, that any citizen of another state or country may remove into this state with his slaves; and so long as he remains with them, they are not "left," within the meaning of the statute, even although he may not intend to return.

What then does the word "left" mean in this statute? We must, when a term has different senses, kept in view the object contemplated by those who use it, in this, as in all other cases which may arise. Thus, if a law forbids the master of a vessel from landing foreigners upon our shores, and leaving them there, without a license, or without bonds, it would be a poor defence, that they had all agreed to return in his ship, at the end of two years, and therefore, he had not *left* them; or that he had not *left* them, because he remained in the country with them. Or, if a law to guard against contagious diseases prohibits the leaving, in any town in this state, of a person having the small-pox, would the fact that the persons who left the infected person in a town, remained with him, be any justification of the act? Or, would not such infected person be *left*, because he who brought him had not departed from him or abandoned him? . . . We think, that the same construction should be given to the word "left" in this statute: no slave shall be brought from any place and suffered to remain in this state.

If it be claimed, that the word "left" is, in this way, made of no effect, we think otherwise, and that it has an important meaning. While the legislature were desirous of preventing the increase of slavery, on the one hand, they were not desirous of doing any thing, which might be considered unkind or unfriendly to the inhabitants of adjoining states, on the other. New York and Massachusetts were then both slave states. It was not a time to provoke controversies with such powerful neighbours. While, therefore, this state exercised its undoubted right to prevent the increase of slavery among us, they meant to do it in such a manner as not to give offence to our sister states, by impeding their citizens in travelling through this state, with their servants or slaves; but those slaves were not to be *left*, or suffered to remain here. In this way, slavery would not be increased among us, to the injury of the poor; nor would our friends from abroad be prevented from coming among us, and passing through our state, with their families.

If it be asked, how long they might continue here, before they could be said to be *left*, it is answered, that a liberal construction should be given to the term, depending upon circumstances, though two years could not be allowed, under any circumstances, except of imperious necessity. . . .

A slave, then, brought from another state or country into this state, may, in our opinion, be considered as *left* in this state, although the owner does not intend to reside here permanently himself, or to suffer such slave permanently to remain here. So long as he is a traveller, passing through the state, he cannot be said to have *left* her here. But when he and his family are residing here, for years; and when he has suffered his slave to remain here, for almost two years; he cannot claim the privilege of a traveller, even although he intended, at some future time, to return with his family to his former residence. . . .

In the opinion of a majority of the court, it follows, that this slave has been brought and left in this state, contrary to the act of 1774; and therefore, that she cannot be claimed or treated as a slave, under our laws.

The statute of 1784, follows up and completes the system of abolition. The preamble shows the views of the legislature: "And whereas sound policy requires, that the abolition of slavery should be effected as soon as may be consistent with the rights of individuals and the public safety and welfare; therefore, *Be it enacted*, that no negro or mulatto child, that shall, after the 1st day of *March*, 1784, be born within this state, shall be held in servitude longer than until they arrive at the age of 25 years, notwithstanding the mother or parent of such child was held in servitude, at the time of its birth; but such child, at the age aforesaid, shall be free; any law, usage or custom to the contrary, notwithstanding." The former law had declared the increase of slavery injurious to the poor and inconvenient; and it was evidently intended to prevent the *increase* of slaves. This statute declares, that sound policy requires the abolition of slavery, as soon as consistent with public safety and individual rights. It was evidently intended to destroy the system entirely; and to effect this, the legislature declare, that no coloured children, born in this state, shall be slaves. If the words "within this state" had been omitted, then this statute would, of itself, have operated so as that there could remain no such thing as slavery in this state, after the extinction of those slaves, who were born before the year 1784. The legislature, in their enactments, ordinarily intend to confine their operation to this state. It is for this state they legislate, and not for the world. . . . If, in this case, it had been said, no child born after *March*, 1784, shall be a slave after 25 years of age, it might have had the appearance of legislating for others—of proclaiming liberty to all born in the country after that time. The language might have seemed at least offensive. The legislature, therefore, used language, not uncommon at that time, similar to that used in other statutes, which would have received precisely the same construction whether containing those words or not. Is it too much to say, that those words meant no more in this case than in the cases cited above; and that when they were attempting to abolish slavery, they may be fairly understood to mean, that persons born after that time shall not be held as slaves after they arrive at a certain age? Had the language of the statute been; whereas sound policy requires, that slavery should be abolished, as soon as is consistent with the public safety and individual rights, no person hereafter born shall be held in servitude in this state, after he is 25 years of age; the words *within this state* would then be held superfluous, as they must be in many other cases; and it would give complete effect to the object in view. Without however giving a definite opinion upon the point, there is another view of the subject, which, upon principles conceded in this case, we think conclusive.

The respondent, it has been conceded, can claim nothing by the law of comity, and nothing under the constitution of the United States. From the law, as settled in *Somerset's* case, that a foreigner who brings his slave into a country where slavery is not permitted, cannot hold him, it would seem to result, that upon this subject at least, an inhabitant of another state or country could claim no other or greater privileges than the inhabitants of that state or country into which he removed. . . .

[I]f one citizen could hold no person but those under 25 years of age as slaves, by a parity of reasons, no others among us could hold them for a longer period. If our law abolishes slavery entirely, as it respects our citizens, it has not been denied, that its operation would be to prevent others from holding slaves among us. If then from regard to supposed existing rights and public safety, they have abolished it in part, or a certain extent, among our citizens, why should not this restriction operate to the same extent that it does upon our own citizens? . . .

The result, therefore, to which a majority of the court have arrived is, that these statutes were designed to terminate slavery in Connecticut, and that they are sufficient for that purpose. The act of 1774 aimed a blow at the increase of slaves; that of 1784, struck at the existence of slavery. The former was intended to weaken the system; the latter, to destroy it. The former lopped off a limb from the trunk; the latter struck a deadly blow at the root; and ever since it has withered and decayed; and with the exception of here and there a dying limb, slavery has disappeared from our state, and will, in a short time, be known only in our history; unless indeed, it is to revive and flourish, by the construction we shall now give to the statutes. To us it appears as if there was nothing in the intent of the legislature, or in the words of the act, which requires such a construction.

We feel therefore bound to say, that we know of no law of this state, under which this woman can be holden in slavery; and therefore advise, that she be discharged.

HUNTINGTON and WAITE, Js. were of the same opinion.

BISSELL, J. . . .

It is deeply to be regretted, that, in a case involving consequences of more than ordinary magnitude; affecting, as this
does, not only our own institutions, but our intercourse with
our sister states; the usual harmony should not prevail among
the members of the court. I find myself compelled to dissent
from the opinions held by a majority of my brethren; and I
feel bound, in justice to myself, to state the reasons on which
my own opinion is founded. . . .

Now, by the laws of Georgia, the individual brought up, on
this writ, is the slave and property of the respondent; and it is
admitted, that by those laws, her condition is not affected, by her
temporary residence among us. If she return with him to
Georgia, she will still continue to be his slave and his property.
Is this relation destroyed, and is this respondent divested of his
rights, by the operation of our laws? Do the claims set forth
on this return so far *"clash with the rights of our citizens;"* and
are they so opposed to the institutions, and the essential interests
of this community, as that the law of the domicil must yield?
This, as it seems to me is the whole enquiry; and it lies within
very narrow limits.

The discussion has, however, taken a wide range, and many
considerations have been urged upon us, which, in my judgment, has very little to do with the case to be decided. Much has
been said of the injustice and immorality of slavery; and both
moral and political writers have been summoned to our bar, to
bear testimony to the enormities of the system.

Those considerations might very properly be urged, and have
their influence, elsewhere. They might, with propriety, and
should have been addressed to our pilgrim fathers, when they
were about to introduce the system, and to bring this foul stain
upon our otherwise free institutions. They may properly enough
be urged upon the legislative department of the government.
And I am not about to deny the propriety of urging them upon
the moral sense and feelings of the community. With these topics,
and with the excitement that is abroad on this subject, whether
favorable or adverse to the present claim, I can have nothing to
do. Sitting here to administer the law, I cannot undertake to be
wiser than the laws and constitution of my country, nor purer
than those great and good men, by whom they were ordained. As
a citizen and as a man, I may admit the injustice and immorality
of slavery; that its tendencies are all bad; that it is productive
of evil, and of evil only. But as a jurist, I must look at that
standard of morality, which the law prescribes. . . .

If then, the claims of the respondent are repugnant, neither to our unwritten law, nor to our constitution, it only remains that we enquire whether they conflict with any of the statutes to which I have adverted.

It has been supposed, that the case falls within the spirit and meaning of the acts providing for the gradual abolition of slavery. These statutes, as we have seen, are confined, *in terms*, to persons *born in this state*. And I confess, I hardly know upon what principle of interpretation it is, that we are called upon to extend the provision of these acts to persons *born elsewhere*. Is it to carry into effect the general intention of the legislature? That the great and leading object was, entirely to abolish slavery in this state, I most readily admit. But still, regard was had to individual interests, as well as the public welfare. The legislature did not intend to break in upon the rights of our own citizens, or upon those of the citizens of other states. And having provided, that no slaves should be brought into the state, to be disposed of, left or sold within the same; and that persons thereafter born *in the state*, should be free; they doubtless supposed, they had done all that could consistently be done. And it never could have been their intention, as I maintain, to extend these acts to persons *born out of the state*. Since the act of 1784, our statutes have passed through three deliberate revisions; and in all, the provision in question has been confined, as at the first, to persons born in the state. In the meantime, it could not but be well known, that our Southern brethren were in the constant practice of visiting us, as the respondent has done, bringing their slaves with them, and taking them back to their own states, whenever it suited their convenience. And if this had been felt to be an evil, to militate against the spirit of our laws, would not the legislature have applied the remedy? And would they have thrown upon courts of justice the invidious task of torturing the language of the act from its plain and unequivocal meaning, in order to carry out their intention? It is more than half a century since these emancipating acts have been in force; and never I believe, until the present experiment, have they been supposed to apply to a case like this. Now, I confess, I do not feel at liberty, and especially, in the face of this practical construction, to say, that when the legislature speak of persons born *in this state*, they really mean persons born somewhere else.

It is, however, said, that upon the construction contended for, we allow to citizens of other states, a privilege which we deny to our own. I do not admit this conclusion. We allow to our citizens the right of holding *their own slaves;* and why should we deny to citizens of other states, the right of holding *theirs?*

It is true, that persons born *in this state*, after the first of *March*, 1784, are not, and never were, slaves. Nobody is divested of a property in them for they never were the subjects of property. But not so in this case. The individual claimed was the property of the respondent. Has he become divested of it? And if so, by what law?

But it is said, that this view of the case will sanction the introduction here of slaves, born in other states; that our own citizens may bring and hold them here, with impunity; and especially, that the citizens of the slave-holding states may come here and acquire a domicil, bringing their slaves along with them, and holding them in perpetual servitude, contrary to the whole scope and spirit of our laws. Neither can I admit the correctness of this conclusion: and if it followed—if in this respect, there be a defect in our legislation,—I submit that the correction does not appertain to this branch of the government. Our concern is with the laws as they are; and if they are not so framed, as upon a fair construction, to carry out the whole intent of the makers, it were better that they should be corrected, in the proper place, than that courts of justice should resort to novel modes of interpretation, for the purpose of supplying the deficiency. But were I called upon to decide the case put, I should say, that they fell much more clearly within the equity of the 4th and 5th sections of the statute, than of the one now under consideration. It will, however, be sufficient to decide such a case, when it shall arise. Of this, however, there would seem to be little danger; as neither our own citizens, nor those of other states have ever supposed, that they were at liberty to bring slaves here, to be held in perpetual servitude.

Again; it has been objected, and much reliance is placed upon the objection, that the facts set forth in the return show, that the slave *Nancy* was brought here *to be left*, and has been *left*, within the meaning of the 4th section of the statute. That section I will again advert to. It is in these words: "No indian, negro or mulatto slave, shall be brought or imported into this state, by sea or by land, from any place whatever, to be disposed of, left or sold within the same." I have already adverted to the facts stated in the return, and they seem to me to furnish quite as strong evidence, that this slave was brought here to be *sold* or *disposed of*, as that she was brought here *to be left*. "To leave," says Dr. *Webster*, (and with him agrees every English lexicographer,) signifies *"to withdraw* or depart from," "to forsake," "desert, abandon," "to suffer to remain," "not to take or remove." Now, this slave has ever been in the service of the respondent's family, and under his protection and control. He has not *"with-*

drawn from her." She has neither been *forsaken, deserted* nor *abandoned;* and so far from suffering her to remain, he states his intention to be to take her with him to his domicil and hers. Now, is here any evidence that this slave was brought here *to be left,* within either the grammatical or popular meaning of the term? The respondent has come into this state, for the purpose of educating the younger members of his family; and when that object is accomplished, he means to return with them to their common home.

Would any man acquainted with the facts say, that he had brought his family here *to be left?* And would not this be a perversion of language? I, however, understand it to be claimed, that to leave a slave in the state, within the meaning of the act, it is not necessary that he should be abandoned, but that it is sufficient if he *stop here with his master:* and that *to be left,* is used in the statute, only in contradistinction to a mere *transit* or passage through the state: that in the one case, the rights of the master are preserved, and in the other lost, although the place of the domicil be the object in both cases. I am unable to feel the force of this distinction; or to see why it is, that in the one case, we are to have regard to the law of the domicil, and suffer it to govern, and not in the other. Can any thing depend on mere length of stay, so long as the domicil is unchanged, and the *animus revertendi, bona fide* remains? . . .

It was very properly contended, at the bar, that by the energy of our laws, this slave became free, the moment she touched the soil of Connecticut. This claim has, at least, the merit of consistency, and I can feel its force. But the argument here, does not proceed upon any such ground. It distinctly admits, that when the slave *Nancy* came into this state, she was the slave and property of the respondent; and that had she merely passed with him through the state, she might have remained his slave and property still; but that *by stopping with him,* in the state, she has, by the operation of this statute, become free. How this has been accomplished; at what time this process of emancipation commenced, and when it was consummated; I have not been able, very clearly, to comprehend.

If the respondent has brought his slave here *to be left,* in violation of the statute, I can readily see the propriety of visiting him with the penalty which the statute prescribes; but I am not able to see upon what authority it is, that we superadd to this, a forfeiture of his property. . . .

Upon the best consideration I have been able to give to this case, I am constrained to say, that in my judgment, the return is sufficient; and that the demurrer ought to be overruled. At the same time, I must be permitted to say, that it is a source of gratification both to my learned brother who concurs with me, and to myself, to know, that if our views on this subject are erroneous, their effect will not be unjustly to deprive a fellow-being of her liberty.

CHURCH, J., concurred in this opinion.

QUESTIONS

The Connecticut Legislature had enacted two statutes, in 1774 and 1784, similar to the "gradual abolition" legislation in other states, see p. 41 *supra*. The result reached in *Jackson v. Bulloch*—that a slave owner from Georgia could not hold his slave in the condition of slavery in Connecticut during a limited but substantial stay—was based both on interpretation of those statutes and declaration of common-law principles. The majority opinion illustrates the interstitial declaration of law by the court in those areas not covered by legislatively declared law.

1. The 1774 statute: statutory interpretation.—This statute provided that no slave should thereafter be brought or imported into Connecticut "from any place or places whatsoever, to be disposed of, left or sold within this state." The statute provided that any person who violated this provision "shall forfeit and pay to the Treasurer of this state, the sum of three hundred and thirty four dollars for every slave so imported . . . [or] brought into this state. . . ." Two issues can be isolated with respect to the effect of this statute in *Jackson v. Bulloch*: (a) whether it was a violation of the statute to bring a slave into Connecticut and hold him as a slave, when the owner intended to stay in Connecticut for a limited period (as distinguished from simply traveling through the state on the one hand, or intending to stay permanently on the other) and, (b) if it was a violation of the statute to do so, whether the owner should be held to have lost his right to dominion over the slave, in addition to being subjected to the statutory fine of $334.

a. The "plain meaning" v. the "mischief" rule.—The first of these issues required the court to give meaning to the word "left." In his dissenting opinion Justice Bissell said that it was not within the "grammatical" meaning of the word, and would be a "perversion" of language, to hold that "left" meant anything other than to permit the slave to remain permanently in Connecticut without staying with her. This was a variation on the theme of "plain meaning," was it not? Compare the approach to interpretation of the statute in Chief Justice Williams's opinion for the majority: "[I]t is the business of the court to give such construction to the statute as to suppress the mischief and advance the remedy." Williams here referred to a 1584 decision of the English Court of the Exchequer, Heydon's Case, 76 Eng. Rep. 637. The full discussion in *Heydon's Case* should be included here, for it is an ideal description of the function of a court in interpreting a statute:

> And it was resolved by them that for the sure and true interpretation of all statutes in general (be they penal or beneficial, restrictive or enlarging of the common law,) four things are to be discerned and considered:—
>
> 1st. What was the common law before the making of the Act.
>
> 2nd. What was the mischief and defect for which the common law did not provide.
>
> 3rd. What remedy the Parliament hath resolved and appointed to cure the disease of the commonwealth.
>
> And, 4th. The true reason of the remedy; and then the office of all the Judges is always to make such construction as shall suppress the mischief, and advance the remedy, and to suppress subtle inventions and evasions for continuance of the mischief, and *pro privato commodo*, and to add force and life to the cure and remedy, according to the true intent of the makers of the Act, *pro bono publico*. 76 Eng. Rep. at 638.

The word "left" could mean to "suffer to remain" either permanently or for a limited period of time. How should the court select which of those meanings will prevail? Chief Justice Williams's opinion is a good example of purpose-oriented interpretation, looking to the reasons why the statutory principle was adopted, and determining the extent to which those reasons are present in the specific case before the court. Why would the Connecticut Legislature in 1774 enact a statute prohibiting the importation of slaves to be "left" *permanently* in the state? Among the reasons asserted at the time were the following: (a) a conclusion that some effort should be made to lessen the increase in the slave population of the state because slavery was becoming less necessary as a source of labor, and was becoming a source of discontent among whites seeking employment in occupations filled by slaves; (b) fear of slave revolts if the slave population continued to increase; (c) the prevailing religious, ethical and political arguments against slavery (prohibition of importation being regarded as a first step toward abolition); and (d) an economic judgment that slavery had now become unprofitable.[25] To what extent were these reasons present in the case of an importation of a slave into Connecticut to be "left" for a limited period of time? Did the majority of the court correctly conclude that exclusion of the limited-period case "would greatly enervate the statute"?

In *Jackson v. Bulloch* the slave had been in Connecticut with the owner's family for two years, and the family apparently was planning to stay until the education of the children had been completed. The majority inquired how long a stay might continue in the state before the slave would be said to be "left," and answered that that would turn on the circumstances, "though two years could not be allowed, under any circumstances, except of imperious necessity." Would it have been a proper exercise of the judicial function if the court had said: "We have now decided that 'left' does not refer to travelers going through the state, but does refer to stays for limited periods. In order to make this determination as clear as possible for the guidance of all concerned, we shall be quite specific. The word 'left' in the statute refers to a stay in Connecticut for more than two weeks [or two months or one year]"? The majority in *Jackson* said only that a stay of two years violated the statute, but it might be that periods shorter than two years would also constitute a violation. Would it be proper for the court to declare the applicable law in such specific terms as those suggested, or is that type of precise lawmaking the sole province of the legislature?

The majority in *Jackson v. Bulloch* was of the view that "left" did not include an owner who brought a slave into Connecticut while traveling through the state. Did the majority correctly conclude that exclusion of the in-transit case would not "greatly enervate the statute"?

b. (i) Canons of construction: strict construction of penal statutes.—The dissent, p. 70 *supra,* said that Nancy Jackson had not been "left" in Connecticut within the "popular" meaning of the term. Three questions are suggested by this statement: (1) What is the relevant populace in determining a popular meaning? The entire population? Slave owners? Slaves? Abolitionists? (2) In determining the popular meaning should we consider the term in the abstract or in its statutory context? (3) Why would the popular meaning of the term be relevant to the court's interpretation of the statute?

---

25 *See generally* A. ZILVERSMIT, THE FIRST EMANCIPATION: THE ABOLITION OF SLAVERY IN THE NORTH (1967), and materials referred to therein.

Was it important that the statute carried a fine as the sanction for violation? In the discussion of *Somerset v. Stewart* we asked how much weight should have been given to the reliance interests of the owners whose slaves would now be emancipated. The dissenting opinion in *Jackson*, in referring to the "popular" meaning of the word "left" in the statute, may in effect have been asking, "How did this defendant read the statute? Was it his understanding that by bringing a slave into Connecticut under these circumstances he would be committing a crime?" Courts frequently refer, in interpreting criminal statutes, to a so-called canon of construction that such statutes should be "strictly construed." The point of that canon is sometimes said to be that ambiguity in a criminal statute should be resolved in favor of the accused, because a man should have fair warning that his conduct would violate a criminal statute. Is this a sound principle? Is there good reason to limit it to criminal statutes? Of course, an interpretation suggested by application of the fair-warning principle may conflict with an interpretation that would better effectuate the purposes of the statute. In fact, courts do not automatically hold for the defendant in a criminal prosecution just because he demonstrates some ambiguity in the statutory language. This policy is one among many considerations that influence a court's interpretation of a statute. If this policy is founded on the prevention of unfair surprise, should it be required, in order for the accused to invoke the policy, that he demonstrate that he read the statute beforehand, and then went ahead with his conduct, having concluded it would not violate the statute? But would he not then be on notice that the conduct *might* violate the statute? And if a court later so holds, has the accused been unfairly surprised?

These questions suggest that another policy may also lie behind the canon of strict construction of penal statutes. Does that canon firmly recognize the lawmaking function performed by a court in attributing meaning to the words of a statute, and seek to limit courts' lawmaking powers with respect to criminal offenses? Consider the statement that common-law crimes are not recognized in the United States. When a court interprets a criminal statute to apply to the past conduct of the accused, has the court indulged in ex post facto lawmaking?

The canon of strict construction of penal statutes is an example of what Professors Henry Hart and Albert Sacks call "policies of clear statement" in judicial interpretation of statutes. "In effect, these presumptions all say to the legislature, 'If you mean *this*, you must say so plainly.'" H. HART, JR., & A. SACKS, THE

LEGAL PROCESS: BASIC PROBLEMS IN THE MAKING AND APPLICA-
TION OF LAW 1235, 1240 (tent. ed. 1958). Professor Morris Cohen
described the purpose of such canons of interpretation:

> Consider the rules of statutory interpretation laid down
> in any textbook, for example, that penal statutes, or stat-
> utes in derogation of the common law, should be strictly
> construed, that remedial statutes should be liberally con-
> strued, and that there is an almost conclusive presumption
> against an unreasonable or inconvenient intention on the
> part of the legislator. These are not scientific rules for the
> discovery of actual intentions or the meanings of words, but
> *maxims of public policy to guide judges in the process of
> making law out of statutes.* M. COHEN, LAW AND THE SO-
> CIAL ORDER 131 (1933), reprinted in M. COHEN & F. COHEN,
> READINGS IN JURISPRUDENCE AND LEGAL PHILOSOPHY 506
> (1951).

Chief Justice Williams's opinion in *Jackson* reflects these concerns when he says, in effect, that the approach to statutory interpretation in *Heydon's Case* is a policy of clear statement: "Must
it be shewn, that the slave imported was to be *permanently* left
in this state? Such a construction would greatly enervate the
statute; and ought not, therefore, to be given, unless the language
imperiously demands it." P. 63 *supra*.

The Connecticut statute imposed a fine for violation of the
prohibition on bringing slaves into the state. The majority in
Jackson held that because the owner violated the statute, he
could not exercise dominion over the slave in Connecticut. Did
the court improperly add to the sanction the legislature had provided for violation of the statute? Was the court here interpreting the statute, or declaring a common-law principle? It
appears that it was doing both. The first question was one of
statutory interpretation: Was imposition of the fine the sole
effect which could be given under Connecticut law to the importation of a slave in violation of the statute? If the answer
to that question was "No," the next question was one on which
the court would declare the law: Could an owner who had violated the statute still exercise the rights of a slave owner in
Connecticut? How should each of these questions have been
answered? These questions about the impact of criminal law
standards on private rights and obligations are encountered in
a variety of contexts. One notable example is the doctrine of
"negligence per se," studied in the course on torts.

(ii) **Canons of construction: "noscitur a sociis" ("it is known from its associates") and "ejusdem generis" ("of the same kind").—** Courts frequently refer to a canon that the meaning of a word is or may be known from the accompanying words. The Connecticut statute in *Jackson v. Bulloch* prohibited importation of a slave into the state to be "disposed of, left or sold" within the state. Of what utility would this canon be in attributing meaning to the word "left"? It might be contended that because "disposed of" and "sold" refer to situations in which the slave owner will no longer have any relationship to the slave, and may no longer be present, the word "left" should be given that meaning which would be most closely analogous to the factual situations connoted by "disposed of" and "sold." Would there be any sound policy ground for using such a process of thinking to resolve the ambiguity in the meaning of "left"? Compare this canon with that of "strict construction of penal statutes." As Professor Morris Cohen stated in the extract quoted, p. 75 *supra*, that canon is a maxim "of public policy to guide judges. . . ." It reflects policies both of preventing unfair surprise and limiting the lawmaking function of courts. The canon that the meaning of a word is or may be known from the accompanying words is of a different sort—it purports only to state a custom of English usage: that *one* of the meanings a word can carry is a meaning analogous to those of accompanying words. It should not be understood, should it, to state which of several meanings *ought to* prevail? Its utility would be, would it not, solely to help to isolate those meanings which the word "left" could bear, not to determine which of several possible meanings ought to be attributed to the word? See H. HART & A. SACKS, THE LEGAL PROCESS: BASIC PROBLEMS IN THE MAKING AND APPLICATION OF LAW 1412 (tent. ed. 1958).

2. **The 1784 statute: statutory principles as a foundation for judge-made law.—** The 1784 Connecticut statute provided that no child "born within this state" after March 1, 1784, should be held as a slave beyond the age of twenty-five (later, by amendment, age twenty-one). The majority of the court suggested (without deciding the question) that this statute could be interpreted to apply in *Jackson*, where the alleged slave had not been born in Connecticut. The words "born within this state," under such an interpretation, were "superfluous." Alternatively, they were to be interpreted to mean, "who comes to this state though not born here." To the dissenting justices this was "torturing the language of the act from its plain and unequivocal mean-

ing." Having banned the importation of slaves in 1774, the next step in "gradual abolition" was to make slaves free after age twenty-five. Why limit the statement of that principle to those born in Connecticut? The explanation would appear to lie in the legal doctrine concerning the status of slavery. A child had the same status as his mother, and the 1784 statute said that a child who heretofore would have been a slave for his entire life under Connecticut law would be free at age twenty-five (later twenty-one). If the 1774 statute in effect freed slaves who were imported into Connecticut, then there was no need in the 1784 statute to deal, so far as the future was concerned, with slaves of owners in other states. Hence it may be questioned whether the 1784 statute should have been found to have anything to do with slaves from other states. Assume, however, that there had been no 1774 statute. Would it then have been appropriate for the court to say: "The 1784 statute makes slaves free at age twenty-five. When we consider the mischief which the statute was designed to prevent, we can see no good reason why that policy should apply only to persons born in this state. The slave population of Connecticut has included some persons who were born here and some who were born elsewhere. Hence we conclude that the words 'born within this state' should be considered to be superfluous, having probably been inserted as a result of carelessness. The statute as drafted left a gap which it made no sense to leave, and we interpret the words of the statute so as to close that gap"?

Was not the court's actual ruling on the effect of the 1784 statute more sound? We paraphrase: "Slavery has been abolished to a limited extent within Connecticut by the 1784 statute, and it is abolished, by a rule of common law declared by the court, in cases which do not fall within the language of the statute but which do fall within the reasons for the statutory principle and other analogous reasons." The problem resembles the two-part issue concerning an owner's forfeiture of his slave for violation of the 1774 statute: (a) Does the 1784 statute abolish slavery only with respect to persons born in Connecticut, precluding the courts from declaring abolition with respect to other persons? (b) If the court is free to decide the abolition issue with respect to persons not born in Connecticut, what should the result be as a matter of common-law decision? In making the latter decision, what weight should the court give to the "precedent" provided by the statute in the area of its appropriate application?

Chief Justice Roger Traynor of the California Supreme Court has recently written about this question:

A judge's responsibility is the greater now that legislatures fabricate laws in such volume. The endless cases that proceed before him increasingly involve the meaning or applicability of a statute, or, on occasion, its constitutionality. Such statutes, reflecting their sponsors or draftsmen or author-legislators, are of infinite variety in purpose, range, and quality. Except for constitutional limitations, legislators innovate them with a freedom unknown to judges, who must ordinarily stay within the confines of precedent and articulate the reasons for their rules. A statute may be a fat code or a thin paragraph or a starveling sentence. It may cast a heavy shadow on the common law or a light one, or it may idly plane until some incident sends it careening into action. The hydraheaded problem is how to synchronize the unguided missiles launched by legislatures with a going system of common law.

. . . .

Long before the eighteenth century, common-law judges made their way by fits and starts, sometimes by leaps and bounds, to conglomerate mergers that worked wonders in the law. If statutes in English law did not invariably have so large a role as in Roman law, they nonetheless served now and again to change the course of common law. Long before the discovery of America, a doctrine so sweetly named as *equity of the statute* was imaginatively conceived and utilized by judges in a manner described by Professor Page as "somewhere between a genuine, though very free, construction, and a disguised use of analogy in the creation of common law principles, rules and standards taken from the provisions of statutes which, by their terms, applied to like cases but not to the particular case in question."[26]

Chief Justice Traynor concluded his article by observing that "The real problem is not whether judges should make use of statutes, but how they can make optimum use of them." One of the questions he suggested as relevant to the determination of how to make "optimum use" of statutes was "how can judges immersed in mounting litigation ferret out potentially good statutes for use in their own law-making from among the host of inferior ones"?[27] If courts can, or should, make use of statutes in

---

[26] Traynor, *Statutes Revolving in Common-Law Orbits,* 17 CATHOLIC U.L. REV. 401-02, 403 (1968). Copyright © Catholic University of America Press, Inc.

[27] *Id.* at 426, 427.

the process of judicial lawmaking, should courts feel as free to disregard an "inferior" statute as they might reject, or overrule, a judicial precedent which is concluded no longer to be sound?

3. Should the views of dissenting judges be recorded?—There were five judges on the Connecticut Supreme Court of Errors at the time of the decision in *Jackson v. Bulloch,* and they split 3-2 in deciding the case. The two dissenting judges agreed upon an opinion explaining their conclusion. Is the practice of publishing dissenting opinions sound? Does this practice have any effect in making more, or less, acceptable in society the performance by courts of their law-declaring function? Are dissenting judges, because their views do not control the decision, likely to be less restrained than the majority judges in deciding and discussing the issues in a case? Note the last sentence in Justice Bissell's dissenting opinion in *Jackson v. Bulloch.* What do you think Justices Bissell and Church would have done if, before the decision was finally reached in the case, it had become apparent that at least one other judge was ready to concur in Justice Bissell's opinion?

Commonwealth v. Aves and *Jackson v. Bulloch* dealt with issues that were parallel to the issue that had arisen in England in *Somerset v. Stewart.* There were also decisions in the United States that paralleled *The Slave, Grace.* Because slavery was valid in some states and invalid in others, the issue arose as to the status, in a slave state, of a person who had been a slave in a slave state, had been taken by the owner to a free state, and had then been returned to the slave state. Lord Stowell in *The Slave, Grace,* in 1827, decided that if, under the law of the colony to which the individual was returned, he was a slave, that status would control in spite of his earlier presence in free territory. There were decisions in some state courts after the adoption of the United States Constitution which reached the opposite result. In two states, Maryland and Virginia, it was held that rights of property over a slave could not be resumed when the former slave returned to the state after having been in a free state with the consent of the owner. If this result were not reached, the Maryland Court of Appeals said, the statute prohibiting importation of slaves "would be liable to great evasion."[28] A Louis-

---

[28] Bland and Woolfolk v. Negro Dowling, 9 Gill & Johnson 19, 30 (Md. 1837); *see also* Betty v. Horton, 32 Va. (5 Leigh) 615 (1833). In the Virginia case the report states that the slave brought the suit *in forma pauperis* and was represented by assigned counsel.

iana decision holding a returned slave to be free was followed
by an enactment of the state legislature: ". . . from the passage
of this act, no slave shall be entitled to his or her freedom, under
the pretence that he or she has been, with or without the consent
of his or her owner, in a country where slavery does not exist, or
in any of the States where slavery is prohibited."[29] This same
issue came before the United States Supreme Court in *Dred Scott
v. Sandford,* one of the milestones on the road to civil war.

The *Dred Scott* case was a "test case," brought not so much to
settle the rights of the parties to the action as to settle the state
of the law. Scott, as everyone conceded, had been a slave of
Emerson while both resided in Missouri. Emerson took Scott
first to reside in Illinois, and then to reside at Fort Snelling in
the upper part of the Louisiana Territory (in what is now St.
Paul, Minnesota). In 1838, Emerson and Scott returned to Missouri. Emerson died, and in 1846 suit was brought in a Missouri
state court on behalf of Scott against Emerson's widow, alleging
that Scott's residence in Illinois (a free state) and upper Louisiana (where slavery had been abolished by Congress in the Missouri Compromise of 1820) had emancipated him. Scott prevailed in the trial court, on the basis of established precedent in
Missouri case law, which precedent was contrary to the rule in
The Slave, Grace. On appeal to the Missouri Supreme Court,
however, Scott's judgment was reversed by a 3-2 vote, and the
earlier decisions overruled. Whatever Scott's status might have
been in Illinois or the Louisiana Territory, the court said, he
had come back to Missouri voluntarily, and was a slave under
Missouri law. Scott v. Emerson, 15 Mo. 576 (1852).

While this appeal was pending, Mrs. Emerson had remarried.
Her new husband, Chaffee, was an abolitionist from Massachusetts. He saw in Scott's case a chance to get a ruling from
the federal courts that a slave taken by his owner to a free state
or territory was thereby emancipated once and for all. Perhaps
to conceal the fact that he owned a slave, but more importantly
to create the diversity of citizenship that would support federal-
court jurisdiction, Chaffee transferred Scott to his brother-in-law,
John Sanford, a resident of New York. (The report of the case
incorrectly calls the defendant Sandford.) In 1853, an action was
again brought on behalf of Scott, this time against Sanford in
the federal district court in Missouri, claiming damages for battery and false imprisonment. Sanford, according to the agreed

---

29 Act No. 189, May 30, 1846. The judicial decision was Smith v. Smith,
13 La. 441, 11 La. Rep. 211 (1839). Another case, holding the same way
seemingly after enactment of the 1846 statute, was Josephine v. Poultney,
1 La. Ann. 329, 21 La. Rep. 279 (Nov. 1846).

statement of facts, "laid his hands upon said plaintiff, . . . and imprisoned [him], doing in this respect, however, no more than what he might lawfully do" if Scott were a slave. The trial court rejected Sanford's plea in abatement, holding that Scott was not prevented from being a "citizen" for purposes of federal jurisdiction by virtue of his admitted descent from slaves. On the merits, however, the trial court agreed with the recent decision of the Supreme Court of Missouri, and directed a verdict that Scott was still a slave. It was this judgment that came on for review by the United States Supreme Court.

Chief Justice Taney's opinion would be hard to understand if it were not placed in the context of mid-nineteenth century political history.[30] The Missouri Compromise was an act of Congress in 1820. It provided, among other things, that slavery was prohibited in portions of the Louisiana Territory north of Missouri, and that new states formed in that zone would be free. Southerners in the Congress were reluctant to support the admission of new free states to the Union, because they feared that the political balance in the Congress would swing against slavery. Of the nine states admitted between the Missouri Compromise and the time of the *Dred Scott* decision, five were free (Maine, Michigan, Iowa, Wisconsin, and California) and four permitted slavery (Missouri, Arkansas, Florida, and Texas). Many westerners, anxious to secure southern support for western development and the admission of new states, supported the repeal of the Missouri Compromise in 1854, which was accomplished as part of the Kansas-Nebraska Act. Abolitionists were incensed at the repeal, and agitated for the reestablishment of the principle that would forbid slavery in the territories, and particularly in the northern territories. The southern response was that the Missouri Compromise had been unconstitutional in any event, as would be any future federal legislation to prevent the spread of slavery in the territories.

This issue came to be a key question in the presidential election campaign of 1856, which pitted James Buchanan, the Democrat, against the Republican John C. Frémont and former President Millard Fillmore, the nominee of the Old Line Whigs and the "Know Nothing" party's southern faction. Buchanan was elected, and thought that his mission was to save the Union:

He and his friends attributed [his election] to popular hostility to sectionalism, to abolitionism, and to all movements

---

[30] This summary is taken largely from C. SWISHER, ROGER B. TANEY 476-523 (1936).

on the part of northerners which antagonized the South by
efforts to prevent the spread of slavery. C. SWISHER, ROGER
B. TANEY 493 (1936).

Buchanan and his allies hoped for a sweeping constitutional
opinion in the *Dred Scott* case that would put such southern
fears to rest.

The Supreme Court had put off the decision of the case, by
now well celebrated in the national press, until after the November, 1856 election. The case was reargued in December, but the
Justices' conference on the decision was not held until February
of 1857. At that time, it was decided to hold that Scott was still
a slave, on the relatively narrow ground that Missouri law governed his status upon his return to Missouri. The issue of the
constitutionality of the Missouri Compromise would not be
reached, and Justice Nelson would write the opinion. The dissenters, however, let it be known that they planned to write
opinions that would demonstrate the validity of the Missouri
Compromise and congressional power to forbid slavery in the
territories. The majority Justices, faced with the prospect of
wide publicity to the dissenters' views in the abolitionist press,
determined not to let those views go unanswered. Chief Justice
Taney would write the opinion for the Court, and would include a section to the effect that the Missouri Compromise was
unconstitutional.

The opinion went beyond holding that Scott was still a slave.
It further stated that the entire Negro race was excluded from
citizenship, although not all the majority Justices were of the
view that this issue was properly before the Court. It also placed
the official stamp of the Supreme Court's approval on a theory of
racial inferiority and degradation. There were many blacks in
the north who regarded the opinion as a refreshing bit of candor
about the reality of race relations. A resolution to this effect was
offered by Robert Purvis to a meeting held at Israel Church, in
Philadelphia, a few weeks after the Supreme Court's decision:

> *Resolved,* That this atrocious decision furnishes final con-
> firmation of the already well known fact that under the Con-
> stitution and Government of the United States, the colored
> people are nothing, and can be nothing but an alien, dis-
> franchised and degraded class.
>
> *Resolved,* That to attempt, as some do, to prove that
> there is no support given to Slavery in the Constitution and
> essential structure of the American Government, is to argue
> against reason and common sense, to ignore history and shut

our eyes against palpable facts;[31] and that while it must suit
white men who do not feel the iron heel, to please themselves with such theories, it ill becomes the man of color
whose daily experience refutes the absurdity, to indulge in
any such idle phantasies.

Resolved, That to persist in supporting a Government
which holds and exercises the power, as distinctly set forth
by a tribunal from which there is no appeal, to trample a
class under foot as an inferior and degraded race, is on the
part of the colored man at once the height of folly and the
depth of pusillanimity. . . .

Questions from the audience reflected the viewpoint to which
Purvis had alluded in his resolution's second paragraph. He was
asked "if he had not been acknowledged and treated as an American citizen." He replied that he had, indeed, been issued a passport, but only after the personal intervention of a political
leader; he was indebted for his passport "not to the American
Constitution or to the spirit of the American Government, but
to the generous impulses of General Andrew Jackson," who was
President at the time. Purvis was followed by Charles L.
Remond, of Massachusetts, who offered a similar resolution. In
the debate, Remond was quoted by a reporter:

People might talk to him of "patience." He had no patience
to submit quietly to chains and oppression. Let others bare
their backs to the lash, and meekly and submissively wear
their chains. That was not his idea of duty, of manhood, or
of self-respect.

The resolutions were carried by the meeting, which was reported
in *The Liberator*, William Lloyd Garrison's abolitionist newspaper, in its issue of April 10, 1857. The article is reprinted in
1 A DOCUMENTARY HISTORY OF THE NEGRO PEOPLE IN THE UNIT-
ED STATES 392 (H. Aptheker ed. 1951; paperbound ed. 1965).

The aftermath of the decision in *Dred Scott* was anything but
a lessening of northern abolitionist agitation. The major political result of the decision was a bitter and prolonged attack on
the Supreme Court in the north. Lincoln made the decision one
of his targets during his debates with Stephen Douglas in the

---

[31] One such attempted proof had appeared in 1854: R. HILDRETH,
DESPOTISM IN AMERICA: AN INQUIRY INTO THE NATURE, RESULTS, AND LEGAL
BASIS OF THE SLAVE-HOLDING SYSTEM IN THE UNITED STATES (1854). See
Hildreth's comment on the reception he anticipated to his argument in n.23,
p. 43 *supra*. [*Eds. note.*]

senatorial campaign of 1858, arguing that the effect of the decision should be limited to the status of Scott himself, and rejecting the decision as "a political rule." The decision, he suggested in his 1861 inaugural address, might someday be overruled. 3 THE COLLECTED WORKS OF ABRAHAM LINCOLN 255 (R. Basler ed. 1953); 6 MESSAGES AND PAPERS OF THE PRESIDENTS 5, 9-10 (J. Richardson ed. 1897).

But the Supreme Court never overruled *Dred Scott v. Sandford*. Scott himself was set free soon after the case was decided, and the decision was overruled by war and constitutional amendment.

DRED SCOTT v. SANDFORD
Supreme Court of the United States
60 U.S. (19 How.) 393 (1857)

The counsel filed the following agreed statement of facts, viz:

In the year 1834, the plaintiff was a negro slave belonging to Dr. Emerson, who was a surgeon in the army of the United States. In that year, 1834, said Dr. Emerson took the plaintiff from the State of Missouri to the military post at Rock Island, in the State of Illinois, and held him there as a slave until the month of April or May, 1836. At the time last mentioned, said Dr. Emerson removed the plaintiff from said military post at Rock Island to the military post at Fort Snelling, situate on the west bank of the Mississippi river, in the Territory known as Upper Louisiana, acquired by the United States of France, and situate north of the latitude of thirty-six degrees thirty minutes north, and north of the State of Missouri. Said Dr. Emerson held the plaintiff in slavery at said Fort Snelling, from said last-mentioned date until the year 1838.

In the year 1835, Harriet, who is named in the second count of the plaintiff's declaration, was the negro slave of Major Taliaferro, who belonged to the army of the United States. In that year, 1835, said Major Taliaferro took said Harriet to said Fort Snelling, a military post, situated as hereinbefore stated, and kept her there as a slave until the year 1836, and then sold and delivered her as a slave at said Fort Snelling unto the said Dr. Emerson hereinbefore named. Said Dr. Emerson held said Harriet in slavery at said Fort Snelling until the year 1838.

In the year 1836, the plaintiff and said Harriet at said Fort Snelling, with the consent of said Dr. Emerson, who then claimed to be their master and owner, intermarried, and took each other for husband and wife. Eliza and Lizzie, named in the third count of the plaintiff's declaration, are the fruit of that marriage. Eliza is about fourteen years old, and was born on board the steamboat Gipsey, north of the north line of the State of Missouri, and upon the river Mississippi. Lizzie is about seven years old, and was born in the State of Missouri, at the military post called Jefferson Barracks.

In the year 1838, said Dr. Emerson removed the plaintiff and said Harriet and their said daughter Eliza, from said Fort Snelling to the State of Missouri, where they have ever since resided.

Before the commencement of this suit, said Dr. Emerson sold and conveyed the plaintiff, said Harriet, Eliza, and Lizzie, to the defendant, as slaves, and the defendant has ever since claimed to hold them and each of them as slaves.

At the times mentioned in the plaintiff's declaration, the defendant, claiming to be owner as aforesaid, laid his hands upon said plaintiff, Harriet, Eliza, and Lizzie, and imprisoned them, doing in this respect, however, no more than what he might lawfully do if they were of right his slaves at such times. . . .

Mr. Chief Justice TANEY delivered the opinion of the court.

This case has been twice argued. After the argument at the last term, differences of opinion were found to exist among the members of the court; and as the questions in controversy are of the highest importance, and the court was at that time much pressed by the ordinary business of the term, it was deemed advisable to continue the case, and direct a re-argument on some of the points, in order that we might have an opportunity of giving to the whole subject a more deliberate consideration. It has accordingly been again argued by counsel, and considered by the court; and I now proceed to deliver its opinion.

There are two leading questions presented by the record:

1. Had the Circuit Court of the United States jurisdiction to hear and determine the case between these parties? And

2. If it had jurisdiction, is the judgment it has given erroneous or not?

The plaintiff in error, who was also the plaintiff in the court below, was, with his wife and children, held as slaves by the defendant, in the State of Missouri; and he brought this action in the Circuit Court of the United States for that district, to assert the title of himself and his family to freedom.

The declaration is in the form usually adopted in that State to try questions of this description, and contains the averment necessary to give the court jurisdiction; that he and the defendant are citizens of different States; that is, that he is a citizen of Missouri, and the defendant a citizen of New York.

The defendant pleaded in abatement to the jurisdiction of the court, that the plaintiff was not a citizen of the State of Missouri, as alleged in his declaration, being a negro of African descent, whose ancestors were of pure African blood, and who were brought into this country and sold as slaves. . . . [T]he plea in abatement is necessarily under consideration; and it becomes, therefore, our duty to decide whether the facts stated in the plea are or are not sufficient to show that the plaintiff is not entitled to sue as a citizen in a court of the United States.

This is certainly a very serious question, and one that now for the first time has been brought for decision before this court. But it is brought here by those who have a right to bring it, and it is our duty to meet it and decide it.

The question is simply this: Can a negro, whose ancestors were imported into this country, and sold as slaves, become a member of the political community formed and brought into existence by the Constitution of the United States, and as such become entitled to all the rights, and privileges, and immunities, guarantied by that instrument to the citizen? One of which rights is the privilege of suing in a court of the United States in the cases specified in the Constitution.

It will be observed, that the plea applies to that class of persons only whose ancestors were negroes of the African race, and imported into this country, and sold and held as slaves. The only matter in issue before the court, therefore, is, whether the descendants of such slaves, when they shall be emancipated, or who are born of parents who had become free before their birth, are citizens of a State, in the sense in which the word citizen is used in the Constitution of the United States. And this being the only matter in dispute on the pleadings, the court must be understood as speaking in this opinion of that class only, that is, of those persons who are the descendants of Africans who were imported into this country, and sold as slaves. . . .

The words "people of the United States" and "citizens" are synonymous terms, and mean the same thing. They both describe the political body who, according to our republican institutions, form the sovereignty, and who hold the power and conduct the Government through their representatives. They are what we familiarly call the "sovereign people," and every citizen is one of this people, and a constituent member of this sovereignty. The question before us is, whether the class of persons described in the plea in abatement compose a portion of this people, and are constituent members of this sovereignty? We think they are not, and that they are not included, and were not intended to be included, under the word "citizens" in the Constitution, and can therefore claim none of the rights and privileges which that instrument provides for and secures to citizens of the United States. On the contrary, they were at that time considered as a subordinate and inferior class of beings, who had been subjugated by the dominant race, and, whether emancipated or not, yet remained subject to their authority, and had no rights or privileges but such as those who held the power and the Government might choose to grant them.

It is not the province of the court to decide upon the justice or injustice, the policy or impolicy, of these laws. The decision of that question belonged to the political or law-making power; to those who formed the sovereignty and framed the Constitution. The duty of the court is, to interpret the instrument they have framed, with the best lights we can obtain on the subject, and to administer it as we find it, according to its true intent and meaning when it was adopted.

It becomes necessary, therefore, to determine who were citizens of the several States when the Constitution was adopted. And in order to do this, we must recur to the Governments and institutions of the thirteen colonies, when they separated from Great Britain and formed new sovereignties, and took their places in the family of independent nations. We must inquire who, at that time, were recognised as the people or citizens of a State, whose rights and liberties had been outraged by the English Government; and who declared their independence, and assumed the powers of Government to defend their rights by force of arms.

In the opinion of the court, the legislation and histories of the times, and the language used in the Declaration of Independence, show, that neither the class of persons who had been imported as slaves, nor their descendants, whether they had become free or not, were then acknowledged as a part of the people, nor intended to be included in the general words used in that memorable instrument. . . .

The brief preamble sets forth by whom it was formed, for what purposes, and for whose benefit and protection. It declares that it is formed by the *people* of the United States; that is to say, by those who were members of the different political communities in the several States; and its great object is declared to be to secure the blessings of liberty to themselves and their posterity. It speaks in general terms of the *people* of the United States, and of *citizens* of the several States, when it is providing for the exercise of the powers granted or the privileges secured to the citizen. It does not define what description of persons are intended to be included under these terms, or who shall be regarded as a citizen and one of the people. It uses them as terms so well understood, that no further description or definition was necessary.

But there are two clauses in the Constitution which point directly and specifically to the negro race as a separate class of persons, and show clearly that they were not regarded as a portion of the people or citizens of the Government then formed.

One of these clauses reserves to each of the thirteen States the right to import slaves until the year 1808, if it thinks proper. And the importation which it thus sanctions was unquestionably of persons of the race of which we are speaking, as the traffic in slaves in the United States had always been confined to them. And by the other provision the States pledge themselves to each other to maintain the right of property of the master, by delivering up to him any slave who may have escaped from his service, and be found within their respective territories. By the first above-mentioned clause, therefore, the right to purchase and hold this property is directly sanctioned and authorized for twenty years by the people who framed the Constitution. And by the second, they pledge themselves to maintain and uphold the right of the master in the manner specified, as long as the Government they then formed should endure. And these two provisions show, conclusively, that neither the description of persons therein referred to, nor their descendants, were embraced in any of the other provisions of the Constitution; for certainly these two clauses were not intended to confer on them or their posterity the blessings of liberty, or any of the personal rights so carefully provided for the citizen. . . .

The legislation of the States therefore shows, in a manner not to be mistaken, the inferior and subject condition of that race at the time the Constitution was adopted, and long afterwards, throughout the thirteen States by which that instrument was framed; and it is hardly consistent with the respect due to these States, to suppose that they regarded at that time, as fellow-citizens and members of the sovereignty, a class of beings whom they had thus stigmatized; whom, as we are bound, out of respect to the State sovereignties, to assume they had deemed it just and necessary thus to stigmatize, and upon whom they had impressed such deep and enduring marks of inferiority and degradation; or, that when they met in convention to form the Constitution, they looked upon them as a portion of their constituents, or designed to include them in the provisions so carefully inserted for the security and protection of the liberties and rights of their citizens. It cannot be supposed that they intended to secure to them rights, and privileges, and rank, in the new political body throughout the Union, which every one of them denied within the limits of its own dominion. More especially, it cannot be believed that the large slaveholding States regarded them as included in the word citizens, or would have consented to a Constitution which might compel them to receive them in that character from another State. For if they were so received, and entitled to the privileges and immunities of citizens, it would exempt them from the operation of the special laws and from the police regulations which they considered to be necessary for their own safety. It would give to persons of the negro race, who were recognised as citizens in any one State of the Union, the right to enter every other State whenever they pleased, singly or in companies, without pass or passport, and without obstruction, to sojourn there as long as they pleased, to go where they pleased at every hour of the day or night without molestation, unless they committed some violation of law for which a white man would be punished; and it would give them the full liberty of speech in public and in private upon all subjects upon which its own citizens might speak; to hold public meetings upon political affairs, and to keep and carry arms wherever they went. And all of this would be done in the face of the subject race of the same color, both free and slaves, and inevitably producing discontent and insubordination among them, and endangering the peace and safety of the State. . . .

No one, we presume, supposes that any change in public opinion or feeling, in relation to this unfortunate race, in the civilized nations of Europe or in this country, should induce the court to give to the words of the Constitution a more liberal construction in their favor than they were intended to bear when the instrument was framed and adopted. Such an argument would be altogether inadmissible in any tribunal called on to interpret it. If any of its provisions are deemed unjust, there is a mode prescribed in the instrument itself by which it may be amended; but while it remains unaltered, it must be construed now as it was understood at the time of its adoption. It is not only the same in words, but the same in meaning, and delegates the same powers to the Government, and reserves and secures the same rights and privileges to the citizen; and as long as it continues to exist in its present form, it speaks not only in the same words, but with the same meaning and intent with which it spoke when it came from the hands of its framers, and was voted on and adopted by the people of the United States. Any other rule of construction would abrogate the judicial character of this court, and make it the mere reflex of the popular opinion or passion of the day. This court was not created by the Constitution for such purposes. Higher and graver trusts have been confided to it, and it must not falter in the path of duty.

What the construction was at that time, we think can hardly admit of doubt. We have the language of the Declaration of Independence and of the Articles of Confederation, in addition to the plain words of the Constitution itself; we have the legislation of the different States, before, about the time, and since, the Constitution was adopted; we have the legislation of Congress, from the time of its adoption to a recent period; and we have the constant and uniform action of the Executive Department, all concurring together, and leading to the same result. And if anything in relation to the construction of the Constitution can be regarded as settled, it is that which we now give to the word "citizen" and the word "people."

And upon a full and careful consideration of the subject, the court is of opinion, that, upon the facts stated in the plea in abatement, Dred Scott was not a citizen of Missouri within the meaning of the Constitution of the United States, and not entitled as such to sue in its courts; and, consequently, that the Circuit Court had no jurisdiction of the case, and that the judgment on the plea in abatement is erroneous.

We are aware that doubts are entertained by some of the members of the court, whether the plea in abatement is legally before the court upon this writ of error; but if that plea is regarded as waived, or out of the case upon any other ground, yet the question as to the jurisdiction of the Circuit Court is presented on the face of the bill of exception itself, taken by the plaintiff at the trial; for he admits that he and his wife were born slaves, but endeavors to make out his title to freedom and citizenship by showing that they were taken by their owner to certain places, hereinafter mentioned, where slavery could not by law exist, and that they thereby became free, and upon their return to Missouri became citizens of that State.

Now, if the removal of which he speaks did not give them their freedom, then by his own admission he is still a slave; and whatever opinions may be entertained in favor of the citizenship of a free person of the African race, no one supposes that a slave is a citizen of the State or of the United States. If, therefore, the acts done by his owner did not make them free persons, he is still a slave, and certainly incapable of suing in the character of a citizen.

The principle of law is too well settled to be disputed, that a court can give no judgment for either party, where it has no jurisdiction; and if, upon the showing of Scott himself, it appeared that he was still a slave, the case ought to have been dismissed, and the judgment against him and in favor of the defendant for costs, is, like that on the plea in abatement, erroneous, and the suit ought to have been dismissed by the Circuit Court for want of jurisdiction in that court. . . .

In considering this part of the controversy, two questions arise: 1. Was he, together with his family, free in Missouri by reason of the stay in the territory of the United States hereinbefore mentioned? And 2. If they were not, is Scott himself free by reason of his removal to Rock Island, in the State of Illinois, as stated in the above admissions?

We proceed to examine the first question.

The act of Congress, upon which the plaintiff relies, declares that slavery and involuntary servitude, except as a punishment for crime, shall be forever prohibited in all that part of the territory ceded by France, under the name of Louisiana, which lies north of thirty-six degrees thirty minutes north latitude, and not included within the limits of Missouri. And the difficulty which meets us at the threshold of this part of the inquiry is, whether Congress was authorized to pass this law under any of the powers granted to it by the Constitution; for if the authority is not given by that instrument, it is the duty of this court to declare it void and inoperative, and incapable of conferring freedom upon any one who is held as a slave under the laws of any one of the States. . . .

. . . The power to expand the territory of the United States by the admission of new States is plainly given; and in the construction of this power by all the departments of the Government, it has been held to authorize the acquisition of territory, not fit for admission at the time, but to be admitted as soon as its population and situation would entitle it to admission. It is acquired to become a State, and not to be held as a colony and governed by Congress with absolute authority; and as the propriety of admitting a new State is committed to the sound discretion of Congress, the power to acquire territory for that purpose, to be held by the United States until it is in a suitable condition to become a State upon an equal footing with the other States, must rest upon the same discretion. . . .

But until that time arrives, it is undoubtedly necessary that some Government should be established, in order to organize society, and to protect the inhabitants in their persons and property; and as the people of the United States could act in this matter only through the Government which represented them, and through which they spoke and acted when the Territory was obtained, it was not only within the scope of its powers, but it was its duty to pass such laws and establish such a Government as would enable those by whose authority they acted to reap the advantages anticipated from its acquisition, and to gather there a population which would enable it to assume the position to which it was destined among the States of the Union. . . .

But the power of Congress over the person or property of a citizen can never be a mere discretionary power under our Constitution and form of Government. The powers of the Government and the rights and privileges of the citizen are regulated and plainly defined by the Constitution itself. . . .

A reference to a few of the provisions of the Constitution will illustrate this proposition.

For example, no one, we presume, will contend that Congress can make any law in a Territory respecting the establishment of religion, or the free exercise thereof, or abridging the freedom of speech or of the press, or the right of the people of the Territory peaceably to assemble, and to petition the Government for the redress of grievances.

Nor can Congress deny to the people the right to keep and bear arms, nor the right to trial by jury, nor compel any one to be a witness against himself in a criminal proceeding.

These powers, and others, in relation to rights of person, which it is not necessary here to enumerate, are, in express and positive terms, denied to the General Government; and the rights of private property have been guarded with equal care. Thus the rights of property are united with the rights of person, and placed on the same ground by the fifth amendment to the Constitution, which provides that no person shall be deprived of life, liberty, and property, without due process of law. And an act of Congress which deprives a citizen of the United States of his liberty or property, merely because he came himself or brought his property into a particular Territory of the United States, and who had committed no offence against the laws, could hardly be dignified with the name of due process of law. . . .

Upon these considerations, it is the opinion of the court that the act of Congress which prohibited a citizen from holding and owning property of this kind in the territory of the United States north of the line therein mentioned, is not warranted by the Constitution, and is therefore void; and that neither Dred Scott himself, nor any of his family, were made free by being carried into this territory; even if they had been carried there by the owner, with the intention of becoming a permanent resident.

We have so far examined the case, as it stands under the Constitution of the United States, and the powers thereby delegated to the Federal Government.

But there is another point in the case which depends on State power and State law. And it is contended, on the part of the plaintiff, that he is made free by being taken to Rock Island, in the State of Illinois, independently of his residence in the territory of the United States; and being so made free, he was not again reduced to a state of slavery by being brought back to Missouri.

Our notice of this part of the case will be very brief; for the principle on which it depends was decided in this court, upon much consideration, in the case of Strader et al. *v.* Graham, reported in 10th Howard, 82. In that case, the slaves had been taken from Kentucky to Ohio, with the consent of the owner, and afterwards brought back to Kentucky. And this court held that their *status* or condition, as free or slave, depended upon the laws of Kentucky, when they were brought back into that State, and not of Ohio; and that this court had no jurisdiction to revise the judgment of a State court upon its own laws. This was the point directly before the court, and the decision that this court had not jurisdiction turned upon it, as will be seen by the report of the case.

So in this case. As Scott was a slave when taken into the State of Illinois by his owner, and was there held as such, and brought back in that character, his *status*, as free or slave, depended on the laws of Missouri, and not of Illinois.

It has, however, been urged in the argument, that by the laws of Missouri he was free on his return, and that this case, therefore, cannot be governed by the case of Strader et al. *v.* Graham, where it appeared, by the laws of Kentucky, that the plaintiffs continued to be slaves on their return from Ohio. But whatever doubts or opinions may, at one time, have been entertained upon this subject, we are satisfied, upon a careful examination of all the cases decided in the State courts of Missouri referred to, that it is now firmly settled by the decisions of the highest court in the State, that Scott and his family upon their return were not free, but were, by the laws of Missouri, the property of the defendant; and that the Circuit

Court of the United States had no jurisdiction, when, by the laws of the State, the plaintiff was a slave, and not a citizen. . . .

Upon the whole, therefore, it is the judgment of this court, that it appears by the record before us that the plaintiff in error is not a citizen of Missouri, in the sense in which that word is used in the Constitution; and that the Circuit Court of the United States, for that reason, had no jurisdiction in the case, and could give no judgment in it. Its judgment for the defendant must, consequently, be reversed, and a mandate issued, directing the suit to be dismissed for want of jurisdiction.

[In addition to the Chief Justice's opinion for the Court, six concurring and two dissenting opinions were filed. The entire case occupies 241 pages in Howard's Reports. All of the separate opinions are omitted, except for the following brief extracts from the dissenting opinion of Mr. Justice Curtis.]

Mr. Justice CURTIS, dissenting:[32]

The conclusions at which I have arrived [on the issue of jurisdiction] are:

First. That the free native-born citizens of each State are citizens of the United States.

Second. That as free colored persons born within some of the States are citizens of those States, such persons are also citizens of the United States.

Third. That every such citizen, residing in any State, has the right to sue and is liable to be sued in the Federal courts, as a citizen of that State in which he resides.

Fourth. That as the plea to the jurisdiction in this case shows no facts, except that the plaintiff was of African descent, and his ancestors were sold as slaves, and as these facts are not inconsistent with his citizenship of the United States, and his residence in the State of Missouri, the plea to the jurisdiction was bad, and the judgment of the Circuit Court overruling it was correct.

I dissent, therefore, from that part of the opinion of the majority of the court, in which it is held that a person of African descent cannot be a citizen of the United States; and I regret I must go further, and dissent both from what I deem their assumption of authority to examine the constitutionality of the act of Congress commonly called the Missouri compromise

---

[32] Twenty-one years earlier, Curtis had represented the slave owner in *Commonwealth v. Aves,* p. 44 *supra.* His brother represented Dred Scott in the second argument before the United States Supreme Court in *Dred Scott v. Sandford.* [*Eds.* note.]

act, and the grounds and conclusions announced in their opinion. . . .

But as, in my opinion, the Circuit Court had jurisdiction, I am obliged to consider the question whether its judgment on the merits of the case should stand or be reversed.

The residence of the plaintiff in the State of Illinois, and the residence of himself and his wife in the territory acquired from France lying north of latitude thirty-six degrees thirty minutes, and north of the State of Missouri, are each relied on by the plaintiff in error. As the residence in the territory affects the plaintiff's wife and children as well as himself, I must inquire what was its effect.

The general question may be stated to be, whether the plaintiff's *status*, as a slave, was so changed by his residence within that territory, that he was not a slave in the State of Missouri, at the time this action was brought.

In such cases, two inquiries arise, which may be confounded, but should be kept distinct.

The first is, what was the law of the Territory into which the master and slave went, respecting the relation between them?

The second is, whether the State of Missouri recognises and allows the effect of that law of the Territory, on the *status* of the slave, on his return within its jurisdiction.

As to the first of these questions, the will of States and nations, by whose municipal law slavery is not recognised, has been manifested in three different ways.

One is, absolutely to dissolve the relation, and terminate the rights of the master existing under the law of the country whence the parties came. This is said by Lord Stowell, in the case of the slave Grace, (2 Hag. Ad. R., 94,) and by the Supreme Court of Louisiana in the case of Maria Louise *v.* Marot, (9 Louis. R., 473,) to be the law of France; and it has been the law of several States of this Union, in respect to slaves introduced under certain conditions. . . .

The second is, where the municipal law of a country not recognising slavery, it is the will of the State to refuse the master all aid to exercise any control over his slave; and if he attempt to do so, in a manner justifiable only by that relation, to prevent the exercise of that control. But no law exists, designed to operate directly on the relation of master and slave, and put an end to that relation. This is said by Lord Stowell, in the case above mentioned, to be the law of England, and by Mr. Chief Justice Shaw, in the case of the Commonwealth *v.* Aves, (18 Pick., 193,) to be the law of Massachusetts.

The third is, to make a distinction between the case of a master and his slave only temporarily in the country, *animo non manendi*, and those who are there to reside for permanent or indefinite purposes. This is said by Mr. Wheaton to be the law of Prussia, and was formerly the statute law of several States of our Union. It is necessary in this case to keep in view this distinction between those countries whose laws are designed to act directly on the *status* of a slave, and make him a freeman, and those where his master can obtain no aid from the laws to enforce his rights.

It is to the last case only that the authorities, out of Missouri, relied on by defendant, apply, when the residence in the non-slaveholding Territory was permanent. In the Commonwealth *v.* Aves, (18 Pick., 218,) Mr. Chief Justice Shaw said: "From the principle above stated, on which a slave brought here becomes free, to wit: that he becomes entitled to the protection of our laws, it would seem to follow, as a necessary conclusion, that if the slave waives the protection of those laws, and returns to the State where he is held as a slave, his condition is not changed." It was upon this ground, as is apparent from his whole reasoning, that Sir William Scott [Stowell] rests his opinion in the case of the slave Grace. To use one of his expressions, the effect of the law of England was to put the liberty of the slave into a parenthesis. If there had been an act of Parliament declaring that a slave coming to England with his master should thereby be deemed no longer to be a slave, it is easy to see that the learned judge could not have arrived at the same conclusion. This distinction is very clearly stated and shown by President Tucker, in his opinion in the case of Betty *v.* Horton, (5 Leigh's Virginia R., 615.).
. . .
To avoid misapprehension on this important and difficult subject, I will state, distinctly, the conclusions at which I have arrived. They are:

First. The rules of international law respecting the emancipation of slaves, by the rightful operation of the laws of another State or country upon the *status* of the slave, while resident in such foreign State or country, are part of the common law of Missouri, and have not been abrogated by any statute law of that State.

Second. The laws of the United States, constitutionally enacted, which operated directly on and changed the *status* of a slave coming into the Territory of Wisconsin with his master, who went thither to reside for an indefinite length of time, in the performance of his duties as an officer of the United States, had a rightful operation on the *status* of the slave, and it is in conformity with the rules of international law that this change of *status* should be recognised everywhere.

Third. The laws of the United States, in operation in the Territory of Wisconsin at the time of the plaintiff's residence there, did act directly on the *status* of the plaintiff, and change his *status* to that of a free man.

Fourth. The plaintiff and his wife were capable of contracting, and, with the consent of Dr. Emerson, did contract a marriage in that Territory, valid under its laws; and the validity of this marriage cannot be questioned in Missouri, save by showing that it was in fraud of the laws of that State, or of some right derived from them; which cannot be shown in this case, because the master consented to it.

Fifth. That the consent of the master that his slave, residing in a country which does not tolerate slavery, may enter into a lawful contract of marriage, attended with the civil rights and duties which belong to that condition, is an effectual act of emancipation. And the law does not enable Dr. Emerson, or any one claiming under him, to assert a title to the married persons as slaves, and thus destroy the obligation of the contract of marriage, and bastardize their issue, and reduce them to slavery.

But it is insisted that the Supreme Court of Missouri has settled this case by its decision in Scott *v.* Emerson, (15 Missouri Reports, 576;) and that this decision is in conformity with the weight of authority elsewhere, and with sound principles. If the Supreme Court of Missouri had placed its decision on the ground that it appeared Dr. Emerson never became domiciled in the Territory, and so its laws could not rightfully operate on him and his slave; and the facts that he went there to reside indefinitely, as an officer of the United States, and that the plaintiff was lawfully married there, with Dr. Emerson's consent, were left out of view, the decision would find support in other cases, and I might not be prepared to deny its correctness. But the decision is not rested on this ground. The domicil of Dr. Emerson in that Territory is not questioned in that decision; and it is placed on a broad denial of the operation, in Missouri, of the law of any foreign State or country upon the *status* of a slave, going with his master from Missouri into such foreign State or country, even though they went thither to become, and actually became, permanent inhabitants of such foreign State or country, the laws whereof acted directly on the *status* of the slave, and changed his *status* to that of a freeman.

To the correctness of such a decision I cannot assent. In my judgment, the opinion of the majority of the court in that case is in conflict with its previous decisions, with a great weight of judicial authority in other slaveholding States, and with fundamental principles of private international law. . . .

But it is further insisted we are bound to follow this decision. I do not think so. In this case, it is to be determined what laws of the United States were in operation in the Territory of Wisconsin, and what was their effect on the *status* of the plaintiff. Could the plaintiff contract a lawful marriage there? Does any law of the State of Missouri impair the obligation of that contract of marriage, destroy his rights as a husband, bastardize the issue of the marriage, and reduce them to a state of slavery?

These questions, which arise exclusively under the Constitution and laws of the United States, this court, under the Constitution and laws of the United States, has the rightful authority finally to decide. And if we look beyond these questions, we come to the consideration whether the rules of international law, which are part of the laws of Missouri until displaced by some statute not alleged to exist, do or do not require the *status* of the plaintiff, as fixed by the laws of the Territory of Wisconsin, to be recognised in Missouri. Upon such a question, not depending on any statute or local usage, but on principles of universal jurisprudence, this court has repeatedly asserted it could not hold itself bound by the decisions of State courts, however great respect might be felt for their learning, ability, and impartiality. (See Swift *v.* Tyson, 16 Peters's R., 1; . . .).

Sitting here to administer the law between these parties, I do not feel at liberty to surrender my own convictions of what the law requires, to the authority of the decision in 15 Missouri Reports.

I have thus far assumed, merely for the purpose of the argument, that the laws of the United States, respecting slavery in this Territory, were constitutionally enacted by Congress. It remains to inquire whether they are constitutional and binding laws. . . .

[Justice Curtis went on to argue that the provisions of the Missouri Compromise, outlawing slavery in the area that included Fort Snelling, were within the constitutional power of Congress.]

QUESTIONS

1. A genuine controversy or a collusive suit?—Chief Justice Charles Evans Hughes of the United States Supreme Court once said that *Dred Scott* was one of the Court's "self-inflicted wounds." Consider the following comments of Professor Paul Freund, referring to Chief Justice Hughes's remark:

> Sometimes issues have been decided of the gravest importance which a court, if better advised, could with propriety have left undecided, and which the judgment of history suggests should have been left for decision at a later date and perhaps by other arbiters. . . . No graver issue was ever decided by the Supreme Court than that in the *Dred Scott* case; and it was presented in circumstances which suggested that the Court had no business dealing with it at all. A colorable transfer of ownership of Scott from his Missouri master to a brother-in-law in New York was relied on to create diversity of citizenship between Scott and the defendant and so to provide a basis for relitigating in a federal circuit court the issue which a Missouri court had decided adversely to Scott. This maneuver proved successful, so far as jurisdiction was concerned, and the case was presented on an agreed statement of facts, though it would seem that, in a genuine lawsuit, evidence would have been introduced to show the character of the transfer and to indicate that Dred Scott was simply a pawn in a jurisdictional game. . . .
>
> [This was a case in which counsel were] . . . perhaps too eager for a settlement of burning issues. P. FREUND, ON UNDERSTANDING THE SUPREME COURT 83-84 (1951).

In general, courts in the United States will refuse to decide collusive suits or cases which have become moot, and will refuse to give "advisory opinions" on issues which are not presented in the format of an adversary proceeding. That is, a court in the United States generally refuses to perform its function of declaring law unless that function is to be performed in the course of resolving a real dispute before the court. (This position has a constitutional basis in the case of federal courts, whose judicial power is limited by Article III of the Constitution to "Cases" or "Controversies.") Is this a wise view of the nature of the judicial function in the American legal system? In *Dred Scott*, should the Supreme Court have declined to exercise its lawmaking function?

2. The conflict between Missouri and Illinois law.—On the issue parallel to the one decided in *The Slave, Grace,* Chief Justice

Taney held in *Dred Scott,* following an earlier decision of the Supreme Court, that Missouri, as a state in the federal union, was free to decide for itself whether Scott's former presence in Illinois should leave him free upon his return with his master to Missouri. The fugitive-slave provision of the Constitution, interpreted in *Commonwealth v. Aves,* applied only to slaves who fled to free states, and did not purport to deal with the case of the non-fugitive slave who returned to a slave state. And the effect of the holding in *Dred Scott* was to say that no other provision of the Federal Constitution controlled the content of the law of slave states on this issue. Missouri, along with a few other states (see p. 79 *supra*), had previously held that a slave who had resided in a free state would be free upon his return, but in Scott's suit in a Missouri state court (which preceded the federal court action that was ultimately decided by the Supreme Court), the Missouri Supreme Court departed from its earlier decisions and held that Scott would again be a slave upon his return to the state. There is a provision of the Constitution which might have been the basis for an argument that the Constitution did control the decision of this issue: the full faith and credit clause, Article IV, section 1, which provides that "Full faith and credit shall be given in each state to the public acts, records, and judicial proceedings of every other state."[33] If we assume that Illinois law would have considered Scott emancipated (as distinguished from merely suspending the master-slave relationship while Scott and his owner were in Illinois), then should this clause require Missouri to recognize Scott's emancipated status? Or should the clause instead require Illinois to permit the owner to exercise dominion over Scott? The Supreme Court has, in general, concluded that this clause of the Constitution does not determine which state's law should prevail when state laws conflict with each other. Was *Dred Scott* a stronger or weaker case for application of the result in *The Slave, Grace?* Compare the nature of the federal system, created by the Constitution, with the relationship of the British colonies to England when *The Slave, Grace* was decided. Was it a sound result, in the American federal system, to conclude that Missouri could decide for itself whether Dred Scott was a slave? What was Justice Curtis's view on this question? Would it have been a better result if the Supreme Court had decided that the question of Scott's status was controlled in all states either by the law of Illinois or by the law of Missouri? Would that be an issue appropriate for the

---

[33] In his dissent, Justice Curtis suggested a similar use for the contract clause, Art. I, § 10. cl. 1, which provides: "No State shall . . . pass any . . . Law impairing the Obligation of Contracts. . . ."

Court, as distinguished from Congress, to decide, in view of the "political" nature of the issue—reconciliation of the conflicting interests of Missouri and Illinois? Questions like these are studied in the course in conflict of laws.

3. Limitations on the legislature's lawmaking power in the American legal system: the constitutional issues in Dred Scott.— Up to this point we have seen some of the limitations which have been developed on the lawmaking powers of courts—the necessity of making law only in the process of resolving a genuine dispute, the doctrine of *stare decisis*, canons of statutory construction such as that calling for strict construction of penal statutes. The *Dred Scott* case illustrates an institutional limitation, in the American legal system, on the lawmaking powers of legislatures. The United States Constitution, and the constitutions of the states, allocate lawmaking powers to legislatures and articulate express limitations on those powers. Stemming from Chief Justice Marshall's opinion in Marbury v. Madison, 1 Cranch 137 (1803), the principle has been established that the United States Supreme Court has the power to decide whether acts of the Congress fall within Congress's delegated powers or exceed the constitutional limitations on Congress's powers. Similar recognition of the power of "judicial review" has taken place with respect to the validity of acts of state legislatures under the federal and state constitutions. In these materials we shall not explore the bases for the doctrine of judicial review; that doctrine is studied in the courses in constitutional law. But we will study examples of the application of this doctrine in practice, for understanding judicial review is an integral part of an understanding of the legal system. Determination by a court of the constitutionality of a statute enacted by a legislature involves the process of interpretation of the words of the constitution, and therefore, as we have seen in *Aves*, involves lawmaking by the court.

In *Dred Scott* there were two constitutional issues relating to the validity of the Missouri Compromise of 1820: whether the powers delegated to Congress included authorization to prohibit slavery in the territories of the United States, and, assuming that Congress had a constitutional basis for imposing such a prohibition, whether the due process clause of the Fifth Amendment ("No person shall . . . be deprived of life, liberty, or property, without due process of law. . . .") nevertheless precluded Congress from enacting such a prohibition of slavery. Note the contrasting interpretive problems before the Connecticut court in *Jackson v. Bulloch*, where the court's function was to attribute meaning to the word "left" in the statute, and before the United States Supreme Court in *Dred Scott* with respect to the meaning of the words "due process of law." Chief Justice Taney did not spell out in any detail why the Missouri Compromise was in violation of the Fifth Amendment, and we shall not here explore that issue. But it should be noted, as an introduction to the performance of the court's function in interpreting such phrases of the Constitution as "due process of law," that there is a range of possible meanings which might be attributed here to "due process." The phrase might refer solely to whether the proper procedure was followed by the Congress in adopting the statute, without regard to the substantive content of the statute. Or "due process" could be interpreted as requiring that there be some "due" basis for the statute—that Congress have had some sufficient basis for enacting the statute. And if due process is to be understood as imposing some such requirement of "due" basis on legislative lawmaking, another question arises: Should the Court make its own determination of the justification for the statute as if it were the primary lawmaker, or should it merely scrutinize the statute to determine whether the legislature acted within a broad range of possible "reasonable" positions? What was Chief Justice Taney's interpretation of the due process clause in *Dred Scott*? His opinion fails to build to any doctrinal bridge to his conclusion that the Missouri Compromise violated the Fifth Amendment. This was the first time the Supreme Court had held an act of Congress unconstitutional since 1803, when *Marbury v. Madison* was decided. In view of the political setting of the case, Taney was certain to be charged with deciding first and rationalizing afterwards. Should he have given a fuller explanation? Recall the range of possible meanings suggested above which "due process" might have.

The cases in Chapter 2 will provide an opportunity for detailed consideration of the interpretation of another broad phrase of the Constitution: "the equal protection of the laws."

4. The Fourteenth Amendment and Negro citizenship.—One of the central points in Chief Justice Taney's opinion in *Dred Scott* was overruled in 1868, with the adoption of the Fourteenth Amendment. Section 1 of the amendment provides, in part: "All persons born or naturalized in the United States, and subject to the jurisdiction thereof, are citizens of the United States and of the State wherein they reside."

THE EMANCIPATION PROCLAMATION:
LAWMAKING BY THE EXECUTIVE

The abolition of slavery in the United States culminated in the issuance of the Emancipation Proclamation[34] by President Lincoln in 1863 and the adoption of the Thirteenth Amendment to the Constitution in 1865.

The Emancipation Proclamation designated states and parts of states "wherein the people thereof respectively, are this day in rebellion against the United States," and continued: ". . . I do order and declare that all persons held as slaves within said designated States, and parts of States, are, and henceforward shall be free; and that the Executive government of the United States, including the military and naval authorities thereof, will recognize and maintain the freedom of said persons."

This proclamation was an awesome exercise of lawmaking power by the executive branch of government, as contrasted with the judicial and legislative law-declaration illustrated in the materials thus far. Law-declaration by the executive branch in the American legal system is a common and essential function. It is a regular part of the administrative process, by which much of the day-to-day functioning of government is carried on, effectuating policies in statutes enacted by the legislature. Lincoln's Emancipation Proclamation, however, was outside the normal pattern for the exercise of executive power. There was no specific statutory basis for his action, and its legality was widely debated. The proclamation stated the basis for the presidential authority:

> . . . I, Abraham Lincoln, President of the United States, by virtue of the power in me invested as Commander-in-Chief, of the Army and Navy of the United States in time of actual rebellion against authority and government of the United States, and as a fit and necessary war measure for suppressing said rebellion. . . .

Later in the proclamation came this phrase: "And upon this act, sincerely believed to be an act of justice, warranted by the Constitution, upon military necessity. . . ." The United States Constitution "vests" all "legislative" powers in the Congress, all "executive" powers in the President, and all "judicial" powers in the Supreme Court and other federal courts established by Congress. (State constitutions use similar terminology.) The legal basis for the Emancipation Proclamation had to be found within

---

[34] 12 STAT. 1267, 1268 (1862, 1863).

the "executive" powers of the President. There was no assertion that the President was empowered in time of peace to abolish slavery everywhere within the United States. Lincoln invoked the powers of the President as commander-in-chief of the armed forces, and carefully limited the proclamation's effect to states and parts of states which were "in rebellion against the United States." Thus there were slaveholding areas within the United States which did not fall within the scope of the proclamation.

Some of the legal issues raised concerning the validity of the proclamation are suggested in the following extracts from Welling, *The Emancipation Proclamation,* 130 No. Am. Rev. 163, 176-81 (1880):

The questions presented by the Proclamation of January 1, 1863, in the shape actually given to it by Mr. Lincoln, are these:

Firstly. Had the President of the United States, in the exercise of his war powers, a right, under the Constitution and by public law, to decree, on grounds of military necessity, the emancipation and perpetual enfranchisement of slaves in the insurgent States and parts of States?

Secondly. Did such proclamation work, by its own vigor, the immediate, the unconditional, and the perpetual emancipation of all slaves in the districts affected by it?

Thirdly. Did such proclamation, working *proprio vigore,* not only effect the emancipation of all existing slaves in the insurgent territory, but, with regard to slaves so liberated, did it extinguish the status of slavery created by municipal law, insomuch that they would have remained forever free, in fact and law, provided the Constitution and the legal rights and relations of the States under it had remained, on the return of peace, what they were before the war? . . .

1. . . . [I]t would seem that, as a question of law, the first interrogatory must be answered in the negative. Slaves temporarily captured to weaken the enemy and to conquer a peace are not lawful prize of war by military proceedings alone—proclamation, capture, and deportation. The more fully it be conceded that international law, in time and fact of war, knows the slave only as a person, the more fully must it be conceded that this law, by purely military measures, can take no cognizance of him as a chattel, either to

preserve or to destroy the master's property right under municipal law. It leaves questions about the chattel to be settled in another forum, and by another judicature than the wager of battle. . . .

2. No principle of public law is clearer than that which rules the war rights of a belligerent to be correlative and commensurate only with his war powers. . . . It is only so far as and so fast as the conquering belligerent reclaims "enemy territory" and gets possession of "enemy property" that his belligerent rights attach to either. . . .

3. Since the decision of Lord Stowell in the case of the slave Grace, it has been an accepted doctrine of jurisprudence that the slave character of a liberated slave—liberated by residing on free soil—is redintegrated [restored, reestablished] by the voluntary return of such slave to the country of the master. . . . [E]ach State, under the Constitution as it stood, had a right, in the matter of slavery, to order and control its own domestic institutions according to its own judgment exclusively; and the nation, by the conquest of its own territory, "could acquire no new sovereignty, but merely maintain its previous rights." The Proclamation proposed to leave the institution of slavery undisturbed in certain States and parts of States, while destroying it in certain other States and parts of States. Hence, on the supposition that the paper was to have full force and effect after the war, while our civil polity remained the same, a new distribution of powers as between certain States and parts of States on the one hand, and the Federal Government on the other, would have been created by edict of the Executive. Without any express change in the constitution of the United States, and without any express change in the constitutions of the insurgent States, the status of persons on one side of a State line, or even on one side of a county line, would have depended on municipal law; on the other side of such State or county line it would have depended on a military decree of the President. . . . [T]o suppose that the civil courts, in the ordinary course of judicial decision, could have recognized such anomalies, while the rights of the States under the Constitution were still defined by that instrument, is to suppose that judges decree justice without law, without rule, and without reason. It is safe, therefore, to say that the third question above indicated must equally be answered in the negative. . . . And even if it be held that the President's

want to power to issue the Proclamation . . . were cured by actual conquest under it on the part of the Government, and by actual submission to it on the part of the seceded States, insomuch that it would have operated the extinction of the slave status in those States, it still remains the less clear that, without a change in the Constitution of the United States prohibiting slavery in the South, the Proclamation must have failed, with the rights of plenary conquest limited by the Constitution, to insure the perpetual freedom of the slaves liberated under it; for what, under the rights still reserved to the States, would have prevented the future reestablishment of slavery at the South after the return of peace?

The third argument in the preceding extract had been made in a pamphlet, *Executive Power*, by Benjamin R. Curtis, who had resigned from the Court shortly after the *Dred Scott* decision. In October, 1862, a month after Lincoln had promulgated the "preliminary proclamation" that announced his intention to issue the proclamation the next January first, Curtis wrote:

This proclamation, then, by an executive decree, proposes to repeal and annul valid State laws which regulate the domestic relations of their people. Such is the mode of operation of the decree. . . . [T]he President hereby assumes to himself the power to denounce it as a punishment against the entire people of a State, that the valid laws of that State which regulate the domestic condition of its inhabitants shall become null and void, at a certain future date, by reason of the criminal conduct of a governing majority of its people. . . .

It must be obvious to the meanest capacity that, if the President of the United States has an implied constitutional right, as commander-in-chief of the army and navy in time of war, to disregard any one positive prohibition of the Constitution, or to exercise any one power not delegated to the United States by the Constitution, because, in his judgment, he may thereby "best subdue the enemy," he has the same right, for the same reason, to disregard each and every provision of the Constitution, and to exercise all power needful, in his opinion, to enable him "best to subdue the enemy."

It has never been doubted that the power to abolish slavery within the States was not delegated to the United States by the Constitution, but was reserved to the States. If the President, as commander-in-chief of the army and navy in time of war, may, by an executive decree, exercise this power to abolish slavery in the States, which power was reserved to the States, because he is of [the] opinion that he may thus "best subdue the enemy," what other power, reserved to the States or to the people, may not be exercised by the President, for the same reason that he is of [the] opinion he may thus best subdue the enemy? And, if so, what distinction can be made between powers not delegated to the United States at all, and powers which, though thus delegated, are conferred by the Constitution upon some department of the Government other than the Executive? . . .

Whence, then, do these edicts spring? They spring from the assumed power to extend martial law over the whole territory of the United States,—a power for the exercise of which by the President there is no warrant whatever in the Constitution; a power which no free people could confer upon an executive officer and remain a free people. . . . B. CURTIS, 2 A MEMOIR OF BENJAMIN ROBBINS CURTIS, LL.D. 306, 315, 318-19, 329 (1879).

Some of these arguments equally would have denied power to the Congress to enact a statute containing the substance of the Emancipation Proclamation. It should be emphasized that the narrower issue raised here concerns the power of the President, as distinguished from the power of Congress, to declare the law contained in the proclamation. No judicial decisions ever dealt with the validity of the Emancipation Proclamation, for the Thirteenth Amendment settled the question in 1865.

There have been numerous instances of presidential lawmaking without specific statutory authority, but few judicial decisions on the subject. See Comment, *Presidential Legislation by Executive Order*, 37 U. COLO. L. REV. 105 (1964). These issues fall primarily within the domain of those lawyers who are legal advisors to executive officers of the government. The most recent decision in this area by the United States Supreme Court followed President Truman's 1952 seizure of most of the steel mills in the Nation. The President was seeking to avert what the Department of Justice argued would have been a national catastrophe resulting from an imminent nationwide steel strike while the Korean War was in progress. The Court held the seizure to be invalid, some of the Justices saying that lawmaking power was vested by the Constitution in the Congress, not the President, and that executive lawmaking must have congressional authorization. Three dissenting Justices were of the view that the President had been empowered to deal with the national emergency as he did. Youngstown Sheet & Tube Co. v. Sawyer, 343 U.S. 579 (1952).

The first efforts of the federal government to deal with racial discrimination in employment took the form of presidential executive orders, beginning in 1941, requiring fair employment practices by firms contracting with the government. See Pasley, *The Nondiscrimination Clause in Government Contracts*, 43 VA. L. REV. 837 (1957). During the 1960 presidential campaign Senator John F. Kennedy stated that he, with a "stroke of a Presidential pen," would issue regulations dealing with racial discrimination in housing. The executive order he ultimately issued, in 1962, required nondiscrimination by specified categories of individuals and firms who had received federal assistance; the order was less sweeping than many had argued for, leaving out a wide range of federally regulated mortgage lenders, and the restriction in the order's scope resulted in part from government lawyers' conclusions as to the President's legal authority to impose such nondiscrimination requirements. See Sloane & Freedman, *The Executive Order on Housing: The Constitutional Basis for What It Fails To Do*, 9 HOW. L.J. 1 (1963).

During the years 1961-64 (before the enactment of Title VI of the Civil Rights Act of 1964, which prohibited racial discrimination in programs supported by federal funds), there was considerable discussion whether the President should (or could), by executive order, impose a nondiscrimination condition on public school districts which received federal funds and which had been operating racially segregated schools. In these federal programs Congress had set forth specific requirements which, if met, entitled school districts to federal grants; there was no requirement of nonsegregation. The Secretary of Health, Education, and Welfare concluded that there was no legal authority for the executive to impose a nonsegregation requirement. *Hearings Before the Subcommittee on Integration in Federally Assisted Public Education Programs of the Committee on Education and Labor, House of Representatives*, 87th Cong., 2d Sess., H.R. 6890, Feb. 27, 1962, at 15, 18, 38, 653. It was not until the action of Congress, in the Civil Rights Act of 1964, that such a requirement was made a part of federal grant programs. This requirement will be studied in Chapter 3, *infra*.

The issue of the scope of the lawmaking powers of the executive branch of government in the American legal system raises heady questions. It arises most dramatically in times of emergency. On those occasions in which the power has been invoked, it has always been justified as a power allocated by the Constitution, not a power finding its source elsewhere. As Professor John Hope

Franklin points out in THE EMANCIPATION PROCLAMATION 145 (Anchor ed. 1963):

> Lincoln wrote the Emancipation Proclamation amid severe psychological and legal handicaps. Unlike Jefferson, whose Declaration of Independence was a clean break with a legal and constitutional system that had hitherto restricted thought and action, Lincoln was compelled to forge a document of freedom for the slaves within the existing constitutional system and in a manner that would give even greater support to that constitutional system.

THE THIRTEENTH AMENDMENT

The Thirteenth Amendment to the Constitution, adopted in 1865, completed the abolition process and mooted the debate over the validity of the Emancipation Proclamation. It provides:

> Sec. 1. Neither slavery nor involuntary servitude, except as a punishment for crime whereof the party shall have been duly convicted, shall exist within the United States, or any place subject to their jurisdiction.

> Sec. 2. Congress shall have power to enforce this article by appropriate legislation.

Though Lincoln had sought to persuade Congress to adopt some method of compensation for slave owners, no such plan was accepted. While the 1833 Act abolishing slavery in the British colonies had included both compensation and a process of "gradual abolition," and while abolition in some of the northern states had been gradual, the Thirteenth Amendment required immediate and uncompensated abolition.

Chapter 2

SEGREGATION IN THE PUBLIC SCHOOLS: THE FIRST CENTURY

The abolition of slavery was an intense human experience, raising issues of the highest importance for society. Abolition was an economic issue, a political issue, a moral issue. But the accomplishment of abolition necessarily took the form of lawmaking, for slavery had been above all a legal status—a relationship established, defined and protected by law. In Chapter 1 we dealt with a variety of forms of lawmaking that contributed to abolition: constitutions and constitutional amendments, statutes, executive orders, and judge-made rules. In this chapter, we concentrate on judges, for it was judges who built the "separate but equal" formula and judges who undermined and finally discarded it. This chapter, more than any other in these materials, explores substantive legal doctrine—specifically, the doctrine of the equal protection clause of the Fourteenth Amendment to the United States Constitution. The chapter's principal objective, however, is to examine the process of the growth of law through judicial decision-making. The chapter therefore concentrates on a single subject area over a substantial period of time.

That subject is racial segregation in the public schools. While the subject of slavery and its abolition covered the entire range of relationships between white owner and black slave, school segregation is only one aspect of post-abolition race relations. It is necessary for purposes of study to narrow our inquiry at this point, and we leave to other courses the study of the legal ingredient in other phases of the "second abolition"—notably the ending of racial discrimination in voting, housing, employment, public accommodations, and the administration of criminal justice by police and by courts. It is appropriate to select school segregation as the principal subject of this course, both because it touches all aspects of the legal process and because of its symbolic importance to the present generation's black revolution.

A. POST-ABOLITION SEGREGATION AND "SEPARATE BUT EQUAL"

The abolition of slavery by no means produced an immediate full equality of rights for the black man as a member of society. Instead, abolition was followed—in the north and west before the Civil War, and in the south afterwards—by the creation of a subordinate form of citizenship for the Negro. In various states of the north and west, after abolition (in the period before the Civil War), there persisted such legal disabilities for the black man as these: denial of the right to vote, disqualification to be a witness in a judicial proceeding in which a white man was a party, exclusion from jury service, and prohibition on holding real property. Additionally, the races were segregated by more informal means in a great many aspects of public life:

> While statutes and customs circumscribed the Negro's political and judicial rights, extralegal codes—enforced by public opinion—relegated him to a position of social inferiority and divided northern society into "Brahmins and Pariahs." In virtually every phase of existence, Negroes found themselves systematically separated from whites. They were either excluded from railway cars, omnibuses, stagecoaches, and steamboats or assigned to special "Jim Crow" sections; they sat, when permitted, in secluded and remote corners of theaters and lecture halls; they could not enter most hotels, restaurants, and resorts, except as servants; they prayed in "Negro pews" in the white churches, and if partaking of the sacrament of the Lord's Supper, they waited until the whites had been served the bread and wine. Moreover, they were often educated in segregated schools, punished in segregated prisons, nursed in segregated hospitals, and buried in segregated cemeteries. L. LITWACK, NORTH OF SLAVERY: THE NEGRO IN THE FREE STATES 1790-1860, 97 (Phoenix ed. 1965).

In the north and west, the gradual abandonment of these forms of segregation began before the Civil War, but many of them lasted until well into the twentieth century, and some persist today.

Our subject is racial segregation in the public schools, which began, naturally enough, in areas where there *were* public schools in substantial numbers. Our first case, therefore, comes not from the deep south of Jim Crow, but from pre-Civil War New England. The case of *Roberts v. City of Boston*, which follows, was the first judicial declaration of the "separate but equal" principle, and the opinion was written by Chief Justice Shaw, who had previously written for the court in *Commonwealth v. Aves*. By the middle of the nineteenth century, Massachusetts' railroads had given up their practice of racial segregation, and the state had repealed its statutory prohibition on interracial marriages. The separation of white and black children in public schools had been abolished in some parts of the state. Boston, however, continued to maintain a system of racially segregated public schools. Negroes in Boston held a number of mass meetings seeking to bring about the elimination of separate schools. A resolution adopted by a group in 1844 stated:

Whereas, we, the colored citizens of the city of Boston, have recently sent a petition to the School Committee, respectfully praying for the abolition of the separate schools for colored children, and asking for the rights and privileges extended to other citizens in respect to the common school system—viz. the right to send our children to the schools established in the respective districts in which we reside; and

Whereas, the School Committee, at their last meeting, passed a vote saying, in substance, that the prayer of our petition would not be granted, and that the separate schools for colored children would be continued; and

Whereas, we believe, and have the opinion of eminent counsel, that the institution and support of separate schools, at the public charge, for any one class of the inhabitants in exclusion of any other class, is contrary to the laws of this Commonwealth; therefore,

Resolved, That we consider the late action of the School Committee, in regard to our petition asking for the entire abolition of separate schools for colored children, as erroneous and unsatisfactory.

Resolved, That while we would not turn aside from our main object, the abolition of the separate colored schools, we cannot allow this occasion to pass without an expression of our surprise and regret at the recent acquittal by the School Committee of Abner Forbes, Principal of the Smith School [for Negroes], and of our deep conviction that he is totally unworthy of his present responsible station; and that the colored parents of this city are recommended to withdraw their children from the exclusive school established in contravention of that equality of privileges which is the vital principle of the school system of Massachusetts.

Resolved, That a copy of the above preamble and resolutions be sent to the Chairman of the School Committee, with a request that the petition heretofore presented may be reconsidered, and that we be allowed a hearing on said petition before them. . . . Quoted in A. BLAUSTEIN & R. ZANGRANDO, CIVIL RIGHTS AND THE AMERICAN NEGRO— A DOCUMENTARY HISTORY 111-12 (1968).

When another petition for abolition of separate schools was rejected by the School Committee in 1846, Benjamin Roberts sought to enroll his five-year-old daughter in a white primary school in the district where they lived. After being rejected in four attempts over a period of two years, Roberts retained Charles Sumner, a white lawyer, and Robert Morris, a Negro lawyer, to bring suit against the school officials.[1]

ROBERTS v. CITY OF BOSTON
Supreme Judicial Court of Massachusetts
59 Mass. (5 Cush.) 198 (1850)

This was an action on the case, brought by Sarah C. Roberts, an infant, who sued by Benjamin F. Roberts, her father and next friend, against the city of Boston, under the statute of 1845, c. 214, which provides that any child, unlawfully excluded from public school instruction in this commonwealth, shall recover damages therefor against the city or town by which such public instruction is supported. . . .

C. Sumner and *R. Morris, Jr.,* for the plaintiff.

Mr. Sumner argued as follows:—

1. According to the spirit of American institutions, and especially of the constitution of Massachusetts, (Part First, Arti-

---

[1] Later, as a United States Senator, Sumner was a fervent advocate of abolition, and then of strong federal civil rights legislation. Morris was one of the Secretaries of the group which adopted the 1844 resolution quoted in the text. For the background of *Roberts v. City of Boston,* see L. LEVY, THE LAW OF THE COMMONWEALTH AND CHIEF JUSTICE SHAW 109-17 (1957); Levy & Phillips, *The Roberts Case: Source of the "Separate but Equal" Doctrine,* 56 AM. HIST. REV. 510 (1951); Ruchames, RACE AND EDUCATION IN MASSACHU-SETTS, THE NEGRO HISTORY BULLETIN 53 (Dec. 1949), reprinted in FREEDOM Now 61 (Westin ed. 1964).

cles I. and VI.,) all men, without distinction of color or race,
are equal before the law. . . .

4. The exclusion of colored children from the public schools,
which are open to white children, is a source of practical inconvenience to them and their parents, to which white persons
are not exposed, and is, therefore, a violation of equality.

5. The separation of children in the public schools of Boston,
on account of color or race, is in the nature of caste, and is a
violation of equality. . . .

6. The school committee have no power, under the constitution and laws of Massachusetts, to make any discrimination on
account of color or race, among children in the public schools. . . .

The regulations and by-laws of municipal corporations must
be reasonable, or they are inoperative and void. . . . It is clear,
that the committee may classify scholars, according to age and
sex, for these distinctions are inoffensive, and recognized as legal
. . .; or according to their moral and intellectual qualifications,
because such a power is necessary to the government of schools.
But the committee cannot assume, without individual examination, that an entire race possess certain moral or intellectual
qualities, which render it proper to place them all in a class by
themselves.

But it is said, that the committee, in thus classifying the
children, have not violated any principle of equality, inasmuch
as they have provided a school with competent instructors for
the colored children, where they enjoy equal advantages of
instruction with those enjoyed by the white children. To this
there are several answers: . . . 2d. It is not in fact an equivalent.
It is the occasion of inconveniences to the colored children, to
which they would not be exposed if they had access to the nearest public schools; it inflicts upon them the stigma of caste; and
although the matters taught in the two schools may be precisely
the same, a school exclusively devoted to one class must differ
essentially, in its spirit and character, from that public school
known to the law, where all classes meet together in equality.
3d. Admitting that it is an equivalent, still the colored children
cannot be compelled to take it. They have an equal right with
the white children to the general public schools.

7. The court will declare the by-law of the school committee, making a discrimination of color among children entitled

to the benefit of the public schools, to be unconstitutional and illegal, although there are no express words of prohibition in the constitution and laws. Slavery was abolished in Massachusetts, by virtue of the declaration of rights in our constitution, without any specific words of abolition in that instrument, or in any subsequent legislation. *Commonwealth v. Aves*, 18 Pick. 193, 210. The same words, which are potent to destroy slavery, must be equally potent against any institution founded on caste. . . . If there should be any doubt in this case, the court should incline in favor of equality; as every interpretation is always made in favor of life and liberty. Rousseau says that "it is precisely because the force of things tends always to destroy equality, that the force of legislation ought always to tend to maintain it." In a similar spirit the court should tend to maintain it.

The fact, that the separation of the schools was originally made at the request of the colored parents, cannot affect the rights of the colored people, or the powers of the school committee. The separation of the schools, so far from being for the benefit of both races, is an injury to both. It tends to create a feeling of degradation in the blacks, and of prejudice and uncharitableness in the whites.

P. W. Chandler, city solicitor, for the defendants. [Mr. Chandler's argument is omitted in the published report of this case.] . . .

SHAW, C.J. The plaintiff, a colored child of five years of age, has commenced this action, by her father and next friend, against the city of Boston, upon the statute of 1845, c. 214, which provides, that any child unlawfully excluded from public school instruction, in this commonwealth, shall recover damages therefor, in an action against the city or town, by which such public school instruction is supported. The question therefore is, whether, upon the facts agreed, the plaintiff has been unlawfully excluded from such instruction.

By the agreed statement of facts, it appears, that the defendants support a class of schools called primary schools, to the number of about one hundred and sixty, designed for the instruction of children of both sexes, who are between the ages of four and seven years. Two of these schools are appropriated by the primary school committee, having charge of that class of schools, to the exclusive instruction of colored children, and the residue to the exclusive instruction of white children.

The plaintiff, by her father, took proper measures to obtain admission into one of these schools appropriated to white children, but pursuant to the regulations of the committee, and in conformity therewith, she was not admitted. Either of the schools appropriated to colored children was open to her; the nearest of which was about a fifth of a mile or seventy rods more distant from her father's house than the nearest primary school. It further appears, by the facts agreed, that the committee having charge of that class of schools had, a short time previously to the plaintiff's application, adopted a resolution, upon a report of a committee, that in the opinion of that board, the continuance of the separate schools for colored children, and the regular attendance of all such children upon the schools, is not only legal and just, but is best adapted to promote the instruction of that class of the population.

The present case does not involve any question in regard to the legality of the Smith school, which is a school of another class, designed for colored children more advanced in age and proficiency; though much of the argument, affecting the legality of the separate primary schools, affects in like manner that school. But the question here is confined to the primary schools alone. The plaintiff had access to a school, set apart for colored children, as well conducted in all respects, and as well fitted, in point of capacity and qualification of the instructors, to advance the education of children under seven years old, as the other primary schools; the objection is, that the schools thus open to the plaintiff are exclusively appropriated to colored children, and are at a greater distance from her home. Under these circumstances, has the plaintiff been unlawfully excluded from public school instruction? Upon the best consideration we have been able to give the subject, the court are all of opinion that she has not. . . .

The great principle, advanced by the learned and eloquent advocate of the plaintiff, is, that by the constitution and laws of Massachusetts, all persons without distinction of age or sex, birth or color, origin or condition, are equal before the law. This, as a broad general principle, such as ought to appear in a declaration of rights, is perfectly sound; it is not only expressed in terms, but pervades and animates the whole spirit of our constitution of free government. But, when this great principle comes to be applied to the actual and various conditions of persons in society, it will not warrant the assertion, that men and women are legally clothed with the same civil and political powers, and that children and adults are legally to have the same functions and be subject to the same treatment;

but only that the rights of all, as they are settled and regulated by law, are equally entitled to the paternal consideration and protection of the law, for their maintenance and security. What those rights are, to which individuals, in the infinite variety of circumstances by which they are surrounded in society, are entitled, must depend on laws adapted to their respective relations and conditions.

Conceding, therefore, in the fullest manner, that colored persons, the descendants of Africans, are entitled by law, in this commonwealth, to equal rights, constitutional and political, civil and social, the question then arises, whether the regulation in question, which provides separate schools for colored children, is a violation of any of these rights.

Legal rights must, after all, depend upon the provisions of law; certainly all those rights of individuals which can be asserted and maintained in any judicial tribunal. The proper province of a declaration of rights and constitution of government, after directing its form, regulating its organization and the distribution of its powers, is to declare great principles and fundamental truths, to influence and direct the judgment and conscience of legislators in making laws, rather than to limit and control them, by directing what precise laws they shall make. The provision, that it shall be the duty of legislatures and magistrates to cherish the interests of literature and the sciences, especially the university at Cambridge, public schools, and grammar schools, in the towns, is precisely of this character. Had the legislature failed to comply with this injunction, and neglected to provide public schools in the towns, or should they so far fail in their duty as to repeal all laws on the subject, and leave all education to depend on private means, strong and explicit as the direction of the constitution is, it would afford no remedy or redress to the thousands of the rising generation, who now depend on these schools to afford them a most valuable education, and an introduction to useful life.

We must then resort to the law, to ascertain what are the rights of individuals, in regard to the schools. By the Rev. Sts. c. 23, the general system is provided for. . . .

The statute, after directing what length of time schools shall be kept in towns of different numbers of inhabitants and families, provides (§ 10) that the inhabitants shall annually choose, by ballot, a school committee, who shall have the general charge and superintendence of all the public schools in such towns. . . .

In the absence of special legislation on this subject, the law has vested the power in the committee to regulate the system of distribution and classification; and when this power is reasonably exercised, without being abused or perverted by color-able pretences, the decision of the committee must be deemed conclusive. The committee, apparently upon great delibera-tion, have come to the conclusion, that the good of both classes of schools will be best promoted, by maintaining the separate primary schools for colored and for white children, and we can perceive no ground to doubt, that this is the honest result of their experience and judgment.

It is urged, that this maintenance of separate schools tends to deepen and perpetuate the odious distinction of caste, founded in a deep-rooted prejudice in public opinion. This prejudice, if it exists, is not created by law, and probably cannot be changed by law. Whether this distinction and prejudice, existing in the opinion and feelings of the community, would not be as ef-fectually fostered by compelling colored and white children to associate together in the same schools, may well be doubted; at all events, it is a fair and proper question for the committee to consider and decide upon, having in view the best interests of both classes of children placed under their superintendence, and we cannot say, that their decision upon it is not founded on just grounds of reason and experience, and in the results of a discriminating and honest judgment.

The increased distance, to which the plaintiff was obliged to go to school from her father's house, is not such, in our opin-ion, as to render the regulation in question unreasonable, still less illegal.

On the whole the court are of opinion, that upon the facts stated, the action cannot be maintained.

Plaintiff nonsuit.

QUESTIONS

1. Limitations on the legislature's lawmaking power: the court's interpretation of general constitutional language.—Sumner and Morris based their argument for Roberts on the following pro-vision of the Massachusetts Constitution: "All men are born free and equal, and have certain natural, essential, and unalien-able rights; among which may be reckoned the right of enjoying and defending their lives and liberties; that of acquiring, posses-sing, and protecting property; . . . ." MASS. CONST. art. 1. The contention was that Boston's racial classification of children into separate schools was not equal treatment before the law. Chief Justice Shaw's response to that argument illustrates the way in which courts in the United States, until very recent years, typically have interpreted constitutional guarantees of equality. Shaw's response was, in effect, that the racially separate schools were equal in quality, and that the racial separation was based on a "reasonable" classification:

> . . . The committee, apparently upon great deliberation, have come to the conclusion, that the good of both classes of schools will be best promoted, by maintaining the separate primary schools for colored and for white children, and we can perceive no ground to doubt, that this is the honest result of their experience and judgment.
>
> It is urged, that this maintenance of separate schools tends to deepen and perpetuate the odious distinction of caste, founded in a deep-rooted prejudice in public opinion. . . . [I]t is a fair and proper question for the committee to consider and decide upon, having in view the best interests of both classes of children placed under their superintendence, and we cannot say, that their decision upon it is not founded on just grounds of reason and experience, and in the results of a discriminating and honest judgment.

Thus the schools, though separate, met the constitutional requirement of equality.

Why did the court decide, in interpreting a constitutional provision said to require equal treatment of people by the government, that it would go no further than to inquire whether the classification made by governmental officials was "founded on just grounds of reason and experience, and in the results of a discriminating and honest judgment"? Was an alternative approach open to the court in interpreting the "free and equal" clause of the constitution? For example: Even though there were grounds of reason and experience for racially segregated schools, and even though the school committee had exercised a discriminating and honest judgment, were the deleterious effects on the freedom and equality of the plaintiff child such that the requirement of separate schools should be held to violate the constitutional provision? Until recently, courts have generally said that constitutional requirements of equality are satisfied so long as there is a reasonable basis for the classification made by law; that is, the courts have exhibited great deference to the legislative body's judgment that there should be a specific classification in the law. There are understandable reasons why the courts have used such an approach in interpreting such constitutional provisions as the "free and equal" clause. The generality of the language to be interpreted is one reason; a search for purposes, and an attribution of meaning so as to effectuate those purposes, are progressively less feasible as the language becomes more general. Compare, for example, the purpose-oriented approach followed by Chief Justice Shaw in *Commonwealth v. Aves*, p. 44 *supra*, in determining whether Massachusetts common law (which would free the slave) violated the relatively specific language of Article IV, section 2, of the United States Constitution (the fugitive slave, "escaping into," provision). It would be more difficult, would it not, to write an opinion in *Roberts* in purpose-oriented terms?

There is another reason for deference to the legislative body's decision, when the issue is raised whether it has exceeded constitutional limitations such as the "free and equal" clause. The legislative branch of government, after all, has exercised its lawmaking powers. The judges have little or no direct responsibility to the electorate, and they have only a limited lawmaking power in the total legal system. If they hold invalid a statute that has a *reasonable* basis, are they properly chargeable with substituting their own views about social policy for those of the elected representatives of the people? Are judges better informed on the subject-matter of statutes than are legislators? Are judges better qualified to make fundamental policy choices? If we assume a negative answer to the last two rhetorical questions, what is the alternative? Granting the difficulty of giving specific meaning to standards like "free and equal," are not the courts the designated agencies in government for determining the content of our constitutions? "[W]e act in these matters," Justice Jackson once said, "not by authority of our competence but by force of our commissions." West Virginia State Board of Education v. Barnette, 319 U.S. 624, 640 (1943).

It may help to make the preceding comments more specific. Sumner and Morris argued in *Roberts v. City of Boston* that racial segregation in the public schools (a) inflicted upon Negro children "the stigma of caste," (b) subjected them to inconveniences to which white children were not subjected, and (c) gave them an inferior educational opportunity because "a school exclusively devoted to one class must differ essentially, in its spirit and character, from that public school known to the law, where all classes meet together in equality." The court's response followed the reasonable-basis approach; the opinion can be distilled down to this: "The reasons the plaintiff urges are, indeed, arguments for not requiring segregated schools. But so long as the popularly elected lawmaking agency had 'grounds of reason and experience' for requiring segregated schools, its action did not violate the Constitution." Chief Justice Shaw did not make perfectly clear what those "grounds of reason and experience" were; perhaps he thought the grounds were that considering the nature of race relations in the community and "the best interests of both classes of children" segregation was desirable. The question here is whether the court should have ended its inquiry by determining that some "grounds of reason and experience" were present, or should have gone on to inquire whether the "grounds of reason and experience" for requiring school segregation, whatever they were, were outweighed by the asserted harm to the black children, so that segregation violated the constitutional requirement of equality.[2]

2. The sources of Chief Justice Shaw's views about the relation of law to racial prejudice.—Note specifically Chief Justice Shaw's response to the argument of Sumner and Morris that "maintenance of separate schools tends to deepen and perpetuate the odious distinction of caste, founded in a deep-rooted prejudice in public opinion." There were, Shaw said, "grounds of reason" to require segregation in the face of this argument: (a) this ". . . prejudice, if it exists, is not created by law, and probably cannot be changed by law"; and (b) racially integrated schools might in fact foster this prejudice. Should Shaw have felt compelled to cite recognized sources of information to support these two conclusions about social psychology? Are there effective means by which data on such questions can be placed before a court, given the nature of the adversary system of litigation? Would not such data have been helpful to the court in *Roberts* in deciding on the reasonableness of the School Committee's legislative decision to require segregation? Many towns in Massachusetts had racially integrated schools in 1850, and that experience might have thrown light on both of Shaw's "grounds of reason."

3. In 1855 the Massachusetts legislature prohibited racial segregation in public schools throughout the state. Mass. Laws 1855, ch. 256, § 1.

---

[2] In paragraph 6 of their argument, Sumner and Morris noted the long-standing rule of English and American common law that the regulations of municipal corporations must be reasonable. In applying the standard of reasonableness in this context, courts traditionally have felt more free to substitute their legislative judgment for that of municipal bodies than they have when dealing with the question of the constitutionality of acts of a state legislature. Shaw's opinion did not discuss this argument.

THE BLACK CODES, THE CIVIL RIGHTS ACT OF 1866 AND THE FOURTEENTH AMENDMENT

In the south, emancipation was soon followed by the enactment of the "Black Codes," which wrote into law a systematic and thorough set of disabilities designed to maintain black men in a status that approached slavery almost as closely as the Thirteenth Amendment would allow. The Black Codes imposed disabilities to own or convey property, to inherit or purchase, or to have access to the courts. Other rules governing the employment relation gave an employer rights similar to those previously enjoyed by a slave owner. Perhaps the worst abuse of the legal system was the convict-lease (chain gang) system, which resulted in something that might be called de facto slavery for many thousands of black men:

> To provide an abundant supply of convict labor, the criminal code was revised to make petty offenders subject to very little sympathy from the courts. The legislature was generous in granting to vested interests, planters and politicians, long term leases extending from ten to thirty years, from which concessions they reaped immense profits. Bacote, *Negro Proscriptions, Protests, and Proposed Solutions in Georgia, 1880-1908*, in THE NEGRO IN THE SOUTH SINCE 1865 at 149, 162 (Wynes ed.; Harper paperbound ed. 1968).

In some states, the convict-lease system persisted well into the twentieth century. Some of the Black Codes were repealed or considerably softened by Reconstruction legislatures that sat while federal troops occupied the southern states. But enough of this legislation remained for the Reconstruction Congress to take a hand. The Civil Rights Act of 1866 was designed in major part to abolish the disabilities imposed by the Black Codes. It provided:

> That all persons born in the United States and not subject to any foreign power, . . . are hereby declared to be citizens of the United States; and such citizens, of every race and color, without regard to any previous condition of slavery or involuntary servitude . . . shall have the same right, in every State and Territory in the United States, to make and enforce contracts, to sue, be parties, and give evidence, to inherit, purchase, lease, sell, hold, and convey real and personal property, and to full and equal benefit of all laws and proceedings for the security of person and property, as

is enjoyed by white citizens, and shall be subject to like punishment, pains, and penalties, and to none other, any law, statute, ordinance, regulation, or custom, to the contrary notwithstanding. 14 STAT. 27.

This bill was passed by Congress on March 13, 1866, but was returned to Congress by President Andrew Johnson. He was of the view that Congress did not have power delegated by the Constitution to enact the statute. The only possible basis of such power was section 2 of the Thirteenth Amendment, which empowered Congress to "enforce" by appropriate legislation the abolition of slavery within the United States. The rights declared in the statute were not, in his view, sufficiently related to abolition to fall within the power of Congress under section 2.[3] Declaration of such rights therefore remained solely within the legislative powers of the states. The veto message included the following language:

I do not say that this bill repeals State laws on the subject of marriage between the races, for as the whites are forbidden to intermarry with the blacks, the blacks can only make such contracts as the whites themselves are allowed to make, and therefore can not under this bill enter into the marriage contract with the whites. I cite this discrimination, however, as an instance of the State policy as to discrimination, and to inquire whether if Congress can abrogate all State laws of discrimination between the two races in the matter of real estate, of suits, and of contracts generally Congress may not also repeal the State laws as to the contract of marriage between the two races. Hitherto every subject embraced in the enumeration of rights contained in this bill has been considered as exclusively belonging to the States. They all relate to the internal police and economy of the respective States. They are matters which in each State concern the domestic condition of its people, varying in each according to its own peculiar circumstances and the safety and well-being of its own citizens. . . . If it be granted that Congress can repeal all State laws discriminating between whites and blacks in the subjects covered by this bill, why, it may be asked, may not Congress

---

[3] In Jones v. Alfred H. Mayer Co., 392 U.S. 409 (1968), the Supreme Court held that Congress was empowered under the Thirteenth Amendment to enact the portion of the Civil Rights Act of 1866 relating to acquisition of real and personal property, because Congress could rationally conclude that racial barriers to acquisition of property were badges and incidents of slavery.

repeal in the same way all State laws discriminating between the two races on the subjects of suffrage and office? If Congress can declare by law who shall hold lands, who shall testify, who shall have capacity to make a contract in a State, then Congress can by law also declare who, without regard to color or race, shall have the right to sit as a juror or as a judge, to hold any office, and finally to vote "in every State and Territory of the United States." 6 MESSAGES AND PAPERS OF THE PRESIDENTS 405, 407-08 (J. Richardson ed. 1897).

Congress enacted the Civil Rights Act over the President's veto on April 9, 1866. During the debate on the bill, however, even some ardent radical reconstructionists expressed constitutional concerns like those later expressed by President Johnson. Because many members of Congress doubted that the Thirteenth Amendment provided a sufficient constitutional basis for congressional power, it was proposed to offer to the states a new amendment that would, among other things, validate the 1866 Act. The result was the Fourteenth Amendment, which occupied the attention of Congress from the time of adoption of the Civil Rights Act of 1866 until June 13, 1866, when the House of Representatives adopted the Senate version, and the amendment went to the state legislatures for ratification. The amendment became law in 1868. Section 1 of the Fourteenth Amendment provides:

> All persons born in the United States, and subject to the jurisdiction thereof, are citizens of the United States and of the State wherein they reside. No State shall make or enforce any law which shall abridge the privileges or immunities of citizens of the United States; nor shall any State deprive any person of life, liberty, or property, without due process of law; nor deny to any person within its jurisdiction the equal protection of the laws.

The Fifteenth Amendment, adopted in 1870, completed the cycle of the Civil War Amendments by forbidding a state or the United States to deny or abridge the right to vote "on account of race, color, or previous condition of servitude."

The voluminous congressional debates on the Fourteenth Amendment have been analyzed exhaustively by a number of writers, who have reached varying conclusions on the question whether the Amendment was thought by its framers to apply to such matters as racial segregation. See Bickel, *The Original*

Understanding and the Segregation Decision, 69 HARV. L. REV.
1, 58 (1955); Frank & Munro, *The Original Understanding of
"Equal Protection of the Laws,"* 50 COLUM. L. REV. 131 (1950).

EARLY JUDICIAL INTERPRETATIONS OF THE FOURTEENTH AMENDMENT

The Supreme Court's first decision interpreting the Fourteenth
Amendment came in 1873, in the Slaughter-House Cases, 83
U.S. (16 Wall.) 6. A statute of Louisiana had created a monopoly
of the business of slaughtering cattle in a specified area in the
state, including New Orleans. The statute was challenged by
some New Orleans butchers on the grounds that it violated both
the Thirteenth and Fourteenth Amendments. (The "servitude"
argument drew an analogy to some of the monopolistic incidents
of feudal relations between lord and serf, and was quickly rejected by the Supreme Court, which limited the Thirteenth
Amendment to cases of bondage to personal service.) The Court
rejected the challenge based on the Fourteenth Amendment,
(a) saying that the Amendment's privileges and immunities clause
was limited to the protection of privileges and immunities that
were peculiar to national citizenship, as distinguished from
state citizenship, and (b) denying that national citizenship conferred any immunity from state economic regulation. The bulk
of the opinion dealt with this issue. The Court also rejected the
butchers' claims based on the due process and equal protection
clauses of the Amendment. The latter argument was dismissed,
since "the evil to be remedied by this clause" was racial discrimination. "We doubt very much," said Mr. Justice Miller for the
Court, "whether any action of a state not directed by way of discrimination against the negroes as a class, or on account of their
race, will ever be held to come within the purview of this provision." 16 Wall. at 81. Thus was born the "Negro race theory"
of the Fourteenth Amendment.

The life of that theory was short. By the end of the century,
the Supreme Court had turned the doctrine in the *Slaughter-
House Cases* upside down. The Fourteenth Amendment was
made to do service as a bulwark against "unreasonable." economic regulation, and in a good many cases "unreasonable"
seemed to mean nothing more than that the Justices thought the
laws unwise. During the same period, the Court put aside any
notion that the Fourteenth Amendment imposed a national
rule of racial nondiscrimination on the states. This was the period of national reconciliation, and the price of the south's re-
entry into the Union was nothing less than northern abandon-

ment of the goal of a nationwide standard of racial equality. The most important judicial contribution to this process came in the Civil Rights Cases, 109 U.S. 3 (1883), in which the Supreme Court gave the Nation's blessing to the agreement to turn over the subject of race relations to the states. The Court knew what it was doing, as this passage from Mr. Justice Bradley's opinion shows:

> When a man has emerged from slavery, and by the aid of beneficent legislation has shaken off the inseparable concomitants of that state, there must be some stage in the progress of his elevation when he takes the rank of a mere citizen, and ceases to be the special favorite of the laws, and when his rights as a citizen, or a man, are to be protected in the ordinary modes by which other men's rights are protected. 109 U.S. at 25.

Professor Ralph Gabriel's evaluation of the case's historical importance is not excessive:

> The central political fact of Reconstruction was the assumption by the central government of the power to determine throughout the nation the legal frame which should govern the relations between the races. The freedman became the temporary ward of the United States. Racial equality in civil and in political rights was written into the Constitution by the Fourteenth and Fifteenth Amendments. So long as federal soldiers remained in the South to enforce the will of a determined United States, Southern intransigence was inevitable and Southern loyalty to the national Union difficult. The resolution of the difficulty began in 1877 with the withdrawal of the army.
>
> Of equal if not greater importance than this event was the decision which the Supreme Court handed down on October 15, 1883, in the Civil Rights cases. The Court was considering the Civil Rights Act of March 1, 1875, the purpose of which had been to give force to the Fourteenth Amendment. That amendment had been formulated to enable the central government to protect the colored man. The act had made it a crime for any person to deny to all persons full and equal accommodation at inns, in public conveyances, or in places of public amusement. Mr. Justice Bradley for the Court declared that the Fourteenth Amendment did not invest Congress with power to legislate on subjects which are within the domain of the state or to

create a code of municipal law. He denied that refusal to accommodate any citizen at an inn pinned upon him the badge of slavery. The essence of the decision, however, is not to be found in the general principles which it laid down but, rather, in the reality which it accomplished. By it the Court, in effect, turned over to local Southern communities the solution of the all-important race problem, subject to the limitation that chattel slavery should not be re-established. The Civil War had been fought, in the opinion of the South, over the question of where the control over the arrangements which governed the relations between the races should lie. In 1883, only eighteen years after the surrender of Lee, the Court accepted Calhoun's principle that the disposition of the race problem should be denied to the central government and be left to the local community. The decision, measured by its results, is one of the most important in the history of the national tribunal.

The ultimate sanction behind the decision was its acceptance in the North. There were objections from the intellectual descendants of the Abolitionists. But the mass of the Northern people acquiesced. The reason for this approval was to be found in the fact that, as early as 1883, Northern folkways in the matter of race relations were developing similar, though not identical, patterns to those of the post-war South. In both regions a caste system had crystallized. The Court's decision was a tacit recognition of this system.

Important as was the decision in the Civil Rights cases, still another achievement was necessary before obstacles impeding in the South the development of a true national sentiment were cleared away. This was the creation, by the pragmatic process of trial and error, of a discipline which would be as effective as slavery in maintaining Negro subordination to the white race. By the 1890's such discipline had been achieved, although not perfected in all its details. R. GABRIEL, THE COURSE OF AMERICAN DEMOCRATIC THOUGHT 135-36 (1940).*

The discipline to which Professor Gabriel refers was called Jim Crow. It included a wide range of official and unofficial means to separate the black man from southern white society, and to maintain white supremacy. Historians differ as to the

---

* Copyright © 1940, The Ronald Press Company, New York.

origins of Jim Crow. For a selection of contrasting views, see
THE ORIGINS OF SEGREGATION (J. Williamson ed. 1968). Professor C. Vann Woodward, in his book *The Strange Career of*
Jim Crow, takes the position that Jim Crow was largely the
product of the political bargain that was sealed by the Compromise of 1877, in which conservative Republicans and southern
Democrats agreed to settle the Tilden-Hayes electoral dispute by
making Rutherford B. Hayes President. Federal troops were
withdrawn from the south; and, as Professor Gabriel noted, the
federal judiciary cooperated in turning over the question of the
status of the Negro to the states. Jim Crow, says Professor Woodward, was founded on this legal base. Until around 1890, Negroes
voted in large numbers in southern states; during this period,
there were black legislators in southern statehouses; *after* Reconstruction had ended, ten black congressmen were elected to
represent southern districts.

Professor Woodward's thesis is that Jim Crow resulted from
the removal of northern and national pressure on the south,
combined with the political need of the conservative leadership
of the Democratic Party in the south to placate an aggressive
radical movement. Professor Woodward concludes:

> If the psychologists are correct in their hypothesis that
> aggression is always the result of frustration, then the South
> toward the end of the 'nineties was the perfect cultural
> seedbed for aggression against the minority race. Economic,
> political, and social frustrations had pyramided to a climax
> of social tensions. . . . There had to be a scapegoat. And
> all along the line signals were going up to indicate that the
> Negro was an approved object of aggression. These "per-
> missions-to-hate" came from sources that had formerly de-
> nied such permission. They came from the federal courts
> in numerous opinions, from Northern liberals eager to
> conciliate the South, from Southern conservatives who had
> abandoned their race policy of moderation in their struggle
> against the Populists, from the Populists in their mood of
> disillusionment with their former Negro allies, and from a
> national temper suddenly expressed by imperialistic ad-
> ventures and aggressions against colored peoples in distant
> lands. C. WOODWARD, THE STRANGE CAREER OF JIM CROW
> 81-82 (2d rev. ed. 1966).

Racial segregation of railroad passengers was the first type of
Jim Crow law to be adopted widely. The constitutionality of
Louisiana's law was challenged in *Plessy v. Ferguson,* the first

case in which the Supreme Court was faced with a decision on the validity of Jim Crow. It was only after the *Plessy* decision that Jim Crow legislation was extended to every feature of southern public life: separate telephone booths for Negroes in Oklahoma; separate storage for textbooks used by black schoolchildren in North Carolina and Florida; separate elevators for black passengers in Atlanta; separate Bibles for swearing Negro witnesses in Georgia. *Plessy v. Ferguson* was decided only nineteen years after the withdrawal of federal troops from the south, only twenty-three years after the *Slaughter-House Cases*, only thirty-one years after Appomattox.

PLESSY v. FERGUSON
Supreme Court of the United States
163 U.S. 537 (1896)

Mr. Justice BROWN, after stating the case, delivered the opinion of the court.

This case turns upon the constitutionality of an act of the General Assembly of the State of Louisiana, passed in 1890, providing for separate railway carriages for the white and colored races. Acts 1890, No. 111, p. 152.[4]

The first section of the statute enacts "that all railway companies carrying passengers in their coaches in this State, shall provide equal but separate accommodations for the white, and colored races, by providing two or more passenger coaches for each passenger train, or by dividing the passenger coaches by a partition so as to secure separate accommodations: *Provided*, That this section shall not be construed to apply to street railroads. No person or persons, shall be admitted to occupy seats in coaches, other than, the ones, assigned, to them on account of the race they belong to."

By the second section it was enacted "that the officers of such passenger trains shall have power and are hereby required to assign each passenger to the coach or compartment used for the

---

4 Plessy was prosecuted in the criminal court of Orleans Parish for violation of the Louisiana law described in Justice Brown's opinion. He sought a writ of prohibition in the Supreme Court of Louisiana against Ferguson, the judge of the criminal court, prohibiting him from proceeding further with the trial of the criminal case. The Supreme Court of Louisiana denied the writ, upholding the constitutionality of the statute. *Ex parte* Plessy, 45 La. Ann. 80, 18 L.R.A. 639 (1893). A writ of error to the United States Supreme Court was allowed by the Chief Justice of the Supreme Court of Louisiana. [*Eds.* note.]

race to which such passenger belongs; any passenger insisting on going into a coach or compartment to which by race he does not belong, shall be liable to a fine of twenty-five dollars, or in lieu thereof to imprisonment for a period of not more than twenty days in the parish prison, and any officer of any railroad insisting on assigning a passenger to a coach or compartment other than the one set aside for the race to which said passenger belongs, shall be liable to a fine of twenty-five dollars, or in lieu thereof to imprisonment for a period of not more than twenty days in the parish prison; and should any passenger refuse to occupy the coach or compartment to which he or she is assigned by the officer of such railway, said officer shall have power to refuse to carry such passenger on his train, and for such refusal neither he nor the railway company which he represents shall be liable for damages in any of the courts of this State."

The third section provides penalties for the refusal or neglect of the officers, directors, conductors and employes of railway companies to comply with the act, with a proviso that "nothing in this act shall be construed as applying to nurses attending children of the other race." The fourth section is immaterial.

The information filed in the criminal District Court charged in substance that Plessy, being a passenger between two stations within the State of Louisiana, was assigned by officers of the company to the coach used for the race to which he belonged, but he insisted upon going into a coach used by the race to which he did not belong. Neither in the information nor plea was his particular race or color averred.

The petition for the writ of prohibition averred that petitioner was seven eighths Caucasian and one eighth African blood; that the mixture of colored blood was not discernible in him, and that he was entitled to every right, privilege and immunity secured to citizens of the United States of the white race; and that, upon such theory, he took possession of a vacant seat in a coach where passengers of the white race were accommodated, and was ordered by the conductor to vacate said coach and take a seat in another assigned to persons of the colored race, and having refused to comply with such demand he was forcibly ejected with the aid of a police officer, and imprisoned in the parish jail to answer a charge of having violated the above act.

The constitutionality of this act is attacked upon the ground that it conflicts both with the Thirteenth Amendment of the Constitution, abolishing slavery, and the Fourteenth Amendment, which prohibits certain restrictive legislation on the part of the States.

1. That it does not conflict with the Thirteenth Amendment, which abolishes slavery and involuntary servitude, except as a punishment for crime, is too clear for argument. Slavery implies involuntary servitude—a state of bondage; the ownership of mankind as a chattel, or at least the control of the labor and services of one man for the benefit of another, and the absence of a legal right to the disposal of his own person, property and services. . . .

A statute which implies merely a legal distinction between the white and colored races—a distinction which is founded in the color of the two races, and which must always exist so long as white men are distinguished from the other race by color— has no tendency to destroy the legal equality of the two races, or reestablish a state of involuntary servitude. Indeed, we do not understand that the Thirteenth Amendment is strenuously relied upon by the plaintiff in error in this connection.

2. By the Fourteenth Amendment, all persons born or naturalized in the United States, and subject to the jurisdiction thereof, are made citizens of the United States and of the State wherein they reside; and the States are forbidden from making or enforcing any law which shall abridge the privileges or immunities of citizens of the United States, or shall deprive any person of life, liberty or property without due process of law, or deny to any person within their jurisdiction the equal protection of the laws. . . .

The object of the amendment was undoubtedly to enforce the absolute equality of the two races before the law, but in the nature of things it could not have been intended to abolish distinctions based upon color, or to enforce social, as distinguished from political equality, or a commingling of the two races upon terms unsatisfactory to either. Laws permitting, and even requiring, their separation in places where they are liable to be brought into contact do not necessarily imply the inferiority of either race to the other, and have been generally, if not universally, recognized as within the competency of the state legislatures in the exercise of their police power. The most common instance of this is connected with the establishment of separate schools for white and colored children, which has been held to be a valid exercise of the legislative power even by courts of States where the political rights of the colored race have been longest and most earnestly enforced.

One of the earliest of these cases is that of *Roberts v. City of Boston*, 5 Cush. 198, in which the Supreme Judicial Court of Massachusetts held that the general school committee of Boston had power to make provision for the instruction of colored children in separate schools established exclusively for them, and to prohibit their attendance upon the other schools. "The great principle," said Chief Justice Shaw, p. 206, "advanced by the learned and eloquent advocate for the plaintiff," (Mr. Charles Sumner,) "is, that by the constitution and laws of Massachusetts, all persons without distinction of age or sex, birth or color, origin or condition, are equal before the law. . . . But, when this great principle comes to be applied to the actual and various conditions of persons in society, it will not warrant the assertion, that men and women are legally clothed with the same civil and political powers, and that children and adults are legally to have the same functions and be subject to the same treatment; but only that the rights of all, as they are settled and regulated by law, are equally entitled to the paternal consideration and protection of the law for their maintenance and security." It was held that the powers of the committee extended to the establishment of separate schools for children of different ages, sexes and colors, and that they might also establish special schools for poor and neglected children, who have become too old to attend the primary school, and yet have not acquired the rudiments of learning, to enable them to enter the ordinary schools. Similar laws have been enacted by Congress under its general power of legislation over the District of Columbia, Rev. Stat. D.C. §§ 281, 282, 283, 310, 319, as well as by the legislatures of many of the States, and have been generally, if not uniformly, sustained by the courts. . . .

Laws forbidding the intermarriage of the two races may be said in a technical sense to interfere with the freedom of contract, and yet have been universally recognized as within the police power of the State. . . .

[I]t is also suggested by the learned counsel for the plaintiff in error that the same argument that will justify the state legislature in requiring railways to provide separate accommodations for the two races will also authorize them to require separate cars to be provided for people whose hair is of a certain color, or who are aliens, or who belong to certain nationalities, or to enact laws requiring colored people to walk upon one side of the street, and white people upon the other, or requiring white men's houses to be painted white, and colored men's black, or their vehicles or business signs to be of different colors, upon the theory that one side of the street is as good as the other, or that a house or vehicle of one color is as good as one of another color. The reply to all this is that every exercise of the police power must be reasonable, and extend only to such laws as are enacted in good faith for the promotion for the public good, and not for the annoyance or oppression of a particular class. Thus in *Yick Wo v. Hopkins*, 118 U.S. 356, it was held by this court that a municipal ordinance of the city of San Francisco, to regulate the carrying on of public laundries within the limits of the municipality, violated the provisions of the Constitution of the United States, if it conferred upon the municipal authorities arbitrary power, at their own will, and without regard to discretion, in the legal sense of the term, to give or withhold consent as to persons or places, without regard to the competency of the persons applying, or the propriety of the places selected for the carrying on of the business. It was held to be a covert attempt on the part of the municipality to make an arbitrary and unjust discrimination against the Chinese race. While this was the case of a municipal ordinance, a like principle has been held to apply to acts of a state legislature passed in the exercise of the police power. . . .

So far, then, as a conflict with the Fourteenth Amendment is concerned, the case reduces itself to the question whether the statute of Louisiana is a reasonable regulation, and with respect to this there must necessarily be a large discretion on the part of the legislature. In determining the question of reasonableness it is at liberty to act with reference to the established usages, customs and traditions of the people, and with a view to the promotion of their comfort, and the preservation of the public peace and good order. Gauged by this standard, we cannot say that a law which authorizes or even requires the separation of the two races in public conveyances is unreasonable, or more obnoxious to the Fourteenth Amendment than the acts of Congress requiring separate schools for colored children in the District of Columbia, the constitutionality of which does not seem to have been questioned, or the corresponding acts of state legislatures.

We consider the underlying fallacy of the plaintiff's argument to consist in the assumption that the enforced separation of the two races stamps the colored race with a badge of inferiority. If this be so, it is not by reason of anything found in the act, but solely because the colored race chooses to put that construction upon it. The argument necessarily assumes that if, as has been more than once the case, and is not unlikely to be so again, the colored race should become the dominant power in the state legislature, and should enact a law in precisely similar terms, it would thereby relegate the white race to an inferior position. We imagine that the white race, at least, would not acquiesce in this assumption. The argument also assumes that social prejudices may be overcome by legislation, and that equal

rights cannot be secured to the negro except by an enforced commingling of the two races. We cannot accept this proposition. If
the two races are to meet upon terms of social equality, it must
be the result of natural affinities, a mutual appreciation of each
other's merits and a voluntary consent of individuals. As was
said by the Court of Appeals of New York in *People v. Gallagher*,
93 N.Y. 438, 448, "this end can neither be accomplished nor promoted by laws which conflict with the general sentiment of the
community upon whom they are designed to operate. When the
government, therefore, has secured to each of its citizens equal
rights before the law and equal opportunities for improvement
and progress, it has accomplished the end for which it was organized and performed all of the functions respecting social advantages with which it is endowed."[5] Legislation is powerless to
eradicate racial instincts or to abolish distinctions based upon
physical differences, and the attempt to do so can only result in
accentuating the difficulties of the present situation. If the civil
and political rights of both races be equal one cannot be inferior
to the other civilly or politically. If one race be inferior to the
other socially, the Constitution of the United States cannot put
them upon the same plane. . . .

It is true that the question of the proportion of colored blood
necessary to constitute a colored person, as distinguished from a
white person, is one upon which there is a difference of opinion
in the different States, some holding that any visible admixture
of black blood stamps the person as belonging to the colored
race, (*State v. Chavers*, 5 Jones, [N.C.] 1, p. 11); others that
it depends upon the preponderance of blood, (*Gray v. State*, 4
Ohio, 354; *Monroe v. Collins*, 17 Ohio St. 665); and still others
that the predominance of white blood must only be in the proportion of three fourths. (*People v. Dean*, 14 Michigan, 406;
Jones v. Commonwealth, 80 Virginia, 538.) But these are questions to be determined under the laws of each State and are not
properly put in issue in this case. Under the allegations of his
petition it may undoubtedly become a question of importance
whether, under the laws of Louisiana, the petitioner belongs to
the white or colored race.

The judgment of the court below is, therefore,

Affirmed. . . .

---

[5] The *Gallagher* decision in 1883 upheld racial segregation in the Brook-
lyn schools, under the terms of an 1864 New York statute which permitted
local boards to adopt a segregation policy. Most school segregation in New
York was eliminated by a 1900 law; the last vestiges of authorization were
repealed in 1938. See the summary in Bickel, *The Original Understanding
and the Segregation Decision*, 69 HARV. L. REV. 1, 37 n.71 (1955). [*Eds.* note.]

Mr. Justice HARLAN dissenting. . . .

In respect of civil rights, common to all citizens, the Constitution of the United States does not, I think, permit any public authority to know the race of those entitled to be protected in the enjoyment of such rights. Every true man has pride of race, and under appropriate circumstances when the rights of others, his equals before the law, are not to be affected, it is his privilege to express such pride and to take such action based upon it as to him seems proper. But I deny that any legislative body or judicial tribunal may have regard to the race of citizens when the civil rights of those citizens are involved. Indeed, such legislation, as that here in question, is inconsistent not only with that equality of rights which pertains to citizenship, National and State, but with the personal liberty enjoyed by every one within the United States.

The Thirteenth Amendment does not permit the withholding or the deprivation of any right necessarily inhering in freedom. It not only struck down the institution of slavery as previously existing in the United States, but it prevents the imposition of any burdens or disabilities that constitute badges of slavery or servitude. It decreed universal civil freedom in this country. This court has so adjudged. But that amendment having been found inadequate to the protection of the rights of those who had been in slavery, it was followed by the Fourteenth Amendment, which added greatly to the dignity and glory of American citizenship, and to the security of personal liberty, by declaring that "all persons born or naturalized in the United States, and subject to the jurisdiction thereof, are citizens of the United States and of the State wherein they reside," and that "no State shall make or enforce any law which shall abridge the privileges or immunities of citizens of the United States; nor shall any State deprive any person of life, liberty or property without due process of law, nor deny to any person within its jurisdiction the equal protection of the laws." These two amendments, if enforced according to their true intent and meaning, will protect all the civil rights that pertain to freedom and citizenship. Finally, and to the end that no citizen should be denied, on account of his race, the privilege of participating in the political control of his country, it was declared by the Fifteenth Amendment that "the right of citizens of the United States to vote shall not be denied or abridged by the United States or by any State on account of race, color or previous condition of servitude."

These notable additions to the fundamental law were welcomed by the friends of liberty throughout the world. They removed the race line from our governmental systems. They had, as this court has said, a common purpose, namely, to secure "to a race recently emancipated, a race that through many generations have been held in slavery, all the civil rights that the superior race enjoy." They declared, in legal effect, this court has further said, "that the law in the States shall be the same for the black as for the white; that all persons, whether colored or white, shall stand equal before the laws of the States, and, in regard to the colored race, for whose protection the amendment was primarily designed, that no discrimination shall be made against them by law because of their color." We also said: "The words of the amendment, it is true, are prohibitory, but they contain a necessary implication of a positive immunity, or right, most valuable to the colored race—the right to exemption from unfriendly legislation against them distinctively as colored— exemption from legal discriminations, implying inferiority in civil society, lessening the security of their enjoyment of the rights which others enjoy, and discriminations which are steps towards reducing them to the condition of a subject race." It was, consequently, adjudged that a state law that excluded citizens of the colored race from juries, because of their race and however well qualified in other respects to discharge the duties of jurymen, was repugnant to the Fourteenth Amendment. . . .

It was said in argument that the statute of Louisiana does not discriminate against either race, but prescribes a rule applicable alike to white and colored citizens. But this argument does not meet the difficulty. Every one knows that the statute in question had its origin in the purpose, not so much to exclude white persons from railroad cars occupied by blacks, as to exclude colored people from coaches occupied by or assigned to white persons. Railroad corporations of Louisiana did not make discrimination among whites in the matter of accommodation for travellers. The thing to accomplish was, under the guise of giving equal accommodation for whites and blacks, to compel the latter to keep to themselves while travelling in railroad passenger coaches. No one would be so wanting in candor as to assert the contrary. The fundamental objection, therefore, to the statute is that it interferes with the personal freedom of citizens. "Personal liberty," it has been well said, "consists in the power of locomotion, of changing situation, or removing one's person to whatsoever places one's own inclination may direct, without imprisonment or restraint, unless by due course of law." 1 Bl. Com. *134. If a white man and a black man choose to occupy the same public conveyance on a public highway, it is their right to do so, and no government, proceeding alone on grounds of race, can prevent it without infringing the personal liberty of each.

It is one thing for railroad carriers to furnish, or to be required by law to furnish, equal accommodations for all whom they are under a legal duty to carry. It is quite another thing for government to forbid citizens of the white and black races from travelling in the same public conveyance, and to punish officers of railroad companies for permitting persons of the two races to occupy the same passenger coach. If a State can prescribe, as a rule of civil conduct, that whites and blacks shall not travel as passengers in the same railroad coach, why may it not so regulate the use of the streets of its cities and towns as to compel white citizens to keep on one side of a street and black citizens to keep on the other? Why may it not, upon like grounds, punish whites and blacks who ride together in street cars or in open vehicles on a public road or street? Why may it not require sheriffs to assign whites to one side of a court-room and blacks to the other? And why may it not also prohibit the commingling of the two races in the galleries of legislative halls or in public assemblages convened for the consideration of the political questions of the day? Further, if this statute of Louisiana is consistent with the personal liberty of citizens, why may not the State require the separation in railroad coaches of native and naturalized citizens of the United States, or of Protestants and Roman Catholics?

The answer given at the argument to these questions was that regulations of the kind they suggest would be unreasonable, and could not, therefore, stand before the law. Is it meant that the determination of questions of legislative power depends upon the inquiry whether the statute whose validity is questioned is, in the judgment of the courts, a reasonable one, taking all the circumstances into consideration? A statute may be unreasonable merely because a sound public policy forbade its enactment. But I do not understand that the courts have anything to do with the policy or expediency of legislation. A statute may be valid, and yet, upon grounds of public policy, may well be characterized as unreasonable. . . .

The white race deems itself to be the dominant race in this country. And so it is, in prestige, in achievements, in education, in wealth and in power. So, I doubt not, it will continue to be for all time, if it remains true to its great heritage and holds fast to the principles of constitutional liberty. But in view of the Constitution, in the eye of the law, there is in this country no superior, dominant, ruling class of citizens. There is no caste here. Our Constitution is color-blind, and neither knows nor tolerates classes among citizens. In respect of civil rights, all citizens are equal before the law. The humblest is the peer of the most powerful. The law regards man as man, and takes no account of his surroundings or of his color when his civil rights as guaranteed by the supreme law of the land are involved. It is, therefore, to be regretted that this high tribunal, the final expositor of the fundamental law of the land, has reached the conclusion that it is competent for a State to regulate the enjoyment by citizens of their civil rights solely upon the basis of race.

In my opinion, the judgment this day rendered will, in time, prove to be quite as pernicious as the decision made by this tribunal in the *Dred Scott case*. It was adjudged in that case that the descendants of Africans who were imported into this country and sold as slaves were not included nor intended to be included under the word "citizens" in the Constitution, and could not claim any of the rights and privileges which that instrument provided for and secured to citizens of the United States; that at the time of the adoption of the Constitution they were "considered as a subordinate and inferior class of beings, who had been subjugated by the dominant race, and, whether emancipated or not, yet remained subject to their authority, and had no rights or privileges but such as those who held the power and the government might choose to grant them." 19 How. 393, 404. The recent amendments of the Constitution, it was supposed, had eradicated these principles from our institutions. But it seems that we have yet, in some of the States, a dominant race—a superior class of citizens, which assumes to regulate the enjoyment of civil rights, common to all citizens, upon the basis of race. The present decision, it may well be apprehended, will not only stimulate aggressions, more or less brutal and irritating, upon the admitted rights of colored citizens, but will encourage the belief that it is possible, by means of state enactments, to defeat the beneficent purposes which the people of the United States had in view when they adopted the recent amendments of the Constitution, by one of which the blacks of this country were made citizens of the United States and of the States in which they respectively reside, and whose privileges and immunities, as citizens, the States are forbidden to abridge. Sixty millions of whites are in no danger from the presence here of eight millions of blacks. The destinies of the two races, in this country, are indissolubly linked together, and the interests of both require that the common government of all shall not permit the seeds of race hate to be planted under the sanction of law. What can more certainly arouse race hate, what more certainly create and perpetuate a feeling of distrust between these races, than state enactments, which, in fact, proceed on the ground that colored citizens are so inferior and degraded that they cannot be allowed to sit in public coaches occupied by white citizens? That, as all will admit, is the real meaning of such legislation as was enacted in Louisiana.

The sure guarantee of the peace and security of each race is the clear, distinct, unconditional recognition by our governments, National and State, of every right that inheres in civil freedom, and of the equality before the law of all citizens of the United States without regard to race. State enactments, regulating the enjoyment of civil rights, upon the basis of race, and cunningly devised to defeat legitimate results of the war, under the pretence of recognizing equality of rights, can have no other result than to render permanent peace impossible, and to keep alive a conflict of races, the continuance of which must do harm to all concerned. This question is not met by the suggestion that social equality cannot exist between the white and black races in this country. That argument, if it can be properly regarded as one, is scarcely worthy of consideration; for social equality no more exists between two races when travelling in a passenger coach or a public highway than when members of the same races sit by each other in a street car or in the jury box, or stand or sit with each other in a political assembly, or when they use in common the streets of a city or town, or when they are in the same room for the purpose of having their names placed on the registry of voters, or when they approach the ballot-box in order to exercise the high privilege of voting. . . .

The arbitrary separation of citizens, on the basis of race, while they are on a public highway, is a badge of servitude wholly inconsistent with the civil freedom and the equality before the law established by the Constitution. It cannot be justified upon any legal grounds.

If evils will result from the commingling of the two races upon public highways established for the benefit of all, they will be infinitely less than those that will surely come from state legislation regulating the enjoyment of civil rights upon the basis of race. We boast of the freedom enjoyed by our people above all other peoples. But it is difficult to reconcile that boast with a state of the law which, practically, puts the brand of servitude and degradation upon a large class of our fellow-citizens, our equals before the law. The thin disguise of "equal" accommodations for passengers in railroad coaches will not mislead any one, nor atone for the wrong this day done. . . .

I am of opinion that the statute of Louisiana is inconsistent with the personal liberty of citizens, white and black, in that State, and hostile to both the spirit and letter of the Constitution of the United States. If laws of like character should be enacted in the several States of the Union, the effect would be in the highest degree mischievous. Slavery, as an institution tolerated by law would, it is true, have disappeared from our country, but there would remain a power in the States, by sinister legislation, to interfere with the full enjoyment of the blessings of freedom; to regulate civil rights, common to all citizens, upon the basis of race; and to place in a condition of legal inferiority a large body of American citizens, now constituting a part of the political community called the People of the United States, for whom, and by whom through representatives, our government is administered. Such a system is inconsistent with the guarantee given by the Constitution to each State of a republican form of government, and may be stricken down by Congressional action, or by the courts in the discharge of their solemn duty to maintain the supreme law of the land, anything in the constitution or laws of any State to the contrary notwithstanding.

For the reasons stated, I am constrained to withhold my assent from the opinion and judgment of the majority.

QUESTIONS

1. **The Court's legislative decisions.**—*Plessy v. Ferguson* interpreted the equal protection clause of the Fourteenth Amendment as *Roberts v. City of Boston* had interpreted the free and equal clause of the Massachusetts Constitution:

> . . . [T]he case reduces itself to the question whether the statute of Louisiana is a reasonable regulation, and with respect to this there must necessarily be a large discretion on the part of the legislature. In determining the question of reasonableness it is at liberty to act with reference to the established usages, customs and traditions of the people, and with a view to the promotion of their comfort, and the preservation of the public peace and good order. Gauged by this standard, we cannot say that a law which . . . requires the separation of the two races in public conveyances is unreasonable. . . . (P. 134 *supra*.)

The Supreme Court in *Plessy* thus uses the formula of reasonableness as the measure of its deference to the legislative judgment. There is a presumption that the legislature's classification is valid, and "we cannot say" that the presumption of constitutionality has been overcome.

In our discussion of *Roberts v. City of Boston* we saw some of the reasons why courts tend to uphold legislative classifications that have some reasonable basis. Now we need to ask some further questions about the meaning of "reasonable" in this usage. Reasonable, we may ask without impertinence, with respect to what?

A court that decides a constitutional issue, or any issue of law, is not simply deciding which of the litigants before it should prevail; it is making law, a rule that it expects to apply to other cases that may come before it in the future. In performing this legislative task, the court must make choices among competing interests. In *Plessy v. Ferguson,* Justice Brown's opinion notes the justifications for the regulation (in the passage quoted above), and then minimizes the arguments against it:

> We consider the underlying fallacy of the plaintiff's argu-
> ment to consist in the assumption that the enforced separa-
> tion of the two races stamps the colored race with a badge
> of inferiority. If this be so, it is not by reason of anything
> found in the act, but solely because the colored race chooses
> to put that construction upon it.

In other words, the Court has asked itself, with respect to this law: What good will it do? What harm will it do? These questions go beyond the particular interests of either Plessy or the State of Louisiana in where Plessy shall sit when he rides the railroad. The interests that compete for the Court's legislative preference, in other words, are social interests, and not just the interests of the parties. It is an examination of the social good, and the social harm, that the law may cause, that produces the Court's judgment on the question of the law's "reasonableness." But that judgment is tempered by the Court's sense of its own place in the institutional scheme, and the need to permit even unwise legislative choices, so long as they are based on considerations that are not unreasonable. In other words, the Court in *Plessy* did not make a wholly independent legislative balance in deciding a constitutional case, but instead made its decision in the light of the presumption of constitutionality.

How did the *Plessy* Court reach the twin conclusions (a) that there were justifications for segregation in the "established usages, customs, and traditions of the people," and in the need for "promotion of their comfort, and the preservation of the public peace and good order," and (b) that segregation stamps Negroes with a badge of inferiority only "because the colored race chooses to put that construction upon it"? Both conclusions are mixtures of fact and value, are they not? With respect to the customs and traditions of Louisiana, the Court's statement suggests that it has inquired into the facts, and has determined what the customs are. Further, the statement implicitly accepts those deep-south customs as something the Louisiana legislature can legitimately protect, even after the Civil War. Our question—how did the Court reach its conclusions on the legislative questions—must therefore be fragmented further: Where did the Court get its factual information? Where did it get its value preferences?

2. The legislative facts.—We may take as our starting point this famous statement in Justice Brown's opinion:

> The argument [that state-compelled segregation marks the segregated Negroes with a badge of inferiority] also assumes that social prejudices may be overcome by legislation, and that equal rights cannot be secured to the negro except by an enforced commingling of the two races. We cannot accept this proposition. If the two races are to meet on terms of social equality, it must be the result of natural affinities, a mutual appreciation of each other's merits and a voluntary consent of individuals. . . . Legislation is powerless to eradicate racial instincts or to abolish distinctions based upon physical differences, and the attempt to do so can only result in accentuating the difficulties of the present situation. . . . If one race be inferior to the other socially, the Constitution of the United States cannot put them upon the same plane.

No evidence is cited in support of the various factual conclusions contained in this passage, nor did the briefs of the parties provide any such evidence. Was it therefore improper for the Court to rest its decision on such factual judgments? What alternatives were available to the Court? Could it refuse to decide? Should it have remanded the case for a "trial" of the issues of legislative fact in the lower court? Should it have ordered reargument and the submission of new briefs on these issues? *See* Karst, *Legislative Facts in Constitutional Litigation*, 1960 SUP. CT. REV. 75.

What the Court did was typical of what most appellate courts have done under similar circumstances; it simply decided the issues of legislative fact on the basis of the Justices' own education, experience and insight. The conclusions reached were not markedly different from those that would have been expected if more formal means had been used to inform the Court's judgment. The conclusions, in other words, were in accord with the views that prevailed among social scientists in the late nineteenth century. William Graham Sumner's *Folkways* was not published until 1906, but the work reflected the thought of the preceding generation. The folkways, said Sumner, are customary modes of action, produced by

> the frequent repetition of petty acts, often by great numbers acting in concert or, at least, acting in the same way when face to face with the same need. (p. 3)[6] [T]he folkways take on a philosophy of right living and a life policy for welfare. Then they become mores, and they may be developed by inferences from the philosophy or the rules in the endeavor to satisfy needs without pain. (p. 34) [T]he folkways are the widest, most fundamental, and most important operation by which the interests of men in groups are served, and . . . the process by which folkways are made is the chief one to which elementary societal or group phenomena are due. The life of society consists in making folkways and applying them. (p. 34) The mores of the masses admit of no . . . sudden and massive modification by doctrinal teaching. The process of assimilation is slow, and it is attended by modifying influences at every stage. (p. 46) Legislation . . . has to seek standing ground on the existing mores, and it soon becomes apparent that legislation, to be strong, must be consistent with the mores. (p. 55) To this point all projects of missions and reform must come. It must be recognized that what is proposed is an arbitrary action on the mores. Therefore nothing sudden or big is possible. The enterprise is possible only if the mores are ready for it. . . . That is why the agitator, reformer, prophet, reorganizer of society, who has found out "the truth" and wants to "get a law passed" to realize it right away, is only a mischiefmaker. He has won considerable prestige in the last hundred years, but if the cases are examined it will be found that when he had success it was because he took up something for which the mores were ready. Wilberforce[7] did not overthrow slavery. Natural forces reduced to the service of man and the discovery of new land set men "free" from great labor, and new ways suggested new sentiments of humanity and ethics. The mores changed and all the wider deductions in them were repugnant to slavery. (pp. 113-14)

Specifically directing himself to the subject of our inquiry, Sumner said:

---

6 These page citations are to W. G. SUMNER, FOLKWAYS (1906).

7 Wilberforce was a leader of the anti-slavery movement in the British Parliament in the early nineteenth century. [*Eds.* note.]

In our southern states, before the civil war, whites and blacks had formed habits of action and feeling towards each other. They lived in peace and concord, and each one grew up in the ways which were traditional and customary. The civil war abolished legal rights and left the two races to learn how to live together under other relations than before. The whites have never been converted from the old mores. . . . The two races have not yet made new mores. Vain attempts have been made to control the new order by legislation. The only result is the proof that legislation cannot make mores. . . . There is a trend in the mores now as they begin to form under the new state of things. It is not at all what the humanitarians hoped and expected. The two races are separating more than ever before. . . . Some are anxious to interfere and try to control. They take their stand on ethical views of what is going on. It is evidently impossible for anyone to interfere. We are like spectators at a great natural convulsion. The results will be such as the facts and forces call for. (pp. 77-78)

Sumner summed up his philosophy on the subject of social reform in an article published in *The Forum* in 1894. The article's title is itself a good summary: "The Absurd Effort to Make the World Over." (Reprinted in W. G. SUMNER, WAR AND OTHER ESSAYS at 195 (1919).)

Gunnar Myrdal criticized Sumner in his classic study of the Negro in the United States, *An American Dilemma*. In a "Methodological Note on Facts and Valuations in Social Science," Myrdal commented that social scientists such as Sumner

could not have reached their negative views on planned and induced social change unless guided by a set of general assumptions in their selection and interpretation of the empirical data. This implies that they have introduced valuations along with facts in deriving conclusions relative to what can be and should be the nature of man's practical efforts. . . . When our premises consist exclusively of facts, only a factual conclusion can result. If we proceed otherwise, and if we, further, denounce valuations, we are thus constantly attempting the logically impossible: From certain observations concerning the causation of a social phenomenon we jump to the valuational conclusion that we can do nothing to change this phenomenon because it has such and such a causation. G MYRDAL, AN AMERICAN DILEMMA 1052 (1944).

In 1896, however, it is clear that the view of society implicit in the *Plessy* opinion had impressive professional support among scientists in the young field of sociology. The Court's conclusion, however, seems not to be compelled even by its views on "enforced commingling" of the races. Was Plessy contending that the Court should impose a rule of enforced commingling? Would not a rule permitting railroad passengers to choose their own seats in fact permit the passengers to work out their own folkways, rather than being channeled by law into these racial patterns of transitory association? Indeed, was not the Louisiana statute an effective way to channel folkways toward segregation? See C. Woodward, The Strange Career of Jim Crow 106 (2d rev. ed. 1966):

> Whether railways qualify as folkways or stateways, black man and white man once rode them together and without a partition between them. Later on the stateways apparently changed the folkways—or at any rate the railways—for the partitions and Jim Crow cars became universal. And the new seating arrangement came to seem as normal, unchangeable, and inevitable as the old ways.

For differing views as to the extent of racial segregation in the south in the first three decades after the Civil War see The Origins of Segregation 1-49 (J. Williamson ed. 1968).

A more recent text typifies the view of the majority of today's social scientists on the power of law to change "the mores":

> Attitudes are never changed directly or immediately by laws. Attitudes are predispositions to want or to oppose something, and we neither begin nor stop wanting things because someone else orders us to. But attitudes do not arise in a vacuum. They arise out of experience as a person relates things and conditions in his environment to his own states of drive. Among the most important "conditions in the environment," as we have repeatedly seen, are those shared influences called social norms. Attitudes not only arise but also persist *in response to conditions* in the individual's environment. If these conditions are changed, attitudes are altogether likely to change, too.
>
> Changed conditions concerning segregation are likely to have both short-run and long-run effects. If certain segregation practices are stopped, by legislation or in other ways, then one of the conditions which supports prejudice has been removed. The practice of segregation is, of course, not

the only support of prejudice. But many people's attitudes of approving segregation—especially attitudes that are not very strong—are supported mainly by observing the practice of segregation, as tangible evidence of what constitutes the social norms. If this support is removed, their attitudes are likely to be weakened. If, in addition to the removal of this support, the opposed attitude is now supported by the prestige of "the law," many people's attitudes toward segregation will be changed. In these *indirect* ways legislation may serve to change attitudes, almost as soon as it begins to be enforced. T. NEWCOMB, SOCIAL PSYCHOLOGY 609 (1950).*

Would a modern judge be justified in taking his view of the effect of legislation on attitudes from Professor Newcomb's book? Even though the opposing party in the lawsuit had no opportunity to cross-examine Professor Newcomb about his views or his professional qualifications?

3. The choice of values.—When we leave the question of a court's inquiry into the factual background for legislation and turn to the weighing of values, we enter upon exceedingly slippery ground. One man's conclusion of fact may be another's hidden value preference; indeed, the very language we use to frame our questions of fact will conceal a great many assumptions about values. But, even if we assume that it is possible to separate the two kinds of questions, there are some formidable obstacles to rational choice. In *Plessy v. Ferguson*, for example, let us assume that the Justices were in general agreement on the factual background of the Louisiana segregation law—that they agreed on the degree to which the law imposed an inferior status on black men, and on the degree of danger of disorder or other evil that the law avoided. There would remain the problem of weighing those two incommensurable considerations on an imaginary scale. How much inequality is justified by the avoidance of eleven moderately small racial altercations and one middling riot? In 1942, Judge Learned Hand, a great judge by the standards of any age, eloquently agonized to an audience of lawyers about the problems faced by a court that must interpret phrases like "due process of law" or "the equal protection of the laws":**

But American constitutions always go further. Not only do they distribute the powers of government, but they as-

---

* Copyright © 1950, Holt, Rinehart and Winston, Inc. For references to empirical studies supporting Newcomb's statement, see T. NEWCOMB, R. TURNER & P. CONVERSE, SOCIAL PSYCHOLOGY 455-57 (1965).

** From THE SPIRIT OF LIBERTY, by Learned Hand. Published 1952 by Alfred A. Knopf, Inc. Reprinted by permission.

sume to lay down general principles[8] to insure the just exercise of those powers. This is the contribution to political science of which we are proud, and especially of a judiciary of Vestal unapproachability which shall always tend the Sacred Flame of Justice. Yet here we are on less firm ground. It is true that the logic which has treated these like other provisions of a constitution seems on its face unanswerable. Are they not parts in the same document? Did they not originally have a meaning? Why should not that meaning be found in the same way as that of the rest of the instrument? Nevertheless there are vital differences. Here history is only a feeble light, for these rubrics were meant to answer future problems unimagined and unimaginable. Nothing which by the utmost liberality can be called interpretation describes the process by which they must be applied. Indeed if law be a command for specific conduct, they are not law at all; they are cautionary warnings against the intemperance of faction and the first approaches of despotism. The answers to the questions which they raise demand the appraisal and balancing of human values which there are no scales to weigh. Who can say whether the contributions of one group may not justify allowing it a preference? How far should the capable, the shrewd or the strong be allowed to exploit their powers? When does utterance go beyond persuasion and become only incitement? How far are children wards of the state so as to justify its intervention in their nurture? What limits should be imposed upon the right to inherit? Where does religious freedom end and moral obliquity begin? As to such questions one can sometimes say what effect a proposal will have in fact, just as one can foretell how much money a tax will raise and who will pay it. But when that is done, one has come only to the kernel of the matter, which is the choice between what will be gained and what will be lost. The difficulty here does not come from ignorance, but from the absence of any standard, for values are incommensurable. It is true that theoretically, and sometimes practically, cases can arise where courts might properly intervene, not indeed because the legislature has appraised the values wrongly, for it is hard to see how that can be if it has honestly tried to appraise them at all; but because that is exactly what it has failed to do, because its action has been nothing but the

---

[8] Judge Hand was referring to such constitutional limitations as the due process and equal protection clauses of the Fourteenth Amendment. [*Eds.* note.]

patent exploitation of one group whose interests it has altogether disregarded. But the dangers are always very great. What seems to the losers mere spoliation usually appears to the gainers less than a reasonable relief from manifest injustice. Moreover, even were there a hedonistic rod by which to measure loss or gain, how could we know that the judges had it; or—what is more important—would enough people think they had, to be satisfied that they should use it? So long as law remains a profession (and certainly there is no indication that its complexities are decreasing) judges must be drawn from a professional class with the special interests and the special hierarchy of values which that implies. And even if they were as detached as Rhadamanthus himself, it would not serve unless people believed that they were. But to believe that another is truly a Daniel come to judgment demands almost the detachment of a Daniel; and whatever may be properly said for the judges, among whom there are indeed those as detached as it is given men to be, nobody will assert that detachment is a disposition widespread in any society.

It is not true, as you may be disposed at first blush to reply, that all this can be said with equal force of any other decision of a court. Constitutions are deliberately made difficult of amendment; mistaken readings of them cannot be readily corrected. Moreover, if they could be, constitutions must not degenerate into vade mecums or codes; when they begin to do so, it is a sign of a community unsure of itself and seeking protection against its own misgivings. And this is especially true of such parts of a constitution as I am talking about; these particularly must be left imprecise. If a court be really candid, it can only say: "We find that this measure will have this result; it will injure this group in such and such ways, and benefit that group in these other ways. We declare it invalid, because after every conceivable allowance for differences of outlook, we cannot see how a fair person can honestly believe that the benefits balance the losses." Hand, *The Contribution of an Independent Judiciary to Civilization*, in THE SPIRIT OF LIBERTY at 172, 177-79 (Dilliard ed. 1952).

Judge Hand's conclusion, expressed here and also in *The Bill of Rights* (1958), was that judges should use the greatest caution in exercising the power of judicial review of the constitutionality of legislation. For Judge Hand, the presumption of constitutionality was strong. Do you agree that the incommensurability of competing values implies great judicial deference to a legislative judgment? Should the courts adopt a variable standard for the presumption of constitutionality, so that some kinds of legislative judgments might be paid great deference, but others second-guessed more readily? What kinds of decisions of a legislature should be scrutinized most closely? Which decisions should receive the greatest respect (and thus the least judicial scrutiny)? On such a scale, where would you place legislative judgments that create distinctions based on race?

4. Justice Harlan and the "color-blind" Constitution.—Was Justice Harlan's dissent based on a factual disagreement with the majority on the questions of social psychology discussed above? Did he base his dissent on a conclusion that the state statute created an "unreasonable" classification? What did he mean when he said, p. 138 *supra,* that the Constitution is "color-blind"?

B.   THE CONSTITUTIONAL ATTACK ON SEGREGATION

As late as the 1950s, twenty-one states and the District of Columbia either required or permitted racial segregation in public schools. The doctrine of "separate but equal," adopted by the Supreme Court in *Plessy v. Ferguson,* was the theoretical underpinning for all these systems, and had been employed regularly by state courts (both before and after *Plessy*) to uphold school segregation against constitutional attack. But during the half century between *Plessy* and *Brown v. Board of Education,* the United States Supreme Court never explicitly examined the issues inherent in an application of "separate but equal" in the context of public education. Some of the Court's decisions gave the principle lateral support, and some rested on an assumption of its validity. But the whole fabric of school segregation remained unsupported by a Supreme Court opinion that disposed of the constitutional arguments.

Just three years after *Plessy,* the Supreme Court decided its first case relating to a system of separate public schools for white and black children. In Cumming v. Richmond County Board of Education, 175 U.S. 528 (1899), three Negro citizens, who were also parents and taxpayers, sued in a state court to enjoin a Georgia school board from maintaining a high school for white children without also maintaining one for Negro children. The board had been maintaining, out of general tax funds to which the plaintiffs had contributed, two high schools: one for black children, charging ten dollars per year tuition, and one for white girls, charging an annual tuition of fifteen dollars. There were in the county a private high school for white boys, also charging a tuition of fifteen dollars per year, and three private sectarian high schools that accepted Negro students. In the face of a serious shortage of educational facilities for Negro children in the primary grades, the board decided "for the present" to convert the Negro high school into four primary schools. In the absence of other funds to provide for the needed primary-school facilities, said the board in its answer to the plaintiffs' petition, "it would be unwise and unconscionable to keep up a high school for 60 pupils and turn away 300 little negroes who are asking to be taught their alphabet and to read and write. No part of the funds of this board accrued or accruing and no property appropriated to the education of the negro race has been taken from them." 175 U.S. at 533. The lower court granted an injunction restraining the board from operating any high school for white children until it also provided equal high school facilities for Negroes. The Georgia Supreme Court, however, reversed the lower court's decision, and ordered the case dismissed. On appeal to the United States Supreme Court, the plaintiffs argued that they had been denied the equal protection of the laws, but once again they lost. Not only did the Court fail to consider the doctrine of "separate but equal"; it also refused to pronounce on the degree of equality that would satisfy that formula. Justice Harlan, who had dissented in *Plessy v. Ferguson*, wrote for a unanimous Court:

> It was said at the argument that the vice in the common-school system of Georgia was the requirement that the white and colored children of the state be educated in separate schools. But we need not consider that question in this case. No such issue was made in the pleadings. Indeed, the plaintiffs distinctly state that they have no objection to the tax in question so far as levied for the support of primary, intermediate, and grammar schools, in the management of which the rule as to the separation of races is enforced. We must dispose of the case as it is presented by the record.
>
> The plaintiffs in error complain that the board of education used the funds in its hands to assist in maintaining a high school for white children without providing a similar school for colored children. The substantial relief asked is an injunction that would either impair the efficiency of the high school provided for white children or compel the board to close it. But if that were done, the result would only be to take from white children educational privileges enjoyed by them, without giving to colored children addi-

tional opportunities for the education furnished in high schools. The colored school children of the county would not be advanced in the matter of their education by a decree compelling the defendant board to cease giving support to a high school for white children. The board had before it the question whether it should maintain, under its control, a high school for about 60 colored children or withhold the benefits of education in primary schools from 300 children of the same race. It was impossible, the board believed, to give educational facilities to the 300 colored children who were unprovided for if it maintained a separate school for the 60 children who wished to have a high-school education. Its decision was in the interest of the greater number of colored children, leaving the smaller number to obtain a high-school education in existing private institutions at an expense not beyond that incurred in the high school discontinued by the board.

We are not permitted by the evidence in the record to regard that decision as having been made with any desire or purpose on the part of the board to discriminate against any of the colored school children of the county on account of their race. But if it be assumed that the board erred in supposing that its duty was to provide educational facilities for the 300 colored children who were without an opportunity in primary schools to learn the alphabet and to read and write, rather than to maintain a school for the benefit of the 60 colored children who wished to attend a high school, that was not an error which a court of equity should attempt to remedy by an injunction that would compel the board to withhold all assistance from the high school maintained for white children. If, in some appropriate proceeding instituted directly for that purpose, the plaintiffs had sought to compel the board of education, out of the funds in its hands or under its control, to establish and maintain a high school for colored children, and if it appeared that the board's refusal to maintain such a school was in fact an abuse of its discretion and in hostility to the colored population because of their race, different questions might have arisen in the state court.

The state court did not deem the action of the board of education in suspending temporarily and for economic reasons the high school for colored children a sufficient reason why the defendant should be restrained by injunction from maintaining an existing high school for white children. It rejected the suggestion that the board pro-

ceeded in bad faith or had abused the discretion with which
it was invested by the statute under which it proceeded or
had acted in hostility to the colored race. Under the circumstances disclosed, we cannot say that this action of the state
court was, within the meaning of the Fourteenth Amendment, a denial by the state to the plaintiffs and to those
associated with them of the equal protection of the laws
or of any privileges belonging to them as citizens of the
United States. We may add that while all admit that the
benefits and burdens of public taxation must be shared by
citizens without discrimination against any class on account
of their race, the education of the people in schools maintained by state taxation is a matter belonging to the respective states, and any interference on the part of Federal
authority with the management of such schools cannot be
justified except in the case of a clear and unmistakable
disregard of rights secured by the supreme law of the land.
We have here no such case to be determined; and as this
view disposes of the only question which this court has
jurisdiction to review and decide, the judgment is *affirmed.*

QUESTIONS

**1. The "temporary" closing of the Negro high school and the
interests of children then enrolled.**—Was the "temporary" nature
of the suspension of the Negro high school an important factor
in the decision in *Cumming?* When the claim is being made on
behalf of children whose high school careers would normally
last only a few years, what is the difference between a permanent
closing of the school and a temporary one? Is there a clue to the
Court's reasoning in its reference to the board's statement, quoted
above, that no funds or property devoted to the education of
Negroes "has been taken from *them*"? (Emphasis added.) Do
rights under the Fourteenth Amendment accrue to individuals
or to groups? Later in this chapter we shall consider this question
in relation to the "all deliberate speed" formula in *Brown v.
Board of Education.*

**2. Should a court limit its decision to issues and arguments
properly raised by the parties' attorneys?**—Why did the Court
refuse to consider the questions (a) whether the separation of
the races in Georgia's public schools itself violated the Fourteenth Amendment and (b) whether, assuming the validity of
"separate but equal," the plaintiffs were entitled at least to have

a separate public high school for black children? Apparently plaintiffs' counsel raised the issue of the validity of "separate but equal" for the first time in the litigation in his oral argument before the Supreme Court. With respect to the plaintiffs' right to have (at least) a separate high school, Justice Harlan said that if the plaintiffs had raised this contention "in some appropriate proceeding instituted directly for that purpose, . . . different questions might have arisen in the state court." Apparently this was an unenlightening reference to the way in which the case had come to the Supreme Court. *Two* proceedings had been brought in the state court: one sought an injunction against maintaining the public high school for whites, and the other a writ of mandamus, apparently to require provision of a high school for blacks. Brief for Defendant in Error at 20, Cumming v. Richmond County Board of Education. The trial judge granted relief in the injunction suit, and denied relief in the mandamus action. The state supreme court reversed the trial court's grant of injunctive relief, and affirmed the denial of mandamus. Plaintiffs appealed to the United States Supreme Court only from the state supreme court's judgment in the injunction proceeding. (The state supreme court opinion in *Cumming* is at 103 Ga. 641 (1898). The state supreme court decision in the mandamus action is in Blodgett v. Board of Education of Richmond County, 105 Ga. 463 (1898).) Were these procedural grounds (relating to the way the issues were raised) sufficient reasons for the Supreme Court's refusal to go into the issues? Does a court adequately perform its dispute-resolving function if it fails to consider an issue, raised by the parties or not, which may be relevant to resolving the dispute? Should a court refrain from inquiring into an issue which would decide the case in favor of one party because the attorney for that party has mistakenly failed to place the issue before the court in an adequate manner?

3. Achieving equality by "leveling up" or "leveling down."— The Court seems to assume in *Cumming* that the only possible result of an injunction such as the one granted by the trial court would be the indefinite closing of the public high school for white girls. Suppose that assumption were valid; should the courts refuse to grant the requested relief, on the ground that the injunction would harm white children without giving any corresponding advantage to Negro children? Suppose that (in 1899) a school board uses all its funds to establish a complete system of schools for white children, and provides no schools at all for black children. Should an 1899 court enjoin the continued operation of the white schools? Does this hypothetical case differ significantly from the *Cumming* case? Justice Harlan's opinion suggests that a different case would be presented if the plaintiffs were to sue to compel the school board to use available funds to establish a Negro high school, assuming that the board's previous failure to do so had been based on a purposeful racial discrimination. The question of legislative motive aside, however, why should there be a distinction between ordering the white high school closed and ordering a Negro high school opened? Would one likely result of an injunction in the former case be the early establishment of a Negro high school, in response to the pressure of white parents? Can a court legitimately rely on such a prediction in framing its decree? In Chapter 3 we shall consider a case in which a school board closed all of its schools in response to a desegregation decree.

4. Judicial examination of legislative motive.—Is a court equipped to inquire into the motives of the members of a school board, to determine whether their failure to open a Negro high school was the result of a purpose to discriminate against Negroes, or was rather the result of "economic reasons"? Would it not be easy for a sophisticated board to conceal an improper motive behind "economic reasons"? If the board spent all its remaining funds on additional facilities for the education of white children, might a court order the board to raise more funds for Negro education? Would such an order be more fitting for a court or less fitting than a simple injunction against maintenance of a white high school so long as no Negro high school is provided?

5. Justice Harlan's opinions in Cumming and Plessy.—Is Justice Harlan's opinion for the Court in *Cumming* consistent with his dissent in *Plessy*? If the constitutional validity of school segregation had been properly raised and argued in *Cumming*, could Justice Harlan consistently vote to deny the injunction? Reconsider his dissent in *Plessy*, substituting references to schools for references to railroad accommodations. Can a distinction be found in the compulsory features of school laws? Even if private schools are available? Even if railroad transportation, in some cases, may be a necessity? Some background to Justice Harlan's positions in *Plessy* and *Cumming* is provided in the following description of his campaign in 1871 for the governorship of Kentucky:

. . . Democratic orators . . . advanced the argument . . . that the Republicans were advocating "social equality" between whites and Negroes. Harlan's reaction to the charge was to deny it. "What do they mean by this cry of Negro equality? Do you suppose that any law of the State can regulate social intercourse of the citizen? . . . We do not declare as the Democratic orators well know, in favor of social equality. No law ever can or will regulate such relations. Social equality can never exist between the two races in Kentucky." Stressing that what he advocated was the full legal equality of Negroes with whites, Harlan illustrated the distinction by saying that, in the public schools, it was obviously "right and proper" to keep "whites and blacks separate." Westin, *John Marshall Harlan and the Constitutional Rights of Negroes: The Transformation of a Southerner,* 66 YALE L.J. 637, 662-63 (1957).

GONG LUM v. RICE
Supreme Court of the United States
275 U.S. 78 (1927)

Mr. Chief Justice TAFT delivered the opinion of the Court.

This was a petition for mandamus filed in the state Circuit Court of Mississippi for the First Judicial District of Bolivar County.

Gong Lum is a resident of Mississippi, resides in the Rosedale Consolidated High School District, and is the father of Martha Lum. He is engaged in the mercantile business. Neither he nor she was connected with the consular service or any other service of the government of China, or any other government, at the time of her birth. She was nine years old when the petition was filed, having been born January 21, 1915, and she sued by her next friend, Chew How, who is a native born citizen of the United States and the State of Mississippi. The petition alleged that she was of good moral character and between the ages of five and twenty-one years, and that, as she was such a citizen and an educable child, it became her father's duty under the law to send her to school; that she desired to attend the Rosedale Consolidated High School; that at the opening of the school she appeared as a pupil, but at the noon recess she was notified by the superintendent that she would not be allowed to return to the school; that an order had been issued by the Board of Trustees, who are made defendants, excluding her from attending the school solely on the ground that she was of Chinese descent and not a member of the white or Caucasian race, and that their order had been made in pursuance to instructions from the

State Superintendent of Education of Mississippi, who is also made a defendant.

The petitioners further show that there is no school maintained in the District for the education of children of Chinese descent, and none established in Bolivar County where she could attend.

. . . . The petition alleged that, in obedience to . . . [the state] Constitution, the legislature has provided for the establishment and for the payment of the expenses of the Rosedale Consolidated High School, and that the plaintiff, Gong Lum, the petitioner's father, is a taxpayer and helps to support and maintain the school; that Martha Lum is an educable child, is entitled to attend the school as a pupil, and that this is the only school conducted in the District available for her as a pupil; that the right to attend it is a valuable right; that she is not a member of the colored race nor is she of mixed blood, but that she is pure Chinese; that she is by the action of the Board of Trustees and the State Superintendent discriminated against directly and denied her right to be a member of the Rosedale School; that the school authorities have no discretion under the law as to her admission as a pupil in the school, but that they continue without authority of law to deny her the right to attend it as a pupil. For these reasons the writ of mandamus is prayed for against the defendants commanding them and each of them to desist from discriminating against her on account of her race or ancestry and to give her the same rights and privileges that other educable children between the ages of five and twenty-one are granted in the Rosedale Consolidated High School.

The petition was demurred to by the defendants on the ground, among others, that the bill showed on its face that plaintiff is a member of the Mongolian or yellow race, and therefore not entitled to attend the schools provided by law in the State of Mississippi for children of the white or Caucasian race.

The trial court overruled the demurrer and ordered that a writ of mandamus issue to the defendants as prayed in the petition.

The defendants then appealed to the Supreme Court of Mississippi, which heard the case. *Rice v. Gong Lum,* 139 Miss. 760. In its opinion, it directed its attention to the proper construction of § 207 of the State Constitution of 1890, which provides:

"Separate schools shall be maintained for children of the white and colored races."

The Court held that this provision of the Constitution divided the educable children into those of the pure white or

Caucasian race, on the one hand, and the brown, yellow and black races, on the other, and therefore that Martha Lum of the Mongolian or yellow race could not insist on being classed with the whites under this constitutional division. The Court said:

"The legislature is not compelled to provide separate schools for each of the colored races, and, unless and until it does provide such schools and provide for segregation of the other races, such races are entitled to have the benefit of the colored public schools. Under our statutes a colored public school exists in every county and in some convenient district in which every colored child is entitled to obtain an education. These schools are within the reach of all the children of the state, and the plaintiff does not show by her petition that she applied for admission to such schools. On the contrary the petitioner takes the position that because there are no separate public schools for Mongolians that she is entitled to enter the white public schools in preference to the colored public schools. . . .

"If the plaintiff desires, she may attend the colored public schools of her district, or, if she does not so desire, she may go to a private school. The compulsory school law of this state does not require the attendance at a public school, and a parent under the decisions of the Supreme Court of the United States has a right to educate his child in a private school if he so desires. But plaintiff is not entitled to attend a white public school."

. . . .

The case then reduces itself to the question whether a state can be said to afford to a child of Chinese ancestry born in this country, and a citizen of the United States, equal protection of the laws by giving her the opportunity for a common school education in a school which receives only colored children of the brown, yellow or black races.

The right and power of the state to regulate the method of providing for the education of its youth at public expense is clear. In *Cumming v. Richmond County Board of Education*, 175 U.S. 528, 545, persons of color sued the Board of Education to enjoin it from maintaining a high school for white children without providing a similar school for colored children which had existed and had been discontinued. Mr. Justice Harlan, in delivering the opinion of the Court, said:

"Under the circumstances disclosed, we cannot say that this action of the state court was, within the meaning of the Fourteenth Amendment, a denial by the State to the plaintiffs and to those associated with them of the equal protection of the laws, or of any privileges belonging to them as citizens of the United States. We may add that while all admit that the benefits and burdens of public taxation must be shared by citizens without discrimination against any class on account of their race, the education of the people in schools maintained by state taxation is a matter belonging to the respective States, and any interference on the part of Federal authority with the management of such schools can not be justified except in the case of a clear and unmistakable disregard of rights secured by the supreme law of the land."

The question here is whether a Chinese citizen of the United States is denied equal protection of the laws when he is classed among the colored races and furnished facilities for education equal to that offered to all, whether white, brown, yellow or black. Were this a new question, it would call for very full argument and consideration, but we think that it is the same question which has been many times decided to be within the constitutional power of the state legislature to settle without intervention of the federal courts under the Federal Constitution. *Roberts v. City of Boston*, 5 Cush. (Mass.) 198, 206, 208, 209; [and citations to the decisions of nine state courts and three lower federal courts].

. . . .

In *Plessy v. Ferguson*, 163 U.S. 537, 544, 545, in upholding the validity under the Fourteenth Amendment of a statute of Louisiana requiring the separation of the white and colored races in railway coaches, a more difficult question than this, this Court, speaking of permitted race separation, said:

"The most common instance of this is connected with the establishment of separate schools for white and colored children, which has been held to be a valid exercise of the legislative power even by courts of States where the political rights of the colored race have been longest and most earnestly enforced."

The case of *Roberts v. City of Boston, supra,* in which Chief Justice Shaw of the Supreme Judicial Court of Massachusetts, announced the opinion of that court upholding the separation of colored and white schools under a state constitutional injunction of equal protection, the same as the Fourteenth Amendment, was then referred to, and this Court continued:

"Similar laws have been enacted by Congress under its general power of legislation over the District of Columbia, Rev. Stat. D.C.

§§ 281, 282, 283, 310, 319, as well as by the legislatures of many of the States, and have been generally, if not uniformly, sustained by the Courts," citing many of the cases above named.

Most of the cases cited arose, it is true, over the establishment of separate schools as between white pupils and black pupils, but we can not think that the question is any different or that any different result can be reached, assuming the cases above cited to be rightly decided, where the issue is as between white pupils and the pupils of the yellow races. The decision is within the discretion of the state in regulating its public schools and does not conflict with the Fourteenth Amendment. The judgment of the Supreme Court of Mississippi is affirmed.

QUESTIONS

1. Had prior precedent settled the issue of the validity of school segregation?—If the question of the validity of school segregation were a new one, said Chief Justice Taft, "it would call for very full argument and consideration, ..." Why was this question not a new one? The cited decisions were not decisions of the United States Supreme Court. Many of them did not deal with the Fourteenth Amendment; *Roberts v. City of Boston*, for example, had been decided before the adoption of the Fourteenth Amendment, and even before the Nation had fought a long and costly war in considerable part over the issue of the status of the Negro. And *Plessy v. Ferguson* involved not education but railroad cars. After *Gong Lum v. Rice* the validity of school segregation clearly was settled. Is it fair to conclude that this question *never* received "full argument and consideration" in the Supreme Court?

2. The comparison to Plessy v. Ferguson.—What did Chief Justice Taft mean in saying that *Plessy v. Ferguson* raised "a more difficult question" than the question before the Court in *Gong Lum*? One possible interpretation might be that *Plessy* had furnished a precedent for *Gong Lum*. A more likely meaning is that *Plessy* was a more difficult case on the constitutional merits. Is the interest of the Negro railroad passenger in freedom from discrimination weightier than the corresponding interest of the Chinese schoolchild? Is the state's interest in segregation greater in the case of schools than in the case of railroad accommodations? Is Mississippi's compulsory school law relevant to the latter question?

3. "A clear and unmistakable disregard" of constitutional rights: a prerequisite to judicial invalidation?—The Court quotes from Justice Harlan's opinion in *Cumming*. Is that case appropriately cited as a precedent for this one? The language from *Cumming* about "a clear and unmistakable disregard" of constitutional rights appears to be designed to introduce Chief Justice Taft's citations to the various state court decisions upholding school segregation. May these paragraphs, taken together, be read to say something like the following?

> We cannot invalidate a state's scheme for operating its schools unless that scheme is obviously unconstitutional. These numerous cases, decided over a period of three generations, show that the question is, at the very least, debatable, and so we must not interpose a federal judicial veto in the name of the Constitution, however we might treat this question as an original proposition.

Should the intervention of the Supreme Court be limited to cases of "clear and unmistakable disregard" of constitutional rights? Is there something special about the responsibility of the states for public education? Or should this rule of decision be made applicable to all constitutional questions?

4. School segregation of American Indians and Mexican-Americans.—Two cases involving California public schools illustrate the extent to which racial and ethnic segregation in public schools was imposed by governmental action during the regime of "separate but equal." In Piper v. Big Pine School District, 193 Cal. 664, 226 Pac. 926 (1924), the California Supreme Court held invalid as a denial of equal protection of the laws the exclusion from the district's schools of an American Indian child on the ground that the child had available a United States Government school for Indians within the district. The exclusion of the plaintiff child, on the ground that other schooling was available, raised issues similar to those in *Cumming* and *Missouri ex rel. Gaines v. Canada*, p. 163 *infra*. The California statutory pattern, combining categories of children in a manner revealing of the thinking of the times when the statute was enacted (1921), provided that "the governing body of the school district shall have power to exclude children of filthy or vicious habits, or children suffering from contagious or infectious diseases, and also to establish separate schools for Indian children and for children of Chinese, Japanese or Mongolian parentage . . .," and that if the United States established an Indian school within a school district's boundaries "the Indian children of the district . . . may not be admitted to the district school." Cal. Stats., 1921, ch. 685, p. 1160. These statutes were repealed in 1947. Cal. Stats., 1947, ch. 737, p. 1792, § 1.

In 1947 the Court of Appeals for the Ninth Circuit held invalid the segregation in several school districts in Orange County, California, of children of "Mexican and Latin descent." The holding was based on invalidity under California law—state statutes then permitted segregation only of Indian, Chinese, Japanese, and Mongolian children—without reaching the Fourteenth Amendment claims of the plaintiffs. Westminster School District of Orange County v. Mendez, 161 F.2d 774 (9th Cir. 1947).

5. Inequalities in resources allocated to racially separate schools.
—The "separate but equal" formula as applied to education often resulted in fact in gross inequalities in the resources allocated to educational opportunities for blacks and for whites. As early as 1909, at the national conference that resulted in the organization of the National Association for the Advancement of Colored People, one of the principal demands, in the language of Dr. W. E. B. Du Bois, was "That there be equal educational opportunities for all and in all the states, and that public school expenditure be the same for the Negro and white child." See 2 A DOCUMENTARY HISTORY OF THE NEGRO PEOPLE IN THE UNITED STATES 924, 926 (H. Aptheker ed. 1951; paperbound ed. 1964). This demand reflected the undoubted fact that school expenditures, particularly in southern states, were far from equal. A few figures make the point: In 1911-13, in the four states of Virginia, North Carolina, South Carolina and Georgia, annual salaries of teachers in white schools averaged $287.29; for black schools, the figure was $127.88. In 1915, the school term for white pupils in South Carolina was 133 days long; the comparable figure for Negro schools was 67 days. In the same state, the student-teacher ratio for white schools was 36; for Negro schools, 64. The expenditure per enrolled pupil was $16.22 per white child, and $1.13 per black child. These figures are taken from L. HARLAN, SEPARATE AND UNEQUAL: PUBLIC SCHOOL CAMPAIGNS AND RACISM IN THE SOUTHERN SEABOARD STATES 1901-1915, at 208, 257 (rev. ed. 1968).

Similar disparities in resources allocated to the education of white and black children in southern and border states persisted a generation later. In the school year 1943-44, per-pupil annual expenditures in Alabama were $70.20 in white schools, and $25.65 in Negro schools. For the same year, the comparable figures for North Carolina were $71.60 and $50.07; for Louisiana, $121.32 and $40.25; for Mississippi, $71.65 and $11.96. NEGRO YEAR BOOK 76 (10th ed., J. Guzman ed., 1947). For an example of the persistence of such disparities as late as 1967-68, see United States v. Bertie County Board of Education, 293 F. Supp. 1276, 1279 (E.D. N.C. 1968) (per-pupil valuation of school property: predominantly white schools, $817.91; Negro schools, $473.33.)

MISSOURI *ex rel.* GAINES V. CANADA, 305 U.S. 337 (1938). This decision was the first in which the Supreme Court established any minimum content for equality within the "separate but equal" formula. A Negro plaintiff sought mandamus to compel the Curators of the University of Missouri to admit him to that University's law school, from which he had been excluded on grounds of race, in accordance with state law. A Missouri statute authorized payment from state funds of tuition fees for Negro students to attend universities in adjacent states to study subjects not offered by Lincoln University, the Missouri university for Negroes. Lincoln did not have a law school, and the plaintiff was offered support if he should wish to attend law school in a neighboring state; state university law schools were open to the plaintiff in Kansas, Nebraska, Iowa and Illinois, all of which border on Missouri. The state courts denied relief, but the United States Supreme Court reversed. Chief Justice Hughes, writing for the majority, noted that "furnishing equal facilities in separate schools [is] a method the validity of which has been sustained by our decisions." 305 U.S. at 344. But, he said, "The admissibility of laws separating the races in the enjoyment of privileges by the State rests wholly upon the equality of the privileges which the laws give to the separated groups within the State." 305 U.S. at 349. The provision of tuition fees for out-of-state education for Negroes was not sufficient to meet the requirements of substantial equality; Negro students could not constitutionally be put to the burden of having to leave the state to attend law school.

On remand, the Missouri Supreme Court directed the trial court that if, by the next term, the law school facilities at Lincoln University were substantially the equal of those at the University of Missouri, the writ of mandamus should be denied; otherwise, the writ should be granted. A Missouri statute the next year made it obligatory for the Curators of Lincoln University to reorganize Lincoln "so that it shall afford to the negro people of the state opportunity for training up to the standard furnished at the State University of Missouri." Mo. Rev. Stat. § 10774 (1939).

Before the decision in the *Gaines* case, there had been little effort by black pupils and their parents to challenge local school boards for their failure to live up to the "equal" part of "separate but equal." Decisions like *Cumming* and *Gong Lum* had given them little encouragement. But *Gaines* promised an increased willingness on the part of the Supreme Court, and thus the federal judiciary generally, to police at least the outer boundaries of educational inequality. The *Carter* case, which follows, raises only some of the wide range of questions that a conscientious school board or court might have to face in determining whether the education offered to a black child was substantially equal to that offered to white children in the district. As you read the opinion, ask yourself (a) whether there are other factors, not mentioned by the court, that might also be relevant to the question of substantial equality, and (b) why the court makes no reference to the reasonableness of the state's scheme of classification.

CARTER v. SCHOOL BOARD OF ARLINGTON COUNTY
United States Court of Appeals, Fourth Circuit
182 F.2d 531 (1950)

Before PARKER, Chief Judge, and SOPER and DOBIE, Circuit Judges.

SOPER, Circuit Judge.

This case again brings to our attention the right of Negro students in state schools to the same or substantially equivalent privileges of education as white students. The difficulties inherent in the practice of segregation are again emphasized. The schools in question are high schools located in Arlington County, Virginia, where the Negroes of school age constitute only a small percentage of the school population, so that the expense involved in affording to the small minority in a separate school every course of study and every kind of equipment and recreational facility that are given the majority is proportionately very great. Washington-Lee High School for white students is predominantly a senior high school with a total of 2,377 students of which 1,881 are in the senior and 496 in the junior high school.

Hoffman-Boston High School for Negro students is predominantly an elementary-junior high school with 48 senior high
school pupils, 13 boys and 35 girls, and a total enrollment of 270.
In 1946-1947 and in 1947-1948 high school students numbered 12
and 18 respectively of which only 3 were boys. The burden upon
the county authorities became more onerous when in recent
years the schools in the District of Columbia imposed a tuition
fee upon students from Arlington County and discontinued the
practice of admitting Negro high school students from the county
free of charge. Negro students who desired to attend the Washington schools to obtain courses and facilities available to whites
but not to Negroes in Arlington County applied to the Arlington
County School Board to pay their tuition, and this was done
during the 1946-1947 and 1947-1948 sessions. In 1948-49, however, payment of tuition was refused to all Negro students except
those who had completed three years of work in the District of
Columbia schools.

These circumstances led to the present suit which was instituted by Constance Carter, a Negro high school student, by her
mother and next friend, on her own behalf and on behalf of 300
colored students in Arlington County similarly situated. Subsequently, two other high school students, Julius Brevard and
Peggy Council, were permitted to intervene. It was alleged that
each of the plaintiffs applied for and was refused certain courses
and educational advantages afforded to white students at Washington-Lee but not given to colored students at Hoffman-
Boston. The suit was resisted by the school authorities on the
ground that the educational advantages offered at Hoffman-Boston are substantially equivalent to those given at Washington-
Lee, and this view was taken by the District Judge in an opinion
reported at D.C., 87 F. Supp. 745.

In our view, this position is untenable since the evidence indicates that in plant facilities and courses of education the white
students of Washington-Lee enjoy advantages which are not
offered to the students at the colored high school. The differences
between the two schools are sufficiently illustrated by the following facts which support the conclusion that discrimination actually exists. The physical plant and equipment at Hoffman-
Boston in important respects compares unfavorably with that at
Washington-Lee. Each school has a shop annex but the white
high school has seven separate shop rooms or areas with adequate
equipment for the training of students in various skills. It has a
general machine shop, an automobile mechanics shop, mechan-
ical drawing room, machine shop, sheet metal shop, printing
shop and wood shop. The cost of the shop building was $110,000

and the cost of its equipment $21,000. Hoffman-Boston has a single general shop in one room with a variety of equipment, but no machines or tools for instruction in automobile mechanics or printing and no machines for instruction in machine shop, sheet metal, or wood shop. The cost of the shop building, which also houses the Home Economics Department, was $37,500, and the cost of the equipment was $2,000.

Washington-Lee has four science laboratories, that is, a physics laboratory, a chemistry laboratory and two biology laboratories with adequate furniture and equipment which cost $34,501. Hoffman-Boston has only one science room in which all the sciences given at the school are taught. The equipment is less substantial and varied than that at Washington-Lee and cost $1,934.

The library at Washington-Lee consists of a reading and lending room and a reference room. It contains 8,682 books and 90 subscriptions to periodicals. The books cost $12,000. The library at Hoffman-Boston consists of one room made by combining two rooms of class room size, and is not so well adapted for library purposes as the rooms at Washington-Lee. It contains 1,077 books which cost $1,921 and twenty-one subscriptions to magazines.

Washington-Lee has two rooms especially equipped for instruction in music. It has also an auditorium designed for band and orchestra instruction, with a stage, music stands, and storage room. Hoffman-Boston has no special auditorium or room for instruction in music. For this purpose it uses its main auditorium for choral and instrumental music and a small class room formerly occupied as the principal's office.

Washington-Lee has two large rooms especially equipped for instruction in typewriting, which is furnished with typewriters, special tables and chairs, mimeograph machine and a mimeoscope. Hoffman-Boston uses one small room, which is equipped with some typewriters but no mimeograph machine or mimeoscope.

Washington-Lee has two gymnasiums, one for girls and one for boys. Each gymnasium is well equipped with a basket ball court, dressing rooms, locker rooms, shower rooms, &c. Each room can be used for a variety of games and athletic contests. Hoffman-Boston has no gymnasium. Its auditorium is convertible for use in calisthenics and some gymnasium equipment is furnished; but the room is not suitable for gymnasium purposes and structural columns interfere with games. It has no basket ball court, dressing rooms, lockers or shower facilities.

Washington-Lee has a large well arranged cafeteria in which lunches are served. Hoffman-Boston has no cafeteria or lunch room facilities but plans have been made for a cafeteria to open in September, 1950.

Washington-Lee has an infirmary equipped with six beds and first aid equipment. Hoffman-Boston has no infirmary clinic or first aid room but a nurse spends three afternoons a week there.

There are many subjects taught at Washington-Lee that are not given at Hoffman-Boston. The list of these subjects includes courses in speech, journalism, solid geometry, commercial arithmetic, bookkeeping, automobile mechanics, woodworking, printing, &c.

Washington-Lee is accredited by the well recognized regional accrediting agency, the Southern Association of Colleges and Secondary Schools, and by the Virginia State Department of Education. Hoffman-Boston was accredited by the latter for the first time in 1948-1949 on a probationary basis but has never been accredited by the former.

The white pupils at Washington-Lee enjoy various extracurricular activities, such as glee clubs, choruses, cadet corps, publication staffs, Hi-Y organizations, a debating club and various athletic teams, and are eligible for nomination to the National Honorary Scholastic Society and for the receipt of the Bausch and Lomb Honorary Science award. None of these activities and awards are available to the colored pupils at Hoffman-Boston. The failure to provide these opportunities cannot be defended on the ground that their absence is mainly attributable to the size or location of the school.

It is contended that many courses are not given at Hoffman-Boston because they have not been requested or desired by the students; and that to provide for such a demand, if it should arise, a survey is made in the spring of each year to ascertain what subjects the students will desire for the following session. Interrogatories are issued to the students in attendance as to their desires for the next session and inquiries are made at public meetings of parents in Parents and Teachers Associations and similar organizations; and it is said that if any course is found needed, it is provided. This procedure, however, is not followed at Washington-Lee where all courses in the curriculum are available each year to every eligible pupil without previous demand or request. This difference in procedure cannot be sustained. It places a burden upon the colored student and deprives him of the opportunity of taking a course of instruction unless he has determined to take it months in advance, whereas the white student may apply at the opening of the session and obtain the desired instruction. The point was touched upon by the Supreme Court in the Oklahoma Law School case, Sipuel v. Board of Regents of University of Okl., 332 U.S. 631, 68 S. Ct. 299, 92 L. Ed. 247, and Fisher v. Hurst, 333 U.S. 147, 68 S. Ct. 389, 92 L. Ed. 604, in which the court held that the refusal of admission of a Negro student to the state law school could not be upheld on the ground that the student had failed in advance to demand the establishment of a separate law school and admission thereto.

In further defense of the failure to furnish certain courses to the students at Hoffman-Boston, it is pointed out that the School Authorities of Arlington County have adopted the policy of sending Negro vocational pupils to the Manassas Regional school which is situated twenty-five miles distant in Prince William County, Virginia. Only one Negro student has availed himself of this opportunity. It does not offer in our opinion an equivalent advantage for colored students desiring courses which are given to white students at Washington-Lee in Arlington County. We had occasion to consider a similar situation in Corbin v. County School Board of Pulaski County, 4 Cir., 177 F.2d 924, where the inconvenience and loss of time imposed by transportation to the regional school were pointed out.

The above recital of existing conditions at the two schools is not intended to cover the whole field of physical plant and instruction, but rather to demonstrate by illustration that discrimination in the treatment accorded the students of the two races undoubtedly prevails. We append in the footnote a recapitulation of advantages and disadvantages by the District Judge in his opinion which led him to the conclusion, balancing one against the other, that no discrimination exists.[9] It is established,

---

[9] The evidence shows that each school has some advantages over the other, and each school has disadvantages not suffered by the other, but a summary of them discloses that Hoffman-Boston and Washington-Lee give substantially the same treatment to each of their high school students.

Washington-Lee offers courses in auto mechanics and printing; Hoffman-Boston gives a course in bricklaying, Washington-Lee does not. The home economics instruction facilities at Hoffman-Boston far exceed the corresponding facilities at Washington-Lee.

Hoffman-Boston offers physical education to all of its high school students, but none is offered at Washington-Lee to the students of the 11th and 12th grades, some 900 in number.

Washington-Lee is so overcrowded that its corridors must be made into one-way-traffic arteries; study hours there must be spent in the rear of rooms then being used for class instruction; Hoffman-Boston has no such overcrowding.

At Hoffman-Boston two teachers of physical education are provided for 375 children, while at Washington-Lee four must handle 1,100 children.

The library at Hoffman-Boston will accommodate all of its senior high school at one time, while at Washington-Lee only 6% or 7% of its students may be so accommodated. Thus the student at Washington-Lee has very limited library access, but the Hoffman-Boston student has easy and unrestricted enjoyment and benefit of the library.

however, that the right of the individual student to the privilege of public instruction equivalent to that given by the state to the individual student of another race, is a personal one and equivalency cannot be determined by weighing the respective advantages furnished to the two groups of which the individuals are members. In Corbin v. County School Board of Pulaski County, 4 Cir., 177 F.2d 924, 926, we said: ". . . the question cannot be decided by averaging the facilities provided for the two classes of pupils throughout the county and comparing one with the other, since the rights created by the Fourteenth Amendment are individual and personal and the prohibitions of the Amendment are observed only when the same or equivalent treatment is accorded to persons of different races similarly situated. Mitchell v. United States, 313 U.S. 80, 61 S. Ct. 873, 85 L. Ed. 1201; Shelley v. Kraemer, 334 U.S. 1, 68 S. Ct. 836, 92 L. Ed. 1161, 3 A.L.R.2d 441." . . .

See also State of Missouri ex rel. Gaines v. Canada, 305 U.S. 337, 350, 59 S. Ct. 232, 83 L. Ed. 208.

The view was expressed by the trial court that the differences between the two high schools are not discriminations outlawed by the Fourteenth Amendment, but only such variations as might be expected to exist between any two schools, springing from differences of size, location or methods of instruction; and that the state need not furnish the same or similar treatment to its citizens, but may vary the form of its benefits provided all citizens receive shares of equal value. Again it was said that differences may exist between the provisions made for white and for colored citizens without fouling the amendment, if the differences result only from unattentive stewardship or faulty judgment, and that such shortcomings are defects of administration to be corrected

---

Again, the sizes of the classes at Hoffman-Boston are far more favorable. As an average Hoffman-Boston has between 20 and 25 to a class; at Washington-Lee a great many of the classes contain more than 35.

As we have already explained, the location of Hoffman-Boston is by far the better, having no constant traffic hazards as does Washington-Lee. The grounds are more spacious at Hoffman-Boston for each student, the available play ground greater.

It is fair to say that in classroom instruction the opportunities and facilities offered to the high school student at Hoffman-Boston are greater than those provided at Washington-Lee. This is because, with the physical equipment equal, the Hoffman-Boston boy or girl receives a more individual instruction, enjoys a closer personal relationship to the teacher, is subject to a closer study by the teacher for counsel and guidance, receives instruction under a coordination and correlation of subjects, rather than through a departmentalized form of instruction too often delaying the realization of the relationship of all subjects of study. Then, too, at Hoffman-Boston the individuality of the pupil is not "lost in the crowd". These are but the usual advantages to be gained from a school where the scholars are few. [Footnote in original, renumbered.]

by the responsible authorities and are not constitutional defects for judicial interference.

These holdings may not be taken as safe guides by the school authorities or student population of Virginia. The differences between the two schools are not merely unimportant variations incident to the maintenance of separate establishments, but constitute unlawful discriminations against pupils of the colored race; and it is no defense that they flow in part from variations in the size of the respective student bodies or locations of the buildings. The burdens inherent in segregation must be met by the state which maintains the practice. Nor can it be said that a scholar who is deprived of his due must apply to the administrative authorities and not to the courts for relief. An injured person must of course show that the state has denied him advantages accorded to others in like situation, but when this is established, his right of access to the courts is absolute and complete. . . .

The judgment of the District Court is reversed and the case is remanded for further proceedings.

Reversed and remanded.

SWEATT v. PAINTER
Supreme Court of the United States
339 U.S. 629 (1950)

Mr. Chief Justice VINSON delivered the opinion of the Court.

This case and *McLaurin v. Oklahoma State Regents,* . . . present different aspects of this general question: To what extent does the Equal Protection Clause of the Fourteenth Amendment limit the power of a state to distinguish between students of different races in professional and graduate education in a state university? Broader issues have been urged for our consideration, but we adhere to the principle of deciding constitutional questions only in the context of the particular case before the Court. We have frequently reiterated that this Court will decide constitutional questions only when necessary to the disposition of the case at hand, and that such decisions will be drawn as narrowly as possible. . . . Because of this traditional reluctance to extend constitutional interpretations to situations or facts which are not before the Court, much of the excellent research and detailed argument presented in these cases is unnecessary to their disposition.

In the instant case, petitioner filed an application for admission to the University of Texas Law School for the February, 1946 term. His application was rejected solely because he is a Negro. Petitioner thereupon brought this suit for mandamus against the appropriate school officials, respondents here, to compel his admission. At that time, there was no law school in Texas which admitted Negroes.

The state trial court recognized that the action of the State in denying petitioner the opportunity to gain a legal education while granting it to others deprived him of the equal protection of the laws guaranteed by the Fourteenth Amendment. The court did not grant the relief requested, however, but continued the case for six months to allow the State to supply substantially equal facilities. At the expiration of the six months, in December, 1946, the court denied the writ on the showing that the authorized university officials had adopted an order calling for the opening of a law school for Negroes the following February. While petitioner's appeal was pending, such a school was made available, but petitioner refused to register therein. The Texas Court of Civil Appeals set aside the trial court's judgment and ordered the cause "remanded generally to the trial court for further proceedings without prejudice to the rights of any party to this suit."

On remand, a hearing was held on the issue of the equality of the educational facilities at the newly established school as compared with the University of Texas Law School. Finding that the new school offered petitioner "privileges, advantages, and opportunities for the study of law substantially equivalent to those offered by the State to white students at the University of Texas," the trial court denied mandamus. The Court of Civil Appeals affirmed. 210 S.W.2d 442 (1948). Petitioner's application for a writ of error was denied by the Texas Supreme Court. We granted certiorari, 338 U.S. 865 (1949), because of the manifest importance of the constitutional issues involved.

The University of Texas Law School, from which petitioner was excluded, was staffed by a faculty of sixteen full-time and three part-time professors, some of whom are nationally recognized authorities in their field. Its student body numbered 850. The library contained over 65,000 volumes. Among the other facilities available to the students were a law review, moot court facilities, scholarship funds, and Order of the Coif affiliation. The school's alumni occupy the most distinguished positions in the private practice of the law and in the public life of the State. It may properly be considered one of the nation's ranking law schools.

The law school for Negroes which was to have opened in February, 1947, would have had no independent faculty or library. The teaching was to be carried on by four members of the University of Texas Law School faculty, who were to maintain their offices at the University of Texas while teaching at both institutions. Few of the 10,000 volumes ordered for the library had arrived; nor was there any full-time librarian. The school lacked accreditation.

Since the trial of this case, respondents report the opening of a law school at the Texas State University for Negroes. It is apparently on the road to full accreditation. It has a faculty of five full-time professors; a student body of 23; a library of some 16,500 volumes serviced by a full-time staff; a practice court and legal aid association; and one alumnus who has become a member of the Texas Bar.

Whether the University of Texas Law School is compared with the original or the new law school for Negroes, we cannot find substantial equality in the educational opportunities offered white and Negro law students by the State. In terms of number of the faculty, variety of courses and opportunity for specialization, size of the student body, scope of the library, availability of law review and similar activities, the University of Texas Law School is superior. What is more important, the University of Texas Law School possesses to a far greater degree those qualities which are incapable of objective measurement but which make for greatness in a law school. Such qualities, to name but a few, include reputation of the faculty, experience of the administration, position and influence of the alumni, standing in the community, traditions and prestige. It is difficult to believe that one who had a free choice between these law schools would consider the question close.

Moreover, although the law is a highly learned profession, we are well aware that it is an intensely practical one. The law school, the proving ground for legal learning and practice, cannot be effective in isolation from the individuals and institutions with which the law interacts. Few students and no one who has practiced law would choose to study in an academic vacuum, removed from the interplay of ideas and the exchange of views with which the law is concerned. The law school to which Texas is willing to admit petitioner excludes from its student body members of the racial groups which number 85% of the population of the State and include most of the lawyers, witnesses, jurors, judges and other officials with whom petitioner will inevitably be dealing when he becomes a member of the Texas Bar. With such a substantial and significant segment of society excluded, we cannot conclude that the education offered petitioner is substantially equal to that which he would receive if admitted to the University of Texas Law School.

It may be argued that excluding petitioner from that school is no different from excluding white students from the new law school. This contention overlooks realities. It is unlikely that a member of a group so decisively in the majority, attending a school with rich traditions and prestige which only a history of consistently maintained excellence could command, would claim that the opportuities afforded him for legal education were unequal to those held open to petitioner. That such a claim, if made, would be dishonored by the State, is no answer. "Equal protection of the laws is not achieved through indiscriminate imposition of inequalities." *Shelley v. Kraemer*, 334 U.S. 1, 22 (1948).

It is fundamental that these cases concern rights which are personal and present. This Court has stated unanimously that "The State must provide [legal education] for [petitioner] in conformity with the equal protection clause of the Fourteenth Amendment and provide it as soon as it does for applicants of any other group." *Sipuel v. Board of Regents*, 332 U.S. 631, 633 (1948). That case "did not present the issue whether a state might not satisfy the equal protection clause of the Fourteenth Amendment by establishing a separate law school for Negroes." *Fisher v. Hurst*, 333 U.S. 147, 150 (1948). In *Missouri ex rel. Gaines v. Canada*, 305 U.S. 337, 351 (1938), the Court, speaking through Chief Justice Hughes, declared that "petitioner's right was a personal one. It was as an individual that he was entitled to the equal protection of the laws, and the State was bound to furnish him within its borders facilities for legal education substantially equal to those which the State there afforded for persons of the white race, whether or not other negroes sought the same opportunity." These are the only cases in this Court which present the issue of the constitutional validity of race distinctions in state-supported graduate and professional education.

In accordance with these cases, petitioner may claim his full constitutional right: legal education equivalent to that offered by the State to students of other races. Such education is not available to him in a separate law school as offered by the State. We cannot, therefore, agree with respondents that the doctrine of *Plessy v. Ferguson*, 163 U.S. 537 (1896), requires affirmance of the judgment below. Nor need we reach petitioner's contention that *Plessy v. Ferguson* should be reexamined in the light of contemporary knowledge respecting the purposes of the Fourteenth Amendment and the effects of racial segregation. . . .

We hold that the Equal Protection Clause of the Fourteenth Amendment requires that petitioner be admitted to the University of Texas Law School. The judgment is reversed and the cause is remanded for proceedings not inconsistent with this opinion.

Reversed.

McLAURIN v. OKLAHOMA STATE REGENTS
FOR HIGHER EDUCATION
Supreme Court of the United States
339 U.S. 637 (1950)

Mr. Chief Justice VINSON delivered the opinion of the Court.

In this case, we are faced with the question whether a state may, after admitting a student to graduate instruction in its state university, afford him different treatment from other students solely because of his race. We decide only this issue; see *Sweatt v. Painter.* . . .

Appellant is a Negro citizen of Oklahoma. Possessing a Master's Degree, he applied for admission to the University of Oklahoma in order to pursue studies and courses leading to a Doctorate in Education. At that time, his application was denied, solely because of his race. The school authorities were required to exclude him by the Oklahoma statutes, 70 Okla. Stat. (1941) §§ 455, 456, 457, which made it a misdemeanor to maintain or operate, teach or attend a school at which both whites and Negroes are enrolled or taught. Appellant filed a complaint requesting injunctive relief, alleging that the action of the school authorities and the statutes upon which their action was based were unconstitutional and deprived him of the equal protection of the laws. Citing our decisions in *Missouri ex rel. Gaines v. Canada,* 305 U.S. 337 (1938), and *Sipuel v. Board of Regents,* 332 U.S. 631 (1948), a statutory three-judge District Court held that the State had a Constitutional duty to provide him with the education he sought as soon as it provided that education for applicants of any other group. It further held that to the extent the Oklahoma statutes denied him admission they were unconstitutional and void. On the assumption, however, that the State would follow the constitutional mandate, the court refused to grant the injunction, retaining jurisdiction of the cause with full power to issue any necessary and proper orders to secure McLaurin the equal protection of the laws. 87 F. Supp. 526.

Following this decision, the Oklahoma legislature amended these statutes to permit the admission of Negroes to institutions of higher learning attended by white students, in cases where such institutions offered courses not available in the Negro schools. The amendment provided, however, that in such cases the program of instruction "shall be given at such colleges or institutions of higher education upon a segregated basis." Appellant was thereupon admitted to the University of Oklahoma Graduate School. In apparent conformity with the amendment, his admission was made subject to "such rules and regulations as to segregation as the President of the University shall consider to afford to Mr. G. W. McLaurin substantially equal educational opportunities as are afforded to other persons seeking the same education in the Graduate College," a condition which does not appear to have been withdrawn. Thus he was required to sit apart at a designated desk in an anteroom adjoining the classroom; to sit at a designated desk on the mezzanine floor of the library, but not to use the desks in the regular reading room; and to sit at a designated table and to eat at a different time from the other students in the school cafeteria.

To remove these conditions, appellant filed a motion to modify the order and judgment of the District Court. That court held that such treatment did not violate the provisions of the Fourteenth Amendment and denied the motion. 87 F. Supp. 528. This appeal followed.

In the interval between the decision of the court below and the hearing in this Court, the treatment afforded appellant was altered. For some time, the section of the classroom in which appellant sat was surrounded by a rail on which there was a sign stating, "Reserved For Colored," but these have been removed. He is now assigned to a seat in the classroom in a row specified for colored students; he is assigned to a table in the library on the main floor; and he is permitted to eat at the same time in the cafeteria as other students, although here again he is assigned to a special table.

It is said that the separations imposed by the State in this case are in form merely nominal. McLaurin uses the same classroom, library and cafeteria as students of other races; there is no indication that the seats to which he is assigned in these rooms have any disadvantage of location. He may wait in line in the cafeteria and there stand and talk with his fellow students, but while he eats he must remain apart.

These restrictions were obviously imposed in order to comply, as nearly as could be, with the statutory requirements of Oklahoma. But they signify that the State, in administering the facilities it affords for professional and graduate study, sets McLaurin apart from the other students. The result is that appellant is handicapped in his pursuit of effective graduate instruction. Such restrictions impair and inhibit his ability to study, to engage in discussions and exchange views with other students, and, in general, to learn his profession.

Our society grows increasingly complex, and our need for trained leaders increases correspondingly. Appellant's case represents, perhaps, the epitome of that need, for he is attempting to obtain an advanced degree in education, to become, by definition, a leader and trainer of others. Those who will come under his guidance and influence must be directly affected by the education he receives. Their own education and development will necessarily suffer to the extent that his training is unequal to that of his classmates. State-imposed restrictions which produce such inequalities cannot be sustained.

It may be argued that appellant will be in no better position when these restrictions are removed, for he may still be set apart by his fellow students. This we think irrelevant. There is a vast difference—a Constitutional difference—between restrictions imposed by the state which prohibit the intellectual commingling of students, and the refusal of individuals to commingle where the state presents no such bar. *Shelley v. Kraemer,* 334 U.S. 1, 13-14 (1948). The removal of the state restrictions will not necessarily abate individual and group predilections, prejudices and choices. But at the very least, the state will not be depriving appellant of the opportunity to secure acceptance by his fellow students on his own merits.

We conclude that the conditions under which this appellant is required to receive his education deprive him of his personal and present right to the equal protection of the laws. See *Sweatt v. Painter. . . .* We hold that under these circumstances the Fourteenth Amendment precludes differences in treatment by the state based upon race. Appellant, having been admitted to a state-supported graduate school, must receive the same treatment at the hands of the state as students of other races. The judgment is

Reversed.

QUESTIONS

1. The "broader issues" in Sweatt and McLaurin.—The "broader issues" which the Court did not reach in the *Sweatt* and *Mc-Laurin* cases, as the Court notes, centered on the "contention that *Plessy v. Ferguson* should be reexamined in the light of contemporary knowledge respecting the purposes of the Fourteenth

Amendment and the effects of racial segregation." An elaborate brief in the *Sweatt* case had argued that separation was inherently unequal. Why did the Court refuse to decide that question? Did the Court avoid deciding a constitutional issue? In what sense are these two decisions "narrower" than a decision that segregation necessarily implies inequality? Do these opinions throw any light on the "broader issues"? Was the Court's refusal to decide the "broader issues" in these two cases subject to the criticism, suggested earlier, of Justice Harlan's refusal to decide the validity of "separate but equal" in the *Cumming* case?

2. Was there a "rational basis" for a separate Negro law school?— *Plessy v. Ferguson* rested on the conclusion that the Fourteenth Amendment permits classification that is "reasonable." Was the decision of the Texas legislature to establish a separate law school for Negroes an unreasonable one, within the meaning of *Plessy?* In the *Sweatt* and *McLaurin* opinions, does the Court give any consideration to the state's objectives in segregating professional and graduate students by race? Is it possible that some "reasonable" (not arbitrary) classifications are nonetheless unconstitutional?

3. The basis for the conclusions about inequality of educational opportunity.—The two opinions focus on the loss that would be caused to the complaining students if they were not granted the relief sought. Since all the Justices were graduates of law schools and men of considerable experience in the legal profession, they were well qualified in *Sweatt* to evaluate "those qualities . . . which make for greatness in a law school." What qualified them for the judgment made in the *McLaurin* case that the various forms of segregation imposed on the plaintiff would impair his education? Does the *McLaurin* decision rest on such a conclusion? Could you reach the same result without reference to the question of equality of educational opportunity? How would your alternative opinion read? Would such an opinion require the overruling of *Plessy v. Ferguson?*

J. GREENBERG, RACE RELATIONS AND AMERICAN LAW 35-39 (1959)*

[In 1934 the National Association for the Advancement of Colored People received a grant of $10,000 from the Garland Fund "for a campaign of legal action and public education against unequal apportionment of public funds for education and

discrimination in public transportation." 1934 NAACP ANNUAL
REPORT 22. The NAACP hired Nathan R. Margold to make a
"study of the legal aspects and background" of these and other
problems. *Ibid.*]

Before Margold was appointed the Garland Fund had had a
memorandum prepared which proposed an initial attack on the
civil rights issue. He quoted the following portion of the memorandum in his study.

> It is proposed that taxpayers' suits be brought to force
> *equal* if separate accommodations for Negroes as well as
> whites. The minimum cost of such taxpayers' suits, includ-
> ing attorney's fees, travelling expenses, printing of briefs and
> other legal documents, would average $2,000 per suit. It is
> suggested that seven (7) suits in the worst states, as follows,
> be instituted: South Carolina, Georgia, Mississippi, Louisi-
> ana, Florida, Alabama, Arkansas. . . .
>
> Such taxpayers' suits, it is believed, will (a) make the cost
> of a dual school system so prohibitive as to speed the abolish-
> ment of segregated schools; (b) serve as examples and give
> courage to Negroes to bring similar actions; (c) cases will
> likely be appealed by city authorities, thus causing higher
> court decisions to cover wider territory; (d) focus as nothing
> else will public attention north and south upon the vicious
> discrimination in the apportionment of public schools funds
> so far as Negroes are concerned, in certain of these states.

Margold himself, however, would have preferred an all-out attack on segregation itself—based upon *Yick Wo*[10]—which he
believed would gain not only the improvements suggested by the
memorandum, but probably more. His report urged:

> It would be a great mistake to fritter away our limited
> funds on sporadic attempts to force the making of equal
> divisions of school funds in the few instances where such
> attempts might be expected to succeed. At the most, we
> could do no more than eliminate a very minor part of the
> discrimination during the year our suits are commenced.
> We should not be establishing any new principles, nor bring-
> ing any sort of pressure to bear which can reasonably be ex-
> pected to retain the slightest force beyond that exerted by the
> specific judgment or order that we might obtain. And we

10 See the description of *Yick Wo v. Hopkins* in the opinion of the Court
in *Plessy v. Ferguson*, p. 134 *supra*. [*Eds*. note.]

should be leaving wholly untouched the very essence of the existing evils.

On the other hand if we boldly challenge the constitutional validity of segregation if and when accompanied irremediably by discrimination, we can strike directly at the most prolific sources of discrimination.

We can transform into an authoritative adjudication the principle of law, now only theoretically inferable from *Yick Wo v. Hopkins*, that segregation coupled with discrimination resulting from administrative action permitted but not required by state statute, is just as much a denial of equal protection of the laws as is segregation coupled with discrimination required by express statutory enactment. And the threat of using the adjudication as a means of destroying segregation itself, would always exert a very real and powerful force at least to compel enormous improvement in the Negro schools through voluntary official action.

In fact, the aspect of elementary and high school education segregation which Margold proposed to assail was not approached seriously by participants in the campaign he helped to map out until about 1950. Under Charles H. Houston's guidance the actual casework was launched in the 1930s with suits against graduate and professional schools. The reasoning behind this tack appears to have been that inequality in higher education could be proved with ease. There were virtually no public Negro graduate and professional schools in the South, and judges would readily understand the shortcomings of separate legal education, which some of the cases concerned. Since it would be financially impossible to furnish true equality—both tangible and intangible—desegregation would be the only practicable way to fulfill the constitutional obligation of equal protection. Small numbers of mature students were involved, undercutting opposing arguments based on violence and widespread social revolution. Finally, Negro leadership would be augmented whether there was desegregation or enriched separate schools.

While schools were the primary interest in this undertaking, cases involving restrictive covenants, public accommodations, interstate travel, recreation, the rights of criminal defendants, voting, and other activities were also brought or defended as part of a coordinated effort to create civil rights precedents in the courts. Most of these legal actions were conducted under the aegis of Houston or his successor, Thurgood Marshall, who took charge of the NAACP's legal work in 1938. The Garland Fund contributions ultimately amounted to only $20,700, so the association alone almost wholly supported the court program until the incorporation in 1939 of the NAACP Legal Defense and Educational Fund, which still aids and directs litigation in the civil rights field. At least fifty-five cases decided by the United States Supreme Court in the race relations area have been suits presented by lawyers connected with the NAACP or the Legal Defense Fund. . . . [These cases include the *Gaines, Sweatt, McLaurin* and *Brown* cases, all included in this chapter.—Eds.]

There were also numerous other suits supported by the association and the Legal Defense Fund in various lower courts, and other groups aided in similar suits. Moreover, a large number of *amicus curiae* briefs were filed by other sympathetic associations.[11] Of even greater significance were the *amicus* briefs and arguments of the United States Department of Justice in support of the Negro plaintiffs in a number of the cases cited above, including the *School Segregation Cases*. In addition, some significant civil rights decisions were achieved which had not been organizationally underwritten. . . .

It would be highly misleading to imply that all of the suits which were part of what might be called the NAACP program were planned with precision. How and when plaintiffs sought relief and the often unpredictable course of litigation were frequently as influential as any blueprint in determining the sequence of cases, the precise issues they posed, and their outcome. But we cannot elaborate on this here, for it would take perhaps a volume the size of this one to tell the whole story of the litigation program.

Actually, as it turned out, the greatest significance of the Margold and related studies preceding the lawsuits, which were to a large extent conducted pragmatically, was that their scholarly, thorough, and thoughtful approach underscored the need for a

---

11 The following organizations filed *amicus* briefs in discrimination cases before the Supreme Court from 1938 up to and including the *School cases:* American Association for the United Nations, American Civil Liberties Union, American Federation of Labor, American Federation of Teachers, American Indian Citizens League of California, American Jewish Committee, American Jewish Congress, American Unitarian Association, American Veterans Committee, Civil Liberties Department of Grand Lodge of Elks I.B.P.O.E.W., Civil Rights Defense Union of Northern California, Congress of Industrial Organizations, Executive Committee of General Council of Congregational Christian Churches of the United States, Human Rights Commission of Protestant Council of the City of New York, Japanese-American Citizens League, National Bar Association, National Lawyers Guild, Non-Sectarian Anti-Nazi League To Champion Human Rights, Workers Defense League.

In 1949 Rule 42 of Rev. R. U.S. Sup. Ct. sharply curtailed the number of *amicus* briefs by requiring consent of both sides or the Court's permission before they may be filed. [Footnote in original, renumbered.]

program which would employ the highest skills, build precedent, and treat each case in a context of jurisprudential development, not as an isolated private lawsuit. This was combined with a realistic view of how great a next step the courts could be expected to take, the lawyers being always mindful that courts may be persuaded to move ahead or to hesitate not only by the letter of the law but by awareness of social factors often unmentioned in opinions.

The NAACP supported the litigation in the cases decided under the name of *Brown v. Board of Education*. These cases were widely perceived as the culmination of the strategy that began in 1934. While it was understood that a number of alternatives were open to the Supreme Court in deciding these cases, the Court's own treatment of them, outlined below by the late Judge Loren Miller, raised the expectation that they would be landmark decisions. The article of Professors Robert Leflar and Wylie Davis, which is extracted following the passage from Judge Miller's book, was published in January, 1954, one month after final argument of the segregation cases and four months before the decision.

L. MILLER, THE PETITIONERS 344-46 (1967)*

There was more to this carefully stage-managed selection of cases for review than meets the naked eye. The Kansas case concerned grade-school children in a northern state with a permissive segregation statute; the Virginia case involved high-school students in a state having compulsory laws and located in the upper tier of southern states; South Carolina represented the Deep South, and Delaware the border states. The state cases all presented the issue of the application of the equal-protection-of-law clause of the Fourteenth Amendment, and the Court could have reached and decided that question in any one of them, but the wide geographical range gave the anticipated decision a national flavor and would blunt any claim that the South was being made a whipping boy. Moreover, the combination of cases included Kansas with its permissive statute, while other cases concerned the state constitutional provisions as well as statutes with mandatory segregation requirements. Grade-school students were involved in the Kansas case; high-school students in the Virginia

---

case, and all elementary and secondary students in the Delaware and South Carolina cases. The District of Columbia case drew due process of law into the cases as an issue, in distinction to the equal-protection-of-law clause, and also presented an opportunity for inquiry into the congressional power to impose racial segregation. The NAACP had touched all bases.

Initial arguments were made on December 9, 1952, two-and-a-half years after the *Sweatt* decision. But the Court reached no decision on the basis of the first briefs and arguments. On June 8, 1953, it issued an order setting the case for reargument that fall, submitting a series of questions to the litigants, and inviting the United States Attorney General to participate in the arguments.

The Court's first question asked what evidence there was that the Congress which submitted and the states which ratified the Fourteenth Amendment contemplated that the amendment would abolish school segregation. It then asked whether Congress had the power to abolish all school segregation, regardless of whether the framers or ratifying states believed that the amendment required its immediate abolition, and what was the reach of the Court's power under those circumstances. Its third inquiry was the extent of the Court's power to abolish school segregation in the event that the answers to the first two questions were inconclusive. The fourth question was that of whether a decree favoring the Negro plaintiffs would carry with it an order directing their immediate admission to state-supported schools or whether the Court could devise a gradualistic scheme for their enrollment—a very obvious, and very curious, inquiry as to whether the rights of Negro grade-school students to attend public schools were *personal and present* (as all constitutional rights are) or whether their exercise could be delayed until a more propitious time. The fifth question concerned the form the decree should take, if the Court decided on a gradualistic abolition of segregation.

Thurgood Marshall, counsel and director of the NAACP Legal Defense & Educational Fund, convoked sessions of lawyers, law school professors, and historians from all over the nation to help find answers to the Court's questions and to fashion briefs and arguments. The hard-pressed states hired John W. Davis, one-time Democratic candidate for the presidency of the United States and one of the nation's leading constitutional lawyers, to head an imposing array of counsel.

Reargument began on December 8, 1953 and continued for three days. Then the Court took all of the cases under submission for later decision.

LEFLAR & DAVIS, SEGREGATION IN THE PUBLIC SCHOOLS—1953
67 Harvard Law Review 377, 387-92 (1954)*

Without guessing what position the Court will ultimately take in deciding the pending cases [*Brown v. Board of Education* and its companion cases], it is possible to list most of the positions which it *might* take, and perhaps all of them. Some of those suggested are highly improbable and deserve inclusion only because they come within the historical framework of the race problem in America or because they represent points of view that may influence the Court, even negatively. It is reasonable to expect that all tenable approaches are being considered by the Court, at least in its analysis of the issues. The actual decision could combine two or more of the possibilities. Eleven are listed:—

1. If procedurally possible, the Court might avoid passing on the segregation issue at all. This would depend on the availability of less delicate grounds upon which each of the cases could be decided,[12] under the rule that the Court will not anticipate a question of constitutional law in advance of the necessity of deciding it.

---

12 The District of Columbia case might be disposed of through statutory interpretation, without reaching the Fifth Amendment, since the maintenance of school segregation in the District depends upon authority putatively conferred by congressional acts which arguably do not confer it. Bolling v. Sharpe, No. 11,018, D.C. Cir., *cert. granted,* 344 U.S. 873 (1952). See First Brief for United States as *Amicus Curiae,* pp. 15-17. In the Virginia and Delaware cases it might be found that the plaintiffs are entitled to the same relief under the "separate but equal" doctrine as they would be if segregation were held unconstitutional. Davis v. County School Board of Prince Edward County, 103 F. Supp. 337 (E.D. Va.), *probable jurisdiction noted,* 344 U.S. 1 (1952); Gebhart v. Belton, 91 A.2d 137 (Del.), *cert. granted,* 344 U.S. 891 (1952) (on reargument, Jackson and Frankfurter, JJ., indicated that the Court could not order permanent desegregation inasmuch as plaintiffs, admitted by [the] Delaware court to white schools temporarily, had failed to file cross-petition for Supreme Court review. See St. Louis Post-Dispatch, Dec. 11, 1953, p. 1E, col. 3). In the Kansas case, segregation was the only issue left inasmuch as equality of facilities was proved. Brown v. Board of Educ. of Topeka, 98 F. Supp. 797 (D. Kan. 1951), *probable jurisdiction noted,* 72 Sup. Ct. 1070 (1952). Subsequently, however, in September 1953, the Topeka School Board voted to admit Negroes on an unsegregated basis, so that this case may possibly be deemed moot. New York Times, Sept. 5, 1953, p. 13, col. 5. *Cf.* Gray v. Board of Trustees of U. of Tenn., 97 F. Supp. 463, 100 F. Supp. 113 (E.D. Tenn. 1951), *dismissed as moot,* 342 U.S. 517 (1952); Bond v. Tij Fung, 148 Miss. 462, 114 So. 332 (1927), *rev'd per curiam with direction to dismiss as moot,* 279 U.S. 818 (1928). But in the South Carolina case it appears that equality of facilities was conceded on the second trial, so that segregation as such is the only issue left in that case also. Briggs v. Elliott, 98 F. Supp. 529 (E.D.S.C. 1951), *vacated and remanded with directions,* 342 U.S. 350, *reaff'd on rehearing,* 103 F. Supp. 920 (E.D.S.C.), *probable jurisdiction noted,* 72 Sup. Ct. 1078 (1952). [Footnote in original, renumbered.]

2. The "separate but equal" doctrine is still the law, and the Court will accept lower court fact-findings of "substantial equality" such as were characteristic of the older state cases, which really meant only nominal equality. Some of the lower federal courts, however, and a few state tribunals too, following the lead of *Gaines,* . . . *Sweatt,* and *McLaurin,* have already held that under the "separate but equal" concept real equality is now required.

3. The "separate but equal" doctrine is still the law, and when the separate facilities are unequal the Court will allow additional time for bringing them to a state of substantial equality (which means real equality), under the direction of the lower courts.[13]

4. The "separate but equal" doctrine is still the law, but when separate facilities are unequal the Court will require immediate admission of Negroes to the white schools pending achievement of actual equality in the Negro facilities.[14]

5. Recognizing that the constitutionality of a particular state activity involving sociological relationships like segregated public schools may change with the times, and that the once valid "separate but equal" doctrine is diminishing in validity, the Court may yet conclude that it is not ready to condemn the doctrine as presently invalid but will undertake to wait a while longer before doing so.[15] Although the Court would not of course state such a position in so many words, it might practically do the same thing by promulgating a compromise dressed up in nicely chosen legalisms.

6. The "separate but equal" doctrine is still the law, but in special situations segregation is inconsistent with equality. The practice might be allowable only in some but not all phases of the educational process. Thus it might be held that segregation in the major scholastic work of the classroom produces unconstitutional inequality, whereas it remains permissible in extracurricular activities not materially affecting academic advancement. The opposite conclusion might also stem from the idea that psychological harm to young minds would accrue more from discrimination in extracurricular programs than from classroom segregation. Or it might be held that the validity of segregation

---

13 Or the Supreme Court might retain direct supervisory control itself, possibly with the aid of a master, as suggested by the Court's question number 5. . . . [Footnote in original, renumbered.]

14 This was the relief ordered by the state court in the Delaware case. [Footnote in original, renumbered.]

15 "Presumably the Court looks forward to years of peeling layers off the onion and at last arriving at the place where nothing remains." Roche, *Education, Segregation and the Supreme Court—A Political Analysis,* 99 U. OF PA. L. REV. 949, 950 (1951). [Footnote in original, renumbered.]

depends on the field or type of education involved, full association with one's fellows being of great importance in some fields and less important in other.

7. Whether segregation in a given case amounts to unconstitutional inequality is a question of fact, to be decided like other questions of fact in the trial court. This would permit different results from case to case, the variances possibly being influenced by whatever local social or emotional factors operate upon fact finders, whether judges or jurors, to produce divergent findings from substantially similar evidence.

8. The "separate but equal" doctrine is no longer valid and the Equal Protection Clause forbids public school segregation, but the Court will not itself undertake elaborate implementation; rather it will limit itself to minimum personal relief to the parties before it, leaving to Congress the duty of enacting general remedial legislation which will prescribe detailed rules for the future. The Court habitually regards some questions as primarily "political" in nature, by reason of their complex social and economic as well as emotional ramifications, particularly if decision calls for new rules to govern the future conduct of large numbers of persons in a new area of regulation. The legislative branch is better qualified to handle such questions than is the judicial, and so the Court remits them to the Congress.

9. The "separate but equal" doctrine is no longer valid and the Equal Protection Clause forbids public school segregation, but a gradual correction of the unlawful situation extending over a period of time will be permitted, the Supreme Court giving general directions only as to the broad plan and the time within which a changeover is to be made, leaving the formulation of detailed orders and the supervision thereof to the lower courts.

10. Same as 9, above, except that with the aid of a master the Court itself would issue detailed orders, either retaining jurisdiction in the cases during the time fixed for compliance and presumably exercising its supervisory power through the appointed master, or returning the cases to the lower courts for continuing supervision of the compliance details.

11. The "separate but equal" doctrine is no longer valid and the Equal Protection Clause forbids public school segregation, which must end at once. In all cases before the Court, Negroes must be admitted to white schools, or the school systems in some other way racially integrated, forthwith, and state or local laws providing for separate schools are no longer to be enforced.

BROWN v. BOARD OF EDUCATION
Supreme Court of the United States
347 U.S. 483 (1954)

Mr. Chief Justice WARREN delivered the opinion of the Court.

These cases come to us from the States of Kansas, South Carolina, Virginia, and Delaware. They are premised on different facts and different local conditions, but a common legal question justifies their consideration together in this consolidated opinion.[16]

---

[16] In the Kansas case, *Brown* v. *Board of Education*, the plaintiffs are Negro children of elementary school age residing in Topeka. They brought this action in the United States District Court for the District of Kansas to enjoin enforcement of a Kansas statute which permits, but does not require, cities of more than 15,000 population to maintain separate school facilities for Negro and white students. Kan. Gen. Stat. § 72-1724 (1949). Pursuant to that authority, the Topeka Board of Education elected to establish segregated elementary schools. Other public schools in the community, however, are operated on a nonsegregated basis. The three-judge District Court, convened under 28 U.S.C. §§ 2281 and 2284, found that segregation in public education has a detrimental effect upon Negro children, but denied relief on the ground that the Negro and white schools were substantially equal with respect to buildings, transportation, curricula, and educational qualifications of teachers. 98 F. Supp. 797. The case is here on direct appeal under 28 U.S.C. § 1253.

In the South Carolina case, *Briggs* v. *Elliott*, the plaintiffs are Negro children of both elementary and high school age residing in Clarendon County. They brought this action in the United States District Court for the Eastern District of South Carolina to enjoin enforcement of provisions in the state constitution and statutory code which require the segregation of Negroes and whites in public schools. S.C. Const., Art. XI, § 7; S.C. Code § 5377 (1942). The three-judge District Court, convened under 28 U.S.C. §§ 2281 and 2284, denied the requested relief. The court found that the Negro schools were inferior to the white schools and ordered the defendants to begin immediately to equalize the facilities. But the court sustained the validity of the contested provisions and denied the plaintiffs admission to the white schools during the equalization program. 98 F. Supp. 529. This Court vacated the District Court's judgment and remanded the case for the purpose of obtaining the court's views on a report filed by the defendants concerning the progress made in the equalization program. 342 U.S. 350. On remand, the District Court found that substantial equality had been achieved except for buildings and that the defendants were proceeding to rectify this inequality as well. 103 F. Supp. 920. The case is again here on direct appeal under 28 U.S.C. § 1253.

In the Virginia case, *Davis* v. *County School Board*, the plaintiffs are Negro children of high school age residing in Prince Edward County. They brought this action in the United States District Court for the Eastern District of Virginia to enjoin enforcement of provisions in the state constitution and statutory code which require the segregation of Negroes and whites in public schools. Va. Const., § 140; Va. Code § 22-221 (1950). The three-judge District Court, convened under 28 U.S.C. §§ 2281 and 2284, denied the requested relief. The court found the Negro school inferior in physical plant, curricula, and transportation, and ordered the defendants forthwith to provide substantially equal curricula and transportation and to "proceed with all reasonable diligence and dispatch to remove" the inequality in physical plant. But, as in the South Carolina case, the court sustained the validity of the contested provisions and denied the plaintiffs admission to the white schools during the

In each of the cases, minors of the Negro race, through their legal representatives, seek the aid of the courts in obtaining admission to the public schools of their community on a nonsegregated basis. In each instance, they had been denied admission to schools attended by white children under laws requiring or permitting segregation according to race. This segregation was alleged to deprive the plaintiffs of the equal protection of the laws under the Fourteenth Amendment. In each of the cases other than the Delaware case, a three-judge federal district court denied relief to the plaintiffs on the so-called "separate but equal" doctrine announced by this Court in *Plessy* v. *Ferguson*, 163 U.S. 537. Under that doctrine, equality of treatment is accorded when the races are provided substantially equal facilities, even though these facilities be separate. In the Delaware case, the Supreme Court of Delaware adhered to that doctrine, but ordered that the plaintiffs be admitted to the white schools because of their superiority to the Negro schools.

The plaintiffs contend that segregated public schools are not "equal" and cannot be made "equal," and that hence they are deprived of the equal protection of the laws. Because of the obvious importance of the question presented, the Court took jurisdiction. Argument was heard in the 1952 Term, and reargument was heard this Term on certain questions propounded by the Court.

Reargument was largely devoted to the circumstances surrounding the adoption of the Fourteenth Amendment in 1868. It covered exhaustively consideration of the Amendment in

---

equalization program. 103 F. Supp. 337. The case is here on direct appeal under 28 U.S.C. § 1253.

In the Delaware case, *Gebhart* v. *Belton*, the plaintiffs are Negro children of both elementary and high school age residing in New Castle County. They brought this action in the Delaware Court of Chancery to enjoin enforcement of provisions in the state constitution and statutory code which require the segregation of Negroes and whites in public schools. Del. Const., Art. X, § 2; Del. Rev. Code § 2631 (1935). The Chancellor gave judgment for the plaintiffs and ordered their immediate admission to schools previously attended only by white children, on the ground that the Negro schools were inferior with respect to teacher training, pupil-teacher ratio, extracurricular activities, physical plant, and time and distance involved in travel. 87 A.2d 862. The Chancellor also found that segregation itself results in an inferior education for Negro children . . . , but did not rest his decision on that ground. *Id.*, at 865. The Chancellor's decree was affirmed by the Supreme Court of Delaware, which intimated, however, that the defendants might be able to obtain a modification of the decree after equalization of the Negro and white schools had been accomplished. 91 A.2d 137, 152. The defendants, contending only that the Delaware courts had erred in ordering the immediate admission of the Negro plaintiffs to the white schools, applied to this Court for certiorari. The writ was granted, 344 U.S. 891. The plaintiffs, who were successful below, did not submit a cross-petition. [Footnote in original, renumbered.]

Congress, ratification by the states, then existing practices in racial segregation, and the views of proponents and opponents of the Amendment. This discussion and our own investigation convince us that, although these sources cast some light, it is not enough to resolve the problem with which we are faced. At best, they are inconclusive. The most avid proponents of the post-War Amendments undoubtedly intended them to remove all legal distinctions among "all persons born or naturalized in the United States." Their opponents, just as certainly, were antagonistic to both the letter and the spirit of the Amendments and wished them to have the most limited effect. What others in Congress and the state legislatures had in mind cannot be determined with any degree of certainty.

An additional reason for the inconclusive nature of the Amendment's history, with respect to segregated schools, is the status of public education at that time. In the South, the movement toward free common schools, supported by general taxation, had not yet taken hold. Education of white children was largely in the hands of private groups. Education of Negroes was almost nonexistent, and practically all of the race were illiterate. In fact, any education of Negroes was forbidden by law in some states. Today, in contrast, many Negroes have achieved outstanding success in the arts and sciences as well as in the business and professional world. It is true that public school education at the time of the Amendment had advanced further in the North, but the effect of the Amendment on Northern States was generally ignored in the congressional debates. Even in the North, the conditions of public education did not approximate those existing today. The curriculum was usually rudimentary; ungraded schools were common in rural areas; the school term was but three months a year in many states; and compulsory school attendance was virtually unknown. As a consequence, it is not surprising that there should be so little in the history of the Fourteenth Amendment relating to its intended effect on public education.

In the first cases in this Court construing the Fourteenth Amendment, decided shortly after its adoption, the Court interpreted it as proscribing all state-imposed discriminations against the Negro race. The doctrine of "separate but equal" did not make its appearance in this Court until 1896 in the case of *Plessy v. Ferguson, supra,* involving not education but transportation.[17] American courts have since labored with the doctrine

---

17 The doctrine apparently originated in *Roberts* v. *City of Boston,* 59 Mass. 198, 206 (1850), upholding school segregation against attack as being violative of a state constitutional guarantee of equality. Segregation in

for over half a century. In this Court, there have been six cases involving the "separate but equal" doctrine in the field of public education. In *Cumming v. County Board of Education*, 175 U.S. 528, and *Gong Lum v. Rice*, 275 U.S. 78, the validity of the doctrine itself was not challenged. In more recent cases, all on the graduate school level, inequality was found in that specific benefits enjoyed by white students were denied to Negro students of the same educational qualifications. *Missouri ex rel. Gaines v. Canada*, 305 U.S. 337; *Sipuel v. Oklahoma*, 332 U.S. 631; *Sweatt v. Painter*, 339 U.S. 629; *McLaurin v. Oklahoma State Regents*, 339 U.S. 637. In none of these cases was it necessary to re-examine the doctrine to grant relief to the Negro plaintiff. And in *Sweatt v. Painter, supra,* the Court expressly reserved decision on the question whether *Plessy v. Ferguson* should be held inapplicable to public education.

In the instant cases, that question is directly presented. Here, unlike *Sweatt v. Painter*, there are findings below that the Negro and white schools involved have been equalized, or are being equalized, with respect to buildings, curricula, qualifications and salaries of teachers, and other "tangible" factors.[18] Our decision, therefore, cannot turn on merely a comparison of these tangible factors in the Negro and white schools involved in each of the cases. We must look instead to the effect of segregation itself on public education.

In approaching this problem, we cannot turn the clock back to 1868 when the Amendment was adopted, or even to 1896 when *Plessy v. Ferguson* was written. We must consider public education in the light of its full development and its present place in American life throughout the Nation. Only in this way can it be determined if segregation in public schools deprives these plaintiffs of the equal protection of the laws.

Today, education is perhaps the most important function of state and local governments. Compulsory school attendance laws

---

Boston public schools was eliminated in 1855. Mass. Acts 1855, c. 256. But elsewhere in the North segregation in public education has persisted in some communities until recent years. It is apparent that such segregation has long been a nationwide problem, not merely one of sectional concern. [Footnote in original, renumbered.]

[18]In the Kansas case, the court below found substantial equality as to all such factors. 98 F. Supp. 797, 798. In the South Carolina case, the court below found that the defendants were proceeding "promptly and in good faith to comply with the court's decree." 103 F. Supp. 920, 921. In the Virginia case, the court below noted that the equalization program was already "afoot and progressing" (103 F. Supp. 337, 341); since then, we have been advised, in the Virginia Attorney General's brief on reargument, that the program has now been completed. In the Delaware case, the court below similarly noted that the state's equalization program was well under way. 91 A.2d 137, 149. [Footnote in original, renumbered.]

and the great expenditures for education both demonstrate our recognition of the importance of education to our democratic society. It is required in the performance of our most basic public responsibilities, even service in the armed forces. It is the very foundation of good citizenship. Today it is a principal instrument in awakening the child to cultural values, in preparing him for later professional training, and in helping him to adjust normally to his environment. In these days, it is doubtful that any child may reasonably be expected to succeed in life if he is denied the opportunity of an education. Such an opportunity, where the state has undertaken to provide it, is a right which must be made available to all on equal terms.

We come then to the question presented: Does segregation of children in public schools solely on the basis of race, even though the physical facilities and other "tangible" factors may be equal, deprive the children of the minority group of equal educational opportunities? We believe that it does.

In *Sweatt v. Painter, supra,* in finding that a segregated law school for Negroes could not provide them equal educational opportunities, this Court relied in large part on "those qualities which are incapable of objective measurement but which make for greatness in a law school." In *McLaurin v. Oklahoma State Regents, supra,* the Court, in requiring that a Negro admitted to a white graduate school be treated like all other students, again resorted to intangible considerations: ". . . his ability to study, to engage in discussions and exchange views with other students, and, in general, to learn his profession." Such considerations apply with added force to children in grade and high schools. To separate them from others of similar age and qualifications solely because of their race generates a feeling of inferiority as to their status in the community that may affect their hearts and minds in a way unlikely ever to be undone. The effect of this separation on their educational opportunities was well stated by a finding in the Kansas case by a court which nevertheless felt compelled to rule against the Negro plaintiffs:

> Segregation of white and colored children in public schools has a detrimental effect upon the colored children. The impact is greater when it has the sanction of the law; for the policy of separating the races is usually interpreted as denoting the inferiority of the negro group. A sense of inferiority affects the motivation of a child to learn. Segregation with the sanction of law, therefore, has a tendency to [retard] the educational and mental development of negro chil-

dren and to deprive them of some of the benefits they would receive in a racial[ly] integrated school system.[19]

Whatever may have been the extent of psychological knowledge at the time of *Plessy v. Ferguson*, this finding is amply supported by modern authority.[20] Any language in *Plessy v. Ferguson* contrary to this finding is rejected.

We conclude that in the field of public education the doctrine of "separate but equal" has no place. Separate educational facilities are inherently unequal. Therefore, we hold that the plaintiffs and others similarly situated for whom the actions have been brought are, by reason of the segregation complained of, deprived of the equal protection of the laws guaranteed by the Fourteenth Amendment. This disposition makes unnecessary any discussion whether such segregation also violates the Due Process Clause of the Fourteenth Amendment.

Because these are class actions,[21] because of the wide applicability of this decision, and because of the great variety of local conditions, the formulation of decrees in these cases presents problems of considerable complexity. On reargument, the consideration of appropriate relief was necessarily subordinated to the primary question—the constitutionality of segregation in public education. We have now announced that such segregation is a denial of the equal protection of the laws. In order that we may have the full assistance of the parties in formulating decrees, the cases will be restored to the docket, and the parties are requested

---

19 A similar finding was made in the Delaware case: "I conclude from the testimony that in our Delaware society, State-imposed segregation in education itself results in the Negro children, as a class, receiving educational opportunities which are substantially inferior to those available to white children otherwise similarly situated." 87 A.2d 862, 865. [Footnote in original, renumbered.]

20 K.B. Clark, Effect of Prejudice and Discrimination on Personality Development (Midcentury White House Conference on Children and Youth, 1950); Witmer and Kotinsky, Personality in the Making (1952), c. VI; Deutscher and Chein, The Psychological Effects of Enforced Segregation: A Survey of Social Science Opinion, 26 J. Psychol. 259 (1948); Chein, What are the Psychological Effects of Segregation Under Conditions of Equal Facilities?, 3 Int. J. Opinion and Attitude Res. 229 (1949); Brameld, Educational Costs, in Discrimination and National Welfare (MacIver, ed., 1949), 44-48; Frazier, The Negro in the United States (1949), 674-681. And see generally Myrdal, An American Dilemma (1944). [In the original, this was the Court's famous Footnote 11.—*Eds.* note.]

21 In a class action, the plaintiff sues on behalf of himself and other persons similarly situated. In each of the cases before the Court in 1954, the class consisted of all black school children in the district governed by the defendant school board. For our present purposes, it is important to note that the class did *not* include all black school children in the south. [*Eds.* note.]

to present further argument on Questions 4 and 5 previously propounded by the Court for the reargument this Term. The Attorney General of the United States is again invited to participate. The Attorneys General of the states requiring or permitting segregation in public education will also be permitted to appear as *amici curiae* upon request to do so by September 15, 1954, and submission of briefs by October 1, 1954.

It is so ordered.

BOLLING v. SHARPE
Supreme Court of the United States
347 U.S. 497 (1954)

Mr. Chief Justice WARREN delivered the opinion of the Court.

This case challenges the validity of segregation in the public schools of the District of Columbia. The petitioners, minors of the Negro race, allege that such segregation deprives them of due process of law under the Fifth Amendment. They were refused admission to a public school attended by white children solely because of their race. They sought the aid of the District Court for the District of Columbia in obtaining admission. That court dismissed their complaint. The Court granted a writ of certiorari before judgment in the Court of Appeals because of the importance of the constitutional question presented. . . .

We have this day held that the Equal Protection Clause of the Fourteenth Amendment prohibits the states from maintaining racially segregated public schools. The legal problem in the District of Columbia is somewhat different, however. The Fifth Amendment, which is applicable in the District of Columbia, does not contain an equal protection clause as does the Fourteenth Amendment which applies only to the states. But the concepts of equal protection and due process, both stemming from our American ideal of fairness, are not mutually exclusive. The "equal protection of the laws" is a more explicit safeguard of prohibited unfairness than "due process of law," and, therefore, we do not imply that the two are always interchangeable phrases. But, as this Court has recognized, discrimination may be so unjustifiable as to be violative of due process.

Classifications based solely upon race must be scrutinized with particular care, since they are contrary to our traditions and hence constitutionally suspect. As long ago as 1896, this Court declared the principle "that the Constitution of the United States, in its present form, forbids, so far as civil and political rights are concerned, discrimination by the General Government, or by the States, against any citizen because of his race." And in *Buchanan v. Warley*, 245 U.S. 60, the Court held that a statute which limited the right of a property owner to convey his property to a person of another race was, as an unreasonable discrimination, a denial of due process of law.

Although the Court has not assumed to define "liberty" with any great precision, that term is not confined to mere freedom from bodily restraint. Liberty under law extends to the full range of conduct which the individual is free to pursue, and it cannot be restricted except for a proper governmental objective. Segregation in public education is not reasonably related to any proper governmental objective, and thus it imposes on Negro children of the District of Columbia a burden that constitutes an arbitrary deprivation of their liberty in violation of the Due Process Clause.

In view of our decision that the Constitution prohibits the states from maintaining racially segregated public schools, it would be unthinkable that the same Constitution would impose a lesser duty on the Federal Government. We hold that racial segregation in the public schools of the District of Columbia is a denial of the due process of law guaranteed by the Fifth Amendment to the Constitution.

For the reasons set out in *Brown v. Board of Education,* this case will be restored to the docket for reargument on Questions 4 and 5 previously propounded by the Court. . . .

It is so ordered.

QUESTIONS

1. The use of precedent in Brown.—The Court's opinion in *Brown* cites three cases that we have studied on segregation in graduate-level higher education (*Gaines, Sweatt,* and *McLaurin*), and in varying degrees treats those decisions as authoritative precedent for its conclusion that public-school segregation is unconstitutional. The reasoning proceeds by analogy; some features of the earlier cases are identified as important for purposes of the present decision. From those features of the earlier cases, the Court derives principles on a higher level of abstraction, which principles are then applied to the cases before the Court. What are the doctrinal principles that the Court derives from the named decisions? What does *Gaines* mean with respect to the constitutionally-required content of equality in state-provided educational opportunity? How do *Sweatt* and *McLaurin* add to that content? Can you express a doctrinal formula that leads from those three decisions to the conclusion that "Separate educational facilities are inherently unequal"?

What was the authoritative principle of *Plessy v. Ferguson*, viewed from the standpoint of the Court that decided *Brown v. Board of Education*? Can the holding of a case be defined in the abstract, or is it necessary to know the purposes for which a later court inquires into the holding of an earlier case? Is it a fair characterization of the *Brown* opinion to say that it reads *Sweatt* and *McLaurin* for the most that can be found in them, and *Plessy* for the least? The eleven possible results listed by Professors Leflar and Davis in advance of the *Brown* decision illustrate that thoughtful lawyers know that normally both sides to a doctrinal dispute are able to draw analogies to precedents that support their positions. In fact, it has been said that reasoning by analogy is at the heart of most legal reasoning. See generally E. LEVI, AN INTRODUCTION TO LEGAL REASONING (rev. ed. 1962).

In what sense was *Plessy* an obstacle to the holding in *Brown*? In *Brown* the Court said that compulsory racial segregation in elementary and secondary schools "generates a feeling of inferiority," which in turn impairs the motivation of Negro children to learn. "Whatever may have been the extent of psychological knowledge at the time of *Plessy v. Ferguson*," the Court said, "this finding is amply supported by modern authority. Any language in *Plessy v. Ferguson* contrary to this finding is rejected." Was there any language in *Plessy* contrary to the Court's finding in *Brown*? In *Plessy* the majority said, p. 134 *supra*: "the underlying fallacy of the plaintiff's argument [is] . . . the assumption that the enforced separation of the two races stamps the colored race with a badge of inferiority. If this be so, it is not by reason of anything found in the act, but solely because the colored race chooses to put that construction on it." Did this statement in *Plessy* deny that segregation generates a feeling of inferiority? Or was the majority in *Plessy* saying that even if segregation created feelings of inferiority it was not unconstitutional for the state to require segregation? If the latter interpretation be accurate, what findings would be necessary to support a conclusion that imposition of a badge of inferiority was to be "found in the act"? Would such a conclusion necessarily rest on a finding that the enacting legislature was motivated by a desire to harm black people?

2. The social science issues in Brown.—To what extent does the Court's decision in *Brown* rest upon a factual judgment such as that which the Court quotes from the lower court's opinion in the Kansas case? Footnote 11 (here renumbered as footnote 20) to the Court's opinion was cited by southern critics of the decision as evidence that the Court had attempted to write into the Constitution its own sociological preferences. And others, sympathetic to the outcome of the case, were unhappy over these references in the opinion. One well known criticism is that of Professor Edmond Cahn:

> . . . I would not have the constitutional rights of Negroes —or of other Americans—rest on any such flimsy foundation as some of the scientific demonstrations in these records. . . . [S]ince the behavioral sciences are so very young, imprecise, and changeful, their findings have an uncertain expectancy of life. Today's sanguine asseveration may be cancelled by tomorrow's new revelation—or new technical fad. It is one thing to use the current scientific findings, however ephemeral they may be, in order to ascertain whether the legislature has acted reasonably in adopting some scheme of social or economic regulation; deference here is not so much to the findings as to the legislature. It would be quite another thing to have our fundamental rights rise, fall, or change along with the latest fashions of psychological literature. Cahn, *Jurisprudence*, 30 N.Y.U.L. REV. 150, 157-58, 167 (1955).

Would there be any way to decide *Brown v. Board of Education* without making some fundamental psychological findings or assumptions? Consider, for example, the position that racial classifications are invalid per se under the equal protection clause. Does not that position also rest on implicit factual conclusions about human beings? Was Professor Cahn concerned with legal standards flowing from such factual bases in general, or with the specific social psychological finding upon which the Court relied in *Brown*?

Suppose it should be concluded by respectable social scientists that the racial composition of schools or classrooms does not affect the achievement of black students. Should a statute requiring school segregation be upheld on the basis of these new findings? Soon after the *Brown* decision, some courts in the south sought to justify racial segregation on the ground that some social scientists had concluded that it would be educationally harmful to black children from disadvantaged environments to force them into competition with relatively advantaged white children. One notable example is Stell v. Savannah-Chatham County Board of Education, 220 F. Supp. 667 (S.D. Ga. 1963), in which Judge Scarlett allowed an intervention by minor white school children in a school desegregation suit. The intervenors presented the testimony of several social scientists from the Universities of Georgia, North Carolina, and Virginia and from New York University, along with that of a psychologist on the staff of the Children's Court in New York City. On the basis of this testimony, and concluding that the *Brown* decision rested on the findings of fact in that case, Judge Scarlett issued the following findings of fact, conclusions of law, and judgment:

FINDINGS

. . . .

Student Test Grouping

4. All pupils in three significant grades of the Savannah-Chatham County school system have been tested annually since 1954 for psychometric intelligence and correlative academic achievement through a battery of nationally accepted tests administered by local personnel, supervised and processed by the University of Georgia. This program was initiated prior to May, 1954 at the request of the Superintendent of Schools for Savannah-Chatham County as part of a comprehensive study of mental growth and school achievement for pupil placement and course selection and content recommendations. The result of this testing program has been considered by the Savannah-Chatham County Board of Education in arranging school curricula responsive to the abilities and learning characteristics of the two student groups.

5. The psychometric test results have conclusively demonstrated that the differences between white and Negro students in learning capabilities and school performance vary in increasing degree from the pre-school period through the completion of high school. The differences between white and Negro students were consistent on all types of tests and increased with chronological age at a predictable and constant rate. The Negro overlap of the median white scores dropped from approximately 15% in the lowest grades to 1-2% in the highest and indicated that the Negro group reached an educational plateau as much as four years before the white group. When a special control group was se-

lected for identity of age and intelligence quotient in the lower grades, the Negro students lagged by two to four years when the entire group reached the 12th grade.

6. The tests covered general intelligence, reading and arithmetic achievement, and mental maturity. On the last, the white average was 22 points above the Negro average. The achievement tests showed major ability pattern differences. On reading comprehension and arithmetic fundamentals there was virtually no overlap between the two groups.

Basis of Test Variations

7. These differences in test results in Savannah-Chatham County are not the result of the educational system or of the social or economic differences in status or in environment of the students. These test results agree on a point for point basis with substantially identical results obtained from similar tests made in other areas of this country and abroad and in both segregated and integrated situations. Additionally, quantitative and qualitative distinctions in Savannah-Chatham County and other test results have shown the same variation in learning rates between the two ethnic groups even after the socio-economic factors of the test students had been equated.

8. All the evidence before the Court was to the effect that the differences in test results between the white and Negro students is attributable in large part to hereditary factors, predictably resulting from a difference in the physiological and psychological characteristics of the two races. The evidence establishes and the Court so finds that of the twenty-point difference in maturity test results between Negro and white students in Savannah-Chatham County a negligible portion can be attributed to environmental factors. Furthermore no evidence whatsoever was offered to this Court to show that racial integration of the schools could reduce these differences. Substantially all the difference between these two groups of children is inherent in the individuals and must be dealt with by the defendants as an unchangeable factor in programming the schools for the best educational results.

Group Integration

9. The students in Savannah-Chatham County schools are 60% white, 40% Negro. A school class mixed on this basis would

have a median progress rate 12 points below that of the former white class, and 8 points above the progress rate of the comparable former Negro class. Two thirds of the Negro students would fail in this situation, particularly in the upper grades. This would place in the same schoolroom Negro students two to four years older in chronological age than the white students. White students in such a class lose any challenge to further academic accomplishment.

10. Failure to attain the existing white standards would create serious psychological problems of frustration on the part of the Negro child, which would require compensation by attention-creating antisocial behavior. In other cities this effect has created serious discipline problems for the teachers and school administrators with consequent loss of schooltime. In New York 37% of Negro truants questioned in a study stated that they had run away from home because of failure to keep up in school.

11. The congregation of two substantial and identifiable student groups in a single classroom, under circumstances of distinct group identification and varying abilities, would lead to conflict impairing the educational process. It is essential for an individual to identify himself with a reference group for healthy personality development. Physical and psychological differences are the common basis of group identification, indeed they compel such self-identification. To increase this divisive tendency, it has been established without contradiction, that selective association is a universal human trait; that physically observable racial differences form the basis for preferential association and that patterns of racial preference are formed and firmly established at a preschool age.

12. The effects of intergroup association are reasonably predictable on the basis of that branch of psychology known as social dynamics. In the case of two identifiable groups in the same classroom, intergroup tensions and conflicts result. These become substantial when the groups have a high identification index in a situation where the difference between them is as great as that existing between white and Negro children in the Savannah-Chatham County schools.

13. In each city referred to in the evidence where large scale integration had taken place or had existed continuously, the predicted level or even a greater degree of conflict existed and substantially impaired the efficacy of the entire educational system.

14. Total group integration as requested by plaintiffs would seriously injure both white and Negro students in the Savannah-Chatham County schools and adversely affect the educational standards and accomplishments of the public school system.

Selective Integration

15. Throughout the trial, counsel for plaintiffs emphasized the conceded ability of certain superior Negro children to meet the progress norms of the white classes and implied that at least selective transfers of such student to white schools would not cause injury similar to the effects of group integration. The Court finds that such selective integration would cause even greater psychological harm to the individual Negro children involved and to the balance of their group.

16. Negro children so transferred would not only lose their right of achievement in their own group but would move to a class where they would be inescapably conscious of total social rejection by the dominant group. Such children must try to identify themselves with the white children while unable to free themselves from continuing identification with other Negro children. Additionally, the children involved, while able to maintain the rate of the white class at first, would, according to all of the test results, thereafter tend to fall further back in each succeeding term.

17. The effects on the remaining Negro children would be even more injurious. The loss of the better group members would greatly increase any existing sense of inferiority. The competitive drive to educational accomplishment for those not transferred would be taken away. The Court finds that selective integration would cause substantial and irremovable psychological injury both to the individual transferee and to other Negro children.

Segregation Injury

18. Plaintiffs' assumption of injury to Negro students by the continuance of segregated schools is not supported by any evidence in this case. Whatever psychological injury may be sustained by a Negro child out of his sense of rejection by white children is increased rather than abated by forced intermixture, and this increase is in direct proportion to the number and extent of his contacts with white children.

19. Each study presented to the Court, confirmed by the opinions of the witnesses showed that the damaging assumptions of inferiority increase whenever the child is brought into forced association with white children. The principal author of the studies relied on by the Supreme Court in the Brown case came to the conclusion that compulsory intermixture rather than racial separation in school was the principal source of the damaging loss of race identification.

20. The adverse effects of compulsory congregation are particularly harmful in the early formative school years. Intervenors' witnesses noted that the adverse effects of educational integration at higher levels lessens to some degree. The findings herein are limited to children of primary and secondary school ages.

CONCLUSIONS

1. The white and Negro school children have equivalent rights before this court, and are equally entitled to be considered in determining the scope and content of constitutional rights.

2. A reasonable classification within the meaning of the equal protection clause of the Constitution would be one which secures the maximum result in the educational process for all students and the minimum injury to any.

3. The classification of children in the Savannah-Chatham County schools by division on the basis of coherent groups having distinguishable educability capabilities is such a reasonable classification.

JUDGMENT

1. The injunction prayed for by the plaintiffs in this case is denied and the complaint is dismissed. . . .[22]

---

[22] Judge Scarlett's decision was reversed by the Court of Appeals for the Fifth Circuit in an opinion that dealt quite summarily with the effort to turn the social-science language in *Brown* to a different conclusion. The Supreme Court's determination that segregated education was inherently unequal was said to be binding on lower federal courts. The court also rejected the argument that school children were being assigned on the basis of ability groupings, which happened to coincide with racial differences. Stell v. Savannah-Chatham County Board of Education, 333 F.2d 55 (5th Cir.), *cert. denied sub nom.* Roberts v. Stell, 379 U.S. 933 (1964). [*Eds.* note.]

3. The measure of educational opportunity.—Should equality of educational opportunity be measured by the resources the state devotes to the education of white and black students? By the achievement of children in the two racial groups as measured by their scores on standardized tests? In the *Brown* opinion, the Court speaks mostly of the damage that segregation can do to the outcome of a Negro child's education, but the Court's solution was simply to order desegregation, as a means of equalizing the educational resources provided to white and black children. The assumption seemed to be that enforcing equality of educational inputs would lead to a corresponding equality of outputs (achievement). Social scientists agree that a student's achievement is associated with his socio-economic status. Does the *Brown* opinion, which treats desegregation as an instrument to produce an equal chance at achievement in school, now demand that school boards take steps to provide educational programs that will compensate for a student's disadvantaged environment? These issues, and other related questions, are explored in Chapter 4.

4. An "unreasonable" classification?—In the Court's analysis of school segregation in the *Brown* opinion, what became of the question of the reasonableness of the state's classification scheme? A variety of justifications for school segregation had been argued to the Court: avoidance of racially motivated violence in the schools; differences between the races in average levels of educational achievement; differences between the races in average health; even maintenance of a traditional "way of life," including the avoidance of social contacts that might produce interracial marriages. If you were writing the *Brown* opinion, would you omit (as the Court did) all reference to such considerations? If not, how would you respond to the argument that the separation of the races was not arbitrary or unreasonable, given the argued considerations? Would your response be aided by repeating the passage from the *Gaines* opinion that the Court quoted in *Sweatt v. Painter*, concerning the personal nature of the right to equal protection? Did the Court satisfy its obligation to explain this aspect of the *Brown* decision by its statement in *Bolling v. Sharpe* that public school segregation "is not reasonably related to any proper governmental objective"?

Did not the Court silently overrule *Plessy v. Ferguson* on this question of inquiry into the reasonableness of the classification? Recall that in *Plessy* the majority opinion stated that "the case reduces itself to the question whether the statute of Louisiana is a reasonable regulation. . . . In determining the question of reasonableness it [the state legislature] is at liberty to act with reference to the established usages, customs and traditions of the people, and with a view to the promotion of their comfort, and the preservation of the public peace and good order." P. 134 *supra*. The only reference in *Brown* to *Plessy* concerned the factual question whether segregation creates feelings of inferiority, and on that issue perhaps, as suggested in paragraph 1, p. 194 *supra*, *Plessy* should be read as having said nothing.

5. The holding of Brown.—All of the foregoing questions about *Brown* are variations on a question we now ask directly: What does *Brown v. Board of Education* hold? One way to give focus to the inquiry is to put a few cases, and to ask how they should be decided, under the rule of the *Brown* case. (Recall the discussion, p. 34 *supra*, of the precedent of *Somerset v. Stewart* as it bore on the decision in *The Slave, Grace*.) The purpose in putting these hypothetical cases is not to begin a thorough exploration of all their implications, but merely to suggest some of the possible (or arguable) implications of the *Brown* decision. Consider these four cases:

(a) A city ordinance compels segregated seating on buses chartered to operate in the city, and a black passenger is successfully prosecuted for sitting in a "white" section of the bus; he appeals.

(b) A state statute forbids the purchase of liquor by American Indians, and an Indian is successfully prosecuted for buying whiskey; he appeals. (Justice William O. Douglas, in his book, *We, the Judges: Studies in American and Indian Constitutional Law from Marshall to Mukherjea* (1956), says (p. 399): "Experience shows that liquor has a devastating effect on the North American Indian and Eskimo. . . . [W]hat at first blush may seem to be an invidious discrimination may on analysis be found to have plausible grounds justifying it.")[23]

---

23 A California statute enacted in 1872 and amended in 1873 made it a misdemeanor to sell liquor to an habitual drunkard and a felony to sell liquor to an Indian. The California Supreme Court upheld the statute as applied to a sale of liquor to an Indian in People v. Bray, 105 Cal. 344, 38 P. 731 (1894). The statute was repealed in 1953. Cal. Stat., 1953, ch. 146, p. 918, amending Penal Code § 397. A similar Idaho statute was sustained against equal protection attack in a 3-2 decision in State v. Rorvick, 76 Idaho 58, 277 P.2d 566 (1954); the statute was repealed in 1955. Idaho Stat., 1955, ch. 262, § 1, p. 630. In the Idaho case the majority referred to the historical background of laws prohibiting the sale of intoxicants to Indians; the dissenters viewed this historical background as "mythology and folklore." [*Eds.* **note.**]

(c) An integration-minded city council orders that apartments in a city-operated housing development be assigned on the basis of a "benign quota," according to the racial composition of the community at large. A black applicant, otherwise qualified for admission to an apartment, is refused housing because the Negro quota is filled; he sues to compel his admission, and loses; he appeals.[24]

(d) The board of education of a large city, determined to end de facto segregation of the city's schools, embarks on a program of bussing children to schools, on the basis of race, to assure that each school's racial composition reflects the ratio of the city's black and white populations. Two parents (one black and one white) sue to enjoin the bussing of their children. Each loses and he appeals. (This problem is considered in Chapter 4, *infra*.)

Another way to inquire into the principles of the *Brown* decision would be to ask whether the case stands for the proposition that, as the first Justice Harlan said, "Our Constitution is color-blind. . . ." But even so simple a phrase as "color-blind" may take on various meanings. The phrase might describe (a) a rule of absolute prohibition on racial classifications by a state, (b) a prohibition against intentionally harmful racial classifications, (c) a prohibition on racial classification if it can be shown that in fact one race is disadvantaged by the scheme, or (d) a presumptive invalidity of a racial classification, unless the state can make a showing that justifies its scheme. See Fiss, *Racial Imbalance in the Public Schools: The Constitutional Concepts*, 78 HARV. L. REV. 564, 591-93 (1965). Which of these did Justice Harlan have in mind when he used the phrase "color-blind" in his *Plessy* dissent? Is any of these meanings an adequate statement of the principle of *Brown*? Or does *Brown* stand for the more modest proposition that a state must provide equality of educational opportunity for black and white children in its public schools and that segregated schools are inherently unequal? See Fiss, *supra*.

Plessy v. Ferguson was silently overruled in 1956 in Gayle v. Browder, 352 U.S. 903, which held invalid an Alabama statute requiring segregated seating on buses. There was no reference to *Plessy*; the Court's per curiam opinion[25] consisted of a citation

---

[24] For a comprehensive discussion of the benign quota issue see Bittker, *The Case of the Checker-Board Ordinance: An Experiment in Race Relations*, 71 YALE L.J. 1387 (1962).

[25] "Per curiam" means "by the court." A per curiam opinion is not signed by an individual judge, but is at least formally the product of the whole court. *See* Brown, *Foreword: Process of Law, The Supreme Court, 1957 Term*, 72 HARV. L. REV. 77 (1958).

to *Brown*. In the decade following 1954, the Supreme Court has, by similarly unexplained per curiam decisions citing *Brown*, held invalid every form of state-compelled racial segregation to come before it: seating in courtrooms; participation in athletic contests; use of city golf courses and public beaches; seating in a city auditorium. Should the Supreme Court in 1954, anticipating these cases, have written an opinion broadly invalidating state-compelled segregation of any kind? See paragraph 7 *infra*. Would your answer be affected by the possibility that such a broad opinion might not receive the unanimous support of all of the Justices? The unanimity of the *Brown* decision, and the fact that there were no concurring opinions to dilute the strength of the opinion of the Court, seem to have been calculated. Justice Jackson had been seriously ill before the *Brown* case was decided (he died later in the year), but on the Monday when the opinion was read, he took his place on the bench for the first time since he had become ill, as if to emphasize the Court's unanimity.

6. The justifications for overruling precedent.—What are the considerations that justify a court in overruling a previous decisional rule? Should a court be influenced by its view as to the degree of unsoundness of the precedent? By the degree to which interests have been built up in reliance on the earlier rule? By the availability to the court of techniques for minimizing the damage done by surprise? In the *Brown* decision and in the succeeding decisions outlawing all state-compelled racial segregation, did the Supreme Court give proper weight to these considerations, or others you think relevant to the propriety of overruling? See Israel, *Gideon v. Wainwright: The "Art" of Overruling*, 1963 SUP. CT. REV. 211, 215-29.

Would it be appropriate for the Supreme Court to overrule an established decisional rule simply because changes in the society had left that rule outdated? Justice Douglas, speaking for the Court in the decision that invalidated the use of the poll tax as a condition on voting in state elections, Harper v. Virginia State Board of Elections, 383 U.S. 663, at 669-70 (1966), said this:

> Notions of what constitutes equal treatment for purposes of the Equal Protection Clause *do* change. This Court in 1896 held that laws providing for separate public facilities for white and Negro citizens did not deprive the latter of the equal protection and treatment that the Fourteenth Amendment commands. *Plessy v. Ferguson*, ... Seven of eight Justices then sitting subscribed to the Court's opin-

ion, thus joining in expressions of what constituted unequal and discriminatory treatment that sound strange to a
contemporary ear. When, in 1954—more than half a century
later—we repudiated the "separate-but-equal" doctrine of
Plessy as respects public education we stated: "In approaching this problem, we cannot turn the clock back to 1896
when *Plessy v. Ferguson* was written." *Brown v. Board of
Education,* . . . .

In dissent in the *Harper* case, Justice Black chastised the majority
for "consulting its own notions rather than following the original
meaning of the Constitution." He expressed his dismay at the
theory "that to save the country from the original Constitution
the Court must have constant power to renew it and keep it
abreast with this Court's more enlightening theories of what is
best for our society." In a footnote to this last statement, Justice
Black added a statement that recalls the language of Chief Justice
Taney in *Dred Scott* on the subject of fidelity to the purpose of
the framers:

In *Brown v. Board of Education* . . . the Court today purports to find precedent for using the Equal Protection Clause
to keep the Constitution up to date. I did not vote to hold
segregation in public schools unconstitutional on any such
theory. I thought when *Brown* was written, and I think now
that Mr. Justice Harlan was correct when he dissented from
Plessy v. Ferguson, . . . which held that it was not a discrimination prohibited by the Equal Protection Clause for state
law to segregate white and colored people in public facilities,
there railroad cars. I did not join the opinion of the Court
in *Brown* on any theory that segregation where practiced in
the public schools denied equal protection in 1954 but did
not similarly deny it in 1868 when the Fourteenth Amendment was adopted. In my judgment the holding in *Brown*
against racial discrimination was compelled by the purpose
of the Framers of the Thirteenth, Fourteenth and Fifteenth
Amendments completely to outlaw discrimination against
people because of their race or color. See the *Slaughter-
House Cases,* 16 Wall. 36, 71-72; . . . . [383 U.S. at 677-78.]

Which of these views found clearer expression in the *Brown*
opinion? Which is more appropriate for a court that is confronted with a constitutional issue?

7. The "neutrality" of the principles in Brown.[26]—In his 1959 Holmes Lecture at Harvard Law School, Professor Herbert Wechsler criticized the *Brown* opinion for its failure to state "grounds of adequate neutrality and generality, tested not only by the instant application but by others that the principles [implied]." While he expressed approval of the result in the cases, Professor Wechsler thought that the decision's stated grounds were inadequate.

WECHSLER, TOWARD NEUTRAL PRINCIPLES OF CONSTITUTIONAL LAW
73 Harvard Law Review 1, 14-17, 19, 31-34 (1959)

REPRINTED IN H. WECHSLER, PRINCIPLES, POLITICS,
AND FUNDAMENTAL LAW 3, 21-24, 27, 43-47 (1961)*

All I have said, you may reply, is something no one will deny, that principles are largely instrumental as they are employed in politics, instrumental in relation to results that a controlling sentiment demands at any given time. Politicians recognize this fact of life and are obliged to trim and shape their speech and votes accordingly, unless perchance they are prepared to step aside; and the example that John Quincy Adams set somehow is rarely followed.

That is, indeed, all I have said but I now add that whether you are tolerant, perhaps more tolerant than I, of the *ad hoc* in politics, with principle reduced to a manipulative tool, are you not also ready to agree that something else is called for from the courts? I put it to you that the main constituent of the judicial process is precisely that it must be genuinely principled, resting with respect to every step that is involved in reaching judgment on analysis and reasons quite transcending the immediate result that is achieved. To be sure, the courts decide, or should decide, only the case they have before them. But must they not decide on grounds of adequate neutrality and generality, tested not only by the instant application but by others that the principles imply? Is it not the very essence of judicial method to insist upon

---

26 A beginning law student may find the materials in this note to be very difficult. The materials are included at this point in order to introduce—not resolve—some fundamental questions about the judicial process, which questions will arise frequently in other law courses, and are treated more fully in the courses in constitutional law.

attending to such other cases, preferably those involving an opposing interest, in evaluating any principle avowed?

Here too I do not think that I am stating any novel or momentous insight. But now, as Holmes said long ago in speaking of
"the unrest which seems to wonder vaguely whether law and
order pay," we "need education in the obvious." We need it
more particularly now respecting constitutional interpretation,
since it has become a commonplace to grant what many for so
long denied: that courts in constitutional determinations face
issues that are inescapably "political"—political in the third
sense that I have used that word—in that they involve a choice
among competing values or desires, a choice reflected in the
legislative or executive action in question, which the court must
either condemn or condone.

I should be the last to argue otherwise or to protest the emphasis upon the point in Mr. Justice Jackson's book, throughout
the Marshall conference, and in the lectures by Judge Hand. I
have, indeed, insisted on the point myself. But what is crucial,
I submit, is not the nature of the question but the nature of the
answer that may validly be given by the courts. No legislature
or executive is obligated by the nature of its function to support
its choice of values by the type of reasoned explanation that I
have suggested is intrinsic to judicial action—however much we
may admire such a reasoned exposition when we find it in those
other realms.

Does not the special duty of the courts to judge by neutral
principles addressed to all the issues make it inapposite to contend, as Judge Hand does, that no court can review the legislative
choice—by any standard other than a fixed "historical meaning"
of constitutional provisions—without becoming "a third legislative chamber"? Is there not, in short, a vital difference between
legislative freedom to appraise the gains and losses in projected
measures and the kind of principled appraisal, in respect of values that can reasonably be asserted to have constitutional dimension, that alone is in the province of the courts? Does not the
difference yield a middle ground between a judicial House of
Lords and the abandonment of any limitation on the other
branches—a middle ground consisting of judicial action that embodies what are surely the main qualities of law, its generality
and its neutrality? This must, it seems to me, have been in Mr.
Justice Jackson's mind when in his chapter on the Supreme
Court "as a political institution" he wrote in words that I find
stirring, "Liberty is not the mere absence of restraint, it is not a
spontaneous product of majority rule, it is not achieved merely

by lifting underprivileged classes to power, nor is it the inevitable by-product of technological expansion. It is achieved only by a rule of law." Is it not also what Mr. Justice Frankfurter must mean in calling upon judges for "allegiance to nothing except the effort, amid tangled words and limited insights, to find the path through precedent, through policy, through history, to the best judgment that fallible creatures can reach in that most difficult of all tasks: the achievement of justice between man and man, between man and state, through reason called law"?

You will not understand my emphasis upon the role of reason and of principle in the judicial, as distinguished from the legislative or executive, appraisal of conflicting values to imply that I depreciate the duty of fidelity to the text of the Constitution, when its words may be decisive—though I would certainly remind you of the caution stated by Chief Justice Hughes: "Behind the words of the constitutional provisions are postulates which limit and control." Nor will you take me to deny that history has weight in the elucidation of the text, though it is surely subtle business to appraise it as a guide. Nor will you even think that I deem precedent without importance, for we surely must agree with Holmes that "imitation of the past, until we have a clear reason for change, no more needs justification than appetite." But after all, it was Chief Justice Taney who declared his willingness "that it be regarded hereafter as the law of this court, that its opinion upon the construction of the Constitution is always open to discussion when it is supposed to have been founded in error, and that its judicial authority should hereafter depend altogether on the force of the reasoning by which it is supported." Would any of us have it otherwise, given the nature of the problems that confront the courts?

At all events, is not the relative compulsion of the language of the Constitution, of history and precedent—where they do not combine to make an answer clear—itself a matter to be judged, so far as possible, by neutral principles—by standards that transcend the case at hand? . . .

Let me repeat what I have thus far tried to say. The courts have both the title and the duty when a case is properly before them to review the actions of the other branches in the light of constitutional provisions, even though the action involves value choices, as invariably action does. In doing so, however, they are bound to function otherwise than as a naked power organ; they participate as courts of law. This calls for facing how determinations of this kind can be asserted to have any legal quality. The answer, I suggest, inheres primarily in that they are—or are obliged to be—entirely principled. A principled decision, in the sense I have in mind, is one that rests on reasons with respect to all the issues in the case, reasons that in their generality and their neutrality transcend any immediate result that is involved. When no sufficient reasons of this kind can be assigned for overturning value choices of the other branches of the Government or of a state, those choices must, of course, survive. Otherwise, as Holmes said in his first opinion for the Court, "a constitution, instead of embodying only relatively fundamental rules of right, as generally understood by all English-speaking communities, would become the partisan of a particular set of ethical or economical opinions. . . ." . . .

The problem for me, I hardly need to say, is not that the Court departed from its earlier decisions holding or implying that the equality of public educational facilities demanded by the Constitution could be met by separate schools. I stand with the long tradition of the Court that previous decisions must be subject to reexamination when a case against their reasoning is made. Nor is the problem that the Court disturbed the settled patterns of a portion of the country; even that must be accepted as a lesser evil than nullification of the Constitution. Nor is it that history does not confirm that an agreed purpose of the fourteenth amendment was to forbid separate schools or that there is important evidence that many thought the contrary; the words are general and leave room for expanding content as time passes and conditions change. Nor is it that the Court may have miscalculated the extent to which its judgment would be honored or accepted; it is not a prophet of the strength of our national commitment to respect the judgments of the courts. Nor is it even that the Court did not remit the issue to the Congress, acting under the enforcement clause of the amendment. That was a possible solution, to be sure, but certainly Professor Freund is right that it would merely have evaded the claims made.

The problem inheres strictly in the reasoning of the opinion, an opinion which is often read with less fidelity by those who praise it than by those by whom it is condemned. The Court did not declare, as many wish it had, that the fourteenth amendment forbids all racial lines in legislation, though subsequent per curiam decisions may, as I have said, now go that far. Rather, as Judge Hand observed, the separate-but-equal formula was not overruled "in form" but was held to have "no place" in public education on the ground that segregated schools are "inherently unequal," with deleterious effects upon the colored children in implying their inferiority, effects which retard their educational and mental development. So, indeed, the district court had found as a fact in the Kansas case, a finding which the Supreme

Court embraced, citing some further "modern authority" in its support.

Does the validity of the decision turn then on the sufficiency of evidence or of judicial notice to sustain a finding that the separation harms the Negro children who may be involved? There were, indeed, some witnesses who expressed that opinion in the Kansas case, as there were also witnessess in the companion Virginia case, including Professor Garrett of Columbia, whose view was to the contrary. Much depended on the question that the witness had in mind, which rarely was explicit. Was he comparing the position of the Negro child in a segregated school with his position in an integrated school where he was happily accepted and regarded by the whites; or was he comparing his position under separation with that under integration where the whites were hostile to his presence and found ways to make their feelings known? And if the harm that segregation worked was relevant, what of the benefits that it entailed: sense of security, the absence of hostility? Were they irrelevant? Moreover, was the finding in Topeka applicable without more to Clarendon County, South Carolina, with 2,799 colored students and only 295 whites? Suppose that more Negroes in a community preferred separation than opposed it? Would that be relevant to whether they were hurt or aided by segregation as opposed to integration? Their fates would be governed by the change of system quite as fully as those of the students who complained.

I find it hard to think the judgment really turned upon the facts. Rather, it seems to me, it must have rested on the view that racial segregation is, in principle, a denial of equality to the minority against whom it is directed; that is, the group that is not dominant politically and, therefore, does not make the choice involved. For many who support the Court's decision this assuredly is the decisive ground. But this position also presents problems. Does it not involve an inquiry into the motive of the legislature, which is generally foreclosed to the courts? Is it alternatively defensible to make the measure of validity of legislation the way it is interpreted by those who are affected by it? In the context of a charge that segregation *with equal facilities* is a denial of equality, is there not a point in *Plessy* in the statement that if "enforced separation stamps the colored race with a badge of inferiority" it is solely because its members choose "to put that construction upon it"? Does enforced separation of the sexes discriminate against females merely because it may be the females who resent it and it is imposed by judgments predominantly male? Is a prohibition of miscegenation a discrimination against the colored member of the couple who would like to marry?

For me, assuming equal facilities, the question posed by state-enforced segregation is not one of discrimination at all. Its human and its constitutional dimensions lie entirely elsewhere, in the denial by the state of freedom to associate, a denial that impinges in the same way on any groups or races that may be involved. I think, and I hope not without foundation, that the Southern white also pays heavily for segregation, not only in the sense of guilt that he must carry but also in the benefits he is denied. In the days when I was joined with Charles H. Houston in a litigation in the Supreme Court, before the present building was constructed, he did not suffer more than I in knowing that we had to go to Union Station to lunch together during the recess. Does not the problem of miscegenation show most clearly that it is the freedom of association that at bottom is involved, the only case, I may add, where it is implicit in the situation that association is desired by the only individuals involved? I take no pride in knowing that in 1956 the Supreme Court dismissed an appeal in a case in which Virginia nullified a marriage on this ground, a case in which the statute had been squarely challenged by the defendant, and the Court, after remanding once, dismissed per curiam on procedural grounds that I make bold to say are wholly without basis in the law.[27]

But if the freedom of association is denied by segregation, integration forces an association upon those for whom it is unpleasant or repugnant. Is this not the heart of the issue involved, a conflict in human claims of high dimension, not unlike many others that involve the highest freedoms—conflicts that Professor Sutherland has recently described.[28] Given a situation where the state must practically choose between denying the association to those individuals who wish it or imposing it on those who would avoid it, is there a basis in neutral principles for holding that the Constitution demands that the claims for association should prevail? I should like to think there is, but I confess that I have not yet written the opinion. To write it is for me the challenge of the school-segregation cases.

The publication of this lecture was immediately greeted with a spate of replies in the law journals. Alternative opinions for *Brown* were suggested in two of these replies. Professor (later

---

27 *See* Ham Say Naim v. Naim, 197 Va. 80, 87 S.E.2d 749, *vacated*, 350 U.S. 891 (1955), *on remand*, 197 Va. 734, 90 S.E.2d 849, *appeal dismissed*, 350 U.S. 985 (1956). [Footnote in original, renumbered.]

28 *See* SUTHERLAND, THE LAW AND ONE MAN AMONG MANY 35-62 (1956). [Footnote in original, renumbered.]

Dean) Louis Pollak would have an opinion that rested on a presumptive invalidity of state racial classifications, following these two dicta of the Supreme Court in cases dealing with the restrictions imposed on citizens of Japanese ancestry during World War II:

> Distinctions between citizens solely because of their ancestry are by their very nature odious to a free people whose institutions are founded upon the doctrine of equality. Hirabayashi v. United States, 320 U.S. 81, 100 (1943).

> . . . [A]ll legal restrictions which curtail the civil rights of a single racial group are immediately suspect. That is not to say that all such restrictions are unconstitutional. It is to say that courts must subject them to the most rigid scrutiny. Pressing public necessity may sometimes justify the existence of such restrictions; racial antagonism never can. Korematsu v. United States, 323 U.S. 214, 216 (1944).

Since the states had not provided an adequate countervailing justification for racial segregation in the public schools, Professor Pollak would conclude that the segregation is unconstitutional. What becomes of the presumption of constitutionality under this analytical scheme? See Pollak, *Racial Discrimination and Judicial Integrity: A Reply to Professor Wechsler*, 108 U. PA. L. REV. 1 (1959). Professor Charles Black would approach the cases from the assumption, founded on his experience as a southerner, that segregation in the schools was only one part of an elaborate system by which the community in a variety of ways maintained Negroes in a subordinate position—a system which the post-Civil War amendments to the Constitution were designed to forbid. Black, *The Lawfulness of the Segregation Decisions*, 69 YALE L.J. 421 (1960).

Professor Wechsler was using the *Brown* opinion to illustrate his more general point about the desirability of a genuinely principled process of decision in constitutional cases, "resting with respect to every step that is involved in reaching judgment on analysis and reasons quite transcending the immediate result that is achieved." Professors Addison Mueller and Murray Schwartz addressed their reply to this more fundamental concern about the way constitutional cases are decided, and decisions explained.

MUELLER & SCHWARTZ, THE PRINCIPLE OF NEUTRAL PRINCIPLES
7 U.C.L.A. Law Review 571, 577-82 (1960)*

To begin with, where does an analysis of the terms "adequately general" and "adequately neutral" lead if we consider the standard meanings of those terms? Certainly, "generality" leads nowhere. A decision holding a statute which forbids all Negroes to drive automobiles unconstitutional because it discriminates against Negroes enunciates a reason which is general. The question is: Is it adequately general? The next question must be: Adequate for what purpose? The answer would seem to be: General enough to be neutral.

"Neutral," then, is the controlling term, and "neutral" is a no-nonsense sort of word; it means "not taking sides." How does our "it discriminates against Negroes" reason meet the test of neutrality? If it is tested by *future* applications by the Court in terms of whether or not it will permit the Court to take sides either for or against a Negro appellant, it is completely neutral and hence certainly adequately neutral. But if it is tested in terms of its *initial formulation*, it is not completely neutral since it rather clearly takes sides for Negroes and against the legislature which passed the statute.

The search, therefore, must be for a neutrality test that meets the challenge of such original formulation. Is complete neutrality in such a case possible? It would seem not, for *some* side-taking is essential in every case unless all choice is abdicated. This, then, is too extreme a meaning of "neutrality." Perhaps what we are after is a reason that will permit this initial and essential choice but will still be "neutral" in the sense that it will prevent judges from taking sides in the process of deciding which side to take. Such neutrality, again, would certainly be adequate. A reason of this kind in the case of our "no Negroes shall drive" statute would seem to be: A state may not deprive only some persons of the privilege to drive because such action denies equal protection of the laws. This treats all persons alike; it is neutral in this very meaningful sense.

But now what happens to the numerous state laws regulating the privilege to drive? Application of the above reason would make them all unconstitutional. Hence again we seem to have adopted too extreme a meaning of "neutrality," for we know that a state may deny the privilege to drive to less than all, so long as the denial is based on proper grounds. The constitutional question, then, turns on the propriety of these grounds, and obviously within this area again a court must have choice. But here again the choice must be neutral. And now we are at a point where neutrality as a strict limiting concept collapses because the areas of choice become too complex.

Professor Wechsler's use of "adequate" now comes into focus: adequate neutrality can only mean sufficient neutrality to curb a court's power without crippling it in areas where choice is essential. What reasons for any given decision, then, will be sufficiently neutral? Professor Wechsler's answer is: Reasons which are equally applicable to indistinguishable cases and hence leave no room for significant doubt as to their soundness. Since every case is distinguishable on *some* ground, this leaves the question: How distinguishable is distinguishable enough to take a case out from under the scope of the neutrality test (*i.e.*, eliminate it as a doubt-creator) in any given instance? This, of course, cannot be decided in the abstract; it must be decided on a case by case basis, with the Court both the formulator and the applier of the test.

Another way of talking about the principle is to approach it from the standpoint of what a judicial opinion must contain to qualify as a "principled" decision. At the very least, of course, it must contain some reason for the result. A court cannot merely say that a statute is unconstitutional without giving a reason. For such an opinion gives no proper clue as to the basis for decision and our legal system is built on such clues.

Next, the reason given must be related to the facts in the case which presents the constitutional problem. A statement that a statute prohibiting all Negroes from driving cars is unconstitutional because the Court was offended or irritated by the attorney arguing for its constitutionality fails to qualify, not because this is not a possible reason for the decision, but because this reason bears no observable relationship to any facts in the controversy presented for decision.

The reason given must not only be related to a fact in the controversy presented for decision, it must be related to the constitutional problem itself. Thus if a statute prohibiting all Negroes from driving cars is a Mississippi statute and a suit challenging the statute is brought by a Negro man who lives in Jackson, Mississippi, a statement that the statute is unconstitutional because the plaintiff lives in Jackson, Mississippi, fails to satisfy the standard. This is not because it is not directed to a fact of legal significance in the case (*e.g.*, for jurisdiction or venue purposes), but because the reason seems to have nothing to do with any principle involved in a constitutional consideration of the statute.

Finally, the reason given must not only be related to the constitutional problem involved, it must transcend the case at hand. This means that other "similar" cases must be covered by the same reason and thus, in effect, they must be pre-judged in the sense that we can predict with confidence that they will be similarly decided. This, of course, is the essence of our legal system. But this still leaves the question: How do we determine what cases are to be included in the "similar" category?

It is hard to think of a reason related to a question involved in a case which does not to at least *some* extent transcend the case in which it is given. What we are looking for, therefore, is a definition of the extent of the required extension. Professor Wechsler provides that definition; he states that the reason must transcend the case at hand far enough to cover, without significant conflict, other cases which the principle based upon this reason implies. Thus a statement that a statute which prohibits all Negroes from driving cars is unconstitutional because it denies equal protection to Negroes as a class might not qualify, not because it does not enunciate a reason which transcends the case at hand, but because it also disposes of possible statutes which would deny the privilege of driving to females as a class, or to residents over the age of sixty as a class, or to residents under the age of eighteen as a class, and this denial for at least the last of these classes not only has been, but will continue to be, permitted.

Each of those classes, of course, is different in some degree. Are they *sufficiently* different so that they can be put outside the implications of the deciding principle in the "Negroes shall not drive" case? This depends on whether or not the reasons for discrimination are the same. If the "Negroes shall not drive" statute is based on legislative findings of intellectual and emotional deficiency as a class, and if the basis for a "women shall not drive" statute or a "minors shall not drive" statute would be the same, it would seem that the "Negroes shall not drive" statute must be found constitutional if it would appear to the Court deciding the case that it would let any of the other "related" statutes stand. For such a conclusion should raise sufficient doubt in the Court's mind as to cause it to bow to the legislative decision being questioned—unless, of course, the Court could find some *other* reason to support a decision of unconstitutionality that would pass the neutrality test.

This, then, brings us to the conclusion that a decision is correct (*i.e.*, is a "principled" decision) only if it is based on reasons which can be applied to those cases which the deciding court must decide in the same way, and it must decide in the same way those cases which are so similar to the case involved that they cannot be sufficiently distinguished. This, again, of course, cannot be determined in the abstract; it must be determined on a case by case basis with the Court both the formulator and the applier of the test.

These ways of talking about the principle of "neutrality" may not exhaust the verbal possibilities. But perhaps they make a crucial question abundantly clear. That question is: To what standard is the Court to be held in its construction of the neutrality test in any given case, to say nothing of the correctness of its application of that test, once formulated? Is the Court required (1) to foresee all of the major doubt-creating situations later seen by its critics and to resolve all of those doubts, or (2) to resolve at least the doubts created by those situations presented in arguments of the case at all levels of adjudication, or (3) to resolve only those doubts created by "obviously" similar cases? Professor Wechsler's guiding instruction is to look to those other cases that the principles *imply*. Apparently, then, there is implicit an understanding that *any* principle necessarily and obviously suggests cases which all will agree come within its ambit and which then must be used to test the reasons for the initial principle. . . .

[The authors turn to a discussion of the post-*Brown* per curiam decisions invalidating state-compelled segregation in areas other than education.]

Professor Wechsler's argument on this point has two different aspects. The first is that the use of the per curiam makes it impossible to determine the principle in the case actually being decided. The second is that the use of the per curiam indicates that the original case cited as controlling in the per curiam must have been based upon an inadequate principle, for otherwise the Court would not have hesitated to spell out the relationship in a full opinion.

The attack on the per curiam does not lack for precedent, and one not privy to the Court's deliberations can only speculate as to whether these attacks are well-founded. But the Court does cite a "controlling" case in the per curiam order, so that there is at least reason to believe that the Court is of the opinion that there is a principle and that it is controlling. The argument seems to be that the first principle just *can't* be controlling, that there are too many distinguishing relevant factors. The only disagreement then would seem to be between the critics and the Court as to whether there are distinguishing relevant factors.

On this point, too, the "institutional" aspect of the Court, particularly in the *Segregation Cases*, cannot be ignored. If, as is quite possible, there was disagreement among the Court in the post-*Brown* cases as to the basis for the judgments, but agreement as to the judgments, the desirability of a united front on the result—without the dilution of opinion controversy—cannot be ignored.

On the second point, that the per curiam indicates that the principle of the first case was inadequate, surely the logic goes the other way, *i.e.*, that the Court is of the opinion that there is no distinguishing relevant factor.

This problem of the per curiam points up another, more basic aspect of the "generality and neutrality" controversy. To expect nine men with the rich and diverse backgrounds and experience of the members of the Court to agree completely in any controversial case on a single set of premises and values is to expect the impossible. Accordingly, there are at least these alternatives: (1) never to invalidate a statute because there is no single set of reasons which can be agreed upon—a consummation not to be wished if *Marbury* is to retain any validity; (2) to print all of the differing opinions—in direct contradiction of the hoped-for results of Professor Hart's "mature deliberation";[29] or (3) to negotiate, compromise and qualify so as to obtain agreement on a common exposition—which may or may not comport with true generality and neutrality.

LEFLAR & DAVIS, SEGREGATION IN THE PUBLIC SCHOOLS—1953
67 Harvard Law Review 377, 387, 392 (1954)

[This passage begins with a reference to questions 4 and 5 posed by the Supreme Court upon the reargument of *Brown v. Board of Education* during the 1953 Term, before the Court's initial decision in those cases. These two questions (sets of questions) were once again set down for reargument during the 1954 Term, and decided by the Court in 1955 in the second phase of *Brown v. Board of Education*, which follows this extract. The text of the two questions appears in footnote 31, *infra*.]

The Court's last two questions assume that segregation is unconstitutional and ask whether this conclusion would nevertheless permit a gradual rather than immediate changeover from existing segregated school systems, and if so whether the details of the adjustment should be formulated by the Court itself, perhaps with the aid of a master, or by the lower courts after the Supreme Court remands the cases to them with general directions. One major significance of these questions is of course the fact that the

---

29 *See* Hart, *Foreword: The Time Chart of the Justices, The Supreme Court, 1958 Term*, 73 HARV. L. REV. 84 (1959). [*Eds.* note.]

Court is seriously attentive to the possibilities explicit in them. A necessary implication is that the Court is regarding the cases before it as having somewhat the character of "class suits," in fact if not in form, affecting the rights not only of the parties but also of the many others similarly situated. And a corollary is that less emphasis may be put on the "present" (immediate) and "personal" nature of rights protected by the Fourteenth Amendment than has appeared in some other cases where the less-involved interests of fewer persons were at stake.[30] If the Court concludes that segregation in the schools is unconstitutional but that a gradual adjustment to the requirement of desegregation is permissible, the administrative details that may be devised under federal equity powers (or adapted to a state's judicial machinery), either by the Supreme Court or in the lower courts, are limited only by the ingenuity of the courts, exercised of course within the confines of whatever is determined to be the law. . . .

Regardless of what the Court's decision may be, it will almost surely seem to the layman more far-reaching than it really is, since the ensuing orders will be directly applicable only in the cases and to the parties actually before the Court. Unless criminal proceedings be initiated, even United States marshals will not move in to enforce the Court's rulings. Voluntary compliance may be anticipated in some, perhaps in many, districts. In other districts, new litigation will have to be brought if compliance with pronouncements that go at all beyond the limits of present practices is to be achieved. In some sections of the country political and social pressures will probably forestall lawsuits for years to come, just as these pressures have done in most districts of the South in years gone by despite a general realization that the legal rights of Negroes even under the "separate but equal" doctrine were being denied.

BROWN v. BOARD OF EDUCATION
Supreme Court of the United States
349 U.S. 294 (1955)

Mr. Chief Justice WARREN delivered the opinion of the Court.

These cases were decided on May 17, 1954. The opinions of that date, declaring the fundamental principle that racial discrimination in public education is unconstitutional, are incor-

---

30 *See* McLaurin v. Oklahoma State Regents, 339 U.S. 637, 642 (1950); Sweatt v. Painter, 339 U.S. 629, 635 (1950); Sipuel v. Board of Regents of U. of Okla., 332 U.S. 631, 633 (1948); Missouri *ex rel.* Gaines v. Canada, 305 U.S. 337, 351 (1938). [Footnote in original, renumbered.]

porated herein by reference. All provisions of federal, state, or local law requiring or permitting such discrimination must yield to this principle. There remains for consideration the manner in which relief is to be accorded.

Because these cases arose under different local conditions and their disposition will involve a variety of local problems, we requested further argument on the question of relief.[31] In view of the nationwide importance of the decision, we invited the Attorney General of the United States and the Attorneys General of all states requiring or permitting racial discrimination in public education to present their views on that question. The parties, the United States, and the States of Florida, North Carolina, Arkansas, Oklahoma, Maryland, and Texas filed briefs and participated in the oral argument.

These presentations were informative and helpful to the Court in its consideration of the complexities arising from the transition to a system of public education freed of racial discrimination. The presentations also demonstrated that substantial steps to eliminate racial discrimination in public schools have already been taken, not only in some of the communities in which these cases arose, but in some of the states appearing as *amici curiae*, and in other states as well. Substantial progress has been made in the District of Columbia and in the communities in Kansas and Delaware involved in this litigation. The defendants in the cases coming to us from South Carolina and Virginia are awaiting the decision of this Court concerning relief.

Full implementation of these constitutional principles may require solution of varied local school problems. School authorities

---

[31] Further argument was requested on the following questions, 347 U.S. 483, 495-496, n.13, previously propounded by the Court:

"4. Assuming it is decided that segregation in public schools violates the Fourteenth Amendment

"(a) would a decree necessarily follow providing that, within the limits set by normal geographic school districting, Negro children should forthwith be admitted to schools of their choice, or

"(b) may this Court, in the exercise of its equity powers, permit an effective gradual adjustment to be brought about from existing segregated systems to a system not based on color distinctions?

"5. On the assumption on which questions 4 (a) and (b) are based, and assuming further that this Court will exercise its equity powers to the end described in question 4 (b),

"(a) should this Court formulate detailed decrees in these cases;

"(b) if so, what specific issues should the decrees reach;

"(c) should this Court appoint a special master to hear evidence with a view to recommending specific terms for such decrees;

" (d) should this Court remand to the courts of first instance with directions to frame decrees in these cases, and if so what general directions should the decrees of this Court include and what procedures should the courts of first instance follow in arriving at the specific terms of more detailed decrees? [Footnote in original, renumbered.]

have the primary responsibility for elucidating, assessing, and solving these problems; courts will have to consider whether the action of school authorities constitutes good faith implementation of the governing constitutional principles. Because of their proximity to local conditions and the possible need for further hearings, the courts which originally heard these cases can best perform this judicial appraisal. Accordingly, we believe it appropriate to remand the cases to those courts.

In fashioning and effectuating the decrees, the courts will be guided by equitable principles. Traditionally, equity has been characterized by a practical flexibility in shaping its remedies and by a facility for adjusting and reconciling public and private needs. These cases call for the exercise of these traditional attributes of equity power. At stake is the personal interest of the plaintiffs in admission to public schools as soon as practicable on a nondiscriminatory basis. To effectuate this interest may call for elimination of a variety of obstacles in making the transition to school systems operated in accordance with the constitutional principles set forth in our May 17, 1954, decision. Courts of equity may properly take into account the public interest in the elimination of such obstacles in a systematic and effective manner. But it should go without saying that the vitality of these constitutional principles cannot be allowed to yield simply because of disagreement with them.

While giving weight to these public and private considerations, the courts will require that the defendants make a prompt and reasonable start toward full compliance with our May 17, 1954, ruling. Once such a start has been made, the courts may find that additional time is necessary to carry out the ruling in an effective manner. The burden rests upon the defendants to establish that such time is necessary in the public interest and is consistent with good faith compliance at the earliest practicable date. To that end, the courts may consider problems related to administration, arising from the physical condition of the school plant, the school transportation system, personnel, revision of school districts and attendance areas into compact units to achieve a system of determining admission to the public schools on a nonracial basis, and revision of local laws and regulations which may be necessary in solving the foregoing problems. They will also consider the adequacy of any plans the defendants may propose to meet these problems and to effectuate a transition to a racially nondiscriminatory school system. During this period of transition, the courts will retain jurisdiction of these cases.

The judgments below, except that in the Delaware case, are accordingly reversed and the cases are remanded to the District

Courts to take such proceedings and enter such orders and de-crees consistent with this opinion as are necessary and proper to admit to public schools on a racially nondiscriminatory basis with all deliberate speed the parties to these cases. The judgment in the Delaware case—ordering the immediate admission of the plaintiffs to schools previously attended only by white children—is affirmed on the basis of the principles stated in our May 17, 1954, opinion, but the case is remanded to the Supreme Court of Delaware for such further proceedings as that Court may deem necessary in light of this opinion.

It is so ordered.

QUESTIONS

1. The Court's answers to its own remedial questions.—Look again at questions 4 and 5, propounded by the Court for reargument in the 1954 Term. What were the answers that emerged from the 1955 *Brown* decision? Which of the projec-tions of Professors Leflar and Davis (numbers 8 through 11), p. 185 *supra,* was the closest to the Court's remedial choice? Do the Court's answers adequately inform the lower courts as to what they must now do? If you were the trial judge in, say, the South Carolina case, what order would you issue to the school board?

2. Gradualism v. immediate compliance: the timing of deseg-regation.—Must the school board in any of these cases do any-thing immediately? What is the content of the phrase "a prompt and reasonable start toward full compliance"?

a. "All deliberate speed."—The source of this phrase seems to have been Justice Frankfurter, who borrowed it from Justice Holmes, who may have developed it from the phrase "all con-venient speed" in English Equity practice. See A. LEWIS, POR-TRAIT OF A DECADE 27 (Bantam ed. 1965); Thaler, "*With All Deliberate Speed,*" 27 TENN. L. REV. 510 (1960). The phrase nibbles at the edge of paradox, and so is susceptible to more than one interpretation. What meaning do you think the phrase was intended to convey?

b. The analogy to "prospective overruling."—Occasionally an appellate court, in overruling a precedent, will limit the effect of its newly declared rule to transactions and cases arising in the future. There was an analogy to this practice of "prospective overruling" in the second *Brown* decision. In appraising the "all deliberate speed" decree in *Brown* it may be useful to consider three factors which a court, having decided to overrule a prior precedent, must take into account in deciding whether the overruling should be only prospective: whether it would be unfair to apply the "new" rule to the defendant; whether the plaintiff should be denied the benefit of the new rule; and whether the court would be exceeding a wise limitation on the scope of its lawmaking power. See generally Schaefer, *The Control of "Sunbursts": Techniques of Prospective Overruling*, 42 N.Y.U.L. Rev. 631 (1967); P. MISHKIN & C. MORRIS, ON LAW IN COURTS 272-317 (1965).

If the defendant can demonstrate that he engaged in conduct in reliance on the court's prior precedent, would it be unfair to him to declare a new rule reversing that precedent and permitting the plaintiff to prevail? Such reliance interests are the main reason for resorting to prospective overruling. Given the fact that courts are empowered to overrule precedent, are all persons sufficiently on notice that an existing rule may change after they have pursued a course of conduct in reliance on it? Would it be relevant, in considering such reliance interests, to inquire into the reasonableness of a defendant's reliance—*i.e.*, to consider whether he should have anticipated that a change in the law was forthcoming?

If courts always overruled only prospectively, what would be the effect on potential plaintiffs who might seek to change existing rules through litigation? Would your answer be different in cases involving "institutional" plaintiffs, because their primary goal is to have prior precedent reversed for the benefit of large numbers of individuals? Because such plaintiffs can anticipate future fact situations in which they will have the benefit of the new rule, even though the court does not apply the new rule in the specific litigation before it? Can the problem of the effect on potential plaintiffs be wisely solved by permitting the plaintiff who brought the suit to prevail, but not applying the decision retroactively with respect to anyone else?

When a court declares a new rule, but limits the rule's application to future transactions and litigants, is it behaving too much like a legislature? In such a case it is difficult to argue that the court is making law only for the purpose of settling a dispute. Is the resolution of a dispute before the court an essential condition on the judicial power to make law?

Under the "all deliberate speed" decree, children who were plaintiffs in the cases before the Court in *Brown* were not necessarily assured admission to schools without regard to their race. As we shall see in the next chapter, the pace of desegregation after *Brown* was tortuously slow, and in a sense the decree in *Brown* was prospective in nature. Were there any significant reliance interests which justified the prospective nature of the decree in *Brown?* School boards had borrowed money and constructed school buildings, hired and assigned teachers, and arranged transportation systems in reliance on the "separate but equal" formula. Was that reliance, if otherwise significant, justified after *Gaines?* After *Sweatt* and *McLaurin?* Were the interests of the plaintiffs sufficiently "institutional" in nature so as to justify failing to make the benefits of the new rule available to all of the children involved in the cases before the Court? (Recall that the cases were "class actions," in which the plaintiffs represented all Negro children in the defendant school districts.) Was the principle of "all deliberate speed" declared by the Court in a context too far removed from the resolution of a specific dispute before the Court?

c. **The importance of community attitudes toward desegregation.**—In the Virginia case, counsel for the school board asked the Court to allow the time that was reasonably necessary for the board to comply with the decision, "consistent with the preservation of the school system and local community attitudes." The second *Brown* opinion dismisses community "disagreement" as unimportant. Is that language wholly consistent with the "deliberate speed" formula?

d. **Gradual enforcement and the judicial function.**—Who will carry the burden of supervising the enforcement of desegregation in these cases? During the oral argument on the remedial issues, John W. Davis, representing some of the school boards, said: "Your Honors do not sit, and cannot sit, as a glorified Board of Education for the State of South Carolina or any other State. Neither can the District Court." A. BLAUSTEIN & C. FERGUSON, DESEGREGATION AND THE LAW 171-72 (1957). The brief for the South Carolina board opposed any issuance by the Supreme Court of "criteria for desegregation" as conditions on the approval of any gradual desegregation plan. Such a ruling, said the brief, would not be the exercise of judicial power, but rather a legislative or administrative act. Do you agree? Did the Supreme Court establish "criteria for desegregation" in the second *Brown* opinion? Would it have been more or less of a "judicial" solution to order complete desegregation by a specified date? Compare the immediate judicial abolition of slavery in England in *Somerset v. Stewart* with the gradualism of the 1833 Act abolishing slavery in the colonies.

e. The individual constitutional rights of the plaintiffs.—In *Cumming v. Richmond County Board of Education,* p. 152 *supra,* the Court had noted that the closing of the Negro high school was only temporary. For an individual Negro high school student, however, the closing might just as well have been permanent; he would soon be required to earn a living, and would have great difficulty in taking advantage of a reopening of his school some years in the future. In these desegregation cases, it is even clearer that any harm to the segregated black children will be of a permanent nature, since presumably they will not repeat grades already completed in their segregated schools. In other words, if the constitutional right being vindicated is, as the Court says it is, a "personal interest of the plaintiffs," can it also be an interest "in admission to public schools *as soon as practicable* on a nondiscriminatory basis"? Or is it a right to be admitted immediately to a desegregated school? The brief of counsel for the Negro children in four of the cases rested heavily on this personal-right argument, and called for an order requiring immediate desegregation. The brief identified three types of states:

(a) "Those which have not waited for further directions from the Court, but have undertaken desegregation in varied measure during the current school year." These included Delaware, Kansas, Missouri and West Virginia, plus the District of Columbia.)

(b) "Those which have decided to await a decision on the question of relief but have indicated an intention to obey the Court's directions." (These, said the brief, included Kentucky, Oklahoma and Tennessee.)

(c) "Those which have indicated an intention to circumvent the decision of this Court or interminably delay the enjoyment by Negro children of their constitutionally protected rights not to be segregated in public schools." (These included South Carolina, Mississippi, Virginia and Florida.)

The brief argued that a delay in enforcement of desegregation would serve no good purpose in any of the three classes of states.

f. The argument of the United States as amicus curiae.—The Solicitor General, appearing as "amicus curiae" (friend of the court), asked for a vindication of the plaintiffs' individual rights that would be "as prompt as feasible." Much of the Government's brief was devoted to a catalogue of the kinds of problems that state governments and local school boards would have to face in carrying out an order to desegregate. In conclusion, the Government argued that the Court should give the school boards a choice: either the immediate admission of the Negro children to desegregated schools, or, alternatively, the prompt submission of a plan of desegregation to the trial court, which plan should be approved only on the condition that it call for completion of the desegregation process by a date to be specified by the Supreme Court. The Court's opinion adopted the Government's position, with the exception that no deadlines were set.

g. "Political" limitations on a court's lawmaking power.—Would it have been proper for the Supreme Court to give weight, in deciding on the issue of gradualism in desegregation enforcement, to such broadly political questions as: the power of the judiciary to enforce its decisions; the widespread and deep disagreement with the first *Brown* decision that had been manifested in many southern states; the fact that some twelve million children were attending segregated schools in 1955; the need for ultimate acceptance of desegregation by masses of people in the south? Professor Alexander Bickel considers these questions, along with some of the questions previously raised, in the following passage. (As you read the materials in Chapter 3, think back to Professor Bickel's justifications for the Court's solution to the remedial problem in *Brown*. Do the subsequent events support or weaken Professor Bickel's position?)

A. BICKEL, THE LEAST DANGEROUS BRANCH: THE SUPREME COURT AT THE BAR OF POLITICS 247-54 (1962)*

In the vast majority of cases—barring those that are dismissed outright as not suitable for adjudication—the normal and expected judgment of the Court is a crisp and specific writing which tells one of the parties exactly what he must do, such as pay a judgment, deliver certain real estate, cease from doing something, or, indeed, go to jail. The equivalent in these cases would have been a decree ordering the named children, and perhaps, since these were class actions, all children in the five school districts affected who were similarly situated, to be admitted forthwith to the white schools of their choice. The question is, why should the Court not have issued such a decree? Indeed, one might have asked whether the Court could do other than issue such a decree?

If the Court, at the other extreme from merely composing for the anthologies, sat merely to render *ad hoc* judgments applicable solely to the precise circumstances of a controversy immediately before it, then also it would not be the powerful institution it is, and its function would need no elaborate justification. The matrix paradox of all paradoxes concerning the Court is, as I have noted, that the Court may only decide concrete cases and may not pronounce general principles at large; but it may decide a constitutional issue only on the basis of general principle. In the performance of this function—to use a fittingly lofty phrase of Chief Justice Hughes—the Court's "mental vision embraces distant scenes." Hence, while the cases immediately before the Court exemplified and concretized the issue of principle, they could not be treated as if they involved only the admission of three or four dozen children to a dozen schools. Rather, these five cases did necessarily bring into view the total situation in all the states having school districts which are organized on a segregated basis.

The admission of a few dozen children to a few dozen schools would have presented no very grave difficulties calling for a study of means of gradual adjustment. Seen in its totality, however, as involving some 5,000 school districts, nearly nine million white children and nearly three million colored, the situation exhibited great variety and complexity. To begin with, a vast number of statutes and regulations, incorporating centrally or marginally the rule of segregation, would require change in order to conform to the new principle. In most places, pupils are assigned to schools in accordance with the location of their homes. Where there were two schools, one white and one Negro, residential lines would now have to be drawn purely on a geographical basis, rather than, as previously, in accordance with both geography and race. But the two schools may not have been of equal size or otherwise of equal character. Thus elimination of the racial criterion may create a new and expensive problem before solving the old one. In general, running two segregated school systems is more expensive than running a single integrated one. But that is not to say that the process of integration might not require some immediate additional expenditures. And the cost of money is either money or time. Further complications: New assignments and other administrative arrangements for teachers, including Negro teachers, would have to be made. School transportation would have to be rearranged. No doubt, since Negro schools had seldom been fully equal to white ones, and since many Negro pupils came from economically and culturally depressed families, differences in educational background and aptitudes would be found between Negro and white pupils, and allowance might have to be made for these in the process of integration.

These and yet additional problems varied greatly from place to place, from cities to rural districts, and in relation, among other things, to the ratio of Negro to white pupils in a given district. No solution could be fabricated and made effective overnight, no matter what anyone might wish. Moreover, the Court itself bore some responsibility for the situation it now faced. The practice of segregation was no invention of the Court, to be sure. But segregation had prospered and come to full flower at least partly in reliance upon the Court's decision, in 1896, that it conformed to constitutional principle. No one hearing the late John W. Davis, who argued to the Court in behalf of South Carolina, emphasize how pervasive and how solidly founded the present order was could fail to be sensible of the difficulties to be encountered in uprooting it. "Sometime to every principle," Mr. Davis remarked, "comes a moment of repose when it has been so often announced, so confidently relied upon, so long continued, that it passes the limits of judicial discretion and disturbance." Mr. Davis was intimating that the existing order was no longer subject to judicial change, that no principle of its alteration could now be announced. This was to deny the essence of the Court's function, and on the basis of no more than an inadmissibly static view of society. But the suggestion that judicial alteration of so deep-rooted an order of things raises special problems to which the Court must have due regard—that could not be ignored.

It is unusual but not unheard of for the Court—for all courts, in the general run of business, constitutional and otherwise—to be faced with practical factors that make it impossible to achieve immediately a result called for by the Court's decision. Thus in applying the antitrust laws the Court may find—has in fact found —that a large corporation, the American Tobacco Company, for example, was a near-monopoly and violated the antitrust laws, and that it should be dissolved and split into its component parts. Or the Court may find, as it recently did, that ownership by the DuPont Corporation of a potentially controlling block of shares in the General Motors Corporation violates the antitrust laws, and that the relationship should be severed. But such things cannot be made to happen in a day. Here is the elemental demonstration of the truth that very often society can only strive to attain the rule of principle through a tangle of perverse and intractable existing facts, which are themselves man-made but which are not any the less real for that. Pupil-assignment rules were willfully scrambled by men pursuing racist ends rather than ordained of God; but that does not render them any easier to unscramble overnight, once the racist principle has been extracted. There is embedded in Anglo-American law, quite aside from the peculiar function of constitutional adjudication, the recognition that, on occasion, the law proposes but, for a time at least, the facts of life dispose. The mainstream of Anglo-American legal development has been the common law, administered by judges who evolved and reasoned from principle. But there soon flowed alongside the common law another stream, the equity jurisdiction, whose headwaters were in the discretionary royal prerogative. Equity was a more flexible process, more unprincipled, initially quite *ad hoc*. It often worked the accommodation that made the rigorous principles of the common law fit to live with. Our courts in general now combine both functions—common law and equity—and so does the process of judicial review.

The considerations I have recited are significant and would by themselves have led the Court, in the exercise of equity discretion, to allow southern communities some time in which to comply with the principle of integration; these considerations nevertheless leave out of account the most important factor. This is the unpalatable but undeniable fact that the principle of the integration of the races ran counter to the views and the strong emotions, not merely the customary practice, of a majority of the people to whose way of life it was to be chiefly applicable; that is to say, most southern whites. Despite the prefatory work that had been in progress, as I have indicated, for over a generation, despite many hopeful steps toward the integration of universities in the South, and, in any event, the absence of any concerted political offensive against such integration or against other judicial measures enforcing equal treatment of the races—despite all that, resistance could be expected. This does not mean that the principle of integration was wrong or not suitable for pronouncement by the Court in discharge of the constitutional functions, nor even that the Court should have had more pause before announcing it, fearing that it was not a fundamental presupposition "to which widespread acceptance may fairly be attributed." First, even if the task of the Court were, in Mr. Dooley's phrase, to follow the election returns, surely the relevant returns would be those from the nation as a whole, not from a white majority in a given region. Fragmented returns cannot count, any more than early ones. Secondly, as we have seen, the Court's principles are required to gain assent, not necessarily to have it. Yet the fact of foreseeable opposition, like the fact of confident reliance, "so long continued," that Mr. Davis stressed, could not be ignored; it constituted an additional problem.

The problem was not simply one of enforcement. The task of the Court is to seek and to foster assent, and compliance through assent. Of course, we normally enforce some of our law—the criminal law, for example—forthwith and without recourse. But the analogy from the *Segregation Cases* to criminal statutes and the like fails completely. The latter are generally based on almost universal acceptance and need to be enforced only against an infinitesimal minority, consisting of the irreducible number of the antisocial. When they are not so based, they are commonly ineffective. Witness the great prohibition experiment. Witness also anti-gambling statutes, most sex laws, and other laws policing morals. Indeed, we have built-in devices for ensuring the ineffectiveness of such laws—for example, the discretion of prosecutors, who are most often politically sensitive officers, and the grand and petit jury systems. When we say, as we often do, that government should not try to enforce morality by law, we mean that in our system it cannot enforce it, if it is merely an idiosyncratic morality or a falsely professed morality, not the generally accepted one. It follows that in achieving integration, the task of the law—and all the more, the task of judicial rather than legislative law—was not to punish law breakers but to diminish their number. For what was to be foreseen was the resistance, not of a fringe of misfits, but of a populace. In such circumstances, it may not be prudent to force immediate compliance.

This brings me to a third and very closely connected reason that the Court did not order sudden execution of the principle pronounced in the *Segregation Cases*. The foreseeable opposition was localized, indeed isolated; but, by the same token, it was entrenched in a cluster of states, where it formed a majority. Thus concentrated, it could wield power disproportionate to what its numbers would give it if distributed nationwide. Hence, just possibly, the cooperation of the political branches might be needed in fostering the necessary acceptance; and it could well be looked for, since the Solicitor General of the United States, responding to the Court's request for an expression of views as *amicus curiae*, had appeared and supported the cause of the Negro plaintiffs. Normally, to be sure, the Court relies on its own great and mystic prestige and on the skilled exertion of its educational faculty, and finds them quite sufficient even to overcome or otherwise direct the will of the political branches. But here exceptional circumstances were in prospect. Moreover, there might be, not only resistance to the full reach of the new principle, but even difficulty with the enforcement of specific decrees. In an enforcement crisis of any real proportions, the judiciary is wholly dependent upon the Executive. The Court commands no significant police power of its own. It is true that both in practice and in theory the Executive is obliged to come to the judiciary's support in any such crisis. Good order demands it, regardless of the merits. But there are degrees of enthusiasm in rendering executive support, and there are ways of emphasizing order above, rather than alongside of, the decision that is to be enforced. If, then, one of those rare occasions was to be foreseen when the cooperation of the political institutions might be needed both in fostering consent and quite possibly in administering enforcement, the Court was entitled to consider that those institutions are uncomfortable in the presence of hard and fast principles calling for universal and sudden execution. They respond naturally to demands for compromise, and, of course, they contain within themselves representatives of the opposition that was to be foreseen. They can most readily be expected to exert themselves when some leeway to expediency has been left open. Therefore, time and an opportunity for accommodation were required not only for the other reasons I have mentioned; they were needed also to form part of the invitation that the Court might be extending to the political institutions to join with it in what amounted to a major enterprise of social reform.

It was argued to the Court by the National Association for the Advancement of Colored People, which represented the Negro children, that the task of making the Court's principle accepted and effective would be facilitated by a sort of shock treatment, an order of immediate and sudden execution, rather than by allowing time for accommodation. The argument was that "gradualism, far from facilitating the process, may actually make it more difficult; that, in fact, the problems of transition will be a good deal less complicated than might be forecast. . . . Our submission is that this, like many wrongs, can be easiest and best undone, not by 'tapering off' but by forthright action." Conceivably this might have been so, but certainly it was not a broadly shared view. What the Court was more widely urged to do, especially by the Solicitor General, and what it did was in effect to require the local school boards to submit to the lower federal courts plans providing for a start toward integration—that is, to begin with, the admission of a few children here and there on some staged scheme. Any such plan would have to contain also the promise of eventual full compliance, meaning an eventually unified school system in which children would be assigned to schools without distinction of race, although other criteria, in-

cluding residential ones, might still be effective. The Court set
no deadlines. None was seriously urged, it being realized, as the
Solicitor General pointed out, that conditions vary and "that
maximum periods tend to become minimum periods." The test
for each plan would be whether it was moving in good faith
toward integration "with all deliberate speed." . . .

A phrase, then, that resembles poetry and resembles equity
techniques of discretionary accommodation between principle
and expediency, but that fits precisely one thing only, namely,
the unique function of judicial review in the American system.
The formula does not signify that the process of judicial review
will involve itself in finding expedient compromises for a difficult situation. It means only that the Court, having announced
its principle, and having required a measure of initial compliance, resumed its posture of passive receptiveness to the complaints of litigants. The political institutions might work out
their compromises. Some of these might not return to be litigated
at all. Some would. The Court placed itself in position to engage
in a continual colloquy with the political institutions, leaving it
to them to tell the Court what expedients of accommodation
and compromise they deemed necessary.

3. The function of the amicus curiae brief.—Reference has been
made to the brief of the United States on the question of the
remedy in *Brown v. Board of Education.* Frequently someone
who is not a party to an action will ask the court's permission to
file a brief as a friend of the court, or amicus curiae. Such a brief
is normally filed with an appellate court; occasionally, the court
will invite the submission of such briefs, as it did in the *Brown*
case. (In addition to the United States, six states filed amicus
briefs.) At one time, the theory of an amicus brief was that the
court was obtaining disinterested advice from one who had no
particular interest in the litigation, and that function is still
sometimes performed by such a brief. More typically, however,
the amicus brief has come to be a device by which a person with
an interest related to those before the court can communicate
his arguments to the court. Does not this institution emphasize a
court's legislative function? If it was inappropriate in *Cumming
v. Richmond County Board of Education,* p. 152, *supra,* for the
Supreme Court to rule on a question not raised by a party, why
is it appropriate for the Court to receive briefs from persons who
are not parties?

Abuses of the amicus brief privilege became evident to the
Justices in the 1940s:

In fact, such briefs were no longer presented only by parties with cases or interests similar to or identical with those actually before the Court; they had become a vehicle for propaganda efforts. Far from affording assistance to the Justices, on occasion they did not even mention the decisive issue on which the case turned and which divided the Court. Instead, their emphasis was on the size and importance of the group represented, or on contemporaneous press comment adverse to the ruling of the Court. . . . So the amendment of 1949 [to the Supreme Court's rules] placed restrictions on the right to file such briefs, after which the then Solicitor General almost automatically withheld his approval when asked to consent to a motion for leave to file—a practice that threw upon the Court the burden of scrutinizing such motions, and, in time, called forth the *On Lee* memorandum,[32] in which Mr. Justice Frankfurter severely criticized the Government's policy. After the summer of 1952, the Government's attitude became more liberal, and consent to file was more freely given, except to obvious propaganda groups, and except to groups otherwise represented. Wiener, *The Supreme Court's New Rules*, 68 HARV. L. REV. 20, 80-81 (1954).

The Supreme Court's present rule on the subject is Rule 42, which provides, in relevant part:

Rule 42. Briefs of an amicus curiae. . . .

2. A brief of an *amicus curiae* in cases before the court on the merits may be filed only after order of the court or when accompanied by written consent of all parties to the case and presented within the time allowed for the filing of the party supported.

3. When consent to the filing of a brief of an *amicus curiae* is refused by a party to the case, a motion for leave to file may timely be presented to the court. It shall concisely state the nature of the applicant's interest, set forth facts or questions of law that have not been, or reasons for believing that they will not adequately be, presented by the parties, and their relevancy to the disposition of the case; and it shall in no event exceed five printed pages in length. A party served with such motion may seasonably file an ob-

---

32 On Lee v. United States, 343 U.S. 924 (1952). . . . [Footnote in original, renumbered.]

jection concisely stating the reasons for withholding consent.

4. Consent to the filing of a brief of an *amicus curiae* need not be had when the brief is presented for the United States sponsored by the Solicitor General; for any agency of the United States authorized by law to appear in its own behalf, sponsored by its appropriate legal representative; for a State, Territory, or Commonwealth sponsored by its attorney general; or for a political subdivision of a State, Territory or Commonwealth sponsored by the authorized law officer thereof. . . .

If an amicus brief is designed to aid the Court in its law-making role, why should the parties to the case have even an initial veto over the filing of the brief? Is the answer to be found in the very heavy and increasing burden of the caseload of the Court? On the history of amicus briefs, and their modern use, see Krislov, *Amicus Curiae Brief: From Friendship to Advocacy*, 72 YALE L.J. 694 (1963).

AN ANTICIPATORY EPILOGUE

The two chapters just completed have surveyed the role that law and lawyers have played in the abolition of slavery, and in the rise and fall of the judicial formula of "separate but equal" in public education. We have explored the development of the legal doctrine from *Somerset v. Stewart* to *Brown v. Board of Education*, but only partly for the purpose of understanding that doctrine. More importantly, we have studied these materials in order to arrive at an introductory understanding of the operation of some basic institutions in the American legal process. At this midpoint in the course, we want to look back at some of the ground we have covered in this institutional nature walk. By now a student should be able to identify and to discuss (in a beginning way) such issues in the legal process as these:

1. The role of courts in declaring law. Where does the lawmaking function of courts fit in the legal system's institutional framework for lawmaking? (Recall the contrasting uses of the judicial, legislative, and administrative processes in the abolition of slavery in England.) How does the lawmaking function as performed by courts differ from a legislature's lawmaking function? (Recall the analysis of the process of judicial decision-making in the discussions of *Somerset v. Stewart* and *The Slave, Grace*: the various "inputs" into that process, and the requirement of reasoned grounds for decision.) What limitations are there, and should there be, on the exercise of a court's lawmaking powers? (Recall, for example, the discussions of the rule of stare decisis, prospective overruling, the rule against deciding collusive suits, the canon of strict construction of penal statutes, the potential problems of enforcement of a decree in *Brown v. Board of Education*, and the reluctance of some courts—but not others—to resolve questions of law beyond those necessary to decide a case.) What is the proper role of an amicus curiae in the process of judicial lawmaking? Are the courts properly equipped to acquire the factual information that may be essential to their lawmaking role? (Recall the discussions of this question in connection with cases like *Plessy v. Ferguson* and *Brown v. Board of Education*.) To what extent should a court, in performing its dual function of resolving a dispute and making law, go into issues not raised by the parties? (Recall the discussions of this point in *Cumming v. Richmond County Board of Education* and *Dred Scott v. Sandford.*) What obligation should a court feel to articulate either a narrow or a broad legal principle as the basis for its decision? To what extent should a court feel obligated to explain the sources or motivations behind the doctrinal rules it announces? (Recall the discussion of both these questions in connection with *Somerset v. Stewart, Gong Lum v. Rice* and *Brown v. Board of Education*, along with the per curiam decisions that followed the *Brown* decision.) How do courts use (and how should they use) judicial precedent in deciding the cases before them? (Recall the discussions in connection with *The Slave, Grace* and *Brown v. Board of Education.*) What factors should a court consider in determining whether to depart from an earlier precedent? If a court does decide to depart from precedent, what considerations should influence its choice of techniques for doing so? (Recall the discussions of these questions in connection with both the 1954 and the 1955 decisions in *Brown v. Board of Education.*)

2. The lawmaking role of legislatures. Are there issues which are more appropriate for legislative than for judicial lawmaking? Should courts "defer" such lawmaking to the legislature? (Recall the 1833 British abolition statute, and the discussion of *Somerset v. Stewart.*) How should courts approach the problem of giving meaning to general constitutional limitations on legislative lawmaking powers? To what extent can, and should, courts attempt to weigh values of a constitutional dimension that are incommensurable? (Recall the discussions of these questions in connection with the line of cases from *Roberts v. City of Boston* through *Brown v. Board of Education.*)

3. The function of courts in interpreting law made by the legislature. To what extent is it meaningful to approach this interpretive function by searching for the "plain meaning" of words, or the "intent" of those who used the words? To what extent should this interpretive function be analogized to the exercise of the court's lawmaking function while making use of prior precedent—*i.e.*, to use a "purpose-oriented" approach? How should a court using such an approach go about interpreting a specific statute? What is the appropriate role here for canons of construction such as the "strict construction of penal statutes"? Is there a different role for canons such as "ejusdem generis"? Should courts use statutory principles as "precedents" in declaring judge-made law? In considering all of these questions, recall the discussions in connection with *Commonwealth v. Aves* and *Jackson v. Bulloch*.)

4. The responsibilities of the legal profession. Should a lawyer have an obligation, in general, to accept a client's cause? Is there a serious conflict of interests if a lawyer represents one side of an issue after he has previously represented the other side? (Recall the discussion in connection with John Dunning's actions in *Somerset v. Stewart* and a case which preceded it.)

Much of our discussion has pointed up the wide-ranging freedom of the decision-maker to decide a question of law in accordance with his own value preferences and his own assessment of the factual setting for his doctrinal decision. The same point can be made with respect to all legal subjects; it is by no means peculiar to the subjects of this course. But it would be foolish to assume that for this reason serious attention need not be paid to the professional, analytical ingredient in the lawmaking process. There are professional standards for measuring the quality of a lawyer's argument, a judge's opinion, a legislator's statute. In studying these materials, it is important to keep these considerations in mind as well as the freedom of the decision-maker. The careful lawyer reads with the eye of the skeptic, but also with the eye of the craftsman.

In the remaining two chapters, we shall return to some of the institutional issues already raised, and we shall see some new ones that have been produced by efforts since *Brown* to secure equality of educational opportunity.

Chapter 3

IMPLEMENTATION OF BROWN v. BOARD OF EDUCATION IN THE SOUTH

The desegregation of southern school districts following the *Brown* decision was not characterized by speed, deliberate or otherwise. By the 1968-69 school year 20.3 per cent of Negro students in public schools in eleven southern states were enrolled in schools in which at least 50 per cent of the students were white. Washington Post, Jan. 17, 1969, p. A2, col. 1.[1] The percentages of Negro children in desegregated schools in many of these states did not begin to increase until after enactment by the Congress of the Civil Rights Act of 1964, when eligibility of public schools for federal grants was conditioned on elimination of racial discrimination, and when the Attorney General was authorized to initiate desegregation suits. A decade after *Brown*, in 1964-65, the percentage of Negro students in schools with whites

---

[1] The United States Commission on Civil Rights reported in 1967 that approximately 28 per cent of all Negro *first-grade* pupils in the urban north attended schools in which at least 50 per cent of the students were white. The report contained the following data on percentages of Negro *elementary school* students in majority-white schools in northern and western public school systems:

Chicago, Ill.	3.1	Pittsburgh, Pa.	17.2
Gary, Ind.	5.2	Omaha, Neb.	18.9
Cleveland, Ohio	5.4	Columbus, Ohio	19.2
St. Louis, Mo.	6.3	Boston, Mass.	20.5
Detroit, Mich.	8.5	Denver, Colo.	24.8
Newark, N. J.	9.7	Hartford, Conn.	26.2
Philadelphia, Pa.	9.8	New Haven, Conn.	26.6
Wichita, Kan.	10.9	San Diego, Cal.	26.7
Buffalo, N. Y.	11.3	San Francisco, Cal.	27.7
Cincinnati, Ohio	12.0	Seattle, Wash.	39.6
Los Angeles, Cal.	12.5	Portland, Ore.	40.8
Milwaukee, Wis.	13.2	New York, N. Y.	44.5*
Indianapolis, Ind.	15.8	Minneapolis, Minn.	60.8
Oakland, Cal.	16.8		

* Considering Negro and Spanish-surname students as a group, 15 per cent attended majority-Anglo schools.

(These data were for the 1965-66 school year with the exception of Cleveland, Ohio [1962-63], Los Angeles, Cal. [1963-64], and Seattle, Wash. [1964-65].) 1 U.S. COMM'N ON CIVIL RIGHTS, RACIAL ISOLATION IN THE PUBLIC SCHOOLS 2-3, 4-5 (1967). The legal aspects of de facto segregation are explored in Chapter 4, *infra*.

in the eleven southern states had reached only 2.14 per cent. Southern Education Reporting Service, Southern School News 2 (14th rev. 1964). The fact is that most of the putative beneficiaries of the legal principle declared in *Brown* have been frustrated in the vindication of their rights. A study of the efforts to vindicate these rights can provide insights into the legal process.

Until 1964 most southern school boards would not desegregate unless they were ordered to do so by the courts. Counsel for the boards regularly advised that the orders that accompanied the second *Brown* opinion applied only to those five cases, and that even the "deliberate speed" formula would apply only after a board came under a court order to desegregate.

Constitutional decisions are sometimes called "the law of the land." What does that phrase mean in the context of the *Brown* decision? Consider this comment on articles published in *The Alabama Lawyer*, the "Official Organ" of the State Bar of Alabama:

> Among the unquestioned doctrines most often stated in *The Alabama Lawyer* is the one that Supreme Court decisions like Brown are not the "law of the land." This means, of course, that Alabama lawyers whose writings appear there don't like such decisions. But it is obviously intended to mean more than that. How much more?
>
> Consider a fairly typical statement of the proposition by a favorite author:

> "No federal or state court of record in America has ever held that a decision of the Supreme Court of the United States or that of any other federal court is 'the law of the land' or 'the law of the Union.' Such decision is never anything more than *the law of the case* actually decided by the court and binding only upon the parties to that case and no others."

Does Mr. Pittman really mean what he seems to be saying? Suppose, for example, in an imaginary case of *Doe v. Georgia* the United States Supreme Court has held unconstitutional a state tax claimed from Doe, and suppose the decision rests upon an interpretation of the federal constitution that is flagrantly wrong in Mr. Pittman's judgment. As counsel for taxpayer Roe, identically situated, he obviously would not advise paying the tax unless required to do so by an official agency. Would he, however, as State Attorney General advise that the tax be extracted from Roe until or unless

Roe brought a lawsuit like Doe's? After all, the *Doe* decision is only a precedent, not *res judicata*, for persons not party to it. But one suspects that many people, possibly including Mr. Pittman, would consider such a position of the Attorney General a bold case of official lawlessness. The suspicion may rest upon the lawyer's sense—maybe even the common sense—that a Supreme Court decision is "law" for more than the parties to it, and possibly upon the further notion that officials owe a special duty to respect rights and immunities declared in such a decision. Query, then, whether there may be room for doubts—on intellectual or ethical grounds, or both—concerning the repeated advice of *The Alabama Lawyer* that school officials should ignore *Brown* until or unless they are specifically sued. . . . [We must ask] whether Alabama's lawyers, when they blandly define judicial decisions as less than "law," are nourishing a kind of lawlessness at all levels of society. If officials may properly ignore court pronouncements until they are sued, is it wrong to bomb churches or shoot NAACP officials when the likelihood of being caught—or if caught, convicted—is so slim? This may be a nasty question. But are the answers so clear as to make the question silly? And why, above all, is there such certainty that the decisions of the nation's highest court are less than the "law of the land."? Frankel, *The Alabama Lawyer, 1954-1964—Has the Official Organ Atrophied?*, 64 COLUM. L. REV. 1243, 1249-50 (1964).*

Not all the resistance to *Brown v. Board of Education* was so passive. Some local school boards that voted to desegregate voluntarily, without waiting for a court decree, were subjected to harassment and threats. And even when a court issued its decree, there was no assurance that the decree would be obeyed. *Cooper v. Aaron*, which follows, details one head-on confrontation between the federal judiciary and state officials. It is an unusual case in many ways: the timing of the action of the various courts was accelerated in order to permit disposition of the case to be completed before the school term began; the opinion was signed by all nine of the Justices; the opinion lectures Governor Orval Faubus in a rather personal way, although it does not name him; and the opinion goes out of its way to announce the adherence of three new members of the Court to the *Brown* decision. *Cooper v. Aaron* is notable also in a doctrinal sense, as we shall discuss in the note that follows the opinion. But the confronta-

---

* Copyright 1964, by Directors of Columbia Law Review Association, Inc.

tion in Little Rock had an importance far beyond the judicial decision in this case. The sight, on national television, of a handful of black children, walking into school down a path cleared by police through a mob of screaming adults, solidified public opinion outside the south. Furthermore, the defiance of a federal court order prodded a hitherto reluctant federal executive branch into its first important action supporting desegregation. Those two political consequences of Little Rock, already clear when this case was decided, are worth remembering as you read the brave words of this opinion.

COOPER v. AARON
Supreme Court of the United States
358 U.S. 1 (1958)

Opinion of the Court by THE CHIEF JUSTICE, Mr. Justice BLACK, Mr. Justice FRANKFURTER, Mr. Justice DOUGLAS, Mr. Justice BURTON, Mr. Justice CLARK, Mr. Justice HARLAN, Mr. Justice BRENNAN, and Mr. Justice WHITTAKER.

As this case reaches us it raises questions of the highest importance to the maintenance of our federal system of government. It necessarily involves a claim by the Governor and Legislature of a State that there is no duty on state officials to obey federal court orders resting on this Court's considered interpretation of the United States Constitution. Specifically it involves actions by the Governor and Legislature of Arkansas upon the premise that they are not bound by our holding in *Brown v. Board of Education*, 347 U.S. 483. That holding was that the Fourteenth Amendment forbids States to use their governmental powers to bar children on racial grounds from attending schools where there is state participation through any arrangement, management, funds or property. We are urged to uphold a suspension of the Little Rock School Board's plan to do away with segregated public schools in Little Rock until state laws and efforts to upset and nullify our holding in *Brown v. Board of Education* have been further challenged and tested in the courts. We reject these contentions.

The case was argued before us on September 11, 1958. On the following day we unanimously affirmed the judgment of the Court of Appeals for the Eighth Circuit, 257 F.2d 33, which had reversed a judgment of the District Court for the Eastern District of Arkansas, 163 F. Supp. 13. The District Court had granted the application of the petitioners, the Little Rock School Board and School Superintendent, to suspend for two and one-half years the operation of the School Board's court-approved desegregation program. In order that the School Board might know, without doubt, its duty in this regard before the opening of school, which had been set for the following Monday, September 15, 1958, we immediately issued the judgment, reserving the expression of our supporting views to a later date. This opinion of all of the members of the Court embodies those views.

The following are the facts and circumstances so far as necessary to show how the legal questions are presented.

On May 17, 1954, this Court decided that enforced racial segregation in the public schools of a State is a denial of the equal protection of the laws enjoined by the Fourteenth Amendment. *Brown v. Board of Education,* 347 U.S. 483. The Court postponed, pending further argument, formulation of a decree to effectuate this decision. That decree was rendered May 31, 1955. *Brown v. Board of Education,* 349 U.S. 294. In the formulation of that decree the Court recognized that good faith compliance with the principles declared in *Brown* might in some situations "call for elimination of a variety of obstacles in making the transition to school systems operated in accordance with the constitutional principles set forth in our May 17, 1954, decision." *Id.,* at 300. . . .

Under such circumstances, the District Courts were directed to require "a prompt and reasonable start toward full compliance," and to take such action as was necessary to bring about the end of racial segregation in the public schools "with all deliberate speed." *Ibid.* Of course, in many locations, obedience to the duty of desegregation would require the immediate general admission of Negro children, otherwise qualified as students for their appropriate classes, at particular schools. On the other hand, a District Court, after analysis of the relevant factors (which, of course, excludes hostility to racial desegregation), might conclude that justification existed for not requiring the present nonsegregated admission of all qualified Negro children. In such circumstances, however, the courts should scrutinize the program of the school authorities to make sure that they had developed arrangements pointed toward the earliest practicable completion of desegregation, and had taken appropriate steps to put their program into effective operation. It was made plain that delay in any guise in order to deny the constitutional rights of Negro children could not be countenanced, and that only a prompt start, diligently and earnestly pursued, to eliminate racial segregation from the public schools could constitute good faith compliance. State authorities were thus duty bound to devote every effort toward initiating desegregation and bringing about the elimination of racial discrimination in the public school system.

On May 20, 1954, three days after the first *Brown* opinion, the Little Rock District School Board adopted, and on May 23, 1954, made public, a statement of policy entitled "Supreme Court Decision—Segregation in Public Schools." In this statement the Board recognized that

"It is our responsibility to comply with Federal Constitutional Requirements and we intend to do so when the Supreme Court of the United States outlines the method to be followed."

Thereafter the Board undertook studies of the administrative problems confronting the transition to a desegregated public school system at Little Rock. It instructed the Superintendent of Schools to prepare a plan for desegregation, and approved such a plan on May 24, 1955, seven days before the second *Brown* opinion. The plan provided for desegregation at the senior high school level (grades 10 through 12) as the first stage. Desegregation at the junior high and elementary levels was to follow. It was contemplated that desegregation at the high school level would commence in the fall of 1957, and the expectation was that complete desegregation of the school system would be accomplished by 1963. Following the adoption of this plan, the Superintendent of Schools discussed it with a large number of citizen groups in the city. As a result of these discussions, the Board reached the conclusion that "a large majority of the residents" of Little Rock were of "the belief . . . that the Plan, although objectionable in principle," from the point of view of those supporting segregated schools, "was still the best for the interests of all pupils in the District."

Upon challenge by a group of Negro plaintiffs desiring more rapid completion of the desegregation process, the District Court upheld the School Board's plan, *Aaron v. Cooper*, 143 F. Supp. 855. The Court of Appeals affirmed. 243 F.2d 361. Review of that judgment was not sought here.

While the School Board was thus going forward with its preparation for desegregating the Little Rock school system, other state authorities, in contrast, were actively pursuing a program designed to perpetuate in Arkansas the system of racial segregation which this Court had held violated the Fourteenth Amendment. First came, in November 1956, an amendment to the State Constitution flatly commanding the Arkansas General Assembly to oppose "in every Constitutional manner the Un-constitutional desegregation decisions of May 17, 1954 and May 31, 1955 of the United States Supreme Court," Ark. Const., Amend. 44, and, through the initiative, a pupil assignment law, Ark. Stat. 80-1519 to 80-1524. Pursuant to this state constitutional command, a law relieving school children from compulsory attendance at racially mixed schools, Ark. Stat. 80-1525, and a law establishing a State Sovereignty Commission, Ark. Stat. 6-801 to 6-824, were enacted by the General Assembly in February 1957.

The School Board and the Superintendent of Schools nevertheless continued with preparations to carry out the first stage of the desegregation program. Nine Negro children were scheduled for admission in September 1957 to Central High School, which has more than two thousand students. Various administrative measures, designed to assure the smooth transition of this first stage of desegregation, were undertaken.

On September 2, 1957, the day before these Negro students were to enter Central High, the school authorities were met with drastic opposing action on the part of the Governor of Arkansas who dispatched units of the Arkansas National Guard to the Central High School grounds and placed the school "off limits" to colored students. As found by the District Court in subsequent proceedings, the Governor's action had not been requested by the school authorities, and was entirely unheralded. The findings were these:

"Up to this time [September 2], no crowds had gathered about Central High School and no acts of violence or threats of violence in connection with the carrying out of the plan had occurred. Nevertheless, out of an abundance of caution, the school authorities had frequently conferred with the Mayor and Chief of Police of Little Rock about taking appropriate steps by the Little Rock police to prevent any possible disturbances or acts of violence in connection with the attendance of the 9 colored students at Central High School. The Mayor considered that the Little Rock police force could adequately cope with any incidents which might arise at the opening of school. The Mayor, the Chief of Police, and the school authorities made no request to the Governor or any representative of his for State assistance in maintaining peace and order at Central High School. Neither the Governor nor any other official of the State government consulted with the Little Rock authorities about whether the Little Rock police were prepared to cope with any incidents which might arise at the school, about any need for State assistance in maintaining peace and order, or about stationing the Arkansas National Guard at Central High School." Aaron v. Cooper, 156 F. Supp. 220, 225.

The Board's petition for postponement in this proceeding states: "The effect of that action [of the Governor] was to harden the core of opposition to the Plan and cause many persons who theretofore had reluctantly accepted the Plan to believe there was some power in the State of Arkansas which, when exerted, could nullify the Federal law and permit disobedience of the decree of this [District] Court, and from that date hostility to the Plan was increased and criticism of the officials of the [School] District has become more bitter and unrestrained." The Governor's action caused the School Board to request the Negro students on September 2 not to attend the high school "until the legal dilemma was solved." The next day, September 3, 1957, the Board petitioned the District Court for instructions, and the court, after a hearing, found that the Board's request of the Negro students to stay away from the high school had been made because of the stationing of the military guards by the state authorities. The court determined that this was not a reason for departing from the approved plan, and ordered the School Board and Superintendent to proceed with it.

On the morning of the next day, September 4, 1957, the Negro children attempted to enter the high school but, as the District Court later found, units of the Arkansas National Guard "acting pursuant to the Governor's order, stood shoulder to shoulder at the school grounds and thereby forcibly prevented the 9 Negro students . . . from entering," as they continued to do every school day during the following three weeks. 156 F. Supp., at 225.

That same day, September 4, 1957, the United States Attorney for the Eastern District of Arkansas was requested by the District Court to begin an immediate investigation in order to fix responsibility for the interference with the orderly implementation of the District Court's direction to carry out the desegregation program. Three days later, September 7, the District Court denied a petition of the School Board and the Superintendent of Schools for an order temporarily suspending continuance of the program.

Upon completion of the United States Attorney's investigation, he and the Attorney General of the United States, at the District Court's request, entered the proceedings and filed a petition on behalf of the United States, as *amicus curiae*, to enjoin the Governor of Arkansas and officers of the Arkansas National Guard from further attempts to prevent obedience to the court's order. After hearings on the petition, the District Court found that the School Board's plan had been obstructed by the Governor through the use of National Guard troops, and granted a preliminary injunction on September 20, 1957, enjoining the Governor and the officers of the Guard from preventing the attendance of Negro children at Central High School, and from otherwise obstructing or interfering with the orders of the court in connection with the plan. 156 F. Supp. 220, affirmed, *Faubus v. United States*, 254 F.2d 797. The National Guard was then withdrawn from the school.

The next school day was Monday, September 23, 1957. The Negro children entered the high school that morning under the protection of the Little Rock Police Department and members of the Arkansas State Police. But the officers caused the children to be removed from the school during the morning because they had difficulty controlling a large and demonstrating crowd which had gathered at the high school. 163 F. Supp., at 16. On September 25, however, the President of the United States dispatched federal troops to Central High School and admission of the Negro students to the school was thereby effected. Regular army troops continued at the high school until November 27, 1957. They were then replaced by federalized National Guardsmen who remained throughout the balance of the school year. Eight of the Negro students remained in attendance at the school throughout the school year.

We come now to the aspect of the proceedings presently before us. On February 20, 1958, the School Board and the Superintendent of Schools filed a petition in the District Court seeking a postponement of their program for desegregation. Their position in essence was that because of extreme public hostility, which they stated had been engendered largely by the official attitudes and actions of the Governor and the Legislature, the maintenance of a sound educational program at Central High School, with the Negro students in attendance, would be impossible. The Board therefore proposed that the Negro students already admitted to the school be withdrawn and sent to segregated schools, and that all further steps to carry out the Board's desegregation program be postponed for a period later suggested by the Board to be two and one-half years.

After a hearing the District Court granted the relief requested by the Board. Among other things the court found that the past year at Central High School had been attended by conditions of "chaos, bedlam and turmoil"; that there were "repeated incidents of more or less serious violence directed against the Negro students and their property"; that there was "tension and unrest among the school administrators, the class-room teachers, the pupils, and the latters' parents, which inevitably had an adverse effect upon the educational program"; that a school official was threatened with violence; that a "serious financial burden" had been cast on the School District; that the education of the students had suffered "and under existing conditions will continue to suffer"; that the Board would continue to need "military assistance or its equivalent"; that the local police department would not be able "to detail enough men to afford the necessary protection"; and that the situation was "intolerable." 163 F. Supp., at 20-26.

The District Court's judgment was dated June 20, 1958. The Negro respondents appealed to the Court of Appeals for the Eighth Circuit and also sought there a stay of the District Court's judgment. At the same time they filed a petition for certiorari in this Court asking us to review the District Court's judgment without awaiting the disposition of their appeal to the Court of Appeals, or of their petition to that court for a stay. That we declined to do. 357 U.S. 566. The Court of Appeals did not act on the petition for a stay, but, on August 18, 1958, after convening in special session on August 4 and hearing the appeal, reversed the District Court, 257 F.2d 33. On August 21, 1958, the Court of Appeals stayed its mandate to permit the School Board to petition this Court for certiorari. Pending the filing of the School Board's petition for certiorari, the Negro respondents, on August 23, 1958, applied to Mr. Justice WHITTAKER, as Circuit Justice for the Eighth Circuit, to stay the order of the Court of Appeals withholding its own mandate and also to stay the District Court's judgment. In view of the nature of the motions, he referred them to the entire Court. Recognizing the vital importance of a decision of the issues in time to permit arrangements to be made for the 1958-1959 school year, see *Aaron v. Cooper,* 357 U.S. 566, 567, we convened in Special Term on August 28, 1958, and heard oral argument on the respondents' motions, and also argument of the Solicitor General who, by invitation, appeared for the United States as *amicus curiae,* and asserted that the Court of Appeals' judgment was clearly correct on the merits, and urged that we vacate its stay forthwith. Finding that respondents' application necessarily involved consideration of the merits of the litigation, we entered an order which deferred decision upon the motions pending the disposition of the School Board's petition for certiorari, and fixed September 8, 1958, as the day on or before which such petition might be filed, and September 11, 1958, for oral argument upon the petition. The petition for certiorari, duly filed, was granted in open Court on September 11, 1958, . . . and further arguments were had, the Solicitor General again urging the correctness of the judgment of the Court of Appeals. On September 12, 1958, as already mentioned, we unanimously affirmed the judgment of the Court of Appeals in the *per curiam* opinion. . . .

In affirming the judgment of the Court of Appeals which reversed the District Court we have accepted without reservation the position of the School Board, the Superintendent of Schools, and their counsel that they displayed entire good faith in the conduct of these proceedings and in dealing with the unfortunate and distressing sequence of events which has been outlined. We likewise have accepted the findings of the District Court as to the conditions at Central High School during the 1957-1958 school year, and also the findings that the educational progress of all the students, white and colored, of that school has suffered and will continue to suffer if the conditions which prevailed last year are permitted to continue.

The significance of these findings, however, is to be considered in light of the fact, indisputably revealed by the record before us, that the conditions they depict are directly traceable to the actions of legislators and executive officials of the State of Arkansas, taken in their official capacities, which reflect their own determination to resist this Court's decision in the *Brown* case and which have brought about violent resistance to that decision in Arkansas. In its petition for certiorari filed in this Court, the School Board itself describes the situation in this language: "The legislative, executive, and judicial departments of the state government opposed the desegregation of Little Rock schools by enacting laws, calling out troops, making statements vilifying federal law and federal courts, and failing to utilize state law enforcement agencies and judicial processes to maintain public peace."

One may well sympathize with the position of the Board in the face of the frustrating conditions which have confronted it, but, regardless of the Board's good faith, the actions of the other state agencies responsible for those conditions compel us to reject the Board's legal position. Had Central High School been under the direct management of the State itself, it could hardly be suggested that those immediately in charge of the school should be heard to assert their own good faith as a legal excuse for delay in implementing the constitutional rights of these respondents, when vindication of those rights was rendered difficult or impossible by the actions of other state officials. The situation here is in no different posture because the members of the School Board and the Superintendent of Schools are local officials; from the point of view of the Fourteenth Amendment, they stand in this litigation as the agents of the State.

The constitutional rights of respondents are not to be sacrificed or yielded to the violence and disorder which have followed upon the actions of the Governor and Legislature. As this Court said some 41 years ago in a unanimous opinion in a case involving another aspect of racial segregation: "It is urged that this proposed segregation will promote the public peace by preventing race conflicts. Desirable as this is, and important as is the preservation of the public peace, this aim cannot be accomplished by laws or ordinances which deny rights created or protected by the Federal Constitution." *Buchanan v. Warley*, 245 U.S. 60, 81. Thus law and order are not here to be preserved by depriving the Negro children of their constitutional rights. The record before us clearly establishes that the growth of the Board's difficulties to a magnitude beyond its unaided power to control is the product of state action. Those difficulties, as counsel for the Board forthrightly conceded on the oral argument in this Court, can also be brought under control by state action.

The controlling legal principles are plain. The command of the Fourteenth Amendment is that no "State" shall deny to any person within its jurisdiction the equal protection of the laws. "A State acts by its legislative, its executive, or its judicial authorities. It can act in no other way. The constitutional provision, therefore, must mean that no agency of the State, or of the officers or agents by whom its powers are exerted, shall deny to any person within its jurisdiction the equal protection of the laws. Whoever, by virtue of public position under a State government, . . . denies or takes away the equal protection of the laws, violates the constitutional inhibition; and as he acts in the name and for the State, and is clothed with the State's power, his act is that of the State. This must be so, or the constitutional prohibition has no meaning." *Ex parte Virginia*, 100 U.S. 339, 347. Thus the prohibitions of the Fourteenth Amendment extend to all action of the State denying equal protection of the laws; whatever the agency of the State taking the action, see *Virginia v. Rives*, 100 U.S. 313; *Pennsylvania v. Board of Directors of City Trusts of Philadelphia*, 353 U.S. 230; *Shelley v. Kraemer*, 334 U.S. 1; or whatever the guise in which it is taken, see *Derrington v. Plummer*, 240 F.2d 922; *Department of Conservation and Development v. Tate*, 231 F.2d 615. In short, the constitutional rights of children not to be discriminated against in school admission on grounds of race or color declared by this Court in the *Brown* case can neither be nullified openly and directly by state legislators or state executive or judicial officers, nor nullified indirectly by them through evasive schemes for segregation whether attempted "ingeniously or ingenuously." *Smith v. Texas*, 311 U.S. 128, 132.

What has been said, in the light of the facts developed, is enough to dispose of the case. However, we should answer the premise of the actions of the Governor and Legislature that they are not bound by our holding in the *Brown* case. It is necessary only to recall some basic constitutional propositions which are settled doctrine.

Article VI of the Constitution makes the Constitution the "supreme Law of the Land." In 1803, Chief Justice Marshall, speaking for a unanimous Court, referring to the Constitution as "the fundamental and paramount law of the nation," declared in the notable case of *Marbury v. Madison*, 1 Cranch 137, 177, that "It is emphatically the province and duty of the judicial department to say what the law is." This decision declared the basic principle that the federal judiciary is supreme in the exposition of the law of the Constitution, and that principle has ever since been respected by this Court and the Country as a permanent and indispensable feature of our constitutional system. It follows that the interpretation of the Fourteenth Amendment enunciated by this Court in the *Brown* case is the supreme law of the land, and Art. VI of the Constitution makes it of binding effect on the States "any Thing in the Constitution or Laws of any State to the Contrary notwithstanding." Every state legislator and executive and judicial officer is solemnly committed by oath taken pursuant to Art. VI, cl. 3, "to support this Constitution." Chief Justice Taney, speaking for a unanimous Court in 1859, said that this requirement reflected the framers' "anxiety to preserve it [the Constitution] in full force, in all its powers, and to guard against resistance to or evasion of its authority, on the part of a State. . . ." *Ableman v. Booth*, 21 How. 506, 524.[2]

---

[2] *Ableman v. Booth,* a century earlier, raised constitutional issues similar to those in *Cooper v. Aaron.* It brought before the Court the issue of nullification of federal law by state judicial action. In March, 1854, Booth aided a fugitive slave in Wisconsin to escape from the custody of a United States deputy marshal. Booth was arrested, for trial for violating the federal Fugitive Slave Law. While being held by federal officers he was ordered released by the Wisconsin Supreme Court, on the ground that the Fugitive Slave Law was unconstitutional. He was later convicted in the federal court in Wisconsin of violating the federal statute, and sentenced to a one-month prison term and a fine. After he was imprisoned he again obtained an order from the Wisconsin Supreme Court that he be released because the federal statute was unconstitutional. The United States Supreme Court, Chief Justice Taney writing for a unanimous Court, reversed both decisions of the Wisconsin court. The Fugitive Slave Law, the Court said, was constitutional, and, in any event, state judicial officials could not interfere with federal officers who

No state legislator or executive or judicial officer can war against the Constitution without violating his undertaking to support it. Chief Justice Marshall spoke for a unanimous Court in saying that: "If the legislatures of the several states may, at will, annul the judgments of the courts of the United States, and destroy the rights acquired under those judgments, the constitution itself becomes a solemn mockery. . . ." *United States v. Peters*, 5 Cranch 115, 136. A Governor who asserts a power to nullify a federal court order is similarly restrained. If he had such power, said Chief Justice Hughes, in 1932, also for a unanimous Court, "it is manifest that the fiat of a state Governor, and not the Constitution of the United States, would be the supreme law of the land; that the restrictions of the Federal Constitution upon the exercise of state power would be but impotent phrases. . . ." *Sterling v. Constantin*, 287 U.S. 378, 397-398.

It is, of course, quite true that the responsibility for public education is primarily the concern of the States, but it is equally true that such responsibilities, like all other state activity, must be exercised consistently with federal constitutional requirements as they apply to state action. The Constitution created a government dedicated to equal justice under law. The Fourteenth Amendment embodied and emphasized that ideal. State support of segregated schools through any arrangement, management, funds, or property cannot be squared with the Amendment's command that no State shall deny to any person within its jurisdiction the equal protection of the laws. The right of a student not to be segregated on racial grounds in schools so

---

were enforcing the Law, or with the judgment of a federal court under the Law.

This decision, based on the supremacy of federal law, was hailed by proslavery forces and attacked by abolitionists. The Wisconsin legislature passed resolutions declaring the decision of the Supreme Court to be an act of arbitrary power, "without authority, void, and of no force." States, the legislature said, were the final judges of whether they violated the Federal Constitution (here by allegedly interfering with the enforcement of federal law and the federal judicial system). The case was decided on March 7, 1859. Not until November of that year did the United States Attorney in Wisconsin seek to have the federal court order the re-arrest of Booth. Meanwhile, the state supreme court took no steps to carry out the Supreme Court's decision. In December, federal officials finally arrested Booth. He was imprisoned in a room in the federal building in Milwaukee, and remained in custody after his original one-month sentence had been served because he had not paid the $1000 fine. Booth refused to petition the President for his own release, and remained in custody. At one point a mob unsuccessfully attempted to release him. He was finally freed by a group of abolitionists, and although he remained in the state he was never proceeded against any further by federal officers. This description is from C. SWISHER, ROGER B. TANEY 526-33 (1936). *See also* W. LEWIS, WITHOUT FEAR OR FAVOR: A BIOGRAPHY OF CHIEF JUSTICE ROGER B. TANEY 433-40 (1965). [*Eds.* note.]

maintained is indeed so fundamental and pervasive that it is embraced in the concept of due process of law. *Bolling v. Sharpe*, 347 U.S. 497. The basic decision in *Brown* was unanimously reached by this Court only after the case had been briefed and twice argued and the issues had been given the most serious consideration. Since the first *Brown* opinion three new Justices have come to the Court. They are at one with the Justices still on the Court who participated in that basic decision as to its correctness, and that decision is now unanimously reaffirmed. The principles announced in that decision and the obedience of the States to them, according to the command of the Constitution, are indispensable for the protection of the freedoms guaranteed by our fundamental charter for all of us. Our constitutional ideal of equal justice under law is thus made a living truth.

[The concurring opinion of Justice Frankfurter is omitted.]

THE BROWN DECISION AS "THE LAW OF THE LAND"

The Constitution's supremacy clause says:

> This Constitution, and the Laws of the United States which shall be made in Pursuance thereof; and all Treaties made, or which shall be made, under the Authority of the United States, shall be the supreme Law of the Land; and the Judges in every State shall be bound thereby, any Thing in the Constitution or Laws of any State to the Contrary notwithstanding. Art. VI, cl. 2.

The clause says nothing explicit about judicial decisions interpreting the Constitution. What is the reasoning that supports the statement in the opinion in *Cooper v. Aaron* that "the interpretation of the Fourteenth Amendment enunciated by this Court in the *Brown* case is the supreme law of the land . . ."? Did Governor Faubus violate his oath to support the Constitution by his announced opposition to the *Brown* decision? By his efforts to prevent the Little Rock school board from complying with court decrees in this litigation?

There is a crucial difference between these last two questions; it is the difference between arguing with the umpire and refusing to leave the base when you are called out. One of the ways in which the law of the Constitution can grow and adapt to new social environments is for the political branches of govern-

ment to continue to press the judiciary to consider and reconsider the implications of its constitutional interpretations. That
is what Lincoln had in mind when he referred to the *Dred Scott*
decision in his First Inaugural Address:

> I do not forget the position assumed by some that
> constitutional questions are to be decided by the Supreme
> Court, nor do I deny that such decisions must be binding
> in any case upon the parties to a suit as to the object of that
> suit, while they are also entitled to very high respect and
> consideration in all parallel cases by all other departments
> of the Government. And while it is obviously possible that
> such decision may be erroneous in any given case, still the
> evil effect following it, being limited to that particular
> case, with the chance that it may be overruled and never
> become a precedent for other cases, can better be borne
> than could the evils of a different practice. At the same time,
> the candid citizen must confess that if the policy of the
> Government upon vital questions affecting the whole people
> is to be irrevocably fixed by decisions of the Supreme Court,
> the instant they are made in ordinary litigation between
> parties in personal actions the people will have ceased to
> be their own rulers, having to that extent practically re-
> signed their Government into the hands of that eminent
> tribunal. Nor is there in this view any assault upon the
> court or the judges. It is a duty from which they may not
> shrink to decide cases properly brought before them, and
> it is no fault of theirs if others seek to turn their decisions to
> political purposes. 6 MESSAGES AND PAPERS OF THE PRESI-
> DENTS 1789-1897, pp. 5, 9-10 (J. Richardson, ed. 1897).

A government official or a private citizen does not make "war
against the Constitution" just because he criticizes a court's interpretation. The Supreme Court makes constitutional law, but
it makes law—as any court makes law—by deciding cases. The
disappointed citizen can hope that the next case can be decided
differently. But he can also complain, and hope to influence the
course of decision. Professor Louis Jaffe places the Supreme
Court's political role in the perspective of the entire lawmaking
process:

> There is no area in which criticism at its most intense
> is more appropriate or more to be anticipated than the area
> of constitutional adjudication. There will be and there

should be popular response to the Supreme Court's decision; not just the "informed" criticism of law professors but the deep-felt, emotion-laden, unsophisticated reaction of the laity. This is so because more than any court in the modern world the Supreme Court "makes policy," and is at the same time so little subject to formal democratic control. Where else do nine nonelected lawyers have the power as in the *Reapportionment Case* to remake the political map of the country? The Court is encouraged, is adjured by many to press forward, to exercise leadership. I am myself convinced that there are areas where it should. The *Segregation Cases* were one, and it could be that the *Reapportionment Case* was another. Yet those who urge the Court on to political innovation are outraged when its decisions arouse, as they must, resentment and political attack. At this point they become lawyers marching behind the solemn, sacrosanct banner of the law. These people want it both ways. But a Court which decides *Marbury v. Madison, Dred Scott, Plessy v. Ferguson,* . . . *Brown v. Board of Education, Baker v. Carr* [reapportionment] and *Engel v. Vitale* [school prayers] is deep in the business of government. It is in politics and that in a democracy means that it must be prepared to withstand the angry howls of outraged citizens.

We are told that to criticize the Court in any basic sense, in any way that goes to its general philosophy, its role, and its approach is to play the game of segregationist. To be sure the segregationist may be an incidental beneficiary. Violently expressed hostility to a decision may indeed increase the difficulty of enforcing it, and, of course, significantly affect the shape of its translation into a going system of rules and remedies. Once granting that public opinion is intrinsic to a democratic system its operation cannot be cabined, cribbed, and confined to formal legal paths. We are, of course, deeply shocked where it is not the private citizen but the public official under oath to uphold the law who leads in flouting it. But great political decisions such as desegregation and reapportionment *do* involve major confrontations of political power and the form in which such decisions become viable is inevitably a consequence of the whole political process, a process which involves a great variety and gradation of lawmaking phenomena. It is precisely to conserve its power and prestige in those cases in which it cannot do otherwise that the Supreme Court should be made aware that each and every bold policy decision will bring it into the political arena.

. . . Jaffe, *Impromptu Remarks,* 76 HARV. L. REV. 1111-12 (1963).*

Threats of violence and other reprisals were not the sole deterrents to implementation of the rule in *Brown*. Much of the effort to delay or prevent desegregation of southern schools took the form of action within the legal system—or in any case action that the resistance movement sought to place within the legal system. An appeal to law was written into the "Southern Manifesto," a 1956 document signed by 101 members of Congress from the states of the old Confederacy (excluding only Senators Lyndon Johnson of Texas and Estes Kefauver and Albert Gore of Tennessee). The Manifesto argued that "the Supreme Court, with no legal basis for such action, undertook to exercise their naked judicial power and substituted their personal political and social ideas for the established law of the land," and the signers pledged "to use all lawful means to bring about a reversal of this decision which is contrary to the Constitution." New York Times, March 12, 1956, p. 19, col. 2. The devices adopted, primarily by state legislatures, included, for example, pupil assignment procedures, the closing of schools, tuition grants for children attending private schools, and "freedom of choice" school-attendance plans. A separate phase of litigation thus began as black children and parents sought to have these devices invalidated. The emphasis on litigation in turn produced efforts by some states to reduce the availability of legal counsel to would-be plaintiffs. The remaining materials in this chapter will consider some of these devices for evasion, along with efforts from 1954 to 1964 within the Federal Government to implement *Brown,* and finally some aspects of the Civil Rights Act of 1964, in which Congress responded to the argument that there had been too much deliberateness in the speed with which the principle of *Brown v. Board of Education* had been implemented.

A. PUPIL ASSIGNMENT PROCEDURES

One early response to *Brown v. Board of Education* was the widespread adoption of new procedures for assigning children to schools. The mechanisms for making these assignments provide an illustration of some basic aspects of the administrative process.

By statute, administrative agencies—either existing school boards or newly created state agencies—were delegated legal authority to make pupil assignments. The designated agency was to handle cases individually, assigning each child to a school in accordance with the statutory criteria. A child who was dissatisfied with his assignment could appeal to an administrative appellate agency and ultimately to the state courts. Judicial review was not available until administrative review had been exhausted. The administrative process thus was to be used for the adjudication of a mass of individual claims, by an agency which presumably would be expert in handling the types of claims individual children would make, with judicial review of the validity of the administrative action. From the standpoint of those who sought to delay or prevent desegregation, the administrative process seemed to offer a lengthy procedure with each child's case being handled individually (*i.e.*, the Negro children could not have their cases determined in one comprehensive class action).

A 1957 decision of the United States Court of Appeals for the Fifth Circuit concerning a 1954 Louisiana pupil assignment law illustrates two aspects of the place of the administrative process in the legal system.

ORLEANS PARISH SCHOOL BOARD v. BUSH
United States Court of Appeals, Fifth Circuit
242 F.2d 156 (1957)
cert. denied, 354 U.S. 921 (1957)

Before RIVES, TUTTLE AND BROWN, Circuit Judges.

TUTTLE, Circuit Judge.

This is an appeal in an action on behalf of certain New Orleans Negro school children from a judgment of the District Court for the Eastern District of Louisiana enjoining appellant "from requiring and permitting segregation of the races, in any school under their supervision, from and after such time as may be necessary to make arrangements for admission of children to such schools on a racially non-discriminatory basis with all deliberate speed as required by the decision of the Supreme Court in Brown v. Board of Education of Topeka. . . ."

The principal grounds of appellant's attack on the validity of this order are: . . . (2) The complaint failed to state a claim on which relief could be granted; (3) The court erred in holding that the provisions of Art. XII, Sec. 1 of the Louisiana Constitution-LSA requiring separate schools for white and colored children and that all of Louisiana Act 555 and Section 1 of 556 of 1954 LSA-R.S. 17:81.1, 17:331-17:334, requiring segregation and assignment of pupils respectively in public schools were invalid. . . .

After the first opinion in the Brown case the State Legislature of Louisiana proposed and the people adopted an amendment to Art. XII, Sec. 1 of the State Constitution which had already provided, in effect, that all public elementary and secondary schools should be operated separately for white and colored children by adding that "This provision is made in the exercise of the state police power to promote and protect public health, morals, better education and the peace and good order in the State, and not because of race. The Legislature shall enact laws to enforce the state police power in this regard." The Legislature then promptly enacted Acts 1954, No. 555 and 556. Section 1 of 555 merely repeated the constitutional requirement of separate schools. Sections 2, 3 and 4 provide for penalties to be imposed on local boards and an individual failing to observe the requirements as to separate schools in Section 1. Section 5 is a separability clause. Act 556, adopted at the same time, is the pupil assignment statute. It provides for assignment of each pupil each year by the parish superintendent to a particular school, and, without providing any standards other than those of Act 555 for separation of the races, provides for an appeal to the local board and then to the State Board and thereafter to the state district court.[3]

---

3 Act 556, Sec. 1, in full, appears as follows in L.S.A. 17:

"§ 81.1. Assignment of children to particular schools by parish superintendent; hearings; review by board; appeal

"Each parish superintendent of schools, throughout this state, shall, each year, determine the particular public school within each parish to be attended by each school child applying for admission to public schools. No school child shall be entitled to be enrolled or to enter into a public school until he has been assigned thereto in accordance with the provisions of this Section. In the event of dissatisfaction with the school assignment made by the superintendent, the parents or next of kin to the child affected, within ten days from the date of assignment may apply to the school superintendent for a hearing to have said child assigned to some other public school in the parish, in which case the superintendent shall grant a hearing, and within thirty days after the conclusion of said hearing, the superintendent shall hand down a decision in writing either sustaining his school assignment in question or changing the same. The action of the parish superintendent shall be reviewable by the parish school board upon application of any person paying ad valorem taxes for the support and maintenance of the public schools or on the application of any other party in interest. Any such application for review shall be filed with the parish school board within thirty days from the day the action complained of was taken and within sixty days thereafter, said parish school board shall hold a hearing at which evidence shall be taken down and transcribed, the cost thereof to be paid for by the party making said application prior to submission of the matter to the school board. The school board shall have the right to require applicant to furnish bond for costs within a reasonable sum, properly secured, prior to the

Following the enactment of these laws, appellees petitioned the school board to take immediate steps to reorganize the schools under its jurisdiction on a nondiscriminatory basis. No reply was made to this or to a subsequent petition, but the board engaged counsel to "defend, as special attorney for the Board, both in the trial court and in the Courts of Appeal" the action then pending. Soon thereafter appellees filed a first amended complaint setting up the provisions of the amended constitution and the newly enacted statutes, a prayer for declaratory relief holding them invalid and renewing their prayer for preliminary and permanent injunction against the enforcement by the board of the provisions of the new laws. . . .

The second ground of appellant's motion to dismiss was its contention that the complaint fails to state a claim on which relief can be granted. The first basis for this attack is that, assuming all the allegations as to unconstitutional acts by the defendant to be true, the plaintiffs have not pursued their administrative remedies for relief before filing of their suit. . . .

. . . [T]here is . . . no merit in appellant's argument. Appellees were not seeking specific assignment to particular schools. They, as Negro students, were seeking an end to a local school board rule that required segregation of all Negro students from all white students. As patrons of the Orleans Parish school system they are undoubtedly entitled to have the district court pass on their right to seek relief. . . .

Moreover, so long as assignments could be made under the Louisiana constitution and statutes only on a basis of separate schools for white and colored children to remit each of these minor plaintiffs and thousands of others similarly situated to thousands of administrative hearings before the board for relief that they contend the Supreme Court has held them entitled to, would, as the trial judge said, "be a vain and useless gesture, un-

---

holding of said hearing. The parish school board shall consider the evidence so adduced and as soon as practicable render its decision in writing. Any person, having applied for and secured a hearing by the parish school board who feels aggrieved by the ruling of said board shall have the right to apply to the district court of the domicile of the said board and the right to appeal from the judgment of the district court to the appropriate court of appeal, provided, however, that such right to apply to the district court shall not exist until said party shall have complied with the provisions hereof, and shall have exhausted the administrative remedies provided for herein.

"Each school board throughout the state shall have authority to adopt rules and regulations governing the hearing and appeals provided for herein.

"Wherever reference is made to parish superintendent of schools or school boards the same shall apply to those in the cities of Monroe, Bogalusa and Lake Charles. Added Acts 1954, No. 556, § 1." [Footnote in original, renumbered.]

worthy of a court of equity, . . . a travesty in which this court will not participate." . . .

We next come to the Pupil Assignment Law. Although we have already expressed the view that this statute did not have the effect of preventing the commencement and maintenance of this action, the role it might have in the future disposition of the case by the trial court makes it appropriate for us to answer appellant's contention that that court erred in holding it invalid.

Whatever might be the holding as to the validity of an administrative pupil assignment statute containing reasonably certain or ascertainable standards to guide the official conduct of the superintendent of the local school board and to afford the basis for an effective appeal from arbitrary action, Act 556 is not such a statute. The plaintiffs, seeking to assert their right to attend nonsegregated schools as guaranteed them under the Constitution, would be remitted to an administrative official guided by no defined standards in the exercise of his discretion. In such circumstances no number of hearings or appeals would avail them anything because it would be impossible for them to bring forward any proof bearing on whether they possessed those attributes, qualifications, or characteristics that would bring them within the group of students permitted to attend the particular school or schools. Attempts by statute to give any official the power to assign students to schools arbitrarily according to whim or caprice are legally impermissible, especially if considered in light of the history of assignments made in a manner that has now been held to be unconstitutional and of the recently readopted requirement of the state constitution reaffirming such unconstitutional standards, which is reinforced by the heavy sanctions against any official permitting a departure therefrom contained in a companion statute. Such a statute is unconstitutional either because it has on its face the effect of depriving appellees of their liberty or property without due process of law or as having implied as its only basis for assignments the prohibited standard of race. . . .

The orders of the trial court are

Affirmed.

QUESTIONS

1. **The lack of standards to guide the administrative process.**— The court said that "Attempts by statute to give any official the power to assign students to schools arbitrarily according to whim

or caprice are legally impermissible," and found that the Louisiana pupil assignment law was invalid because the administrative officials charged with carrying it out had "no defined standards in the exercise of [their] discretion." The court thus applied one aspect of the so-called "non-delegation" doctrine in administrative law, invalidating an administrative scheme because of the absence of adequate "standards" in the statute delegating powers to the administrative agency. What purposes are served by requiring the legislature to spell out standards for administrators? Consider the function of the school superintendents and school boards under the Louisiana statute. They were to decide which schools individual children were to attend, and rule on requests for transfers. They were performing an adjudicative function, applying legal principles in deciding individual cases. But what were the principles by which the administrators would decide? Presumably the administrative officials would have to declare these principles (*i.e.*, make law) as they adjudicated individual requests for transfer. They might declare general principles in advance—the "rule-making" function of many administrative agencies. One reason thus emerges for requiring standards in a statutory scheme such as the Louisiana pupil assignment law: to impose some limit on the lawmaking powers of administrative agencies in order to maintain a separation of powers among the branches of government. The legislature, as the lawmaking agency most directly responsible to the electorate, it is said, should make basic policy. The delegation of too wide a scope of lawmaking power to an administrative agency violates this principle. We may ask why similar concerns have not led to similar limitations on the lawmaking powers of courts. What differences are there in the administrative and judicial processes which would account for the more expansive lawmaking powers of courts?

The non-delegation doctrine in administrative law does not have much practical significance today. Both federal and state governments abound with agencies that operate under legislative authorization containing standards no more specific than that the agencies perform their lawmaking and law-applying functions so as to advance or protect the "public interest." Apart from the school segregation overtones of the Louisiana statute, would there be sound reason, on separation of powers grounds, to hold invalid a direction by a legislature that school superintendents and school boards develop criteria for assigning children to school as part of their general authority to administer their school systems?

The court in the Louisiana case also suggested a rather different reason for invalidating the statute for lack of standards:

> . . . no number of hearings or appeals would avail them anything because it would be impossible for them to bring forward any proof bearing on whether they possessed those attributes, qualifications, or characteristics that would bring them within the group of students permitted to attend the particular school or schools.

The emphasis here is on protection against arbitrary governmental action. If the administrative official is not required to stay within some defined bounds, a reviewing court has difficulty determining whether his conduct has been arbitrary. Without adequate standards the entire scheme may then be invalid, not on separation of powers grounds but on due process grounds, relating to the possible use by the school administrator of an arbitrary—*i.e.*, constitutionally impermissible—reason for his assignment decisions. But why is not judicial review an adequate protection against arbitrary administrative action? What is wrong, in due process terms, with the legislature's giving an administrative agency extremely broad authority, as long as judicial review is available? Would all due process questions be resolved if the legislature should say that the agency is limited to "non-arbitrary" exercise of its powers?

2. Exhaustion of the plaintiff's administrative remedies.—The defendants argued that the action should have been dismissed because the plaintiffs had not "pursued their administrative remedies for relief before filing of their suit"—*i.e.*, the plaintiffs had not first "exhausted" the remedies available to them under the pupil assignment law: appeal for reconsideration by the superintendent and appeal to the school board, followed by review by the state district court. Why shouldn't the plaintiffs have been required first to go through the administrative process before resorting to the courts? One of the chief reasons for using the administrative process where there are large numbers of individual claims to be adjudicated is to channel those claims away from the courts to a specialized forum, at least until the stage of judicial review of administrative action provided by the statute. But while there are good reasons for the requirement of exhaustion of administrative remedies, both courts and legislatures have recognized that individuals with grievances may themselves be exhausted by an elaborate administrative process. Such a recognition certainly underlay the Louisiana legislature's establishment of the system of administrative appeals in the pupil assignment law. As long as Louisiana law required racial segregation in the public schools, the pupil assignment administrative procedure in fact offered no remedy to correct a racial assignment. Under those circumstances, was not the court correct in concluding that the plaintiffs need not have exhausted their administrative remedies?

3.   The 1958 Louisiana pupil placement law: a more sophisticated use of the administrative process.—In 1958 the Louisiana legislature adopted a pupil placement law designed to remedy the deficiencies in its first attempt. This statute was similar to those in other southern states. There was no overriding requirement that once the pupil placement process was completed children should nevertheless be assigned to schools on the basis of race, and the statute included a lengthy list of factors to be considered in making assignments. Among these assignment criteria were: available facilities and teachers in the various schools; availability of transportation; adequacy of a pupil's academic preparation for admission to the school of his choice; scores on intelligence tests; psychological qualification of a pupil for the type of teaching and associations he would encounter at a specific school; psychological effect on a pupil of attendance at a specific school; effect of admission of a pupil to a specific school upon academic progress of other pupils in that school; possibility of friction or disorder among pupils or others if a pupil should attend a specific school. LSA-R.S. 17:101-10 (1963).

In 1958 there was litigation in Alabama seeking to enjoin public education officials from enforcing a similar Alabama pupil placement procedure. Plaintiffs attacked the constitutionality of the statute "on its face"—*i.e.*, not in the context of how it had actually been applied, but rather on how it might be applied. The three-judge federal district court held for the defendants, saying:

> The plaintiffs would have us conclude without further ado "that the whole intent is to continue the system of separate schools for Negro and white in the State of Alabama." In dealing with an Act of the legislature of a sovereign State, we cannot lightly reach such a conclusion, nor, indeed, are we permitted to do so except upon the most weighty and compelling of reasons.
>
> In testing constitutionality "we cannot undertake a search for motive." "If the State has the power to do an act, its intention or the reason by which it is influenced in doing it

cannot be inquired into." As there is no one corporate mind of the legislature, there is in reality no single motive.

It is possible for the Act to be applied so as to admit qualified Negro pupils to nonsegregated schools. . . . We cannot say, in advance of its application, that the Alabama Law will not be properly and constitutionally administered.
. . .

All that has been said in this present opinion must be limited to the constitutionality of the law *upon its face*. The School Placement Law furnishes the legal machinery for an orderly administration of the public schools in a constitutional manner by the admission of qualified pupils upon a basis of individual merit without regard to their race or color. We must presume that it will be so administered. If not, in some future proceeding it is possible that it may be declared unconstitutional in its application. Shuttlesworth v. Birmingham Board of Education of Jefferson County, Alabama, 162 F. Supp. 372, 381-382, 384 (N.D. Ala. 1958).

The Supreme Court affirmed per curiam, on "the limited grounds on which the District Court rested its decision." 358 U.S. 101 (1958).

The analogous Louisiana statute was attacked in its application in another chapter of *Bush v. Orleans Parish School Board*. The school officials did not use the pupil placement procedure in making initial school assignments; initial assignments were made on the basis of race. Applications of children who wished to transfer to schools other than those to which they had been assigned initially were acted upon under the criteria in the pupil placement law. Thus, in practice, only Negro children sought transfers. If you were counsel for the Orleans Parish School Board, what argument would you have made that initial racial assignments followed by opportunity to transfer in accordance with arguably non-racial pupil placement criteria were compatible with the equal protection clause? If you were counsel for the plaintiffs, what would have been your argument that this scheme violated the equal protection clause? The Court of Appeals for the Fifth Circuit held that it was unconstitutional to use the pupil placement law in this manner. Bush v. Orleans Parish School Board, 308 F.2d 491 (5th Cir. 1962).

Without initial racial assignments, pupil placement laws did not provide an effective means of maintaining racial segregation. They were too cumbersome, in any event, to be seriously applied in making initial assignments of all children.

See Note, *The Federal Courts and Integration of Southern Schools: Troubled Status of the Pupil Placement Acts*, 62 COLUM. L. REV. 1448 (1962).

4. The issues raised in paragraphs 1 and 2, *supra*, are considered in the course on administrative law.

B. CLOSING THE PUBLIC SCHOOLS

Some state legislatures, in response to *Brown*, authorized the closing of public schools in districts where desegregation was imminent—an "experiment with ignorance," as one federal court characterized the action.[4] With public schools closed in one district but operating elsewhere in the state, a new dimension was added to the constitutional issue of equality of educational opportunity. The constitutional question now related to inter- rather than intra-district differences in the treatment of children. As we shall see in Chapter 4, issues of inter-district equality of educational opportunity have taken on great current significance in the north and the west.

GRIFFIN v. COUNTY SCHOOL BOARD OF PRINCE EDWARD COUNTY
Supreme Court of the United States
377 U.S. 218 (1964)

Mr. Justice BLACK delivered the opinion of the Court.

This litigation began in 1951 when a group of Negro school children living in Prince Edward County, Virginia, filed a complaint in the United States District Court for the Eastern District of Virginia alleging that they had been denied admission to public schools attended by white children and charging that Virginia laws requiring such school segregation denied complainants the equal protection of the laws in violation of the Fourteenth Amendment. On May 17, 1954, ten years ago, we held that the Virginia segregation laws did deny equal protection. . . . On May 31, 1955, after reargument on the nature of relief, we remanded this case, along with others heard with it, to the District Courts to enter such orders as "necessary and proper to admit [complainants] to public schools on a racially nondiscriminatory basis with all deliberate speed. . . ." Brown v. Board of Education. . . .

---

[4] Hall v. St. Helena Parish School Bd., 197 F. Supp. 649, 659 (E.D. La. 1961), *aff'd*, 368 U.S. 515 (1962).

Efforts to desegregate Prince Edward County's schools met with resistance. In 1956 Section 141 of the Virginia Constitution was amended to authorize the General Assembly and local governing bodies to appropriate funds to assist students to go to public or to nonsectarian private schools, in addition to those owned by the State or by the locality. The General Assembly met in special session and enacted legislation to close any public schools where white and colored children were enrolled together, to cut off state funds to such schools, to pay tuition grants to children in nonsectarian private schools, and to extend state retirement benefits to teachers in newly created private schools.[5] The legislation closing mixed schools and cutting off state funds was later invalidated by the Supreme Court of Appeals of Virginia, which held that these laws violated the Virginia Constitution. *Harrison v. Day,* 200 Va. 439, 106 S.E.2d 636 (1959). In April 1959 the General Assembly abandoned "massive resistance" to desegregation and turned instead to what was called a "freedom of choice" program. The Assembly repealed the rest of the 1956 legislation, as well as a tuition grant law of January 1959, and enacted a new tuition grant program. At the same time the Assembly repealed Virginia's compulsory attendance laws and instead made school attendance a matter of local option.

In June 1959, the United States Court of Appeals for the Fourth Circuit directed the Federal District Court (1) to enjoin discriminatory practices in Prince Edward County schools, (2) to require the County School Board to take "immediate steps" toward admitting students without regard to race to the white high school "in the school term beginning September 1959," and (3) to require the Board to make plans for admissions to elementary schools without regard to race. *Allen v. County School Board of Prince Edward County,* 266 F.2d 507, 511 (C.A. 4th Cir. 1959). Having as early as 1956 resolved that they would not operate public schools "wherein white and colored children are taught together," the Supervisors of Prince Edward County refused to levy any school taxes for the 1959-1960 school year, explaining that they were "confronted with a court decree which requires the admission of white and colored children to all the schools of the county without regard to race or color." As a result, the county's public schools did not reopen in the fall of 1959 and have remained closed ever since, although the public

---

[5] This legislative package, together with legislation directed against the activities of the NAACP, constituted Virginia's program of "massive resistance" to *Brown v. Board of Education.* See NAACP v. Patty, 159 F. Supp. 503, 511-15 (E.D. Va. 1958). The attack on the NAACP is considered in section E of this chapter, *infra.* [*Eds.* note.]

schools of every other county in Virginia have continued to operate under laws governing the State's public school system and to draw funds provided by the State for that purpose. A private group, the Prince Edward School Foundation, was formed to operate private schools for white children in Prince Edward County and, having built its own school plant, has been in operation ever since the closing of the public schools. An offer to set up private schools for colored children in the county was rejected, the Negroes of Prince Edward preferring to continue the legal battle for desegregated public schools, and colored children were without formal education from 1959 to 1963, when federal, state, and county authorities cooperated to have classes conducted for Negroes and whites in school buildings owned by the county. During the 1959-1960 school year the Foundation's schools for white children were supported entirely by private contributions, but in 1960 the General Assembly adopted a new tuition grant program making every child, regardless of race, eligible for tuition grants of $125 or $150 to attend a nonsectarian private school or a public school outside his locality, and also authorizing localities to provide their own grants. The Prince Edward Board of Supervisors then passed an ordinance providing tuition grants of $100, so that each child attending the Prince Edward School Foundation's schools received a total of $225 if in elementary school or $250 if in high school. In the 1960-1961 session the major source of financial support for the Foundation was in the indirect form of these state and county tuition grants, paid to children attending Foundation schools. At the same time, the County Board of Supervisors passed an ordinance allowing property tax credits up to 25% for contributions to any "nonprofit, nonsectarian private school" in the county.

In 1961 petitioners here filed a supplemental complaint, adding new parties and seeking to enjoin the respondents from refusing to operate an efficient system of public free schools in Prince Edward County and to enjoin payment of public funds to help support private schools which excluded students on account of race. The District Court, finding that "the end result of every action taken by that body [Board of Supervisors] was designed to preserve separation of the races in the schools of Prince Edward County," enjoined the county from paying tuition grants or giving tax credits so long as public schools remained closed. *Allen v. County School Board of Prince Edward County*, 198 F. Supp. 497, 503 (D.C.E.D. Va. 1961). At this time the District Court did not pass on whether the public schools of the county could be closed but abstained pending determination by the Virginia courts of whether the constitution and laws of Virginia required the public schools to be kept open. Later, however, without waiting for the Virginia courts to decide the question, the District Court held that "the public schools of Prince Edward County may not be closed to avoid the effect of the law of the land as interpreted by the Supreme Court, while the Commonwealth of Virginia permits other public schools to remain open at the expense of the taxpayers." *Allen v. County School Board of Prince Edward County*, 207 F. Supp. 349, 355 (D.C.E.D. Va. 1962). Soon thereafter, a declaratory judgment suit was brought by the County Board of Supervisors and the County School Board in a Virginia Circuit Court. Having done this, these parties asked the Federal District Court to abstain from further proceedings until the suit in the state courts had run its course, but the District Court declined; it repeated its order that Prince Edward's public schools might not be closed to avoid desegregation while the other public schools in Virginia remained open. The Court of Appeals reversed, Judge Bell dissenting, holding that the District Court should have abstained to await state court determination of the validity of the tuition grants and the tax credits, as well as the validity of the closing of the public schools. *Griffin v. Board of Supervisors of Prince Edward County*, 322 F.2d 332 (C.A. 4th Cir. 1963). We granted certiorari, stating:

"In view of the long delay in the case since our decision in the *Brown* case and the importance of the questions presented, we grant certiorari and put the case down for argument March 30, 1964, on the merits, as we have done in other comparable situations without waiting for final action by the Court of Appeals." 375 U.S. 391, 392.

For reasons to be stated, we agree with the District Court that, under the circumstances here, closing the Prince Edward County schools while public schools in all the other counties of Virginia were being maintained denied the petitioners and the class of Negro students they represent the equal protection of the laws guaranteed by the Fourteenth Amendment. . . .

II.

In *County School Board of Prince Edward County v. Griffin*, 204 Va. 650, 133 S.E.2d 565 (1963), the Supreme Court of Appeals of Virginia upheld as valid under state law the closing of the Prince Edward County public schools, the state and county tuition grants for children who attend private schools, and the county's tax concessions for those who make contributions to private schools. The same opinion also held that each county had "an option to operate or not to operate public schools." 204 Va., at 671, 133 S.E.2d, at 580. We accept this case as a definitive and authoritative holding of Virginia law, binding on us, but we cannot accept the Virginia court's further holding, based largely on the Court of Appeals' opinion in this case, 322 F.2d 332, that closing the county's public schools under the circumstances of the case did not deny the colored school children of Prince Edward County equal protection of the laws guaranteed by the Federal Constitution.

Since 1959, all Virginia counties have had the benefits of public schools but one: Prince Edward. However, there is no rule that counties, as counties, must be treated alike; the Equal Protection Clause relates to equal protection of the laws "between persons as such rather than between areas." *Salsburg v. Maryland,* 346 U.S. 545, 551 (1954). Indeed, showing that different persons are treated differently is not enough, without more, to show a denial of equal protection. *Kotch v. Board of River Port Comm'rs,* 330 U.S. 552, 556 (1947). It is the circumstances of each case which govern. *Skinner v. Oklahoma ex rel. Williamson,* 316 U.S. 535, 539-540 (1942).

Virginia law, as here applied, unquestionably treats the school children of Prince Edward differently from the way it treats the school children of all other Virginia counties. Prince Edward children must go to a private school or none at all; all other Virginia children can go to public schools. Closing Prince Edward's schools bears more heavily on Negro children in Prince Edward County since white children there have accredited private schools which they can attend, while colored children until very recently have had no available private schools, and even the school they now attend is a temporary expedient. Apart from this expedient, the result is that Prince Edward County school children, if they go to school in their own county, must go to racially segregated schools which, although designated as private, are beneficiaries of county and state support.

A State, of course, has a wide discretion in deciding whether laws shall operate statewide or shall operate only in certain counties, the legislature "having in mind the needs and desires of each." *Salsburg v. Maryland, supra,* 346 U.S., at 552. A State may wish to suggest, as Maryland did in *Salsburg,* that there are reasons why one county ought not to be treated like another. 346 U.S., at 553-554. But the record in the present case could not be clearer that Prince Edward's public schools were closed and private schools operated in their place with state and county assistance, for one reason, and one reason only: to ensure, through measures taken by the county and the State, that white and colored children in Prince Edward County would not, under any circumstances, go to the same school. Whatever nonracial grounds might support a State's allowing a county to abandon public schools, the object must be a constitutional one, and grounds of race and opposition to desegregation do not qualify as constitutional.

In *Hall v. St. Helena Parish School Board*, 197 F. Supp. 649 (D.C.E.D. La. 1961), a three-judge District Court invalidated a Louisiana statute which provided "a means by which public schools under desegregation orders may be changed to 'private' schools operated in the same way, in the same buildings, with the same furnishings, with the same money, and under the same supervision as the public schools." *Id.*, at 651. In addition, that statute also provided that where the public schools were "closed," the school board was "charged with responsibility for furnishing free lunches, transportation, and grants-in-aid to the children attending the 'private' schools." *Ibid.* We affirmed the District Court's judgment invalidating the Louisiana statute as a denial of equal protection. 368 U.S. 515 (1962). While the Louisiana plan and the Virginia plan worked in different ways, it is plain that both were created to accomplish the same thing: the perpetuation of racial segregation by closing public schools and operating only segregated schools supported directly or indirectly by state or county funds. See *Cooper v. Aaron*, 358 U.S. 1, 17 (1958). Either plan works to deny colored students equal protection of the laws. Accordingly, we agree with the District Court that closing the Prince Edward schools and meanwhile contributing to the support of the private segregated white schools that took their place denied petitioners the equal protection of the laws.

III.

We come now to the question of the kind of decree necessary and appropriate to put an end to the racial discrimination practiced against these petitioners under authority of the Virginia laws. That relief needs to be quick and effective. The parties defendant are the Board of Supervisors, School Board, Treasurer, and Division Superintendent of Schools of Prince Edward County, and the State Board of Education and the State Superintendent of Education. All of these have duties which relate directly or indirectly to the financing, supervision, or operation of the schools in Prince Edward County. The Board of Supervisors has the special responsibility to levy local taxes to operate public schools or to aid children attending the private schools now functioning there for white children. The District Court enjoined the county officials from paying county tuition grants or giving tax exemptions and from processing applications for state tuition grants so long as the county's public schools remained closed. We have no doubt of the power of the court to give this relief to enforce the discontinuance of the county's racially discriminatory practices. It has long been established that actions against a county can be maintained in United States courts in order to vindicate federally guaranteed rights. . . . The injunction against paying tuition grants and giving tax credits while public schools remain closed is appropriate and necessary since those grants and tax credits have been essential parts of the county's program, successful thus far, to deprive petitioners of the same advantages of a public school education enjoyed by children in every other part of Virginia. For the same reasons the District Court may, if necessary to prevent further racial discrimination, require the Supervisors to exercise the power that is theirs to levy taxes to raise funds adequate to reopen, operate, and maintain without racial discrimination a public school system in Prince Edward County like that operated in other counties in Virginia.

The District Court held that "the public schools of Prince Edward County may not be closed to avoid the effect of the law of the land as interpreted by the Supreme Court, while the Commonwealth of Virginia permits other public schools to remain open at the expense of the taxpayers." *Allen v. County School Board of Prince Edward County*, 207 F. Supp. 349, 355 (D.C.E.D. Va. 1962). At the same time the court gave notice that it would later consider an order to accomplish this purpose if the public schools were not reopened by September 7, 1962. That day has long passed, and the schools are still closed. On remand, therefore, the court may find it necessary to consider further such an order. An order of this kind is within the court's power if required to assure these petitioners that their constitutional rights will no longer be denied them. The time for mere "deliberate speed" has run out, and that phrase can no longer justify denying these Prince Edward County school children their constitutional rights to an education equal to that afforded by the public schools in the other parts of Virginia.

The judgment of the Court of Appeals is reversed, the judgment of the District Court is affirmed, and the cause is remanded to the District Court with directions to enter a decree which will guarantee that these petitioners will get the kind of education that is given in the State's public schools. And, if it becomes necessary to add new parties to accomplish this end, the District Court is free to do so.

It is so ordered.

Mr. Justice CLARK and Mr. Justice HARLAN disagree with the holding that the federal courts are empowered to order the reopening of the public schools in Prince Edward County, but otherwise join in the Court's opinion.

QUESTIONS

1. Inter-district inequalities in public education.—Mr. Justice Black's opinion said: "Whatever nonracial grounds might support a State's allowing a county to abandon public schools, the object must be a constitutional one, and grounds of race and opposition to desegregation do not qualify as constitutional." Can you think of any "nonracial grounds" that would "support a State's allowing a county to abandon public schools"? For example, suppose a majority of the electorate in an all-white school district, faced with rising taxes, were to vote, as permitted by state law, to stop levying taxes for public education and to close the district's schools. How should the case be approached under the equal protection clause? What should the decision be? A current variation on this issue, involving not school closing but the quality of educational offerings, is raised by the fact that expenditures per pupil vary widely from school district to school district within a given state, largely because of variances in districts' property tax bases. This issue will be explored in Chapter 4. What result, and based on what reasoning, would Mr. Justice Black likely have reached if the plaintiffs in *Griffin* had been white children, complaining about their lack of opportunity to attend public schools?

2. The courts' power to order the reopening of schools and the levying of taxes.—The Court said that in fashioning its decree the district court could, if necessary, "require the Supervisors to exercise the power that is theirs to levy taxes to raise funds adequate to" reopen and operate the public schools in Prince Edward County, and could, if necessary, order the reopening of the schools. Justices Clark and Harlan noted their disagreement "with the holding that the federal courts are empowered to order the reopening of the schools in Prince Edward County. . . ." Professor Philip Kurland commented on this aspect of the Court's opinion in *Griffin*: "The case represents one of the many factual situations that compels the Court to resort to unbecoming and unfortunate methods for assuring that its will be done."[6] Why is an order that the tax-levying authorities levy taxes and the school-administering authorities reopen and operate schools "unbecoming and unfortunate," or beyond the court's power? Do these comments rest on conceptions of the role of the courts in the legal system? What might those conceptions be? Do the comments rest on conceptions of the nature of the federal system? Was there an appropriate alternative disposition of *Griffin* which would have met the objections of Justices Clark and Harlan and of Professor Kurland? What would that disposition be?

3. Some subsequent history in Prince Edward County.—After the Supreme Court's decision the trial judge ordered the county officials to appropriate such funds "as are reasonably necessary for the opening and maintenance of the public schools on a nondiscriminatory basis." The Board of Supervisors appropriated $189,000 for public schools (anticipating enrollment of 1600 Negro children) and $375,000 in tuition grants for 1600 white children in private schools. The Court of Appeals for the Fourth Circuit in 1964 enjoined payment of tuition grants for children who attended segregated private schools. Griffin v. County School Board of Prince Edward County, 339 F.2d 486 (4th Cir. 1964). (The Supreme Court had held that plaintiffs were entitled to have the court enjoin payment of tuition grants while the public schools were closed. The later decision of the Court of Appeals dealt with tuition grants after the public schools had been reopened. The validity of tuition grants for attendance at private segregated schools while public schools are operating is discussed in the next section of this chapter.)

A report in the spring of 1968 on elementary and secondary education in Prince Edward County stated that at that time there were 1600 students (all but eight of whom were black) in the public schools, and 1200 white students in the private Prince Edward Academy. The Academy was then charging $340 per year elementary school tuition and $365 high school tuition. With state tuition grants no longer being paid, there were 200 white children who were not financially able to attend the private school and who did not attend the public schools. Hotel, motion picture, and restaurant facilities in Farmville, where the schools are located, had been desegregated, following the enactment of the Civil Rights Act of 1964, "because they need the

---

[6] Kurland, *Foreword: "Equal in Origin and Equal in Title to the Legislative and Executive Branches of the Government,"* 78 HARV. L. REV. 143, 158 (1964).

money of Negro customers." Jacoby, *Prince Edward County: Back Where They Started*, Washington Post, March 24, 1968, *Potomac*, p. 22.

Events leading up to the filing of the original desegregation suit in Prince Edward County and the closing of the schools are recounted in B. SMITH, THEY CLOSED THEIR SCHOOLS (1965).

C. TUITION GRANTS

An integral part of patterns of resistance to *Brown* was the effort to move to "private" schools which would be racially segregated and arguably beyond the reach of the Fourteenth Amendment, while also maintaining "desegregated" public schools. The history of this effort in Louisiana, and the judicial response, are set forth in the following opinion.

POINDEXTER v. LOUISIANA FINANCIAL ASSISTANCE COMMISSION
United States District Court, Eastern District of Louisiana
275 F. Supp. 833 (1967)
aff'd per curiam, 389 U.S. 571 (1968)

Before WISDOM and AINSWORTH, Circuit Judges, and CHRISTENBERRY, District Judge.

WISDOM, Circuit Judge:

This class action by Negro schoolchildren and their parents against the Louisiana Financial Assistance Commission and others attacks the constitutionality of Act 147 of 1962. Under that law the Commission administers a program of tuition grants to pupils attending private schools in Louisiana. The United States intervened as a party plaintiff; directors of four private schools for Negro retarded children intervened as parties defendant. . . .

The free lunches and textbooks Louisiana provides for all its school children are the fruits of racially neutral benevolence. Tuition grants are not the products of such a policy. They are the fruits of the State's traditional racially biased policy of providing segregated schools for white pupils. Here that policy has pushed the State to the extreme of using public funds to aid private discrimination endangering the public school system and equal educational opportunities for Negroes in Louisiana.

As certainly as "12" is the next number of a series starting 2, 4, 6, 8, 10, Act 147 fitted into the long series of statutes the Louisiana legislature enacted for over a hundred years to maintain segregated schools for white children. After the Supreme Court's 1954 decision in the School Segregation Cases, the legislature rapidly expanded the series. As fast as the courts knocked out one school law, the legislature enacted another. Each of these laws, whether its objective was obvious or nonobvious, was designed to provide a state-supported sanctuary for white children in flight from desegregated public schools.

Act 147 of 1962 is unconstitutional. The purpose and natural or reasonable effect of this law are to continue segregated education in Louisiana by providing state funds for the establishment and support of segregated, privately operated schools for white children. The United States Constitution does not permit the State to perform acts indirectly through private persons which it is forbidden to do directly. The evidence before the Court shows that the tuition grants have supplied a heavy predominance of funds needed to establish and maintain post-1954 and especially post-1962 private segregated schools. The Commission's recent decision to reduce its aid to less than 50 per cent of the funds required for operating a school fails to take the curse off the Act. Any affirmative and purposeful state aid promoting private discrimination violates the equal protection clause. There is no such thing as the State's legitimately being just a little bit discriminatory.

I.
The Statute

Act 147 of 1962 (LSA-R.S. 17:2951-17:2953) authorizes state tuition grants for children attending "private non-sectarian elementary or secondary schools" in Louisiana. The statute creates the Louisiana Financial Assistance Commission to administer the program. The Commission is composed of three members appointed by the governor. Payments are "by check to the parent or guardian of, or the person standing in loco parentis to, the applicant." The statute is tied in with the public school system in the sense that to receive a grant, the applicants must be "eligible . . . for admission to elementary or secondary schools within the public school system of the state." Applicants must furnish "satisfactory evidence of admissibility to a private non-sectarian . . . school . . . legally constituted and operated under constitution and laws of the state." As thus far administered, each grant amounts to two dollars a day based on an assumed school term of 180 days, or $360, but limited to an amount not to exceed the tuition obligation actually incurred by the applicant.
. . .

II.
Purpose and Motive

We are not unmindful of the distinction courts draw between "purpose" and "motive." We accept the first Justice Harlan's statement, quoted by the defendants: "In a legal sense the object or purpose of legislation is to be determined by its natural and reasonable effect, whatever may have been the motive of the legislature."

Recognition of the distinction between purpose and motive does not prohibit courts from looking beyond the face of the statute. As we said in Hall v. St. Helena, E.D. La. 1961, 197 F. Supp. 649, aff'd 368 U.S. 515, 82 S. Ct. 529, 7 L. Ed. 2d 521, in holding unconstitutional an earlier version of Louisiana's grant-in-aid system:

> Irrespective of the terms of a statute, particularly in the area of racial discrimination, courts must determine its purpose as well as its substance and effect. . . . "[A]cts generally lawful may become unlawful when done to accomplish an unlawful end." Western Union Tel. Co. v. Foster, 247 U.S. 105, 115, 38 S. Ct. 438, 62 L. Ed. 1006. . . .

III.
The Purpose as Shown in the History
and Present Setting of Act 147

We consider first the purpose of Act 147, "in the light of its history and present setting." . . .

. . . The Constitution of 1870 was adopted when the Reconstruction period in Louisiana was far from being over, but in effect the Constitution gave its blessing to the dual system of segregated schools. . . . "By 1877 separate schools had been established for the two races and in that year there were 54,390 pupils in attendance in the public schools, while the number capable of enrollment was 266,033." In 1898, Louisiana, along with other southern states, for the first time specifically adopted Jim Crow provisions. Article 248 of the Constitution of 1898 provided for "free public schools for the white and colored races, separately established." The Constitution of 1913 and the present Constitution of 1921 carried forward similar language.

In 1954, a few months after the Supreme Court decided the first *Brown* case desegregating public schools, Louisiana amended Article XII, Section 1 of the Constitution of 1921. This amendment expressed the state policy on segregated schools:

"All public elementary and secondary schools in the State of Louisiana shall be operated separately for white and colored children. This provision is made in the exercise of the state police power to promote and protect public health, morals, better education and the peace and good order in the State, and not because of race. The Legislature shall enact laws to enforce the state police power in this regard."

The Legislature promptly enacted Acts No. 555 and 556 of 1954. Act 555 carried out the constitutional requirement of separate schools and provided penalties for failing to observe it. Act 556 provided for the assignment to a school of each pupil each year by the superintendent of schools of the district in which the pupil lived. In February 1956 this Court held that both the amendment to Article XII Section 1 and the two statutes were invalid, and enjoined the Orleans Parish School Board from requiring and permitting segregation in the parish public schools. Bush v. Orleans Parish School Board, E.D. La. 1956, 138 F. Supp. 337, aff'd 242 F.2d 156, cert. denied 354 U.S. 921, 77 S. Ct. 1380, 1 L. Ed. 2d 1436.

The Louisiana Legislature immediately enacted a new package of laws. Act 319 of 1956 purported to "freeze" the existing racial status of the public schools in Orleans Parish and to reserve to the legislature the power of racial reclassification of the schools. The Court declared this "legal artifice" unconstitutional on its face. Bush v. Orleans Parish School Board, E.D. La. 1958, 163 F. Supp. 701, aff'd 5 Cir., 268 F.2d 78.

In 1958 the legislature enacted another bundle of school laws. Professor Charles A. Reynard of Louisiana State University has described these as follows:

> Adhering to its steadfast course of circumventing the Supreme Court's decisions forbidding the enforced segregation of the races in public education, the Legislature took steps to provide for the closing of public schools threatened with desegregation and authorized a system of publicly financed private education in lieu thereof. A pupil assignment law, applicable to the public schools, was also adopted. These measures were designed to fill the void created by the decisions of the federal courts invalidating acts adopted at the 1956 session, . . . which, in turn had been adopted to replace legislation passed in 1954, declared unconstitutional by the courts. Reynard, Legislative Symposium: Segregation, 19 La. L. Rev. 114 (1958).

Act 257 provided in detail for the establishment of educational cooperatives. Act 258 established the first Louisiana system of grants-in-aid for "children attending non-sectarian non-public schools." Its purpose was obvious: The aid was conditioned on there being "no racially separate public school" in the parish. The grant system was to be administered jointly by the State Board of Education and the parish or city school boards.

By 1959 it was apparent to all that the Orleans Parish School Board could not take independent action to carry out the Court's order of February 15, 1956, requiring it to desegregate public schools in New Orleans. July 15, 1959, therefore, the Court ordered the Board to file a desegregation plan by March 1, 1960. Later, the Court extended the deadline to May 16, 1960. When the Board failed to file a plan, the Court, on May 16, 1960, entered an order setting forth a plan of desegregation for the Orleans Parish School Board to follow. The plan called for the desegregation of the first grade in September 1960.

The Louisiana Legislature promptly built additional barricades. Act 333 of 1960 prohibited the furnishing of free books, school supplies, school funds or assistance to integrated schools. Act 495 authorized the Governor to close integrated schools. Act 496 purported to "freeze" the racial classification of public schools and reserve to the Legislature the power to change this classification. Act 542 authorized the Governor to close the public schools in case of riots and disorder.

The tempo of resistance increased. July 29, 1960, the Attorney General of Louisiana obtained an injunction in the state courts restraining the Orleans Parish School Board from desegregating its schools. August 17, 1960, the Governor of Louisiana, acting under Act 495 of 1960, took over control of the Orleans public schools. August 27, 1960, a three-judge district court struck down these actions along with Acts 333, 495, 496, and 542 of 1960, Act 555 of 1964, Act 319 of 1956, and Act 256 of 1958. Bush v. Orleans Parish School Board, E.D. La. 1960, 187 F. Supp. 42.

At this point, the Orleans School Board conferred with the district court. In public session the Board adopted a grade-a-year plan, postponed to November 14, 1960, and announced its intention to comply with the Court's orders.

The Board's compliance brought on five extraordinary sessions of the legislature within four months. Among other actions, the Legislature seized the funds of the Orleans Parish School Board; forbade banks to lend money to this Board; removed as fiscal agent for the state the Bank which honored payroll checks issued by the Orleans Board; ordered a school holiday on November 14,

1960; discharged four of the five Orleans Board members; later repealed the Act creating the Board, then twice created a new School Board for Orleans Parish; and still later discharged the Superintendent, dismissed the Board's attorney, and attempted to require that the State Attorney General be counsel for the Board. The courts declared these and other related acts unconstitutional. Bush v. Orleans Parish School Board, E.D. La., Nov. 30, 1960, 188 F. Supp. 916; Bush v. Orleans Parish School Board, E.D. La., March 3, 1961, 191 F. Supp. 871; and Bush v. Orleans Parish School Board, E.D. La., May 4, 1961, 194 F. Supp. 182.

Act 3 of the Second Extraordinary Session of 1960 was the Legislature's second version of grants in aid. This law differs from Act 258 of 1958, which it repealed, in two respects. First, the legislature did away with the provision that availability of tuition grants was dependent on the integration of the public schools in the parish. Second, it restricted grants to non-profit schools. The administration of the grant system continued to be the joint responsibility of the State Board of Education and the parish or city school boards. On the day the Senate passed Act 3, State Senator E. W. Gravolet described the bill as designed to "dove-tail" with Act 257 of 1958, which authorized educational cooperatives, and commented that the grant-in-aid principle had been used successfully for a private school system in Prince Edward County, Virginia. At a meeting of the White Citizen's Council in New Orleans on December 15, 1960, the Secretary of State of Louisiana, Wade O. Martin, predicted that Louisiana would go from public to private schools so that every child would have a check or money to go to the school of his choice; the white schools would accept white students, and the "black schools" would accept Negro students. In the Louisiana House of Representatives, December 21, 1960, Representative Triche of Assumption Parish argued that the grant-in-aid system was the most effective weapon against the integration of public schools and that the tax was needed to continue the fight for a segregated school system in Louisiana.

In 1961 the Court of Appeals for the Fifth Circuit affirmed orders requiring the desegregation of public schools in East Baton Rouge and St. Helena Parishes. On the same day the Governor of Louisiana called the Second Extraordinary Session of the Legislature for 1961. He certified as emergency legislation what became Act 2 of that session. Act 2 masqueraded as a local option law. It gave each parish or municipal school board the "option" to close its schools if a majority of the qualified voters in the parish or municipality voted in favor of such action. The school board was then authorized to dispose of its property for such consideration as it deemed appropriate. Act 257 of 1958 had created educational cooperatives which could acquire the property and then operate schools with the state money furnished by the grant-in-aid program provided for in Act 3 of the Second Extraordinary Session of 1960. In Hall v. St. Helena the Court characterized the option for a poor parish such as St. Helena as an option to attend segregated schools—or no schools. 197 F. Supp. 649, aff'd per curiam, 368 U.S. 515, 82 S. Ct. 529, 7 L. Ed. 2d 521.

Act 9 of the 1961 Second Extraordinary Session of 1961 transferred $2,500,000 from the Public Welfare Fund to the Education Expense Grant Fund for grant-in-aid use. Act 10 of the same session transferred $200,000 monthly from the sales tax collections to the same fund for the same purpose.

In Hall v. St. Helena Parish School Board, E.D. La. 1961, 197 F. Supp. 649, aff'd per curiam, 368 U.S. 515, 82 S. Ct. 529, holding the grants in aid unconstitutional, the Court stated:

> Under Act 3 . . . the parish school boards would continue to supervise the "private" schools, under the State Board of Education, by administering the grant-in-aid program of tuition grants payable from state and local funds. . . .
>
> This analysis of Act 2 and related legislation makes it clear that when the Legislature integrated Act 2 with its companion measures, especially the "private" school acts, as part of a single carefully constructed design, constitutionally the design was self-defeating. Of necessity, the scheme requires such extensive state control, financial aid, and active participation that in operating the program the state would still be providing public education. [The state would not be doing business at the old stand, but the state would participate as the senior and not silent partner in the same sort of business.] The continuance of segregation at the state's public-private schools, therefore, is a violation of the equal protection clause.

This brings us to the 1962 session. First, the legislature repealed outright the state's compulsory school attendance law, Act 128. (Two years before, in Act 28 of 1956, the law was made inapplicable in a parish where the public school system had been ordered to integrate.) Act 342 of 1962 appropriated funds for the schools of St. Bernard Parish to compensate for expenses incurred in providing facilities for pupils who were not residents of St. Bernard; most of these were white students who had left the desegregated schools in neighboring Orleans Parish. Act 67 of 1962 purported to restrict the right to sue parish school boards, except by authorization of the Legislature.

This was the background and setting when the Louisiana Legislature enacted the statute under attack in this case. The Act transfers administration of tuition grants from the Board of Education to the Louisiana Financial Assistance Commission, provides that tuition grants be made directly to the parent rather than to the parent and school jointly and, to attract entrepreneurs, waives the requirement that schools attended by students receiving tuition grants be non-profit organizations. In all other significant respects Act 147 is substantially identical with the 1960 tuition grants statute. . . .

Thus, for a hundred years, the Louisiana legislature has not deviated from its objective of maintaining segregated schools for white children. Ten years after *Brown*, declared policy became undeclared policy. Open legislative defiance of desegregation orders shifted to subtle forms of circumvention—although some prominent sponsors of grant-in-aid legislation have been less than subtle in their public expression. But the changes in means reflect no change in legislative ends.

IV.
Effect of Act 147

The problem of fairly ascertaining the effect of a statute becomes complicated when the degree of a state's involvement in private discrimination is nonobvious. In Burton v. Wilmington Parking Authority, 1961, 365 U.S. 715, 81 S. Ct. 856, 6 L. Ed. 2d 45, the Supreme Court observed, "Only by sifting facts and weighing circumstances can the nonobvious involvement of the State in private conduct be attributed its true significance." 365 U.S. at 722, 81 S. Ct. at 860.

In our earlier opinion in this case we held that "any amount of state support to help found segregated schools or to help maintain such schools is sufficient to give standing to Negro school children to file the kind of complaint filed in this case." 258 F. Supp. at 164. We concluded, however, largely because of *Burton*:

"This case should be decided after a full trial on the facts. The extent to which the tuition grants contributed to the founding of the quasi-public schools, in dollars and as a stimulus, the extent to which the grants now contribute to the support of the quasi-public schools, the extent of state involvement and control, and other factors relevant to state action can be determined only by a trial on the merits."

The inevitable effect of the tuition grants was the establishment and maintenance of a state-supported system of segregated schools for white children, making the state a party to organized private discrimination.

A. There are 67 school districts in Louisiana, 15 of which were not, at the opening of the 1966-67 school year, under court order to desegregate. There are 79 private, nonsectarian schools in nine school districts. . . . Of the 79 schools, 62 are for normal children: 60 for white pupils, two for Negro pupils. Each of these schools is segregated.

Before 1954 there were 16 private schools in the state, all but one located within the New Orleans Metropolitan area. After 1954 but before enactment of the 1960 tuition grant statute, nine additional schools were started. Between enactment of the 1960 law and enactment of Act 147 in July 1962, eight more private schools came into being. Between the enactment of Act 147 and the time of the trial of this case, 36 additional schools for white children began operation. Thus 44 of the 60 private schools for white children were formed after the first desegregation of public schools in 1960.

B. (1) The amounts the newly organized schools charge for tuition show that these schools could not have come into existence and could not have continued to exist without the state's grants in aid. This inference finds especially strong support in the tuition charged by post-1962 schools. The Commission set tuition grants at two dollars a school day for each recipient, or $360 on an assumed school year of 180 days. . . . [Here the court includes a table showing "the close correlation between the amount of the grant and the amount the schools charged for tuition."] . . .

C. The . . . state is becoming increasingly involved in supporting private segregated schools. The total number of recipients of tuition grants has increased from 7,093 in 1962-63 to 15,177 in 1966-67. As noted earlier, Act 147 initially authorized the monthly transfer of $200,000 from the education expense grant fund (Act 10, 2nd Extraordinary Session of 1961, LSA-R.S. 47-318), supported by sales tax deductions, to a fund to be administered by the Commission. In the 1963 fiscal session the legislature increased this amount to $300,000 a month.

D. The directors and principals of thirty-two private schools were deposed and questioned about their admissions policy. All but six were equivocal in their statements. The statements of many of these principals that they maintained no policy as to the admission of Negroes must come as a surprise and shock to the parents who have children attending these schools. We find such statements incredible. . . .

G. In effect the state has established a second system of schools, competitive with the public school system. The public schools no doubt will survive such competition, but only after sustaining severe damage detrimental to the system and to students attending public schools. For example, of the 345 teachers in private schools organized since 1962, 139 teachers or 35% came from the public schools.

There are 5,187 white children in pre-1954 private schools. 3,483 receive grants although many attend expensive, fashionable, endowed schools, such as the Louise McGehee School for Girls, Newman School, and Metairie Park Country Day School.

There are 4,029 students attending private schools formed between 1954 and enactment of Act 147; 3,336 receive grants. Attending schools formed after enactment of Act 147 are 7,376 white children, of whom 6,874 receive grants; 386 Negro children, of whom 366 receive grants. In the seven districts where private schools were formed after 1962, there are 244,158 students enrolled in the public schools; 7,762 students enrolled in the private schools, of whom 7,240 receive grants. *It is a fair inference that these substantial numbers of white students at private schools represent only a small fraction of the number that will enroll in such schools, should the courts bless the state tuition grant program.*

In brief, the evidence produced in court of the actual effect of Act 147 substantiates the view of the purpose and the natural or reasonable effect of the law to be inferred from an understanding of Act 147 in its historical context and legislative setting. The tuition grants authorized under the Act provided the funds indispensable to establishing newly organized private segregated schools for white children. The tuition grants continue to furnish almost all of the funds needed for maintaining these post-Brown schools. What Hall v. St. Helena forbade the State to do directly, it has attempted to accomplish indirectly. The tuition grants damage Negroes by draining students, teachers, and funds from the desegregated public school system into a competitive, segregated "quasi-public" school system. The stamp of State approval of "white" schools perpetuates the open humiliation of the Negro implicit in segregated education.

V.
The Defendants' Authorities . . . .

The defendants insist that Act 147 stands alone, and that it is constitutional on its face and as applied.

A. Defendants' counsel resort to history, going back to colonial times, to trace the record of public assistance to private schools. But as we noted in our discussion of the statutory purpose (Section II of this opinion), the overriding constitutional principle here is that "acts generally lawful may become unlawful when done to accomplish an unlawful end." The unlawful end and necessary effect of the Louisiana tuition grants were to establish and maintain a system of segregated schools for white children, in violation of the equal protection clause. . . .

B. The 1958 program invalidated in Hall v. St. Helena Parish School Board, E.D. La. 1961, 197 F. Supp. 649, aff'd 368 U.S. 515, 82 S. Ct. 529, 7 L. Ed. 2d 521, allowed parish school boards to close public schools under desegregation orders and to lease the buildings to private persons and cooperatives. The present program funnels public funds into the hands of private persons who are thereby enabled to provide different school buildings but count on having the same students and teachers. The 1962 plan has the same purpose and many of the effects of the 1958 plan. . . .

. . . The payment of public funds in any amount through a state commission under authority of a state law is undeniably state action. The question is whether such action in aid of private discrimination violates the equal protection clause.

. . . [D]ecisions on the constitutionality of state involvement in private discrimination do not turn on whether the state aid adds up to 51 per cent or adds up only to 49 per cent of the support of the segregated institution. The criterion is whether the state is so *significantly* involved in the private discrimination as to render the state action and the private action violative of the equal protection clause. (Here the plaintiffs ask only that the state be enjoined from paying the tuition grants; not that the schools be desegregated.)

The courts have wisely not attempted to devise a formula that would include "significant involvement" in all types of private discrimination. In the Little Rock case the Supreme Court said, "State support of segregated schools *through any arrangement*, management, funds, or property cannot be squared with the Fourteenth Amendment's command that no State shall deny to any person within its jurisdiction the equal protection of the laws." Cooper v. Aaron, 1958, 358 U.S. 1, 78 S. Ct. 1401, 3 L. Ed. 2d 5. . . . The constitutional odium of official approval of race discrimination has no necessary relation to the extent of the State's financial support of a discriminatory institution. Any aid to segregated schools that is the product of the State's affirmative, purposeful policy of fostering segregated schools and has the effect of encouraging discrimination is significant state involvement in private discrimination. (We distinguish, therefore, state aid from tax benefits, free schoolbooks, and other products of the State's traditional policy of benevolence toward charitable and educational institutions.) . . .

In Mulkey v. Reitman, 1966, 64 Cal. 2d 529, 50 Cal. Rptr. 881, 413 P.2d 825 (1966) the California Supreme Court impliedly held that § 26 of the California constitution[7] was discriminatory because, by repealing prior legislation forbidding discrimination in housing, the section established an atmosphere conducive to discrimination. The court found that there could be a prohibited state involvement "even where the State can be charged only with encouraging, rather than commanding discrimination." In reaching this result, the court examined § 26 in terms of its "immediate objective," its "ultimate impact," and its "historical context and conditions existing prior to its enactment." The Supreme Court affirmed. Reitman v. Mulkey, 1967, 387 U.S. 369, 87 S. Ct. 1627, 18 L. Ed. 2d 830. Justice White, for the Court, pointed out: The California Court, "armed . . . with the knowledge of the facts and circumstances concerning the passage and the potential impact of § 26, and familiar with the milieu in which that provision would operate," held that the "purpose and intent of § 26 was to authorize private racial discriminations in the housing market. . . . [T]he section would encourage and significantly involve the State in private racial discrimination." Justice Douglas, concurring, put his finger on the crux of the case: "Proposition 14 is a form of sophisticated discrimination whereby the people of California harness the energies of private groups to do indirectly what they cannot under our decisions allow their government to do." Justice Harlan, dissenting, said: "The core of the Court's opinion is that § 26 is offensive to the Fourteenth Amendment because it effectively *encourages* private discrimination." He would approach the "inducement" or "authorization" cases "in terms of the impact and extent of affirmative state governmental activities." Justice Harlan, speaking also for Justices Black, Clark, and Stewart, said: "the state action required to

---

[7] "Proposition 14" on the 1964 California ballot. [*Eds.* note.]

bring the Fourteenth Amendment into operation must be affirmative and purposeful, actively fostering discrimination. Only in such a case is ostensibly 'private' action more properly labelled 'official.' "

Louisiana's tuition grants "encourage and significantly involve [Louisiana] in private racial discrimination" more obviously than California was involved through Proposition 14 and § 26. And Justice Douglas's comment applies as aptly to Act 147 of 1962 as it does to Proposition 14. Moreover, the grants meet Justice Harlan's criteria: they are an "affirmative and purposeful" means of "actively fostering discrimination." The purpose of Louisiana's tuition grant program, however, was not just to encourage and not just to authorize private racial discrimination in the field of education. The purpose was to establish and maintain "private" segregated schools.

As the Supreme Court noted in Reitman v. Mulkey, the "Court has never attempted the 'impossible task' of formulating an infallible test for determining whether the State 'in any of its manifestations' has become significantly involved in private discriminations." The facts must be sifted and weighed on a case-to-case basis. The cases in this area of the law teach, however, that there is no constitutional basis for courts to adopt as a test the predominance of state financial support. . . . In . . . Reitman v. Mulkey, there was no state financial involvement. . . .

We summarize.

The system of private segregated schools the State created and nourishes through Act 147 is in a nascent stage. Its tangible and intangible costs to the State *thus far* are but a drop in the bucket compared with its future costs—should the courts bless the nourishment the private schools receive from the State. The facts this case presents point in only one direction: Unless this system is destroyed, it will shatter to bits the public school system of Louisiana and kill the hope that now exists for equal educational opportunities for all our citizens, white and black.

We hold that the purpose and natural or reasonable effect of Act 147 of 1962 render it unconstitutional on its face. The law was designed to establish and maintain a system of segregated schools. We hold also that Act 147 of 1962 is unconstitutional in its actual effect. The State has predominantly supplied the financial means necessary to establish and maintain the post-1962 private schools and most of the post-1954 private schools in Louisiana. The State is so significantly involved in the discrimination practiced by the private schools in Louisiana that any financial aid from the State to these schools or newly organized schools in the form of tuition grants or similar benefits violates the equal protection clause of the Fourteenth Amendment.

The tuition grants have benefitted certain special schools for handicapped, retarded, and exceptional children. Some of these schools are barely able to exist with the help of tuition grants. But the court cannot rewrite Act 147 so as to provide funds for these schools. That responsibility is the Louisiana Legislature's.

ORDER

In accordance with the findings of fact and conclusions of law in the foregoing opinion,

It is hereby ordered that the defendant Louisiana Financial Assistance Commission, its members, officers, agents, servants, employees and successors in office, and all those who are acting or may act in concert or participation with them are hereby restrained, enjoined and prohibited from enforcing or seeking to enforce by any means the provisions of Act 147 of the 1962 Session of the Louisiana Legislature. . . .

QUESTIONS

1. **Legislative "purpose," "motive" and "intent."**—Was it indispensable in *Poindexter* that the *purpose* of the tuition grants was to create racially segregated "private" schools? Why should it not be sufficient, for a holding that the tuition grants violate the Fourteenth Amendment, that the *effect* of the grants was to create such schools? Did the court hold the act unconstitutional because the legislators tried to perpetuate segregation, or because they succeeded? Is the inquiry into "purpose" really distinguishable from an inquiry into "motive," which the court sought to avoid? (See the discussion in Part II of the opinion, p. 276 *supra.*) Is "purpose," as the court used the term, distinguishable from the "intent" of the legislature as that phrase is sometimes used in discussions of statutory interpretation? As we have seen, the subjective intent of the legislature often is thought to be either nonexistent or unascertainable. Is the *Poindexter* case different, since it is perfectly clear that the Louisiana Legislature did have a collective subjective intent in creating the tuition grant program? Should the question whether a state has denied equal protection of the laws turn on whether the state official or agency responsible for the action had a "bad mind" or a "specific intent"?

2. The problem of "state action."—The legal theory behind the tuition grants resembled the theory behind the pupil assignment statutes: it was argued that any racial segregation which occurred was not the product of state compulsion but of voluntary private choice. With respect to the pupil assignment statutes, the argument was that Negro children could request assignment to integrated schools, so that any segregation which remained was not the state's doing. Similarly it was argued that individuals could choose whether to attend public schools or—with the assistance of tuition grants—private schools that were free to set their own admission policies. The court's opinion in *Poindexter* typifies the conclusion of a great many courts in recent analogous cases: state "involvement" was so significant in the racial segregation produced by the private choices of parents and of operators of private schools that the state involvement violated the equal protection clause. The court's remedy was to enjoin this state involvement; an alternative remedy might have been to desegregate the "private" schools that had been supported by state funds. There is a vast literature on the subject of state action that is related to, or gives effect to, private racial discrimination. The subject is studied in the course in constitutional law. One of the leading cases, *Reitman v. Mulkey*, involving racial discrimination by private owners of housing accommodations, is referred to in our extract from the *Poindexter* opinion. Another variation of the issue will be seen in the next case, involving "freedom of choice" plans adopted by southern school boards as a means of assigning children to public schools.

3. Tuition grants v. other forms of state support for private schools.—Consider the way in which the court distinguished state aid to private schools in the form of tax exemptions and free schoolbooks. These forms of support, the court said, p. 285 *supra*, were "products of the State's traditional policy of benevolence toward charitable and educational institutions," and were not products of the "State's affirmative, purposeful policy of fostering segregated schools." Tax benefits, and similar governmental benefits, to "private" schools can contribute significantly to the viability of such schools. Does not such state aid similarly violate the Fourteenth Amendment if the effect is the support of segregated schools which drain students away from public schools?

4. Should the decree have been tailored to permit grants to schools for the handicapped?—At the end of the *Poindexter* opinion the court noted that the tuition grants had been of crit-

ical significance for private special schools for handicapped, retarded, and exceptional children, and intimated that some form
of state aid to these schools might be constitutional even though
the schools practiced racial discrimination. "But the court cannot rewrite Act 147 so as to provide funds for these schools. That
responsibility is the Louisiana Legislature's." If tuition grants or
other aid for such schools were valid, why should not the court
fashion its holding and its decree so as to sustain the validity of
financial assistance to those schools? Is the judicial function such
that it can operate only in the broad way the court suggests? Or
does the court's conclusion rest on an interpretation of the statute, *i.e.*, that the statute did not contemplate the severability of
the program to aid these special schools?

5. **Louisiana's 1967 tuition grant statute.**—In 1967 the Louisiana
Legislature adopted a program for provision of "financial aid
scholarships to needy children enrolled in private non-sectarian
elementary and secondary schools located in this state whose
parents choose not to enroll said children in the public education facilities of this state." The statute declared that parents, not
the state, should decide "on the type of education ultimately
received by the child," and that the act was designed to assist parents who "lack the finances which would enable them to enroll
their children in private schools." The statute contained a schedule setting forth varying amounts of tuition grants based upon
the income of the family. LSA-R.S. 17:2971 *et seq.* (Supp. 1969).
Did the program, by the shift in emphasis to "needy" children,
then satisfy the equal protection clause? A three-judge federal
district court held the 1967 statute unconstitutional early in 1968,
and the Supreme Court affirmed per curiam in Louisiana Education Commission for Needy Children v. Poindexter, 393 U.S. 17
(1968).

D. FREEDOM OF CHOICE PLANS

Southern school districts, faced with the invalidity of racial
school assignments, generally did not turn to the adoption of
geographical school attendance zones (the "neighborhood
school"). Many districts resorted to "freedom of choice" plans,
under which any child in the district could attend any school
in the district. These plans have been attacked under the equal
protection clause, because the exercise of individual choice within the district has resulted in the continuation of racially segregated schools. The constitutional issues raised by a freedom

of choice plan resemble those we have considered in connection with pupil assignment laws and tuition grant programs.

GREEN v. COUNTY SCHOOL BOARD OF NEW KENT COUNTY
Supreme Court of the United States
391 U.S. 430 (1968)

Mr. Justice BRENNAN delivered the opinion of the Court.

The question for decision is whether, under all the circumstances here, respondent School Board's adoption of a "freedom-of-choice" plan which allows a pupil to choose his own public school constitutes adequate compliance with the Board's responsibility "to achieve a system of determining admission to the public schools on a nonracial basis. . . ." *Brown v. Board of Education*, 349 U.S. 294, 300-301 (*Brown II*).

Petitioners brought this action in March 1965 seeking injunctive relief against respondent's continued maintenance of an alleged racially segregated school system. New Kent County is a rural county in Eastern Virginia. About one-half of its population of some 4,500 are Negroes. There is no residential segregation in the county; persons of both races reside throughout. The school system has only two schools, the New Kent school on the east side of the county and the George W. Watkins school on the west side. In a memorandum filed May 17, 1966, the District Court found that the "school system serves approximately 1,300 pupils, of which 740 are Negro and 550 are white. The School Board operates one white combined elementary and high school [New Kent], and one Negro combined elementary and high school [George W. Watkins]. There are no attendance zones. Each school serves the entire county." The record indicates that 21 school buses—11 serving the Watkins school and 10 serving the New Kent school—travel overlapping routes throughout the county to transport pupils to and from the two schools.

The segregated system was initially established and maintained under the compulsion of Virginia constitutional and statutory provisions mandating racial segregation in public education, Va. Const., Art. IX, § 140 (1902); Va. Code § 22-221 (1950). These provisions were held to violate the Federal Constitution in *Davis v. County School Board of Prince Edward County*, decided with *Brown v. Board of Education*, 347 U.S. 483, 487 (*Brown I*). The respondent School Board continued the segregated operation of the system after the *Brown* decisions, presumably on the authority of several statutes enacted by Virginia in resistance to those decisions. Some of these statutes were held to be unconstitutional on their face or as applied. One statute, the Pupil Placement Act, Va. Code § 22-232.1 *et seq.* (1964), not repealed until 1966, divested local boards of authority to assign children to particular schools and placed that authority in a State Pupil Placement Board. Under that Act children were each year automatically reassigned to the school previously attended unless upon their application the State Board assigned them to another school; students seeking enrollment for the first time were also assigned at the discretion of the State Board. To September 1964, no Negro pupil had applied for admission to the New Kent school under this statute and no white pupil had applied for admission to the Watkins school.

The School Board initially sought dismissal of this suit on the ground that petitioners had failed to apply to the State Board for assignment to New Kent school. However on August 2, 1965, five months after the suit was brought, respondent School Board, in order to remain eligible for federal financial aid, adopted a "freedom-of-choice" plan for desegregating the schools. Under that plan, each pupil may annually choose between the New Kent and Watkins schools and, except for the first and eighth grades, pupils not making a choice are assigned to the school previously attended; first and eighth grade pupils must affirmatively choose a school. After the plan was filed the District Court denied petitioner's prayer for an injunction and granted respondent leave to submit an amendment to the plan with respect to employment and assignment of teachers and staff on a racially nondiscriminatory basis. The amendment was duly filed and on June 28, 1966, the District Court approved the "freedom-of-choice" plan as so amended. The Court of Appeals for the Fourth Circuit, *en banc*, 382 F.2d 326, 338, affirmed the District Court's approval of the "freedom-of-choice" provisions of the plan but remanded the case to the District Court for entry of an order regarding faculty "which is much more specific and more comprehensive" and which would incorporate in addition to a "minimal, objective time table" some of the faculty provisions of the decree entered by the Court of Appeals for the Fifth Circuit in *United States v. Jefferson County Board of Education,* 372 F.2d 836, aff'd *en banc,* 380 F.2d 385 (1967). Judges Soboleff and Winters concurred with the remand on the teacher issue but otherwise disagreed, expressing the view "that the District Court should be directed . . . also to set up procedures for periodically evaluating the effectiveness of the [Board's] 'freedom of choice' [plan] in the elimination of other features of a segregated school system." 382 F.2d, at 330. We granted certiorari, 389 U.S. 1003.

The pattern of separate "white" and "Negro" schools in the New Kent County school system established under compulsion of state laws is precisely the pattern of segregation to which *Brown I* and *Brown II* were particularly addressed, and which *Brown I* declared unconstitutionally denied Negro school children equal protection of the laws. Racial identification of the system's schools was complete, extending not just to the composition of student bodies at the two schools but to every facet of school operations—faculty, staff, transportation, extracurricular activities and facilities. In short, the State, acting through the local school board and school officials, organized and operated a dual system, part "white" and part "Negro."

It was such dual systems that 14 years ago *Brown I* held unconstitutional and a year later *Brown II* held must be abolished; school boards operating such school systems were *required* by *Brown II* "to effectuate a transition to a racially nondiscriminatory school system." 349 U.S., at 301. It is of course true that for the time immediately after *Brown II* the concern was with making an initial break in a long-established pattern of excluding Negro children from schools attended by white children. The principal focus was on obtaining for those Negro children courageous enough to break with tradition a place in the "white" schools. See, *e.g., Cooper v. Aaron*, 358 U.S. 1. Under *Brown II* that immediate goal was only the first step, however. The transition to a unitary, nonracial system of public education was and is the ultimate end to be brought about; it was because of the "complexities arising from the transition to a system of public education freed of racial discrimination" that we provided for "all deliberate speed" in the implementation of the principles of *Brown I*, 349 U.S., at 299-301. Thus we recognized the task would necessarily involve solution of "varied local school problems." *Id.*, at 299. In referring to the "personal interest of the plaintiffs in admission to public schools as soon as practicable on a nondiscriminatory basis," we also noted that "[t]o effectuate this interest may call for elimination of a variety of obstacles in making the transition. . . ." *Id.*, at 300. Yet we emphasized that the constitutional rights of Negro children required school officials to bear the burden of establishing that additional time to carry out the ruling in an effective manner "is necessary in the public interest and is consistent with good faith compliance at the earliest practicable date." *Ibid.* We charged the district courts in their review of particular situations to "consider problems related to administration, arising from the physical condition of the school plant, the school transportation system, personnel, revision of school districts and attendance areas into compact units to achieve a system of determining admission to the public schools on a nonracial basis, and revision of local laws and regulations which may be necessary in solving the foregoing problems. They will also consider the adequacy of any plans the defendants may propose to meet these problems and to effectuate a transition to a racially nondiscriminatory school system." *Id.*, at 300-301.

It is against this background that 13 years after *Brown II* commanded the abolition of dual systems we must measure the effectiveness of respondent School Board's "freedom-of-choice" plan to achieve that end. The School Board contends that it has fully discharged its obligation by adopting a plan by which every student, regardless of race, may "freely" choose the school he will attend. The Board attempts to cast the issue in its broadest form by arguing that its "freedom-of-choice" plan may be faulted only by reading the Fourteenth Amendment as universally requiring "compulsory integration," a reading it insists the wording of the Amendment will not support. But that argument ignores the thrust of *Brown II*. In the light of the command of that case, what is involved here is the question whether the Board has achieved the "racially nondiscriminatory school system" *Brown II* held must be effectuated in order to remedy the established unconstitutional deficiencies of its segregated system. In the context of the state-imposed segregated pattern of long standing, the fact that in 1965 the Board opened the doors of the former "white" school to Negro children and of the "Negro" school to white children merely begins, not ends, our inquiry whether the Board has taken steps adequate to abolish its dual, segregated system. *Brown II* was a call for the dismantling of well-entrenched dual systems tempered by an awareness that complex and multifaceted problems would arise which would require time and flexibility for a successful resolution. School boards such as the respondent then operating state-compelled dual systems were nevertheless clearly charged with the affirmative duty to take whatever steps might be necessary to convert to a unitary system in which racial discrimination would be eliminated root and branch. See *Cooper v. Aaron, supra*, at 7; *Bradley v. School Board*, 382 U.S. 103; cf. *Watson v. City of Memphis*, 373 U.S. 523. The constitutional rights of Negro school children articulated in *Brown I* permit no less than this; and it was to this end that *Brown II* commanded school boards to bend their efforts.

In determining whether respondent School Board met that command by adopting its "freedom-of-choice" plan, it is relevant that this first step did not come until some 11 years after

Brown I was decided and 10 years after *Brown II* directed the making of a "prompt and reasonable start." This deliberate perpetuation of the unconstitutional dual system can only have compounded the harm of such a system. Such delays are no longer tolerable, for "the governing constitutional principles no longer bear the imprint of newly enunciated doctrine." *Watson v. City of Memphis, supra,* at 529; see *Bradley v. School Board, supra; Rogers v. Paul,* 382 U.S. 198. Moreover, a plan that at this late date fails to provide meaningful assurance of prompt and effective disestablishment of a dual system is also intolerable. "The time for mere 'deliberate speed' has run out," *Griffin v. County School Board,* 377 U.S. 218, 234; "the context in which we must interpret and apply this language [of *Brown II*] to plans for desegregation has been significantly altered." *Goss v. Board of Education,* 373 U.S. 683, 689. See *Calhoun v. Latimer,* 377 U.S. 263. The burden on a school board today is to come forward with a plan that promises realistically to work, and promises realistically to work *now.*

The obligation of the district courts, as it always has been, is to assess the effectiveness of a proposed plan in achieving desegregation. There is no universal answer to complex problems of desegregation; there is obviously no one plan that will do the job in every case. The matter must be assessed in light of the circumstances present and the options available in each instance. It is incumbent upon the school board to establish that its proposed plan promises meaningful and immediate progress toward disestablishing state-imposed segregation. It is incumbent upon the district court to weigh that claim in light of the facts at hand and in light of any alternatives which may be shown as feasible and more promising in their effectiveness. Where the court finds the board to be acting in good faith and the proposed plan to have real prospects for dismantling the state-imposed dual system "at the earliest practicable date," then the plan may be said to provide effective relief. Of course, where other, more promising courses of action are open to the board, that may indicate a lack of good faith; and at the least it places a heavy burden upon the board to explain its preference for an apparently less effective method. Moreover, whatever plan is adopted will require evaluation in practice, and the court should retain jurisdiction until it is clear that state-imposed segregation has been completely removed. . . .

We do not hold that "freedom of choice" can have no place in such a plan. We do not hold that a "freedom-of-choice" plan might of itself be unconstitutional, although that argument has been urged upon us. Rather, all we decide today is that in desegregating a dual system a plan utilizing "freedom of choice" is not an end in itself. As Judge Sobeloff has put it,

" 'Freedom of choice' is not a sacred talisman; it is only a means to a constitutionally required end—the abolition of the system of segregation and its effects. If the means prove effective, it is acceptable, but if it fails to undo segregation, other means must be used to achieve this end. The school officials have the continuing duty to take whatever action may be necessary to create a 'unitary, nonracial system.' " *Bowman v. County School Board*, 382 F.2d 326, 333 (C.A. 4th Cir. 1967) (concurring opinion). Accord, *Kemp v. Beasley*, 389 F.2d 178 (C.A. 8th Cir. 1968); *United States v. Jefferson County Board of Education, supra.*

Although the general experience under "freedom of choice" to date has been such as to indicate its ineffectiveness as a tool of desegregation,[8] there may well be instances in which it can serve as an effective device. Where it offers real promise of aiding a desegregation program to effectuate conversion of a state-imposed dual system to a unitary, nonracial system there might be no objection to allowing such a device to prove itself in operation. On the other hand, if there are reasonably available other ways,

---

[8] The views of the United States Commission on Civil Rights, which we neither adopt nor refuse to adopt, are as follows:

"Freedom of choice plans, which have tended to perpetuate racially identifiable schools in the Southern and border States, require affirmative action by both Negro and white parents and pupils before such disestablishment can be achieved. There are a number of factors which have prevented such affirmative action by substantial numbers of parents and pupils of both races:

"(a) Fear of retaliation and hostility from the white community continue to deter many Negro families from choosing formerly all-white schools;

"(b) During the past school year [1966-1967], as in the previous year, in some areas of the South, Negro families with children attending previously all-white schools under free choice plans were targets of violence, threats of violence and economic reprisals by white persons and Negro children were subjected to harassment by white classmates notwithstanding conscientious efforts by many teachers and principals to prevent such misconduct;

"(c) During the past school year, in some areas of the South public officials improperly influenced Negro families to keep their children in Negro schools and excluded Negro children attending formerly all-white schools from official functions;

"(d) Poverty deters many Negro families in the South from choosing formerly all-white schools. Some Negro parents are embarrassed to permit their children to attend such schools without suitable clothing. In some districts special fees are assessed for courses which are available only in the white schools;

"(e) Improvements in facilities and equipment . . . have been instituted in all-Negro schools in some school districts in a manner that tends to discourage Negroes from selecting white schools." Southern School Desegregation, 1966-1967, at 88 (1967). See *id.*, at 45-69; Survey of School Desegregation in the Southern and Border States 1965-1966, at 30-44, 51-52 (U.S. Comm'n on Civil Rights 1966). [Footnote in original, renumbered.]

such for illustration as zoning, promising speedier and more effective conversion to a unitary, nonracial school system, "freedom of choice" must be held unacceptable.

The New Kent School Board's "freedom-of-choice" plan cannot be accepted as a sufficient step to "effectuate a transition" to a unitary system. In three years of operation not a single white child has chosen to attend Watkins school and although 115 Negro children enrolled in New Kent school in 1967 (up from 35 in 1965 and 111 in 1966) 85% of the Negro children in the system still attend the all-Negro Watkins school. In other words, the school system remains a dual system. Rather than further the dismantling of the dual system, the plan has operated simply to burden children and their parents with a responsibility which *Brown II* placed squarely on the School Board. The Board must be required to formulate a new plan and, in light of other courses which appear open to the Board, such as zoning,[9] fashion steps which promise realistically to convert promptly to a system without a "white" school and a "Negro" school, but just schools.

The judgment of the Court of Appeals is vacated insofar as it affirmed the District Court and the case is remanded to the District Court for further proceedings consistent with this opinion.

It is so ordered.[10]

---

9 "In view of the situation found in New Kent County, where there is no residential segregation, the elimination of the dual school system and the establishment of a 'unitary, non-racial system' could be readily achieved with a minimum of administrative difficulty by means of geographic zoning—simply by assigning students living in the eastern half of the county to the New Kent School and those living in the western half of the county to the Watkins School. Although a geographical formula is not universally appropriate, it is evident that here the Board, by separately busing Negro children across the entire county to the 'Negro' school, and the white children to the 'white' school, is deliberately maintaining a segregated system which would vanish with non-racial geographic zoning. The conditions in this county present a classical case for this expedient." *Bowman v. County School Board, supra*, n. 3, at 332 (concurring opinion).

Petitioners have also suggested that the Board could consolidate the two schools, one site (*e.g.*, Watkins) serving grades 1-7 and the other (*e.g.*, New Kent) serving grades 8-12, this being the grade division respondent makes between elementary and secondary levels. Petitioners contend this would result in a more efficient system by eliminating costly duplication in this relatively small district while at the same time achieving immediate dismantling of the dual system.

These are two suggestions the District Court should take into account upon remand, along with any other proposed alternatives and in light of considerations respecting other aspects of the school system such as the matter of faculty and staff desegregation remanded to the court by the Court of Appeals. [Footnote in original, renumbered.]

10 On remand the district court gave the school board until September 1969 to accomplish "total integration." During the 1968-69 school year, there were 136 black children out of a total of 650 children in the New Kent school. News Broadcast, WRC-TV, Washington, D.C., Nov. 5, 1968. [*Eds.* note.]

QUESTIONS

1. Legislative purpose and the law's effects.—In his *New Kent County* opinion, Justice Brennan gave all his attention to the effects of the "freedom of choice" plan in bringing about a transition to a "unitary, non-racial system," without referring to the "purposes" of the plan or the school district's "motives." Compare this approach to determining the constitutionality of the school board's action with that in the tuition grant case, *Poindexter v. Louisiana Financial Assistance Commission,* p. 274 *supra,* where Judge Wisdom emphasized the "purpose" of the program. Should we conclude that an improper "purpose," while it may be a contributing factor, is not indispensable to a holding of denial of equal protection of the laws in cases of this type? Are these questions of purpose and effect really separate? Would proof of a law's effects be one way to establish its purpose?

2. The court's supervision of the details of school administration.—Justice Brennan's opinion stated that the federal district court, in determining the adequacy of the school board's proposed desegregation plan, should consider "any alternatives which may be shown as feasible and more promising [than "freedom of choice"] in their effectiveness." Not only does the Court order the school board to use a method of assigning children to schools that is "feasible and more promising" in bringing about a unitary school system; in footnote 9, *supra,* the Court goes on to set forth two suggestions for the school board to consider. Is the Court here interfering too much in the exercise of legislative or administrative functions by a local governmental body? Is this kind of close judicial supervision the inevitable result of the second *Brown* decision?

3. New Kent County and the problem of de facto segregation in the north and west.—There is no suggestion in the Court's opinion that local governmental officials in any way sought to influence parents and children in the exercise of their "freedom of choice" in determining which schools the children would attend; yet the assignment plan based on such freedom of choice was held to violate the equal protection clause. Does it follow from this case that de facto racial segregation in northern and western cities (segregation resulting from the combination of the neighborhood school with racially segregated neighborhoods) denies black children equal protection of the laws? In the *New Kent County* case the existing racial pattern in the schools was not said to be the product of anything other than individual private choice. The racial population pattern, however, existed in schools that previously had been racially segregated under compulsion of state law, and the Court concluded that "freedom of choice" was not an adequate means of dismantling that dual system. Did the Court's conclusion rest on the fact that past state-compelled racial segregation still permeated the atmosphere in New Kent County, so that any purported exercise of private choice today was made in the context of patterns of behavior molded to a great extent by past state compulsion? If that is the basis of the Court's decision, how can New Kent County cleanse itself of the past, so that individual choice can be said to be sufficiently free from state guidance or encouragement? What criteria can the Court use in making such a determination? Underlying the Court's decision, was there an unstated premise about the "purpose" of the New Kent County plan: that basing school assignments solely on the choices of parents and children is so unwieldy an administrative mechanism that this method of assignment could have been adopted only for the purpose of maintaining as much racial segregation in the schools as would be possible? (Recall the Court's statement, p. 294 *supra*, that "where other, more promising courses of action are open to the board, that may indicate a lack of good faith. . . .") Does this line of inquiry about the Court's decision in *New Kent County* lead to a different measure of Fourteenth Amendment obligation of school boards in the south, as compared with the north and west, to deal with existing (post-*Brown*) patterns of racial segregation in public schools? Is there a neutral principle which would accommodate a holding that in the south, school boards must adopt geographical zones for school assignments, in order to undo de jure segregation, and that in the north and west school boards must abandon geographical zones in order to undo de facto segregation? These questions will be considered further in Chapter 4.

E. AVAILABILITY OF COUNSEL

Until the enactment by Congress of the Civil Rights Act of 1964, implementation of *Brown v. Board of Education* required litigation, except in the relatively few cases where school boards acted voluntarily. School boards throughout the south took the position that they were not obligated to do anything until a court so ordered. The magnitude of the task of vindicating individual rights through litigation was increased by the devices discussed in the preceding sections—pupil placement plans, school closings, tuition grants, "freedom of choice"—the validity of which had to be adjudicated. Since adjudication was performed in the ordinary adversary proceeding, various questions arose with respect to availability of counsel for plaintiffs and the ethical obligations of the legal profession.

The effort to secure attorneys for desegregation plaintiffs

Implementation of *Brown v. Board of Education* required legal counsel in vast numbers, and attorneys in southern communities who would take such cases were, with very rare exceptions, nonexistent. The problem was intensified by the need for counsel to represent persons who were being prosecuted following participation in various forms of civil rights activities. National organizations—the Lawyers' Committee for Civil Rights Under Law, the Lawyers Constitutional Defense Committee, the National Lawyers Guild—in recent years have recruited attorneys from outside the south to establish offices in some southern communities.[11] Since 1964 the Attorney General has been authorized to bring lawsuits to desegregate public schools. But

---

[11] Volunteer attorneys from outside the south have not always been welcomed with open arms by the southern bench and bar. Two 1968 decisions are illustrative:

(a) In 1967, the United States District Court for the Southern District of Mississippi promulgated a rule of court limiting nonresident attorneys to one appearance in any 12-month period, and permitting such attorneys to appear only if they had been admitted to practice in their home states for five years (unless such a nonresident attorney's home-state federal district court permitted Mississippi attorneys to appear on more lenient terms). These requirements were held invalid by the Court of Appeals for the Fifth Circuit, on the ground that they were "unreasonable," and inconsistent with the policy of Congress as expressed in federal civil rights legislation. Sanders v. Russell, 401 F.2d 241 (5th Cir. 1968). *See* Note, *Constitutional Right To Engage an Out-of-State Attorney*, 19 STAN. L. REV. 856 (1967).

(b) In Plaquemines Parish, Louisiana, Richard Sobol, a young Washington lawyer who had come to do volunteer work in civil rights cases, was prosecuted in 1967 for practicing law without a license. He was arrested and jailed for four hours, fingerprinted and photographed several times, and made to give up his belt, his tie, and a briefcase containing papers relating to the defense of a black defendant in a civil-rights-related criminal case. The United States District Court enjoined Sobol's prosecution on the ground that his activities did not constitute the unauthorized practice of law, and that his arrest and prosecution under the circumstances could "only be interpreted as harassment." "This prosecution," said the court, "was meant to show Sobol that civil rights lawyers were not welcome in the parish, and that their defense of Negroes involved in cases growing out of civil rights efforts would not be tolerated. It was meant also as a warning to other civil rights lawyers and to Negroes in the parish who might consider retaining civil rights lawyers to advance their rights to equal opportunity and equal treatment under the Equal Protection Clause of the Fourteenth Amendment." Sobol v. Perez, 289 F. Supp. 392, 402 (E.D. La. 1968).

during the first decade following the *Brown* decision, the burden of providing counsel in desegregation suits fell almost entirely on the NAACP.

There are several explanations for the unavailability of local counsel to represent plaintiffs in school suits: (a) disagreement by attorneys with the principle in *Brown*; (b) the overwhelming unpopularity of a desegregation case, which threatened an attorney with the loss of other clients; and (c) the absence of economic resources to cover the costs of desegregation litigation. With respect to the first two of these explanations, recall A.B.A. Canon 31: "No lawyer is obliged to act either as adviser or advocate for every person who may wish to become his client. He has the right to decline employment." Did Canon 31 serve the ends of justice in the south after 1954? Particularly where the legal rights of individuals have been made as clear as *Brown v. Board of Education* stated, should a member of the legal profession have an obligation to accept a case to enforce such rights? Recall the English practice referred to in the discussion following *Somerset v. Stewart*, p. 21, *supra*: a barrister is, in general, bound to accept any brief offered him. Under the English system would public reaction have been so adverse to lawyers who represented desegregation plaintiffs? What would have been the effect of the "deliberate speed" formula if there had been, in every southern school district in 1955, a lawyer who was willing to represent black children and parents in desegregation litigation? Was the argument of the NAACP at the time of the second *Brown* decision based on an assumption that legal counsel would be in short supply? Perhaps not; even if the Court had ordered immediate desegregation by the defendant school boards, enforcement in other districts would have required litigation, and thus legal counsel.

The other obstacle to the availability of attorneys was the absence of economic resources to bear the costs of litigation. There are several possible responses to this problem. One is for lawyers to volunteer their services, or, in damages actions, to accept contingent fee arrangements. Another, particularly pertinent in the context of school suits in the south, is to require the losing party to pay the prevailing party's counsel fees. This latter possibility may be particularly attractive where the obligations of a school board are relatively clear and where the school board is a governmental entity charged with violating the constitutional rights of individuals. There have been a few school cases in which attorneys' fees were awarded to the plaintiffs. A typical discussion of the question is the following:

It is only in the extraordinary case that such an award of attorneys' fees is requisite. . . . Attorneys' fees are appropriate only when it is found that the bringing of the action should have been unnecessary and was compelled by the school board's unreasonable, obdurate obstinacy. Whether or not the board's prior conduct was so unreasonable in that sense was initially for the District Judge to determine. Undoubtedly he has large discretion in that area, which an appellate court ought to overturn only in the face of compelling circumstances. Bradley v. School Board of the City of Richmond, 345 F.2d 310, 321 (4th Cir. 1965).

On the criteria stated in this extract, should plaintiffs' counsel fees have been assessed against any school board which took the position that it would comply with *Brown* only after a court ordered it to do so? Would it be desirable to adopt as a general principle the concept that the losing party in civil litigation (and perhaps in criminal litigation where the state is the losing party) must pay the other party's attorneys' fees?

Another means of making counsel available to those who cannot afford the costs is through publicly or privately financed legal services programs. For many decades, legal aid programs, financed from private sources, have been a means of employing attorneys to provide legal services to the poor in civil cases, and sometimes in criminal cases as well. Governmental public defender programs in many states provide counsel for indigent defendants in criminal proceedings. More recently the Legal Services Program has been created by the federal Office of Economic Opportunity to support programs for the provision of ·legal services to the poor. The Legal Services Program finances private nonprofit organizations, some of which maintain "neighborhood law offices" for the urban poor, and some of which provide legal services to the poor in rural areas. Lawyers in OEO-funded programs have represented plaintiffs in actions against school districts contending that there were unconstitutional inequalities of educational opportunity in the districts' programs. Primarily because of the activities of an OEO-funded legal services program in California, California Rural Legal Assistance, some public officials have taken the position that it is inappropriate for lawyers in governmentally-financed law offices to represent clients in actions against governmental agencies.[12] Is there a sound basis for this position?

---

[12] A proposal to prohibit such representation, the so-called "Murphy amendment," was defeated in the United States Senate in 1967. 113 CONG. REC. 27871-73 (1967).

The attack on the NAACP and its lawyers

These institutional obstacles to availability of counsel in desegregation cases existed whether or not the states took a hand
in the matter. But some states sought to place additional barriers
in the way of efforts by the NAACP and other organizations to
bring about and support school desegregation suits.[13] One example was Virginia, which attacked the NAACP directly for
"solicitation" of business for lawyers, as part of the state's "massive resistance"[14] to *Brown v. Board of Education.*

NATIONAL ASSOCIATION FOR THE ADVANCEMENT OF COLORED PEOPLE v. BUTTON
Supreme Court of the United States
371 U.S. 415 (1962)

Mr. Justice BRENNAN delivered the opinion of the Court. . . .

There is no substantial dispute as to the facts; the dispute centers about the constitutionality under the Fourteenth Amendment of Chapter 33, as construed and applied by the Virginia
Supreme Court of Appeals to include NAACP's activities within
the statute's ban against "the improper solicitation of any legal
or professional business."[15]
The NAACP was formed in 1909 and incorporated under New
York law as a nonprofit membership corporation in 1911. It
maintains its headquarters in New York and presently has some
1,000 active unincorporated branches throughout the Nation.
The corporation is licensed to do business in Virginia, and has
89 branches there. The Virginia branches are organized into the
Virginia State Conference of NAACP Branches (the Conference),
an unincorporated association, which in 1957 had some 13,500
members. The activities of the Conference are financed jointly
by the national organization and the local branches from contributions and membership dues. NAACP policy, binding upon
local branches and conferences, is set by the annual national
convention.
The basic aims and purposes of NAACP are to secure the
elimination of all racial barriers which deprive Negro citizens
of the privileges and burdens of equal citizenship rights in the

---

13 *See* Note, *Barratry—A Comparative Analysis of Recent Barratry Statutes,* 14 DE PAUL L. REV. 146 (1964).
14 *See* note 5, p. 266 *supra.*
15 The NAACP sued to enjoin the state attorney general from enforcing
Chapter 33 against it. [*Eds.* note.]

United States. To this end the Association engages in extensive educational and lobbying activities. It also devotes much of its funds and energies to an extensive program of assisting certain kinds of litigation on behalf of its declared purposes. For more than 10 years, the Virginia Conference has concentrated upon financing litigation aimed at ending racial segregation in the public schools of the Commonwealth.

The Conference ordinarily will finance only cases in which the assisted litigant retains an NAACP staff lawyer to represent him. The Conference maintains a legal staff of 15 attorneys, all of whom are Negroes and members of the NAACP. The staff is elected at the Conference's annual convention. Each legal staff member must agree to abide by the policies of the NAACP, which, insofar as they pertain to professional services, limit the kinds of litigation which the NAACP will assist. Thus the NAACP will not underwrite ordinary damages actions, criminal actions in which the defendant raises no question of possible racial discrimination, or suits in which the plaintiff seeks separate but equal rather than fully desegregated public school facilities. The staff decides whether a litigant, who may or may not be an NAACP member, is entitled to NAACP assistance. The Conference defrays all expenses of litigation in an assisted case, and usually, although not always, pays each lawyer on the case a per diem fee not to exceed $60, plus out-of-pocket expenses. The assisted litigant receives no money from the Conference or the staff lawyers. The staff member may not accept, from the litigant or any other source, any other compensation for his services in an NAACP-assisted case. None of the staff receives a salary or retainer from the NAACP; the per diem fee is paid only for professional services in a particular case. This per diem payment is smaller than the compensation ordinarily received for equivalent private professional work. The actual conduct of assisted litigation is under the control of the attorney, although the NAACP continues to be concerned that the outcome of the lawsuit should be consistent with NAACP's policies already described. A client is free at any time to withdraw from an action.

The members of the legal staff of the Virginia Conference and other NAACP or Defense Fund [the NAACP Legal Defense and Educational Fund] lawyers called in by the staff to assist are drawn into litigation in various ways. One is for an aggrieved Negro to apply directly to the Conference or the legal staff for assistance. His application is referred to the Chairman of the legal staff. The Chairman, with the concurrence of the President of the Conference, is authorized to agree to give legal assistance in an appropriate case. In litigation involving public school segregation, the procedure tends to be different. Typically, a local NAACP branch will invite a member of the legal staff to explain to a meeting of parents and children the legal steps necessary to achieve desegregation. The staff member will bring printed forms to the meeting authorizing him, and other NAACP or Defense Fund attorneys of his designation, to represent the signers in legal proceedings to achieve desegregation. On occasion, blank forms have been signed by litigants, upon the understanding that a member or members of the legal staff, with or without assistance from other NAACP lawyers, or from the Defense Fund, would handle the case. It is usual, after obtaining authorizations, for the staff lawyer to bring into the case the other staff members in the area where suit is to be brought, and sometimes to bring in lawyers from the national organization or the Defense Fund. In effect, then, the prospective litigant retains not so much a particular attorney as the "firm" of NAACP and Defense Fund lawyers, which has a corporate reputation for expertness in presenting and arguing the difficult questions of law that frequently arise in civil rights litigation.

These meetings are sometimes prompted by letters and bulletins from the Conference urging active steps to fight segregation. The Conference has on occasion distributed to the local branches petitions for desegregation to be signed by parents and filed with local school boards, and advised branch officials to obtain, as petitioners, persons willing to "go all the way" in any possible litigation that may ensue. While the Conference in these ways encourages the bringing of lawsuits, the plaintiffs in particular actions, so far as appears, make their own decisions to become such.

Statutory regulation of unethical and nonprofessional conduct by attorneys has been in force in Virginia since 1849. These provisions outlaw, *inter alia*, solicitation of legal business in the form of "running" or "capping." Prior to 1956, however, no attempt was made to proscribe under such regulations the activities of the NAACP, which had been carried on openly for many years in substantially the manner described. In 1956, however, the legislature amended, by the addition of Chapter 33, the provisions of the Virginia Code forbidding solicitation of legal business by a "runner" or "capper" to include, in the definition of "runner" or "capper," an agent for an individual or organization which retains a lawyer in connection with an action to which it is not a party and in which it has no pecuniary right or liability.[16]

---

16 . . .
"§ 54-78. . . . (1) A 'runner' or 'capper' is any person, corporation, partnership or association acting in any manner or in any capacity as an agent

The Virginia Supreme Court of Appeals held that the chapter's purpose "was to strengthen the existing statutes to further control the evils of solicitation of legal business. . . ." 202 Va., at 154, 116 S.E.2d, at 65. The court held that the activities of NAACP, the Virginia Conference, the Defense Fund, and the lawyers furnished by them, fell within, and could constitutionally be proscribed by, the chapter's expanded definition of improper solicitation of legal business, and also violated Canons 35 and 47 of the American Bar Association's Canons of Professional Ethics, which the court had adopted in 1938. Specifically the court held that, under the expanded definition, such activities on the part of NAACP, the Virginia Conference, and the Defense Fund constituted "fomenting and soliciting legal business in which they are not parties and have no pecuniary right or liability, and which they channel to the enrichment of certain lawyers employed by them, at no cost to the litigants and over which the litigants have no control." 202 Va., at 155; 116 S.E.2d, at 66. . . .

II.

Petitioner challenges the decision of the Supreme Court of Appeals on many grounds. But we reach only one: that Chapter 33 as construed and applied abridges the freedoms of the First Amendment, protected against state action by the Fourteenth. More specifically, petitioner claims that the chapter infringes the right of the NAACP and its members and lawyers to associate for the purpose of assisting persons who seek legal redress for infringements of their constitutionally guaranteed and other rights. . . .

We reverse the judgment of the Virginia Supreme Court of Appeals. We hold that the activities of the NAACP, its affiliates and legal staff shown on this record are modes of expression and

---

for an attorney at law within this State *or for any person, partnership, corporation, organization or association which employs, retains or compensates any attorney at law in connection with any judicial proceeding in which such person, partnership, corporation, organization or association is not a party and in which it has no pecuniary right or liability,* in the solicitation or procurement of business for such attorney at law *or for such person, partnership, corporation, organization or association in connection with any judicial proceedings for which such attorney or such person, partnership, corporation, organization or association is employed, retained or compensated.*

"The fact that any person, partnership, corporation, organization or association is a party to any judicial proceeding shall not authorize any runner or capper to solicit or procure business for such person, partnership, corporation, organization or association or any attorney at law employed, retained or compensated by such person, partnership, corporation, organization or association.

"(2) An 'agent' is one who represents another in dealing with a third person or persons. . . ." [Footnote in original, renumbered.]

association protected by the First and Fourteenth Amendments which Virginia may not prohibit, under its power to regulate the legal profession, as improper solicitation of legal business violative of Chapter 33 and the Canons of Professional Ethics.

A.

We meet at the outset the contention that "solicitation" is wholly outside the area of freedoms protected by the First Amendment. To this contention there are two answers. The first is that a State cannot foreclose the exercise of constitutional rights by mere labels. The second is that abstract discussion is not the only species of communication which the Constitution protects; the First Amendment also protects vigorous advocacy, certainly of lawful ends, against governmental intrusion. . . . In the context of NAACP objectives, litigation is not a technique of resolving private differences; it is a means for achieving the lawful objectives of equality of treatment by all government, federal, state and local, for the members of the Negro community in this country. It is thus a form of political expression. Groups which find themselves unable to achieve their objectives through the ballot frequently turn to the courts. Just as it was true of the opponents of New Deal legislation during the 1930's, for example, no less is it true of the Negro minority today. And under the conditions of modern government, litigation may well be the sole practicable avenue open to a minority to petition for redress of grievances.

We need not, in order to find constitutional protection for the kind of cooperative, organizational activity disclosed by this record, whereby Negroes seek through lawful means to achieve legitimate political ends, subsume such activity under a narrow, literal conception of freedom of speech, petition or assembly. For there is no longer any doubt that the First and Fourteenth Amendments protect certain forms of orderly group activity. Thus we have affirmed the right "to engage in association for the advancement of beliefs and ideas." *NAACP v. Alabama,* [357 U.S. 449, 460]. We have deemed privileged, under certain circumstances, the efforts of a union official to organize workers. *Thomas v. Collins,* [323 U.S. 516]. . . .

The NAACP is not a conventional political party; but the litigation it assists, while serving to vindicate the legal rights of members of the American Negro community, at the same time and perhaps more importantly, makes possible the distinctive contribution of a minority group to the ideas and beliefs of our society. For such a group, association for litigation may be the most effective form of political association.

B. . . .

We conclude that under Chapter 33, as authoritatively construed by the Supreme Court of Appeals, a person who advises another that his legal rights have been infringed and refers him to a particular attorney or group of attorneys (for example, to the Virginia Conference's legal staff) for assistance has committed a crime, as has the attorney who knowingly renders assistance under such circumstances. There thus inheres in the statute the gravest danger of smothering all discussion looking to the eventual institution of litigation on behalf of the rights of members of an unpopular minority. Lawyers on the legal staff or even mere NAACP members or sympathizers would understandably hesitate, at an NAACP meeting or on any other occasion, to do what the decree purports to allow, namely, acquaint "persons with what they believe to be their legal rights and . . . [advise] them to assert their rights by commencing or further prosecuting a suit. . . ." For if the lawyers, members or sympathizers also appeared in or had any connection with any litigation supported with NAACP funds contributed under the provision of the decree by which the NAACP is not prohibited "from contributing money to persons to assist them in commencing or further prosecuting such suits," they plainly would risk (if lawyers) disbarment proceedings and, lawyers and nonlawyers alike, criminal prosecution for the offense of "solicitation," to which the Virginia court gave so broad and uncertain a meaning. It makes no difference whether such prosecutions or proceedings would actually be commenced. It is enough that a vague and broad statute lends itself to selective enforcement against unpopular causes. We cannot close our eyes to the fact that the militant Negro civil rights movement has engendered the intense resentment and opposition of the politically dominant white community of Virginia; litigation assisted by the NAACP has been bitterly fought. In such circumstances, a statute broadly curtailing group activity leading to litigation may easily become a weapon of oppression, however even-handed its terms appear. Its mere existence could well freeze out of existence all such activity on behalf of the civil rights of Negro citizens. . . .

We hold that Chapter 33 as construed violates the Fourteenth Amendment by unduly inhibiting protected freedoms of expression and association. . . .

C. . . .

However valid may be Virginia's interest in regulating the traditionally illegal practices of barratry, maintenance and champerty, that interest does not justify the prohibition of the NAACP activities disclosed by this record. Malicious intent was of the essence of the common-law offenses of fomenting or stirring up litigation. And whatever may be or may have been true of suits against government in other countries, the exercise in our own, as in this case, of First Amendment rights to enforce constitutional rights through litigation, as a matter of law, cannot be deemed malicious. Even more modern, subtler regulations of unprofessional conduct or interference with professional relations, not involving malice, would not touch the activities at bar; regulations which reflect hostility to stirring up litigation have been aimed chiefly at those who urge recourse to the courts for private gain, serving no public interest. Hostility still exists to stirring up private litigation where it promotes the use of legal machinery to oppress: as, for example, to sow discord in a family; to expose infirmities in land titles, as by hunting up claims of adverse possession; to harass large companies through a multiplicity of small claims; or to oppress debtors as by seeking out unsatisfied judgments. For a member of the bar to participate, directly or through intermediaries, in such misuses of the legal process is conduct traditionally condemned as injurious to the public. And beyond this, for a lawyer to attempt to reap gain by urging another to engage in private litigation has also been condemned: that seems to be the import of Canon 28, which the Virginia Supreme Court of Appeals has adopted as one of its Rules.

Objection to the intervention of a lay intermediary, who may control litigation or otherwise interfere with the rendering of legal services in a confidential relationship, also derives from the element of pecuniary gain. Fearful of dangers thought to arise from that element, the courts of several States have sustained regulations aimed at these activities. We intimate no view one way or the other as to the merits of those decisions with respect to the particular arrangements against which they are directed. It is enough that the superficial resemblance in form between those arrangements and that at bar cannot obscure the vital fact that here the entire arrangement employs constitutionally privileged means of expression to secure constitutionally guaranteed civil rights. There has been no showing of a serious danger here of professionally reprehensible conflicts of interest which rules against solicitation frequently seek to prevent. This is so partly because no monetary stakes are involved, and so there is no danger that the attorney will desert or subvert the paramount interests of his client to enrich himself or an outside sponsor. And the aims and interests of NAACP have not been shown to conflict with those of its members and nonmember Negro liti-

gants; compare *NAACP v. Alabama ex rel. Patterson,* 357 U.S.
449, 459, where we said:

"[the NAACP] and its members are in every practical sense
identical. The Association, which provides in its constitution
that '[a]ny person who is in accordance with [its] principles and
policies . . .' may become a member, is but the medium through
which its individual members seek to make more effective the
expression of their own views." See also *Harrison v. NAACP,* 360
U.S. 167, 177.

Resort to the courts to seek vindication of constitutional rights
is a different matter from the oppressive, malicious, or avaricious
use of the legal process for purely private gain. Lawsuits attacking racial discrimination, at least in Virginia, are neither very
profitable nor very popular. They are not an object of general
competition among Virginia lawyers; the problem is rather one
of an apparent dearth of lawyers who are willing to undertake
such litigation. There has been neither claim nor proof that
any assisted Negro litigants have desired, but have been prevented from retaining, the services of other counsel. We realize
that an NAACP lawyer must derive personal satisfaction from
participation in litigation on behalf of Negro rights, else he
would hardly be inclined to participate at the risk of financial
sacrifice. But this would not seem to be the kind of interest or
motive which induces criminal conduct.

We conclude that although the petitioner has amply shown
that its activities fall within the First Amendment's protections,
the State has failed to advance any substantial regulatory interest, in the form of substantive evils flowing from petitioner's
activities, which can justify the broad prohibitions which it has
imposed. Nothing that this record shows as to the nature and
purpose of NAACP activities permits an inference of any injurious intervention in or control of litigation which would constitutionally authorize the application of Chapter 33 to those activities. *A fortiori,* nothing in this record justifies the breadth and
vagueness of the Virginia Supreme Court of Appeals' decree.

A final observation is in order. Because our disposition is
rested on the First Amendment as absorbed in the Fourteenth,
we do not reach the considerations of race or racial discrimination which are the predicate of petitioner's challenge to the statute under the Equal Protection Clause. That the petitioner
happens to be engaged in activities of expression and association
on behalf of the rights of Negro children to equal opportunity
is constitutionally irrelevant to the ground of our decision. The

course of our decisions in the First Amendment area makes plain
that its protections would apply as fully to those who would
arouse our society against the objectives of the petitioner. . . .
For the Constitution protects expression and association without
regard to the race, creed, or political or religious affiliation of
the members of the group which invokes its shield, or to the
truth, popularity, or social utility of the ideas and beliefs which
are offered.

Reversed.

Mr. Justice HARLAN, whom Mr. Justice CLARK and Mr. Justice
STEWART join, dissenting.

No member of this Court would disagree that the validity of
state action claimed to infringe rights assured by the Fourteenth
Amendment is to be judged by the same basic constitutional
standards whether or not racial problems are involved. No worse
setback could befall the great principles established by *Brown v.
Board of Education*, 347 U.S. 483, than to give fair-minded persons reason to think otherwise. With all respect, I believe that
the striking down of this Virginia statute cannot be squared with
accepted constitutional doctrine in the domain of state regulatory
power over the legal profession.

I.

At the outset the factual premises on which the Virginia Supreme Court of Appeals upheld the application of Chapter 33
to the activities of the NAACP in the area of litigation, as well
as the scope of that court's holding, should be delineated.

First, the lawyers who participate in litigation sponsored by
petitioner are, almost without exception, members of the legal
staff of the NAACP Virginia State Conference. (It is, in fact,
against Conference policy to give financial support to litigation
not handled by a staff lawyer.) As such, they are selected by petitioner, are compensated by it for work in litigation (whether or
not petitioner is a party thereto), and so long as they remain on
the staff, are necessarily subject to its directions. As the Court
recognizes, it is incumbent on staff members to agree to abide
by NAACP policies.

Second, it is equally clear that the NAACP's directions, or those
of its officers and divisions, to staff lawyers cover many subjects
relating to the form and substance of litigation. . . .

In short, . . . the form of pleading, the type of relief to be requested, and the proper timing of suits have to a considerable extent, if not entirely, been determined by the Conference in coordination with the national office.

Third, contrary to the conclusion of the Federal District Court in the original federal proceeding, *NAACP v. Patty,* 159 F. Supp. 503, 508-509, the present record establishes that the petitioner does a great deal more than to advocate litigation and to wait for prospective litigants to come forward. In several instances, especially in litigation touching racial discrimination in public schools, specific directions were given as to the types of prospective plaintiffs to be sought, and staff lawyers brought blank forms to meetings for the purpose of obtaining signatures authorizing the prosecution of litigation in the name of the signer.

Fourth, there is substantial evidence indicating that the normal incidents of the attorney-client relationship were often absent in litigation handled by staff lawyers and financed by petitioner. Forms signed by prospective litigants have on occasion not contained the name of the attorney authorized to act. In many cases, whether or not the form contained specific authorization to that effect, additional counsel have been brought into the action by staff counsel. There were several litigants who testified that at no time did they have any personal dealings with the lawyers handling their cases nor were they aware until long after the event that suits had been filed in their names. This is not to suggest that the petitioner has been shown to have sought plaintiffs under false pretenses or by inaccurate statements. But there is no basis for concluding that these were isolated incidents, or that petitioner's methods of operation have been such as to render these happenings out of the ordinary.

On these factual premises, amply supported by the evidence, the Virginia Supreme Court of Appeals held that petitioner and those associated with it

"solicit prospective litigants to authorize the filing of suits by NAACP and Fund [Educational Defense Fund] lawyers, who are paid by the Conference and controlled by NAACP policies . . ." (202 Va., at 159; 116 S.E.2d, at 68-69),

and concluded that this conduct violated Chapter 33 as well as Canons 35 and 47 of the Canons of Professional Ethics of the American Bar Association, which had been adopted by the Virginia courts more than 20 years ago.

At the same time the Virginia court demonstrated a responsible awareness of two important limitations on the State's power to regulate such conduct. The first of these is the long-standing recognition, incorporated in the Canons, of the different treatment to be accorded to those aiding the indigent in prosecuting or defending against legal proceedings. The second . . . is the constitutional right of any person to express his views, to disseminate those views to others, and to advocate action designed to achieve lawful objectives, which in the present case are also constitutionally due. Mindful of these limitations, the state court construed Chapter 33 not to prohibit petitioner and those associated with it from acquainting colored persons with what it believes to be their rights, or from advising them to assert those rights in legal proceedings, but only from "solicit[ing] legal business for their attorneys or any particular attorneys." Further, the court determined that Chapter 33 did not preclude petitioner from contributing money to persons to assist them in prosecuting suits, if the suits "have not been solicited by the appellants [the NAACP and Defense Fund] or those associated with them, and channeled by them to their attorneys or any other attorneys." . . .

II. . . .

. . . [T]he question is whether the particular regulation of conduct concerning litigation has a reasonable relation to the furtherance of a proper state interest, and whether that interest outweighs any foreseeable harm to the furtherance of protected freedoms.

III.

The interest which Virginia has here asserted is that of maintaining high professional standards among those who practice law within its borders. This Court has consistently recognized the broad range of judgments that a State may properly make in regulating any profession. . . . But the regulation of professional standards for members of the bar comes to us with even deeper roots in history and policy, since courts for centuries have possessed disciplinary powers incident to the administration of justice. . . .

The regulation before us has its origins in the long-standing common-law prohibitions of champerty, barratry, and maintenance, the closely related prohibitions in the Canons of Ethics against solicitation and intervention by a lay intermediary, and statutory provisions forbidding the unauthorized practice of law. The Court recognizes this formidable history, but puts it aside in the present case on the grounds that there is here no element of malice or of pecuniary gain, that the interests of the NAACP are not to be regarded as substantially different from those of its members, and that we are said to be dealing here with a matter that transcends mere legal ethics—the securing of federally guaranteed rights. But these distinctions are too facile. They do not account for the full scope of the State's legitimate interest in regulating professional conduct. For although these professional standards may have been born in a desire to curb malice and self-aggrandizement by those who would use clients and the courts for their own pecuniary ends, they have acquired a far broader significance during their long development.

First, with regard to the claimed absence of the pecuniary element, it cannot well be suggested that the attorneys here are donating their services, since they are in fact compensated for **their** work. Nor can it tenably be argued that petitioner's litigating activities fall into the accepted category of aid to indigent litigants. The reference is presumably to the fact that petitioner itself is a nonprofit organization not motivated by desire for financial gain but by public interest and to the fact that no monetary stakes are involved in the litigation.

But a State's felt need for regulation of professional conduct may reasonably extend beyond mere "ambulance chasing." . . .

Underlying this impressive array of relevant precedent is the widely shared conviction that avoidance of improper pecuniary gain is not the only relevant factor in determining standards of professional conduct. Running perhaps even deeper is the desire of the profession, of courts, and of legislatures to prevent any interference with the uniquely personal relationship between lawyer and client and to maintain untrammeled by outside influences the responsibility which the lawyer owes to the courts he serves.

When an attorney is employed by an association or corporation to represent individual litigants, two problems arise, whether or not the association is organized for profit and no matter how unimpeachable its motives. The lawyer becomes subject to the control of a body that is not itself a litigant and that, unlike the lawyers it employs, is not subject to strict professional discipline as an officer of the court. In addition, the lawyer necessarily finds himself with a divided allegiance—to his employer and to his client—which may prevent full compliance with his basic professional obligations. . . .

There has, to be sure, been professional criticism of certain applications of these policies. But the continued vitality of the principles involved is beyond dispute, and at this writing it is hazardous at best to predict the direction of the future. For us, however, any such debate is without relevance, since it raises questions of social policy which have not been delegated to this Court for decision. Our responsibility is simply to determine the extent of the State's legitimate interest and to decide whether the course adopted bears a sufficient relation to that interest to fall within the bounds set by the Constitution.

Second, it is claimed that the interests of petitioner and its members are sufficiently identical to eliminate any "serious danger" of "professionally reprehensible conflicts of interest." . . .

The NAACP may be no more than the sum of the efforts and views infused in it by its members; but the totality of the separate interests of the members and others whose causes the petitioner champions, even in the field of race relations, may far exceed in scope and variety that body's views of policy, as embodied in litigating strategy and tactics. Thus it may be in the interest of the Association in every case to make a frontal attack on segregation, to press for an immediate breaking down of racial barriers, and to sacrifice minor points that may win a given case for the major points that may win other cases too. But in a particular litigation, it is not impossible that after authorizing action in his behalf, a Negro parent, concerned that a continued frontal attack could result in schools closed for years, might prefer to wait with his fellows a longer time for good-faith efforts by the local school board than is permitted by the centrally determined policy of the NAACP. Or he might see a greater prospect of success through discussions with local school authorities than through the litigation deemed necessary by the Association. The parent, of course, is free to withdraw his authorization, but is his lawyer, retained and paid by petitioner and subject to its directions on matters of policy, able to advise the parent with that undivided allegiance that is the hallmark of the attorney-client relation? I am afraid not.

Third, it is said that the practices involved here must stand on a different footing because the litigation that petitioner supports concerns the vindication of constitutionally guaranteed rights.

But surely state law is still the source of basic regulation of the legal profession, whether an attorney is pressing a federal or a state claim within its borders. . . .

There remains to be considered on this branch of the argument the question whether this particular exercise of state regulatory power bears a sufficient relation to the established and substantial interest of the State to overcome whatever indirect impact this statute may have on rights of free expression and association.

Chapter 33 as construed does no more than prohibit petitioner and those associated with it from soliciting legal business for its staff attorneys or, under a fair reading of the state court's opinion and amounting to the same thing, for "outside" attorneys who are subject to the Association's control in the handling of litigation which it refers to them. . . . Such prohibitions bear a strong and direct relation to the area of legitimate state concern. In matters of policy, involving the form, timing, and substance of litigation, such attorneys are subject to the directions of petitioner and not of those nominally their clients. Further, the methods used to obtain litigants are not conducive to encouraging the kind of attorney-client relationships which the State reasonably may demand. There inheres in these arrangements, then, the potentialities of divided allegiance and diluted responsibility which the State may properly undertake to prevent.

The impact of such a prohibition on the rights of petitioner and its members to free expression and association cannot well be deemed so great as to require that it be struck down in the face of this substantial state interest. The important function of organizations like petitioner in vindicating constitutional rights is not of course to be minimized, but that function is not, in my opinion, substantially impaired by this statute. Of cardinal importance, this regulatory enactment as construed does not in any way suppress assembly, or advocacy of litigation in general or in particular. Moreover, contrary to the majority's suggestion, it does not, in my view, prevent petitioner from recommending the services of attorneys who are not subject to its directions and control. . . . And since petitioner may contribute to those who need assistance, the prohibition should not significantly discourage anyone with sufficient interest from pressing his claims in litigation or from joining with others similarly situated to press those claims. It prevents only the solicitation of business for attorneys subject to petitioner's control, and as so limited, should be sustained.

IV.

The Court's remaining line of reasoning is that Chapter 33 as construed (hereafter sometimes simply "the statute") must be struck down on the score of vagueness and ambiguity. I think that this "vagueness" concept has no proper place in this case and only serves to obscure rather than illuminate the true questions presented.

The Court's finding of ambiguity rests on the premise that the statute may prohibit *mere* recommendation of "any particular attorney," whether or not a member of the NAACP's legal staff or otherwise subject to the Association's direction and control. Proceeding from this premise the Court ends by invalidating the entire statute on the basis that this alleged vagueness too readily lends itself to the stifling of protected activity. . . .

Ambiguity in the present statute can be made to appear only at the price of strained reading of the state court's opinion. As construed, the statute contains two types of prohibition relating to solicitation. The first prohibits such groups as the NAACP and the Educational Defense Fund, "their officers, members, affiliates, voluntary workers and attorneys" from soliciting legal business for "their attorneys." And the state court made it clear that "their attorneys" referred to "attorneys whom they [the NAACP and the Fund] pay, and who are subject to their directions." 202 Va., at 164, 116 S.E.2d, at 72. This is the practice with which the state court's opinion is predominantly concerned and which gave rise to the intensive consideration by that court of the relations between petitioner and its legal staff. Surely, there is no element of uncertainty involved in this prohibition. The state court has made it plain that the solicitation involved is not the advocacy of litigation in general or in particular but only that involved in the handling of litigation by petitioner's own paid and controlled staff attorneys. . . .

The second prohibition in the statute is the solicitation by petitioner of legal business for "any particular attorneys" or the channeling of litigation which it supports to "any other attorneys," whether or not they are petitioner's staff attorneys. This language of the state court, coupled primarily with this Court's own notion that Chapter 33 in defining "agents" has departed from common-law principles, leads the majority to conclude that the statute may have been interpreted as precluding organizations such as petitioner from simply advising prospective litigants to engage for themselves particular attorneys, whether members of the organization's legal staff or not.

Surely such an idea cannot be entertained with respect to the state court's discussion of the NAACP and its staff attorneys. The record is barren of all evidence that any litigant, in the type of litigation with which this case is concerned, ever attempted to retain for his own account one of those attorneys, and indeed strongly indicates that such an arrangement would not have been acceptable to the NAACP so long as such a lawyer remained on its legal staff. And the state court's opinion makes it clear that that court was not directing itself to any such situation.

Nor do I think it may reasonably be concluded that the state court meant to preclude the NAACP from recommending "outside" attorneys to prospective litigants, so long as it retained no power of direction over such lawyers. Both in their immediate context and in light of the entire opinion and record below, it seems to me very clear that the phrases "or any particular attorneys" and "or any other attorneys" both have reference only to those "outside" attorneys with respect to whom the NAACP or the Defense Fund bore a relationship equivalent to that existing between them and "their attorneys." It savors almost of disrespect to the Virginia Supreme Court of Appeals, whose opinion manifests full awareness of the considerations that have traditionally marked the line between professional and unprofessional conduct, to read this part of its opinion otherwise. Indeed the ambiguity which this Court now finds quite evidently escaped the notice of both petitioner and its counsel for they did not so much as suggest such an argument in their briefs. Moreover, the kind of approach that the majority takes to the statute is quite inconsistent with the precept that our duty is to construe legislation, if possible, "to save and not to destroy." . . .

V.

Since the majority has found it unnecessary to consider them, only a few words need be said with respect to petitioner's contentions that Chapter 33 deprives it of property without due process of law and denies it equal protection. . . .

As to equal protection, this position is premised on the claim that the law was directed solely at petitioner's activities on behalf of Negro litigants. But Chapter 33 as it comes to us, with a narrowing construction by the state court that anchors the statute firmly to the common law and to the court's own independently existing supervisory powers over the Virginia legal profession, leaves no room for any finding of discriminatory purpose. Petitioner is merely one of a variety of organizations that may come within the scope of the long-standing prohibitions against solicitation and unauthorized practice. It would of course be open to the petitioner, if the facts should warrant, to claim that Chapter 33 was being enforced discriminatorily as to it and not against others similarly circumstanced. See *Yick Wo v. Hopkins*, 118 U.S. 356, 373-374. But the present record is barren of any evidence suggesting such unequal application, and we may not presume that it will occur. . . .

I would affirm.[17]

[Separate opinions of Justice Douglas (concurring) and Justice White (concurring in part and dissenting in part) are omitted.]

QUESTIONS

1. The canons against solicitation and lay intermediaries.— *Button* dealt with the constitutional aspects of several of the A.B.A. Canons (and analogous state statutes) as applied to the activities of the NAACP. There are important issues of policy raised by these Canons, aside from the constitutional issues. Three of the Canons are particularly pertinent to the conduct of attorneys who represent clients through the auspices of an organization like the NAACP in circumstances like those in *Button*:

Canon 27: It is unprofessional to solicit professional employment by circulars, advertisements, through touters or by personal communications or interviews not warranted by personal relations.

Canon 28: It is unprofessional for a lawyer to volunteer advice to bring a lawsuit, except in rare cases where ties of blood, relationship or trust make it his duty to do so. Stirring up strife and litigation is not only unprofessional, but it is indictable at common law. It is disreputable to hunt up . . . causes of action and inform thereof in order to be employed to bring suit . . ., or to breed litigation by seeking out those with . . . grounds of action in order to secure them as clients. . . . A duty to the public and to the profession devolves upon every member of the Bar having knowledge of such practices upon the part of any practitioner immediately to inform thereof, to the end that the offender may be disbarred.

Canon 35: The professional services of a lawyer should not be controlled or exploited by any lay agency, personal or corporate, which intervenes between client and lawyer. A lawyer's responsibilities and qualifications are individual.

---

[17] In Brotherhood of Railroad Trainmen v. Virginia, 377 U.S. 1 (1964), the Virginia State Bar obtained an injunction against activities of the Brotherhood which the Bar characterized as solicitation. The Brotherhood maintained a list of lawyers whom it recommended to its members for prosecution of damages claims for work-related injuries. The Supreme Court, relying on *Button,* vacated the injunction. [*Eds.* note.]

He should avoid all relations which direct the performance of his duties by or in the interest of such intermediary. A lawyer's relation to his client should be personal, and the responsibility should be direct to the client. Charitable societies rendering aid to the indigent are not deemed such intermediaries. . . .[18]

What purposes are served by the canons against solicitation? In *Button* the majority of the Court was of the view that those purposes are not sufficiently weighty to justify (in a constitutional sense) the abridgment of the freedom of speech that resulted from application of the Virginia version of the no-solicitation rule to the NAACP. What is socially undesirable about "stirring up litigation" to enforce an individual's rights against a governmental agency? Does solicitation harm the reputation of the legal profession and thereby impair its effectiveness, or does it harm clients in some way? Is the no-solicitation rule primarily a means of controlling competition within the profession? If an attorney is not being paid by the client, but either is volunteering his services or is being paid by an organization such as the NAACP, should the no-solicitation rules apply to him? See Note, *A Critical Analysis of Rules Against Solicitation by Lawyers*, 25 U. CHI. L. REV. 674 (1958).

Is constitutional litigation different, so that it should be permissible for an attorney to build his lawsuit first, and then go out and find a client? Professor Harry Kalven asks:

Who is the client in a case affecting great constitutional issues?. . . . [O]ften the great constitutional issues involve only modest private interests. . . . There is, therefore, often a great discrepancy between the private interest of the individual litigant which produces the controversy and the large public interest in the issue he raises. To some extent, this public interest has been satisfied by the use of the amicus brief; and in recent years, particularly in the civil-rights cases, the United States itself has played a major role. . . . A *Yale Law Journal* note some years ago aptly called the NAACP a "private attorney general." There is no secret as to what, in fact, its role is; it provides an effective stimulus to the litigating of civil-rights issues; in reality, the NAACP

---

[18] The *Button* opinion refers also to Canon 47, which provides: "No lawyer shall permit his professional services, or his name, to be used in aid of, or to make possible, the unauthorized practice of law by any lay agency, personal or otherwise."

is the client. H. KALVEN, THE NEGRO AND THE FIRST AMEND-
MENT 79-80 (1965).*

Issues such as those in *Button* have arisen with respect to
OEO-funded legal services programs. It has been charged that
lawyers in some of these programs are violating the canons against
solicitation. Consider, for example, the following extracts from a
booklet distributed in California, the cover of which reads, "Farm
Workers, the law can protect you if you . . . demand your
rights!":

> This booklet is a brief description of the laws affecting
> farm workers. It states the law as it is written and not as
> it is enforced. These laws will be enforced only if you de-
> mand your rights. If your complaints are resisted, or if a
> government agency does not help you, then contact a
> lawyer. . . .
> If an employer forces a worker to agree not to join a
> labor union . . . then the employer is breaking the law.
> . . .
> If you think such violations exist . . . then you should
> contact a lawyer immediately. . . .
> If the employer does not provide clean, fresh drinking
> water . . . then he is breaking the law. . . .
> If first aid kits are not on a job site wherever women and
> children are working . . . then the employer is breaking
> the law. . . .
> Any violation of these laws should be reported to your
> union, the local health department, and/or the Division of
> Industrial Welfare, California Department of Industrial
> Relations. . . . You should also contact a lawyer. (See page
> 44 for the office nearest you.) . . .

At the end of the booklet there is a listing of legal services program offices in rural areas throughout the state. Is this booklet in
violation of the canons against solicitation? Should there be a
prohibition against the distribution of the booklet? After *Button*, would such a prohibition be constitutional?
Consider the following:

> Attorney General Nicholas de B. Katzenbach urged the
> legal profession today to meet the needs of the poor by re-

---

laxing its rules against lawyers soliciting clients. . . . In a speech to 550 lawyers at the Administration's national conference on law and poverty, he said that the "historic strictures" of the legal canons of ethics should not be allowed to stand between poor people and legal help. . . . "To be reduced to inaction by ethical prohibitions against profiteering when the client may well be penniless is, on its face, anomalous," Mr. Katzenbach declared, adding: "To be reduced to inaction by ethical prohibitions against promoting litigation when unfair treatment abounds is to let a canon of lawyers serve injustice." . . . Mr. Katzenbach said the American Bar Association should . . . draft canons of ethics that would allow solicitation of poor clients but continue to forbid it when done for profit. N.Y. Times, June 25, 1965, p. 15, reprinted in V. COUNTRYMAN & T. FINMAN, THE LAWYER IN MODERN SOCIETY 575-76 (1966).

What purposes are served by the canon against lay intermediaries? Did the majority in *Button* take too lightly the NAACP rule that prohibited NAACP attorneys from seeking any relief short of desegregation? When the Office of Economic Opportunity funds nonprofit private organizations which employ lawyers who render legal services to the poor, does Canon 35 limit the control that can be exercised by the board of directors of such a corporation over attorneys as they represent their clients? What is the implication of the *Button* decision for the degree of control that state law must permit to the board of directors of such a corporation? The Office of Economic Opportunity has taken the general position that in order to qualify for federal funds such a nonprofit organization must have a majority of lawyers on its board of directors. Is this a wise requirement?

2. The "motive" of the Virginia legislature and the interpretation of the statute.—The statute before the Court in the *Button* case was enacted in 1956 as part of Virginia's legislative program of "massive resistance" to *Brown v. Board of Education.* The statute's sponsors candidly supported it as a means for limiting the activities of the NAACP in Virginia, which activities were characterized as violations of professional ethics. In the *Button* opinion, the Court chose not to rest its decision on any "considerations of race or racial discrimination. . . ." The Court went on: "That the petitioner happens to be engaged in activities of expression and association on behalf of the rights of Negro children to equal opportunity is constitutionally irrelevant to the ground of our decision." Was the question of legislative motive really irrelevant?

The issue of statutory construction that divided Justice Harlan from the majority may reflect the majority's unwillingness to tackle the problem of motive. The majority's reading was that the statute forbade all arrangements by which prospective litigants would be advised to retain particular attorneys. That reading gave the statute a sweep that was both broad and uncertain, and permitted the Court to dispose of the case on First Amendment grounds. Justice Harlan read the statute more narrowly, interpreting it to forbid an organization like the NAACP only to solicit cases for its own attorneys; such a limitation on speech was justified, he argued, by the interests of the state advanced by the canons against solicitation and lay intermediaries. Professor Kalven comments on this disagreement in the following passage:

> Simply as an exercise in reading words, Justice Harlan seems to me to have the better of the argument thus far. . . . [Justice Brennan's] argument now becomes one that, given the climate of opinion in the South in civil-rights litigation, lack of precision in the wording of a statute regulating such litigation is doubly threatening, ...
>
> In this context, Justice Harlan's talk of "savoring of disrespect" to the Virginia court has a hollow ring. This is not an old law regulating legal ethics in Virginia from time immemorial; it is a new law designed in 1956 as part of an elaborate scheme of laws to meet the crisis of the segregation decision. And somehow, as Justice Brennan insists, this fact has something to do with predictions as to how it will be construed. Nor are we persuaded by Justice Harlan's closing admonition that it will, of course, be open to petitioners to show at some later date that the law is being enforced in a discriminatory fashion.
>
> This collision of views on the apparently colorless question of construing a statute indicates once again how pervasive and indeed corrosive the strains and tensions of the race issue are for the legal system. If the Court ignores the motivation of the South in these cases, it risks deciding great issues in a vacuum and giving us a parody of legal wisdom; yet if it acknowledges the motivation of the South, it risks giving constitutional litigation the appearance of civil war and of giving us a parody of legal neutrality. The problem is real because it is of profound importance to the Negro cause that it not merely win its cases in a court but that it

win them from a just court. H. Kalven, The Negro and
the First Amendment 84-85 (1965).*

Professor Kalven is suggesting here that the majority avoided the
necessity of impugning the motives of the legislators by concluding that the statute was unconstitutionally vague, since it failed
to differentiate between conduct which could and could not
constitutionally be prohibited. In view of its conclusion about the
inadequacy of the justifications for the prohibitions against
solicitation and lay intermediaries, was it necessary for the majority to enter into the vagueness discussion?

**3. The presumption of constitutionality and the "preferred po-
sition" of political freedoms.**—The *Button* case raised the question of the Virginia statute's validity under the due process
clause of the Fourteenth Amendment, as that clause has been held
to "incorporate" the freedom of speech protected by the First
Amendment. In recent cases involving freedom of speech, and
related freedoms of political association, the Supreme Court has
often taken the position that restrictive legislation requires a
substantial and persuasive justification by the government (state
or federal) if it is to escape being held invalid—more than a
showing that there was some "reasonable basis" for the regulation. This "preferred position" for speech and related freedoms
results in a standard of review far more stringent than the "reasonable basis" rule that we encountered in the opinions of Chief
Justice Shaw in *Roberts v. City of Boston* and Justice Brown in
Plessy v. Ferguson. The *Button* opinion, following recent free-
speech precedent, more closely resembles the Court's approach in
Brown v. Board of Education: the state's interests in the rules
against solicitation and lay intermediaries are weighed against the
constitutionally protected interest of the NAACP and its clients
to engage in litigation as a form of political activity. It is not
enough to say that the state law has a reasonable basis. Does
Justice Harlan's dissent disagree with this approach to speech
cases? Does the Court's approach result in its acting as a "super-
legislature" as it performs the function of judicial review? Would
Justice Harlan's greater deference to the state legislature's judgment avoid the "super-legislature" problem?

---

* Reprinted from *The Negro and the First Amendment,* by Harry Kalven,
Jr. Copyright © 1965 by the Ohio State University Press. All rights reserved.

F. EFFORTS FROM 1954 TO 1964 WITHIN THE FEDERAL GOVERNMENT TO IMPLEMENT THE PRINCIPLE DECLARED IN BROWN

The preceding sections of this chapter have dealt with implementation of *Brown v. Board of Education* through the process of litigation in actions brought by private individuals. Until the Civil Rights Act of 1964, Congress did nothing to add to the means for vindicating the rights declared in *Brown*. During the period 1954-1960 the major action within the Executive branch of the government, aside from the use of federal troops in Little Rock, consisted of the appearance of the Department of Justice as amicus curiae in school desegregation suits brought by private individuals. No criminal prosecutions were brought under federal civil rights statutes against school officials who refused to afford black children their constitutional right to be free from racial segregation in the schools. Statements by President Eisenhower during this period recalled the language of Justice Brown's majority opinion in *Plessy v. Ferguson*: "I don't believe you can change the hearts of men with laws or decisions."[19]

We have noted earlier that in some parts of the south, for various reasons, private individuals did not sue to desegregate the schools. Beginning in 1961, in the administration of President Kennedy, there was increased federal executive action with respect to a variety of civil rights issues.[20] In the school area attention centered on federal grantees who used racial standards in the administration of their programs. We have seen that Executive branch officials concluded that they could not, by a "stroke of the pen," impose desegregation requirements as eligibility conditions on all the public schools that were entitled to grants under the federal "impacted areas" program. See p. 108 *supra*. This program was then the largest federal aid program for education; under it, federal payments were made to school districts that educated children whose parents were employed on federal installations. Still, some actions were taken under the impacted areas legislation. The Secretary of Health, Education, and Welfare ruled that racially segregated schools did not provide "suitable free public education" for children who lived on federal military installations and attended local public schools. Under the federal statute,[21] if suitable free public education is available to such children, federal funds are paid to the local schools for their education. If the Commissioner of Education determines

---

[19] A. Lewis, Portrait of a Decade 89 (Bantam ed. 1965).
[20] See *id.*, pp. 100-04.
[21] 20 U.S.C. §§ 241, 640; F.C.A. 20 §§ 241, 640.

that suitable free public education is not available in the local schools, he is to make other arrangements for education of the children, and is authorized to build and operate schools on federal installations. As a result of the Secretary's ruling, the statutory authority was used to provide "on-base" schools at some installations; the children affected no longer attended the local schools, and the schools no longer received federal funds for educating these children.[22]

The United States also initiated litigation against a number of school districts to enforce an asserted contractual obligation not to segregate by race the children of military personnel; these districts had received federal "impacted areas" funds for the construction of school facilities. At the time the Government brought these suits the Attorney General was not authorized by statute to bring suits to restrain state violations of individuals' civil rights except in cases relating to voting. The litigation regarding "impacted areas" funds was therefore an attempt to establish some authority for the Attorney General to initiate school desegregation suits. This litigation had only a limited potential, because it could affect only those school districts which received "impacted areas" funds and could bring about desegregation only for "federally-connected" children. Nonetheless, success for the Government in this litigation would have had a significant symbolic value, establishing a federal presence in the desegregation of southern schools. The litigation raised a variety of issues relating to the function of courts in interpreting statutes.

One of the suits was brought against the County School Board of Prince George County, Virginia. The federal district judge held for the United States, and the defendants did not appeal to the Court of Appeals for the Fourth Circuit. The other suits were brought in federal courts in the Fifth Circuit. The defendant school boards prevailed in each of them at the district court level, and the Court of Appeals for the Fifth Circuit affirmed; the Supreme Court denied certiorari. Two of the district court opinions and the Court of Appeals opinion follow.

---

[22] The Secretary's announcement of this ruling appears in *Hearings on H.R. 6890 Before the Subcomm. on Integration in Federally Assisted Public Education Programs of the Comm. on Education and Labor*, 87th Cong., 2d Sess. 453-60 (1962).

UNITED STATES v. BILOXI MUNICIPAL SCHOOL DISTRICT
UNITED STATES v. GULFPORT MUNICIPAL SEPARATE SCHOOL DISTRICT
United States District Court, Southern District of Mississippi
219 F. Supp. 691 (1963)

Mize, District Judge.

This is an action brought by the United States of America seeking to enjoin the Defendants from separating upon the basis of race or color any dependents of military personnel or civilian employees of the Plaintiff in the operation of the public schools of the Gulfport Municipal Separate School District in Harrison County, Mississippi. [The United States brought a similar suit against the Biloxi Municipal School District. The facts alleged in that case are omitted. Judge Mize's opinion dealt with both suits.—Eds.] This relief is sought on the ground that the Defendants have and are violating their Assurances given under Chapter 19 of Title 20, United States Code. . . .

The Plaintiff alleges as a basis for the relief sought the following facts:

1. The United States of America maintains Keesler Air Force Base, a large military installation, and a Veterans Administration Hospital in Harrison County, Mississippi.

2. Approximately 2,000 children of military personnel and government employees attend the schools of the Gulfport Municipal Separate School District, including approximately 130 Negroes. The United States government does not have facilities for the education of these children. . . .

5. The United States Commissioner of Education from 1950 to date has approved and the Plaintiff has paid or agreed to pay grants to the Gulfport Municipal Separate School District in the amount of $1,240,478.35 for the construction and improvement of the schools of the district under Chapter 19 of Title 20, United States Code.

6. A large proportion of these payments under both Chapter 13 and Chapter 19 of Title 20, United States Code, have been made by the Plaintiff since 1954.

7. The Gulfport Municipal Separate School District in connection with each of its applications for grants under Chapter 19 of Title 20, United States Code, has given written Assurances, as required by 20 U.S.C. § 636, that the school facilities of the dis-

trict "will be available to the children for whose education contributions are provided on the same terms, in accordance with the laws of the state in which applicant is situated, as they are available to other children in applicant's school district."

8. It is the policy and practice of the Defendants in operating the public schools of the district to enroll white and Negro students in separate schools maintained and operated exclusively for students who are of the white or Negro race. As a result thereof all Negro school-age dependents of military personnel and civilian employees of the Plaintiff residing within the district attend schools operated exclusively for members of the Negro race. . . .

The . . . question is whether or not the Complaint states a claim upon which relief can be granted on the ground that the Defendants have breached the terms of the Assurances given under 20 U.S.C.A. § 636.

The Court is of the opinion that the language of the statutory Assurances is unambiguous and that there is no need for the application of any rules of construction; that the Assurances merely provide that the Defendants will treat the children of military personnel or civilian employees of the United States government in exactly the same manner as other children in the district are treated, i.e. identical treatment for federal children and non-federal children. If identical treatment for the white and colored children of the military personnel or civilian employees of the government had been intended as a part of the assurance given, it would have been easy for the act requiring the assurance to have so provided. Its omission was not an oversight, but was intentional. All children attending schools in the Defendants' district are admitted on the same terms, i.e. all white children without exception are alleged to go to white schools and all colored children without exception are alleged to go to schools reserved for the Negro race. . . .

This construction of the Assurances is in conformity with the history of the legislation and the executive and administrative interpretation thereof.

The administration of both Chapters 13 and 19 of Title 20, United States Code, is delegated to the Commissioner of Education. Financial assistance has been granted by the Commissioner, and funds have been allocated for school construction by the Commissioner with full knowledge of how the schools in the district were operated, and said funds have been thus granted and allocated consistently since the 1954 decision in Brown v. Board of Education. . . .

In 1958 and again in 1962 an effort was made to amend these Acts so as to specifically provide that the Assurances must provide that the applying school districts would offer the same school facilities to all federal children regardless of race. In each instance the amendments were defeated. During the hearings before the Subcommittee, on April 16th, 1962, on H.R. 10056 Mr. Burke Marshall, as Assistant Attorney General stated: ". . . The apparent congressional purpose was to provide federal funds for the education of children of our military forces and related civilians even though the educational facilities used were racially segregated." Congress refused to enact H.R. 10056, which provided that the applicant should give "assurance that such agency will operate its public schools and admit students thereto on a racially nondiscriminatory basis . . . ."

The Court therefore concludes that neither under the clear language of the statute nor the executive construction thereof nor the congressional intent is there any contractual liability here on the part of the Defendants. . . .

Moreover, had the Defendants breached their Assurances the remedy and the relief that Plaintiff could obtain is specifically provided for in and limited by the statutes themselves. The entire administration of the Acts is delegated to the United States Commissioner of Education, 20 U.S.C. §§ 642(b), 242(b). 20 U.S.C. § 641 provides that where the Commissioner feels that any assurance given is not being carried out that there shall be a hearing after reasonable notice before the Commissioner and that the finding of the Commissioner is subject to judicial review on the record by the United States Court of Appeals. The prescribed administrative remedy is exclusive. . . .

Furthermore, the statutes themselves provide the penalty for a violation of the Assurances or the relief available to the Commissioner. By 20 U.S.C. § 640 the Commissioner can make arrangements for constructing or providing proper school facilities himself. By 20 U.S.C. § 641 the Commissioner after the hearing can stop all payments to the agency as long as there is a failure to comply with the assurance, or if compliance is impossible, require a repayment by the agency of federal moneys diverted or improperly expended and make no further payments until this repayment is made. No right is given the Commissioner to require compliance with the Assurances by injunctive relief.

Where a statute creates a right of action and therein fixes the remedies available, the specified remedies are an integral part of the right and are substantive conditions and as such are exclusive. The statute does not make the assurances contractual promises that can be enforced by specific performance or injunction but merely assurances of a nature that a failure to comply therewith would authorize enforcement of the statutory remedies. . . .

The Court therefore also finds that Plaintiff has failed to state a claim upon which relief can be granted on the ground that the Defendants have failed or refused to perform the Assurances.

Defendants' Motion to Dismiss is sustained.

UNITED STATES v. COUNTY SCHOOL BOARD OF PRINCE GEORGE COUNTY, VIRGINIA
United States District Court, Eastern District of Virginia
221 F. Supp. 93 (1963)

BUTZNER, District Judge.

The United States seeks an injunction requiring the defendants to admit Negro children who are dependents of military and civilian personnel stationed or employed at Fort Lee, Virginia to schools attended only by white pupils.

The United States [contends] that pursuant to P.L. 815, Chapter 19 of Title 20 U.S.C. (20 U.S.C. § 631 et seq.), the Prince George County School Board gave assurance that its school facilities will be available to the federally-connected children on the same terms in accordance with the laws of the State as they are available to local children. The plaintiff urges that this is a contractual obligation or a statutory obligation. . . .

There is little material conflict in the evidence. The Court finds the following facts.

Fort Lee is situated in Prince George County, Virginia. It is the home of the United States Army Quartermaster School and the United States Army Logistical Management Center. Also stationed at the Fort are various other army units.

Approximately 5,000 military personnel are stationed at the Fort, of whom 694 are Negroes. The Army employs about 2,000 civilians there, of whom 350 are Negroes. The school-age dependents of military personnel include 159 Negroes. The school-age dependents of civilian personnel include 426 Negroes.

The Government maintains 1,484 family housing units on the Fort. More than 600 Negroes live on the post, and of these, 57 have families living with them.

None of the facilities and activities on the post is segregated on the basis of race or color.

No educational facilities are maintained on the post for the education of the dependents of the service men except a nursery for pre-school children. Children living on the post obtain their education in public and private schools in the Fort Lee area. . . .

The School Board of Prince George County has applied for and received from the United States under P.L. 815, Chapter 19 of Title 20, U.S.C. (20 U.S.C. § 631 et seq.), the following grants for the construction of schools in Prince George County on account of the federally-connected children attending the Prince George County Schools:

Date of Approval	School	Amount
6/20/51	Prince George Junior-Senior High	$364,008.00
11/ 8/55	Same (addition)	159,695.00
3/22/56	J. E. J. Moore Junior-Senior High	87,685.00
8/24/59	Wm. A. Walton Elementary	600,400.00
1/23/62	New Elementary School	94,500.00
6/27/62	New Elementary School	99,663.50

Pursuant to 20 U.S.C. § 636(b) (1) (F), the County School Board, when applying for each of the foregoing grants, gave assurance that its ". . . school facilities . . . will be available to the children for whose education contributions are provided in Title 2 of Public Law 815 on the same terms, in accordance with the laws of the State in which Applicant is situated, as they are available to other children in Applicant's school district."

In 1950 at the time of the enactment of Chapter 19 of Title 20, U.S.C. (20 U.S.C. § 631 et seq.), the law of the State of Virginia required the segregation of students according to race in public schools. At the time of the institution of this suit, the law of the State of Virginia did not include race as a criterion for the assignment of students in public schools. . . .

At all times pertinent to this litigation the Secretary of Health, Education, and Welfare knew that the School Board of Prince George County was operating separate schools for white and Negro children. . . .

The purpose of P.L. 815, Chapter 19 of Title 20, U.S.C., is stated in 20 U.S.C. § 631, as follows:

"The purpose of this chapter is to provide assistance for the construction of urgently needed minimum school facilities in school districts which have had substantial increases in school membership as a result of new or increased Federal activities. . . ."

The statute sets forth in detail the basis upon which local school boards receive federal funds for school construction. Each application by a school board must contain a description of the proposed construction and site. It must also contain or be supported by a number of specifications and assurances. Among these are that the board has the right to build schools on the site and to operate them for twenty years; that the board has authority to undertake the construction and to finance its share of the cost; that the board will build the school facility within a reasonable time; that minimum wage scales will be observed; that the school facilities of the board will be available to the federally-connected children on the same terms in accordance with the laws of the state as they are available to other children; and that the board will submit reports on the project to the Commissioner of Education.

After the Commissioner of Education has reviewed the application and determined that the requirements of the statute have been met, that the project is not inconsistent with other state plans for school construction and that there are sufficient federal funds available, he "shall approve" the application. No application may be disapproved until the Commissioner of Education has afforded the School Board a hearing. The statute also provides for judicial review of the refusal of the Commissioner to approve an application.

After approving the application, the Commissioner of Education is directed to pay the School Board ten per cent of the federal share of the costs of the project. Thereafter, as the construction progresses, the Commissioner is authorized to pay in installments the remainder of the federal share.

It has long been recognized that federal grants authorized by Congress create binding contracts . . . .

The Court concludes that the arrangement by which the School Board obtained money from the United States for assistance in construction of schools constituted a contract. The United States agreed to make certain payments to the School Board in exchange for certain assurances. The School Board, in order to receive the funds, gave the assurances required by the statute. The United States made the payments, and the contract is executed on its part.

The next issue is the meaning of the assurance, which is one of the terms of the contract. The defendants urge that the assurance is not applicable to racial segregation. The plaintiff insists that it is.

The assurance originates in 20 U.S.C. § 636(b) (1) (F):

"Each application by a local educational agency shall set forth the project for the construction of school facilities for such agency with respect to which it is filed, and shall contain or be supported by— . . . .

"(F) assurance that the school facilities of such agency will be available to the children for whose education contributions are provided in this chapter on the same terms, in accordance with the laws of the State in which the school district of such agency is situated, as they are available to other children in such school district";

The statute and the assurance are clear and unambiguous. Under these circumstances the law is well settled. In Carter v. Carter, 202 Va. 892, 121 S.E.2d 482, 485 (1961), the Supreme Court of Appeals of Virginia stated:

". . . The courts have neither the duty nor the power to make the contracts. It is only their function to construe them. The intention of the parties must be determined from what they actually say and not from what it may be supposed they intended to say. Where the meaning of the language used is clear, a contract needs no interpretation. It speaks for itself. We are bound to adhere to it as the authentic expression of the intention of the parties. . . ."

The statute and the assurance refer to state laws without excepting any of these laws. The Court can not exclude state laws pertaining to race in the assignment of children to school. To make this exclusion, despite the clear language of the statute and assurance, would violate the well established principle expressed in Carter v. Carter, supra.

This conclusion is in harmony with the explanation of the statute given in H.R. 2810, 81st Congress, 2nd Session, page 15 (1950), U.S. Code Congressional Service, p. 3819 as follows:

"This provision is intended as a safeguard against discrimination directed against categories of children mentioned in the bill as such, but it is not intended to disturb classification on jurisdictional or similar grounds or patterns of racial segregation established in accordance with the laws of the State in which the school district is situated."

Thus, it is plain that the statute does deal with racial segregation. Pursuant to the terms of the statute, the question of racial segregation is to be determined by state law. In 1950 Congress intended that segregated facilities should be used for the education of federally-connected children in those states whose laws provided for the separation of the races. In 1951 the School Board, when it gave the assurance, intended to use segregated facilities in compliance with state laws. Both Congress and the School Board, however, clearly stated that state laws were to be the criteria by which the obligation of the assurance was to be discharged. This Court is bound to adhere to the plain language of the statute and assurance "as the authentic expression of the intention of the parties." Carter v. Carter, supra.

Since 1950, the statute has not been changed. The intent of Congress and of the School Board has not changed. They both stated they would be guided by state law. The only thing that has changed is the state law to which the statute and the assurance refer.

The fact that the state law pertaining to racial segregation has changed affords no justification for disregarding the plain language of the statute or the assurance. Obviously the Congress and the School Board realized state laws would change. They can not be held to have intended that all state laws pertaining to education were frozen in the mold of 1950. The statute places no such limitation on the application of state laws. . . .

The Court also concludes that the School Board has breached the assurance. Under the statute and the assurance given pursuant thereto, the law of Virginia is the measure of the School Board's obligation. In argument at the bar of this Court it was not controverted that the law of Virginia excludes the race of a student as a criterion for pupil placement. . . .

The evidence discloses that the County School Board and the Pupil Placement Board assigned the federally-connected children on the basis of their race.

The defendants point out that officials at Fort Lee and the Secretary of Health, Education and Welfare acquiesced in the manner in which Negro children from Fort Lee were assigned to schools. This, however, does not furnish a defense to this suit. In United States v. City and County of San Francisco, 310 U.S. 16, 31, 60 S. Ct. 749, 757, 84 L. Ed. 1050 (1940), the City of San Francisco urged that administrative interpretation of the Department of the Interior supported the City's claim with respect to the sale of electric power. The Court said:

". . . We cannot accept the contention that administrative rulings—such as those here relied on—can thwart the plain purpose of a valid law." . . .

It has been suggested that relief must be initiated by administrative action because of 20 U.S.C. § 641, which provides:

"(a) Whenever the Commissioner of Education, after reasonable notice and opportunity for hearing to a local educational agency, finds (1) that there is a substantial failure to comply with the drawings and specifications for the project, (2) that any funds paid to a local educational agency under this chapter have been diverted from the purposes for which paid, or (3) that any assurance given in an application is not being or cannot be carried out, the Commissioner may forthwith notify such agency that no further payment will be made under this chapter with respect to such agency until there is no longer any failure to comply or the diversion or default has been corrected or, if compliance or correction is impossible, until such agency repays or arranges for the repayment of Federal moneys which have been diverted or improperly expended."

Subsection (b) provides for review by the Court of Appeals.

Provisions of this section are not applicable to the facts proved in this case. Here, the bulk of the funds can not be withheld because they have already been paid and the schools have been built. Administrative action seeking repayment of federal moneys is not appropriate for several reasons. Compliance with the assurance is not impossible. The evidence does not indicate that any federal moneys have been diverted or improperly expended. Limiting relief to the repayment of federal funds would defeat the declaration of purpose of the statute set forth in 20 U.S.C. § 631.

The Court therefore concludes that relief is not limited to administrative action, and that a money judgment against the County is not authorized by the statute and would defeat the intent of Congress. . . .

The defendants point out that Congress has not enacted legislation permitting the Secretary of Health, Education and Welfare to cut off funds to school districts that have not desegregated or planned for desegregation. Officials of the executive department have testified at hearings before congressional committees on H.R. 10056, 87th Cong., 2nd Sess. (1962), that they do not possess this power under existing law. The defendants argue, therefore, that the plaintiff here seeks to do indirectly what it can not do directly. This argument, however, does not reach the cause of action asserted here. The plaintiff in this suit does not seek to enforce the rights of all the children in Prince George County by the general desegregation of the County schools. If the plaintiff were to seek such broad relief, the argument advanced by the defendants would be pertinent. The relief in this case is limited to federally-connected children. It does not encompass all the children in the county. . . .

The relief to which the United States is entitled is measured by the statute and the assurance given by the School Board. The

School Board and the Pupil Placement Board must assign the federally-connected Negro children to schools so that the school facilities of the County will be available to them on the same terms in accordance with the laws of the state as they are available to other children in the County. No more is required of these defendants. Less will not suffice.

It follows that the motions to dismiss the complaint and the School Board's motion for summary judgment must be denied. . . .

UNITED STATES v. MADISON COUNTY BOARD OF EDUCATION
UNITED STATES v. GULFPORT MUNICIPAL SEPARATE SCHOOL DISTRICT
UNITED STATES v. BILOXI MUNICIPAL SEPARATE SCHOOL DISTRICT

United States Court of Appeals, Fifth Circuit
326 F.2d 237 (1964)
cert. denied, 379 U.S. 929 (1964)

Before RIVES and CAMERON, Circuit Judges, and HUNTER, District Judge.

RIVES, Circuit Judge.

These three appeals, though briefed separately, were argued orally at the same time. Each is an appeal from a judgment dismissing a complaint filed by the United States. In each case the United States sought to enjoin the local school board in the operation of the public schools under its jurisdiction from segregating upon the basis of race or color the children of members and civilian employees of the Armed Services. The opinions of the district courts are reported as United States v. Madison County Board of Education, N.D. Ala. 1963, 219 F. Supp. 60; United States v. Biloxi Municipal School District and United States v. Gulfport Municipal Separate School District, S.D. Miss. 1963, 219 F. Supp. 691. An appeal to this Court from a similar ruling in United States v. Bossier Parish School Board, W.D. La. 1963, 220 F. Supp. 243, has not yet been heard. . . .

We think it clear that the defendants are not under such a contractual obligation to the United States as may be specifically enforced by injunction not to assign federally connected children to local schools on the basis of race or color. No one would be so rash as to claim that a local school board in either of the "hard core" States of Alabama or Mississippi would intentionally enter into a contract which it understood to provide for even partial desegregation of the races in the public schools under its jurisdiction. A more improbable official action of such a local school board can scarcely be imagined. Indeed the complaints do not claim that the local boards understood that any such effect would ensue from any contract.

The theory of the complaints is that the acceptance of federal aid for the operation of the public schools and for school construction in areas affected by federal activities and the assurances required as a condition of such aid have so obligated the local educational agencies. We do not agree. . . .

The particular reliance of the United States is upon Assurance (F), and more specifically upon the clause of that Assurance which we italicize below. . . .

"(F) assurance that the school facilities of such agency will be available to the children for whose education contributions are provided in this chapter on the same terms, *in accordance with the laws of the State in which the school district of such agency is situated,* as they are available to other children in such school district; . . . ." . . .

The United States concedes, as it must, that when the statute was originally enacted the assurance in section 636(b) (1) (F) was intended for an almost opposite purpose, as thus explained in the report of the Committee on Education and Labor of the House of Representatives, No. 2810, 81st Cong., 2d Sess., p. 15 (1950):

"This provision is intended as a safeguard against discrimination against categories of children mentioned in the bill as such, but *it is not intended to disturb classification on jurisdictional or similar grounds, or patterns of racial segregation established in accordance with the laws of the State in which the school district is situated.*" (Emphasis added.)

Again, the United States places its emphasis on the last clause just quoted: "in accordance with the laws of the State in which the school district is situated." Its argument is that, as the State law has necessarily changed to conform to the United States Constitution as construed in Brown v. Board of Education, 1954, 347 U.S. 483, 74 S. Ct. 686, 98 L. Ed. 873, the obligation of each local school board under that assurance has also changed.

The doctrine of primary jurisdiction requires that that question be first decided by the federal Commissioner of Education to whom the administration of the statute is confided by section 642(b):

"(b) The Commissioner of Education shall administer this chapter, and he may make such regulations and perform such other functions as he finds necessary to carry out the provisions of this chapter." 20 U.S.C.A. § 642(b).

The only provision of the statute which might possibly indicate a judicial remedy independent of the Commissioner of Education is that providing for repayment of unexpended funds:

"(b) Any funds paid to a local educational agency under this chapter and not expended for the purposes for which paid shall be repaid to the Treasury of the United States." 20 U.S.C.A. § 637(b).

The United States does not seek repayment of any federal funds, but seeks to enjoin the local school board to operate the public schools under its jurisdiction so as not to segregate upon the basis of race or color the children of members and civilian employees of the Armed Services. However commendable may be that purpose, in our system of jurisprudence, the end cannot justify the means.

The only other remedy of which the statute can be said to fairly apprise any local school board is the administrative remedy subject to judicial review provided by section 641: . . . .

[The court here quotes this section, referred to by Judge Mize, p. 328 *supra*.]

The long-established principle is applicable that:

"A general liability created by statute without a remedy may be enforced by an appropriate common-law action. But where the provision for the liability is coupled with a provision for a special remedy, that remedy, and that alone, must be employed." Pollard v. Bailey, 1874, 87 U.S. (20 Wall.) 520, 527, 22 L. Ed. 376.

The United States complains that the statutory remedy is wholly inadequate. That, however, is a matter appropriate for the consideration of Congress, especially in view of its obvious desire not to interfere with local control of the operation of the public schools, and of familiar legislative history that any such attempted control would prevent enactment of the statute, or if enacted, acceptance of the proffered aid by many of the local school boards where the greatest need might exist.

The briefs of counsel cite a wealth of legislative history which reinforces our conclusion, but we think the statutes so clear that this opinion need not be prolonged by a recital of that history.

Clearly, the local school boards have not entered into any specifically enforceable contractual obligation not to assign federally connected children to local schools on the basis of race or color. . . .

Each of the judgments is

Affirmed.

QUESTIONS

Two issues can be isolated with respect to the breach-of-assurance contention made by the United States: the content of the obligation of the defendant school boards under the assurance, and the availability of injunctive relief as a remedy for breach of the assurance.

1. The school boards' obligations under the assurance.—The United States contended that the assurance obligated a school board to treat "federal" children in the same way that state law required that "local" children be treated, and that state law, after the *Brown* decision, prohibited racial segregation in public schools. The school boards contended that the assurance contained no obligations with respect to racial segregation, or, alternatively, that the assurance did not require desegregation with respect to federal children. The boards argued that their obligation under the assurance with respect to segregation was, at most, whatever state law provided in 1950 when the impacted areas grant program was first enacted (*i.e.,* separate but equal), or whatever the actual practice in the state was in 1963.

a. The statute's "unambiguous" language: two contradictory "plain meanings"?—Compare the following extracts from the opinions of Judge Butzner in the Virginia case and Judge Mize in the Mississippi case on these issues of interpretation of the assurance:

Judge Butzner (p. 332 *supra*): "The statute and the assurance are clear and unambiguous. . . . 'Where the meaning of the language used is clear, a contract needs no interpretation.' . . . Thus, it is plain that the statute does deal with racial segregation. Pursuant to the terms of the statute, the question of racial segregation is to be determined by state law. . . . The fact that the state law pertaining to racial segregation has changed affords no justification for disregarding the plain language of the statute or the assurance."

Judge Mize (p. 327 *supra*): "The Court is of the opinion that the language of the statutory Assurances is unambiguous and that there is no need for the application of any rules of construction; that the Assurances merely provide that the Defendants will treat the children of military personnel or civilian employees of the United States government in exactly the same manner as other children in the district are treated . . . . All children attending schools in the Defendant's district are admitted on the same terms, i.e. all white children without exception are alleged to go to white schools and all colored children without exception are alleged to go to schools reserved for the Negro race."

Each judge was of the view that the meaning of the language of the statutory assurance was so clear that no "interpretation" or "construction" was needed. And yet they came to opposite conclusions as to what that meaning was. What light do these opinions shed on the soundness and utility of the so-called "plain meaning" rule in statutory interpretation?

b. The purposes of the statutory provision.—What were the purposes of the assurance? Certainly the basic point was to prevent discrimination by local schools against federal children, without requiring school districts to treat federal children better than local children were treated under state law. For example, was not the assurance designed to prevent local schools from providing certain curricular offerings only to local children? In 1950, during the regime of "separate but equal," would it not have been clear that the assurance would have been violated if a local school segregated children racially and provided "unequal" (as measured by 1950 separate-but-equal standards) educational opportunity for Negro federal children? Suppose, in 1950, that a local school district had failed to make available to *any* children, federal or local, certain course offerings required by state law? Which standard—the district's legal duty or its illegal practice—should have been used to determine whether the assurance had been violated? Which of these interpretations would better advance the purposes of the assurance? Which interpretation would better advance more general policies in the legal system concerning the obligations of government officials to act within the law? Would the purposes underlying such other policies be relevant in attributing meaning to the words of the assurance?

If the measure of a school district's obligation with respect to federal children were concluded to be that of state law, would the purposes of the assurance be advanced by looking to state law as it had been in 1950 when the language of the assurance was first enacted? By looking to the requirements of state law at the time an individual school district accepted federal funds and executed the assurance? By looking to state law as it might stand at the time of a subsequent challenge to the school board's conduct? (In all of the cases discussed here the defendant school districts had received funds and executed the assurance for some school construction projects after 1954.) Given the general purposes of the assurance, would those purposes be best effectuated by attributing to the words "state law" in the assurance the meaning "state law, including future changes in that law"? Would it have made any sense for Congress to measure the obligation owed to federal children by state law only as it was in 1950?

c. **Aids to interpretation.**—All three of the opinions we have just read referred to various aids to interpretation. These aids can conveniently be categorized as pre- and post-enactment aids to interpretation.

i. **Pre-enactment aids: legislative history.**—The report of the committee of the House of Representatives which accompanied the 1950 impacted areas bill contained the following statement about the assurance:

> This provision is intended as a safeguard against discrimination directed against categories of children mentioned in the bill as such, but it is not intended to disturb classification on jurisdictional or similar grounds or patterns of racial segregation established in accordance with the laws of the State in which the school district is situated. H.R. REP. No. 2810, 81st Cong., 2d Sess. 15 (1950).

The primary purpose of committee reports like this one is to explain proposed legislation to members of the legislature. Committee reports, like floor debates and other similar materials produced during the enactment process, have come into common use by courts as aids to their interpretation of legislation. The extent of this practice once caused Justice Frankfurter to caution against easy acceptance of the quip that only when the legislative history is unclear do you go to the words of the statute.[23] There is reason for caution in relying on such materials from the internal legislative history of a statute; the legislature, after all, has not enacted the committee reports, floor debates, or the like; it has enacted the statute. It is by no means certain that legislators who voted for the statutory language were at the same time voting for and agreeing with all of the accompanying background explanation of the statute. Further caution is suggested by the practice of manufacturing legislative history. The Congressional Record abounds with "questions" like this: "Would the Senator not agree that this bill makes no change in the practice, time-honored in my state, of . . .?"

What might properly have been made of the House Committee's quoted statement by the courts that interpreted the assurance? The report is useful, is it not, in understanding the general purposes of the assurance? At the least it provides a starting point for a purpose-oriented interpretation of the statute. Perhaps the report also can serve as an after-check, once the meaning which will best advance the purposes of the statute has been tentatively settled upon. Is there anything in the committee's explanation of the assurance which suggests that Judge Butzner's interpretation—that the assurance obligates a school board to a non-segregation policy—is not the interpretation that will best effectuate the purposes of the assurance? The committee's explanation did not specifically discuss whether "state law" referred only to the law of 1950 or to the law as it might change thereafter; nor did the committee discuss whether the measure of a school district's obligation was the district's legal duty or its actual illegal practice. Sometimes, however, materials from the internal legislative history of a statute do refer quite specifically to issues that are expected to arise later for judicial interpretation. Suppose, for example, that there had been a statement in the committee report, or by a congressman in floor debate, that the obligation of a school district under the assurance was to be measured solely by state law on racial segregation as it stood in 1950, despite any possible future changes in the interpretation of the Fourteenth Amendment. In 1963, what weight should a court give to such a statement?

ii. Post-enactment aids: actual interpretation of the assurance by those affected.—Judge Mize stated that his interpretation, limiting a school board's duty under the assurance, was

---

[23] *See* Frankfurter, *The Reading of Statutes—Some Reflections*, 47 COLUM. L. REV. 527, 543 (1947).

. . . in conformity with . . . the executive and administrative interpretation thereof.

The administration of . . . [the legislation] is delegated to the Commissioner of Education. Financial assistance has been granted by the Commissioner, and funds have been allocated for school construction by the Commissioner with full knowledge of how the schools in the district were operated, and said funds have been thus granted and allocated consistently since the 1954 decision in Brown v. Board of Education . . . .

Judge Rives, in the Court of Appeals decision, referred to the school districts' interpretation of the assurance:

No one would be so rash as to claim that a local school board in either of the "hard core" states of Alabama or Mississippi would intentionally enter into a contract which it understood to provide for even partial desegregation of the races in the public schools under its jurisdiction. A more improbable official action of such a local school board can scarcely be imagined.

Even though a purpose-oriented interpretation might lead a court to the tentative conclusion that school boards have a contractual obligation to the United States not to segregate federal children, should the court nevertheless adopt a contrary interpretation that has been followed by the parties most closely affected by the statute? What is proved by the practice of the parties? Does their practice tell us how to advance the purposes of the statute? Is it ever sound for a court to adopt an interpretation which, in the court's judgment, will not advance the purposes of the statute so effectively as would another linguistically permissible meaning? Would it be sound for a court to depart from a purpose-oriented interpretation in the face of significant reliance interests of someone who has acted on the basis of his own interpretation of the statute?

These questions may be asked in the context of the statutory assurance in the "impacted areas" cases. The post-enactment interpretation of the assurance by the school boards might be significant because of the boards' reliance on their understanding of their obligations; a contrary interpretation might now be said to constitute unfair surprise. After 1954, when a district accepted federal funds and executed the assurance, what understanding could it reasonably have had as to its obligation not to segregate federal children by race? Did not Brown v. Board *of Education* make clear what the obligations of school districts were? In these circumstances, what was the nature of any reliance by a district on its interpretation of the assurance? Could it have been any more than an expectation that while the district might be subject to a desegregation suit by black parents and children, it would not be subject to suit by the United States? Would that reliance be important enough to justify a court's rejection of an interpretation that would better advance the purposes of the statute? Consider also the alleged administrative interpretation of the assurance. From 1954 to 1962, the Commissioner of Education (a subordinate of the Secretary of Health, Education, and Welfare) continued to make grants to school districts known not to be in compliance with *Brown v. Board of Education;* before 1963, the Commissioner had not sought to require compliance with the assurance as the Government now (1963) contended it should be interpreted. Did this course of conduct necessarily rest on the interpretation of the assurance contended for by the school districts? Or might the Commissioner of Education have been assuming the likelihood of private litigation after *Brown v. Board of Education?* Under the latter interpretation, the Commissioner's course of action should be understood, at most, as undue delay in invoking the rights of the United States under the assurance. Suppose the Commissioner of Education had formally interpreted the assurance as not requiring desegregation. Should such an administrative interpretation take precedence over the meaning that the court concludes will better effectuate the purposes of the statute?

iii. Post-enactment aids: failure of Congress to enact proposed legislation requiring desegregation as a condition on eligibility for grants.—Judge Mize's opinion noted that in

> . . . 1958 and again in 1962 an effort was made to amend these Acts so as to specifically provide that the Assurances must provide that the applying school districts would offer the same school facilities to all federal children regardless of race. In each instance the amendments were defeated. . . . Congress refused [in 1962] to enact H.R. 10056, which provided that the applicant should give "assurance that such agency will operate its public schools and admit students thereto on a racially nondiscriminatory basis. . . ."
>
> The Court . . . concludes that . . . under . . . the congressional intent . . . there [is not] any contractual liability here on the part of the Defendants.

Judge Butzner, in the Virginia case, said that

> This argument [based on Congress's failure to enact legislation denying grants to segregated districts], however, does not reach the cause of action asserted here. The plaintiff in this suit does not seek to enforce the rights of all the children in Prince George County by the general desegregation of the County schools. If the plaintiff were to seek such broad relief, the argument advanced by the defendants would be pertinent. The relief in this case is limited to federally-connected children. It does not encompass all the children in the county.

The proposed legislation, popularly called the "Powell Amendment," would have conditioned federal grants on a nonsegregation policy. H.R. 10056, for example, referred to by both Judge Mize and Judge Butzner, was a bill introduced in the House of Representatives in 1962. It would have required an additional undertaking by the grantee district to operate *all* of its schools on a racially nondiscriminatory basis. Because this new assurance extended beyond racial classification of federal children, Judge Butzner concluded that Congress's failure to enact H.R. 10056 was not relevant to an interpretation of the existing statutory language. But, he added, the argument would have been "pertinent" if the lawsuit had involved more than federal children. Suppose that H.R. 10056 had prohibited racial segregation only of federal children. Then how "pertinent" would have been the argument that failure to enact the proposed amendment expressed the Congress's "intent" that the existing statutory language did not require desegregation of federal children? It should be kept in mind, in considering this question, that failure to enact legislation can happen at any point along the road toward enactment, from the lack of introduction of a bill to a presidential or gubernatorial veto of a bill that has been passed by the legislature. In the case of H.R. 10056, the bill was reported by the House Committee on Education and Labor with a recommendation that it be passed,[24] but it never came to the floor of the House for a vote. The argument is that the "silence" or inaction of the legislature is significant—that, in effect, failure to enact specific legislation is equivalent to a legislative adoption of a principle of opposite tenor. Courts in the United States have accepted this argument based on legislative nonhistory to a surprising degree.

---

[24] H.R. Rep. No. 1751, 87th Cong., 2d Sess. (1962).

But as Justice Rutledge pointed out, "There are vast differences between legislating by doing nothing and legislating by positive enactment, both in the processes by which the will of Congress is derived and stated and in the clarity and certainty of the expression of its will."[25]

Consider the significance of the failure of Congress to pass H.R. 10056 in light of Justice Rutledge's statement. If this occurrence (or non-occurrence) were to be taken as expressive of the will of Congress on the issue of interpretation of the assurance, it would be an expression which had not been adopted by the institutional mechanisms ordinarily used, and even prescribed by the Constitution. Most importantly, the entire legislative body would not have participated in the adoption of the principle. And the President would not have had an opportunity to veto the adoption of the principle.

There is a further problem in giving meaning to the inaction of the legislature. Why was H.R. 10056 not enacted? This is an "interpretation" problem of an especially difficult sort. There was no consideration of the matter beyond one committee of one house, and that committee recommended passage. Some northern and western Congressmen at the time were of the view that the "Powell Amendment" jeopardized continuation of federal aid to education in the "impacted areas" program, because southern Congressmen might vote to end the program rather than accept it with the addition of a desegregation requirement. Some Congressmen may have been of the view that the existing statutory language required desegregation of federal children. Perhaps others were of the view that the existing language did not require desegregation of federal children. Some, no doubt, had no opinion at all on the meaning of the existing statutory language. In attributing meaning to the words of the statute which Congress failed to change, can anything sensible be made of the history of H.R. 10056 in 1962?[26]

In his opinion for the Court of Appeals, affirming the dismissals of the complaints in the Mississippi and Alabama impacted areas cases, Judge Rives made no reference to the failure of Congress to enact bills requiring desegregation as a condition on eligibility for federal grants. We can speculate on the reasons for this noncomment on a bit of nonhistory. The school districts had argued that if the assurance meant what the United States contended, there would have been no need for introduc-

---

[25] Concurring in Cleveland v. United States, 329 U.S. 14, 22 (1946).

[26] See Girouard v. United States, 328 U.S. 61 (1946); Willard & MacDonald, *The Effect of an Unsuccessful Attempt to Amend a Statute*, 44 CORNELL L.Q. 336 (1959).

tion in Congress of amendments to prohibit racial segregation by grantee school districts. The Department of Justice, in its reply brief, referred to "the most recent—and therefore most important —indication of Congressional intent."[27] The "indication" came in a report of the House Committee on Education and Labor, dated July 9, 1963, *after* the district court decisions in the Mississippi and Alabama cases, supporting a bill which would, among other provisions, have added a desegregation requirement to the impacted areas legislation. The report stated:

> In the hearings, officials of the Department of Health, Education, and Welfare described the pending litigation in which the United States is seeking to require nonracial assignment of federally connected children in public schools which have received Public Laws 874 and 815 funds. In approving the above-mentioned amendment, the committee does not wish to be understood as expressing any opinion on the issue of interpretation of Public Law 815 and the other issues which are now before the court in that litigation. As the committee understands it, it is contended in that litigation that local educational agencies have an obligation under Public Law 815 not to make racial assignments of federally connected children. The amendments approved by the committee would deny funds to local educational agencies in whose public schools there is racial segregation of any children, not just of the federally connected children. There is, therefore, need for these amendments regardless of the outcome of that litigation. H.R. REP. No. 506, 88th Cong., 1st Sess. 4-5.

Was there not an aura of fantasy about this entire incident—the argument by the school districts that some significant light as to Congress's "intent" as to the meaning of the assurance was shed by the fact that a bill was introduced to make desegregation a condition of eligibility for receipt of a federal grant, and the response that the committee report, hot off the press, showed what the congressional "intent" really was?

iv. Post-enactment aids: reenactment of the statute.—It was pointed out by the defendants in some of the impacted areas cases, though the matter is not referred to in the three opinions discussed here, that Congress had amended, reenacted, and con-

---

[27] Reply Brief for Appellant, United States v. Gulfport Municipal Separate School Dist., *et al.*, 326 F.2d 237 (5th Cir. 1964), at 33.

tinued to appropriate funds under the impacted areas legislation after *Brown v. Board of Education,* without changing the language of the assurance. The school boards argued that Congress thus had indicated an intent to have the assurance continue to require only what had been required before 1954—and that did not include a prohibition of racial segregation. The 1950 legislation was an authorization to expend federal funds during a limited period of years. After the *Brown* decision and before 1963, Congress acted several times to extend the period of authorization. The boards' argument ran this way: If, before each extension, the assurance had been interpreted administratively not to require desegregation, Congress, by extending and in other ways amending the statute while leaving the previously interpreted assurance unchanged, manifested its intention to adopt that administrative interpretation. A similar argument rested on the continued annual appropriation, after 1954, of funds which were being paid to school districts known to maintain segregated schools.

Another form of this argument often has been employed by courts in response to the contention that a prior judicial interpretation of a statute should be overruled. Here the argument is that if a court has attributed a meaning to the words of a statute, and the legislature thereafter has amended or reenacted the statute without changing the words the court has interpreted, that legislative action should be understood as an adoption of the judicial interpretation. This argument resembles the contention that a legislature by failing to enact a specific proposal thereby adopts a contrary principle. Here, however, the legislature has formally acted, and the court seeks to determine the significance of that action with respect to a prior interpretation of the statute.

Is it sound in these cases for courts to conclude that the legislature has adopted prior administrative or judicial interpretations?

Consider the consequences of such a conclusion for the exercise of the legislative function. The courts, in effect, would be saying to the Congress, when extension of the impacted areas grant program is under consideration (along with various proposals for amendment), that the Congress must at that time inquire into every prior administrative or judicial interpretation of the statute. Under the suggested principle, all prior administrative interpretations, if not specifically dealt with at the time of later legislative action, would virtually become part of the statute. Is it practicable for Congress, every time it tinkers with an existing statute, to come to a conclusion about the soundness of every prior interpretation of that statute? Does not this "reenactment rule" risk a judicial conclusion that the legislature has spoken on issues which in fact have not been resolved by the collective judgment of the legislature? Does the "rule" cut off opportunity for reconsideration and possible overruling by the administrative agencies or courts of their prior interpretations? Under the "reenactment rule," what is the significance of the annual appropriation process, under which Congress makes funds available for expenditure pursuant to previously enacted statutory authorizations? Should Congress be understood, in appropriating funds for the next fiscal year, to approve and adopt all administrative and judicial interpretations of the statute which preceded the appropriations act?

Finally, are not these "rules" about reenactment and the inaction of the legislature based on two unrealistic premises: first, that there has been a collective subjective intent of the legislature on the acceptability of all prior interpretations of the statute, and second, that such an intent can accurately be discovered?

2. Injunctive relief as a remedy for breach of the assurance: canons of construction: the canon of "expressio unius."—Judge Mize in the district court and Judge Rives in the court of appeals said that if the school districts had violated the assurance, the sole remedy for that breach was set forth in the statute: "the Commissioner may forthwith notify such agency that no further payment will be made under this chapter with respect to such agency until there is no longer any failure to comply or the diversion or default has been corrected or, if compliance or correction is impossible, until such agency repays or arranges for the repayment of federal moneys which have been diverted or improperly expended." As Judge Mize stated:

> Where a statute creates a right of action and therein fixes the remedies available, the specified remedies are an integral part of the right and are substantive conditions and as such are exclusive. The statute does not make the assurances contractual promises that can be enforced by specific performance or injunction but merely assurances of a nature that a failure to comply therewith would authorize enforcement of the statutory remedies.

Would suit by the United States to require compliance with the assurance, as an additional remedy to withholding future payments or recovering past payments, advance the purposes of the statute—in some cases even better than the specific remedies set forth in the statute? Why then should there be a general principle, relied on by Judges Mize and Rives, that where a statute includes specific remedies for breach of its terms, those remedies are exclusive? Does a legislature's listing of some remedies show an "intent" that remedies not included are not to be available? Are there other possible explanations for the statute's selection of only some of the remedies which the law, in general, would provide for breach of an obligation such as that in the assurance? Should not the presumption be the other way—*i.e.*, that specifically named remedies for breach of a statutory obligation are not the exclusive remedies unless the language of the statute clearly so provides?

The statements in the opinions of Judges Mize and Rives are expressed in a canon of statutory construction: "expressio unius est exclusio alterius"—the expression of one thing implies the exclusion of another. We have already encountered two types of canons, in the discussion of *Jackson v. Bulloch*, p. 73 *supra*. The canon of strict construction of penal statutes has been called a "policy of clear statement" or a "maxim of public policy." "Expressio unius," however, like the canon of "ejusdem generis," purports only to be a principle of linguistic usage. The "parry" to the "thrust" of "expressio unius," a competing principle of linguistic usage, is this: "the language may fairly comprehend many different cases where some only are expressly mentioned by way of example."[28] Is there any utility in the canon "expressio unius"? Should that canon, in interpretation of the assurance in the impacted areas legislation, lead to the conclusion that other remedies than those specifically included in the statute have been excluded by the Congress? Such a conclusion might rule out a form of remedy particularly suited to advance the purposes of the statute. Should the legislature be presumed to enact all statutes against a background of statements of English usage such as "expressio unius," or should statutory interpretation be approached as a problem of effectuating statutory purposes?

Still, the canon "expressio unius" may be of some use to a court that is interpreting the language of the assurance in the impacted areas statute. Does not the canon suggest that the words of the assurance can reasonably bear the meaning of stating the exclusive remedies for breach of the assurance? The canon would not indicate which meaning should prevail; it would, however, help establish that range of meanings from which the court, with a purpose-oriented approach to statutory interpretation, could select the meaning which should prevail. The function of the canon would therefore be to extend the range of interpretive

---

[28] *See* Llewellyn, *Remarks on the Theory of Appellate Decision and the Rules or Canons About How Statutes Are to Be Construed*, 3 VAND. L. REV. 395, 405 (1950).

choices open to the court. The canon would not settle the question of the availability of injunctive relief to enforce the assurance, but it would keep the court aware of its options.

G. THE CIVIL RIGHTS ACT OF 1964

Not until 1964 did Congress act to deal with the problem of school desegregation. In that year, however, ten years after the *Brown* decision, Congress enacted an omnibus Civil Rights Act, and several provisions of the Act were directed at the desegregation of public schools.

In this chapter, we have seen many of the difficulties that attended the efforts to implement *Brown* in the south. Considering those difficulties, it may be useful to survey the range of possible legislative responses. What might Congress have done in 1964 to speed up compliance with the *Brown* decision? Consider, for example, recourse to the processes of the criminal law. Since Reconstruction there had existed provisions in the federal civil rights statutes under which, theoretically at least, school board officials who denied the constitutional rights of Negro children could be prosecuted. Would it have been wise for Congress to amend these provisions as might have been necessary and to enact other legislation that might be needed to subject school board officials who were not proceeding with all deliberate speed, as specifically defined in the statute, to criminal sanctions? What criteria, in general, should govern a legislative decision whether to resort to the criminal law as an instrument of social control? Should the criminal law be the last resort? See generally H. PACKER, THE LIMITS OF THE CRIMINAL SANCTION (1968).

What were the potentialities of the administrative process for achieving desegregation? Would it have been wise, for example, in 1964 to create an administrative agency, on the model of the National Labor Relations Board or the Federal Trade Commission, with the function of case-by-case enforcement of desegregation criteria enacted by the Congress or promulgated by the agency within broad legislative standards? Such an agency might, for example, have been given authority to adjudicate complaints against school districts, either on the petition of an aggrieved individual or on the motion of the agency's staff. Such a proceeding might end with an order to the district to take specific action, and with resort to the courts, if necessary, to enforce the order.

Or consider a less coercive statutory approach: would it have been wise to resort to the federal grant device? That device is used widely to effectuate congressionally declared policy. In our context, Congress might have provided substantial federal funds to school districts which desegregated their schools, *i.e.*, grants not to meet the financial costs of desegregation but as a kind of "bonus" for speedy desegregation, to be spendable for any education-related purpose by the districts.

The Civil Rights Act of 1964 did not adopt any of these approaches. Several provisions of the Act dealt with school desegregation: Title IV authorized the Commissioner of Education (a) to give technical assistance to local school boards in developing and implementing desegregation plans, and (b) to finance institutes and other programs for school personnel to provide training in dealing with problems incident to desegregation. 42 U.S.C. §§ 2000c-2—2000c-4; F.C.A. 42 §§ 2000c-2—2000c-4. Title IV also empowered the Attorney General of the United States, upon receipt of a complaint that a school board was denying the equal protection of the laws, to institute a civil action in a United States district court, in the name of the United States, for appropriate judicial relief. The Attorney General must (i) "believe" the complaint to be "meritorious," and (ii) certify "that the signer or signers of such complaint are unable, in his judgment, to initiate and maintain appropriate legal proceedings for relief and that the institution of an action will materially further the orderly achievement of desegregation in public education. . . ." 42 U.S.C. § 2000c-6; F.C.A. 42 § 2000c-6. "Desegregation," for purposes of the Commissioner of Education's programs and civil actions by the Attorney General, is defined as "the assignment of students to public schools and within such schools without regard to their race, color, religion, or national origin, but 'desegregation' shall not mean the assignment of students to public schools in order to overcome racial imbalance."[29] And Title VI of the 1964 Act provided, in section 601, that "No person . . . shall, on the ground of race, color, or national origin, be excluded from participation in, be denied the benefits of, or be subjected to discrimination under any program or activity receiving Federal financial assistance." 42 U.S.C. § 2000d; F.C.A. 42 § 2000d. Procedures were created for terminating such financial assistance if the federal grantee violated section 601.

---

[29] 42 U.S.C. § 2000c(b); F.C.A. 42 § 2000c(b). Title IX authorized the Attorney General to intervene in actions brought by private plaintiffs in United States courts seeking relief from denial of equal protection of the laws on account of race, color, religion or national origin. The Attorney General must certify that the case is of "general public importance." 42 U.S.C. § 2000h-2; F.C.A. 42 § 2000h-2.

Title VI provided specific statutory authority for refusal by the Department of Health, Education, and Welfare to make grants to school districts which maintained racially segregated schools, authority which the Secretary of HEW said he did not otherwise have. In 1964 the impacted areas program was the major source of federal financial assistance to public schools; federal aid to public schools, and the significance of Title VI, were greatly increased with the enactment of the Elementary and Secondary Education Act of 1965.

Since the school year 1964-65 the percentage of Negro students in eleven southern states in public schools in which more than one-half the students were white has increased from 2.14 per cent to 20.3 per cent (in the school year 1968-69). See p. 239 *supra*. During that period 122 school districts were denied federal funds, for failure to comply with Title VI. Washington Post, Jan. 17, 1969, p. A2, col. 2. Resort to the potential sanction of denial of federal funds, coupled with the use of a specialized administrative agency to carry out this legislative policy, and the authorization of the Attorney General to bring desegregation suits, have proved to be far more effective than lawsuits by private individuals in implementing *Brown v. Board of Education*.

Several of the provisions of the Civil Rights Act of 1964 were considered in *United States v. Jefferson County Board of Education*, which follows. This was a decision of the United States Court of Appeals for the Fifth Circuit on appeals in separate suits against seven school districts in Alabama and Louisiana contending that freedom-of-choice plans adopted by the districts did not meet constitutional requirements. (The United States intervened in these cases, under the authority granted by Title IX of the 1964 Act.) The federal district courts had modified the freedom-of-choice plans to some extent, but the plaintiffs contended on appeal that the plans were still deficient. A panel of three judges heard the appeals, and after the decision of that panel a rehearing was held before all twelve judges of the Fifth Circuit. Much of the opinions and most of the decree dealt with the validity of freedom-of-choice plans, the issue which was later decided by the Supreme Court in *Green v. County School Board of New Kent County*, p. 290 *supra*. *Jefferson County* is of interest as a good example of the interaction of legislative, executive, and judicial lawmaking.

UNITED STATES v. JEFFERSON COUNTY BOARD OF EDUCATION
United States Court of Appeals, Fifth Circuit
372 F.2d 836 (1966)
aff'd en banc, 380 F.2d 385 (1967)
cert. denied sub nom. Board of Education of the City of
Bessemer v. United States, 389 U.S. 840 (1967)

Before WISDOM and THORNBERRY, Circuit Judges, and COX, District Judge.

WISDOM, Circuit Judge:

Once again the Court is called upon to review school desegregation plans to determine whether the plans meet constitutional standards. The distinctive feature of these cases, consolidated on appeal, is that they also require us to reexamine school desegregation standards in the light of the Civil Rights Act of 1964 and the Guidelines of the United States Office of Education, Department of Health, Education, and Welfare (HEW).

When the United States Supreme Court in 1954 decided Brown v. Board of Education, the members of the High School Class of 1966 had not entered the first grade. *Brown I* held that separate schools for Negro children were "inherently unequal." Negro children, said the Court, have the "personal and present" right to equal educational opportunities with white children in a racially nondiscriminatory public school system. For all but a handful of Negro members of the High School Class of '66 this right has been "of such stuff as dreams are made on". . . .

The only school desegregation plan that meets constitutional standards is one that works. By helping public schools to meet that test, by assisting the courts in their independent evaluation of school desegregation plans, and by accelerating the progress but simplifying the process of desegregation the HEW Guidelines offer new hope to Negro school children long denied their constitutional rights. A national effort, bringing together Congress, the executive, and the judiciary may be able to make meaningful the right of Negro children to equal educational opportunities. *The courts acting alone have failed.*

We hold, again, in determining whether school desegregation plans meet the standards of *Brown* and other decisions of the Supreme Court, that courts in this circuit should give "great weight" to HEW Guidelines. Such deference is consistent with the exercise of traditional judicial powers and functions. HEW Guidelines are based on decisions of this and other courts, are formulated to stay within the scope of the Civil Rights Act of 1964, are prepared in detail by experts in education and school administration, and are intended by Congress and the executive to be part of a coordinated national program. The Guidelines present the best system available for uniform application, and the best aid to the courts in evaluating the validity of a school desegregation plan and the progress made under that plan.

HEW regulations provide that schools applying for financial assistance must comply with certain requirements. However, the requirements for elementary or secondary schools "shall be deemed to be satisfied if such school or school system is subject to a final order of a court of the United States for the desegregation of such school or school system. . . ." This regulation causes our decisions to have a twofold impact on school desegregation. Our decisions determine not only (1) the standards schools must comply with under *Brown* but also (2) the standards these schools must comply with to qualify for federal financial assistance. Schools automatically qualify for federal aid whenever a final court order desegregating the school has been entered in the litigation and the school authorities agree to comply with the order. Because of the second consequence of our decisions and because of our duty to cooperate with Congress and with the executive in enforcing Congressional objectives, strong policy considerations support our holding that the standards of court-supervised desegregation should not be lower than the standards of HEW-supervised desegregation. The Guidelines, of course, cannot bind the courts; we are not abdicating any judicial responsibilities. But we hold that HEW's standards are substantially the same as this Court's standards. They are required by the Constitution and, as we construe them, are within the scope of the Civil Rights Act of 1964. In evaluating desegregation plans, district courts should make few exceptions to the Guidelines and should carefully tailor those so as not to defeat the policies of HEW or the holding of this Court. . . .

We approach decision-making here with humility. Many intelligent men of good will who have dedicated their lives to public education are deeply concerned for fear that a doctrinaire approach to desegregating schools may lower educational standards or even destroy public schools in some areas. These educators and school administrators, especially in communities where total segregation has been the way of life from cradle to coffin, may fail to understand all of the legal implications of *Brown*, but they understand the grim realities of the problems that complicate their task.

The Court is aware of the gravity of their problems. (1) Some determined opponents of desegregation would scuttle public education rather than send their children to schools with

Negro children. These men flee to the suburbs, reinforcing urban neighborhood school patterns. (2) Private schools, aided by state grants, have mushroomed in some states in this circuit. The flight of white children to these new schools and to established private and parochial schools promotes resegregation. (3) Many white teachers prefer not to teach in integrated public schools. They are tempted to seek employment at white private schools or to retire. (4) Many Negro children, for various reasons, prefer to finish school where they started. These are children who will probably have to settle for unskilled occupations. (5) The gap between white and Negro scholastic achievements causes all sorts of difficulties. There is no consolation in the fact that the gap depends on the socio-economic status of Negroes at least as much as it depends on inferior Negro schools.

No court can have a confident solution for a legal problem so closely interwoven with political, social, and moral threads as the problem of establishing fair, workable standards for undoing de jure school segregation in the South. The Civil Rights Act of 1964 and the HEW Guidelines are belated but invaluable helps in arriving at a neutral, principled decision consistent with the dimensions of the problem, traditional judicial functions, and the United States Constitution. We grasp the nettle.

I.

"No army is stronger than an idea whose time has come." Ten years after *Brown*, came the Civil Rights Act of 1964. Congress decided that the time had come for a sweeping civil rights advance, including national legislation to speed up desegregation of public schools and to put teeth into enforcement of desegregation. Titles IV and VI together constitute the congressional alternative to court-supervised desegregation. These sections of the law mobilize in aid of desegregation the United States Office of Education and the Nation's purse.

A. Title IV authorizes the Office of Education to give technical and financial assistance to local school systems in the process of desegregation. Title VI requires all federal agencies administering any grant-in-aid program to see to it that there is no racial discrimination by any school or other recipient of federal financial aid. School boards cannot, however, by giving up federal aid, avoid the policy that produced this limitation on federal aid to schools: Title IV authorizes the Attorney General to sue, in the name of the United States, to desegregate a public school or school system. More clearly and effectively than either of the other two coordinate branches of Government, Congress speaks as the Voice of the Nation. *The national policy is plain: formerly de jure segregated public school systems based on dual attendance zones must shift to unitary, nonracial systems—with or without federal funds.* . . .

In April 1965 Congress for the first time in its history adopted a law providing general federal aid—a billion dollars a year— for elementary and secondary schools. It is a fair assumption that Congress would not have taken this step had Title VI not established the principle that schools receiving federal assistance must meet uniform national standards for desegregation.

To make Title VI effective, the Department of Health, Education, and Welfare (HEW) adopted the regulation, "Non-discrimination in Federally assisted Programs." This regulation directs the Commissioner of Education to approve applications for financial assistance to public schools only if the school or school system agrees to comply with a court order, if any, outstanding against it, or submits a desegregation plan satisfactory to the Commissioner.[30]

To make the regulation effective, by assisting the Office of Education in determining whether a school qualifies for federal financial aid and by informing school boards of HEW requirements, HEW formulated certain standards or guidelines. In April 1965, nearly a year after the Act was signed, HEW published its first *Guidelines*, "General Statement of Policies under Title VI of the Civil Rights Act of 1964 Respecting Desegregation of Elementary and Secondary Schools." These *Guidelines* fixed the fall of 1967 as the target date for total desegregation of all grades. In March 1966 HEW issued *"Revised Guidelines"* to correct most of the major flaws revealed in the first year of operation under Title VI.

B. The HEW Guidelines raise the question: To what extent should a court, in determining whether to approve a school desegregation plan, give weight to the HEW Guidelines? We adhere to the answer this Court gave in four earlier cases. The HEW Guidelines are "minimum standards," representing for the most part standards the Supreme Court and this Court established *before the Guidelines were promulgated.* . . .

---

[30] "Every application for Federal financial assistance to carry out a program to which this part applies . . . shall, as a condition to its approval . . ., contain or be accompanied by an assurance that the program will be conducted or the facility operated in compliance with all requirements imposed by or pursuant to this part. . . ." 45 C.F.R. § 80.4(a) (1964). [Footnote in original, renumbered.]

II.

We read Title VI as a congressional mandate for change—change in pace and method of enforcing desegregation. The 1964 Act does not disavow court-supervised desegregation. On the contrary, Congress recognized that to the courts belongs the last word in any case or controversy.[31] But Congress was dissatisfied with the slow progress inherent in the judicial adversary process. Congress therefore fashioned a new method of enforcement to be administered not on a case by case basis as in the courts but generally, by federal agencies operating on a national scale and having a special competence in their respective fields. Congress looked to these agencies to shoulder the additional enforcement burdens resulting from the shift to high gear in school desegregation. . . .

B. The congressional mandate, as embodied in the Act and as carried out in the HEW Guidelines, does not conflict with the proper exercise of the judicial function or with the doctrine of separation of powers. It does however profoundly affect constructive use of the judicial function within the lawful scope of sound judicial discretion. When Congress declares national policy, the duty the two other coordinate branches owe to the Nation requires that, within the law, the judiciary and the executive respect and carry out that policy. Here the Chief Executive acted promptly to bring about uniform standards for desegregation. The judicial branch too should cooperate with Congress and the executive in making administrative agencies effective instruments for supervising and enforcing desegregation of public schools. . . .

C. We must therefore cooperate with Congress and the Executive in enforcing Title VI. The problem is: Are the HEW Guidelines within the scope of the congressional and executive policies embodied in the Civil Rights Act of 1964. We hold that they are.

The Guidelines do not purport to be a rule or regulation or order. They constitute a statement of policy under section 80.4 (c) of the HEW Regulations issued after the President approved

---

[31] Title IV, § 407, 42 U.S.C. § 2000c-6 authorizing the Attorney General to bring suit, on receipt of a written complaint, would seem to imply this conclusion. Section 409 preserves the right of individual citizens "to sue for or obtain relief" against discrimination in public education. HEW Regulations provide: "In any case in which a final order of a court of the United States for the desegregation of such school or school system is entered after submission of such a plan, such a plan shall be revised to conform to such final order, including any future modification of such order." 45 C.F.R. § 80.4(c) (1964). [Footnote in original, renumbered.]

the regulations December 3, 1964. HEW is under no statutory compulsion to issue such statements. It is, however, of manifest advantage to school boards throughout the country and to the general public to know the criteria the Commissioner uses in determining whether a school meets the requirements for eligibility to receive financial assistance.

The Guidelines have the vices of all administrative policies established unilaterally without a hearing. Because of these vices the courts, as the school boards point out, have set limits on administrative regulations, rulings, policies, and practices: an agency construction of a statute cannot make the law; it must conform to the law and be reasonable. To some extent the administrative weight of the declarations depends on the place of such declarations in the hierarchy of agency pronouncements extending from regulations down to general counsel memoranda and inter-office decisions. . . .

It is evident to anyone that the Guidelines were carefully formulated by educational authorities anxious to be faithful to the objectives of the 1964 Act. To the members of this Court, who for years have gone to bed and waked up with school segregation problems on their minds, it is evident that the HEW standards are strikingly similar to the standards the Supreme Court and this Court have established. The Guidelines, therefore, are not run-of-the-mine agency pronouncements low in the hierarchy of administrative declarations. They are not regulations requiring the approval of the President. They may be described as a restatement of the judicial standards applicable to disestablishing de jure segregation in the public schools.

Courts therefore should cooperate with the congressional-executive policy in favor of desegregation and against aiding segregated schools.

D. Because our approval of a plan establishes eligibility for federal aid, our standards should not be lower than those of HEW. Unless judicial standards are substantially in accord with the Guidelines, school boards previously resistant to desegregation will resort to the courts to avoid complying with the minimum standards HEW promulgates for schools that desegregate voluntarily. . . .

The announcement in HEW regulations that the Commissioner would accept a final school desegregation order as proof of the school's eligibility for federal aid prompted a number of schools to seek refuge in the federal courts. Many of these had not moved an inch toward desegregation. In Louisiana alone twenty school boards obtained quick decrees providing for desegregation according to plans greatly at variance with the Guidelines.

We shall not permit the courts to be used to destroy or dilute the effectiveness of the congressional policy expressed in Title VI. There is no bonus for foot-dragging.

E. The experience this Court has had in the last ten years argues strongly for uniform standards in court-supervised desegregation.

The first school case to reach this Court after Brown v. Board of Education was Brown v. Rippy, 5 Cir. 1956, 233 F.2d 796. Since then we have reviewed 41 other school cases, many more than once. The district courts in this circuit have considered 128 school cases in the same period. Reviewing these cases imposes a taxing, time-consuming burden on the courts not reflected in statistics. An analysis of the cases shows a wide lack of uniformity in areas where there is no good reason for variations in the schedule and manner of desegregation. In some cases there has been a substantial time-lag between this Court's opinions and their application by the district courts. In certain cases—cases we consider unnecessary to cite—there has even been a manifest variance between this Court's decision and a later district court decision. A number of district courts still mistakenly assume that transfers under Pupil Placement Laws superimposed on unconstitutional initial assignment satisfy the requirements of a desegregation plan. The lack of clear and uniform standards to govern school boards has tended to put a premium on delaying actions. In sum, the lack of uniform standards has retarded the development of local responsibility for the administration of schools without regard to race or color. What Cicero said of an earlier Athens and an earlier Rome is equally applicable today: In Georgia, for example, there should not be one law for Athens and another law for Rome.

Before HEW published its Guidelines, this Court had already established guidelines for school desegregation: to encourage uniformity at the district court level and to conserve judicial effort at both the district court and appellate levels. We did so by making detailed suggestions to the district courts. . . .

F. We summarize the Court's policy as one of encouraging the maximum legally permissible correlation between judicial standards for school desegregation and HEW Guidelines. This policy may be applied without federal courts abdicating their proper judicial function. The policy complies with the Supreme Court's increasing emphasis on more speed and less deliberation in school desegregation. It is consistent with the judiciary's duty to the

Nation to cooperate with the two other coordinate branches of government in carrying out the national policy expressed in the Civil Rights Act of 1964.

III.

The defendants contend that the Guidelines require integration, not just desegregation; that school boards have no affirmative duty to integrate. They say that in this respect the Guidelines are contrary to the provisions of the Civil Rights Act of 1964 and to constitutional [sic] intent expressed in the Act. . . .

C. The defendants err in their contention that the HEW and the courts cannot take race into consideration in establishing standards for desegregation. "[T]he Constitution is not this colorblind."

The Constitution is both color blind and color conscious. To avoid conflict with the equal protection clause, a classification that denies a benefit, causes harm, or imposes a burden must not be based on race. In that sense, the Constitution is color blind. But the Constitution is color conscious to prevent discrimination being perpetuated and to undo the effects of past discrimination. The criterion is the relevancy of color to a legitimate governmental purpose. . . .

Here race is relevant, because the governmental purpose is to offer Negroes equal educational opportunities. The means to that end, such as disestablishing segregation among students, distributing the better teachers equitably, equalizing facilities, selecting appropriate locations for schools, and avoiding resegregation must necessarily be based on race. School officials have to know the racial composition of their school populations and the racial distribution within the school district. The Courts and HEW cannot measure good faith or progress without taking race into account. "When racial imbalance infects a public school system, there is simply no way to alleviate it without consideration of race. . . . There is no constitutional right to have an inequality perpetuated." . . .

IV.

We turn now to the specific provisions of the Civil Rights Act on which the defendants rely to show that HEW violates the Congressional intent. These provisions are the amendments to Title IV and VI added in the Senate. The legislative history of these amendments is sparse and less authoritative than usual because of the lack of committee reports on the amended version of the bill.

A. Section 401(b) defines desegregation:

" 'Desegregation' means the assignment of students to public schools and within such schools without regard to their race, color, religion, or national origin, but 'desegregation' shall not mean the assignment of students to public schools in order to overcome racial imbalance."

The affirmative portion of this definition, down to the "but" clause, describes the assignment provision necessary in a plan for conversion of a de jure dual system to a unitary, integrated system. The negative portion, starting with "but", excludes assignment to overcome racial imbalance, that is acts to overcome de facto segregation. As used in the Act, therefore, "desegregation" refers only to the disestablishment of segregation in de jure segregated schools. Even if a broader meaning should be given to "assignment . . . to overcome racial imbalance," Section 401 would not mean that such assignments are unlawful. . . .

The prohibition against assignment of students to overcome racial imbalance was added as an amendment during the debates in the House to achieve the same result as the anti-bussing provision in section 407.[32] Some of the difficulty in understanding the Act and its legislative history arises from the statutory use of the undefined term "racial imbalance." It is clear however from the hearings and debates that Congress equated the term, as do the commentators, with "de facto segregation" that is, non-racially motivated segregation in a school system based on a single neighborhood school for all children in a definable area. Thus, Congressman William Cramer who offered the amendment, was concerned that the bill as originally proposed might authorize the government to require bussing to overcome de facto segregation. In explaining the amendment, he said:

"In the hearings before the committee I raised questions on 'racial imbalance' and in the sub-committee we had lengthy discussions in reference to having these words stricken in the title, as it then consisted, and to strike out the words *racial imbalance* proposed by the administration. The purpose is *to prevent any semblance of congressional acceptance or approval of the concept of 'de facto' segregation* or to include in the definition of 'desegregation' *any balancing of school attendance by moving students across school district lines to level off percentages where one race outweighs another."*

---

[32] See Part IV.B. of the opinion, *infra*. [*Eds*. note.]

The neighborhood school system is rooted deeply in American culture. Whether its continued use is constitutional when it leads to grossly imbalanced schools is a question some day to be answered by the Supreme Court, but that question is not present in any of the cases before this Court. As noted in the previous section of this opinion, we have many instances of a heavy concentration of Negroes or whites in certain areas, but always that type of imbalance has been superimposed on total school separation. And always the separation originally was racially motivated and sanctioned by law in a system based on two schools within a neighborhood or overlapping neighborhoods, each school serving a different race. The situations have some similarity but they have different origins, create different problems, and require different corrective action. . . .

B. Section 407(a)(2) of Title IV authorizing the Attorney General to file suit to desegregate, contains the "antibussing" proviso:

". . . nothing herein shall empower any official or court of the United States to issue any order seeking to achieve a racial balance in any school by requiring the transportation of pupils or students from one school to another or one school district to another in order to achieve such racial balance, or otherwise enlarge the existing power of the court to insure compliance with constitutional standards."

First, it should be noted that the prohibition applies only to transportation; and only to transportation across school lines to achieve racial balance. The furnishing of transportation as part of a freedom of choice plan is not prohibited. Second, the equitable powers of the courts exist independently of the Civil Rights Act of 1964. It is not contended in the instant cases that the Act conferred new authority on the courts. And this Court has not looked to the Act as a grant of new judicial authority.

Section 407(a)(2) might be read as applying only to orders issued in suits filed by the Attorney General under Title IV. However, Senator, now Vice President Humphrey, Floor Manager in the Senate, said it was his understanding that the provision applied to the entire bill. In particular, he said that it applies to any refusal or termination of federal assistance under Title VI since the procedure for doing so requires an order approved by the President. . . .

. . . [C]ontinuing his explanation, Senator Humphrey said:

"The bill does not attempt to integrate the schools, but it does attempt to eliminate segregation in the schools. The natural factors, such as density of population, and the distance that students would have to travel are considered legitimate means to determine the validity of a school district, *if the school districts are not gerrymandered, and in effect deliberately segregated.* The fact that there is a racial imbalance per se is not something which is unconstitutional. That is why we have attempted to clarify it with the language of Section 4." (Emphasis added.) . . .

E. As we construe the Act and its legislative history, . . . Congress, because of its hands-off attitude on bona fide neighborhood school systems, qualified its broad policy of nondiscrimination by precluding HEW's requiring the bussing of children across district lines or requiring compulsory placement of children in schools to strike a balance when the imbalance results from de facto, that is, non-racially motivated segregation. As Congressman Cramer said, 'De facto segregation is racial imbalance. But *there is nothing in the language of the Act or in the legislative history that equates corrective acts to desegregate or to integrate a dual school system initially based on de jure segregation with acts to bring about a racial balance in a system based on bona fide neighborhood schools. . . .*

V.

The HEW Guidelines agree with decisions of this circuit and of the similarly situated Fourth and Eighth Circuits. And *they stay within the Congressional mandate.* There is no cross-district or cross-town bussing requirement. There is no provision requiring school authorities to place white children in Negro schools or Negro children in white schools for the purpose of striking a racial balance in a school or school district proportionate to the racial population of the community or school district. The provision referring to percentages is a general rule of thumb or objective administrative guide for measuring progress in desegregation rather than a firm requirement that must be met. . . . Good faith in compliance should be measured by performance, not promises.

In reviewing the effectiveness of an approved plan it seems reasonable to use some sort of yardstick or objective percentage guide. The percentage requirements in the Guidelines are modest, suggesting only that systems using free choice plans for at least two years should expect 15 to 18 per cent of the pupil population to have selected desegregated schools. This Court has frequently relied on percentages in jury exclusion cases. Where the percentage of Negroes on the jury and jury venires is disproportionately low compared with the Negro population of a county, a prima facie case is made for deliberate discrimination against Negroes. Percentages have been used in other civil rights cases. A similar inference may be drawn in school desegregation cases, when the number of Negroes attending school with white children is manifestly out of line with the ratio of Negro school children to white school children in public schools. Common sense suggests that a gross discrepancy between the ratio of Negroes to white children in a school and the HEW percentage guides raises an inference that the school plan is not working as it should in providing a unitary, integrated system. Thus Evans v. Buchanan, D.C. Del. 1962, 207 F. Supp. 820 upheld that this natural inference coupled with the board's possessing but failing to come forth with the probative facts that might rebut the inference created a presumption that the proposed desegregation plan was unconstitutional. . . .

VI.

School authorities in this circuit, with few exceptions, have turned to the "freedom of choice" method for desegregating public schools. The method has serious shortcomings. Indeed, the "slow pace of integration in the Southern and border States is in large measure attributable to the manner in which free choice plans . . . have operated." When such plans leave school officials with a broad area of uncontrolled discretion, this method of desegregation is better suited than any other to preserve the essentials of the dual school system while giving paper compliance with the duty to desegregate. . . .

School officials should consult with Negro and white school authorities before plans are put in final form. They should see that notices of plans and procedures are clear and timely. They should avoid the discriminatory use of tests and the use of birth and health certificates to make transfers difficult. They should eliminate inconvenient or burdensome arrangements for transfer, such as requiring the personal appearance of parents, notarized forms, signatures of both parents, or making forms available at inconvenient times to working people. They should employ forms which do not designate the name of a Negro school as the choice or contain a "waiver" of the "right" to attend white schools. Certainly school officials should not discourage Negro children from enrolling in white schools, directly or indirectly, as for example, by advising them that they would not be permitted to engage or would not want to engage in school activities, athletics, the band, clubs, school plays. If transportation is provided for white children, the schedules should be re-routed to provide for Negro children. Overcrowding should not be used as an excuse to avoid transfers of Negro children. . . .

VII.

We attach a decree to be entered by the district courts in these cases consolidated on appeal. . . .

We have carefully examined each of the records in these cases. In each instance the record supports the decree. However, the provisions of the decree are intended, as far as possible, to apply uniformly throughout this circuit in cases involving plans based on free choice of schools. School boards, private plaintiffs, and the United States may, of course, come into court to prove that exceptional circumstances compel modification of the decree. For example, school systems in areas which let school out during planting and harvesting seasons may find that the period for exercise of choice of schools, March 1-31, should be changed to a different month. . . .

The substantive requirements of the decree derive from the Fourteenth Amendment as interpreted by decisions of the Supreme Court and of this Court, in many instances before the HEW Guidelines were published. For administrative details, we have looked to the Office of Education. For example, those familiar with the HEW Guidelines will note that the decree follows the Guidelines exactly as to the form letters which go to parents announcing the need to exercise a choice of schools, and the forms for exercising that choice are the same. Indeed a close parallel will be noted between much in Parts II through V of the decree and the Guideline provisions.

The great bulk of the school districts in this circuit have applied for federal financial assistance and therefore operate under voluntary desegregation plans. Approval of these plans by the Office of Education qualifies the schools for federal aid. In this opinion we have held that the HEW Guidelines now in effect are constitutional and are within the statutory authority created in the Civil Rights Act of 1964. Schools therefore, in compliance with the Guidelines can in general be regarded as discharging constitutional obligations.

Some schools have made no move to desegregate or have had plans rejected as unsatisfactory by district courts or the HEW. We expect the provisions of the decree to be applied in proceedings involving such schools. Other schools have earlier court-approved plans which fall short of the terms of the decree. On motion by proper parties to re-open these cases, we expect these plans to be modified to conform with our decree. In some cases the parties may challenge various aspects of HEW-approved plans. Our approval of the existing Guidelines and the deference owed to any future Guidelines is not intended to deny a day in court to any person asserting individual rights or to any school board contesting HEW action. In any school desegregation case the issue concerns the constitutional rights of Negroes, individually and as a class, and the constitutional rights of the State—not the issue whether federal financial assistance should be withheld under Title VI of the Civil Rights Act of 1964. . . .

What the decree contemplates, then, is continuing judicial evaluation of compliance by measuring the performance—not merely the promised performance—of school boards in carrying out their constitutional obligation "to disestablish dual, racially segregated school systems and to achieve substantial integration within such systems." District courts may call upon HEW for assistance in determining whether a school board's performance measures up to its obligation to desegregate. If school officials in any district should find that their district still has segregated faculties and schools or only token integration, their affirmative duty to take corrective action requires them to try an alternative to a freedom of choice plan, such as a geographic attendance plan, a combination of the two, the Princeton plan, or some other acceptable substitute, perhaps aided by an educational park. Freedom of choice is not a key that opens all doors to equal educational opportunities. . . .

The Court reverses the judgments below and remands each case to the district court for further proceedings in accordance with this opinion.

[Judge Cox, dissenting, rejected the majority's conclusion "that precedent required the public schools to mix the races rather than desegregate such schools by removing all effects of state action which may have heretofore compelled segregation, so as to permit these schools to be operated upon a proper free choice plan." He also argued that the HEW Guidelines exceeded the authority granted to the Department under the 1964 Civil Rights Act.]

ON PETITIONS FOR REHEARING
EN BANC

Before TUTTLE, Chief Judge, and BROWN, WISDOM, GEWIN, BELL, THORNBERRY, COLEMAN, GOLDBERG, AINSWORTH, GODBOLD, DYER and SIMPSON, Circuit Judges.

PER CURIAM:

1. The Court sitting en banc adopts the opinion and decree filed in these cases December 29, 1966, subject to the clarifying statements in this opinion and the changes in the decree attached to this opinion.

2. School desegregation cases involve more than a dispute between certain Negro children and certain schools. If Negroes are ever to enter the mainstream of American life, as school children they must have equal educational opportunities with white children.

3. The Court holds that boards and officials administering public schools in this circuit have the affirmative duty under the Fourteenth Amendment to bring about an integrated, unitary school system in which there are no Negro schools and no white schools—just schools. Expressions in our earlier opinions distinguishing between integration and desegregation must yield to this affirmative duty we now recognize. In fulfilling this duty it is not enough for school authorities to offer Negro children the opportunity to attend formerly all-white schools. The necessity of overcoming the effects of the dual school system in this circuit requires integration of faculties, facilities, and activities, as well as students. To the extent that earlier decisions of this Court (more in the language of the opinions, than in the effect of the holdings) conflict with this view, the decisions are overruled. . . .

4. Freedom of choice is not a goal in itself. It is a means to an end. A schoolchild has no inalienable right to choose his school. A freedom of choice plan is but one of the tools available to school officials *at this stage* of the process of converting the dual system of separate schools for Negroes and whites into a unitary system. The governmental objective of this conversion is— educational opportunities on equal terms to all. The criterion for determining the validity of a provision in a school desegregation plan is whether the provision is reasonably related to accomplishing this objective.

5. The percentages referred to in the Guidelines and in this Court's decree are simply a rough rule of thumb for measuring the effectiveness of freedom of choice as a useful tool. The percentages are not a method for setting quotas or striking a balance. If the plan is ineffective, longer on promises than performance, the school officials charged with initiating and administering a

unitary system have not met the constitutional requirements of the Fourteenth Amendment; they should try other tools.

6. In constructing the original and revised decrees, the Court gave great weight to the 1965 and 1966 HEW Guidelines. These Guidelines establish minimum standards clearly applicable to disestablishing state-sanctioned segregation. These Guidelines and our decree are within the decisions of this Court, comply with the letter and spirit of the Civil Rights Act of 1964, and meet the requirements of the United States Constitution. Courts in this circuit should give great weight to future HEW Guidelines, when such guidelines are applicable to this circuit and are within lawful limits. We express no opinion as to the applicability of HEW Guidelines in racially imbalanced situations such as occur in some other circuits where it is contended that state action may be found in state tolerance of de facto segregation or in such action as the drawing of attendance boundaries based on a neighborhood school system.

The Court reaffirms the reversal of the judgments below and the remand of each case for entry of the decree attached to this opinion.

The mandate will issue immediately.

CORRECTED DECREE

It is ORDERED, ADJUDGED and DECREED that the defendants, their agents, officers, employees and successors and all those in active concert and participation with them, be and they are permanently enjoined from discriminating on the basis of race or color in the operation of the school system. As set out more particularly in the body of the decree, they shall take affirmative action to disestablish all school segregation and to eliminate the effects of the dual school system:

I.
SPEED OF DESEGREGATION

Commencing with the 1967-68 school year, in accordance with this decree, all grades, including kindergarten grades, shall be desegregated and pupils assigned to schools in these grades without regard to race or color.

II.
EXERCISE OF CHOICE

The following provisions shall apply to all grades:

(a) *Who May Exercise Choice.* A choice of schools may be exercised by a parent or other adult person serving as the student's parent. A student may exercise his own choice if he (1) is exercising a choice for the ninth or a higher grade, or (2) has reached the age of fifteen at the time of the exercise of choice. Such a choice by a student is controlling unless a different choice is exercised for him by his parent or other adult person serving as his parent during the choice period or at such later time as the student exercises a choice. Each reference in this decree to a student's exercising a choice means the exercise of the choice, as appropriate, by a parent or such other adult, or by the student himself.

(b) *Annual Exercise of Choice.* All students, both white and Negro, shall be required to exercise a free choice of schools annually.

(c) *Choice Period.* The period for exercising choice shall commence May 1, 1967 and end June 1, 1967, and in subsequent years shall commence March 1 and end March 31 preceding the school year for which the choice is to be exercised. No student or prospective student who exercises his choice within the choice period shall be given any preference because of the time within the period when such choice was exercised.

(d) *Mandatory Exercise of Choice.* A failure to exercise a choice within the choice period shall not preclude any student from exercising a choice at any time before he commences school for the year with respect to which the choice applies, but such choice may be subordinated to the choices of students who exercised choice before the expiration of the choice period. Any student who has not exercised his choice of school within a week after school opens shall be assigned to the school nearest his home where space is available under standards for determining available space which shall be applied uniformly throughout the system.

(e) *Public Notice.* On or within a week before the date the choice period opens, the defendants shall arrange for the conspicuous publication of a notice describing the provisions of this decree in the newspaper most generally circulated in the community. The text of the notice shall be substantially similar to the text of the explanatory letter sent home to parents. Publication as a legal notice will not be sufficient. Copies of this notice must also be given at that time to all radio and television stations located in the community. Copies of this decree shall be posted in each school in the school system and at the office of the Superintendent of Education.

(f) *Mailing of Explanatory Letters and Choice Forms.* On the first day of the choice period there shall be distributed by first-class mail an explanatory letter and a choice form to the parent (or other adult person acting as parent, if known to the defendants) of each student, together with a return envelope addressed to the Superintendent. Should the defendants satisfactorily demonstrate to the court that they are unable to comply with the requirement of distributing the explanatory letter and choice form by first-class mail, they shall propose an alternative method which will maximize individual notice, e.g., personal notice to parents by delivery to the pupil with adequate procedures to insure the delivery of the notice. The text for the explanatory letter and choice form shall essentially conform to the sample letter and choice form appended to this decree.

(g) *Extra Copies of the Explanatory Letter and Choice Form.* Extra copies of the explanatory letter and choice form shall be freely available to parents, students, prospective students, and the general public at each school in the system and at the office of the Superintendent of Education during the times of the year when such schools are usually open.

(h) *Content of Choice Form.* Each choice form shall set forth the name and location and the grades offered at each school and may require of the person exercising the choice the name, address, age of student, school and grade currently or most recently attended by the student, the school chosen, the signature of *one* parent or other adult person serving as parent, or where appropriate the signature of the student, and the identity of the person signing. No statement of reasons for a particular choice, or any other information, or any witness or other authentication, may be required or requested, without approval of the court.

(i) *Return of Choice Form.* At the option of the person completing the choice form, the choice may be returned by mail, in person, or by messenger to any school in the school system or to the office of the Superintendent.

(j) *Choices not on Official Form.* The exercise of choice may also be made by the submission in like manner of any other writing which contains information sufficient to identify the student and indicates that he has made a choice of school.

(k) *Choice Forms Binding.* When a choice form has once been submitted and the choice period has expired, the choice is binding for the entire school year and may not be changed except in cases of parents making different choices from their children under the conditions set forth in paragraph II (a) of this decree and in exceptional cases where, absent the consideration of race, a change is educationally called for or where compelling hardship is shown by the student. A change in family residence from one neighborhood to another shall be considered an exceptional case for purposes of this paragraph.

(l) *Preference in Assignment.* In assigning students to schools, no preferences shall be given to any student for prior attendance at a school and, except with the approval of court in extraordinary circumstances, no choice shall be denied for any reason other than overcrowding. In case of overcrowding at any school, preferences shall be given on the basis of the proximity of the school to the homes of the students choosing it, without regard to race or color. Standards for determining overcrowding shall be applied uniformly throughout the system.

(m) *Second Choice where First Choice is Denied.* Any student whose choice is denied must be promptly notified in writing and given his choice of any school in the school system serving his grade level where space is available. The student shall have seven days from the receipt of notice of a denial of first choice in which to exercise a second choice.

(n) *Transportation.* Where transportation is generally provided, buses must be routed to the maximum extent feasible in light of the geographic distribution of students, so as to serve each student choosing any school in the system. Every student choosing either the formerly white or the formerly Negro school nearest his residence must be transported to the school to which he is assigned under these provisions, whether or not it is his first choice, if that school is sufficiently distant from his home to make him eligible for transportation under generally applicable transportation rules.

(o) *Officials not to Influence Choice.* At no time shall any official, teacher, or employee of the school system influence any parent, or other adult person serving as a parent, or any student, in the exercise of a choice or favor or penalize any person because of a choice made. If the defendant school board employs professional guidance counselors, such persons shall base their guidance and counselling on the individual student's particular personal, academic, and vocational needs. Such guidance and counselling by teachers as well as professional guidance counsellors shall be available to all students without regard to race or color.

(p) *Protection of Persons Exercising Choice.* Within their authority school officials are responsible for the protection of persons exercising rights under or otherwise affected by this decree. They shall, without delay, take appropriate action with regard to any student or staff member who interferes with the successful operation of the plan. Such interference shall include harassment, intimidation, threats, hostile words or acts, and similar behavior. The school board shall not publish, allow, or cause to be published, the names or addresses of pupils exercising rights or otherwise affected by this decree. If officials of the school system are not able to provide sufficient protection, they shall seek whatever assistance is necessary from other appropriate officials.

III.
PROSPECTIVE STUDENTS

Each prospective new student shall be required to exercise a choice of schools before or at the time of enrollment. All such students known to defendants shall be furnished a copy of the prescribed letter to parents, and choice form, by mail or in person, on the date the choice period opens or as soon thereafter as the school system learns that he plans to enroll. Where there is no pre-registration procedure for newly entering students, copies of the choice forms shall be available at the Office of the Superintendent and at each school during the time the school is usually open.

IV.
TRANSFERS

(a) *Transfers for Students.* Any student shall have the right at the beginning of a new term, to transfer to any school from which he was excluded or would otherwise be excluded on account of his race or color.

(b) *Transfers for Special Needs.* Any student who requires a course of study not offered at the school to which he has been assigned may be permitted, upon his written application, at the beginning of any school term or semester, to transfer to another school which offers courses for his special needs.

(c) *Transfers to Special Classes or Schools.* If the defendants operate and maintain special classes or schools for physically handicapped, mentally retarded, or gifted children, the defendants may assign children to such schools or classes on a basis related to the function of the special class or school that is other than freedom of choice. In no event shall such assignments be made on the basis of race or color or in a manner which tends to perpetuate a dual school system based on race or color.

V.
SERVICES, FACILITIES, ACTIVITIES AND PROGRAMS

No student shall be segregated or discriminated against on account of race or color in any service, facility, activity, or program (including transportation, athletics, or other extracurricular activity) that may be conducted or sponsored by the school in which he is enrolled. A student attending school for the first time on a desegregated basis may not be subject to any disqualification or waiting period for participation in activities and programs, including athletics, which might otherwise apply because he is a transfer or newly assigned student except that such transferees shall be subject to longstanding, non-racially based rules of city, county, or state athletic associations dealing with the eligibility of transfer students for athletic contests. All school use or school-sponsored use of athletic fields, meeting rooms, and all other school related services, facilities, activities, and programs such as commencement exercises and parent-teacher meetings which are open to persons other than enrolled students, shall be open to all persons without regard to race or color. All special educational programs conducted by the defendants shall be conducted without regard to race or color.

VI.
SCHOOL EQUALIZATION

(a) *Inferior Schools.* In schools heretofore maintained for Negro students, the defendants shall take prompt steps necessary to provide physical facilities, equipment, courses of instruction, and instructional materials of quality equal to that provided in schools previously maintained for white students. Conditions of overcrowding, as determined by pupil-teacher ratios and pupil-classroom ratios shall, to the extent feasible, be distributed evenly between schools formerly maintained for Negro students and those formerly maintained for white students. If for any reason it is not feasible to improve sufficiently any school formerly maintained for Negro students, where such improvement would otherwise be required by this paragraph, such school shall be closed as soon as possible, and students enrolled in the school shall be reassigned on the basis of freedom of choice. By October of each year, defendants shall report to the Clerk of the Court pupil-teacher ratios, pupil-classroom ratios, and per-pupil expenditures both as to operating and capital improvement costs, and shall outline the steps to be taken and the time within which they shall accomplish the equalization of such schools.

(b) *Remedial Programs.* The defendants shall provide remedial education programs which permit students attending or who have previously attended segregated schools to overcome past inadequacies in their education.

VII.
New Construction

The defendants, to the extent consistent with the proper operation of the school system as a whole, shall locate any new school and substantially expand any existing schools with the objective of eradicating the vestiges of the dual system.

VIII.
Faculty and Staff

(a) *Faculty Employment.* Race or color shall not be a factor in the hiring, assignment, reassignment, promotion, demotion, or dismissal of teachers and other professional staff members, including student teachers, except that race may be taken into account for the purpose of counteracting or correcting the effect of the segregated assignment of faculty and staff in the dual system. Teachers, principals, and staff members shall be assigned to schools so that the faculty and staff is not composed exclusively of members of one race. Wherever possible, teachers shall be assigned so that more than one teacher of the minority race (white or Negro) shall be on a desegregated faculty. Defendants shall take positive and affirmative steps to accomplish the desegregation of their school faculties and to achieve substantial desegregation of faculties in as many of the schools as possible for the 1967-68 school year notwithstanding that teacher contracts for the 1967-68 or 1968-69 school years may have already been signed and approved. The tenure of teachers in the system shall not be used as an excuse for failure to comply with this provision. The defendants shall establish as an objective that the pattern of teacher assignment to any particular school not be identifiable as tailored for a heavy concentration of either Negro or white pupils in the school.

(b) *Dismissals.* Teachers and other professional staff members may not be discriminatorily assigned, dismissed, demoted, or passed over for retention, promotion, or rehiring, on the ground of race or color. In any instance where one or more teachers or other professional staff members are to be displaced as a result of desegregation, no staff vacancy in the school system shall be filled through recruitment from outside the system unless no such displaced staff member is qualified to fill the vacancy. If, as a result of desegregation, there is to be a reduction in the total professional staff of the school system, the qualifications of all staff members in the system shall be evaluated in selecting the staff member to be released without consideration of race or color. A report containing any such proposed dismissals, and the reasons therefor, shall be filed with the Clerk of the Court, serving copies upon opposing counsel, within five (5) days after such dismissal, demotion, etc., as proposed.

(c) *Past Assignments.* The defendants shall take steps to assign and reassign teachers and other professional staff members to eliminate the effects of the dual school system.

IX.
REPORTS TO THE COURT

(1) *Report on Choice Period.* The defendants shall serve upon the opposing parties and file with the Clerk of the Court on or before April 15, 1967, and on or before June 15, 1967, and in each subsequent year on or before June 1, a report tabulating by race the number of choice applications and transfer applications received for enrollment in each grade in each school in the system, and the number of choices and transfers granted and the number of denials in each grade of each school. The report shall also state any reasons relied upon in denying choice and shall tabulate, by school and by race of student, the number of choices and transfers denied for each such reason.

In addition, the report shall show the percentage of pupils actually transferred or assigned from segregated grades or to schools attended predominantly by pupils of a race other than the race of the applicant, for attendance during the 1966-67 school year, with comparable data for the 1965-66 school year. Such additional information shall be included in the report served upon opposing counsel and filed with the Clerk of the Court.

(2) *Report After School Opening.* The defendants shall, in addition to reports elsewhere described, serve upon opposing counsel and file with the Clerk of the Court within 15 days after the opening of schools for the fall semester of each year, a report setting forth the following information:

(i) The name, address, grade, school of choice and school of present attendance of each student who has withdrawn or requested withdrawal of his choice of school or who has transferred after the start of the school year, together with a description of any action taken by the defendants on his request and the reasons therefor.

(ii) The number of faculty vacancies, by school, that have occurred or been filled by the defendants since the order of this Court or the latest report submitted pursuant to this sub-paragraph. This report shall state the race of the teacher employed to fill each such vacancy and indicate whether such teacher is newly employed or was transferred from within the system. The tabulation of the number of transfers within the system shall indicate the schools from which and to which the transfers were made. The report shall also set forth the number of faculty members of each race assigned to each school for the current year.

(iii) The number of students by race, in each grade of each school.

EXPLANATORY LETTER

(School System Name and Office Address)

(Date Sent)

Dear Parent:

All grades in our school system will be desegregated next year. Any student who will be entering one of these grades next year may choose to attend any school in our system, regardless of whether that school was formerly all-white or all-Negro. It does not matter which school your child is attending this year. You and your child may select any school you wish.

Every student, white and Negro, must make a choice of schools. If a child is entering the ninth or higher grade, or if the child is fifteen years old or older, he may make the choice himself. Otherwise a parent or other adult serving as parent must sign the choice form. A child enrolling in the school system for the first time must make a choice of schools before or at the time of his enrollment.

The form on which the choice should be made is attached to this letter. It should be completed and returned by June 1, 1967. You may mail it in the enclosed envelope, or deliver it by messenger or by hand to any school principal or to the Office of the Superintendent at any time between May 1 and June 1. No one may require you to return your choice form before June 1 and no preference is given for returning the choice form early.

No principal, teacher or other school official is permitted to influence anyone in making a choice or to require early return of the choice form. No one is permitted to favor or penalize any student or other person because of a choice made. A choice once made cannot be changed except for serious hardship.

No child will be denied his choice unless for reasons of overcrowding at the school chosen, in which case children living nearest the school will have preference.

Transportation will be provided, if reasonably possible, no matter what school is chosen. [Delete if the school system does not provide transportation.]

Your School Board and the school staff will do everything we can to see to it that the rights of all students are protected and that desegregation of our schools is carried out successfully.

Sincerely yours,
Superintendent.

Choice Form

This form is provided for you to choose a school for your child to attend next year. You have 30 days to make your choice. It does not matter which school your child attended last year, and does not matter whether the school you choose was formerly a white or Negro school. This form must be mailed or brought to the principal of any school in the system or to the office of the Superintendent, [address], by June 1, 1967. A choice is required for each child.

Name of child ....
                    (Last)   (First)   (Middle)
Address ....
Name of Parent or other
adult serving as parent ....
If child is entering first grade, date of birth:

                ....
                    (Month)   (Day)   (Year)
Grade child is entering ....
School attended last year ....
Choose one of the following schools by marking an X beside
the name.
Name of School   Grade   Location
....
....
....
....
                    Signature ....
                    Date ....
....
....
To be filled in by Superintendent:
                    School Assigned ....[1]

---

[1] In subsequent years the dates in both the explanatory letter and the
choice form should be changed to conform to the choice period.

[Judges Gewin, Bell, Coleman and Godbold all filed dissenting opinions. Judge Gewin emphasized the injustice of interpreting the 1964 Civil Rights Act to require affirmative action to
integrate schools that had been segregated by law while tolerating
de facto segregation. He argued that the HEW Guidelines were
not properly before the court, since they had not been considered
by the district courts in these cases. Additionally, he argued that
the Guidelines should not even be applied to deny funds to any
district (or, by implication, be applied as the majority was applying them), since they were adopted without an administrative hearing. He echoed Judge Cox's dissent on the subject of
"enforced integration," and he objected to the inflexibility of the
majority's model decree. The other dissenting judges made similar arguments, with varying emphasis on one or another of the
points made by Judge Gewin.]

QUESTIONS

1. Was the Jefferson County decree an "advisory opinion," beyond the scope of judicial power?—Judge Wisdom's opinion, adopted by the court of appeals sitting en banc, said (p. 365 *supra*): "We attach a decree to be entered by the district courts in these cases consolidated on appeal . . . . We have carefully examined each of the records in these cases. In each instance the record supports the decree. However, the provisions of the decree are intended, as far as possible, to apply uniformly throughout this circuit in cases involving plans based on free choice of schools. School boards, private plaintiffs, and the United States may, of course, come into court to prove that exceptional circumstances compel modification of the decree." In Hall v. St. Helena Parish, 268 F. Supp. 923 (E.D. La. 1967), the plaintiffs sought changes in desegregation plans previously ordered by the court, to conform those plans to the decree in *Jefferson County*. The district judge, Judge West, stated in his opinion:

> . . . [S]ince neither the record nor the facts involved in the cases now before this Court were before the Court of Appeals when it decided Jefferson, the specific decree rendered therein, is, of course, not necessarily applicable to these cases. For this Court to take the position that it is bound to enter the decree formulated by the Appellate Court in Jefferson, without regard to the proofs offered in the present cases, merely because the Court of Appeals recognized what it believed to be a desirability of uniformity of decrees entered in cases of this sort, would be to recognize a fact which simply does not exist, i.e., that the Court of Appeals has the right to render advisory opinions. It simply does not have this right. A case, such as the ones here involved, is not properly before a Court of Appeals until the issues therein involved have been duly considered and passed upon by the proper District Court. It is the duty of a District Judge to perform his duties "according to the best of *his* abilities and understanding agreeably to the Constitution and laws of the United States." This I intend to do . . . . The function of the Court of Appeals is to review what I have done, to affirm me if they feel I am right, and to reverse me if they believe I am wrong. I respectfully suggest that it is not their function to tell me in advance of hearing a case what decree I must enter therein, regardless of what the proofs may show.

Judge West went on to decide that some provisions of the *Jefferson County* decree were not applicable to the "freedom of choice" plans before him, because he found no evidence of any impediment to the exercise of a free, unfettered choice of schools by all students, no evidence of inadequacy in the notice given to children and parents, and no evidence of improper influence by school officials or others on the exercise of choice of schools.

Judge West was apparently of the view that the *Jefferson County* decree was an "advisory opinion" with respect to "freedom of choice" plans which differed from those before the Fifth Circuit in *Jefferson County,* and that such an advisory opinion was beyond the power of the court of appeals to issue. Courts in the United States have generally held that they are not empowered to issue advisory opinions—for example, at the request of a governmental official for an opinion on a legal question. For federal courts, this limitation has been said to be constitutionally required, because the federal judicial power is limited by Article III of the Constitution to "Cases" and "Controversies." To state this doctrine in a different way, courts are said to be empowered to declare law only in the resolution of adversary disputes. (Recall the discussion of this doctrine in the questions following *Dred Scott v. Sandford,* p. 99 *supra.*) Was the *Jefferson County* decree an advisory opinion in this sense? Consider the following comment on *Jefferson County* in a student note in the *Harvard Law Review*:

> The form of the *Jefferson County* decree—uniform detailed standards applicable to all free choice plans brought before the courts in the Fifth Circuit—represents a novel but justifiable approach to the problem of devising effective desegregation remedies. Normally it is true that the proper role of a court is limited to the adjudication of only those constitutional issues necessary to a resolution of the particular controversy before it, and does not extend to the declaration of a broad, sweeping, quasi-statutory decree governing an entire class of cases. However, after dealing with substantially similar desegregation suits, many involving protracted litigation, in the twelve years since *Brown,* the court was competent to conclude that any differences existing between school districts throughout its jurisdiction could not justify a plan which fell below the Guideline standard. 81 HARV. L. REV. 474, 477 (1967).

Certainly the court of appeals resolved a real dispute in the decision in *Jefferson County.* The issue raised by Judge West was whether the court had also declared law for the resolution of disputes that were different from the one then before the court.

In considering that issue, is anything added by the fact that the court of appeals specifically stated that the *Jefferson County* decree applied to "freedom of choice" plans which would come before the district courts in the future or which were then included in existing district-court-entered plans? Did the court there do anything more "novel" than articulate the principle of stare decisis? And was not Judge West's point, though cast in language about advisory opinions, also based on the principle of stare decisis: that the holding in *Jefferson County* was not applicable in the cases before him because of a significant distinction in the facts of the cases? If in *Jefferson County* all of the "freedom of choice" plans before the court operated in a context where there were impediments to a genuinely free choice, would it necessarily be an impermissible advisory opinion for the court to state that certain criteria must be included in such plans whether or not impediments to freedom of choice were proved in a specific case? Might not the court have been resting its decision on a broad principle in the cases before it, that whether or not impediments to freedom of choice were established, conversion to a unitary system required the inclusion in all such plans of the criteria included in the *Jefferson County* decree? It seems clear that the court was doing the latter, anticipating much of what the Supreme Court said in *New Kent County.* Was Judge West simply refusing to follow a holding that school districts which formerly maintained compulsory segregation must act affirmatively to bring about desegregation?

2. Was the Jefferson County decree an "administrative decree," beyond the scope of judicial power?—Judge West was later ordered by the court of appeals to enter the *Jefferson County* decree in the cases before him.[33] In a later proceeding to determine whether school board officials should be punished for contempt for failure to comply with the decree, Judge West said that the specific terms of the decree, if the court of appeals meant that they be meticulously complied with, amounted to an "administrative decree" rather than a "judicial judgment," and an "act far beyond the Court's judicial powers." 273 F. Supp. at 543. The law review comment quoted in paragraph 1, *supra,* referred, apparently in a similar vein, to the "quasi-statutory" nature of the decree. Why might a decree such as that in *Jefferson County,* with specific forms and time periods to be employed in adminis-

---

33 Williams v. Iberville Parish School Board, 273 F. Supp. 542 (E.D. La. 1967). See Note, *Judicial Performance in the Fifth Circuit,* 73 YALE L.J. 90 (1963), for a study of some district judges' obstruction of the vindication of civil rights in the south.

tering "freedom of choice" plans, be beyond the appropriate scope of the judicial power? Are courts empowered to declare law only in more general terms, leaving more precise lawmaking to legislatures or to administrative agencies functioning within the scope of legislatively-declared standards? Is the problem that the text of the letter to parents, the specific procedures for administering the plan, and the like are not based on the reasoned elaboration of previously established principles, but are instead "arbitrary" lines drawn within a broad range of permissible decisions? Does a problem arise from the generality of the equal protection clause, and the undesirability, as a process of constitutional interpretation, of distilling from that clause such specifics as those in the *Jefferson County* decree?

3. Was the court's order to provide remedial programs beyond the scope of judicial power?—The *Jefferson County* decree contained a provision, p. 374 *supra*, related to "remedial programs": "The defendants shall provide remedial education programs which permit students attending or who have previously attended segregated schools to overcome past inadequacies in their education." Compare the generality of this order to the defendants with the specificity of other parts of the decree, setting forth such requirements as the precise forms of notice to be given to parents and the precise time limits to be observed. Is the portion of the decree related to remedial programs enforceable? What advice might an attorney give to a school board client as to the scope of its obligations under the decree? Is the court, with the entry of such an order, constituting itself a superschool board? Is the problem of enforceability so great that the court should not enter such a decree, even though it is convinced on the merits that the school board has such a constitutional obligation? Or does determination of the content of the constitutional obligation itself require consideration of the issue of enforceability? Certainly there is a strong argument to be made that if in the past a school board has injured children by providing them with constitutionally unequal educational opportunity, the board should now take steps to attempt to repair that injury. Should the court have been more specific in directing what those steps should be? Would it have been wiser for the court to add a phrase, so that its decree would read, "The defendants shall take such steps as are reasonably feasible to provide . . ."?

4. Desegregation as a condition on federal grants: the HEW Guidelines.—Title VI of the Civil Rights Act of 1964 enunciates the policy that "No person in the United States shall, on the ground of race, color, or national origin, be excluded from participation in, be denied the benefits of, or be subjected to discrimination under any program or activity receiving Federal financial assistance." 42 U.S.C. § 2000d; F.C.A. 42 § 2000d. All Federal departments and agencies administering financial assistance programs (other than contracts of insurance or guaranty) are directed to effectuate that policy by issuing "rules, regulations, or orders of general applicability . . . ." The statute requires that such rules, regulations, or orders be approved by the President. The agencies are authorized to secure compliance with any requirement imposed to effectuate the statutory policy by termination of a grant, by refusal of a grant, by refusal to continue financial assistance, or by "any other means authorized by law." Termination or denial of a grant or federal financial assistance to a specific recipient, such as a school board, can be ordered only after an administrative hearing in which a finding is made that the recipient has failed to comply with the requirements promulgated under Title VI. An unusual step was added in the administrative process, indicating the political compromise involved in the enactment of Title VI: the head of a Federal department or agency proposing to refuse or withdraw financial assistance must "file with the committees of the House and Senate having legislative jurisdiction over the program or activity involved a full written report of the circumstances and the grounds for such action." The administrative action cannot become effective until thirty days after the filing of such a report. And, finally, provision is made for judicial review of administrative orders refusing or withholding assistance. 42 U.S.C. §§ 2000d-1, 2000d-2; F.C.A. 42 §§ 2000d-1, 2000d-2.

Pertinent provisions of the Department of Health, Education, and Welfare regulations promulgated under Title VI at the end of 1964 follow:

CODE OF FEDERAL REGULATIONS
Title 45
Revised as of January 1, 1968

PART 80—NONDISCRIMINATION IN FEDERALLY-ASSISTED PROGRAMS OF THE DEPARTMENT OF HEALTH, EDUCATION, AND WELFARE— EFFECTUATION OF TITLE VI OF THE CIVIL RIGHTS ACT OF 1964

§ 80.1 Purpose.

The purpose of this part is to effectuate the provisions of title VI of the Civil Rights Act of 1964 (hereafter referred to as the

"Act") to the end that no person in the United States shall, on the ground of race, color, or national origin, be excluded from participation in, be denied the benefits of, or be otherwise subjected to discrimination under any program or activity receiving Federal financial assistance from the Department of Health, Education, and Welfare.

§ 80.2   Application of this part.

This part applies to any program for which Federal financial assistance is authorized under a law administered by the Department, including the Federally-assisted programs and activities listed in Appendix A of this part. . . .

§ 80.3   Discrimination prohibited.

(a) *General.* No person in the United States shall, on the ground of race, color, or national origin be excluded from participation in, be denied the benefits of, or be otherwise subjected to discrimination under any program to which this part applies.

(b) *Specific discriminatory actions prohibited.* (1) A recipient under any program to which this part applies may not, directly or through contractual or other arrangements, on ground of race, color, or national origin: . . . .

(iii) Subject an individual to segregation or separate treatment in any matter related to his receipt of any service, financial aid, or other benefit under the program; . . . .

(d) *Indian Health and Cuban Refugee programs.* An individual shall not be deemed subjected to discrimination by reason of his exclusion from the benefits of a program limited by Federal law to individuals of a particular race, color, or national origin different from his.

§ 80.4   Assurances required.

(a) *General.* (1) Every application for Federal financial assistance to carry out a program to which this part applies, . . . and every application for Federal financial assistance to provide a facility shall, as a condition to its approval and the extension of any Federal financial assistance pursuant to the application, contain or be accompanied by an assurance that the program will be con-

ducted or the facility operated in compliance with all requirements imposed by or pursuant to this part. . . .

(c) *Elementary and secondary schools.* The requirements of
paragraph (a) . . . of this section with respect to any elementary
or secondary school or school system shall be deemed to be satisfied if such school or school system (1) is subject to a final order
of a court of the United States for the desegregation of such school
or school system, and provides an assurance that it will comply
with such order, including any future modification of such order,
or (2) submits a plan for the desegregation of such school or
school system which the responsible Department official determines is adequate to accomplish the purposes of the Act and this
part, at the earliest practicable time, and provides reasonable
assurance that it will carry out such plan; in any case of continuing Federal financial assistance the responsible Department official may reserve the right to redetermine, after such period as may
be specified by him, the adequacy of the plan to accomplish the
purposes of the Act and the regulations in this part. In any case
in which a final order of a court of the United States for the
desegregation of such school or school system is entered after submission of such a plan, such plan shall be revised to conform to
such final order, including any future modification of such order.
. . .

These excerpts are from a lengthy regulation which covered the
vast array of grant programs administered by the Department of
Health, Education, and Welfare. The excerpted portions are examples of lawmaking or law-declaration by an administrative
agency under statutory authorization. The agency was directed
by the statute to adjudicate individual cases, and the HEW regulation also contained detailed provisions setting up administrative hearing procedures. The legal aspects of this kind of administrative mechanism—adjudication of individual cases—are the
domain of the lawyer employed in the executive branch of government, in this case the Office of the General Counsel in HEW.

Two aspects of the HEW regulations should be emphasized
here. Section 80.4 built part of the enforcement mechanisms
around an "assurance" by a recipient of federal financial assistance
"that the program will be conducted or the facility operated in
compliance with all requirements imposed by or pursuant to"
the regulation, with the assurance to include "provisions which

give the United States a right to seek its judicial enforcement." This assurance was the direct descendant of the assurance in the impacted areas legislation, enforcement of which was sought in the cases we have studied in Section F. As yet there have been no concluded judicial proceedings in which specific enforcement of an assurance has been sought.[34] In section 80.4(c) the regulation referred specifically to elementary and secondary schools. A public school system meets the non-discrimination requirements of the regulation if it "(1) is subject to a final order of a court of the United States for the desegregation of" its schools and "provides an assurance that it will comply with such order . . .," or "(2) submits a plan for the desegregation of such . . . school system which the responsible Department official determines is adequate to accomplish the purposes of the Act . . . at the earliest practicable time, and provides reasonable assurance that it will carry out such plan . . . ."

Through the sanction of withdrawal of federal financial assistance to southern public schools the Department of Health, Education, and Welfare became the focal point for administrative development of school desegregation plans. In April, 1965, a few months after the HEW regulation was promulgated, the Office of Education, in HEW, issued its "Guidelines" spelling out in greater detail the specifics of desegregation plans which would satisfy the regulation. The Guidelines were not considered to be "rules, regulations, or orders" under Title VI, and hence were not carried through the step of approval by the President in the form required by Title VI for such administrative lawmaking. Three types of plans were said to be acceptable: nonracial geographic attendance areas, freedom of choice, and a combination of these.[35]

The Guidelines were amended in 1966 and more detailed procedures for freedom-of-choice plans, such as time and notice requirements, were added; these procedures were included in the *Jefferson County* decree. The 1966 amendments to the Guidelines added provisions the validity of which were discussed in *Jefferson County*. These were the "requirements for effectiveness of free choice plans."[36] This section stated that the Com-

---

[34] See Hoff, *The Courts, HEW, and Southern School Desegregation*, 77 Yale L.J. 321, 331 n.36 (1967) for a description of one such action which ended inconclusively.

[35] See Dunn, *Title VI, the Guidelines and School Desegregation in the South*, 53 Va. L. Rev. 42 (1967).

[36] The 1966 guidelines are published in 45 C.F.R. § 181.1 *et seq.* (1968). They were rewritten in March, 1968, and the current version is published in 33 Fed. Reg. 4955 (Mar. 23, 1968). The "requirements for effectiveness of free choice plans" are at 45 C.F.R. § 181.54.

missioner of Education would "scrutinize with special care the operation" of free choice plans:

> The single most substantial indication as to whether a free choice plan is actually working to eliminate the dual school structure is the extent to which Negro or other minority students have in fact transferred from segregated schools. . . .
>
> As a general matter, for the 1966-67 school year the Commissioner will, in the absence of other evidence to the contrary, assume that a free choice plan is a viable and effective means of completing initial stages of desegregation in school systems in which a substantial percentage of the students have in fact been transferred from segregated schools. . . .
>
> In districts with a sizable percentage of Negro or other minority group students, the Commissioner will, in general, be guided by the following criteria in scheduling free choice plans for review:
>
> (1) If a significant percentage of the students, such as 8 percent or 9 percent, transferred from segregated schools for the 1965-66 school year, total transfers on the order of at least twice that percentage would normally be expected.
>
> (2) If a smaller percentage of the students, such as 4 percent or 5 percent, transferred from segregated schools for the 1965-66 school year, a substantial increase in transfers would normally be expected, such as would bring the total to at least triple the percentage for the 1965-66 school year. . . .
>
> Where there is substantial deviation from these expectations, and the Commissioner concludes, on the basis of the choices actually made and other available evidence, that the plan is not operating fairly, or is not effective to meet constitutional and statutory requirements, he will require the school system to take additional steps to further desegregation. 45 C.F.R. § 181.54 (1968).

Two aspects of the Guidelines as discussed in the *Jefferson County* opinion, are of interest at this point: (a) the weight which the court gave to the Guidelines in framing the decree, and (b) the validity of the provisions of the Guidelines that dealt with progress under freedom-of-choice plans.

a. The weight which the court gave to the Guidelines in framing the decree.—The Guidelines provided that school districts which were under final federal court orders for desegregation would thereby be in compliance with the HEW regulation. The court in *Jefferson County* gave "great weight" to the Guidelines in the performance of its function of interpreting the Fourteenth Amendment and fashioning a decree that would bring about compliance with constitutional requirements. Among other effects, the use of the Guidelines by the court foreclosed efforts by school districts to get the courts to order desegregation plans less onerous than what HEW would require. The pattern created by the adoption by the administrative agency of court decrees and by the courts of administrative guideliness is described in a student comment in the *Yale Law Journal:*

> A complex relationship between different institutions emerges. Local school officials seek to avoid responsibility for having to observe guideline standards by arguing that the courts require it. Arguing that merely the Office of Education requires it is not as effective. Similarly the Office of Education seeks to strengthen its position in the South by arguing that they have both the general support of the courts and now, after *Jefferson,* their specific endorsement. At the same time they avoid any possibility of a politically damaging confrontation with the courts by writing an exception in their regulations for court orders. The courts wish to limit their involvement with the problem for several reasons. Their response has been to enthusiastically endorse the guidelines, though, in part, to draw on the political strength of the United States Congress to justify their stance rather than to expend their own prestige too openly. Their endorsement of the guidelines helps to shift future responsibility back to the federal executive and hopefully reduces their own future involvement. The circle is thus squared. Everybody benefits by the process and no one involved on either side of the controversy must pay by having to publicly assume responsibility for adoption of the guidelines and the desegregation that results. Hoff, *The Courts, HEW, and Southern School Desegregation,* 77 YALE L.J. 321, 362-63 (1967).

In *Jefferson County* the court had before it the claims of individuals under the Fourteenth Amendment. The issue was not the statutory eligibility of the defendant school districts for federal funds. The school districts argued that acceptance by the court of the Guidelines as the measure of the defendants' constitutional obligations would be an abdication of the judicial function; the court, it was argued, was in effect turning over the interpretation of the Constitution to an administrative agency. In Part II.B. of his opinion, p. 357 *supra*, Judge Wisdom said that the congressional mandate in the 1964 Act that the pace of desegregation be increased, amplified by the Guidelines, did not conflict with proper exercise of the judicial function, but did

> profoundly affect constructive use of the judicial function within the lawful scope of sound judicial discretion. When Congress declares national policy, the duty the two other coordinate branches owe to the Nation requires that, within the law, the judiciary and the executive respect and carry out that policy. Here the Chief Executive acted promptly to bring about uniform standards for desegregation. The judicial branch too should cooperate with Congress and the executive in making administrative agencies effective instruments for supervising and enforcing desegregation of public schools.

Was this an adequate answer to the contention that the court was failing to perform its function of interpreting the Constitution? If Title VI and the Guidelines were viewed as legislative and administrative enforcement of the equal protection clause, would that view make more acceptable the "great weight" which the Fifth Circuit gave the Guidelines? (Section 5 of the Fourteenth Amendment provides: "The Congress shall have power to enforce, by appropriate legislation, the provisions of this article.")

b. The validity of the provisions of the Guidelines that dealt with progress under "freedom of choice" plans.—One of the arguments by the school districts in *Jefferson County*, assuming that the Guidelines were to be used as a measure of the districts' constitutional obligations, was that the provisions of the Guidelines on progress under "freedom of choice" plans were invalid because they were beyond the authority of HEW under Title VI. The court's disposition of this argument was an example of judicial review of the decision of an administrative agency on an issue of law. Title VI itself, which was the immediate statutory authority for HEW's regulations and the Guidelines, said nothing about "freedom of choice" plans. It simply declared the policy of nondiscrimination in federally assisted programs, and directed agencies in the Executive branch to effectuate that policy. HEW promulgated criteria for desegregation of schools, including standards for determining the effectiveness of "freedom of choice" plans in eliminating dual systems of school assignment. The school districts' argument was, in effect, that whatever might be the *constitutional* requisites for an acceptable "freedom of choice" plan, Title VI precluded HEW from requiring actual integration as a criterion for continued eligibility for federal funds of a district which adopted freedom of choice. Here an administrative agency interpreted the statute, and then the correctness of the agency's statutory interpretation came before the court. Does the court's function in interpreting a statute in this type of situation differ from its function when there has been no prior administrative interpretation? This question is generally phrased in terms of the "scope" of judicial review of the agency's decision on an issue of law. Should the court approach the issue de novo, or should it give some weight to the agency's interpretation? And, if some weight, how much? What argument can be made that on the facts of *Jefferson County* the court should say this: "However we might interpret Title VI as an original proposition, the administrative interpretation should prevail if it has some reasonable basis"? Consider here the provision in Title VI that federal agencies should effectuate the policy of Title VI by issuing rules and regulations. What scope of lawmaking or law-declaring power was delegated to administrative agencies by Title VI? Questions of this type are considered in the course in administrative law.

Do you agree that HEW could require more than mere abandonment of racial assignments as a condition on accepting a "freedom of choice" plan? Does your reading effectuate the policy set forth in Title VI? More specifically, which meaning would better advance the statutory purpose—that HEW could or could not take race into account in establishing standards for desegregation, requiring some degree of actual desegregation as a guarantee of the plan's effectiveness? There is no difficulty, is there, in answering that question? See the discussion of this question in Part III.C. of Judge Wisdom's opinion, p. 360 *supra*. It was argued, however, that HEW was precluded from considering race as a factor in determining the effectiveness of "freedom of choice" plans, because federal action to remedy "racial imbalance" was specifically prohibited by the statute. Title VI does not contain such language, but in Title IV there are two such provisions: (1) In the provisions relating to technical and other assistance by the Commissioner of Education to school districts in dealing with problems of "desegregation," that term is defined as "the assignment of students to public schools and within such schools without regard to their race, color, religion, or national origin, but 'desegregation' shall not mean the assignment of students to pub-

lic schools in order to overcome racial imbalance." 42 U.S.C.
§ 2000c(b); F.C.A. 42 § 2000c(b). And, (2) the authorization to
the Attorney General to bring suits which "will materially further
the orderly achievement of desegregation" (as defined in the preceding sentence) ends with the proviso that "nothing herein shall
empower any official or court of the United States to issue any
order seeking to achieve a racial balance in any school by requiring the transportation of pupils from one school to another or
one school district to another in order to achieve such racial
balance . . . ." 42 U.S.C. § 2000c-6(a); F.C.A. 42 § 2000c-6(a).
These provisions raise two issues with respect to Title VI: (1)
should Title VI be read as if it included these limitations on dealing with "racial imbalance," and (2) if so, do these limitations
preclude the Guideline provisions which look toward remedying "racial imbalance" under "freedom of choice" plans? Judge
Wisdom refers to the legislative history of the Civil Rights Act
of 1964 in dealing with both these questions, principally statements on the floor of the Senate by the floor manager of the bill,
Senator Humphrey. What weight should be given to Senator
Humphrey's statement, p. 363 *supra,* that the limitations on
remedying racial imbalance in Title IV apply as well to Title VI?
That was not a critical issue in *Jefferson County,* because the
court concluded that the Guideline provisions were designed to
deal with racial imbalance that was the product or legacy of
compulsory, or de jure, racial segregation, while the racial imbalance provisions of Title IV (and perhaps Title VI) were directed at de facto racial segregation in the north and west, where
school segregation patterns were the product of geographical
attendance zones superimposed on racially segregated housing patterns. But finding such racial imbalance limitations in Title VI
would be of critical importance with respect to the application of
Title VI in the north and west and the eligibility for federal
funds of school districts with de facto racially segregated schools.
That issue will be explored in Chapter 4, where the most recent
HEW Guidelines, applicable to the north and west, are examined.

**5. The Attorney General as protector of individual constitu-
tional rights.**—The Civil Rights Act of 1964 authorized the Attorney General of the United States to initiate actions in federal
district courts in the name of the United States, seeking relief
against denials of equal protection by public school boards. The
Attorney General must certify that in his judgment the complainants who petition for him to do so "are unable . . . to
initiate and maintain appropriate legal proceedings for relief and
the institution of such an action will materially further the or-

derly achievement of desegregation in public education." He may deem complainants unable to initiate appropriate legal proceedings if they are "unable, either directly or through other interested persons or organizations, to bear the expense of the litigation or to obtain effective legal representation," or if "he is satisfied that the institution of such litigation would jeopardize the personal safety, employment, or economic standing of such person or persons, their families, or their property." 42 U.S.C. § 2000c-6; F.C.A. 42 § 2000c-6. The Attorney General was also authorized to intervene in the name of the United States in any action which "has been commenced in any court of the United States seeking relief from the denial of equal protection of the laws under the fourteenth amendment . . . on account of race, color, religion, or national origin." He must certify that "the case is of general public importance." The United States is entitled to the same relief as if it had instituted the action. 42 U.S.C. § 2000h-2; F.C.A. 42 § 2000h-2.

Consider the following comments by Professor Bickel on the bill which ultimately became the Civil Rights Act of 1964:

"The administration bill . . . raises serious problems on several levels. It is, obviously, an effort to alter those mechanics of the system . . . which ensure that a rule of constitutional law will become effective only when it is widely assented to. Of course, nothing is likely altogether to alter the system. Given the judicial resources that are available, and given, indeed, the resources that can conceivably be made available to the Attorney General himself, it is still out of the question that desegregation can be achieved wholly or even chiefly through litigation; it is still impossible that desegregation can be achieved if people are not moved by political action to achieve it voluntarily, because it is morally right and because it is, on balance, in their political and material interest. Yet the intention, and no doubt, in some measure, the effect, will be more coercion more promptly.

"If the system were to be altered in this fashion across the board, as was rather light-heartedly proposed in the House this fall; if, that is, the Attorney General were empowered to enforce all existing constitutional rights, and to seek from the courts declaration of new rights, then surely one would be entitled to the gravest of misgivings, because then the delicate balance between authoritarian judicialism and government by consent would indeed be significantly altered. Not only would that process of private litigation which, as I have said, is in its totality something of a political process of measuring the intensity and strength of interests affected by a judicial rule—not only would this process be circumvented, with the result that judicial power would be potentially enhanced quite out of proportion to what it now is or ought to be. The Attorney General would gain and share with the courts, at his option, powers entirely free of the imprecise safeguards that are implicit in our present reliance on private litigating initiative. It would be the Attorney General, in the exercise of a discretion for whose control no machinery exists or is easily conceived, who would choose to make existing rules of constitutional law effective, or explore the possibility of new ones, for he would elect from time to time to concentrate on enforcement in this or that area of constitutional law. This would be quite a revolutionary change. I hope, in some appropriately old-fashioned words of Justice McKenna, that "it is something more than timidity, dread of the new, that makes me fear that it is a step from the deck to the sea—the metaphor suggests a peril in the consequences." The present Attorney General, one is encouraged to note, resists being decorated with any such broad powers.

"But this is an argument at wholesale. The Attorney General already exercises by statute authority to enforce a great deal of law which, in the legislative judgment, needed enforcement beyond what could be expected from private initiative. And so do other administrative officers. There is a difference of more than just degree when the law to be enforced is constitutional rather than statutory. But it can be argued that when Congress passes a statute authorizing the Attorney General to enforce a given rule of constitutional law, the source of that rule is no longer exclusively in the judiciary. And that is so, so long as Congress closely defines what it wishes to see enforced. This is the view that prevailed when the Attorney General was given the authority that he now possesses to enforce the fifteenth amendment's guaranty of an equal vote. There is also a limited criminal statute under which the Attorney General can enforce constitutional rights. But the authority under this statute has been most cautiously and circumspectly limited by the courts, so as to encompass only well-defined and thoroughly established rules of constitutional law. As for the right to vote, there are very special circumstances that make private litigation for its enforcement extremely difficult, indeed almost certainly beyond any private resources. The power to litigate to desegregate public accommodations, also to be conferred by the administration bill, is again a special and different matter. First, the source of the right to be asserted is at most only partly constitutional; essentially, the Attorney General is to enforce, on the basis of a specific statute, something not unlike the Wages and Hours Act. Secondly, the private interest involved is so diffuse, and in any individual case so slight, that the incentive to undergo the ordeal of litigation is in this instance at a minimum, and yet the collective feeling on the subject is known, in the most concrete way, to be quite intense. In school cases, private litigation is a going concern. No superhuman efforts at collecting data fit for a census bureau and in any event not likely to be readily obtained from local officials —no such unusual efforts, which characterize voting cases, are required here. What is perhaps most important, no clear statutory definition of the sort of school segregation—*de jure* and perhaps *de facto*—that Congress may wish to see most efficiently abolished is proposed. Congress, of course, could not be brought to agree on such a definition. Nor is there a definition of remedies. With voting and with public accommodations it is otherwise. Both the objectives and the ways of attaining them are relatively clear, and Congress has stated them. The power to be conferred with respect to schools is, therefore, much more far-ranging, and much more independent.

"If it is conceded that there is a general presumption against executive power to litigate constitutional rights, and that exceptions must justify themselves, then I believe that the argument I have offered suffices. Still, it is a question of judgment, and there is yet more to be said, even if somewhat cumulatively. If the Attorney General is to decide that this or that case will 'materially further the public policy of the United States favoring the orderly achievement of desegregation in public education,' how is he to make this decision? To put the matter quite concretely, when is school desegregation to start in Clarendon County, South Carolina, or in Athens, Georgia, or in Columbia, South Carolina, or in Jackson, or Oxford, Mississippi, and in which of those places should it start first? And is *de facto* segregation to be attacked, and if so, where? And when? As things now stand, private parties, parents locally, local Negro lawyers, if any, the NAACP and its corresponding counsel, and whatever other leadership is present and effective in the Negro community nationwide somehow make the decision. The lawyer in charge of the suit in Clarendon County, South Carolina, has been deciding year after year not to push it. One of these days he may decide that the time has come. He may not be able to articulate the grounds for that decision, and it may be right or wrong as we view it afterwards. If we substitute the Attorney General as the decision-maker, must we not expect from him some more orderly, rational, and articulable process? For his decision will have been made at the expense of a dozen other places which pressed their claims on his resources—the resources of government, to which in principle all are equally entitled. It will be said that we do not displace the private decision-makers by empowering the Attorney General to bring suit, and on the face of things that is no doubt true. But in practice, matters will rest almost entirely in the hands of the Attorney General. Private initiative is bound to be chilled and the flow of private funds is bound to be discouraged and diverted elsewhere, where the help of the federal government is not available. If a private suit is brought, it will inevitably be regarded somewhat suspiciously by the courts and by public opinion, and inevitably be treated as of secondary importance. It will, after all, by hypothesis be a suit that does not necessarily 'materially further the public policy of the United States favoring the orderly achievement of desegregation in public education.'

"It would be a somewhat different matter, I think, if the business of desegregation were seriously taken in hand in administrative fashion. That is, it would be a different matter if the Office of Education, for example, or the Civil Rights Commission, were given adequate statutory standards to formulate plans of desegregation, were then required to hold hearings where there was opposition to the plans proposed, and were authorized to issue orders at the conclusion of those hearings, and to go to court to enforce such orders. Even this sort of more responsible and methodologically different displacement of private and local responsibility would be something to ponder long and carefully. Concerning the proposal as it stands, I cannot free myself of the feeling that those who now favor it most may come to regret it most.

"Quite aside from statutory authorization, there is considerable federal litigating power which is not subject to the misgivings I have voiced. Since before *In re Debs*, the Attorney General has been allowed to go into the courts of the United States in special circumstances to protect not only its material, but its functional interests. There was some language in *In re Debs* that was more sweeping than it needed to be, but on its facts, the objection to that case is that the courts were asked to do—and did—something they were not fit to do, at anyone's behest, not that the Attorney General was an improper party to initiate the suit. Just what a definable functional interest of the United States may be which does not include everything is hard to say. But the point of this line of cases is that occasional authority exists in limited circumstances. In each case some special federal responsibility must be shown. And so long as this is the rule, it may be expected that the decision to exercise inherent litigating power, being rare, will be made responsibly, at the highest executive level. And no derogation of private litigating initiative need be feared, for no announced federal undertaking to litigate is in play, and there can be no expectations. The administration has tried some desegregation suits against impacted-area school districts that receive federal funds, and against airports and hospitals that also receive federal funds, with results that are not yet clear, but certainly not negative. There is better than a good chance that inherent power to sue in such circumstances will be confirmed by the Supreme Court. These and other suits that fall somewhere in the traditional category can be prosecuted to good purpose, without raising the difficulties that inhere in broader statutory authority." Bickel, *The Decade of School Desegregation—Progress and Prospects,* 64 COLUM. L. REV. 193, 219-23 (1964).*

How soundly based are Professor Bickel's misgivings about the use of executive power to vindicate individual constitutional rights in the context of school desegregation litigation?

MACKENZIE, "ALL DELIBERATE SPEED" WAS UNWISE POLICY, BLACK FEELS
Washington Post, Dec. 4, 1968, p. A28, col. 1**

Looking back on the Supreme Court's role in school desegregation, Justice Hugo L. Black said last night that the "all deliberate speed" edict may have been unwise because it "delayed the process of outlawing segregation."

He strongly implied, but stopped short of saying directly, that he had preferred a different approach but had gone along with others on the Court in the spirit of unanimity that attended the historic school decisions of 1954 and 1955.

In a rare departure from Court tradition, the 82-year-old Justice appeared in a nationally televised interview, discussing and defending controversial criminal law and obscenity decisions as well as the basic decision against "separate but equal" public education. . . .

Black . . . shed some new light on the Court's 1955 decision that set the pace of implementing the 1954 ruling. Asked about the consequences of calling for "all deliberate speed" in desegregation, he said:

"Looking back on it now, it seems to me that it delayed the process of outlawing segregation. It seems to me, probably, with all due deference to the opinion and my brethren, all of them, that it would have been better—maybe—I don't say positively—not to have that sentence, to treat that case as an ordinary lawsuit and force that judgment on the counties it affected, that minute. That's true, that it would have only been one school and each case would have been only one case. But that fitted into my ideas of the Court not making policies for the Nation."

Chapter 4

BEYOND DE JURE SEGREGATION: NATIONWIDE PROBLEMS OF INEQUALITY OF EDUCATIONAL OPPORTUNITY

Chapter 3 has focused on a problem that is essentially regional: the undoing of de jure racial segregation in southern public schools. Current issues of equality of educational opportunity range well beyond the south, and well beyond the elimination of conscious racial policies of school assignment. The dimensions of these issues are outlined in the following extracts from the report of the Kerner Commission.

REPORT OF THE NATIONAL ADVISORY COMMISSION ON CIVIL DISORDERS 236-44, 251 (1968)

Education in our democratic society must equip the children of the nation to develop their potential and to participate fully in American life. For the community at large, the schools have discharged this responsibility well. But for many minorities, and particularly for the children of the racial ghetto, the schools have failed to provide the educational experience which could help overcome the effects of discrimination and deprivation. . . .

Several factors have converged to produce this critical situation.

The vast majority of inner-city schools are rigidly segregated. In 75 major central cities surveyed by the U.S. Commission on Civil Rights in its study, "Racial Isolation in the Public Schools," 75 percent of all Negro students in elementary grades attended schools with enrollments that were 90 percent or more Negro. Almost 90 percent of all Negro students attended schools which had a majority of Negro students. In the same cities, 83 percent of all white students in those grades attended schools with 90 to 100 percent white enrollment.[1]

Racial isolation in the urban public schools is the result principally of residential segregation and widespread employ-

---

[1] For percentages in individual cities see the footnote at p. 239 *supra.* [*Eds.* note.]

ment of the "neighborhood school" policy, which transfers segregation from housing to education. The effect of these conditions is magnified by the fact that a much greater proportion of white than Negro students attend private schools. Studies indicate that, in America's twenty largest cities, approximately four out of ten white students are enrolled in nonpublic schools, as compared with only one out of 10 Negro pupils. The differential appears to be increasing.

Urban schools are becoming more segregated. . . . By 1975, it is estimated that, if current policies and trends persist, 80 percent of all Negro pupils in the 20 largest cities, comprising nearly one-half of the Nation's Negro population, will be attending 90 to 100 percent Negro schools.

Segregation has operated to reduce the quality of education provided in schools serving disadvantaged Negro neighborhoods.

Most of the residents of these areas are poor. Many of the adults, the products of the inadequate, rural school systems of the South, have low levels of educational attainment. Their children have smaller vocabularies, and are not as well equipped to learn rapidly in school—particularly with respect to basic literary skills —as children from more advantaged homes.

When disadvantaged children are racially isolated in the schools, they are deprived of one of the more significant ingredients of quality education: exposure to other children with strong educational backgrounds. The Coleman Report and the Report of the Civil Rights Commission establish that the predominant socioeconomic background of the students in a school exerts a powerful impact upon achievement. . . .

Another strong influence on achievement derives from the tendency of school administrators, teachers, parents, and the students themselves to regard ghetto schools as inferior. Reflecting this attitude, students attending such schools lose confidence in their ability to shape the future. The Coleman Report found this factor—destiny control—"to have a stronger relationship to achievement than all the 'school' factors together" and to be related for Negroes, to the proportion of white in the schools. . . .

The schools attended by disadvantaged Negro children commonly are staffed by teachers with less experience and lower qualifications than those attended by middle-class whites. . . .

In virtually every large American city, the inner-city schools attended by Negroes are the most overcrowded. We have cited the vast population exchange—relatively affluent whites leaving the city to be replaced by Negroes—which has taken place over the last decade. The impact on public education facilities has been severe. . . .

Inner-city schools are not only overcrowded; they also tend to be the oldest and most poorly equipped. . . .

The quality of education offered by ghetto schools is diminished further by use of curricula and materials poorly adapted to the life-experiences of their students. . . .

Despite the overwhelming need, our society spends less money educating ghetto children than children of suburban families. . . .

There is evidence that the disparity in educational expenditures for suburban and inner-city schools has developed in parallel with population shifts. In a study of 12 metropolitan areas, the Civil Rights Commission found that, in 1950, 10 of the 12 central cities spent more per pupil than the surrounding suburbs; by 1964, in seven of the 12, the average suburb spent more per pupil than the central city.

This reversal reflects the declining or stagnant city tax base, and increasing competition from nonschool needs (police, welfare, fire) for a share of the municipal tax dollar. Suburbs, where nonschool needs are less demanding, allocate almost twice the proportion of their total budgets to education as the cities. . . .

To meet the urgent need to provide full equality of educational opportunity for disadvantaged youth, we recommend pursuit of the following strategies:

Increasing Efforts to Eliminate de facto Segregation

We have cited the extent of racial isolation in our urban schools. It is great and it is growing. It will not easily be overcome. Nonetheless, we believe school integration to be vital to the wellbeing of this country.

We base this conclusion not on the effect of racial and economic segregation on achievement of Negro students, although there is evidence of such a relationship; nor on the effect of racial isolation on the even more segregated white students, although lack of opportunity to associate with persons of different ethnic and socioeconomic backgrounds surely limits their learning experience.

We support integration as the priority education strategy because it is essential to the future of American society. We have seen in this last summer's disorders the consequences of racial isolation, at all levels, and of attitudes toward race, on both sides, produced by three centuries of myth, ignorance and bias. It is indispensable that opportunities for interaction between the races be expanded. . . .

Provision of Quality Education for Ghetto Schools

We recognize that the growing dominance of pupils from disadvantaged minorities in city school populations will not soon be reversed. No matter how great the effort toward desegregation, many children of the ghetto will not, within their school careers, attend integrated schools.

If existing disadvantages are not to be perpetuated, we must improve dramatically the quality of ghetto education. Equality of results with all-white schools in terms of achievement must be the goal.

We see no conflict between the integration and quality education strategies we espouse. Commitment to the goal of integrated education can neither diminish the reality of today's segregated and unequal ghetto schools nor sanction the tragic waste of human resources which they entail.

Far from being in conflict, the strategies are complementary. The aim of quality education is to compensate for and overcome the environmental handicaps of disadvantaged children. The evidence indicates that integration, in itself, does not wholly achieve this purpose. . . .

In short, compensatory education is essential not only to improve the quality of education provided in segregated ghetto schools, but to make possible both meaningful integration and maximum achievement in integrated schools.

Attainment of this goal will require adoption of a comprehensive approach designed to reconstruct the ghetto child's social and intellectual environment, compensate for disadvantages already suffered and provide necessary tools for development of essential literary skills. This approach will entail adoption of new and costly educational policies and practices beginning with early childhood and continuing through elementary and secondary schools. It will require extraordinary efforts to reconnect parents with the schools. It will also require unique experimentation with new methods to bring back into the educational process street-oriented teenagers and subteenagers who have lost all connection with existing school institutions. . . .

Implementation of These Programs. . . .

We urge that every state reexamine its present method of allocating funds to local school districts, not merely to provide equal funds for all political subdivisions on a per-pupil basis, but to assure more per-student aid to districts having a high proportion of disadvantaged students. Only if equalization formulas reflect the need to spend larger amounts per pupil in schools predominantly populated by disadvantaged students will state aid be allocated on an equitable basis. . . .

THE COLEMAN REPORT AND THE CIVIL RIGHTS COMMISSION'S "RACIAL ISOLATION" REPORT

This chapter will examine some of the legal aspects of the issues raised in the Kerner Commission report.

Social science data are of critical importance in dealing with these legal issues. What factors are relevant in measuring equality of educational opportunity? What is the comparative quality of educational opportunity offered the black or Mexican-American child who attends a de facto segregated school? Is *expenditure* per child a sound measure of equality of educational opportunity in schools within the same school district and from district to district? Is *achievement* of pupils on standardized tests a useful measure of the quality of educational opportunity offered those pupils? Are there ways to measure comparative quality of educational opportunity in different schools with respect to teaching staffs, facilities, and the like? What are the magnitude and significance of any inequalities which these or other measures may indicate? To what extent can "compensatory education" programs or new approaches to education ameliorate such inequalities? Is it feasible to determine the educational "needs" of different categories of children with different backgrounds and environments, and to develop different types of educational programs which will adequately respond to those needs? These, and similar questions, are the analogues to the social science issues involved in *Brown v. Board of Education*. They are questions which are currently the subject of research by social scientists. The data produced by this research have been, and will continue to be, basic elements in the development of legal doctrine by legislatures and courts concerning equality of educational opportunity.

It is not feasible here to attempt to summarize or to reach conclusions concerning all the current social science research relating to equality of educational opportunity. In the past few years, two major efforts, referred to in the extract from the Kerner Commission Report, stand out: (1) *Equality of Educational Opportunity,* published by the United States Office of Education (HEW) in 1966, pursuant to Title IV of the Civil Rights Act of 1964, which directed the Commissioner of Education to "conduct a survey and make a report to the President and the Congress . . . concerning the lack of availability of equal educational opportunities for individuals by reason of race, color, religion, or national origin in public educational institutions at all levels in the United States. . . ." 42 U.S.C. § 2000c-1; F.C.A. 42 § 2000c-1. This report has come to be known as the "Coleman Report." (2) *Racial Isolation in the Public Schools,* a report of the United States Commission on Civil Rights in 1967, which was a comprehensive study of race and education, including chapters on racial isolation in the public schools, causes of racial isolation, remedies, the role of law, and racial isolation and the outcomes of education (based on analysis of the Coleman Report data). An overview of these two reports and current related issues of educational policy is contained in the following article.

PETTIGREW, THE CONSEQUENCES OF RACIAL ISOLATION IN THE PUBLIC SCHOOLS: ANOTHER LOOK[2]

Suppose the racial isolation and segregation of America's public schools had no seriously negative effects upon either Negro or white children. If this were true, the increasing pattern of so-called *de facto* racial segregation of public education throughout the nation need not concern us. . . . Thus, Chapter Three, entitled "Racial Isolation and the Outcomes of Education," of the U. S. Commission on Civil Rights' report on *Racial Isolation in the Public Schools* assumes special importance and deserves another look.

I. The Chief Correlates of Negro Academic Achievement

To evaluate adequately the academic consequences for Negro American children of racial isolation, the findings must be placed in the context of the chief correlates in general of Negro student achievement. Such a context is provided by the much-discussed and often-misinterpreted Coleman Report. Called for by Congress in Title IV of the 1964 Civil Rights Act and supervised by the U. S. Office of Education, this massive study of *Equality of Educational Opportunity* tested over 600,000 children and thousands of teachers and school administrators throughout the country. No short summary of James Coleman's survey can do justice

---

[2] A paper prepared for the National Conference on Equal Educational Opportunity in America's Cities, sponsored by the United States Commission on Civil Rights, November 1967. [*Eds.* note.]

to this complex work. But combined with the extended analyses of the Coleman data later performed by the Commission on Civil Rights, a few generalizations can be ventured about Negro academic achievement in public schools.

Two basic correlates of achievement emerge from the Coleman data: "home background of the child" and "student body quality of the school." Though each of these factors are measured in the report by a number of indicators, both basically involve social class differences and are effectively represented by parents' education. Home background can be tapped by the average of the parents' education of each student; and student body quality can be rated by the education of the parents of all of the students comprising a particular school. Measured in this manner, it is perhaps more accurate to speak of these two major correlates as *individual social class* and *school social class*.

The individual social class factor is often said to be *the* principal correlate of achievement in the Coleman study, but this flat statement requires qualification. Individual social class proved a more important predictor of test scores for white than Negro children. And it proved of declining importance from the sixth to the twelfth grades. As shown in considerable research on adolescents in American society, the influence of the family recedes as the influence of peers strengthens. Consequently, the *school* social class variable becomes particularly powerful in secondary education; and it is a far more important correlate of Negro than white achievement.

These trends can be detailed with data from the metropolitan Northeast. By the twelfth grade, lower-status Negro children attending higher-status schools perform as a group slightly better than higher-status Negro children in lower-status schools. Combining the two variables for the scores of these children, their verbal achievement averages range from slightly below an eighth-grade level for low-status students in lower-status schools to almost an eleventh-grade level for high-status students in higher-status schools—a decisive difference of three full grades.

School social class, then, is easily the most important *school* correlate of achievement scores, white as well as Negro, although Coleman also looked closely at teacher ability and school facility variables. Teacher variables—ranging from years of teaching experience to years of formal education and vocabulary test score of the teacher—prove important, however. In similar ways to the school social class factor, the teacher factor is a stronger correlate of Negro than white student verbal achievement scores and is much more powerful in the secondary than elementary years.

By contrast, school facilities do not relate highly to pupil performance. Once individual social class is controlled, for example, per pupil instructional expenditure in grades six, nine, and twelve is not significantly associated with achievement save in one notable case of marked extremes—Negro children in the South. Nor do such variables as pupil-teacher ratio, library volumes, laboratories, number of extracurricular activities, comprehensiveness of the curriculum, strictness of promotion, ability grouping, and school size reveal any important and consistent relationships with achievement. These essentially negative findings concerning the influence of school facilities have received great attention and have apparently threatened many educators who ponder what chances for success their next school facilities bond referendum will have. Much of this concern, however, is caused by a misreading of these results. The chief finding is that school social class is such a critical achievement correlate that with a gross survey approach it will simply overwhelm any smaller school effects.

Moreover, the Coleman data do *not* mean that school facilities are unimportant. What they do signify is that the range of facilities now found in the nation's public schools is not great enough to explain wide differences in student performance. Consider the pupil-teacher ratio variable. Most American classrooms range between twenty and forty students per teacher. Within this relatively narrow range, Coleman could not show any consistent relationships with achievement scores. Yet one can still reasonably argue that it makes a major difference whether one is teaching five or 500 students; but Coleman could not test this proposition since actual pupil-teacher ratios of five and 500 are virtually non-existent. In short, Coleman could only test the effects of variables as they range in present-day schools. Just where below twenty and above forty pupils-per-teacher the instructional ratio variable becomes crucial for student performance must await more detailed, experimental studies.

II. Racial Composition of the Classroom and Negro Achievement

A key finding of the Coleman Report, then, and one of special importance for this paper . . . is that the most significant school correlate of achievement test scores of all types of children is the social class climate of the school's student body. Measured by the social class origins of all of a school's students, this variable appears most critical in the later grades and somewhat more important for Negro than white children. Put bluntly, children of all backgrounds tend to do better in schools with a predominantly middle-class milieu; and this trend is especially true in the later grades where the full force of peer-group influence is felt. This basic result of the Coleman Report has been vigorously challenged by a number of methodological critics, none of whom seem aware that the identical finding has been obtained by four other studies which employed sharply different measures and samples from those used by Coleman. The racial significance of this fundamental aspect of the Coleman Report becomes obvious as soon as we recall that only about one-fourth at most of the Negro American population can be accurately described as "middle-class."[3] Apart from strictly racial factors, then, extensive desegregation is necessary to provide Negro pupils with predominantly middle-class school settings. On these class grounds alone, Negro children in interracial classrooms would be expected to achieve more than similar Negro children in all-Negro classrooms, and these expectations are supported in the Coleman data. Negro children from "more than half" white classrooms score higher on both reading and mathematical achievement tests than other Negro children; and this effect is strongest among those who began their interracial schooling in the early grades. In addition, Negro students in "more than half" white classrooms yield as a group higher standard deviations in test scores than Negroes in classrooms with fewer whites—that is, their scores deviate more widely from the group average.

But are these achievement benefits of the interracial classroom *completely* a function of the school social class factor? Or are racial composition factors independently related *in addition?* The text of the Coleman Report is equivocal on this point; it speaks of the desegregation effect being ". . . largely, perhaps wholly, related to . . .," or ". . . largely accounted for by . . .," other student body characteristics. The Civil Rights Commission's re-analysis of these data, however, focuses further attention upon this particular question and finds that there *is* indeed a critical racial composition correlate. The re-analysis uncovers relatively large and consistent differences in favor of those twelfth-grade Negroes who are in "more than half" white classrooms even after the two major factors of the Coleman analysis

---

[3] This crude estimate derives from three modest and measurable definitions of "middle class": approximately one-quarter of adult Negroes are high school graduates; slightly more than one-fifth of Negroes in the labor force have white-collar occupations: and about one-quarter of Negro families have an annual income in excess of $6,000. [Footnote in original, renumbered.]

have been controlled—family social class and school social class. The most relevant chart is published on page 90 of *Racial Isolation in the Public Schools* showing the verbal achievement scores of twelfth-grade Negro children in the metropolitan Northeast (the only region with enough Negro children in both segregated and desegregated classrooms to furnish meaningful comparisons). Since this chart presents, perhaps, the most critical data of the entire report, it is reproduced here.

Figure 5. *Average Grade Level Performance of Twelfth Grade Negro Students by Individual Social Class Origin, Social Class Level of School and Proportion White Classmates Last Year; Metropolitan Northeast*

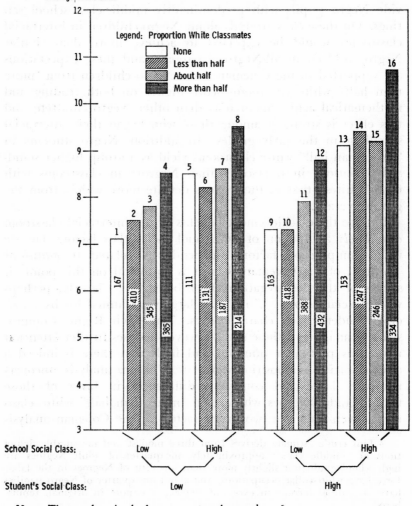

Note: The numbers in the bars represent the number of cases.

Observe several major trends. First, both social class and racial composition of the school are importantly related to the verbal scores. The differences at the extremes for twelfth-graders represent roughly three grade levels of achievement—a most significant contrast. Thus, students in lower social class schools with no white classmates attain only a seventh-grade standing (note bars 1 and 9) compared with nine-and-a-half to ten-and-a-half grade standings for those in higher social class schools with "more than half" white classmates (note bars 8 and 16). Second, within the same student and school social class clusters, the proportion of white classmates still makes a marked difference at the extremes of from one to one-and-a-half grade levels (compare bars 1 with 4, 5 with 8, 9 with 12, and 13 with 16). Third, these apparent benefits for Negro achievement of interracial classrooms are not linear; that is, the test scores do not gradually increase as the percentage of white students increases. Note that Negroes in predominantly-white classrooms score sharply higher than others in each of the four comparisons, but those in classrooms with "less than half" whites tend to do no better than those in all-Negro classrooms. We shall return to this important fact later.

Further aspects of the Commission's re-analysis of the Coleman data extend these results. The importance of interracial education in the primary grades is borne out at numerous points in the Coleman and Commission Reports. The improved Negro academic performance under desegregation, for instance, appears greatest for those Negro children who begin their biracial training in the early grades. Controlling again for both individual and school social class, those ninth-grade Negro children in the metropolitan Northeast who had been in interracial classrooms in the first three grades consistently scored from a half to a full grade above comparable students. . . . As the Commission Report made amply clear, the results of the critical chart on page 90 of the Report are not easily interpreted. A number of explanations can be offered for these findings which maintain that racial composition of the classroom itself is not the crucial variable, but rather other factors which co-vary with racial composition are crucial. Each of these explanations deserves examination. Thus, it could be maintained that even in the metropolitan Northeast, predominantly-Negro and predominantly-white schools vary sharply in school quality, especially teacher quality, and that it is these quality distinctions that are responsible for the improved scores in predominantly-white institutions. This argument could be challenged by the failure of the Coleman study to uncover sharp quality differences between "Negro" and "white" schools in the metropolitan Northeast; but this Coleman finding can itself be questioned. In any event, school quality controls narrow slightly the performance differentials attributable to desegregation, but do not by any means exhaust them.

A second type of explanation involves possible selection biases. One special form of the selection argument involves ability grouping. It can be argued that all the Commission found was that schools in the metropolitan Northeast do a reliable and accurate job of placing Negro students in ability groups or "tracks." Given the social handicaps many Negro children bring to the school situation, goes the argument, only the very brightest do well; and these gifted Negro children eventually are assigned to high-ability groups where most of their classmates are white. But less exceptional Negro students will find themselves assigned to low- or medium-ability groups where many or most of their classmates are other Negroes. Consequently, those Negroes with mostly white classmates score highest on academic achievement tests simply because they were brighter to begin with.

Another form of the selection explanation concerns parental choice of community and school. It maintains that *within a given social class group* more ambitious Negro parents will somehow manage to live in communities with interracial schools. Thus, what appears to be an advantage wrought by interracial schools is actually a result of the self-recruitment of especially motivated children of educationally-minded Negro parents within each Negro social class. A third possible selection argument involving relatively more drop-outs of poorly achieving Negro students from predominantly-white schools is not viable here, because the Commission results can be replicated on ninth-graders before the vast majority of present-day drop-outs have occurred.

These selection explanations receive some empirical support from Wilson's research in Richmond, California conducted for the Commission. He found that ". . . Negro students who attended integrated schools had higher mental maturity test scores in their primary grades, and came from homes better provided with educative materials." Thus, when Wilson held constant the early elementary achievement of these students, he found that the school class effect remained but that "the racial composition of schools, while tending to favor Negro students in integrated schools, does not have a substantial effect."

Wilson's conclusion is limited, however, in four ways. First, it applies to *schools*, not *classrooms*—the principal unit of the Commission's analysis. This is not an unimportant distinction, of course, since formally desegregated schools often have largely segregated classes within them. Second, unlike the Coleman data, the number of Negro students in desegregated schools in Wilson's study of Richmond, California is quite small. The eighth-grade verbal reasoning test data, for example, are available for only 128 Negro children in predominantly-white schools compared with 777 Negro children in predominantly-Negro schools. Third, among these 128 desegregated eighth-graders, only 8 of them (6%) were in lower-status schools; but among the 777 segregated eighth-graders, 378 of them (49%) were in lower-status schools. In other words, there is not enough variance in school social class among desegregated eighth-graders for Wilson's statistical procedures to separate out the school social class and racial composition factors convincingly. Likewise, [fourth,] another type of Negro child critical to Wilson's analysis is in especially short supply. While he has Negro students with both high and low test scores when they entered segregated primary schools and others with high test scores when they entered desegregated schools, he lacks many examples of Negro children with *low* test scores when they entered *desegregated* primary schools. This missing group is the most crucial of all for analytical and practical purposes.

Since the Wilson study leaves open the question about the effects of desegregation upon the more disadvantaged Negro students, the Commission employed Coleman data to check on the effects of interracial classrooms on the verbal scores of less gifted Negro ninth-graders in the metropolitan Northeast. These students had poorly educated parents and reported themselves to be in low- or medium-ability tracks. Both in high and low status high schools, these Negroes who were from predominantly-white classrooms performed on the average from one-half to two-thirds of a grade better than comparable Negroes from predominantly-Negro classrooms.

The ability grouping argument is directed at the finding that predominantly-white *classrooms* are associated with higher Negro scores. But it does not address itself to the additional finding that multiple tracked, predominantly-white *schools* also tend to relate to higher Negro performance. Most importantly, the ability grouping contentions lose force from the time sequence involved. Recall that the largest effects of interracial classrooms occur when the experience begins in the earliest elementary grades. Yet ability grouping does not typically begin in American public schools until the middle school grades and does not become nearly universal until the high school grades. Therefore, desegregation would appear to afford a better explanation for who gets into the high-ability tracks than ability tracks do for desegregation effects. A Negro child of medium ability who begins his education in a desegregated school, for instance, has a far higher probability of being selected later for a high ability track than a Negro child of comparable ability going to a school of similar social status who began his education in an all-Negro school. Ability grouping, then, can serve as a magnifier of the differences already begun by classroom differences in racial composition, a catalyst adding to the cumulative deficits of the segregated Negro.

The parental choice of community and school idea is in some ways the reverse of the ability grouping contention. It aims to account for the fact that predominantly-white *communities and schools* are associated with higher Negro achievement; but it cannot fully account for the fact that the Commission shows interracial *classrooms* are also associated with higher Negro achievement—unless one is willing to assume that there is widespread selection by Negro parents of classrooms as well as communities and schools. There are other assumptions, too, that this particular line of reasoning must make that are at best dubious. Since lower-status, low-ability Negro pupils also benefit from desegregation, these contentions require that poor Negro families possess a sophisticated knowledge of where to go to find the better interracial schools and the funds and freedom of mobility to move accordingly. All that is known about the extreme residential discrimination practiced against Negroes, especially poor Negroes, in American metropolitan areas today make such assumptions most improbable.

Two additional explanations argue that at least some of the apparent racial composition effect revealed by the Commission's re-analysis still reflects the operation of the powerful school social class effect. One chain of reasoning is based on the difficulty of controlling for social class across racial groups. Since the floor of Negro deprivation is below that of whites, for example, it can be maintained that "lower class" Negroes who attend a predominantly-white school comprised largely of "lower class" whites are still benefiting from a higher social class student climate than "lower class" Negroes who attend a predominantly-Negro school comprised of "lower class" Negroes. While there is some merit in this reasoning, it should be remembered that the Commission's differences for twelfth-graders by racial composition of classrooms (averaging about one-and-a-third grades holding the two class variables constant) were approximately 80% as large as those attributable to school social class directly (averaging about one-and-two-thirds grades holding the individual social class and racial composition variables constant). Hence, it would seem that the small school class residual under discussion could account for only a small portion of the racial composition effect.

The other class explanation is limited, but, perhaps, the most subtle of all. It applies only to certain lower-status Negro students who attend predominantly-white, lower-status schools. Even if the lower-status Negro child is of fully equivalent status to that of the whites, he might well benefit from membership in a minority comprised largely of middle-class Negroes. This possibility is not as remote as it may sound, for a larger percentage of middle-class than lower-class Negroes attend predominantly-white schools and the argument assumes only that the Negro minority will serve as a more positive and salient reference group than the white majority. Though of limited scope, this ingenious possibility elegantly illustrates the subtleties and difficulties inherent in this type of research.

None of these counter explanations, taken singly or together, appears to eliminate the relatively large relationship found by the Commission between the racial composition of the classroom and Negro test performance. This means that while the social class composition of the school remains the dominant factor, there is in addition a significant contribution of the interracial classroom upon the Negro child's academic achievement. The lengthy discussion to reach this conclusion had two purposes. One was to illustrate in depth the operation of many of the special problems of interpreting race and education survey research results. A second reason for this discussion is that the issue is in fact of vital theoretical and practical significance. While it is not critical for determining the *need* for desegregated schools, it is crucial for determining the *actual processes* through which desegregation affects both Negro and white children. If it is merely a school social class effect, that fact limits our search to non-racial processes that should not be unique to interracial schools. If, however, there is also a racial composition effect, then our net must be cast wider to include specifically racial considerations. The writer believes the evidence at this point. It points to the operation of both social class and racial composition factors. . . .

III. Useful Definitions of "Segregation," "Desegregation," and "Integration"

The Coleman and Civil Rights Commission results strongly suggest some empirically-based definitional distinctions that could prove clarifying to this semantically confused realm. To begin with, the legal distinctions between *de jure* and *de facto* segregation is of no practical importance for the consequences of racial isolation in the schools. The Commission's data speak to this issue directly; they suggest effects of *de facto* school segregation just as negative as those reported earlier for *de jure* school segregation. The legal distinction has little relevance for the Negro child in the all-Negro school.

Indeed, a realistic look at so-called *de facto* school segregation in cities today calls into question even the legal separation of the two forms of segregation. While *de jure* apartheid has its roots in blatant state legislation, so-called *"de facto"* apartheid generally has its roots in state action, too. Such state action may include anything from school board decisions to urban renewal plans and zoning ordinances. At some future time in American history, as Paul Freund has suggested, the judiciary will have to come to terms with the implications of the state action similarity between *de jure* and *de facto* forms of school segregation.

The Coleman and Commission data also have implications for the question of numbers and percentages. Two major alternatives had been previously proposed. One manner of defining "segregation" and "desegregation" is to peg the definition to the non-white percentage of the area's over-all school population. Thus, if twelve per cent of a system's students are non-white, then ideally each school in the system would approach a non-white student composition of twelve per cent. There are at least two criticisms of this approach: it is often impractical in all but reasonably small areas; and it treats the individual school as a simple reflection of the community, rather than an integumented institution with its own dynamics and requirements.

A second definition of a racially desegregated school attempts to meet these criticisms with a relatively fixed, rather than variable, gauge. On the basis of several social psychological considerations, the ideally desegregated school is one whose student body includes from roughly 20 to 45 per cent non-whites. The disadvantage here is that uniracial schools could still result in systems with fewer than 20 per cent or more than 45 per cent non-white children. The federal studies suggest a simpler set of definitions; a segregated school is one whose student body is predominantly non-white; while a desegregated school is one whose student body is interracial but predominantly white. Such definitions stem from the previously mentioned finding that the beneficial effects of interracial schools for the academic performance of Negro children are not linear; that is, Negro test scores do not rise evenly with increasing percentages of white children in the classroom. Rather, both the Coleman and Commission analyses point to a discontinuity at just past the mid-point with the highest Negro verbal test scores reported from *"more than half"* white classrooms. Indeed, enrollment in classes with "less than half" whites is associated with scores not significantly different from those all-Negro classrooms.

These simpler definitions receive further support from white test performance. . . . Suffice it here to note that, as long as the class is predominantly-white, the achievement levels of white pupils in interracial classrooms do not differ from those of white pupils in all-white classrooms. But attendance in predominantly-Negro classes is associated with lower white test scores. In other words, the same classes relate to higher scores for both Negro and white children; and these classrooms are predominantly-white and may usefully be defined as "desegregated." Similarly, the same classes relate to lower scores for both Negro and white children; and these classrooms are predominantly-Negro and may usefully be defined as "segregated."

The ideological difficulties of such definitions are readily apparent. As mentioned before, Negroes can rightfully argue that such definitions imply that "white is right," that predominantly-Negro schools cannot be "good schools." Commissioner Frankie Freeman of the Civil Rights Commission addressed herself specifically to this issue in a supplementary statement to the Commission report:

> The question is not whether in theory or in the abstract Negro schools can be as good as white schools. In a society free from prejudice in which Negroes were full and equal participants, the answer would clearly be "Yes." But we are forced, rather, to ask the harder question, whether in our present society, where Negroes are a minority which has been discriminated against, Negro children can prepare themselves to participate effectively in society if they grow up and go to school in isolation from the majority group. We must also ask whether we can cure the disease of prejudice and prepare all children for life in a multiracial world if white children grow up and go to school in isolation from Negroes.

The two federal reports also suggest that another useful distinction can and should be made between "desegregated" and "integrated" schools. Note that the definition of desegregation involves only a specification of the racial mix of students—namely, more than half whites. It does not include any description of the *quality* of the interracial contact. Merely desegregated schools can be either effective or ineffective, can boast genuine interracial acceptance or intense interracial hostility. In short, a desegregated school is not necessarily a "good school."

Recall that the Coleman Report revealed consistently larger standard deviations for the test scores of Negro children in desegregated (i.e., "more than half" white) classrooms. Many of these children are doing extremely well, but others are not doing nearly as well. What accounts for these wide differences? The Commission's re-analysis of these Coleman data suggests that the explanatory intervening variable is *interracial acceptance.* In desegregated schools where most teachers report no tension, Negro students evince higher verbal achievement, more definite college plans, and more positive attitudes than students in tense desegregated schools. White students also evince benefits from the interracially harmonious school. . . .

The term "integrated school," then, might usefully be reserved for the desegregated school where interracial acceptance is the norm. With these usages, "desegregation" becomes the prerequisite, but "integration" is the ultimate goal.

IV. *The Non-Academic Consequences of Interracial Education*

While important, high achievement test scores are surely not the only goal of education. Indeed, many advocates argue for integrated education solely in terms of the non-academic benefits of diverse contacts. Preparation for the interracial world of the future, they insist, demands interracial schools today for both white and Negro youth. The Coleman and Commission data speak to this issue, too.

The Coleman Report itself shows that white students who attend public schools with Negroes are the least likely to prefer all-white classrooms and all-white "close friends"; and this effect, too, is strongest among those who begin their interracial schooling in the early grades. Consistent with these results are data from Louisville, Kentucky on Negro pupils. In an open choice situation, Negro children are likely to select predominantly-white high schools only if they are currently attending predominantly-white junior high schools. In short, integration leads to a preference among both white and Negro children for integration, while segregation breeds further segregation.

A Civil Rights Commission survey of urban adults in the North and West discussed in the Report suggests that these trends continue into adulthood. Negro adults who themselves attended desegregated schools as children tend to be more eager to have their children attend such schools and do in fact more often send their children to such schools than comparable Negro adults who attended only segregated schools as children. They are typically making more money and more frequently in white-collar occupations than previously-segregated Negroes of comparable origins. Similarly, white adults who experienced as children integrated schooling differ from comparable whites in their greater willingness to reside in an interracial neighborhood, to have their children attend interracial schools, and to have Negro friends. Thus, the cumulative nature of integration is not limited to just the school career of the child, but tends to span generations.

The consistency of these results and their practical importance commend further and more detailed work in this area. Longitudinal research and more sensitive methods than crude surveys seem indicated. Such future work could give us a clearer conception of the *process* by which these effects are generated. One hint as to a mediating mechanism appears in the Commission's analysis: namely, many of the attitude and behavioral consequences appeared to be mediated by cross-racial friendship. Consistent with the findings and ideas expressed earlier about a truly *integrated* school, many of the adult results were greatly enhanced if the respondent had had interracial schooling *and* a close friend of the other race. Those who had received a desegregated education but who had not had a close friend often showed few if any positive effects. To sum up, it appears that *integrated* schools do in fact prepare their Negro and white products for interracial living as adults.

In addition to improved interracial attitudes, an interesting personality benefit of the biracial classroom emerges in Coleman's data which in turn is directly connected with academic performance. Student personality variables are surprisingly strong independent correlates of test performance in Coleman's data for all groups of children, though different measures predict white and Negro achievement. An "academic self-concept" variable—measured by such items as "How bright do you think you are in comparison with the other students in your grade?"—proves more significant for white performance. But a brief scale of "fate control"—indicated, for example, by disagreeing that "Good luck is more important than hard work for success"—is much more important for Negro performance. The critical point is that this sense of fate control among Negroes tends to be greater in desegregated schools.

Clearly, these personality-achievement findings result from tapping into a complex process involving a two-way causal pattern. Not only do those Negro children with a sense of fate control subsequently do better in their school achievement, but those who do well in school achievement undoubtedly begin to gain a sense of fate control. Nevertheless, it is tempting to speculate with Coleman that each child faces a two-stage problem: first, he must learn that he can within reasonably broad limits act effectively upon his surroundings; and, second, he must then evaluate his own relative capabilities for mastering the environment. The critical stage for white children seems to be the second stage concerning the self-concept, while the critical stage for Negro children seems realistically enough to involve the question of manipulating an often harsh and overpowering environment. In any event, more detailed experimental work along these lines appears warranted.

V. Is Compensatory Education in Segregated Schools an Effective Substitute for Integrated Education?

Since the initiation of the much-touted "Higher Horizons" project in New York City and similar early programs elsewhere, so-called "compensatory education" has been put forward as an effective alternative to racially-integrated education. Now the roughly billion-and-a-half dollars annually invested by the Federal Government into this type of strategy through Title I of the 1965 Elementary and Secondary Education Act makes this alternative even more attractive and widespread. Moreover, it is politically expedient, for it solves—temporarily, at any rate—a real dilemma many school superintendents and boards of education in urban districts face: on the one hand, one must act to change the incredibly-ineffective education of impoverished Negroes that has been occurring for years; but, on the other hand, racial desegregation of public schools is often a controversial and stoutly-resisted action. Compensatory programs allow one to act and to avoid controversy—especially if Federal funds pay the bill.

There is only one difficulty with this "solution": there is no solid evidence that it works. Indeed, there is mounting evidence from throughout the nation that it resoundingly fails. This is not to say that these enthusiastically-initiated programs do not improve for a time the tenor of many ghetto schools—not an unimportant achievement. But it is to say that it remains to be demonstrated that these programs can lead to lasting and significant academic gains. So far the record of these programs is not encouraging.

To account for repeated failures in this realm, one need only recall the chief finding of the Coleman Report: the principal resource a school can offer a disadvantaged child is close association with advantaged children. As we have seen, a major reason why integration leads to lasting significant academic gains for Negro children seems to be the association with middle-class children that it often provides for working-class Negro children. Compensatory programs for disadvantaged youngsters without such contact are, to put it mildly, struggling uphill to achieve meaningful effects with mere curriculum changes under the same isolated conditions as before. One may speculate if this is not one of the reasons for the Coleman Report's unpopularity in some quarters. Striking as it does at the heart of a politically-expedient strategy which is supported by a billion-and-a-half dollars, the Report understandably, perhaps, has been suppressed and irresponsibly criticized. Released late on a rainy Saturday afternoon of a July 4th weekend, the Coleman Report is now out of print and one is cheerfully told by both the U.S. Government Printing Office and the U.S. Office of Education that it will not be reissued.

The Commission Report explores this crucial area further. Though widely misinterpreted as attacking "compensatory education" in general, the Commission expressed skepticism over the efficacy of such programs *in ghetto schools*. It came to this conclusion after studying in detail such programs in St. Louis, New York City, Syracuse, Philadelphia, Berkeley, and Seattle. . . . It noted with interest that comparable Negro children in the last four cities who were bussed out to predominantly-white schools did show sustained academic gains, whereas those who had remained behind in the ghetto schools for special programs did not.

The Commission's conclusion is obvious: Why not have both integration and remedial education as needed? Of course, the two intervention strategies are often pitted against one another as either-or alternatives, since realistically they compete for the same funds, have rival educational ideologies undergirding them, and have different political constituencies. These are political reasons why we do not combine them; in educational terms, there is every reason to coordinate both measures into a single strategy.

Finally, it should be said in fairness that the general failure of ghetto compensatory programs to date does not necessarily mean failure of future and radically different programs. One cannot evaluate a program yet to be tried. It is the responsibility, however, of those who honestly believe that compensatory education can in fact be a viable alternative to racial integration to reject the null hypothesis with rigorous data; that is, the advocates have the burden of proof that it can yet be accomplished.

VI. Practical Implications

By way of recapitulation, the following practical considerations for educational policy can be deduced from the material reviewed in this paper:

(1) Careful attention to the "social class" mix of school student bodies is indicated, for children of all regions, groups, and classes tend to academically perform best in schools characterized by a middle-class milieu.

(2) Teacher quality, but not the typical range of school facilities, relates to student achievement. Special attention to upgrading a system's teachers seems justified, especially in the verbal achievement domain.

(3) Racial composition of the school and classroom is important for academic, attitude, and personality reasons; and it operates in addition as well as in concert with the more powerful school social class factor.

(4) In terms of the achievement consequences for both white and Negro children, it is useful to define a "segregated" school as one that is predominantly Negro, a "desegregated" school as one that is interracial but predominantly white, and an "integrated" school as one that boasts both desegregation and cross-racial acceptance and friendship. . . .

(5) The academic and attitude benefits of integrated education for children of both races are maximized when they begin their interracial experience in the earliest primary grades. It is, of course, politically most difficult to desegregate the elementary level; but it is also true that it is most difficult to achieve real integration—as opposed to desegregation—when the biracial contact begins at the junior high and, particularly, the high school levels.

(6) On the basis of the record of the many popular attempts to date, it does not appear that so-called "compensatory" education in segregated schools is an effective substitute for integrated education. While these programs generally represent an improvement in school morale and climate, they have not led to lasting academic improvement of Negro student achievement. When at all politically and financially feasible, the most attractive possibility is to combine such programs with school desegregation.

A. THE VALIDITY OF GOVERNMENTAL ACTION TO REDUCE DE FACTO SEGREGATION

Legislative and administrative steps have been taken in a few states to require school boards to make efforts to reduce racial imbalance in public schools. The following judicial decision deals with the validity of a 1963 Illinois statute; it also summarizes the decisions of several other courts on similar measures.

TOMETZ v. BOARD OF EDUCATION, WAUKEGAN CITY SCHOOL DISTRICT NO. 61
Supreme Court of Illinois
39 Ill.2d 593, 237 N.E.2d 498 (1968)

WARD, Justice.

On June 13, 1963, the legislature approved an amendment to section 10-21.3 of the Illinois School Code relating to the duties of school boards. (Ill. Rev. Stat. 1967, chap. 122, par. 10-21.3.) This amendment, commonly called the Armstrong Act, provides in part: "As soon as practicable, and from time to time thereafter, the board shall change or revise existing [attendance] units or create new units in a manner which will take into consideration the prevention of segregation and the elimination of separation of children in public schools because of color, race or nationality."

On August 4, 1965, the plaintiffs, seven children, by their respective parents, instituted a suit in the circuit court of Lake County claiming that the Waukegan City School District had violated the Armstrong Act and seeking a mandatory injunction requiring the district to revise the boundaries of its school attendance units. The district and the local board of education were named as defendants.

No boundary changes had been made in the school district since the enactment of the Armstrong Act. At the time suit was filed, the percentages of Caucasian and Negro students in each of the district's attendance units were as follows:

Name of School	Percentage of Caucasians	Percentage of Negroes
Whittier	15%	85%
Clearview	100%	0%
Glen Flora	98%	2%
Glenwood	100%	0%
Hyde Park	100%	0%

After suit had been filed, Dr. McCall, who was then the superintendent of the defendant school district, was requested by the board to make a study of the Whittier and surrounding attendance units. Dr. McCall prepared a comprehensive report, which included four possible revisions of the boundaries for the school district area, which were designated plans 1, 2, 3, and 4. His observations concerning each plan's feasibility and desirability were part of the report. On June 13, 1966, the board considered the report, which, though it described possible boundary changes, recommended that no changes be made, and voted to make no revisions of attendance unit boundaries.

Trial was had on the plaintiffs' complaint and at its conclusion on July 20, 1966, the court found *inter alia* that the racial imbalance in the Whittier School area had not been created by any deliberate conduct on the part of the defendants and that the defendants had not been guilty of any intentional racial discrimination. Also, the trial court held that the Armstrong Act was constitutional and applicable to "so-called *de facto* segregation in schools, i.e., racial imbalance in schools not created by the deliberate intent of a school board." The trial court judged that the defendants' failure to make any change in the boundaries of the district's attendance units was unreasonable under the circumstances and in violation of the Armstrong Act. The court therefore ordered the defendants to submit a plan making reasonable boundary revisions so as to "in some measure ameliorate the racial imbalance" in the attendance units concerned. August 4, 1966, was set for a hearing to consider the plan to be proposed.

On such date the trial court incorporated in its decree plan 2 of the McCall report with certain modifications. These modifications were proposed by Dr. Van Devander, the new school district superintendent, to improve the original plan 2 by avoiding certain traffic hazards and by more acceptably balancing class loads among the schools. Under the court's decree the distribution of Caucasian and Negro school children in the district was to be:

Name of School	Percentage of Caucasians	Percentage of Negroes
Whittier	57.4%	42.6%
Clearview	100%	0%
Glen Flora	83%	17%
Glenwood	83.6%	16.4%
Hyde Park	79.9%	20.1%

In this direct appeal the defendants challenge the constitutionality of the Armstrong Act, alleging that the Act's requirement that race be considered as a factor in changing or forming school attendance unit boundaries, constitutes a racial classification condemned by the equal protection clause and due process clause of the fourteenth amendment to the United States constitution and the due process clause of the Illinois constitution.

To support this claim, the defendants heavily rely on three Federal cases, each of which held, no State law being involved, that a local school board does not have an affirmative constitutional duty to act to alleviate racial imbalance in the schools that it did not cause. (Deal v. Cincinnati Board of Education (6th Cir. 1966) 369 F.2d 55, cert. denied 389 U.S. 847, 88 S. Ct. 39, 19 L. Ed. 2d 114; Downs v. Board of Education of Kansas City (10th Cir. 1964) 336 F.2d 988, cert. denied 380 U.S. 914, 85 S. Ct. 898, 13 L. Ed. 2d 800; Bell v. School City of Gary, Indiana (7th Cir. 1963) 324 F.2d 209, cert. denied 377 U.S. 924, 84 S. Ct. 1223, 12 L. Ed. 2d 216.) However, the question as to whether the constitution requires a local school board, or a State, to act to undo *de facto* school segregation is simply not here concerned. The issue here is whether the constitution permits, rather than prohibits, voluntary State action aimed toward reducing and eventually eliminating *de facto* school segregation.

State laws or administrative policies, directed toward the reduction and eventual elimination of *de facto* segregation of children in the schools and racial imbalance, have been approved by every high State court which has considered the issue. (Pennsylvania—Pennsylvania Human Relations Commission v. Chester School District (Sept. 1967) 427 Pa. 157, 233 A.2d 290; Massachusetts—School Committee of Boston v. Board of Education (June, 1967) Mass., 227 N.E.2d 729, appeal dismissed (Jan. 15, 1968) 389 U.S. 572, 88 S. Ct. 692, 19 L. Ed. 2d 778; New Jersey—Booker v. Board of Education of City of Plainfield, Union County (1965) 45 N.J. 161, 212 A.2d 1, 11 A.L.R.3d 754; Morean v. Board of Education of Town of Montclair (1964) 42 N.J. 237, 200 A.2d 97; California—Jackson v. Pasadena City School District (1963) 59 Cal.2d 876, 31 Cal. Rptr. 606, 382 P.2d 878; New York—Addabbo v. Donovan (1965) 16 N.Y.2d 619, 261 N.Y.S.2d 68, 209 N.E.2d 112, cert. denied 382 U.S. 905, 86 S. Ct. 241, 15 L. Ed. 2d 158; Vetere v. Allen (1965) 15 N.Y.2d 259, 258 N.Y.S. 2d 77, 206 N.E.2d 174; see also Guida v. Board of Education of City of New Haven (1965) 26 Conn. Supp. 121, 213 A.2d 843.) Similarly, the Federal courts which have considered the issue, including Deal v. Cincinnati Board of Education . . ., relied on by the defendants, have recognized that voluntary programs of local school authorities designed to alleviate *de facto* segregation and racial imbalance in the schools are not constitutionally forbidden. . . .

In Springfield School Committee v. Barksdale (1st Cir. 1965) 348 F.2d 261, the school authorities of Springfield, Massachusetts, had passed a resolution to take appropriate action "to eliminate to the fullest extent possible, [*de facto*] racial concentration in the schools within the framework of effective educational procedures." Addressing itself to this resolution, the Court of Appeals for the First Circuit stated at page 266 that: "It has been suggested that classification by race is unlawful regardless of the worthiness of the objective. We do not agree. The defendants' proposed action does not concern race except insofar as race correlates with proven deprivation of educational opportunity. This evil satisfies whatever 'heavier burden of justification' there may be. Cf. McLaughlin v. State of Florida, 1964, 379 U.S. 184, 194, 85 S. Ct. 283, 13 L. Ed. 2d 222. It would seem no more unconstitutional to take into account plaintiffs' special characteristics and circumstances that have been found to be occasioned by their color than it would be to give special attention to physiological, psychological or sociological variances from the norm occasioned by other factors. That these differences hap- pen to be associated with a particular race is no reason for ignor- ing them. Booker v. Board of Education etc., 1965, 45 N.J. 161, 212 A.2d 1, 11 A.L.R.3d 754. . . ."

In Morean v. Board of Education of Town of Montclair (1964) 42 N.J. 237, 200 A.2d 97, the Supreme Court of New Jersey sustained the constitutionality of a school board's plan to assign students from a predominantly Negro junior high school to the town's three remaining junior high schools, even though race had been a consideration. The court stated there that: "The motivation was, to avoid creating a situation at Hillside [school] which would deprive the pupils there of equal educational opportunities and subject them to the harmful consequences of practical segregation. Constitutional color blindness may be wholly apt when the frame of reference is an attack on official efforts toward segregation; it is not generally apt when the attack is on official efforts toward the avoidance of segregation." 200 A.2d at 99; accord, Offermann v. Nitkowski (2d Cir. 1967) 378 F.2d 22, 24. . . .

The test of any legislative classification essentially is one of reasonableness. This court stated in City of Chicago v. Vokes, 28 Ill.2d 475, 193 N.E.2d 40, that neither the fourteenth amendment nor any provision of the Illinois constitution forbids legislative classifications reasonably calculated to promote or serve a proper police-power purpose. "Rather, they invalidate only enactments that are arbitrary, unreasonable and unrelated to the public purpose sought to be attained, or those which, although reasonably designed to promote the public interest, effect classifications which have no reasonable basis and are therefore arbitrary." . . . And, of course, the burden rests upon one assailing a statute or a classification in a law, to show that it does not rest upon any reasonable basis but is essentially arbitrary. . . .

Here, the legislature has directed school boards "as soon as practicable" to fix or revise the boundaries of school attendance units in a manner that "takes into consideration" the prevention and elimination of segregation. We cannot say that the legislature acted arbitrarily and without a reasonable basis in so directing the school boards of this State. . . .

. . . Too, not to be disregarded is article VIII of the constitution which directs the general assembly to "provide a thorough and efficient system of free schools, whereby all children of this state may receive a good common school education." Ill. Const., art. VIII, sec. 1.

When, in Brown v. Board of Education of Topeka (1954) 347 U.S. 483, 74 S. Ct. 686, 98 L. Ed. 873, the Supreme Court declared unconstitutional *de jure* segregation in public schools, it made clear its position that all segregation of children solely on the basis of race deprives children of the minority group of equal educational opportunities. Though *Brown* directly concerned *de jure* segregation, segregation caused by official governmental action, courts since *Brown* have recognized that *de facto* segregation has a seriously limiting influence on educational opportunity. . . .

The fact that children other than Negro children may be deprived of equal educational opportunities does not form a constitutional impediment to the Act concerned. The legislature is not required to choose between legislating against all evils of the same genus or not legislating at all. It may recognize degrees of harm confining itself to where the need seems most acute. . . . Too, the Armstrong Act would apply to the offensive segregation of school children of any "color, race or nationality."

We deem that neither the fourteenth amendment nor any provision of the Illinois constitution deprives the legislature of the authority to require school boards "as soon as practicable" to fix or change the boundaries of school attendance units "in a manner which will take into consideration" the prevention and eventual elimination of segregation.

It is apparent from what we have said that our view is that the Armstrong Act was designed to apply to *de facto* school segregation. Illinois has never been classified as a *de jure* segregation State. School authorities in Illinois were forbidden from separating or excluding school children based on race or color as early as 1874. . . . In 1954, the United States Supreme Court in Brown v. Board of Education of Topeka, 347 U.S. 483, 74 S. Ct. 686, 98 L. Ed. 873, declared *de jure* school segregation by State action unconstitutional. Since then the unconstitutionality of *de jure* segregation has been clear. It would be unreasonable

that our legislature, in 1963, in enacting the statute here concerned would be directing its attention superfluously to *de jure*
rather than *de facto* school segregation, as defendants maintain.
. . . We concur in the trial court's interpretation that the reference in the Armstrong Act to the "elimination of separation of
children in the public schools because of color" is intended to
apply to *de facto* segregation. . . .

The defendants also argue that the trial court improperly overruled the school board, which had concluded, based on considerations of traffic hazards, walking distances, finances and classroom
capacity, that existing attendance unit boundaries should not
be revised.

As stated, the Act provides that "as soon as practicable" a
school board shall revise attendance unit boundaries "taking
into consideration" the prevention and elimination of segregation.
Here, a full hearing was conducted by the trial court at which
the parties presented detailed evidence. At its conclusion, the
trial court ruled *inter alia* that the defendants were in violation
of the Armstrong Act and directed the alteration of school
boundaries as described.

As the defendants state, the trial judge said that under the
Act racial imbalance is a paramount consideration in drawing
school attendance unit boundaries. However, it is clear from the
opinion of the trial judge that he considered and did not disregard other relevant factors in arriving at his decision. The trial
judge stated: "Defendants' evidence concerning traffic, distances
of students from school, finances and classroom capacity are not
determinative of the issues in the case at bar. In making this
statement, the Court does not mean to intimate that in a given
case these factors could not be the determining factors and would
override any factor of racial consideration. In a certain situation
the Court feels this could be true. However, in the instant case,
the Court is of the opinion that the evidence on these factors
was not conclusive, and did not prove that a serious problem, or
even one of very large proportions, existed in any of these categories: namely, traffic, distance, finance or classroom capacity."
Later the court observed: ". . . in the case at hand, all of the
attendance units involved are contiguous and in a general
sense, constitute a neighborhood in the larger sense of the term.
This is not an instance where units are separate, nor where any
busing or transportation problems are involved."

The trial court found that no serious problems existed with
reference to the so-called traditional considerations and that such
considerations were outweighed by the factor of racial imbalance in the attendance units concerned.

We are not prepared, following a review of the record, to declare that the holding of the trial court was manifestly against the weight of the evidence or clearly unreasonable.

Accordingly, the judgment of the circuit court of Lake County is affirmed.

Judgment affirmed.

House, Justice (dissenting).

What is particularly disturbing about the Armstrong Act is the fact that school authorities are, for the first time in the history of this State, told to make decisions based upon race and nationality. The majority opinion holds that racial discrimination under the Act is constitutionally permissible because it is for the benign purpose of equalizing the educational opportunity between Negroes and Caucasians. I am of the opinion, however, that "the fundamental principle that racial discrimination in public education is unconstitutional" (Brown v. Board of Education of Topeka, 349 U.S. 294, 75 S. Ct. 753, 99 L. Ed. 1083), prevents a State legislature or school board from deciding what is benign and what is not benign with respect to racial discrimination in public education.

The opening statements of the Supreme Court in Brown v. Board of Education of Topeka, 349 U.S. 294, 75 S. Ct. 753, 99 L. Ed. 1083, (Brown II) were "These cases were decided on May 17, 1954. The opinions of that date . . . declaring *the fundamental principle that racial discrimination in public education is unconstitutional* [emphasis added], are incorporated herein by reference. All provisions of federal, state, or local law requiring or permitting such discrimination must yield to this principle." In the third paragraph of the opinion the court mentions "a system of public education freed of racial discrimination" and "steps to eliminate racial discrimination in public schools."

Racial discrimination is, of course, the act of making distinctions based on race. A reading of *Brown II* indicates that the principle announced in *Brown I* is a neutral principle like the neutral principles of freedom of speech, freedom of the press, freedom of religion and freedom of assembly. Just as these principles prohibit government from deciding what is benign or not benign with respect to speech, the press, religion or assembly, so the "fundamental principle that racial discrimination in public education is unconstitutional" prohibits government from deciding when racial discrimination in public education is benign and when it is not.

The Armstrong Act has the effect of ordering school boards to enter the field of racial classification. In 1874, this court ruled that "The free schools of the State are public institutions, and in their management and control the law contemplates that they should be so managed that all children within the district . . . regardless of race or color, shall have equal and the same right to participate in the benefits to be derived therefrom. While the directors, very properly, have large and discretionary powers in regard to the management and control of schools, in order to increase their usefulness, they have no power to make class distinctions. . . ." . . . Thus, from 1874 until the passage of the Armstrong Act there has been no doubt that school authorities in this State had no power to make class distinctions.

During this same period the fourteenth amendment has been construed as not prohibiting school authorities from making racial classifications (Plessy v. Ferguson, 163 U.S. 537, 16 S. Ct. 1138, 41 L. Ed. 256), and then as prohibiting school authorities from making racial classifications. (Brown v. Board of Education of Topeka, 349 U.S. 294, 75 S. Ct. 753, 99 L. Ed. 1083.) History paints a sorry picture for the period when school authorities were permitted to make decisions based on race. The very gist of Plessy v. Ferguson was that racial discrimination resulting in segregation was benign as long as the separate facilities were equal. Experience, of course, proved this proposition wrong.

Several States have again entered the field of racial classification in education albeit for what they now consider a proper governmental goal. As one commentator has pointed out, "This is exactly what the plaintiffs' attorneys urged the Supreme Court to prohibit in the *Brown* case, and for good reason. Although today a court might rule that the state is required to consider race in a benign way, tomorrow this might well prove a precedent for a much less happy result. Moreover, even today it is not easy to decide whether a given racial classification is benign." Kaplan, Segregation Litigation and the Schools—Part II: The General Northern Problem, 58 Nw. U.L. Rev. 157, 188 (1963).

Unfortunately the battle for equal educational opportunity is being fought as a racial one. This tends to generate heat rather than light. Even the strongest exponents for elimination of racial imbalance in the schools recognize and admit that denial of equal education opportunity is not limited to the Negroes. (See e.g., Fiss, Racial Imbalance in the Public Schools: The Constitutional Concepts, 78 Harv. L. Rev. 564 (1963).) I believe that programs to create equal educational opportunities must,

under the equal-protection clause of the fourteenth amendment
(Brown v. Board of Education of Topeka, 347 U.S. 483, 74 S.
Ct. 686, 98 L. Ed. 873), and under section 22 of article IV of our
constitution, be administered without regard to race. Chase v.
Stephenson, 71 Ill. 383.

Several commentators have recognized the desirability of employing our traditional concept of general laws without regard
to race to reach the problems of the disadvantaged in general,
and Negroes in particular. For example, Professor Freund has
stated, "Is not the constitution color blind? Can a preferential
treatment of Negroes be squared with the requirement of equal
protection of the laws? Is it not an unconstitutional discrimination in reverse? A head on clash of principle can be averted, in
most cases wisely in my judgment, by framing programs of aid
in terms of reaching the most disadvantaged segment of the community, whether economically, or politically. And if these happen to be in fact predominantly Negroes, no principle of race-
creed classification has been violated." (Freund, Civil Rights and
the Limits of Law, 14 Buffalo L. Rev. 199, 204 (1964)). The
Anti-Poverty Programs of the Federal government and our Public Aid Programs are good examples of the point. . . .

For the preceding reasons, I would hold the Armstrong Act
unconstitutional.

KLINGBIEL and KLUCZYNSKI, JJ., join in this dissent.

QUESTIONS

1. **The issue of statutory interpretation: did the statute apply to
de facto segregation?**—The Illinois statute referred to prevention
of "segregation" and elimination of "separation . . . because of
. . . race. . . ." Defendants argued that the statute should be
interpreted to apply only to de jure segregation. The majority's
response was that "It would be unreasonable that our legislature,
in 1963 [89 years after Illinois forbade school segregation and
nine years after *Brown v. Board of Education*], . . . would be directing its attention superfluously to *de jure* rather than *de facto*
school segregation. . . ." Why would it be unreasonable to conclude that the state legislature did a "superfluous" act? Should
there be a canon of statutory construction that unless the language clearly otherwise requires, a court should attribute a meaning to a statute which would make the legislature's action not
"superfluous"? Could such a canon soundly rest on the suggestion

of Professors Hart and Sacks that in interpreting a statute a court
"should assume, unless the contrary unmistakably appears, that
the legislature was made up of reasonable persons pursuing
reasonable purposes reasonably"? H. HART & A. SACKS, THE
LEGAL PROCESS: BASIC PROBLEMS IN THE MAKING AND APPLICA-
TION OF LAW 1415 (tent. ed. 1958).

**2. The validity of racial classifications designed to bring about
integration.**—The Illinois statute directs school boards to consider the race of children in drawing school attendance zones.
Should such action by a school board, which in practice results in
assigning children to schools on the basis of race, be held to
deny such children equal protection of the laws? Is it feasible to
distinguish racial assignments for a benign purpose from those
for an improper purpose? Recall the beneficent purposes which
were argued to underlie racial assignments in the southern states
—to prevent threats to the public peace, and the like. Is the
decision in *Tometz* contrary to the holding in *Brown v. Board
of Education?*

In the view of the dissenting judges, whose constitutional rights
were infringed by the statute? Children who might have to travel
greater distances to school? Black parents and children who prefer separate schools? White parents and children who prefer
separate schools? Others? Did the majority, in its adoption of the
rational basis standard to determine the validity of the racial
classification (*i.e.,* in failing to weigh the interests of those who
might be harmed by the statute), use the approach that was followed in *Plessy v. Ferguson* and rejected in *Brown?*

Is the argument for constitutional validity stronger in the case
of the Illinois statute, which directs school boards to consider
the racial composition of neighborhoods, than it would be if
school boards were directed to assign each child to a school
based on his race, providing transportation where necessary, so
as to end up with racially balanced schools?

Would it be constitutional for a state university to assign a
specified number of places in its entering freshman class to
black or Mexican-American students, excluding qualified white
or Anglo applicants from consideration for those places, in order
to have a racially and ethnically integrated student body? How
does this problem differ from the problem in *Tometz?* See
generally Bittker, *The Case of the Checker-Board Ordinance: An
Experiment in Race Relations,* 71 YALE L.J. 1387 (1962).

**3. Statutory approaches to improving racial balance in public
schools: the Illinois and Massachusetts statutes.**—The dissenting

judges in *Tometz,* in a portion of Justice House's opinion not included here, expressed the view that the Illinois statute was invalid as an "unlawful delegation of legislative power" because the statute did not adequately define the terms under which school boards were to exercise discretion in implementing the statutory policy. Aside from the issue of the constitutional validity of the statute, was it wise for the legislature to be as general as it was? Consider these phrases in the statute: "as soon as practicable," "in a manner which will take into consideration," "prevention of segregation," "separation of children . . . because of color, race or nationality." Should there, for example, have been more definite time requirements and standards of racial balance? Would it have been wise to make use of a state-wide administrative agency to enforce the statutory policy? What methods of enforcement of the statutory policy could have been provided? Consider the 1965 Massachusetts "Act Providing for the Elimination of Racial Imbalance in the Public Schools," MASS. ANN. LAWS, ch. 71, §§ 37C-37D (1967 Supp.), held constitutional in School Committee of Boston v. Board of Education, 352 Mass. 693, 227 N.E.2d 729 (1967). This statute requires each local school board annually to submit a racial census of its schools to the state board of education: if the state agency finds that "racial imbalance" exists in a school, the local board is to adopt a plan, approved by the state board, to "eliminate" the imbalance. "Racial imbalance" is "deemed to exist when the percent of nonwhite students in any public school is in excess of fifty percent of the total number of students in such school." A local board, in preparing a plan, "must take into consideration on an equal basis . . . the safety of the children involved in traveling from home to school and from school to home." State aid is to be withheld from local districts which do not "show progress within a reasonable time in eliminating racial imbalance" in their schools. Local boards can obtain judicial review of decisions of the state board. MASS. ANN. LAWS, ch. 15, §§ 1I, 1J (1967 Supp.).

Given the legislative policy implicit in the Massachusetts and Illinois statutes, what are the criteria for determining which statute was a better job of lawmaking? Which of these statutory approaches, for example, is better designed to effectuate the statutory policy that racial balance be improved? Which of these statutory approaches makes the better allocation of functions among the available lawmaking and law applying agencies (administrative and judicial)? In *Tometz* the local school board had considered several plans and had voted to make no revisions of attendance unit boundaries. What is the appropriate scope of judicial review of that type of determination by a school board?

Should a court be empowered to make its own de novo determination whether, at the time the board acted, attendance zones could be revised in order to achieve a better racial balance? What of the other factors which the board presumably considered, such as traffic hazards, distances to schools, classroom sizes, and the like? Should the court weigh those factors de novo? Does the use of more general statutory standards for implementation by an administrative agency create a greater likelihood that a court will become a super-school board in reviewing school administrators' decisions? Consider the following extracts from the trial judge's opinion in the *Tometz* case:

> A reasonable application of the Act to the de facto situation presented by this record leads to the conclusion that there is no reasonable ground outweighing the State directive contained in the "Armstrong Act" for not making some change in the attendance units within the district . . . in order to correct or improve in some measure the admittedly flagrant racial imbalance in the attendance units in question. It might well be that in another and different geographical situation, reason might call for a contrary application of the Act, but, in the case at hand, all of the attendance units involved are contiguous and in a general sense, constitute a neighborhood in the large sense of the term. This is not an instance where units are separated, nor where any bussing or transportation problems are involved. While there may be some problems in connection with traffic, room capacity, finance and possibly even walking distance, they would seem to be of a minor nature as compared to the very marked racial imbalance in the Whittier unit, and, in a collective sense, in all of the units involved.
>
> In the Court's opinion, the defendants would have to show by much stronger evidence than they have, a lack of a suitable alternative to making some change in the boundaries to correct the obvious imbalance. Certainly, the Act seems to call for some type of action—something beyond investigation, consideration and meditation. . . . The Court somewhat reluctantly feels called upon to make the observation that the cause of defendants' problems appears to emanate from "attitude" more than anything else. It is clear from the evidence that the approach has been: "what do we have to do," not "what can we do" to correct the admitted problem. 11 Race Relations L. Rep. 1742, 1745-46 (Cir. Ct. Ill. 1966).

Did the trial judge make his own weighing of all of the factors relevant to a decision under the statute on whether attendance zones should be redrawn, or did he only test whether the school board's decision to do nothing was a permissible decision under the statute? In a practical sense is it likely that a judge can limit himself only to the latter? Should he so limit himself? If the Illinois statute had been differently drafted, in the pattern of the Massachusetts statute, would there have been in fact a better allocation of functions between administrators and judges?

4. Residential segregation and de facto school segregation: a causal circle?—a relevant consideration in Tometz?—Consider the following:

A final reason why the community may be justified in placing benign quotas on Negroes in the public schools is that de facto segregation seems to be a cause as well as a result of segregated housing patterns. It is well-known that when neighborhoods change from white to Negro, the schools change far more rapidly and that, often, transitional neighborhood integration exists only because white families without children, or with children in parochial schools, have chosen to remain while those with public school children have moved out. Middle-class white parents with school-age children seem to be most sensitive to the racial composition of their schools, and they tend to leave precipitously to avoid the disadvantages they feel flow from predominantly Negro and lower-class schools. Moreover, the desirability of the neighborhood school influences other white families to avoid moving into an area served by what they think is or will become a poor (or heavily Negro) school. A policy of applying benign quotas to Negroes in schools not only assures these parents that their schools will not become too heavily Negro, but, perhaps more important, by spreading Negroes throughout the school system, makes it clear that if they move elsewhere in the city they cannot expect to find a sufficiently lower percentage of Negroes. Kaplan, *Equal Justice in an Unequal World: Equality for the Negro— The Problem of Special Treatment,* 61 Nw. U.L. Rev. 363, 400 (1966).

If a factual demonstration of this point had been made in the *Tometz* case, would it have been appropriate for the Illinois Supreme Court to give weight to this consideration in determining the validity of the statute?

B. A CONSTITUTIONAL OBLIGATION TO REDUCE DE FACTO SEGREGATION?

The preceding section considered whether a school board can constitutionally take steps to end or to reduce de facto segregation. In this section, our concern is not with what a board *can* do, but rather with what it *must* do. Is there, in other words, a constitutional requirement under the equal protection clause for a school board to act to reduce segregation, even when the segregation has not resulted from purposive action by the board specifically intended to bring about that result? Answering that question requires us to explore still further the implications of *Brown v. Board of Education.* The two opinions which follow—one from Pasadena, California (placed in perspective by Professor William Cohen) and one from Cincinnati, Ohio—only partly reflect the difficulty of the doctrinal and factual questions that have agonized school boards and courts throughout the north and west. As you read the two opinions, consider these questions, which we shall take up again in the material following the opinions: Does *Brown* stand only for the principle that racial classifications resulting in compulsory school segregation are invalid, or also for a principle of equal educational opportunity? If the latter principle was also declared in *Brown,* what is the content of "equal educational opportunity"? Does it imply only equality of "input"—the state resources devoted to educating black children—or does it imply equality of the product (*e.g.,* homogeneity between racial averages in scores on achievement tests)? Is adoption of the no-racial-classifications principle a suitable way for judges to escape the social-science jungle?

COHEN, RACIAL IMBALANCE IN THE PASADENA PUBLIC SCHOOLS
2 Law & Society Review 42-49 (1967)*

[A 1965 report to the United States Office of Education, as condensed by the staff of the *Law & Society Review*]

PASADENA, CALIFORNIA, LOCATED roughly ten miles northeast of downtown Los Angeles, had a public school enrollment of slightly more than 31,000 during the 1964-65 school year. The racial distribution was 68.9% Caucasian, 21.1% Negro, and 9.9% Mexican-American and Japanese. The surrounding communities have essentially no minority group population and it is expected that migration of minority group members will continue to be

---

* Copyright © 1967 by the Law and Society Association.

concentrated in Pasadena. The residentially segregated pattern of the typical Northern city is conspicuous in Pasadena. The all-Negro neighborhood is present as is the totally white neighborhood. The intermediate areas contain various degrees of segregation.

The Negro population of Pasadena—constituting 20% of the city's population—is worse off both economically and educationally than the white. The Negro median income in 1960 was $4,821, while that for the entire city was $6,922. (One of the all-white neighborhoods, Linda Vista, had a median income of $14,170.) Nonwhite Pasadenians, twenty-five years or older, at the median had completed 11.5 years of school, compared to 12.4 years for the city and 14.9 years for the Linda Vistans. There is, however, a significant Negro middle and upper-middle class element present which has provided effective leadership for civil rights activities within the city.

The neighborhood school concept is fully operative in Pasadena, hence the school enrollments reflect the composition of the neighborhoods and range from essentially all-Negro to fully white. In 1965, 19 of the 28 elementary schools had less than 10% Negro enrollment (10 had less than 1%), 5 had over 60% Negro enrollment, and the remainder ranged from 27% to 39%. With the rapid growth of the Negro population in Pasadena, this racial imbalance will increase unless the neighborhood school concept is modified.

In 1965 the total enrollment in the five junior high schools was just over 7,000, of which 20% were Negro. The Negro enrollment in these five schools ranged from zero to 67%. At the time of the controversies to be described, there were only two high schools in Pasadena (since then a third has been built), with a combined enrollment of approximately 7,000. The percentages of Negro enrollment were 5.5% and 29.3% (of the 460 tenth graders attending the new school, 22% were Negro). In general, the high schools are highly regarded educational institutions.

The racial controversy in the Pasadena public schools had its origins in the early 1950s. In mid-1953 the local branch of the NAACP demanded that the Pasadena Board of Education refrain from a program of (1) expanding the capacity of the all-Negro elementary schools while white schools operated at less than capacity, (2) allowing broad transfer policies, and (3) maintaining "neutral zones" where students were permitted their choice of schools. These neutral zones, which had originally been designed to permit adaptation to population growth, permitted the white students to "escape" those schools with higher Negro enrollment.

For instance, white students living within attendance zones of the three predominantly Negro schools were freely allowed to transfer out.

In response to these demands of the NAACP, the School Board approached the County Counsel for his opinion on the legality of its transfer and neutral zone policies. County Counsel, considering the policies in light of *Brown v. Board of Education* (which had been handed down in the interim period) warned that the Board would be in violation of the Constitution if its policies contributed to the separation of the races in the public schools. He advised that the Board take action "to render its position less vulnerable from a legal standpoint." Apparently, the Board's response was to adopt compact and defensible elementary school attendance zones, with restrictive and objective interdistrict transfer policies. This application, however, of a more rigid neighborhood school policy led many families to move away from the high Negro attendance areas or enroll their children in private schools.

The late 1950s saw a rapid increase in the Negro population of the Pasadena School District, with a corresponding increase of racial imbalance in the schools. By 1961 it was clear that not merely one or two but a tier of elementary schools across the western end of the city were, or were becoming, predominantly Negro.

THE LINDA VISTA CONTROVERSY

In 1960 the all-white La Canada area withdrew from the Pasadena Unified School District. Linda Vista, a well-to-do all-white section of Pasadena, had traditionally sent its children to the La Canada Junior High School. As of July 1961, however, these children would have to attend some other Pasadena junior high school. The Pasadena Board of Education, at the request of the Linda Vista PTA Fathers' Council, called a meeting at the Linda Vista Elementary School for November 29, 1960. The agenda concerned the future placement of Linda Vista's junior high students.

The facts were developed as follows: the Washington School, 2.5 miles from Linda Vista, was operating at capacity and busing would take approximately 26 minutes; McKinley, 3.7 miles from Linda Vista, had room for expansion and busing would take roughly 25 minutes. Washington, however, was 50% Negro, while McKinley was only 7% Negro. Although relative distances and busing times were the most discussed issues, a number of parents' frank reference to the racial makeup of the schools betrayed the primary concern of many. Many of the white and well-to-do parents were concerned about the possibility of their children attending the heavily Negro Washington School, even though it was a mile closer to the area than McKinley. On the other hand, busing the Linda Vistans to the predominantly white and more distant McKinley School would worsen an already unbalanced racial distribution between the two schools and violate the neighborhood concept. Then the Superintendent, Dr. Jenkins, outlined a third alternative whereby some of the Washington students could be assigned to the McKinley School while the Linda Vistans would be sent to the closer Washington School. This could be worked to improve the racial balance at both locations and minimize the distances for the children. While no decision was made at the meeting, it was clear that three of the five Board members wished to assign the Linda Vistans to the predominantly white McKinley School and leave the existing attendance zones unchanged.

Two weeks later, at the mid-December meeting of the Board, Mrs. LaMotte read a prepared statement to her fellow Board members. In it she said (1) that while she had a personal moral commitment, and the Board a legal commitment, for integration, there was no problem since both McKinley and Washington were integrated, there being Negro and white pupils in each school; (2) that assignments to schools should not be decided on the basis of race; and (3) that the additional distance of one mile to McKinley was not relevant, since the children would have to be transported by bus in either event. With ethnic composition and transportation irrelevant considerations, and since she opposed any major redistricting unless absolutely necessary, Mrs. LaMotte favored assigning Linda Vista children to McKinley.

Mr. Shatford, another member of the Board, responded that the Board would have to consider racial makeup of school attendance districts if it was to further its announced policy of doing nothing to promote segregation, that the presence of Negroes at both schools did not mean there was no racial imbalance, and that the Board had an obligation to correct racial imbalance between McKinley and Washington.

At the next meeting, on January 4, 1961, in response to a proposal by Mr. Taylor of the NAACP Education Committee, Mrs. LaMotte announced: "This is an area where no one has any business debating the percentage of colored and white children, as it makes no difference; and to make any move to increase integration or segregation is equally wrong."

At this point Mr. Shatford made it plain that he did not question the sincerity of other members of the Board who advocated a color-blind policy, but he questioned whether the arguments would have been the same if McKinley had been a Negro school and Washington white. Still no decision was reached, but the Superintendent, Dr. Jenkins, read a letter from the County of Los Angeles Commission on Human Relations, expressing a concern about the divisiveness of the racial issue and recommending that the Board defer action until community groups could be brought together to discuss the problem. The Board unanimously endorsed the proposal and authorized the Superintendent to appoint a "conference-type committee" to study the rezoning problem and make recommendations. The Superintendent thereupon spent three weeks organizing a "balanced" citizens committee of sixteen community leaders, including several Negroes. It met a number of times with various groups and professionals. Although the Committee then unanimously issued a statement urging a policy of ". . . the widest possible distribution of the various racial, ethnic and cultural groups in each school, on as wide a basis as possible, [as] a desirable educational objective," it nevertheless recommended that the Linda Vista students and a portion of Washington students be sent to the white McKinley School. A Negro group committeeman presented the report in order to "show the unanimity of spirit." When the report was presented to the Board, the three members who opposed the integration plans agreed to it, stating that though it was a "compromise," it would be acceptable. Mr. Shatford and one other Board member opposed the report because it failed to confront the problem of racial balancing, and offered at best only a vague policy statement in place of an effective solution to an urgent and important problem. On March 21, 1961, the Committee's plan was put to a vote and approved 3 to 2 by the Board. No Board member had changed his mind since the initial meeting in November of 1960.

THE HIGH SCHOOL CONTROVERSY

The NAACP and other Negro groups were hardly well-pleased by the resolution of the Linda Vista problem, and continued to press for the school district to take widespread affirmative action, particularly in the high schools. On June 5, 1962, the School Board authorized the Superintendent to reactivate the Citizens' Advisory Committee on Redistricting—the Committee which had proposed the policy in the Linda Vista controversy. After five months of meetings the Committee presented a report and proposed a plan for redistricting whereby no high school would become more than 30% Negro or 40% non-Caucasian. The report pointed out that whereas, if lines were not redrawn Muir High School would have 38.1% ethnic minority students and Pasadena High School would have only 7.4%, the proposed rezoning would redistribute the racial balance to 29% and 11% respectively. These recommendations, which presumed the continual existence of only two high schools, deliberately sought both to transfer Caucasian neighborhoods into the Muir attendance zone and to transfer some Negro neighborhoods into the Pasadena zone. Also, the Committee relied upon the June 1962 Declaration of Policy of the California State Board of Education which directed local boards to give "serious and thoughtful consideration" to the policy of "elimination of existing segregation and curbing any tendency toward its growth."

The Board received the report and recommendations on April 2, and scheduled its next meeting on the evening of April 16 so that interested citizens could attend. In the interim, considerable opposition began to be organized in the white neighborhoods which [were] to be rezoned into the Muir attendance district. On April 16, four of the five Board members began the meeting by proposing as "individuals" that plans for a third high school be initiated. This would have the effect of postponing the policy of racial balancing until the plans for the third high school were resolved. Mr. Shatford, however, opposed this postponement and urged immediate adoption and implementation of the Committee's proposals. Some in the audience argued that the proposed "instant" third high school was a means of subverting the Committee's recommendations. However, Dr. Jenkins, the Superintendent, came out in favor of the third high school, and emphasized that it would allow for an even better ethnic balance than provided for in the Committee's plan. He thereupon introduced a plan suggested by a U.S.C. professor, which would distribute the ethnic minorities equally among the three schools. Caucasians would be zoned on a geographic basis and there would be open enrollment for all Negroes, to the extent that they were equally distributed and space was sufficient. It was projected that after three years each of the schools would have from 13 to 18% Negro enrollment. The plan met with the general approval of four of the five Board members, with only Mr. Shatford objecting on grounds that it would mean extensive transportation for only Negro students. Instead, he proposed a plan to deploy children from neighborhoods having more than 50% Negro concentration.

Both of these plans were submitted to the County Counsel in June 1963, and his opinion was that they were both illegal "ratio or quota plans based on color," which violated equal protection under the fourteenth amendment. With this the Superintendent amended his plan to provide for open districts for all persons living in specified areas (which just happened to be Negro neighborhoods). His estimated attendance figures for this plan showed Negro percentages ranging from 13% to 18% in each of the three high schools. The Superintendent worked quietly for a month to bring the Board members and civil rights groups together to secure unanimous adoption without undue publicity or organized opposition. He felt that the only way to secure passage of [a] school bond issue was to minimize opposition by creating a united front. The Superintendent's modified plan was adopted by the Board on June 11 but detailed implementation was postponed until after the bond election to keep down the level of public conflict. The bond issue was passed, without difficulty, in the fall of 1963. On January 7, 1964, the Superintendent made a presentation of detailed plans for implementing his proposal.

However, by March 25, 1964, the date selected for making the assignment of pupils to high schools, so many students had moved from the Muir and third high school areas to the Pasadena area that only 48 open places remained at Pasadena instead of the anticipated 195. Consequently, the Negro enrollment in the three high schools would range from 3% to 30% instead of the projected 13% to 18%. When Dr. Jenkins reported these figures to the Board on April 7, the NAACP bitterly accused him of breaking faith. By April 17, however, Dr. Jenkins and the NAACP agreed on a plan providing a projected range of 10% to 23% Negro in the three high schools. As part of this agreement the NAACP volunteered to recruit as many students as possible to fill 125 places at Pasadena High School. The NAACP was successful as 97 Negro pupils were recruited. In spite of this, the actual fall enrollment figures indicated a range of 5% to 30% Negro in the three schools.

THE JACKSON LITIGATION

In August 1961, Jay Jackson—a Negro student at Washington Junior High—petitioned to the Board of Education for permission to attend Eliot Junior High School on the sole ground that Washington was segregated and therefore inferior. When the request was denied, an attorney-member of the NAACP, who was working full-time in the Los Angeles office of the California Corporations Commission, filed a petition for writ of mandate on behalf of Jay Jackson against the Board to compel the granting of the motion for transfer. The complaint alleged that the Washington Junior High School attendance zone had been established "for the sole purpose of relegating to a single junior high school zone a substantial proportion of all Negro pupils of junior high school age." He argued that the handling of the Linda Vista situation clearly demonstrated such a policy.

The Board Counsel demurred, and the superior court sustained the demurrer, commenting that it was "common knowledge" that the allegations of gerrymander were false. The case was appealed by Jackson to the district court of appeals. The opinion of the district court of appeals, handed down in December 1962, followed the original arguments of the County Counsel for the School Board. It too held that there was no segregation in the schools.

This decision was appealed to the California state supreme court and petition for hearing was granted. Here Jackson's briefs were joined by amicus curiae briefs from Herbert Bernhard of the American Jewish Congress and Deputy Attorney General Robert Burke. County Counsel, on behalf of the Pasadena Board of Education, reiterated his same arguments, that "school boards should determine attendance at the public schools *not on the basis* of race, creed or color, but rather, upon considerations which tend to promote and maximize the educational opportunities. . . . To ask for ['affirmative integration' is to ask for] discrimination on the basis of race."

JACKSON v. PASADENA CITY SCHOOL DISTRICT
Supreme Court of California
59 Cal.2d 876, 382 P.2d 878, 31 Cal. Rptr. 606 (1963)

GIBSON, C.J.—Jay Jackson, a 13-year-old Negro boy, brought this mandamus proceeding to compel defendants to permit him to transfer from the Washington Junior High School to the Eliot Junior High School. Defendants' demurrer was sustained without leave to amend, and this appeal is from the ensuing judgment. The allegations of the complaint are summarized below.

Prior to July 1961 the Pasadena City School District contained a number of junior high school zones, including Washington, McKinley, and Eliot. The McKinley zone is immediately south of Washington, and Eliot is immediately north of Washington. Extending along the western boundary of the Washington zone and, to a lesser extent, along a portion of the western boundary of the McKinley zone was the Linda Vista Elementary School zone. Because of the withdrawal from the Pasadena district of a junior high school which pupils of the Linda Vista area formerly attended, it became necessary to determine which junior high school they would attend in the Pasadena district. The Linda Vista area is in the main closer to Washington than to any other junior high school in the district. Certain residents of Linda Vista became alarmed at the possibility that pupils from that area, none of whom was a Negro, might be required to attend Washington, which has an enrollment predominantly of Negroes and members of other minority groups. They urged defendant board to assign the Linda Vista pupils to McKinley, which contains a considerably smaller proportion of Negroes, and threatened to seek withdrawal of Linda Vista from the district if this were not done. In July 1961 the board adopted zone boundaries for junior high schools, and, instead of placing the Linda Vista area in the Washington zone, the board arbitrarily gerrymandered the McKinley zone to include that area. This was done for the purpose of instituting, maintaining, and intensifying racial segregation at Washington, relegating to a single junior high school a substantial proportion of all Negro pupils, and permitting most white pupils to avoid attendance at schools where substantial numbers of Negroes are enrolled. As so established, Washington is a racially segregated school which is inherently inferior to other junior high schools in the district. Plaintiff, who resides in the Washington zone, is required by the board to attend the Washington school, with the result that he is denied equal opportunity for public school education. Plaintiff's request for a transfer to Eliot, which is convenient for him to attend, was denied by the board.

In support of the contention that the complaint does not state a cause of action it is argued that the allegations that Washington is a racially segregated school and that the McKinley zone was gerrymandered to include the Linda Vista area within it are conclusions of law which are not admitted by demurrer. The distinction between ultimate facts and conclusions of law involves at most a matter of degree. The particularity required in pleading facts depends on the extent to which the defendant in fairness needs detailed information that can be conveniently provided by the plaintiff; less particularity is required where the defendant may be assumed to have knowledge of the facts equal to that possessed by the plaintiff. . . .

The averments with respect to racial segregation and gerrymandering should be treated on general demurrer as allegations of ultimate facts and not mere conclusions of law.

A local board of education has power, in the exercise of reasonable discretion, to establish school attendance zones within the district, to determine the area that a particular school shall serve, and to require the students in that area to attend that school. (Ed. Code, § 984, subd. (a); see 29 Ops. Cal. Atty. Gen. 63 (1957); Ops. Cal. Atty. Gen. No. 7800 (Nov. 3, 1931).) It is obvious, however, that the general powers of the board with respect to attendance zones are subject to the constitutional guaranties of equal protection and due process.

The segregation of school children into separate schools because of their race, even though the physical facilities and the methods and quality of instruction in the several schools may be equal, deprives the children of the minority group of equal opportunities for education and denies them equal protection and due process of the law. (*Brown v. Board of Education of Topeka*, 347 U.S. 483, 493-495 [74 S. Ct. 686, 98 L. Ed. 873, 880-881, 38 A.L.R.2d 1180, 1186-1187]; *Bolling v. Sharpe*, 347 U.S. 497, 499-500 [74 S. Ct. 693, 98 L. Ed. 884, 886-887].) In view of the importance of education to society and to the individual child, the opportunity to receive the schooling furnished by the state must be made available to all on an equal basis. Because of intangible considerations relating to the ability to learn and exchange views with other students, segregated professional schools have been held not to provide equal educational opportunities, and such considerations apply with added force to children in grade and high schools. The separation of children from others of similar age and qualifications solely because of race may produce a feeling of inferiority which can never be removed and which has a tendency to retard their motivation to learn and their mental development. (*Brown v. Board of Education of Topeka*, 347 U.S. 483, 493-494 [74 S. Ct. 686, 98 L. Ed. 873, 880, 38 A.L.R.2d 1180, 1186-1187].)

The constitutional rights of children not to be discriminated against in school admission on the grounds of race or color cannot be nullified by state action either openly and directly or indirectly by evasive schemes for segregation, and the Fourteenth Amendment is violated where zoning is merely a subterfuge for producing or perpetuating racial segregation in a school. (*Cooper v. Aaron* . . .; cf. *Gomillion v. Lightfoot*, 364 U.S. 339, 341 et seq. [81 S. Ct. 125, 5 L. Ed. 2d 110, 113].) Although in general the federal cases have been concerned with instances of complete or almost complete segregation, it is not decisive that absolute segregation is not present.

Improper discrimination may exist notwithstanding attendance by some white children at a predominantly Negro school or attendance by some Negro children at a predominantly white school.

The boundaries of school zones are normally fixed on a neighborhood basis, and where racial imbalance exists in California schools it is usually caused by the fact that the Negro population tends to concentrate in certain areas due to economic factors and discrimination in housing. Thus, some schools may have a disproportionately high percentage of Negro students even though there is no intent by school authorities to discriminate against them. Here, however, it is alleged that the existing imbalance has been intensified by purposeful and unreasonable action on the part of the board. The fact that the gerrymandering of the McKinley zone is not alleged to have changed the physical boundaries of Washington or its racial composition does not mean that the gerrymandering did not constitute discrimination against plaintiff and the other Negro pupils at Washington. A racial imbalance may be created or intensified in a particular school not only by requiring Negroes to attend it but also by providing different schools for white students who, because of proximity or convenience, would be required to attend it if boundaries were fixed on a nonracial basis.

Although it is alleged that the board was guilty of intentional discriminatory action, it should be pointed out that even in the absence of gerrymandering or other affirmative discriminatory conduct by a school board, a student under some circumstances would be entitled to relief where, by reason of residential segregation, substantial racial imbalance exists in his school. So long as large numbers of Negroes live in segregated areas, school authorities will be confronted with difficult problems in providing Negro children with the kind of education they are entitled to have. Residential segregation is in itself an evil which tends to frustrate the youth in the area and to cause antisocial attitudes and behavior. Where such segregation exists it is not enough for a school board to refrain from affirmative discriminatory conduct. The harmful influence on the children will be reflected and intensified in the classroom if school attendance is determined on a geographic basis without corrective measures. The right to an equal opportunity for education and the harmful consequences of segregation require that school boards take steps, insofar as reasonably feasible, to alleviate racial imbalance in schools regardless of its cause. Our State Board of Education has adopted regulations which encourage transfers to avoid and eliminate racial segregation (Cal. Admin. Code, tit. 5, §§ 2010, 2011[4]), and transfers for that purpose are provided for in New

---

[4] California Administrative Code, title 5, section 2010, provides: "STATE BOARD POLICY. It is the declared policy of the State Board of Education that persons or agencies responsible for the establishment of school attendance

York City and elsewhere (see 1961 U.S. Commission on Civil Rights Report, Book 2, Education, pp. 104-107).

School authorities, of course, are not required to attain an exact apportionment of Negroes among the schools, and consideration must be given to the various factors in each case, including the practical necessities of governmental operation. For example, consideration should be given, on the one hand, to the degree of racial imbalance in the particular school and the extent to which it affects the opportunity for education and, on the other hand, to such matters as the difficulty and effectiveness of revising school boundaries so as to eliminate segregation and the availability of other facilities to which students can be transferred.

It follows from what we have said that the demurrer should have been overruled.

The judgment is reversed.

COHEN, RACIAL IMBALANCE IN THE PASADENA PUBLIC SCHOOLS
2 Law & Society Review 49-52 (1967)*

This opinion of the California supreme court was handed down on June 27, 1963, over two years after the decision to place the Linda Vista students in white McKinley School and a year after Jay Jackson had graduated from Washington Junior High.

It is interesting to note the impact—or more appropriately, lack of impact—of the *Jackson* decision. While the *Jackson* decision did not spell out very clearly precisely what obligations school boards had, it did at least indicate that boards need not

---

centers or the assignment of pupils thereto shall exert all effort to avoid and eliminate segregation of children on account of race or color."

California Administrative Code, title 5, section 2011, provides: "ESTABLISH-MENT OF SCHOOL ATTENDANCE AREAS AND SCHOOL ATTENDANCE PRACTICES IN SCHOOL DISTRICTS. For the purpose of avoiding, insofar as practicable, the establishment of attendance areas and attendance practices which in practical effect discriminate upon an ethnic basis against pupils or their families or which in practical effect tend to establish or maintain segregation on an ethnic basis, the governing board of a school district in establishing attendance areas and attendance practices in the district shall include among the factors considered the following: (a) The ethnic composition of the residents in the immediate area of the school. (b) The ethnic composition of the residents in the territory peripheral to the immediate area of the school. (c) The effect on the ethnic composition of the student body of the school based upon alternate plans for establishing the attendance area or attendance practice. (d) The effect on the ethnic composition of the student body of adjacent schools based upon alternate plans for establishing an attendance area or an attendance practice. (e) The effect on the ethnic composition of the student body of the school and of adjacent schools of the use of transportation presently necessary and provided either by a parent or the district." [Footnote in original, renumbered.]

* Copyright © 1967 by the Law and Society Association.

accept a "color-blind" policy in zoning and, in fact, should "take steps, insofar as reasonably feasible" (although no criteria for reasonable feasibility were supplied) to alleviate de facto school segregation. Despite this decision the Pasadena Board of Education and County Counsel continued to "ignore" racial considerations, defending their position, in part, by claiming they had no constitutional or legal alternative. This can be seen in a controversy arising one year after the California supreme court handed down the *Jackson* opinion. Upon receiving a letter from a Caucasian boy requesting to be transferred from Pasadena High School to Muir High School—because the boy believed the racial balance between the two schools would be better equalized if he attended Muir and a Negro were selected in his place to attend Pasadena High School—Dr. Jenkins sought an advisory opinion from the County Counsel, and was told: ". . . a policy allowing attendance from the selected Open District to another school, only if it contributes to better ethnic distribution, would be violative of the equal protection clause of the 14th Amendment of the U. S. Constitution."

Following this opinion at the Board meeting, Mr. Shatford read a hastily drafted reply, arguing that this was what the *Jackson* decision had decided against.

> It is my opinion that at least a majority of lawyers would now be satisfied, after the *Jackson* case, that a school board could most certainly employ ethnic considerations in drawing district lines, and it is not necessary for a school board to engage in a verbal minuet mincing back and forth and sideways, talking of capacity of school facilities, geographical considerations, etc. while slowly and surely progressing toward its real goal: compliance with the declared policy which requires alleviation of racial imbalance.

Nevertheless, the Board seemed to ignore Mr. Shatford's arguments. The Superintendent said he would comply with current Board policy and deny the requested transfer unless the Board directed otherwise. There was no motion to do so.

ELEMENTARY REDISTRICTING

After the bond election, the three-member majority of the Board was opposed to reactivating the Citizens Advisory Committee on Redistricting, on the grounds that it was the Board's responsibility to redistrict and that there was no need to consider a comprehensive policy for elementary and junior high school redistricting. The unspoken fear was that the Committee would recommend, as it had in the high school report, that the Board commit itself to a similar policy of putting a ceiling on ethnic concentration in the elementary schools. Predictably, the Board voted (with the now familiar 3-2 division) not to have the Committee reactivated. Community integrationist groups decided to wait and see what the Board and Superintendent would propose.

In January 1964, Dr. Jenkins proposed only slight modifications of existing boundaries, which barely reduced the percentages of Negroes in the heavily Negro elementary schools (*e.g.*, from 75% to 69%). The three members of the Board majority, again restating their good intentions and opposition to race as a criterion for pupil assignment, agreed to the Superintendent's plan. On the other hand, the other two members of the Board, members of the Citizens Committee, and the officers of the NAACP criticized the plan. The Board's continued commitment to the neighborhood concept, it was argued, would entail increased segregation as neighborhoods developed. All agreed that the Citizens Committee should be reactivated, but Mr. Shatford's motion to this effect lost 3 to 2.

Dr. Jenkins proposed that eight town-hall meetings be held with the Board present to discuss in public proposals for redistricting. During this period, when many ideas and views were publicly aired, Dr. Jenkins was quietly drawing up a comprehensive plan for the elementary schools. It called for a voluntary transfer of students in certain (heavily Negro) areas, but—unlike the partially involuntary high school plan—it did not provide for transportation. Other plans to consolidate and pair schools were proposed by integrationists, but little came of them.

Another telling development of the community response to the issues was seen toward the end of the time period discussed here. In the spring of 1965 the terms of three school board members expired; all three filed for reelection. Two of these incumbents, including Mrs. LaMotte, formed a slate with a third person, who was running against Mr. Shatford. All three members of this slate, which campaigned on a platform of "preserving neighborhood schools" and promoting "quality education," were elected, thus defeating Mr. Shatford.

An Overview

Committed to maintaining ethnic balance among its three high schools, the Pasadena Unified School District has consciously chosen to live, for the foreseeable future, with seven or more segregated elementary schools and one segregated junior high school. Why the difference in community attitude toward the two problems? An obvious reason is that the neighborhood school concept does not befog the issue: high school attendance areas and the high schools themselves are traditionally large and the pupils relatively mobile. A less obvious, but equally important, reason is that the Muir High School had never been written off by the community, as had been the Washington Junior High School, as a "Negro school." In other words, large numbers of Caucasians in the western portions of Pasadena had an interest in stemming the rising percentage tide of Negro enrollment at Muir, to maintain an excellent and integrated high school on the west side of town. Would the community have done as much if Muir's minority group enrollment had, for example, been in excess of 90% for the last five years?

Most of Pasadena's whites have simply concluded that solution of the integration problem in the elementary and junior high schools is not so serious a community problem that it merits the price that feasible solutions might require them and their children to pay. The only current source for the additional funds which might be necessary for any ambitious plan to correct racial imbalance at the elementary and junior high school levels is the District's taxpayers, who are already about to be asked to approve bond issues for new school construction. Pasadena has a problem which is nonexistent in other San Gabriel Valley communities without substantial ethnic minority populations, largely because Pasadena is a city to which Negroes can move. There is some justice to a claim that, to the extent to which the problem is financial, it is unfair to place the cost of removing school segregation which flows from residential segregation on the community into which Negroes may move. In other words, it is a considerable strain on the altruism of Pasadena's taxpayers to ask them to provide funds, not necessary in adjoining districts, for the solution of a state-wide and national problem.

DEAL v. CINCINNATI BOARD OF EDUCATION
United States Court of Appeals, Sixth Circuit
369 F.2d 55 (1966)
cert. denied, 389 U.S. 847 (1967)

Before WEICK, Chief Judge, and O'SULLIVAN and PHILLIPS, Circuit Judges.

WEICK, Chief Judge.

The suit in the District Court was a class action against the Board of Education of the City of Cincinnati, brought by the parents and next friends of Negro pupils enrolled in the public schools of the city, to enjoin the operation of allegedly racially segregated public schools, to enjoin the construction of new schools on sites which would increase and harden alleged existing patterns of racial segregation, and for declaratory and other relief.

The Board denied that it created, operated or maintained racially segregated schools, and alleged that the only genuine issue in the case was whether it violated the constitutional rights of the plaintiffs by refusing to adopt and enforce an affirmative policy of balancing the races in the Cincinnati Public School System.[5]

The evidence in the case consisted of a number of lengthy stipulations, exhibits, and oral testimony. At the close of plaintiffs' evidence defendants moved for judgment, which motion was taken under advisement by the Court. Defendants presented their entire case except for expert testimony. The Court then granted defendants' motion for judgment without considering the evidence offered by the defendants. He handed down an opinion which he adopted as findings of fact and conclusions of law under Rules 41(b) and 52(a), Fed. R. Civ. Proc. In essence, the Court held that there was no constitutional duty incumbent upon the Board to balance the races in the public school system, and that there was a failure of proof on the part of the plaintiffs to establish a policy of segregation or gerrymandering on the part of the Board.

Was There A Constitutional Duty On The Part Of The Board To Balance The Races In The Cincinnati Public Schools

---

[5] On March 9, 1964, after the commencement of the present action, the Board of Education adopted the following policy statement to guide its officers and employees:

"(1) As a matter of policy, the Board would like to avoid predominantly Negro schools to the extent that the Board has any control over the causes which create such predominance. But in exercising any control in this area the Board will not deviate from the long established neighborhood school plan or the requirement of Section 3313.48 R.C. that schools be located where they will be most convenient for the largest number of students.

"The Board is willing to make race of students one of the elements to be considered in the establishment of school attendance zone lines so long as this can be done consistently with the neighborhood school policy, the requirements of Section 3313.48, and the numerous factors which have always been considered in establishing such zone lines as—safety of children, travel distance and capacity of school.

"(2) The Board does not accept the concept of de facto segregation and will not agree to any proposal to bus students, to transfer classes or any other program to attempt to balance races as such." [Footnote in original, renumbered.]

Where The Imbalance Was Not Caused By Any Act Of Discrimination On Its Part?

At the outset it should be pointed out that the State of Ohio abolished segregation in the public schools on February 22, 1887, which was more than 67 years before the United States Supreme Court barred it on constitutional grounds in the momentous decision of Brown v. Board of Education, 347 U.S. 483, 74 S. Ct. 686, 98 L. Ed. 873 (1954).

The so-called neighborhood plan for the location of public schools is authorized by statute under which Ohio School Boards are required to—

". . . provide for the free education of the youth of school age within the district under its jurisdiction, at such places as will be convenient for the attendance of the largest number thereof." Ohio Rev. Code § 3313.48.

We think the legislature had the power to enact this statute. The Cincinnati Board of Education has complied with it.

Appellants contend that the maintenance of a public school system in which racial imbalance exists is a violation of their constitutional right to the equal protection of the law. They assert that because the Negro student population is not spread uniformly throughout the Cincinnati school system, without a showing of deliberate discrimination or even racial classification, there is a duty of constitutional dimensions imposed on the school officials to eliminate the imbalance. Appellants claim that it is harmful to Negro children to attend a racially imbalanced school and this fact alone deprives them of equal educational opportunity.

The essence of the *Brown* decision was that the Fourteenth Amendment does not allow the state to classify its citizens differently solely because of their race. While the detrimental impact of compulsory segregation on the children of the minority race was referred to by the Court, it was not indispensable to the decision. Rather, the Court held that segregation of the races was an arbitrary exercise of governmental power inconsistent with the requirements of the Constitution.

A finding of educational or other harm is not essential to strike down enforced segregation. This is shown by many subsequent cases nullifying separate facilities of all kinds with no evidence of harm.

In summarizing this principle, the Court said that classifications based on race violate the Fourteenth Amendment because

they are obviously invidious and irrelevant. Goss v. Board of
Education, 373 U.S. 683, 687, 83 S. Ct. 1405, 10 L. Ed. 2d 632
(1963).

Thus it is not necessary that a victim of racial discrimination
prove that he was harmed in any specific material sense in order
to invalidate state-imposed racial distinctions. See Johnson v. State
of Virginia, 373 U.S. 61, 83 S. Ct. 1053, 10 L. Ed. 2d 195 (1963)
(seating in courtrooms); Watson v. City of Memphis, 373 U.S.
526, 83 S. Ct. 1314, 10 L. Ed. 2d 529 (1963) (municipal parks);
Burton v. Wilmington Parking Authority, 365 U.S. 715, 81 S.
Ct. 856, 6 L. Ed. 2d 45 (1961) (restaurants in public buildings);
Dawson v. Mayor and City Council of Baltimore, 220 F.2d 386
(4th Cir. 1955) aff'd 350 U.S. 877, 76 S. Ct. 133, 100 L. Ed. 774
(1955) (public beaches and bathhouses).

In Bolling v. Sharpe, 347 U.S. 497, 74 S. Ct. 693, 98 L. Ed. 884
(1954), which is a companion case to *Brown*, and which involved
the validity of school segregation in the District of Columbia,
the Court held that the Fifth Amendment was violated. The
Court emphasized that it was the fact of discriminatory classification by the government that violated the Constitution, and
looked no further for evidence of educational or psychological
injury, saying—

"Classifications based solely upon race must be scrutinized
with particular care, since they are contrary to our traditions
and hence constitutionally suspect." Bolling v. Sharpe, supra,
at 499, 74 S. Ct. at 694.

The principle thus established in our law is that the state may
not erect irrelevant barriers to restrict the full play of individual
choice in any sector of society. Since it is freedom of choice that
is to be protected, it is not necessary that any particular harm
be established if it is shown that the range of individual options
had been constricted without the high degree of justification
which the Constitution requires. It is harm enough that a citizen
is arbitrarily denied choices open to his fellows.

Conversely, a showing of harm alone is not enough to invoke
the remedial powers of the law. If the state or any of its agencies
has not adopted impermissible racial criteria in its treatment of
individuals, then there is no violation of the Constitution. If
factors outside the schools operate to deprive some children of
some of the existing choices, the school board is certainly not
responsible therefor.

Appellants, however, argue that the state must take affirmative steps to balance the schools to counteract the variety of

private pressures that now operate to restrict the range of choices presented to each school child. Such a theory of constitutional duty would destroy the well-settled principle that the Fourteenth Amendment governs only state action. Under such a theory, all action would be state action, either because the state itself had moved directly, or because some private person had acted and thereby created the supposed duty of the state to counteract any consequences.

The standard to be applied is "equal educational opportunity." The Court in *Brown* cast its decision thus because it recognized that it was both unnecessary and impossible to require that each child come through the complex process of modern education with the same end result. This approach grants due respect for the unavoidable consequences of variations in individual ability, home environment, economic circumstances, and occupational aspirations. Equal opportunity requires that each child start the race without arbitrary official handicaps; it does not require that each shall finish in the same time.

Appellants, however, pose the question of whether the neighborhood system of pupil placement, fairly administered without racial bias, comports with the requirements of equal opportunity if it nevertheless results in the creation of schools with predominantly or even exclusively Negro pupils. The neighborhood system is in wide use throughout the nation and has been for many years the basis of school administration. This is so because it is acknowledged to have several valuable aspects which are an aid to education, such as minimization of safety hazards to children in reaching school, economy of cost in reducing transportation needs, ease of pupil placement and administration through the use of neutral, easily determined standards, and better home-school communication. The Supreme Court in *Brown* recognized geographic districting as the normal method of pupil placement and did not foresee changing it as the result of relief to be granted in that case. Brown v. Board of Education, 347 U.S. 483, 495 note 13, question 4(a), 74 S. Ct. 686, 98 L. Ed. 873; Brown v. Board of Education, 349 U.S. 294, 300-301, 75 S. Ct. 753, 99 L. Ed. 1083 (1955). But see Blocker v. Board of Education of Manhasset, 226 F. Supp. 208, 221-222 (E.D. N.Y. 1964).

Because of factors in the private housing market, disparities in job opportunities, and other outside influences, (as well as positive free choice by some Negroes), the imposition of the neighborhood concept on existing residential patterns in Cincinnati creates some schools which are predominantly or wholly of one race or another. Appellants insist that this situation, which they concede is not the case in every school in Cincinnati, presents the same separation and hence the same constitutional violation condemned in *Brown*. We do not accept this contention. The element of inequality in *Brown* was the unnecessary restriction on freedom of choice for the individual, based on the fortuitous, uncontrollable, arbitrary factor of his race. The evil inherent in such a classification is that it fails to recognize the high value which our society places on individual worth and personal achievement. Instead, a racial characterization treats men in the mass and is unrelated to legitimate governmental considerations. It fails to recognize each man as a unique member of society.

In the present case, the only limit on individual choice in education imposed by state action is the use of the neighborhood school plan. Can it be said that this limitation shares the arbitrary, invidious characteristics of a racially restrictive system? We think not. In this situation, while a particular child may be attending a school composed exclusively of Negro pupils, he and his parents know that he has the choice of attending a mixed school if they so desire, and they can move into the neighborhood district of such a school. This situation is far removed from *Brown*, where the Negro was condemned to separation, no matter what he as an individual might be or do. Here, if there are obstacles or restrictions imposed on the ability of a Negro to take advantage of all the choices offered by the school system, they stem from his individual economic plight, or result from private, not school, prejudice.[6] We read *Brown* as prohibiting only enforced segregation.

The School Board, in the operation of the public schools, acts in much the same manner as an administrative agency exercising its accumulated technical expertise in formulating policy after balancing all legitimate conflicting interests. If that policy is one conceived without bias and administered uniformly to all who fall within its jurisdiction, the courts should be extremely wary of imposing their own judgment on those who have the technical knowledge and operating responsibility for the educational sys-

---

[6] The District Court correctly excluded evidence of alleged discrimination in the public and private housing markets. Such discrimination is caused, if in fact it does exist, by persons who are not parties to this case and the Board has no power to rectify that situation. If appellants have any valid claim for infringement of their rights by public housing or urban renewal officials, they may obtain appropriate relief against them under the Fourteenth Amendment. With respect to private actions amounting to discriminatory practice, while there is no federal constitutional right available to appellants, they may seek relief from the state Civil Rights Commission or in the state courts, if relief is denied, under the provisions of the Ohio Fair Housing Law. Ohio Rev. Code § 4112.01-.07. [Footnote in original, renumbered.]

tem. Thus, whereas such a geographical principle might be totally unacceptable in the administration of facilities such as beaches, parks, restaurants, or golf courses (see desegregation cases cited above), the school system presents problems of an altogether different nature and the fair minded judgment of the school officials is entitled to full consideration in determining whether freedom of choice has been preserved for the children within the limits necessary for effective educational practice. See Watson v. City of Memphis, supra, 373 U.S. at 531–532, 83 S. Ct. 1314.

We hold that there is no constitutional duty on the part of the Board to bus Negro or white children out of their neighborhoods or to transfer classes for the sole purpose of alleviating racial imbalance that it did not cause, nor is there a like duty to select new school sites solely in furtherance of such a purpose.

The bussing of pupils away from the neighborhoods of their residences may create many special problems for boards of education. These include the providing of adequate transportation and proper facilities and personnel for the supervision, education and well being of *all* pupils. All of this must be accomplished within the Board's budget.

Although boards of education have no constitutional obligation to relieve against racial imbalance which they did not cause or create, it has been held that it is not unconstitutional for them to consider racial factors and take steps to relieve racial imbalance if in their sound judgment such action is the best method of avoiding educational harm. . . .

In dealing with the multitude of local situations that must be considered and the even greater number of individual students involved, we believe it is the wiser course to allow for the flexibility, imagination and creativity of local school boards in providing for equal opportunity in education for all students. It would be a mistake for the courts to read *Brown* in such a way as to impose one particular concept of educational administration as the only permissible method of insuring equality consistent with sound educational practice. We are of the view that there may be a variety of permissible means to the goal of equal opportunity, and that room for reasonable men of good will to solve these complex community problems must be preserved. See Freund, Civil Rights and the Limits of Law, 14 Buffalo L. Rev. 199, 205 (1964). . . .

Appellants' right to relief depends on a showing of more than mere statistical imbalance in the Cincinnati schools. They must also expose that added quantum of discriminatory state action which deprives them of their constitutional right to freedom of choice. If the school officials, through overt practice or by subterfuge, have treated students differently solely because of race, then they not only must cease doing so, but also must take affirmative action to remedy the condition which they have caused. Thus, even if the Negro students were distributed uniformly in the schools, if other forms of discrimination were used against them they would still be entitled to the aid of the law. When no discrimination is shown, racial imbalance alone is no warrant for relief.

Did The Board of Education Intentionally Cause Racial Imbalance In The Cincinnati Public Schools, Deprive Negro Children Of Equal Educational Opportunities, And Discriminate Against Negroes In The Hiring And Assignment Of Teachers?

In their "Statement of Questions Involved" appellants assert that they have sufficiently shown that the Board of Education has *intentionally* caused, and then failed to eliminate, serious racial imbalance in the Cincinnati public schools, has afforded Negro children who are confined to segregated schools, inferior educational programs and facilities, and has provided school faculties and personnel which reflect the racial patterns of students. They state that children who attend racially imbalanced schools suffer injury constituting a denial of equal educational opportunity. . . .

At the trial level this case confronted the District Court with an enormous amount of evidence in the form of detailed maps, charts, statistical tables, sociological studies, and historical accounts, in addition to a substantial amount of oral testimony, expert and otherwise. To his credit, the District Judge succeeded to a great degree in expediting the trial through the extensive use of many stipulations and effective pre-trial procedures, which sharpened the issues. However, in his opinion he adopted as fair the following statement taken verbatim from the School Board's brief:

"The Cincinnati Public School System includes a number of schools which are attended almost entirely by Negro pupils, a number of schools attended entirely by white pupils, and a number of schools attended by both Negro and white pupils in various percentages of each of the races; the racial composition of each school is simply a result of the racial composition of the neighborhoods which they serve."

Then, after discussing the issue of imbalance, he stated:

"Their [appellants'] failure to produce evidence to establish a policy of segregation or gerrymandering on the part of defendants strongly suggests that such practices have not been engaged in. It is here found that plaintiffs have failed to establish a deprivation of rights under the law or under the Constitution of the United States by the requisite degree of proof. . . ."

In dealing with the issue of discrimination in the context of a great metropolitan education complex, these general findings do not present an adequate basis for review by this Court.

The District Court's finding on the racial composition of the schools in Cincinnati reveals that the schools are indeed racially imbalanced. In other words, the Negro student population is not spread uniformly among the individual schools, mainly because of the operation of the neighborhood school policy in conjunction with the residential concentration of Negroes in some areas. As the District Court held, and we affirmed above, this fact by itself gives rise to no relief. However, the crucial fact to be found is whether the racial imbalance was intentionally caused by gerrymandering or by other alleged discriminatory practices on the part of the Board. On that point the District Judge said only that appellants had failed to produce evidence to establish gerrymandering or other discriminatory practice and that this failure strongly suggested that such practices did not exist. Such a general finding must be supported by subsidiary findings of fact. . . .

Appellants, through extensive use of discovery techniques, adduced vast quantities of information concerning matters such as alleged discrimination in school attendance zoning, transportation policies, teacher selection and assignment, comparative test results, and policies on transfers and overcrowding of students. Some of their contentions with respect thereto are answered by appellees on appeal here, but some are not. This is due partly to the truncated status of the case at the time of the District Court's decision on the motion to dismiss, and partly because the Court considered only appellants', and not the School Board's, evidence in ruling on the motion.

An example of such unanswered and unaccounted for situations is the districting of the Sawyer Junior High School where the enrollment is mostly Negro. The fact is that its boundaries exclude children who live across the street from it in a largely white neighborhood. The School Board in its brief offered no explanation for this situation or for the selection of the Sawyer site so close to the existing Withrow Junior High School.

We have stated above that a showing of impairment of a Negro student's capacity to learn, arising from his school's racial imbalance, does not, standing alone, make out a case of constitutional deprivation. Evidence of such harm, however, may indeed be relevant to the issues of the case before us. Appellants offered expert evidence on this subject. The School Board offered no opposing expert testimony, no doubt because the Court granted the Board's motion to dismiss, made at the close of plaintiffs' proofs. Our review would be helped by a finding as to whether the District Judge considered plaintiffs' expert testimony of such relevance, weight or probative value as to make an issue calling for rebuttal proof by defendant.

No findings were made on these disputed issues. Without findings we are unable to determine whether discrimination existed with respect to specific schools and programs. . . .

The judgment of the District Court is affirmed on the issue of racial imbalance not intentionally caused by the Board, and the case is remanded for further findings on the issues of claimed discrimination in specific schools and programs and claimed harm to Negro students, allegedly caused by racially imbalanced schools, and for the taking of such additional relevant evidence as either party may offer. . . .

QUESTIONS

1. **Racial gerrymanders and legislative motive.**—Both the *Deal* case and the *Jackson* case were remanded for trial on the question of racial gerrymandering. Both courts assumed that a finding that district lines were drawn on a racial basis would support the relief sought. Even the *Jackson* court assumed that a showing of a racial gerrymander would present an easier case for the plaintiff black child than would a simple showing of racial imbalance in the district's schools. What *is* a racial gerrymander? Why is it invalid? The court in *Deal* distinguished *Brown* from the de facto segregation case, because in *Brown* "the Negro was condemned to separation," while in the de facto case he might move to a mixed-school neighborhood. If that is the controlling distinction, would it not follow that even a deliberate drawing of attendance zones on racial lines would be valid, since a black child might move to another zone? Is it unconstitutional for the line between two school zones to be the same as a line that divides a "white" neighborhood from a "black" neighborhood? Or does invalidity rest on a showing of improper motive on the part of the legislative (or administrative) body that drew the line?

The United States Supreme Court has not spoken directly to this issue in a school-zones case. The Court has, however, decided two cases involving alleged racial gerrymanders relating to the political process. In Gomillion v. Lightfoot, 364 U.S. 339 (1960), the Alabama legislature redrew the boundaries of the City of Tuskegee, so as to exclude all but a handful of the city's former black residents, who numbered upwards of 400. The Court reversed a lower court's dismissal of an action by some of the excluded Negroes to enjoin the execution of the new boundary statute, holding that the allegation of the foregoing facts was sufficient to state a cause of action under the Fifteenth Amendment, which prohibits a state from denying the right to vote on grounds of race. In Wright v. Rockefeller, 376 U.S. 52 (1964) (7-2 decision), on the other hand, the Court affirmed the dismissal of a complaint alleging that the New York legislature had drawn the lines of Manhattan's congressional districts so as to assure that Harlem and its environs would be represented by one—and only one—congressman. Dismissal of this complaint was grounded on the three-judge trial court's (2-1) finding that the plaintiffs had not shown an intentional shaping of the districts on racial lines.[7] The following quotations from the two opinions throw some dark on the definition of a racial gerrymander:

> *Gomillion*: "The essential inevitable *effect* of this redefinition of Tuskegee's boundaries is to remove from the city all save only four or five of its 400 Negro voters while not removing a single white voter. The *result* of the Act is to deprive the Negro petitioners discriminatorily of the benefits of residence in Tuskegee, including, *inter alia,* the right to vote in municipal elections.
>
>   . . . If these allegations upon a trial remained uncontradicted or unqualified, the conclusion would be irresistible, tantamount for all practical purposes to a mathematical dem-

---

[7] The racial and ethnic breakdown of the four congressional districts was reported by Justice Goldberg in the following chart:

District	White %	Non-White and Puerto Rican Origin %
17th	94.9	5.1
18th	13.7	86.3
19th	71.5	28.5
20th	72.5	27.5

Dissenting opinion of Justice Goldberg, 376 U.S. 67, at 72 (quoting the opinion of the dissenting judge in the trial court).

onstration, that the legislation *is solely concerned* with segregating white and colored citizens by fencing Negro citizens out of town so as to deprive them of their pre-existing municipal vote. 364 U.S. at 341. (Emphasis added.)

Wright: We accept the findings of the majority of the District Court that appellants failed to prove that the New York Legislature was *either motivated* by racial considerations *or in fact drew* the districts on racial lines. Compare *Gomillion v. Lightfoot,* . . . . It is plain to us that the District Court was not compelled to find that these districts were the product of a state *contrivance to discriminate* against colored or Puerto Rican voters. 376 U.S. at 56-57. (Emphasis added.)

In Tuskegee, before the redrawing of the city's boundaries, Negro voters had been increasing in numbers, as voter-registration drives succeeded. The Alabama legislature had seemingly reacted to this change. But the evidence in the *Wright* case, as the dissenters emphasized, showed a 1961 adjustment of the boundaries of the Harlem district and the adjoining "silk stocking" district that increased the racial purity of both districts. Was the *effect* of the law in *Gomillion* what made it unconstitutional, or did the case rest on a finding of discriminatory *motive?* Is *Wright* distinguishable because there may be an electoral advantage to Harlem in being assured of one black congressman? In other words, did *Wright* involve a "benign quota"? (Congressman Powell, who represented the Harlem district, intervened in the action to support the existing system of districting.)[8] Or is *Wright* chiefly distinguishable because New York is New York and Alabama is Alabama? Do inquiries into legislative motive in cases of alleged

---

[8] The problem in the *Wright* case appeared in inverted form in Ince v. Rockefeller, 290 F. Supp. 878 (S.D. N.Y. 1968). The plaintiffs complained that the black population of an area in Queens County known as East Elmhurst had been divided and assigned to two larger assembly districts, with the result that there was no black majority in either district. They sought a redistricting that would create a separate district for East Elmhurst —and thus an assurance of representation like that which the congressional districting of Harlem had produced. The federal court refrained from exercising jurisdiction, and deferred the question for initial decision by the state courts. The court did, however, make its views known on the merits of the complaint:

Stripped of its conclusory allegations, the complaint appears as an unabashed plea for segregation in the composition of Assembly Districts, for color consciousness rather than color blindness. Speaking in a different context, Mr. Justice Douglas has emphasized the repugnance of such a plea to the principles of democracy: "Racial boroughs [like rotten boroughs], are . . . at war with democratic standards." Wright v. Rockefeller, 376 U.S. 52, 62, . . . (1964) (dissenting opinion). 290 F. Supp. at 884.

racial discrimination necessarily mean that the Constitution means different things in different regions of the Nation?

The *Jackson* case was never tried. If it had been tried, how should counsel have gone about proving a racial gerrymander? Is there anything in the condensed version of Professor Cohen's report that supports this charge against the Pasadena school board? What factors in the case would be relevant to a determination of this issue? The near equality in projected costs to the district of providing school buses from the Linda Vista area to McKinley and to Washington? The fact that Linda Vista children live, for the most part, a mile closer to Washington than to McKinley? The odd shape of the McKinley district with the Linda Vista area added to it? The desire of the Linda Vista parents for their children to go to McKinley? The fact that assignment of the Linda Vista children to Washington would have required moving a good many children from Washington to McKinley? The nearly unanimous approval of the board's decision by a citizens' committee that included substantial black representation? In Professor Cohen's full report, he notes all these factors and concludes, "Objective evidence to sustain the gerrymander charge seems to be lacking." Here he was assuming one of the possible meanings of "gerrymander": "It would have been difficult to prove the gerrymander charge, since it required proof that the Board acted from improper motives." After noting that many whites in Pasadena were resentful of the charge of gerrymandering, Professor Cohen makes a point that has importance far beyond the context of this case: "Had the case been tried, a finding of gerrymander—right or wrong—would hardly have been a firm basis on which Pasadena could build continuing healthy inter-racial community relationships." Should a lawyer litigate to protect his client's here-and-now interests if the lawyer believes that such litigation would be destructive of "healthy inter-racial community relationships" in the future?

The *Deal* opinion noted with some suspicion that there was one "mostly Negro" junior high school whose boundaries excluded the white children living across the street. Is that a sufficient showing of a racial gerrymander? Look again at the quoted language from the Supreme Court's opinion in *Gomillion*.

Recall the following language from the Supreme Court's opinion in *Green v. County School Board of New Kent County*, p. 294 *supra*: "[W]here other, more promising courses of action are open to the board, that may indicate a lack of good faith; and at the least it places a heavy burden upon the board to explain its preference for an apparently less effective method." If a school board (a) knows the racial residential patterns in its community,

(b) draws attendance zones which in fact produce racial imbalance in the schools, and (c) is aware of alternative ways to draw zones which would produce less racial imbalance, would that combination of circumstances "indicate a lack of good faith" on the part of the board, the equivalent of a racial gerrymander? In other words, does every case of racial imbalance constitute a gerrymander, when the school board has alternatives that would result in significantly less imbalance?

2. The school board's constitutional duty to reduce de facto segregation.—If a showing of racial imbalance is not always sufficient to prove a gerrymander, there remains the question whether a school board nevertheless has a constitutional obligation to reduce the imbalance. The courts that decided *Deal* and *Jackson* differed in their conclusions on this issue. The Sixth Circuit in *Deal* flatly rejected the argument that the Cincinnati board had such a constitutional obligation, while the California Supreme Court stated that in some circumstances "substantial racial imbalance" would entitle the student to relief. Both opinions purport to draw on *Brown v. Board of Education.* In their doctrinal disagreement, they raise a number of questions about the legal process.

a. The implications of Brown for de facto segregation: herein of a lower court's interpretation of a Supreme Court decision, and the analogy to statutory interpretation.—"The essence of the *Brown* decision was that the Fourteenth Amendment does not allow the state to classify its citizens differently solely because of their race." So said the Sixth Circuit in the *Deal* opinion. "While the detrimental impact of compulsory segregation on the children of the minority race was referred to by the Court, it was not indispensable to the decision." Is that your reading of *Brown?* Compare the interpretation of *Brown* by the California Supreme Court: "The segregation of school children into separate schools because of their race . . . deprives the children of the minority group of equal opportunities for education and denies them equal protection . . . of the law. (*Brown v. Board of Education.* . . .) . . . Where [residential] segregation exists it is not enough for a school board to refrain from affirmative discriminatory conduct. The harmful influence on the children will be reflected and intensified in the classroom if school attendance is determined on a geographic basis without corrective measures. The right to an equal opportunity for education and the harmful consequences of segregation require that school boards take steps, insofar as reasonably feasible, to alleviate racial imbalance in schools regardless of its cause." Was it the harm segregation caused to black children that made it unconstitutional in *Brown*, or did *Brown* simply declare a flat prohibition on racial classifications by the state, regardless of a showing of harm?

We deal now with the interpretation by a lower court of a higher court's decision. Here the analogy is perhaps as close to statutory interpretation as it is, say, to the interpretation of *Plessy v. Ferguson* by the Supreme Court itself in 1954. It is not surprising that we encounter "aids" to interpretation that parallel the aids to statutory construction.

i.   "Legislative history"; the arguments that had been addressed to the Court in the Brown case.—There is an analogy to legislative history in the arguments that were made to the higher court that decided the precedent case. Neither the *Jackson* opinion nor the *Deal* opinion isolates this factor as one that influences either court's interpretation of *Brown*, and it may be that neither the Sixth Circuit nor the California Supreme Court gave the matter any weight. There have been cases (and even series of cases), however, in which the Supreme Court has obviously gone to some length to avoid deciding the central issues that have been argued before it. If those cases are widely publicized, it is not hard for lower courts to get the message that the Supreme Court is disinclined to rest decision on the ground that has been pressed upon it. (A notable example in the race relations area has been the series of cases following *Shelley v. Kraemer,* 334 U.S. 1 (1948), which held unconstitutional a state court's enforcement of a racially restrictive covenant against a would-be Negro buyer of a house in a "restricted" neighborhood. Succeeding cases pressed upon the Supreme Court the sweeping logic of the decision: that the state could not constitutionally enforce any private racial discrimination. The Court has managed to protect Negro rights in a variety of analogous contexts, from access to "private" parks to sit-in demonstrations, but has studiously avoided the heroic issue left hanging by *Shelley*.) Thus the absence, in the *Brown* opinion, of any discussion of the broad question of a state's power to make racial classifications may be a significant omission in light of the arguments that had been addressed to the Court.

We have already seen that the records in the *Brown* cases contained considerable evidence supporting a claim of harm to Negro children from school segregation. The social science brief that was filed also concentrated on this contention. Professor John Kaplan, however, uses the oral argument in *Brown* to support another reading of the Court's decision:

Indeed it was the racial classification rather than the inequality of schools that was the ground most vigorously argued by the attorneys for the plaintiffs before the Supreme Court. For instance, Robert L. Carter, General Counsel of the NAACP and the attorney who tried most of the *Gary* case, at the first argument of *Brown* in 1952 was asked by Justice Black whether the Kansas court's finding, that the segregated Negro schools were not equal to the white schools, referred merely to the community in question or was a more general finding. Mr. Carter answered, "I think I agree that the finding refers to Kansas and to these appellants and to Topeka. Of course, under our theory, you do not have to reach the findings, because we maintain that this is an unconstitutional classification."

Thurgood Marshall, while arguing a companion case the same day, stated:

[This case is just another] attack on a classification statute. This court laid down the rule in many cases that it must be shown that there is a difference between the two classes and, too, that the state must show that the difference has a significance with the subject matter being legislated.

In the reargument of the segregation cases in 1953, Spottswood W. Robinson, who shared with Thurgood Marshall the argument for the plaintiffs from South Carolina and Virginia, asserted that the purpose of the fourteenth amendment was to prevent the imposition of "governmental caste distinctions, predicated upon race." Thurgood Marshall then summarized the argument of the plaintiffs, stating:

Our argument is that the state is deprived of any power to make any racial classification in any governmental field . . . . I can conceive of some governmental action—such as census taking—in which a separation of the races could be made. But in any area which touches the individuals concerned in any form or fashion, it is clear to me under the Fourteenth Amendment that you cannot separate people or denote that one is to go here and one is to go there even if the facilities are absolutely equal.

Lastly, at the final argument in these cases in 1955 when the Court was concerned only with the mandate ordering the end of segregation, Thurgood Marshall declared,

> [T]he only thing that the Court is dealing with is whether race can be used . . . . What we want is the striking down of race . . . . It is no problem to put dumb colored children with dumb white children and smart colored children with smart white children.

Kaplan, *Segregation Litigation and the Schools—Part II: The General Northern Problem,* 58 Nw. U.L. Rev. 157, 173–74 (1963).*

ii. The language of the Brown opinion.—Both the Sixth Circuit and the California Supreme Court referred to the words of the *Brown* opinion, but neither court quoted extensively from *Brown*. Here we see a sharp contrast to the practice of courts in interpreting statutes. There is no parsing of sentences or combing of dictionaries. The precedent—the *rule* of the earlier decision—is to be gleaned from a consideration of the whole case, including the facts and the doctrinal setting of the case as well as the language of the opinion. The *Jackson* opinion, however, uses the words of *Brown*, without quotation marks, to support its conclusion that the key to *Brown* was segregation's harm to the education of the black child. The *Deal* opinion does refer, p. 452 *supra*, to a standard of "equal educational opportunity"— which we have identified with the *Jackson* view—but concludes that a showing of harm to the Negro child is irrelevant, as would be a contrary showing. The *Deal* court supports its position with a quotation from the opinion in *Bolling v. Sharpe*, the companion case to *Brown* that came from the District of Columbia. That language, however, was addressed to the doctrinal problem of finding justification for a no-segregation rule in the Fifth Amendment's due process clause. Finally, the *Deal* opinion supports its conclusions about the constitutional validity of the neighborhood school pattern with a reference to question 4 (a) posed in 1954 by the Supreme Court for argument in the second phase of *Brown*, which question seemed to assume a continuation of geographic districting. (Question 4(a) is in footnote 31, p. 219 *supra*.) What response would you make to this latter argument based on the language of the Court's question to counsel?

---

* Reprinted with special permission from the Northwestern University Law Review. Copyright © 1963 by the Northwestern University School of Law. Volume 58, Number 2.

What is your view as to the proper implication to be drawn from the words of the *Brown* opinion and applied to these cases of de facto segregation? That opinion devotes its key paragraphs to its factual conclusions about the relation of state-enforced segregation to the educational process. The language may not be conclusive (remember Professor Wechsler: "I find it hard to think the judgment really turned upon the facts"), but it is most difficult to conclude from the language that the Court in *Brown* meant to decide on anything other than the quality of the education that states were offering to the segregated black children.

iii.   **The implications of the post-Brown decisions.**—But the *Brown* opinion is by no means the end of the story. The *Deal* court noted that the Supreme Court went on in the years immediately after 1954 to strike down all forms of state-compelled racial segregation that came before it—never with a discussion of the harm caused by segregation, and always with a citation to *Brown v. Board of Education*. In some of these cases, as we have noted, the citation to *Brown* was the entire opinion; for example, that was how *Plessy v. Ferguson* was overruled without being mentioned. (See the reference to *Gayle v. Browder*, p. 203 *supra*.) The clear implication is, as the *Deal* court says, that the state cannot constitutionally segregate its citizens, and that "it is not necessary that a victim of racial discrimination prove that he was harmed in any specific material sense in order to invalidate state-imposed racial distinctions." The Sixth Circuit goes on, however, to draw a negative implication from these post-*Brown* decisions: "Conversely, a showing of harm alone is not enough to invoke the remedial powers of the law." Can that implication fairly be drawn from the "post-'enactment' aids" of the later Supreme Court decisions applying *Brown*? The *Jackson* court solves this problem by silence, making no reference to the decisions applying *Brown* to segregated parks and buses and courtrooms.

iv.   **Professional commentary on Brown.**—The decisions of the United States Supreme Court are subjected to the most exhaustive and rigorous professional scrutiny. The publication of comments and analyses in professional journals can also be of considerable persuasive value in interpreting a precedent. In the case of the great issues, however, it seems fair to say that the influence of the law reviews is minimal as a post-"enactment" aid to interpretation. On the great questions of constitutional life and death, every judge—indeed, every citizen—is apt to regard himself as his own expert guide. Be that as it may, the volume of professional writing about the *Brown* decision is staggering, and much of it has been of the highest quality. With respect to our question—the duty of a school board to act to reduce de facto segregation—we reprint here brief extracts from the opposing conclusions of two thoughtful treatments, both of which make use of the same kinds of materials used in the *Jackson* and *Deal* opinions for interpreting the meaning of *Brown*. (Incidentally, one of these authors owns, even wears, a tiger suit. Which one?)

KAPLAN, SEGREGATION LITIGATION AND THE SCHOOLS—PART II: THE GENERAL NORTHERN PROBLEM
58 Northwestern University Law Review 157, 171-73 (1963)*

[The author is criticizing the argument that a school board has a constitutional duty to remedy de facto segregation. The "first proposition" to which he refers is the proposition that the "Supreme Court held in the *Brown* case that separate Negro schools are harmful to Negro children and therefore unconstitutional." After acknowledging the language in the *Brown* opinion about the relation between segregation and feelings of racial inferiority, Professor Kaplan continues:]

On the other hand, one need not enter the debates concerning "neutral principles" to assert that this language may not be the basis of the Court's holding. To say that the Supreme Court found as a psychological and sociological fact that separate schools were harmful to Negro children and were therefore unconstitutional is to blur the distinctions among the possible rationales open to the Court. The language in the Court's opinion which can be read as implying that inequality, as distinguished from mere separation, caused the unconstitutionality must be considered in the light of the Supreme Court's treatment of segregation over the years. Since the Court apparently was not prepared flatly to overrule *Plessy v. Ferguson* at that time, it was necessary to show that even under the *Plessy* rule the plaintiffs in *Brown* and the other segregation cases would have to prevail. The stipulation of the parties, however, that the Negro and white schools were equal with respect to all tangible facilities limited the Court to consideration of intangibles of the type discussed in *Sweatt v. Painter* and in *McLaurin v. Oklahoma State Regents*. It was in this context that the Court found separate schools inherently

---

unequal and the separate but equal doctrine hence inapplicable in the field of public education. One should remember that, under *Plessy,* only equality of facilities saved the segregation from being unconstitutional. The Court there was not concerned with what it regarded as unequal treatment and went to some pains to show that the Negro was being treated equally, even though he was segregated because he was a Negro. When this equality did not exist—as it did not, in *Brown*—it was the differential treatment accorded to Negroes as Negroes, not the inequality of facilities, that violated the fourteenth amendment.

A reference to the facts of the case of *McLaurin v. Oklahoma State Regents* makes this reasoning somewhat more clear. In *McLaurin,* all facilities were equal, indeed identical, except for the fact that school authorities on the basis of race prevented the plaintiff from normal contact with his schoolmates. Certainly, the mere fact that one person is denied the right to associate in school with other persons cannot be said to be a constitutional violation. Unless a school authority operates only one school it must always divide the school population in some way or other and thus prevent some students from having contact with some others. In some ways a student in one school might even be harmed by his inability to associate with students in another. But even such harm would not mean that the separation was constitutionally prohibited. The *McLaurin* case merely stood for the principle that, at least in higher education, *race* might not be made the criterion for separation of one group of students from another. The practical positions of the two races in the United States made it clear that this very separation made the two groups unequal, and thus outside of the rule of *Plessy v. Ferguson.* In the *Brown* case, the Court merely took the view that the *McLaurin* principle was equally applicable to segregated education in the grade and high schools, and that, as in *McLaurin,* it was the racial separation, rather than any inequality of facilities or other educational benefits, that was the essence of the plaintiffs' claim. This view explains the Court's language that "such considerations apply with added force" to children in grade and high schools because of the psychological harm these children suffer. The Court was asserting that *Brown* was in a sense an easier case than *McLaurin* and *Sweatt v. Painter,* where this type of harm to young children was not to be expected, rather than to show that harm to Negro children or inequality of schools was the essence of the constitutional violation. To highlight this principle one might ask, "Since when are unequal schools per se unconstitutional?" The Supreme Court has never held that in the absence of some racial classification the mere inequality of one school compared with another involves a constitutional violation. In many communities one school is clearly better in terms of faculty, student body, physical facilities, and prestige, than others, yet no one has suggested that this inequality raises a federal constitutional question. If pure inequality were the essence of the constitutional violation, such schools might in some ways be much more unequal and inferior than many Negro schools segregated by force of law.

This view of *Brown* is reinforced by examining the type of evidence that was available to the Court on the question of the actual harm visited upon Negro children by school segregation. Several commentators have pointed out that though a large quantity of expert testimony was introduced as evidence in the cases and in briefs, it was by no means sufficiently definite, unambiguous, uncontradicted, or sweeping to allow the Court to find as a fact, irrefutable in all future cases, that regardless of the area or social climate, even deliberate state-imposed segregation in schools would work such harm on Negro children as to require a finding of unconstitutionality. Subsequent cases disposed of by the Court without a written opinion support this view of the *Brown* case even more clearly. These cases, striking down segregation on golf courses and in parks, where not an iota of evidence indicated the existence of the harm described in the *Brown* case, seem to indicate that it was not the inequality of facilities or the harm which caused the constitutional violation, but rather the separateness by state classification. Thus, *Plessy* held that racial classifications did not offend the Constitution so long as they did not cause some type of harm. *McLaurin* and *Brown* found the necessary harm inherent in the separation by racial classification in education, and subsequent cases have dispensed with the necessity for showing any harm at all so long as racial classifications are drawn by state authority.

[Professor Kaplan goes on to summarize portions of the oral argument in *Brown*; see p. 463 *supra*.]

FISS, RACIAL IMBALANCE IN THE PUBLIC SCHOOLS: THE CONSTITUTIONAL CONCEPTS
78 Harvard Law Review 564, 588-95 (1965)*

[Professor Fiss poses the question whether school boards have a constitutional obligation to act to remedy de facto segregation:]

If this question is to be resolved affirmatively, when the school board's policy is merely one of approval or disregard, a principle requiring equality of educational opportunity must be abstracted from the equal protection clause, for the protest against the creation and maintenance of imbalanced schools essentially consists of a claim that the educational opportunity afforded Negro children required to attend such schools is unequal to that afforded children attending the other public schools of the community. If such a constitutional principle can be established it would require the justification of unequal educational opportunity and in the absence of such a justification, equal educational opportunity. Thus, two critical judgments must be made by a court applying the principle. First, a court must make the empirical judgment whether the opportunity afforded Negro children is significantly and systematically inferior to that afforded others. When this inequality of educational opportunity exists it will sometimes be apparent from an examination of the government's action or law "on its face," as when admission to public schools is restricted to a certain class of people. In other instances, however, the government will nominally treat all members of the relevant class equally. Yet, such nominal equality may, in fact, disguise unequal treatment. In making the empirical judgment a court is required to probe below the nominal level to determine whether this factual inequality exists. Second, a court must make the normative judgment whether there is an adequate justification for any existing substantial difference in educational opportunity. This section of the article examines the extent to which courts have made such judgments, that is, the extent to which the principle of equality of educational opportunity can be said to have taken root in American constitutional law.

[Here Professor Fiss reviews the *Sweatt, McLaurin,* and *Brown* opinions.]

. . . The Court in *Sweatt, McLaurin,* and *Brown* explicitly made the empirical judgment necessary to expose the substantial inequality, and impliedly made the normative judgment that this unequal treatment was not justified by the accident of color or the desire of whites not to associate with Negroes.

The constitutional status of the equal-educational-opportunity principle, not the correctness of these normative and empirical judgments, is being asserted here. However, it has been suggested that the Court could have decided these cases without assessing the quality of a segregated educational opportunity, that instead of employing the equal-educational-opportunity principle the

Court might have relied on the more "neutral" or "general" principle that race is an inherently arbitrary classification. Two points are often overlooked by the proponents of this alternative explanation of *Brown*: first, that the inherently-arbitrary-classification principle is compatible with the equal-opportunity principle; and second, that regardless of the grounds on which *Brown* and its predecessors might have been decided there is no doubt of the ground on which they were decided.

The inherently-arbitrary-classification principle has taken on several different meanings, although each is consistent with the no less "general" and "neutral" (whatever those words mean) principle of equality of educational opportunity. For Professor Pollak, the principle merely creates a presumption that a law that "draws racial lines" treats the racial minority unequally. The application of this presumption would have relieved the Court from probing below the nominal level of the Jim Crow education laws and from having to rely openly on the empirical judgment that segregation disadvantages the minority. The Court would have had to rely on its "amateur wisdom" only to determine whether the presumption of unequal treatment had been rebutted and whether this unequal treatment could be justified. As such, the inherently-arbitrary-classification principle is merely a technique for facilitating the application of the equal-opportunity principle.

The inherently-arbitrary-classification principle could also be interpreted as stating a flat constitutional prohibition against racial discrimination: differences in race do not justify differences in treatment by government. This version of the principle could complement the equal-opportunity principle in the sense that a difference in educational opportunity could not be justified simply because the child is a Negro. This use of the inherently-arbitrary-classification principle would not, however, relieve the court from making an empirical judgment that the Negro is harmed or disadvantaged by the segregated education, since it is only state treatment resulting in systematic inequality that must be justified at the risk of being proscribed by the equal protection clause. Relying on its assessment of an individual's emotional or psychological reaction to imposed separation, the Court in *Brown* could have found the inequality of treatment in the personal hurt, the insult, the humiliation, and the stigma, without elaborating on the educational significance of the harm. Yet, there was no reason to ignore the likely impairment of the educational opportunity of a child compelled to go to a Negro school and the Court did not ignore it.

A third interpretation of the inherently-arbitrary-classification principle views it as a prohibition on governmental interference with the liberty of individuals solely on the basis of their color or race. The restriction on the individual's liberty, rather than his reaction to the restriction, creates the burden that must be justified. This version of the principle is rooted primarily in the due process clause, and the plaintiff is thus relieved from showing that his liberty is being restricted unequally. It does not contradict the equal-opportunity principle, but rather renders the principle unnecessary for the disposition of *Brown* and its predecessors. Such a displacement would have been possible but seems artificial, for a restriction on an individual liberty was not at the heart of *Brown.* . . .

A fourth version of the inherently-arbitrary-classification principle has been suggested by Professor John Kaplan: Any law that contains a "racial classification" is so "completely arbitrary and irrational" that it necessarily violates the equal protection clause regardless of actual or presumed harm, or unequal treatment in any factual sense. The "essence of the constitutional violation" of a law that places children of different races in different schools is not that such a law treats Negroes unequally in any factual sense, but rather that it treats "Negroes as Negroes." Assuming that this version of the principle does not consist in whole or in part of any of the other three, it is fundamentally inadequate. It is not a restatement of the principle of constitutional color blindness since that principle, which rejects race as such as a sufficient basis for unequal treatment, is properly invoked only if state treatment of Negroes results in systematic inequality in some factual sense. Professor Kaplan thus leaves the critical question unanswered: Why cannot Negroes be treated as Negroes, if there is no inequality in any sense other than that they are treated as Negroes and if racial considerations are not used to justify restrictions on individual liberty? Conceivably, some laws may be so "absurd" or "irrational" on their face that they hardly partake of the quality of laws. Certainly, this was not the case with the laws at stake in *Brown*: in 1954, seventeen states and the District of Columbia had laws requiring segregation and four states had legislation explicitly permitting segregation at the option of the local authorities.[9]

The second point often overlooked is that regardless of whether *Brown* could have been decided on "other grounds," it—as well as *Sweatt* and *McLaurin*—was decided on the basis of the equal-educational-opportunity principle. The language of the opinion, and the Court's familiarity with an alternative approach, which

---

[9] N.Y. Times, May 18, 1954, at 21, col. 2. In 1954, 40% of public school pupils in the United States were in areas where the laws required segregation. [Footnote in original, renumbered.]

was used to decide the two cases that sandwich *Brown* in 347 U.S.,[10] leave no doubt that the Court deliberately chose the principle of equal educational opportunity even though the application of this principle required the Court to assess the total social impact of the institution of segregated education. The reasons for the choice are speculative although the fact of the choice is not. The Court may have decided that it would be unconvincing to announce abruptly that race is an inherently arbitrary classification when certain American institutions had been based on racial separation for several hundred years. Or it may have felt itself obliged to continue the debate in the terms set by *Plessy v. Ferguson,* namely that segregation did not disadvantage the Negro except for his choice to "put that construction upon it." Perhaps the Court simply believed that equality of educational opportunity was the principle most deeply involved in these cases and boldly stated so in order to permit that principle's fullest growth. The Court's willingness to decide summarily other cases involving noneducational facilities by citing *Brown* does not necessarily indicate a subsequent rejection of the principle; these summary dispositions can be viewed as the development of a per se rule embodying a judgment that governmental segregation in facilities other than schools—even if attendance is not compulsory —unjustifiably treats the Negro unequally. The refusal to reassess the social impact of segregation in each public facility, and in each community, does involve some rather heavyhanded treatment of state government. Perhaps such treatment can be explained by the Court's lack of respect for a political process from which Negroes have been effectively excluded and in which it is reasonable to assume racial bigotry played a significant role. It can also be explained as a concession to the interest of judicial economy and as an attempt to make the law an effective instrument of social reform.

Can both Professors Kaplan and Fiss be right? Should *Brown* be viewed as having declared two principles: one dealing with racial classifications and one dealing with equality of educational opportunity?

v. What happened to the "legislative purpose" of Brown?— Our analogy to the issues in statutory interpretation would not be

----

10 Hernandez v. Texas, 347 U.S. 475 (1954); Bolling v. Sharpe, 347 U.S. 497 (1954). The Court in *Brown* made it clear that its "disposition makes unnecessary any discussion whether such segregation also violates the Due Process Clause of the Fourteenth Amendment." 347 U.S. at 495. [Footnote in original, renumbered.]

complete without some acknowledgment that there was little effort in either the *Jackson* opinion or the *Deal* opinion to make a "purpose-oriented" interpretation of the *Brown* decision. Of course both courts reasoned by analogy, with the California court finding the educational harm from segregation to be the most significant feature of *Brown,* and the Sixth Circuit finding instead a principle forbidding states to make racial classifications.

Does it make any sense to ask what the purpose of a judicial decision was? The main task in *Brown* was certainly to dispose of the cases before the Court. A subsidiary task was to decide the cases according to principle—to announce a rule that would dispose of the case, and that the Court was willing to live with for the foreseeable future. There is plenty of reason for thinking that the Court deliberately talked about educational harm in order to avoid pronouncing a broad rule forbidding state segregation laws. Professor Wechsler's criticism of *Brown,* p. 209 *supra,* was that the Court—or a majority—really had the latter rule in mind when it spoke of educational harm to the segregated children. Is it possible to state what the purpose of the *Brown* decision was? Or must we always inquire into the meaning of a previous decision by reference to the issue now before us? These questions might also be asked, not cynically, about cases of statutory interpretation. Is it not true that much of the talk about "the statutory purpose" turns out to be talk about the purposes of the court in deciding the case at hand? A court may ask, concerning a statute no less than a precedent decision, "What are the purposes *now* to be served by this rule adopted by my legislative superiors in the past?"

b. The analytical framework for determining the constitutional validity of de facto segregation.—The preceding subsection has asked whether *Brown* held that an interest in equality of educational opportunity (as distinguished from an interest in freedom from racial separation) is among the interests protected by the equal protection clause. Even if *Brown* did not declare such a principle of equality of educational opportunity, it is still arguable that the equal protection clause requires substantial equality in the public educational offerings made available to children, in the absence of compelling justifications for any harmful inequalities which may exist. A constitutional principle of equality of educational opportunity would require, in the case of de facto segregation, an inquiry into the educational harm caused by racial imbalance in public schools, and into the justifications asserted by the state for so administering its schools.

c. The harmful effects of de facto segregation.—The stigma caused by assigning children to neighborhood schools in racially segregated neighborhoods arguably is not so great as the stigma resulting from the use of a racial classification in the statutes and regulations governing school assignments. In the case of de facto segregation perhaps it is harder to establish that a badge of inferiority has adversely affected a student's educational experience. The most recent studies by social scientists demonstrate that it is far from clear that racial imbalance in itself produces substantial negative effects on the achievement of black students. (Recall the discussion of these issues in Professor Pettigrew's paper, pp. 406-13 *supra*.) If a court is persuaded that racial isolation does not significantly impair the achievement of black students, what should be the court's conclusion as to the constitutional duty of the school board? Are there still some arguments that the board must act, arguments based on the principle of equality of educational opportunity?

One such argument based on achievement can be derived from the Coleman Report's conclusions about the effects of the socioeconomic makeup of a pupil's classroom on his achievement, combined with the high correlation between race and socioeconomic class—*i.e.*, a predominantly Negro school probably is a predominantly low-socioeconomic-class school.

Furthermore, in *McLaurin v. Oklahoma State Regents,* p. 174 *supra,* we saw that the Supreme Court was concerned with certain intangible factors in the education of a graduate student, particularly the student's opportunity to exchange views with other students. Presumably the Court was concerned with the *education* of the student, and not simply with his examination scores. So also in *Brown* the Court spoke of education as the "foundation of good citizenship," and as "a principal instrument in awakening the child to cultural values, in preparing him for later professional training, and in helping him to adjust normally to his environment." (Recall Professor Pettigrew's discussion of the effect of segregation on the black pupil's "sense of fate control," p. 417 *supra*.) It may be that none of those aspects of education is measured by the standard achievement tests, although they are of great importance to the student.

d. Harm to American society: an appropriate measure of a school board's duty to seek integration?—The Kerner Commission, it will be remembered, supported efforts to end de facto segregation, not on the basis of any showing of an effect on the achievement of Negro students, but because integration "is essential to the future of American society. We have seen in this last summer's disorders the consequences of racial isolation, at all levels, and of attitudes toward race, on both sides, produced by three centuries of myth, ignorance and bias. It is indispensable that opportunities for interaction between the races be expanded." The Civil Rights Commission's report, *Racial Isolation in the Public Schools,* contains an appendix that compiles some data documenting changes in attitudes of children who have attended integrated classrooms. (Recall Professor Pettigrew's discussion, p. 416 *supra*.) Suppose it should be established that school integration would help to make our society less racist. Would such a showing —absent any showing of other educational harm to black children from de facto segregation—suffice to support the conclusion of the California Supreme Court in *Jackson?* Should a black child or parent have the right to assert that community interest when he sues a school board? Can he, or a white child or parent, show an identifiable personal interest in nudging American society just a little further toward healthy attitudes about race? Is private litigation an appropriate means for achieving such goals? Compare the language of Justice Brown in *Plessy v. Ferguson,* p. 134 *supra*, on the limits of law as an instrument for changing attitudes.

e. **The justifications for tolerating de facto segregation: another look at a school board's motive and the "neighborhood school" pattern.**—The question of the motive of a school board has already been considered in the discussions of racial gerrymandering and of *New Kent County,* pp. 297, 457, *supra.* We have left until now, however, a consideration of the way an inquiry into legislative motive may affect a court's conclusion as to the weight to be given to the state's interest in the constitutional balance. If we assume that de facto segregation causes some substantial harm to black children in black schools, then ordinary constitutional analysis would require a showing of some justification for that harm, however great the presumption of constitutionality might be. (Even a "reasonable basis" approach to the equal protection clause would reach this conclusion, for causing harm to a class of citizens without *any* justification is arbitrary by any test. If Dean Pollak's presumptive-invalidity standard, p. 212 *supra*, is the rule for cases of racial classification, the state is obviously required to justify its action.) If the court concludes that the legislative body's motive is an impermissible one, then the court will hold that the state has not justified the harm it has caused to the constitutionally protected interest (here, the black children's interest in equality of educational opportunity). Correspondingly, evidence showing a legitimate justification for the board's action will tend to negative any implication of an improper motive. The Supreme Court may have had the question of motive in mind when it said, in *Bolling v. Sharpe*, p. 193 *supra*, "Segregation in public education is not reasonably related to any *proper* governmental objective. . . ." (Emphasis added.) But in *Bolling* the Court had before it a case of government-compelled segregation. Should we reach the same conclusion about de facto segregation?

The principal values supporting the maintenance of schools that are segregated in fact are the values associated with "the neighborhood school." Particularly for children in elementary schools, there are reasonable arguments to be made for keeping the schools close to where the children live; some of the arguments are summarized in the *Deal* opinion, p. 452 *supra*. It is doubtful that a court would say that the pattern of neighborhood schools lacks any rational basis. But, as we have seen in cases such as *Brown, New Kent County,* and *NAACP v. Button,* a "rational basis" for a state's policy does not necessarily mean that that policy meets constitutional requirements.

f. Striking the constitutional balance.—We come finally to the point of decision—is it a denial of equal protection of the laws for a school district to maintain racially imbalanced schools, given the available arguments concerning the degree of harm to children and the justifications for using neighborhood school attendance zones? Professor Kaplan, in the article quoted above, asks these questions: "How can the courts weigh the value of a 30 percent increase in integration against a requirement that students cross a dangerous traffic artery or walk five extra blocks? How could the courts weigh the achievement of integration through bussing children against the greater cost and a somewhat larger class size?" Kaplan, p. 466 *supra*, at 183. In the *Jackson* case the California Supreme Court stated that under some circumstances school boards must "take steps, insofar as reasonably feasible, to alleviate racial imbalance in schools regardless of its cause." P. 444 *supra*. Did the California court succeed in weighing incommensurable values? Or did the court decide the case without having to make the kind of value judgment described by Professor Kaplan?

The key portion of the California court's disposition of the issue is the phrase "reasonably feasible." The court does not say that racial imbalance must be eliminated whatever countervailing considerations there may be, nor does it say that neighborhood attendance zones are permissible whatever the severity of the racial imbalance and consequent harm. "[C]onsideration should be given," the court said, p. 445 *supra*, "on the one hand, to the degree of racial imbalance in the particular school and the extent to which it affects the opportunity for education and, on the other hand, to such matters as the difficulty and effectiveness of revising school boundaries so as to eliminate segregation and the availability of other facilities to which students can be transferred." What value judgment did the court make, implicit in its conclusion that the justifications for neighborhood attendance zones would not always be sufficient to make such zones permissible? Did not the court, at a minimum, conclude that, because of the harm to children which can be caused by de facto segregation, school boards must take into consideration the prevention of such harm in assigning children to school? Did the court go further, concluding that, because of the magnitude of such potential harm, school boards must give extra weight to the prevention of such harm in school assignment policies? We have seen a principle of the latter sort in *New Kent County*, p. 295 *supra*, where the Supreme Court said that freedom-of-choice plans violate the equal protection clause "if there are reasonably available other ways, such for illustration as zoning, promising speedier and more effective conversion to a unitary, nonracial school system." *Jackson's* "reasonably feasible" and *New Kent County's* "reasonably available" are examples of requiring resort to "less onerous alternatives," when such alternatives can be reasonably resorted to and will enable the pursuit of governmental objectives with less harmful impact on individuals. Were the values weighed by the California court in coming to the "reasonably feasible" conclusion less incommensurable than Professor Kaplan viewed them to be?

Compare the Sixth Circuit's opinion in *Deal*. Why did that court conclude that the equal protection clause did not require the school board to make efforts to alleviate racial imbalance? Are the court's reasons sufficient to outweigh the arguments for the "reasonably feasible" solution in *Jackson*?

What exactly does the decision in *Jackson* require school boards to do? There are various administrative steps which a school board can consider, in order to reduce racial imbalance: redraw attendance zones; permit black children to transfer from de facto segregated schools; pair elementary schools in adjoining attendance zones, so that all children in both zones attend, for example, the first three grades in one school and the last three grades in the other; select new school sites so as to promote racially balanced school populations; close racially imbalanced schools, distributing their children to other schools; construct "educational parks" which will draw children from large geographical zones; or assign children so as to have racially balanced schools, transporting black and white children across neighborhood zone lines as may be necessary. Some of these steps obviously have limited utility in large urban school systems. And "reasonably feasible" may not be an altogether clear guide for a school board. Consider the following observation by Professor Frank Goodman:

Whether a particular course of action is "feasible" depends largely upon which elements of the situation are assumed to be fixed and unalterable and which, on the other hand, are regarded as freely variable. If, for example, one accepts as a "given" the basic validity of the neighborhood school concept and the existing facilities and financial resources of the school district, the range of "feasible" desegregation measures is apt to be rather limited. Drop these assumptions and the range of feasibilities becomes broader. Assume, finally, that money is no obstacle, and that proximity to schools can be dismissed as a mere matter of "convenience," and nearly *everything* becomes feasible. F. GOODMAN, RACIAL IMBALANCE IN THE OAKLAND PUBLIC SCHOOLS: A LEGAL ANALYSIS 69 (1966).

In effect, the California court seems to have declared the principle that school boards must make a good faith effort to reduce racial imbalance. For that purpose, is "reasonably feasible" a workable standard? Consider, for example, a case in which a school board considers all of the factors referred to by the court in *Jackson* and then takes some steps toward reducing racial imbalance, following which parents in the district contend in a lawsuit that the board did not do enough. How is a court to decide such an issue? Would the court then be driven to weighing incommensurable values as Professor Kaplan suggested? Or could the court still avoid such a specific weighing of values by confining its inquiry to whether the board had in good faith tried to alleviate the racial imbalance?

This inquiry into striking the constitutional balance in the de facto segregation problem illustrates again the difficult task presented to a court which is called upon to decide whether law made by another branch of government amounts to a denial of the equal protection of the laws. Is there any better approach to the exercise of the judicial function in these cases than for the court to appraise the nature and magnitude of the harm to each complainant, the justifications for government's subjecting him to that harm, and the availability of "less onerous" ways in which those governmental objectives might be sought? Does this type of inquiry require a court so to weigh "legislative" values that it is more desirable for the court to limit itself to determining whether the other lawmaking agency had a "rational" basis for what it did? Under the latter approach how would *Brown v. Board of Education* be decided?

g. Racial imbalance in schools in one school district as compared with schools in another district.—School districts are, under state law, separate legal entities which function independently of other districts. Recall in Professor Cohen's description of the events leading up to the *Jackson* case, p. 436 *supra*, the statement that "In 1960 the all-white La Canada area withdrew from the Pasadena Unified School District" into an independent district. What argument can be made, under *Jackson*, supporting a suit to enjoin such a transfer by white parents from one school district to another? Would your argument also support an injunction preventing the establishment of a separate school district to serve, and be controlled by, a ghetto community? Would a Negro parent have a cause of action, under *Jackson*, to require adjoining school districts to merge, or otherwise to take cooperative action, in order to alleviate racial imbalance in one of the districts?

C. BEYOND INTEGRATION: CONSTITUTIONAL DIMENSIONS OF OTHER INEQUALITIES OF EDUCATIONAL OPPORTUNITY

The Kerner Commission Report, p. 399 *supra*, described the full scope of inequalities in public educational opportunity today in the United States: racial (and socioeconomic class) imbalance in urban public school student bodies, and differences in such factors as teacher qualifications, quality of facilities, and expenditures in schools attended by children who live in urban ghettos as compared with other children. The Commission also emphasized the need for improving the quality of educational opportunity offered to children from disadvantaged minorities in urban schools:

> We recognize that the growing dominance of pupils from disadvantaged minorities in city school populations will not soon be reversed. No matter how great the effort toward desegregation, many children of the ghetto will not, within their school careers, attend integrated schools.
>
> If existing disadvantages are not to be perpetuated, we must improve dramatically the quality of ghetto education. Equality of results with all-white schools in terms of achievement must be the goal. . . .

Far from being in conflict, the strategies [of integration and quality education] are complementary. The aim of quality education is to compensate for and overcome the environmental handicaps of disadvantaged children. The evidence indicates that integration, in itself, does not wholly achieve this purpose. . . .

In short, compensatory education is essential not only to improve the quality of education provided in segregated ghetto schools, but to make possible both meaningful integration and maximum achievement in integrated schools.

The constitutional dimensions of all these aspects of inequality of educational opportunity were analyzed in *Hobson v. Hansen*, which involved the public schools of the District of Columbia. Judge Wright's opinion covers 114 pages in the printed reports, 84 of which are devoted to findings of fact that amount to a comprehensive study of the entire school system. In the extracts from the opinion which follow, the section on findings of fact is omitted. The findings are summarized at the beginning of the opinion, and are discussed in the "Opinion of Law."

HOBSON v. HANSEN
United States District Court, District of Columbia
269 F. Supp. 401 (1967)

J. Skelly Wright, Circuit Judge[11]:

Summary

In Bolling v. Sharpe, 347 U.S. 497, 74 S. Ct. 693, 98 L. Ed. 884 (1954), the Supreme Court held that the District of Columbia's racially segregated public school system violated the due process clause of the Fifth Amendment. The present litigation, brought in behalf of Negro as well as poor children generally in the District's public schools, tests the current compliance of those schools with the principles announced in *Bolling*, its companion case, Brown v. Board of Education of Topeka, 347 U.S. 483, 74 S. Ct. 686, 98 L. Ed. 873 (1954), and their progeny. The basic question presented is whether the defendants, the Superintendent of Schools and the members of the Board of Education, in the operation of the public school system here, unconstitutionally deprive the District's Negro and poor public school children of

----
[11] Sitting by designation pursuant to 28 U.S.C. § 291(c). [All footnotes to this opinion are footnotes in the original and have been renumbered.]

their right to equal educational opportunity with the District's white and more affluent public school children. This court concludes that they do.

In support of this conclusion the court makes the following principal findings of fact:

1. Racially and socially homogeneous schools damage the minds and spirit of all children who attend them—the Negro, the white, the poor and the affluent—and block the attainment of the broader goals of democratic education, whether the segregation occurs by law or by fact.

2. The scholastic achievement of the disadvantaged child, Negro and white, is strongly related to the racial and socioeconomic composition of the student body of his school. A racially and socially integrated school environment increases the scholastic achievement of the disadvantaged child of whatever race.

3. The Board of Education, which is the statutory head of the public schools in the District, is appointed pursuant to a quota system which, until 1962, for over half a century had limited the Negro membership of the nine-man Board to three. Since 1962 the Negro quota on the Board has been four, one less than a majority. The city of Washington, which is the District of Columbia, presently has a population over 60% Negro and a public school population over 90% Negro.

4. Adherence to the neighborhood school policy by the School Board effectively segregates the Negro and the poor children from the white and the more affluent children in most of the District's public schools. This neighborhood school policy is relaxed by the Board through the use of optional zones for the purpose of allowing white children, usually affluent white children, "trapped" in a Negro school district, to "escape" to a "white" or more nearly white school, thus making the economic and racial segregation of the public school children more complete than it would otherwise be under a strict neighborhood school assignment plan.

5. The teachers and principals in the public schools are assigned so that generally the race of the faculty is the same as the race of the children. Thus most of the schools can be identified as "Negro" or "white," not only by reference to the predominant race of the children attending, but by the predominant race of the faculty as well. The heaviest concentration of Negro faculty, usually 100%, is in the Negro ghetto schools.

6. The median annual per pupil expenditure ($292) in the predominantly (85–100%) Negro elementary schools in the District of Columbia has been a flat $100 below the median annual per pupil expenditure for its predominantly (85–100%) white schools ($392).

7. Generally the "white" schools are underpopulated while the "Negro" schools generally are overcrowded. Moreover, all of the white elementary schools have kindergartens. Some Negro schools are without kindergartens entirely while other Negro schools operate kindergartens in shifts or consecutive sessions. In addition to being overcrowded and short on kindergarten space, the school buildings in the Negro slums are ancient and run down. Only recently, through the use of impact aid and other federal funds, have the Negro slum schools had sufficient textbooks for the children's use.

8. As they proceed through the Washington school system, the reading scores primarily of the Negro and poor children, but not the white and middle class, fall increasingly behind the national norm. By senior high school the discrepancy reaches several grades.

9. The track system as used in the District's public schools is a form of ability grouping in which students are divided in separate, self-contained curricula or tracks ranging from "Basic" for the slow student to "Honors" for the gifted.

10. The aptitude tests used to assign children to the various tracks are standardized primarily on white middle class children. Since these tests do not relate to the Negro and disadvantaged child, track assignment based on such tests relegates Negro and disadvantaged children to the lower tracks from which, because of the reduced curricula and the absence of adequate remedial and compensatory education, as well as continued inappropriate testing, the chance of escape is remote.

11. Education in the lower tracks is geared to what Dr. Hansen, the creator of the track system, calls the "blue collar" student. Thus such children, so stigmatized by inappropriate aptitude testing procedures, are denied equal opportunity to obtain the white collar education available to the white and more affluent children.

Other incidental, but highly indicative, findings are as follows:
a. The June 1964—December 1965 study by the Office of the

Surgeon General, Army, shows that 55.3% of the 18-year-olds from the District of Columbia failed the Armed Services mental test, a higher percentage than any of the 50 states. b. The average per pupil expenditure in the District's public schools is only slightly below the national average. The 1964-65 Bureau of the Census Report on Governmental Finances shows, however, that the District of Columbia spends less per capita on education generally than all states except Arkansas and Tennessee. c. The same report shows that the District of Columbia spends more per capita on police protection than all states without exception. In fact, the District of Columbia spends more than double any state other than Nevada, New York, New Jersey and California. The inferences, including those bearing on the relationship of the quality of education to crime, which rise from these findings are obvious. Indeed, the National Crime Commission's Task Force Report: Juvenile Delinquency and Youth Crime indicates that the very deficiencies in the District's public school system noted by the record in this case—prejudging, through inappropriate testing, the learning abilities of the disadvantaged child as inferior to the white middle class child; placing the child in lower tracks for reduced education based on such tests, thus implementing the self-fulfilling prophecy phenomenon inherent in such misjudgments; placing inferior teachers in slum schools; continuing racial and economic segregation of pupils; providing textbooks unrelated to the lives of disadvantaged children; inadequate remedial programs for offsetting initial psychological and social difficulties of the disadvantaged child—all have contributed to the increase in crime, particularly juvenile crime.

In sum, all of the evidence in this case tends to show that the Washington school system is a monument to the cynicism of the power structure which governs the voteless capital of the greatest country on earth.

Remedy

To correct the racial and economic discrimination found in the operation of the District of Columbia public school system, the court has issued a decree attached to its opinion ordering: 1. An injunction against racial and economic discrimination in the public school system here. 2. Abolition of the track system. 3. Abolition of the optional zones. 4. Transportation for volunteering children in overcrowded school districts east of Rock Creek Park to underpopulated schools west of the Park. 5. The defendants, by October 2, 1967, to file for approval by the court a plan for pupil assignment eliminating the racial and economic discrimination found to exist in the operation of the Washington public school system. 6. Substantial integration of the faculty of each school beginning with the school year 1967-68. 7. The defendants, by October 2, 1967, to file for approval by the court a teacher assignment plan fully integrating the faculty of each school.

The United States is invited to intervene in these proceedings to assist in implementing the decree, to suggest changes in the decree, and to take whatever other steps it deems appropriate in the interest of public education in the District of Columbia. . . .

OPINION OF LAW

I. PREVIEW

A preliminary matter concerns identification of the governing constitutional principles. In Bolling v. Sharpe, 347 U.S. 497, 74 S. Ct. 693, 98 L. Ed. 884 (1954), the companion to Brown v. Board of Education, 347 U.S. 483, 74 S. Ct. 686, 98 L. Ed. 873 (1954), the Supreme Court held that the equal protection clause's proscription against *de jure* school segregation—segregation directly intended or mandated by law or otherwise issuing from an official racial classification—was an element of due process of law under the Fifth Amendment, thereby applicable in the District of Columbia. In so doing the Court postponed consideration of which additional doctrines of equal protection due process includes, at least insofar as the District of Columbia is concerned. . . .

In the meantime the equal protection clause has consolidated its position as the cutting edge of our expanding constitutional liberty. . . .

From these considerations the court draws the conclusion that the doctrine of equal educational opportunity—the equal protection clause in its application to public school education—is in its full sweep a component of due process binding on the District under the due process clause of the Fifth Amendment.

To fathom and apply the content of the principle of equal educational opportunity is the court's next project. As every student of the Constitution knows, the intense debate over racial segregation in the schools has clustered around two seminal concepts: *de jure* and *de facto* segregation. The first of these, as already indicated, adverts to segregation specifically mandated by law or by public policy pursued under color of law; this is the segregation unequivocally denounced by *Bolling* and *Brown*. School segregation is *de facto* when it results from the action of pupil assignment policies not based on race but upon social or other conditions for which government cannot be held responsible;[12] whether segregation so occasioned does fall within *Brown's* proscription the Supreme Court has not yet considered or decided. A third equal protection approach to the problems presented by this case questions whether the principle of equal educational oppor- tunity does not require that schools must be materially equal whenever, for whatever reasons, these schools are substantially seg- regated racially or economically.

After briefly treating and rejecting plaintiffs' unseasonable argument invoking the requirement that formerly (before 1954) *de jure* school systems affirmatively "disestablish" segregation, the court holds that a separate-but-equal rule, a variation perhaps of Plessy v. Ferguson, 163 U.S. 537, 16 S. Ct. 1138, 41 L. Ed. 256 (1896), does apply, and that violations of this rule have been re- corded here in the District. The court then turns to the optional zones and teacher segregation, concluding that these practices are condemned by *de jure* reasoning. Next, the court assesses the *de facto* segregation question and holds that the District's neighbor- hood school policy, as presently administered at least, results in harm to Negro children and to society which cannot constitu- tionally be fully justified. Finally, the court finds that the effect of the track system is to deny a majority of District students their right to equal educational opportunities.

II. DISESTABLISHING DE JURE
SEGREGATION

Until 1954 the District of Columbia's public schools were seg- regated by law. The question arises of what relevance this fact has to a segregation suit launched in 1966.

Plaintiffs press the argument that effectively to "disestablish" *de jure* segregation—no matter what the law on *de facto* segre- gation—a school board must adopt an assignment system which will achieve substantial *actual* integration. Indeed, considerable apparent support in precedent can be marshalled in defense of this position, including the Office of Education desegregation guidelines, which in some cases require minimum percentages of actual integration, 45 C.F.R. § 181.54 (Supp. 1957); the accent in all the recent cases on a desegregation plan that "works" and gets "objective" results, *e.g.,* United States v. Jefferson County, 5 Cir., 372 F.2d 836, 847 (1967). . . .

---

12 *See* Dowell v. School Board, W.D. Okl., 244 F. Supp. 971, 976 (1965), *affirmed, sub nom.* Board of Ed. of Oklahoma City, etc. v. Dowell, 10 Cir., 375 F.2d 158 (1967), *cert. denied,* 387 U.S. 931, 87 S. Ct. 2054, 18 L. Ed. 2d 993 (May 29, 1967), holding segregation unconstitutional in part because the residential conditions which produced it had been "initiated by law."

All this learning, however, has been applied primarily in situations where not only the condition of segregation persists, but the same students attend the very schools they were attending before "desegregation." The courts have shown less inclination to apply it to situations in which a complete revamping of the school system into neighborhood schools proves to have segregatory effects. *See, e.g.*, Davis v. Board of School Comm'rs, 5 Cir., 364 F.2d 896, 900 n. la (1966). The Office of Education percentage guidelines themselves do not apply to desegregation plans entailing establishment of neighborhood schools. *See* 45 C.F.R. §§ 181.31-181.35 (Supp. 1967).

The argument can be made, however, that even in these situations the court has the power, though not necessarily the duty, to insist on a degree of actual integration. Twin considerations could be thought to underlie such a remedy. One, the court is entitled to real assurance that the school board has abandoned its earlier unconstitutional policy of segregation, assurance which only the objective fact of actual integration can adequately provide, inasmuch as only that is "clearly inconsistent with a continuing policy of compulsory racial segregation." Gibson v. Board of Public Instruction, 5 Cir., 272 F.2d 763, 766 (1959). Two, the entire community, white and black, whose own attitude toward Negro schools is what stigmatizes those schools as inferior, must be disabused of any assumption that the schools are still officially segregated, an assumption it might cling to if after supposed "desegregation" the schools remained segregated in fact.

But whatever the merits of the argument in the large, the court is not disposed to grant relief on its basis in this case, for two reasons. First, there is a failure of proof. Plaintiffs have not supplied the court with the necessary data as to the degree of actual integration in the years immediately following *Bolling*, which obviously under this theory form the crucial period. Although substantial segregation was an inevitable result of adoption of the neighborhood plan in 1954, without hard figures the court cannot be assured that actual integration was then so minor as to justify relief.

Second, the argument is untimely. This suit was begun 12 years after the institution of the neighborhood school policy, making the policy older than most of the students today attending the local schools. Many concurrent causes have combined with the Board's 1954 decisions in the evolution of present reality. If the segregation in the District's schools is not currently objectionable under either an independent *de facto* or *de jure* rationale, it would be very difficult to strike it down merely because the neighborhood school policy failed to produce sufficient integration when it replaced an overt *de jure* system 13 years ago.

III. SEPARATE BUT UNEQUAL

[The findings of fact state] the court's conclusions respecting the comparative inferiority which vexes the typical predominantly Negro school in the District. The major findings can be briefly restated here. First, the school system's most ancient and dilapidated buildings can be found in the low income areas—which in Washington means in the Negro ghettos. There the typical school building is nearly 60 years old; the median building age elsewhere in the city is approximately 40 years.

The predominantly (*i.e.* 85–100%) Negro schools suffer from drastic student overcrowding (the median in 1965–66 for the 107 predominantly Negro elementary schools: 115% of capacity, which qualifies as an emergency situation), even while the 85–100% white schools flourish with empty seats and classrooms (their median: 77%). The distinction is almost systematic, in the sense that virtually every predominantly Negro school is more crowded than the majority of predominantly white schools.

By virtue of the compound of several individual ingredients of imbalance, the teachers at the predominantly white schools are a clear class above predominantly Negro school faculties in quality. Teachers at these latter schools have had much less teaching experience than their colleagues in the predominantly white schools, and more than twice as many of them have only temporary licenses, signifying their failure to compile the qualifications demanded by the school system for tenured positions; indeed, almost all the schools except those predominantly white must deal with a surfeit of temporary teachers. The large number of teachers with graduate degrees in the predominantly white schools is a feature the predominantly Negro schools do not equal. The fact that median per pupil expenditure in the predominantly Negro elementary schools has been a clear $100 below the figure for predominantly white schools, and $132 below the schools west of the Park, summarizes all the inequalities above, and perhaps significant others.

Every student within the boundaries of predominantly white schools gets a chance to attend kindergarten in his neighborhood school; the comparable opportunity is available in the predominantly Negro neighborhoods only if classroom space is available —and often it is not. In view of society's growing awareness that the children of the slums absolutely must be brought into the culturally rich atmosphere of the school at the earliest age—

three or four if possible—this failure in many Negro neighborhoods to provide even kindergarten training, freely available in
the white districts, cannot but be disquieting. . . .

Taking what has been called "a 'new' approach to litigation
over racial imbalance,"[13] the court considers whether these docu-
mented inequalities in the predominantly Negro schools deny
the children who are assigned by defendants to attend them
equal educational opportunity and equal protection of the law.
However the Supreme Court ultimately decides the question of
a school board's duty to avoid pupil-assignment policies which
lead to *de facto* segregation by race and class, it should be clear
that if whites and Negroes, or rich and poor, are to be consigned
to separate schools, pursuant to whatever policy, the minimum
the Constitution will require and guarantee is that for their objectively measurable aspects these schools be run on the basis of
real equality, at least unless any inequalities are adequately justified.

To invoke a separate-but-equal principle is bound to stir
memories of the bygone days of Plessy v. Ferguson, 163 U.S. 537,
16 S. Ct. 1138 (1896). To the extent that *Plessy's* separate-but-
equal doctrine was merely a condition the Supreme Court attached to the states' power deliberately to segregate school children by race, its relevance of course does not survive *Brown.*
Nevertheless, to the extent the *Plessy* rule, as strictly construed
in cases like Sweatt v. Painter, 339 U.S. 629, 70 S. Ct. 848, 94 L.
Ed. 1114 (1950), is a reminder of the responsibility entrusted to
the courts for insuring that disadvantaged minorities receive
equal treatment when the crucial right to public education is
concerned,[14] it can validly claim ancestry for the modern rule
the court here recognizes. It was in the latter days of *Plessy* that
the rule of actual equality began regularly to be applied. At that
time *de jure* segregation was of very shaky status, morally, socially
and constitutionally; so it is with *de facto* segregation today. If
in either circumstance school boards choose not to integrate, it

---

13 *See* T. EMERSON, D. HABER & N. DORSEN, POLITICAL AND CIVIL RIGHTS
IN THE UNITED STATES 1779 (3d ed. 1967). *See also* Rousselot, *Achieving
Equal Educational Opportunity for Negroes in the Public Schools of the
North and West: The Emerging Role for Private Constitutional Litigation,*
35 GEO. WASH. L. REV. 698, 712-718 (1967); Horowitz, *Unseparate but Unequal—The Emerging Fourteenth Amendment Issue in Public School Education,* 13 U.C.L.A. L. REV. 1147 (1966).

14 The crime which *Plessy* committed was that in applying its standard
it concluded that *de jure* segregated facilities were or could be equal. The
Court, ruling in *Brown* that deliberately segregated schools were *inherently*
unequal, implicitly accepted the separate but equal frame of reference,
exploding it from the inside so far as its application to *de jure* schools was
concerned.

is just and right that courts hold these segregated schools to standards of material equality. Of course, however, there are important differences between the doctrines old and new. Under *Plessy's* provisions once a court discovered a substantial inequality between white and Negro schools its inquiry apparently came to an end: even strong justification underlying the inequality could not deprive the Negro student of his right to judicial relief. No court would advance so absolutist an approach outside the *de jure* framework.

The constitutional principle from which this modern separate-but-equal rule draws its sustenance is, of course, equal protection. Orthodox equal protection doctrine can be encapsulated in a single rule: government action which without justification imposes unequal burdens or awards unequal benefits is unconstitutional. The complaint that analytically no violation of equal protection vests unless the inequalities stem from a deliberately discriminatory plan is simply false. Whatever the law was once, it is a testament to our maturing concept of equality that, with the help of Supreme Court decisions in the last decade, we now firmly recognize that the arbitrary quality of thoughtlessness can be as disastrous and unfair to private rights and the public interest as the perversity of a willful scheme.[15]

Theoretically, therefore, purely irrational inequalities even between two schools in a culturally homogeneous, uniformly white suburb would raise a real constitutional question. But in cases not involving Negroes or the poor, courts will hesitate to enforce the separate-but-equal rule rigorously. Through use of a generous *de minimis* rule or of a relaxed justification doctrine, or simply in the name of institutional comity, courts will tolerate a high degree of inequality-producing play, and delay, in the joints of the educational system. But the law is too deeply committed to the real, not merely theoretical (and present, not deferred) equality of the Negro's educational experience to compromise its diligence for any of these reasons when cases raise the rights of the Negro poor. Further, the inequality of a predominantly Negro school is most often no mere random fortuity unlikely to persist or recur, as these proposed rules impliedly regard

---

15 See Baker v. Carr, 369 U.S. 186, 226, 82 S. Ct. 691, 715, 7 L. Ed. 2d 663 (1962): discrimination-in-fact is bad when it "reflects *no* policy, but simply arbitrary and capricious action." (Justice Brennan's emphasis.) The record here indicates, moreover, that not all the inequalities have been thoughtless.

The government classification in this case results from the neighborhood policy which assigns students according to residential zones, and also from the numerous but deliberate government allocative decisions the sum of which represents the inequalities the court has found.

it. It is instead just one more exemplification of a disheartening and seemingly inexorable principle: segregated Negro schools, however the segregation is caused, are demonstrably inferior in fact. This principle is unanimously attested to by reports from every quarter. *E.g.,* U.S. COMM'N ON CIVIL RIGHTS, PUBLIC SCHOOLS NORTH AND WEST 216–226 (1962); SILBERMAN, CRISIS IN BLACK AND WHITE 262–263 (1965); NATIONAL ASS'N OF INTERGROUP RELATIONS OFFICIALS (NAIRO), PUBLIC SCHOOL SEGREGATION IN THE NORTH 34-35 (1963); Dentler, *Barriers to Northern School Desegregation,* in THE NEGRO AMERICAN 472, 473 (K. Clark & T. Parsons ed. 1966); Peck & Cohen, *The Social Context of De Facto School Segregation,* 16 W. RES. L. REV. 572, 590, 593–594 (1965). . . .

And here, too, there is an absence of convincing justification for the discriminations. The school system's failure to keep up with burgeoning population in the Negro neighborhoods explains several of the inequalities, thereby showing that the Board cannot be charged with having schemed their eventuation. But the element of deliberate discrimination is, as indicated above, not one of the requisites of an equal protection violation; and, given the high standards which pertain when racial minorities and the poor are denied equal educational opportunity, . . . justification must be in terms not of excusing reasons of this stripe but of positive social interests protected or advanced. A related line of defense is that the school administration, through its six-year building plan, is moving to close at least the most glaring inequalities. But that a party is in process of curing illegality, although that circumstance may affect the relief which equity finally grants, does not oust the court from its jurisdiction to declare the constitutional wrong. . . .

The failure to justify the teacher inequalities can also be confirmed. The attributes of individual schools' faculties are natural outgrowths of the methods by which teachers are assigned to the schools. And the court has already found that teacher assignment has been characterized by unconstitutional racial considerations. Absent strong evidence, the court will not assume that the superiorities in the qualifications of the predominantly white schools' faculties are unrelated to the infirmities in the appointment process.

The final question concerns the remedy to be administered for relief of the inequalities here identified. Once the showing of inequality is completed, it may be that until it is eliminated the Negro student has the right to transfer to one of the advantaged white schools, as he did during *Plessy's* reign under similar circumstances. *See* Missouri ex rel. Gaines v. Canada, 305 U.S. 337,

59 S. Ct. 232, 83 L. Ed. 208 (1938). He certainly is entitled to appropriate injunctive relief directed at phasing out the inequality. These two considerations coalesce in the remedy the court is ordering for overcrowding: that the Board transport volunteering Negro students from the city's overcrowded elementary schools into the partly vacant white schools west of the Park. . . . Implicit in the court's choice of remedy is the judgment that the Board's open transfer policy . . . as relief from the disparate overcrowding is unacceptably meagre. The transfer right which places the burden of arranging and financing transportation on the elementary schoolchildren is, particularly for the poor, a sterile right, one of form only.

The court should add that the integration implications of this remedy are obvious; as such, it gets cumulative support from the court's *de facto* segregation holding spelled out in Section V, where its equities are more thoroughly explored.

The teacher inequalities need no direct rectification at this time. Pursuant to one section of this court's order entered for reasons apart from separate-but-equal, the school system will soon be integrating its faculties. Compliance with this provision will necessarily encompass the reassignment of a number of white teachers currently serving at predominantly white schools. Since in general these are the best educated, longest-experienced and highest salaried teachers in the system, integration will also serve as a vehicle for equalizing faculty. The court will therefore defer formulation of specific provisions for faculty equalization at least until the dust surrounding this fall's "substantial" teacher integration settles.

IV. DE JURE SEGREGATION

[The court held that there was de jure segregation in the creation of a few "optional zones" that permitted children to choose their schools: "The theme which the court finds runs through these and other optional zones recently abolished is the school system's reluctance to make white students attend primarily Negro schools." De jure segregation was also found in the assignment of teachers and principals.]

V. DE FACTO SEGREGATION

One of the court's findings of fact is that elements in the school administration, though not necessarily on the Board, are affirmatively satisfied with the segregation which the local neighborhood school policy spawns. . . . But this finding falls somewhat short of showing the kind of actual intent needed if the policy is to be censured under *de jure* principles. Therefore the court approaches the more generalized question of whether the *de facto* or adventitious segregation in Washington is itself unconstitutional. In Washington, as in other Northern cities, this question arises in the context of a neighborhood policy which, superimposed on segregated urban housing, effectively separates white from Negro in the public schools.

It would be wrong to ignore or belittle the real social values which neighborhood schools doubtlessly promote. But due appreciation of these values must not obscure the fact that the price society pays for neighborhood schools, in Washington and other urban centers, is in racially segregated public education. As the court's Findings . . . indicate, school segregation, whatever its genesis, typically imposes a twofold disadvantage.

One, the Negro schools provide their Negro students with an education inferior to that which others, white and Negro alike, receive in integrated or predominantly white education settings. This the court finds from the evidence adduced at trial. This finding is confirmed by the Supreme Court in *Brown I*, which, besides noting that "separate" schools are inherently unequal and psychologically harmful to Negro school children, approved the finding entered by the lower court explicitly stating that even unmandated segregation has a "detrimental effect" on Negroes.[16] The court can judicially note that corroborating views can also be found in the conclusions of the federal agency commissioned by Congress to investigate racial questions;[17] in the decisions of federal courts, and of state legislatures and education officers and committees;[18] and in the experienced judgments of American educators and psychologists expert in race relations,[19] who make it clear that the damage segregation causes stems from the sense of confinement it imparts, together with the low esteem which the

---

[16] This finding reads: "Segregation of white and colored children in public schools has a detrimental effect upon the colored children. The impact is greater when it has the sanction of law. . . ." 347 U.S. 483, at 494, 74 S. Ct. 686, at 691, 98 L. Ed. 873.

[17] 1 U. S. COMM'N ON CIVIL RIGHTS, RACIAL ISOLATION IN THE PUBLIC SCHOOLS ch. 3 (1967). The Commission's statistical methods have been criticized. Bowles & Levin, *Equality of Educational Opportunity: A Critical Appraisal* (1967) (unpublished).

[18] *E.g.*, MASS. GEN. LAWS ch. 71, §§ 37C-37D; ch. 15, §§ 1I-1K (1965); *Memorandum of New York State Commissioner of Education*, 8 RACE REL. L. REP. 738 (1963); *see Resolution of Baltimore City Board of School Commissioners*, *id.* at 1226-1227. The *Report of the Advisory Committee on Racial Imbalance and Education to the Massachusetts Board of Education* has been published as BECAUSE IT IS RIGHT—EDUCATIONALLY (1965).

[19] Pettigrew & Pajonas, *Social Psychological Considerations of Racially-Balanced Schools;* Seaholes, *Impact of Racial Imbalance and Balance*, both appendices to BECAUSE IT IS RIGHT—EDUCATIONALLY, *supra* n.[18]; Fischer, *Race and Reconciliation: The Role of the School*, in THE NEGRO AMERICAN

predominantly Negro school naturally draws from the white[20] as well as the Negro community.

In addition, segregation in the schools precludes the kind of social encounter between Negroes and whites which is an indispensable attribute of education for mature citizenship in an interracial and democratic society. Segregation "perpetuates the barriers between the races; stereotypes, misunderstandings, hatred, and the inability to communicate are all intensified."[21] Education, which everyone agrees should include the opportunity for biracial experiences, carries on, of course, in the home and neighborhood as well as at school.[22] In this respect residential segregation, by ruling out meaningful experiences of this type outside of school, intensifies, not eliminates, the need for integration within school. . . .

In the District, moreover, *de facto* segregation results in even additional harm to Negro students, for here the neighborhood policy enters into alliance with deliberate teacher segregation, with optional zones manifesting the school administration's unwillingness to make white students attend Negro schools, and with the objective inequalities between white and Negro schools recapitulated in Section III *supra*.[23] . . .

De facto segregation in the District, in sum, redounds to the academic detriment of Negro students and seriously sets back the

---

491 (K. Clark & T. Parsons ed. 1966). *See also* the reports of the testimony of Professor Pettigrew in Barksdale v. Springfield School Comm., D. Mass., 237 F. Supp. 543, 546, *rev'd on other grounds*, 1 Cir., 348 F.2d 261 (1965) ("[R]acially imbalanced schools are not conducive to learning"), of Dr. Kenneth B. Clark in Matter of Skipwith, 14 Misc. 2d 325, 337-338, 180 N.Y.S.2d 852, 855-866 (Northern segregated conditions "depress the ability of children to learn"), and of professors of education and sociology in Deal v. Cincinnati Board of Education, S.D. Ohio, 244 F. Supp. 572, 580-581 (1965), *aff'd*, 6 Cir., 369 F.2d 55 (1966) ("[A] racially unbalanced school seriously affects a child's ability to learn").

20 The record in this case affirmatively shows that predominantly Negro schools are held in very low repute by white teachers and parents. . . .

21 Fiss, *Racial Imbalance in the [Public] Schools: The Constitutional Concepts*, 78 HARV. L. REV. 564, 570 (1965).

22 *See* B. BAILYN, EDUCATION IN THE FORMING OF AMERICAN SOCIETY 9, 15 (1960); S. KIMBALL & J. McCLELLAN, EDUCATION AND THE NEW AMERICA 39-40 (1962), for the primacy of the school as the institution which mediates between a child's family and neighborhood and the adult outside world.

23 The other side of the coin is the situation to the west of the Park. There the neighborhood policy produces student bodies which, in the northern half, are all 85-100% white and, in the south, are more than two-thirds white in each of the elementary schools. No other school anywhere in the District is currently so much as 67% white. And these white student bodies combine with the segregatory assignment of white teachers, the inbreeding of white principals, a depth of trained, experienced teachers, and a luxury of extra space. The upshot is a cluster of schools, physically set apart by the Park, primarily white and objectively superior, essentially constituting a school system unto itself.

working out of racial prejudices. These facts, however, do not conclusively determine its unconstitutionality, for with every inequality-producing classification there remains the question of justification. Indeed, ordinary statutory classifications resulting in inequalities economic in nature are traditionally upheld whenever the reviewing court can imagine a reasonable or rational basis supporting the classification.

But the Supreme Court has been vigilant in erecting a firm justification principle against every legal rule which isolates for differential treatment a disadvantaged minority, whether defined by alienage, Takahashi v. Fish & Game Comm'n, 334 U.S. 410, 68 S. Ct. 1138, 92 L. Ed. 1478 (1948); nationality, Oyama v. State of California, 332 U.S. 633, 68 S. Ct. 269, 92 L. Ed. 249 (1948); or race, Korematsu v. United States, 323 U.S. 214, 65 S. Ct. 193, 89 L. Ed. 194 (1944). While entitled before they succumb to judicial invalidation to a hearing on the justification question, these classifications come freighted with "a heavy burden of justification." McLaughlin v. State of Florida, 379 U.S. 184, 196, 85 S. Ct. 283, 13 L. Ed. 2d 222 (1965). That is, the objectives they further must be unattainable by narrower or less offensive legislative courses; and even if so, those objectives must be of sufficient magnitude to override, in the court's judgment, the evil of the inequality which the legislation engenders. These rules are allowed to relax not even when the right at stake is one which the law itself disfavors. E.g., McLaughlin, supra (out-of-wedlock cohabitation).

Next—to shift the focus—regardless of the identity of the injured party, when it is a critical personal right which the classification invades, that law too must be remitted to the gauntlet of a judicial review searching for adequate justification. . . .

This need for investigating justification is strengthened when the practice, though not explicitly singling out for special treatment any of the groups for which the Constitution has a special solicitude, operates in such a way that one such group is harshly and disproportionately disadvantaged. See Griffin v. People of State of Illinois, 351 U.S. 12, 76 S. Ct. 585 (1956), and its progeny, all involving the right to appeal in criminal cases, where practices directed specifically at those who do not pay certain fees were held invalid because of the injury they inflicted on those who cannot pay them. See also Harper v. Virginia Bd. of Elections, 383 U.S. 663, 86 S. Ct. 1079, 16 L. Ed. 2d 169 (1966) (poverty and the poll tax).[24]

---

[24] The cases listed in the above paragraphs, while not all written in exactly these terms, have long been understood as reasoning in the direction

The explanation for this additional scrutiny of practices which, although not directly discriminatory, nevertheless fall harshly on such groups relates to the judicial attitude toward legislative and administrative judgments. Judicial deference to these judgments is predicated in the confidence courts have that they are just resolutions of conflicting interests. This confidence is often misplaced when the vital interests of the poor and of racial minorities are involved. For these groups are not always assured of a full and fair hearing through the ordinary political processes, not so much because of the chance of outright bias, but because of the abiding danger that the power structure—a term which need carry no disparaging or abusive overtones—may incline to pay little heed to even the deserving interests of a politically voiceless and invisible minority.[25] These considerations impel a closer judicial surveillance and review of administrative judgments adversely affecting racial minorities, and the poor, than would otherwise be necessary.

This reasoning, as applied to *de facto* segregation, leads the court to conclude that it must hazard a diligent judicial search

---

indicated. *See* Horowitz, *Unseparate but Unequal—The Emerging Fourteenth Amendment Issue in Public [School] Education,* 13 U.C.L.A. L. REV. 1147, 1155-1159 (1966); Van Alstyne, *Student Academic Freedom and the Rule-Making Powers of Public Universities: Some Constitutional Considerations,* 2 LAW IN TRANS. Q. 28 (1965); McKay, *Political Thickets and Crazy Quilts, Reapportionment and Equal Protection,* 61 MICH. L. REV. 645, 664-676 (1963); Comment, *Equal Protection and the Indigent Defendant: Griffin and Its Progeny,* 16 STAN. L. REV. 394, 397-405 (1964); Casenotes, 80 HARV. L. REV. 176 (1966), 70 HARV. L. REV. 126 (1956). *And see Harper, supra,* 383 U.S. at 680-686, 86 S. Ct. 1079 (Harlan, J., dissenting).

That the equal protection standards to be applied in cases dealing with racial classifications and laws infringing fundamental rights are thus similar does no offense to the assumption that the former are the far more uniformly unconstitutional. This difference comes, however, less from the governing standards themselves than from the pattern of results of the standards as applied. Not until another national emergency arises, *see* Korematsu v. United States, 323 U.S. 214, 65 S. Ct. 193 (1944), will outright racial discriminations be backed by a legitimate, let alone overriding, governmental purpose; but such purposes may frequently be discoverable in the case of evenhanded laws which, unavoidably, touch vital personal interests.

25 While in the District it is whites who are the minority, Negroes are unable to translate their superior numbers into political power, for the obvious reason that citizens in the District are disenfranchised with respect to local government. Ultimate responsibility for the District's schools is lodged in the Congress and its District Committees; immediate responsibility in a Board of Education on which until last week Negroes had only a minority vote, and only a one-third vote when the basic decisions on desegregation were reached in 1954. And since they are neither elected nor reelected, but appointed by the judges of the District Court, Negro Board members are neither responsive nor responsible to the public will of the local, largely poor Negro community.

Compare Fiss, *supra* n.[21], at 610-611.

for justification. If the situation were one involving racial imbalance but in some facility other than the public schools, or unequal educational opportunity but without any Negro or poverty
aspects (e.g., unequal schools all within an economically homogeneous white suburb), it might be pardonable to uphold the
practice on a minimal showing of rational basis. But the fusion
of these two elements in de facto segregation in public schools
irresistibly calls for additional justification. What supports this
call is our horror at inflicting any further injury on the Negro,
the degree to which the poor and the Negro must rely on the
public schools in rescuing themselves from their depressed cultural and economic condition, and also our common need for the
schools to serve as the public agency for neutralizing and normal-
izing race relations in this country. With these interests at stake,
the court must ask whether the virtues stemming from the Board
of Education's pupil assignment policy (here the neighborhood
policy) are compelling or adequate justification for the considerable evils of de facto segregation which adherence to this policy
breeds. . . .

In their application, these principles require the illumination
of concrete expedients or alternatives, the question being whether
in view of these alternatives the Board's obeisance to its neighborhood school policy can be justified. One such alternative which
cannot fail to arrest the school official eager to explore ways of
reducing segregation in the schools would be to transfer and
transport volunteering Negro students stuck in overcrowded
elementary schools in their neighborhoods into the partly empty
white schools west of the Park. From the vantage point of conquering the evils of de facto segregation this proposal has much
appeal. It is capable of achieving an integrated educational experience for as many as a thousand Negro students—and, it
should not be forgotten, for more than two thousand white students. It does so under circumstances which will leave the white
students in a clear but not overwhelming majority in the schools,
since the typical school in the west has a present enrollment of
200 or 225 against a capacity of 300; many educators feel these
are optimal conditions for the success of an integration project.[26]

Arrayed against these social and educational virtues are very
few countervailing arguments of any merit. True, the volunteering Negro students would themselves forsake the advantages

---

[26] E.g., Pettigrew & Pajonas, supra n.[19], at 104. This remedy also
serves as a temporary measure for the relief of the disparate overcrowding
in the Negro schools. See Section III, supra. In gauging its advisability, the
court balances against its costs its cumulative power to improve two unconstitutional conditions.

of the neighborhood schools; but who can doubt that these advantages are susceptible to waiver by Negro parents and students who deem that school integration is of greater value. It may be accurate that the school itself gleans some benefit from its proximity to the homes of its students; even if so, this certainly is a clear case in which the school's slight interest in preserving the status quo is transcended by the student's right to obtain an integrated educational experience. Moreover, this transportation remedy clearly entails no depression of the valid interests of the white students west of the Park. They will remain in the schools in their neighborhoods. These schools will give up only the volume of superfluous space which assuredly they have little real need for presently. And, indeed, the white students will themselves number among those profiting from the access to integrated schooling. . . .

The only respectable demerit to the transportation plan is its cost in the purely budgetary sense. The court notes Dr. Hansen's own argument that public transportation at low fares is available to students, and that the expenses entailed in busing would become "excessive" only if the program is very greatly enlarged; it also is impressed that Baltimore introduced a busing plan of apparently equal ambition when the only end sought was the extenuation of overcrowding. Even if transportation costs do climb to moderate levels, the court cannot conclude that they cancel out the wisdom of a policy so abundant in its integrating potential.

For at least this one alternative, therefore, the resulting social gains far exceed the costs of any and every kind. This confirms that the Board's generally strict adherence to the neighborhood policy is beyond justification in this one instance, which supports the assumption that other proposals can also be framed the net advantages of which in integration terms will also be clear. In light of this great likelihood, the court has decided to in effect remand these proceedings to the Board of Education for its formulation of an integration "plan" which carefully assesses the virtues and costs of the spectrum of integration strategies as they could be carried out here in the District. The primary focus, of course, should be on junior and senior high schools, which the court's present injunctive order does not affect. . . .

Additionally, as Dr. Hansen himself testified at trial, the division of the District from its Maryland and Virginia suburbs is, in terms of education, "artificial. . . ." This truth is underlined by the fact that many of the families living in the white suburban "noose" are emigres from the District whose flight may have been prompted in part by their dissatisfaction with the District's school system, for whatever reasons. In many urban areas in the East urban school officials are studying or launching steps which move in the direction of metropolitanizing educational systems. As defendants argue, not more than a minority of Washington's Negroes can be afforded access to integrated education within the present constraints of the District's schools, with their diminished white enrollment. Yet, despite this, there is no evidence that the school administration has devoted more than very minor efforts to contacting the schools in these surrounding suburbs. . . . The court need not here even remotely consider what the provisions ought to be of any metropolitan school alliance; indeed, the court disavows any power to dictate those terms, or even compel the suburbs to come to the conference table. But none of this alters the fact that the Board of Education seems to have everything to gain . . . and nothing to lose in seeking to initiate negotiations. . . .

VI. THE TRACK SYSTEM

Plaintiffs' attack on the track system, Superintendent Hansen's special form of ability grouping, touches yet another phase of the District's administration of the public schools, here the concern being specifically the kind of educational opportunities existing within the classroom. The evidence amassed by both parties with regard to the track system has been reviewed in detail in Part IV of the Findings, where the court has already had occasion to note the critical infirmities of that system. The sum result of those infirmities, when tested by the principles of equal protection and due process, is to deprive the poor and a majority of the Negro students in the District of Columbia of their constitutional right to equal educational opportunities.

At the outset it should be made clear that what is at issue here is not whether defendants are entitled to provide different kinds of students with different kinds of education. Although the equal protection clause is, of course, concerned with classifications which result in disparity of treatment, not all classifications resulting in disparity are unconstitutional. If classification is reasonably related to the purposes of the governmental activity involved and is rationally carried out, the fact that persons are thereby treated differently does not necessarily offend.

Ability grouping is by definition a classification intended to discriminate among students, the basis of that discrimination being a student's capacity to learn.[27] Different kinds of educational

---

27 "Capacity to learn"—rather than "ability"—is a more precise description of the trait looked to in ability grouping. Although present ability is

opportunities are thus made available to students of differing abilities. Whatever may be said of the concept of ability grouping in general, it has been assumed here that such grouping can be reasonably related to the purposes of public education. Plaintiffs have eschewed taking any position to the contrary. Rather the substance of plaintiffs' complaint is that in practice, if not by design,[28] the track system—as administered in the District of Columbia public schools—has become a system of discrimination founded on socioeconomic and racial status rather than ability, resulting in the undereducation of many District students.

As the court's findings have shown, the track system is undeniably an extreme form of ability grouping. Students are early in elementary school sorted into homogeneous groups or tracks (and often into subgroups within a track), thereby being physically separated into different classrooms. Not only is there homogeneity, in terms of supposed levels of ability[29]—the intended result—but as a practical matter there is a distinct sameness in terms of socioeconomic status as well. More importantly, each track offers a substantially different kind of education, both in pace of learning and in scope of subject matter. At the bottom there is the slow-paced, basic (and eventually almost purely low-skill vocational) Special Academic Track; at the top is the intense and challenging Honors program for the gifted student. For a student locked into one of the lower tracks, physical separation from those in other tracks is of course complete insofar as classroom relationships are concerned; and the limits on his academic progress, and ultimately the kind of life work he can hope to attain after graduation, are set by the orientation of the lower curricula. Thus those in the lower tracks are, for the most part, molded for various levels of vocational assignments; those in the upper tracks, on the other hand, are given the opportunity to prepare for the higher ranking jobs and, most significantly, for college.

In theory, since tracking is supposed to be kept flexible, relatively few students should actually ever be locked into a single

---

one element considered, the concept of ability grouping is to provide students with an education designed to help them realize their maximum potential—*i.e.*, to progress as fast and as far as possible according to their innate capacity to learn. . . .

28 Although plaintiffs have alleged that in origin and in present administration defendants through the track system were and are intentionally discriminating against the Negro students contrary to the mandate of Bolling v. Sharpe, 347 U.S. 497, 74 S. Ct. 693 (1954), the evidence does not sustain them. . . .

Of course, the track system is not insulated from constitutional infirmity simply because its motivation is not one of intended racial discrimination. *See* n.[15] *supra* and accompanying text.

29 Abilities that, as it turns out, are not real at all. . . .

track or curriculum. Yet, in violation of one of its principal tenets, the track system is not flexible at all. Not only are assignments permanent for 90% or more of the students but the vast majority do not even take courses outside their own curriculum. Moreover, another significant failure to implement track theory —and in major part responsible for the inflexibility just noted— is the lack of adequate remedial and compensatory education programs for the students assigned to or left in the lower tracks because of cultural handicaps. Although one of the express reasons for placing such students in these tracks is to facilitate remediation, little is being done to accomplish the task. Consequently, the lower track student, rather than obtaining an enriched educational experience, gets what is essentially a limited or watered-down curriculum.

These are, then, the significant features of the track system: separation of students into rigid curricula, which entails both physical segregation and a disparity of educational opportunity; and, for those consigned to the lower tracks, opportunities decidedly inferior to those available in the higher tracks.

A precipitating cause of the constitutional inquiry in this case is the fact that those who are being consigned to the lower tracks are the poor and the Negroes, whereas the upper tracks are the provinces of the more affluent and the whites. Defendants have not, and indeed could not have, denied that the pattern of grouping correlates remarkably with a student's status, although defendants would have it that the equation is to be stated in terms of income, not race. However, as discussed elsewhere, to focus solely on economics is to oversimplify the matter in the District of Columbia where so many of the poor are in fact the Negroes. And even if race could be ruled out, which it cannot, defendants surely "can no more discriminate on account of poverty than on account of religion, race, or color." Griffin v. People of State of Illinois, 351 U.S. 12, 17, 76 S. Ct. 585, 590, 100 L. Ed. 891 (1951). As noted before, the law has a special concern for minority groups for whom the judicial branch of government is often the only hope for redressing their legitimate grievances; and a court will not treat lightly a showing that educational opportunities are being allocated according to a pattern that has unmistakable signs of invidious discrimination. Defendants, therefore, have a weighty burden of explaining why the poor and the Negro should be those who populate the lower ranks of the track system.

Since by definition the basis of the track system is to classify students according to their ability to learn, the only explanation defendants can legitimately give for the pattern of classification found in the District schools is that it does reflect students' abilities. If the discriminations being made are founded on anything other than that, then the whole premise of tracking collapses and with it any justification for relegating certain students to curricula designed for those of limited abilities. While government may classify persons and thereby effect disparities in treatment, those included within or excluded from the respective classes should be those for whom the inclusion or exclusion is appropriate; otherwise the classification risks becoming wholly irrational and thus unconstitutionally discriminatory. It is in this regard that the track system is fatally defective, because for many students placement is based on traits other than those on which the classification purports to be based.

The evidence shows that the method by which track assignments are made depends essentially on standardized aptitude tests which, although given on a system-wide basis, are completely inappropriate for use with a large segment of the student body. Because these tests are standardized primarily on and are relevant to a white middle class group of students, they produce inaccurate and misleading test scores when given to lower class and Negro students. As a result, rather than being classified according to ability to learn, these students are in reality being classified according to their socio-economic or racial status, or—more precisely—according to environmental and psychological factors which have nothing to do with innate ability.

Compounding and reinforcing the inaccuracies inherent in test measurements are a host of circumstances which further obscure the true abilities of the poor and the Negro. For example, teachers acting under false assumptions because of low test scores will treat the disadvantaged student in such a way as to make him conform to their low expectations; this acting out process— the self-fulfilling prophecy—makes it appear that the false assumptions were correct, and the student's real talent is wasted. Moreover, almost cynically, many Negro students are either denied or have limited access to the very kinds of programs the track system makes a virtual necessity: kindergartens; Honors programs for the fast-developing Negro student; and remedial and compensatory education programs that will bring the disadvantaged student back into the mainstream of education. Lacking these facilities, the student continues hampered by his cultural handicaps and continues to appear to be of lower ability than he really is. Finally, the track system as an institution cannot escape blame for the error in placements, for it is tracking that places such an emphasis on defining ability, elevating its importance to the point where the whole of a student's education and future are made to turn on his facility in demonstrating his qualifications for the higher levels of opportunity. Aside from the fact that this makes the consequences of misjudgments so much the worse, it also tends to alienate the disadvantaged student who feels unequal to the task of competing in an ethnocentric school system dominated by white middle class values; and alienated students inevitably do not reveal their true abilities—either in school or on tests.

All of these circumstances, and more, destroy the rationality of the class structure that characterizes the track system. Rather than reflecting classifications according to ability, track assignments are for many students placements based on status. Being, therefore, in violation of its own premise, the track system amounts to an unlawful discrimination against those students whose educational opportunities are being limited on the erroneous assumption that they are capable of accepting no more.

REMEDY

The remedy to be provided against the discriminatory policies of the defendants' school administration must center primarily on pupil assignment, teacher assignment and the track system. The overcrowding in the Negro schools results from pupil assignment and the difference in the per pupil expenditure results in the main from the assignment of the more highly paid teachers to the predominantly white schools. Consequently, corrective measures designed to reduce pupil and teacher racial segregation should also reduce overcrowding in the Negro schools as well as the pupil expenditure differential favoring the white children. Pending the implementation of such measures, the court will require that the defendants provide transportation to volunteering children from the overcrowded schools east of the Park to the underpopulated schools west of the Park.

As to the remedy with respect to the track system, the track system simply must be abolished. In practice, if not in concept, it discriminates against the disadvantaged child, particularly the Negro. Designed in 1955 as a means of protecting the school system against the ill effects of integrating with white children the Negro victims of *de jure* separate but unequal education, it has survived to stigmatize the disadvantaged child of whatever race relegated to its lower tracks—from which tracks the possibility of switching upward, because of the absence of compensatory education, is remote.

Even in concept the track system is undemocratic and discriminatory. Its creator admits it is designed to prepare some children for white-collar, and other children for blue-collar, jobs.

Considering the tests used to determine which children should receive the blue-collar special, and which the white, the danger of children completing their education wearing the wrong collar is far too great for this democracy to tolerate. Moreover, any system of ability grouping which, through failure to include and implement the concept of compensatory education for the disadvantaged child or otherwise, fails in fact to bring the great majority of children into the mainstream of public education, denies the children excluded equal educational opportunity and thus encounters the constitutional bar.

As has been shown, the defendants' pupil placement policies discriminate unconstitutionally against the Negro and the poor child whether tested by the principles of separate-but-equal, *de jure* or *de facto* segregation. The use by the defendants of the neighborhood school policy, intentionally manipulated in some instances to increase segregation, is the primary cause of the pupil assignment discrimination. Because of the 10 to one ratio of Negro to white children in the public schools of Washington and because the neighborhood policy is accepted and is in general use throughout the United States, the court is not barring its use here at this time.

In preparing the plan to alleviate pupil segregation which the court is ordering the defendants to file, however, the court will require that the defendants consider the advisability of establishing educational parks, particularly at the junior and senior high school levels, school pairing, Princeton and other approaches toward maximum effective integration. Where because of the density of residential segregation or for other reasons children in certain areas, particularly the slums, are denied the benefits of an integrated education, the court will require that the plan include compensatory education sufficient at least to overcome the detriment of segregation and thus provide, as nearly as possible, equal educational opportunity to all schoolchildren. Since segregation resulting from pupil assignment is so intimately related to school location, the court will require the defendants to include in their plan provision for the application of the principles herein announced to their $300,000,000 building program.

The plan, too, should anticipate the possibility that integration may be accomplished through cooperation with school districts in the metropolitan suburbs. There is no reason to conclude that all Washingtonians who make their homes in Virginia or Maryland accept the heresy that segregated public education is socially realistic and furthers the attainment of the goals of a democratic society. Certainly if the jurisdictions comprising the Washington metropolitan area can cooperate in the establishment of a metropolitan transit authority (see 1 D.C. Code §§ 1401-1416 (1961)), the possibility of such cooperation in the field of education should not be denied—at least not without first sounding the pertinent moral and social responsibilities of the parties concerned. . . .

PARTING WORD

It is regrettable, of course, that in deciding this case this court must act in an area so alien to its expertise. It would be far better indeed for these great social and political problems to be resolved in the political arena by other branches of government. But these are social and political problems which seem at times to defy such resolution. In such situations, under our system, the judiciary must bear a hand and accept its responsibility to assist in the solution where constitutional rights hang in the balance. So it was in Brown v. Board of Education, Bolling v. Sharpe, and Baker v. Carr. So it is in the South where federal courts are making brave attempts to implement the mandate of *Brown*. So it is here.

The decree is attached to, and made part of, this opinion.

DECREE

It is ORDERED, ADJUDGED and DECREED that the defendants, their agents, officers, employees and successors, and all those in active concert and participation with them be, and they are hereby, permanently enjoined from discriminating on the basis of racial or economic status in the operation of the District of Columbia public school system.

It is FURTHER ORDERED, ADJUDGED and DECREED that the defendants be, and they are hereby, permanently enjoined from operating the track system in the District of Columbia public schools. It is FURTHER ORDERED that on October 2, 1967, the defendants file in the record in this case a report of their compliance with this order of the court.

It is FURTHER ORDERED, ADJUDGED and DECREED that on October 2, 1967, the defendants herein file in the record in this case for approval by the court a plan of pupil assignment complying with the principles announced in the court's opinion and the instructions contained in the part styled REMEDY thereof.

It is FURTHER ORDERED, ADJUDGED and DECREED that the defendants, beginning with the school year 1967-68, provide transportation for volunteering children in overcrowded school districts east of Rock Creek Park to underpopulated schools west of the Park. It is FURTHER ORDERED that on October 2, 1967, the defendants file in the record in this case a report of their compliance with this order of the court.

It is FURTHER ORDERED, ADJUDGED and DECREED that, beginning with the school year 1967-68, the following optional zones be abolished: Wilson-Western-Roosevelt; Cardozo-Western; Dunbar-Western; Gordon-MacFarland; Gordon-Banneker; Powell-Hearst. It is FURTHER ORDERED that on October 2, 1967, the defendants file in the record in this case a report of their compliance with this order of the court.

It is FURTHER ORDERED, ADJUDGED and DECREED that the defendants, beginning with the school year 1967-68, provide substantial teacher integration in the faculty of each school. It is FURTHER ORDERED that on October 2, 1967, the defendants file in the record in this case a report of their compliance with this order of the court.

It is FURTHER ORDERED, ADJUDGED and DECREED that on October 2, 1967, the defendants file in the record in this case for approval by the court a plan of teacher assignment which will fully integrate the faculty of each school pursuant to the principles announced in the court's opinion and the instructions contained in the part styled REMEDY thereof.

It is FURTHER ORDERED, ADJUDGED and DECREED that the United States be, and it is hereby, invited to intervene in these proceedings to assist in the implementation of the decree, to suggest amendments to the decree, and to take whatever other steps it deems appropriate in the interest of public education in the District of Columbia. It is FURTHER ORDERED that the United States be served with a copy of this decree in the manner prescribed by Rule 4(d) (4), FEDERAL RULES OF CIVIL PROCEDURE. The parties, of course, may suggest amendments to this decree at any time.

This decree is without costs.

———————

The District of Columbia Board of Education voted (6-2) not to appeal the decision in *Hobson v. Hansen*. However, ex-Superintendent Hansen (he had resigned after Judge Wright's decision), one member of the Board of Education (Carl C. Smuck), and a group of parents sought to appeal. The United States Court of Appeals for the District of Columbia held that Hansen and Smuck did not have standing to appeal, but that the parents could intervene as appellants. At the time of the appeal a new (elected) board of education had replaced the old (appointed) board. "This Court cannot ignore the importance of assuring that the new school board should not be straitjacketed by an order not rooted in constitutional requirements. We conclude that the parents were properly allowed to intervene of right in order to appeal those provisions of the decree which curtail the freedom of the school board to exercise its discretion in deciding upon educational policy." Smuck v. Hobson, 408 F.2d 175 (D.C. Cir. 1969).

The Court of Appeals affirmed (4-3) on the merits those portions of Judge Wright's decree (p. 504 *supra*) which required the school board to provide transportation for volunteering children to underpopulated schools, to abolish optional zones, and to provide substantial teacher integration in the faculty of each school. The majority also affirmed those portions of Judge Wright's decree which required the school board to prepare a plan for pupil assignment (including compensatory education programs to the extent that integration was not feasible), and to abolish the track system. But the majority expressed no view on the merits of the constitutional issues raised by the portions of the decree relating to pupil assignment and the track system. On these questions, the majority said, Judge Wright's decree did not "materially limit the discretion of the School Board, and . . . accordingly the parents lack standing to challenge the factual and legal bases underlying these provisions of the decree . . . ."

Three dissenting judges were of the view that the concerns expressed by Judge Wright in his "Parting Word," p. 504 *supra*, should have been controlling, and that the decree should be vacated because the issues involved—particularly since an elected school board was now charged with dealing with those issues—were not suitable for resolution by the judiciary.

QUESTIONS

1. **Measuring equality of educational opportunity: an "input" or "output" standard?**—Judge Wright stated in his opinion, p. 488 *supra*, that "it should be clear that if whites and Negroes, or rich and poor, are to be consigned to separate schools, pursuant to whatever policy, the minimum the Constitution will require

and guarantee is that for their objectively measurable aspects these schools be run on the basis of real equality, at least unless any inequalities are adequately justified." Included in the "objectively measurable aspects" of the schools were the following: "the school system's most ancient and dilapidated buildings can be found in the low income areas—which in Washington means in the Negro ghettos"; "The predominantly . . . Negro schools suffer from drastic student overcrowding . . ., even while the . . . white schools flourish with empty seats and classrooms"; "the teachers at the predominantly white schools are a clear class above predominantly Negro school faculties in quality"; "median per pupil expenditure in the predominantly Negro elementary schools has been a clear $100 below the figure for predominantly white schools, and $132 below the schools west of the Park"; "Every student within the boundaries of predominantly white schools gets a chance to attend kindergarten in his neighborhood school; the comparable opportunity is available in the predominantly Negro neighborhoods only if classroom space is available —and often it is not."

The factors referred to by Judge Wright are some of the *inputs,* or resources, devoted by a school system to its educational programs. Do significant inequalities in these factors themselves constitute violations of equal protection requirements, or is it also necessary to demonstrate that the quality of educational opportunity has been adversely affected in some other way? Should it be necessary, for example, to establish that such inequalities are reflected in differences in *achievement* of children? In his "Summary" Judge Wright stated: "As they proceed through the Washington school system, the reading scores primarily of the Negro and poor children, but not the white and middle class, fall increasingly behind the national norm. By senior high school the discrepancy reaches several grades." P. 482 *supra.* There is a good deal of information on comparative achievement of children who attend ghetto (*i.e.,* de facto segregated) and non-ghetto schools. The Coleman Report states:

> With some exceptions—notably Oriental Americans— the average minority pupil scores distinctly lower on these tests at every level than the average white pupil. The minority pupils' scores are as much as one standard deviation below the majority pupils' scores in the 1st grade. At the 12th grade, results of tests in the same verbal and nonverbal skills show that, in every case, the minority scores are farther below the majority than are the 1st-graders. For some groups, the relative decline is negligible; for others, it is large. . . .

For most minority groups, then, and most particularly the Negro, schools provide little opportunity for them to overcome this initial deficiency; in fact they fall farther behind the white majority in the development of several skills which are critical to making a living and participating fully in modern society. Whatever may be the combination of nonschool factors—poverty, community attitudes, low educational level of parents—which put minority children at a disadvantage in verbal and nonverbal skills when they enter the first grade, the fact is the schools have not overcome it. Coleman Report, p. 21.

Studies in specific cities show similar results. The Report of the Governor's Commission on the Los Angeles Riots (the McCone Commission), for example, showed the following comparative data on average reading achievement, in tests that were administered nationally in 1965, of students in three grades in the Los Angeles city schools:[30]

Average Reading Performance in Comparison Areas

Area	Reading Vocabulary Ranking[31]	Reading Comprehension Ranking
Grade B5		
Citywide	48	48
Non-ghetto	81	75
Ghetto	18-20	19-24
Grade B8		
Citywide	49	47
Non-ghetto	79	77
Ghetto	13-16	15-20
Grade B11		
Citywide	63	55
Non-ghetto	82	73
Ghetto	27-34	24-30

[30] Summarized from GOVERNOR'S COMMISSION ON THE LOS ANGELES RIOTS, VIOLENCE IN THE CITY—AN END OR A BEGINNING? 50-51 (1965). We have used the word "ghetto" as a shorthand term for what the Commission called "disadvantaged areas," referring to areas predominantly populated by Negroes and Mexican-Americans. [Eds. note.]

[31] These rankings are percentiles of the national test population.

The conclusions of the Coleman Report as to the relationship between the objectively measurable factors referred to by Judge Wright and these achievement data are discussed by Professor Pettigrew in his article, p. 404 *supra*. Some of these factors appear to have no relationship to achievement; note, for example, the statement in Professor Pettigrew's article that "per pupil instructional expenditure in grades six, nine, and twelve is not significantly associated with achievement save in one notable case of marked extremes—Negro children in the South." P. 406 *supra*. Other input factors do relate to achievement, but to a degree far less than does the factor of the socioeconomic backgrounds and aspirations of a child's fellow students. And all of the correlations between in-school factors and achievement must be appraised in light of this statement in the Coleman Report: ". . . schools bring little influence to bear on a child's achievement that is independent of his background and general social context; and . . . this very lack of an independent effect means that the inequalities imposed on children by their home, neighborhood, and peer environment are carried along to become the inequalities with which they confront adult life at the end of school. For equality of educational opportunity through the schools must imply a strong effect of schools that is independent of the child's immediate social environment, and that strong independent effect is not present in American schools." Coleman Report, p. 325. The issue then arises whether inequalities in factors which have little (or relatively little) relationship to achievement should be held to be unconstitutional inequalities. What justifications or explanations are there for these differences in inputs that might lead to holding them to be constitutionally permissible, assuming alternatively that their impact on achievement is (a) demonstrable or (b) not demonstrable?

See generally Cohen, *Defining Racial Equality in Education,* 16 U.C.L.A. L. Rev. 255 (1969).

2. Are compensatory education programs constitutionally required?—Judge Wright referred, in a portion of his opinion omitted here, to another factor in the input of the school system to pupils' educational opportunity: "It is because of the high proportion of disadvantaged children in the District school system that it is imperative that special programs outside the regular curriculum be adopted so that the disadvantaged child has a real opportunity to achieve at his maximum level of ability." (269 F. Supp. at 471.) One of the reasons for his holding the track system invalid was the failure to provide adequate compensatory education programs: "Moreover, any system of ability grouping

which, through failure to include and implement the concept of
compensatory education for the disadvantaged child or otherwise,
fails in fact to bring the great majority of children into the mainstream of public education denies the children excluded equal
educational opportunity. . . ." P. 503 *supra.* And with respect
to the remedy for de facto segregation, Judge Wright said:
"Where because of the density of residential segregation or for
other reasons children in certain areas, particularly the slums, are
denied the benefits of an integrated education, the court will require that the plan include compensatory education sufficient at
least to overcome the detriment of segregation and thus provide,
as nearly as possible, equal educational opportunity to all schoolchildren." P. 503 *supra.* Part VI of the decree in *United States v.
Jefferson County Board of Education,* p. 374 *supra,* ordered a similar remedy: "The defendants shall provide remedial education
programs which permit students attending or who have previously
attended segregated schools to overcome past inadequacies in
their education." The factor of equality of educational opportunity here isolated is that of "opportunity to achieve at his
maximum level of ability." In order for educational opportunity
to be equal in this sense, students with differing educational
needs should have differing educational programs. Equality of
educational opportunity is here measured by the degree of response to the differing educational needs of children. The *same*
educational programs for all children, in other words, will not
necessarily amount to the provision of *constitutionally equal*
programs.[32] This may mean, among other consequences, that in
order to provide equal educational opportunity, a school board
must spend more for some children's educational programs than
for others.

This measure of equality of educational opportunity raises two
types of problems: (1) What forms of "compensatory" programs
are thus required? Professor Pettigrew states in his article, p. 418
supra, "that it remains to be demonstrated that these programs
can lead to lasting and significant academic gains. So far the
record of these programs is not encouraging." What degree of
support should a judge be able to find in social science data before he finds that the constitution requires "compensatory" and

---

[32] "The schools in the disadvantaged areas do not provide a program
that meets the unique educational needs of culturally disadvantaged children. . . . The same educational program for children of unequal background does not provide an equal opportunity for children to learn." Governor's Commission on the Los Angeles Riots, Violence in the City—An
End or a Beginning? 58 (1965). *See* Horowitz, *Unseparate but Unequal—
The Emerging Fourteenth Amendment Issue in Public Education,* 13
U.C.L.A. L. Rev. 1147, 1166-72 (1966).

"remedial" programs? (2) How effectively can a court bring about compliance with such a constitutional requirement? Does the District of Columbia school board have sufficient guidance in Judge Wright's opinion and decree to determine when it has complied with the decree? Recall the similar questions with respect to the Illinois statutory provision involved in *Tometz v. Waukegan City School District No. 61*, p. 421 *supra*, requiring school districts, "as soon as practicable," to draw attendance zones "which will take into consideration the prevention of segregation and the elimination of separation of children in public schools because of color, race or nationality."

This measure of equality also suggests an exploration of the constitutional duty of school systems serving students from ethnic minorities to respond to the special educational needs of such students. For example, is *Hobson v. Hansen* the basis for an argument that schools should provide instruction in English as a second language and general classroom instruction in Spanish for bilingual or Spanish-speaking children?[33] Is *Hobson v. Hansen* the basis for an argument that schools must provide teaching materials and curricula that will better portray the history of the minority groups of which the school children are members? How might a court word its decrees in such cases?

Hobson v. Hansen was relied on in an action brought in 1968 against the Santa Ana, California, Unified School District. (In this action, the plaintiffs were represented by lawyers working with an OEO-funded legal services program.) That school district had refused to make use of federal funds available to it under the Elementary and Secondary Education Act of 1965 for programs "which are designed to meet the special educational needs of educationally deprived children in school attendance areas having high concentrations of children from low-income families." 20 U.S.C. § 241 *et seq.*; F.C.A. 20 § 241 *et seq.* (Supp. 1968). The district had refused over $1,000,000 in federal funds by the time the suit was brought. The complaint alleged that the district did not "offer any significant compensatory education programs designed to deal with the special educational problems of educationally deprived children in attendance areas having high concentration of children from low-income families," and that "other children in . . . [the] district receive an educational opportunity more responsive to their educational needs than do educationally

---

[33] For an analysis of the relationship between the language spoken at home and the achievement of Mexican-American pupils in the Los Angeles City School System, see C. GORDON, A. SCHWARTZ, R. WENKERT, & D. NASATIR, EDUCATIONAL ACHIEVEMENT AND ASPIRATIONS OF MEXICAN-AMERICAN YOUTH IN A METROPOLITAN CONTEXT (1968).

deprived children in areas having high concentration of low-income families." The prayer was for an order that the district use
all funds available to it for compensatory education programs
under the Elementary and Secondary Education Act of 1965, or,
in lieu thereof, "utilize other resources available to . . . [the dis-
trict] so as to provide such compensatory programs, comparable
to those which would be provided by utilization" of the federal
funds. The suit was dismissed as moot after the district developed
a compensatory education project and applied for the federal
funds. Los Angeles Times, July 10, 1968, part II, p. 8. *Silvas v.
Santa Ana Unified School District,* No. M-0945, Superior Court,
Orange County, California (1968). Recalling *Jackson v. Pasadena
City School District,* p. 441 *supra,* a California Supreme Court decision, how would you have argued the *Silvas* case for the plaintiffs?

3. De facto social-class segregation.—The Coleman Report concluded that the school-related factors most significantly related to
educational opportunity are the socioeconomic status and aspirations of a child's classmates. To the extent that a school system
has any control over this aspect of the make-up of school student
bodies, this factor can be considered to be one of the inputs of
the school system to the quality of educational opportunity offered to children. Should it be held that a school district denies
equal educational opportunity to a low-socioeconomic-status
child if the district does not (at least) take all "reasonably feasible" steps available to it to provide socioeconomic integration
of classrooms? Is not the case for this result stronger than that
for a constitutional obligation to improve racial balance or to
provide compensatory education programs?

**4. The desirability of leaving to other branches of govern-
ment the resolution of these problems of unequal educational
opportunity.**—Consider Judge Wright's "Parting Word" at the
close of his opinion: "It would be far better indeed for these
great social and political problems to be resolved in the political
arena by other branches of government." The dissenting judges
in the court of appeals in *Hobson v. Hansen* argued that Judge
Wright's decree should be vacated because the issues were not
suitable for resolution by a court. The reasons for this concern have been suggested previously in several places in these
materials: the incomplete or controversial nature of the social
science data upon which judgments must be based; the broad
sweep of some of the educational policy issues which are raised;

the difficulty in shaping decrees that are sufficiently specific for meaningful administration and enforcement; the undesirability of involving courts in the day-to-day administration of school systems. We return to a question with which we began in *Somerset v. Stewart*, p. 19 *supra*: Are these issues such that the court should refrain from exercising its law-declaring function (here, interpretation of the Constitution)? There are two ways in which the court might respond to such concern about the nature of the problems in these equality-of-educational-opportunity cases: (1) The court might conclude that the question of the constitutionality of a specific aspect of the operation of a school system was so unfit for judicial resolution that its resolution, if any, must come from the legislative branch. This solution would place the constitutional issue in the ever-dwindling realm of what the United States Supreme Court has called "political questions." We shall not here explore the concept of the political, *i.e.*, non-justiciable question. We raise the point only in order to contrast the problem in *Hobson v. Hansen* with that in *Somerset v. Stewart*. In *Somerset*, if there had been sound grounds to "defer" to the legislature, the court would have been deferring a lawmaking question—the validity of slavery—which was typical of the lawmaking issues customarily considered by the legislative branch. "Deferring" the issues in *Hobson v. Hansen* would be an abstention from exercising the judicial function on an issue of constitutional interpretation, a far less typical kind of lawmaking issue for disposition by the legislature alone. (2) The court might simply hold that there is no denial of equal protection of the laws in the fact situation before the court.

Which of these alternative conclusions would be the better way for the court to dismiss the plaintiffs' action in a case like *Hobson v. Hansen*, if the court were of the view that although there were significant inequalities of educational opportunity in the case before it, the case was not a fit one for exercise of the judicial function? Would the plaintiffs and similarly situated individuals be likely to distinguish the first from the second? Should it be of significance to the court in considering the disposition of the case that those affected by the decision would not distinguish the first from the second? Was Judge Wright correct, p. 504 *supra*, in saying: "these are social and political problems which seem at times to defy such [political] resolution. In such situations, under our system, the judiciary must bear a hand and accept its responsibility to assist in the solution where constitutional rights hang in the balance"?

Consider the following comments by Professor Bickel on Judge Wright's decision in *Hobson v. Hansen*:

Judge Wright's remedy for conditions that he found to be unconstitutional is still in an early stage of development, but it is reasonably clear that he, no more than anyone else, has a remedy or can put one into effect. What then is the use of such judgments? What is the use of a hortatory constitutional pronouncement urging Washington, D.C., to solve its social and economic problems? Judge Wright's opinion might have been a document issued by some group of civic leaders, or some foundation or research organization, and whatever disagreement one might have had with this or that aspect of it, one would have welcomed its attention to the school problem. But the Constitution and the judges who guard it have a well-defined role to play, which no one else can play. They are to address themselves to those features of the society with which law can deal, by defining rights, obligations and goals. No charitable organization and no study group can do that job, can invoke the power of government to those ends. It is no service to any worthy cause to saddle legal institutions with functions they cannot discharge, and to issue in the name of law promises the courts cannot redeem. Bickel, *Skelly Wright's Sweeping Decision*, The New Republic, July 8, 1967, pp. 11, 12.

Recall the discussion at p. 476 *supra*, of the "reasonably available" language in *New Kent County* and the "reasonably feasible" language in *Jackson v. Pasadena City School District.* If, for example, Judge Wright's orders to alleviate de facto segregation and to institute compensatory education programs were qualified by a "reasonably available" or "reasonably feasible" standard, would his judgment on these issues be only "a hortatory constitutional pronouncement" and only "promises the courts cannot redeem"? Recall the Illinois statute in *Tometz v, Board of Education, Waukegan City School District No. 61*, p. 421 *supra*, requiring that school boards "as soon as practicable" create attendance zones which "will take into consideration" the prevention of segregation. Is that only a hortatory pronouncement which the courts, as the final enforcement agency, cannot redeem?

Consider also the following reply by Professor Michael Tigar to Professor Bickel's comments:

Let us consider Judge Wright's response to these problems in the context of the District of Columbia's unique governmental structure. The District's citizens do not govern themselves. The Congress, in which they have neither voice nor vote, legislates for them. . . . Thus, the District's citizens have no political body which is responsive to their criticisms and complaints, except, it now appears, an enlightened court. . . .

What then, of Judge Wright's opinion? A "jeremiad," "hortatory," says Professor Bickel. The courts, he says, cannot redeem Judge Wright's promises. Judge Wright, one should be careful to note, does not promise to rescue the District school system. He promises only to see that certain constitutional decencies are respected: Don't discriminate on the basis of race or wealth in the allocation of funds; don't use an irrational ethnocentric value system in classifying children; integrate faculties; use underutilized classrooms to aid integration, and so on. The Board and the Superintendent will draw plans to meet these commands. Judge Wright will either approve or disapprove and in the end certain guidelines will be set down in a final decree. By this means, constitutional and legal minima will be set. The Board is free to do better than it is ordered to, to do more than it must, to remedy the schools' ugly state.

Professor Bickel's error is in assuming that a judge cannot denounce the conduct of litigants unless he is able to provide a complete remedy. As Professor Bickel's own writings have well-recognized, however, one great purpose of revolutionary judicial utterance—like *Brown v. Board of Education*—is to set at large with official imprimatur ideas which have theretofore gone unspoken. This hortatory function of judging serves at times to legitimize struggle elsewhere in society to attain the ends and put into practice the ideas first set out by judges. Certainly this has been one salutary effect of *Brown*. Tigar, *In Defense of Skelly Wright*, The New Republic, Aug. 5, 1967, pp. 42-43.

Professor Tigar's suggestion about the "hortatory function" of judicial law-making is seconded by Robert L. Carter, the former General Counsel of the NAACP. In reviewing the record of the Warren Court since *Brown v. Board of Education,* he concludes that the principal impact of *Brown* has been indirect, in its encouragement of an attitude among blacks that equality was something to be demanded as a right, not petitioned for as a favor. Carter, *The Warren Court and Desegregation*, 67 MICH. L. REV. 237, 246-48 (1968).

Finally, consider Gunnar Myrdal's observations on this subject, made with the race problem specifically in view:

Americans are accustomed to inscribe their ideals in laws ranging from their national Constitution to their local traffic rules. American laws thus often contain, in addition to the actually enforced rules (that is, "laws" in the ordinary technical meaning of the term), other rules which are not valid or operative but merely express the legislators' hopes, desires, advice or dreams. . . .

The "function," from the legislator's point of view, of legislating national ideals is, of course, a pedagogical one of giving them high publicity and prestige. Legislating ideals has also a "function" of dedicating the nation to the task of gradually approaching them. MYRDAL, AN AMERICAN DILEMMA 14 (1944).

5. Inter-district inequalities of educational opportunity.—In the section of his opinion entitled "Remedy," Judge Wright said that in preparing a desegregation plan the school board "should anticipate the possibility that integration may be accomplished through cooperation with school districts in the metropolitan suburbs." P. 503 *supra.* Attention has only recently come to be focused on the issue of inequalities in educational opportunity among school districts, as distinguished from the issues of intra-district inequalities involved in all of the cases we have considered in these materials. Judge Wright was referring to inequalities stemming from de facto segregation in District of Columbia Schools as compared with schools in surrounding Virginia and Maryland. Inequalities in educational opportunity may be found among school districts in the same state, by all of the measures of inequality discussed above in the context of *Hobson v. Hansen.* Where these conditions are found within a single state, the possibility arises of constitutional attack under the fourteenth amendment. Particular concern has come now to be focused on the unequal resources, measured on a dollars-per-year-per-child basis or on the basis of each child's educational needs, expended in inner-city schools as compared with more wealthy suburban districts. The following article from the *Wall Street Journal* describes recent litigation raising constitutional issues concerning the financing of public education.

NIKOLAIEFF, CITY SCHOOL DISTRICTS, STRAPPED FOR MONEY, ASK COURTS FOR RELIEF
Wall Street Journal, July 16, 1968, p. 1*

DETROIT—Big city public schools, tired of wringing money from an overburdened property tax and grudging state legislators, are trying a new approach—through the courts.

Their demands for more money could result in a basic re-organization of state aid to primary and secondary education, which totaled $12 billion last year. Victory for the cities "could have an impact on education comparable in its significance to the Supreme Court's 1954 decision on desegregation," says Harold Howe II, U.S. Commissioner of Education.

Suits already have been filed in two cities, Detroit and Chicago, and at least 40 other cities are closely watching the legal maneuvering. Observers say that if the cities win, state aid to suburban schools probably would suffer. Then many suburbs, already highly taxed, would be forced to consider tax increases. The resulting outcry ultimately could affect Federal aid-to-education policy.

Plaintiffs in the suits are the Detroit board of education and a group of Chicago ghetto parents and children. The Chicagoans are getting legal help from the antipoverty program. The plaintiffs argue that existing formulas for allocating state aid ignore the needs of individual districts, perpetuate an uneven distribution of funds and therefore deprive some children of the equal opportunities promised by the 14th Amendment. They urge the courts to order the state legislatures to devise new formulas more closely attuned to the needs of individual districts.

The pupils big city districts must educate are often poor and culturally deprived. Many are members of minority groups; about 60% of the children in the Detroit district are Negro. The districts themselves must compete with other desperately needed local programs for money from the property tax base.

A study by the Carnegie Foundation shows that in the 1964-65 school year the nation's 37 largest cities had $121 per pupil less to spend than the outlying districts. Two years before the gap had been only $62 per pupil, and experts believe it is still widening. They note, for example, that in the past school year Detroit could spend only $600 per pupil, while its wealthy suburban neighbor, Grosse Pointe, spent about $900. All-Negro Willow-brook district, near Watts in Los Angeles, spent $613 per pupil, including $219 from Federal assistance funds, while plush Beverly Hills spent $1,017.

With few exceptions, school districts rely for their support largely on a combination of local property taxes and state aid. Last year local taxes provided $15.3 billion of the $31 billion bill for primary and secondary education, state aid provided $12 billion and the rest came mainly from the Federal government. Today, "property taxes are exhausted," says Joel Cogen, assistant to the mayor of New Haven, Conn. "You can't raise them any more."

The reason, the educators say, is that other local services also supported by the property tax cost more in the core city than in the suburbs, due to big-city congestion and higher labor costs; in addition, cities usually spend more than suburbs for such things as cultural activities and transportation facilities. Another Carnegie study found that in 1966 New York City residents paid $44.26 per $1,000 of tax valuation for municipal services, compared with $21.83 for four surrounding suburban counties.

Nor have urban districts been very successful when they've turned for relief to the state legislatures. . . .

Most state school aid formulas, including those in Michigan and Illinois, where the test suits were filed, already favor the poorer districts. For example, Detroit's state aid last year totaled $230.35 a student, while Grosse Pointe got only $145. But the city educators say the extra aid isn't enough.

They argue that most state constitutions and the 14th Amendment require the state not just to support public schools but to treat all students equally—even if it means spending more per pupil in city schools than suburban schools for such things as special courses to improve reading and study skills. "The states assumed the responsibility for equitable public education, and they've got to pay for it," says Zane Cohn, attorney for the group that filed the Chicago suit.

Both the Chicago and Detroit suits attack state aid formulas based on property values within the school district. Michigan's formula is typical. It starts by allowing each district the same gross aid per pupil: $280.50. From this figure, after adjustments for various factors such as transportation costs, the state then deducts an amount based on the total property valuation in the district. Because the wealthier suburbs have higher per-capita property valuations, they normally get less aid per pupil than the city districts.

In theory, the Michigan formula equalizes school aid because it penalizes the districts best equipped to raise money through the property tax. But critics say it doesn't help big city districts enough and argue that its basic assumption is wrong. "State money should be handed out on the basis of what it takes to provide a decent education instead of how big and fancy the houses are in the school district," says Stephen Schlossberg, counsel for United Auto Workers union, which has filed a brief in support of the Detroit suit.

Neither suit proposes specific alternatives to present aid plans; the critics assume new plans, in accordance with court guidelines, could be worked out later. But urban education experts mention four possible alternatives.

Under one, the city school board would prepare its budget based on needs and present it to a state agency for certification; the state would then supplement local revenues to the extent needed. Another plan would create a special metropolitan agency for education, akin to existing transportation authorities, with power to tax and to supplement money raised by the school board. A third concept would relieve local boards of one burden by requiring capital financing of new construction through statewide-bond issues. A fourth envisions a complete take-over by the state of all educational financing.

Attorneys for both Michigan and Illinois are trying to have the suits dismissed. Argues an attorney for Michigan: "It seems to me the legislature has the authority to spend the tax money in any way it sees fit."

Supporters of the suits say they will carry their fight to the Supreme Court if necessary. . . .

———

The litigation described in this article sought declarations of invalidity, on equal protection grounds, of patterns of education finance common to most states. Under these patterns, local school districts finance their operations from locally assessed property taxes, plus varying forms of supplements out of state funds. Typically there are very great differentials in property tax bases from district to district within a state. State-aid formulas normally go only part of the way toward equalizing the resources of the districts. The result is that some districts spend much more per child than do others. Furthermore, taxpayers in some districts pay property taxes at much higher rates than do taxpayers in other districts, just to be able to spend (per child) as much as, or less than, those other districts do.[34]

———

[34] In Serrano v. Priest, No. 938254, Superior Court, Los Angeles County, California, filed August 23, 1968, the following data are included in the complaint as examples of inter-district inequalities under California's method of financing public education, which method is alleged to violate the equal protection clause: (1) In Los Angeles County in 1966-67, *assessed valuation per pupil* (the tax base for local school district property taxes) ranged from $5,000 to $94,000 in elementary schools in unified (first through twelfth grade) school districts, and from $16,000 to $135,000 in high schools in such districts; assessed valuation per pupil in elementary school districts in Los Angeles County ranged from $2,100 to $220,700, and in high school districts from $18,100 to $53,500; in districts in other counties in the state, in 1965-66, the range was $3,698 to $306,077 in elementary districts, $18,607 to $212,655 in high school districts, $6,087 to $134,811 in elementary schools in unified districts, and $12,105 to $257,353 in high schools in unified districts. (2) *Property tax rates* for school purposes per $100 of assessed valuation in Los Angeles County, in 1967-68, ranged from $1.94 to $5.33 in unified districts, from $0.88 to $3.21 in elementary school districts, and from $1.62

Assume that such differentials in expenditure are shown to reflect significant inequalities in educational opportunity, or that other inter-district inequalities in educational opportunity can be established, such as the degree of response of educational programs to the needs of children, or by other measures of quality discussed at pp. 506-09, *supra*. What argument can be developed, based solely upon cases included in these materials, that those inter-district inequalities constitute a denial of the equal protection of the laws? Recall *Griffin v. County School Board,* p. 265 *supra; Green v. County School Board of New Kent County,* p. 290 *supra; Jackson v. Pasadena City School District,* p. 441, *supra;* and *Hobson v. Hansen,* p. 480 *supra.* What relief should plaintiffs seek in suits based on this theory? Who should be the defendants in such actions? Are there especially strong arguments here for a court's refraining from deciding the constitutional issue? See Horowitz & Neitring, *Equal Protection Aspects of Inequalities in Public Education and Public Assistance Programs From Place to Place Within a State,* 15 U.C.L.A. L. REV. 787 (1968); Kirp, *The Poor, the Schools, and Equal Protection,* 38 HARV. EDUC. REV. 635 (1968); Kurland, *Equal Educational Opportunity: The Limits of Constitutional Jurisprudence Undefined,* 38 U. CHI. L. REV. 583 (1968).

One of the cases referred to in the preceding article in the *Wall Street Journal* has been decided by the United States Supreme Court. McInnis v. Shapiro, 293 F. Supp. 327 (E.D. Ill. 1968), involved the financing of public schools in Illinois. A three-judge federal district court dismissed the complaint, concluding that "no cause of action is stated for two principal reasons: (1) the Fourteenth Amendment does not require that public school expenditures be made only on the basis of pupils' educational needs, and (2) the lack of judicially manageable standards makes this controversy non-justiciable." 293 F. Supp. at 329. The Supreme Court affirmed summarily, without oral argument and without a written opinion. McInnis v. Ogilvie, 89 S. Ct. 1197 (1969).

D. THE CIVIL RIGHTS ACT OF 1964

In Chapter 3 we have already considered Title VI of the Civil Rights Act of 1964, providing for withholding of federal funds from grantees which conduct racially discriminatory programs,

---

to $2.85 in high school districts. (3) In Los Angeles County, in 1966-67, *expenditures per child* in elementary districts ranged from $428.34 to $1,317.64, in high school districts from $639.05 to $777.64, and in unified districts from $465.74 to $1,014.35.

and the HEW regulation and Guidelines promulgated under the authority of Title VI. Our concern in Chapter 3 centered on school segregation that was compelled by law or official policy in southern states. In March 1968, HEW issued a new policy statement, amending and superseding the 1966 Guidelines. The 1968 "Policies on Elementary and Secondary School Compliance with Title VI of the Civil Rights Act of 1964"[35] contain new provisions designed to reach problems of equality of educational opportunity other than those related to de jure racial segregation:

SUBPART B. GENERAL COMPLIANCE POLICIES

8. Equal Educational Opportunity

School systems are responsible for assuring that students of a particular race, color, or national origin are not denied the opportunity to obtain the education generally obtained by other students in the system. Providing equal educational opportunity does not, however, require school systems to offer an identical educational program for each student, or to fund each school, curriculum, course, or activity on the same basis, if the variations in programs and funding do not deny educational opportunities to students on the ground of race, color, or national origin.

9. Inferior Educational Facilities and Services

Where there are students of a particular race, color, or national origin concentrated in certain schools or classes, school systems are responsible for assuring that these students are not denied equal educational opportunities by practices which are less favorable for educational advancement than the practices at schools or classes attended primarily by students of any other race, color, or national origin. Examples of disparities between such schools and classes which may constitute a denial of equal educational opportunities include, but are not limited to:

—Comparative overcrowding of classes, facilities, and activities
—Assignment of fewer or less qualified teachers and other professional staff

---

[35] 33 Fed. Reg. 4955 (March 23, 1968).

—Provision of less adequate curricula and extracurricular activities or less adequate opportunities to take advantage of the available activities and services

—Provision of less adequate student services (guidance and counseling, job placement, vocational training, medical services, remedial work)

—Assigning heavier teaching and other professional assignments to school staff

—Maintenance of higher pupil-teacher ratios or lower per pupil expenditures

—Provision of facilities (classrooms, libraries, laboratories, cafeterias, athletic, and extracurricular facilities), instructional equipment and supplies, and textbooks in a comparatively insufficient quantity

—Provision of buildings, facilities, instructional equipment and supplies, and textbooks which, comparatively, are poorly maintained, outdated, temporary or otherwise inadequate.

QUESTIONS

1. The 1968 Guidelines and de facto segregation.—Under paragraphs 8 and 9 of the 1968 "Policies," would a school system that maintained racially imbalanced schools be ineligible for federal funds? Would HEW be authorized under Title VI of the Civil Rights Act of 1964 to enforce such a limitation? Title VI provides that "No person in the United States shall, on the ground of race, color, or national origin, be excluded from participation in, be denied the benefits of, or be subjected to discrimination under any program or activity receiving Federal financial assistance." Would a racial-imbalance limitation advance the purposes of Title VI? Will the words of Title VI bear such a meaning, or do they, at most, refer to de jure racial segregation?[36]

---

[36] The HEW appropriations act for the fiscal year July 1, 1968-June 30, 1969, enacted in October 1968 and appropriating funds for all HEW-administered grant programs, contained the following two provisions:

§ 409: No part of the funds contained in this Act may be used to force busing of students, abolishment of any school, or to force any student attending any elementary or secondary school to attend a particular school against the choice of his or her parents or parent *in order to overcome racial imbalance.*

§ 410: No part of the funds contained in this Act shall be used to force busing of students, the abolishment of any school or the attendance of students at a particular school *in order to overcome racial imbalance* as a condition precedent to obtaining Federal funds otherwise available to any State, school district, or school . . . . P.L. 90-557, 82 Stat. 969 (Oct. 11, 1968). (Emphasis added.)

What weight should be given to the statements of Senator Humphrey, the floor manager of the bill (referred to earlier in the discussion of the *Jefferson County opinion*, p. 391 *supra*), that the limitations on remedying racial imbalance in Title IV apply as well to Title VI? Recall the suggestion, p. 461 *supra*, that racial imbalance may be indistinguishable from de jure segregation, when a school board has alternatives that would significantly lessen the imbalance.

2. The 1968 Guidelines and other inequalities of educational opportunity.—The 1968 policy statement specifically refers to examples of disparities which may constitute a denial of equal educational opportunities. Does Title VI authorize HEW to impose the requirements contained in paragraph 9? Under paragraph 9 could a school system be required to provide compensatory education programs for "students of a particular race, color, or national origin concentrated in certain schools or classes"? Would HEW be authorized under Title VI to enforce such a requirement?

Southern congressmen sought to have these provisions included, without the phrases "in order to overcome racial imbalance," apparently wishing to do away with HEW's power under Title VI to withhold funds from southern school districts which maintained "freedom of choice" plans. Proponents of the "racial imbalance" phrases equated "racial imbalance" with constitutionally permissible de facto segregation, and argued that the statutory language as finally enacted would continue to make unconstitutionally (de jure) segregated districts ineligible for federal funds under Title VI. See 114 CONG. REC. H9439 (October 3, 1968). Assuming the continued enactment of these provisions in future appropriations acts, is it now clear that HEW is not empowered under Title VI to withhold funds from de facto segregated school districts?

Index